Dear Precepts Customer,

It is our privilege to present the 2017–2018 *Precepts For Living*® commentary. As you encounter God's Word through these lessons, we anticipate that you will find this resource to be indispensable.

Precepts For Living® comes to you in three versions: the Personal Study Guide (the workbook), the online version, and a large print edition. You will also notice that the biblical text for each lesson includes the New Living Translation in addition to the King James Version. This contemporary translation will enhance your textual understanding when you compare it side by side to the classic English translation. It is very helpful in illuminating your understanding of the text.

Precepts For Living® is designed to be a witness through our learning and sharing more of the Bible. Our intent is to facilitate innovative ways for pursuing a deeper understanding and practice of God's Word. One of the ways we strive to do this is by highlighting the larger narrative of God's work in salvation as a key part of understanding each biblical passage. We believe it is important to help you understand not only the particulars of the text but also the broad extent of God's revelation to us as well. This panoramic approach enhances our ability to witness to others about the saving power of Jesus Christ.

This year we explore the themes of covenant with God, faith, worship, and justice. Each year of Bible study offers great potential for a more intimate and transformative walk with God.

We want to continually refine *Precepts For Living*® as we endeavor to meet our customers' needs. We are always looking for ways to enhance your study of the Bible, and your comments and feedback are vital in helping us. If you have questions or suggestions, we encourage you to please e-mail us at precepts@urbanministries.com or mail your comments to UMI, *Precepts For Living*®, PO Box 436987, Chicago, IL 60643-6987.

May God draw you closer to the fullness of life with Him through this book.

God's blessings to you,

Adonijah Okechukwu Ogbonnaya

Adonijah Okechukwu Ogbonnaya, Advanced Teachers' Certificate, B.A. Bible and Philosophy, M.A. Theological Studies, M.A. Religion, Ph.D. Theology and Personality
Editor

Uncovering the Benefits of Precepts

It is a great privilege to participate in Christian education and play a significant role in the spiritual formation of fellow Christians in our churches. *Precepts For Living*® is a resource that is designed to help you lead others toward greater knowledge and practice of following Jesus Christ. To that end, please take full advantage of the substantive offerings provided to you in this year's commentary. From the standpoint of your vocation as a teacher, it is very important to be aware of the great responsibility that goes along with your position. James 3:1 reminds us that we have such an important opportunity in front of us that we run the risk of greater judgment if we are derelict in our duties. This is a strong word that helps us understand the great influence we have when we help our students learn about God's Word.

Being a teacher means participating in one of the church's greatest tasks, one that the ancient church called "catechesis." While this word is often associated with particular denominations and with a form of teaching that relies upon a systematic question-and-answer format, the central meaning of the word is teaching. It carries with it the idea of imparting the entirety of the faith to Christians. While many might not be familiar with this word, the truth is that every time we help others learn about God's Word and ways, we are participating in this great task of the church that has been with us from the beginning. Our participation in catechesis is central to the life of the church. As a teacher, you have an opportunity to energize or revitalize this aspect of your church's ministry. Reflect on how you have prepared for the challenge.

What is the goal when you use *Precepts For Living*® to open up the riches of the Bible to your students? It is beyond the mere acquisition of "spiritual data." Certainly we want our students to grow in knowledge, but the knowledge we seek to pass on does not solely comprise Bible facts but includes a larger sense of transformation where the information and doctrine conveyed is oriented toward a faithful life of discipleship. It is very important that we enable our students to deepen their devotion to God and encourage them to better embody that devotion in a way that makes their lives a living witness to the world. Our hope from every lesson should be to inspire students to become the best living examples of the Scriptures with the understanding that their lives may be the only Bible some people ever read.

To best take advantage of this commentary and enhance the classroom experience, utilize the essays highlighting notable African Americans to emphasize quarterly themes.

The People, Places, and Times; Background; In Depth; and More Light on the Text sections are there to help you provide insight and understanding of the text. But the sections include more than a simple compilation of information. In each lesson, you will also see In Focus stories and Lesson in Our Society and Make It Happen sections serving as catalysts for applying the biblical text to life situations.

We believe this commentary is a great tool to help form fully devoted followers of Christ, and we invite you to wholeheartedly partake in all of the resources provided here. May God be glorified as you play your part in this great task of the church!

Creative Teaching

• **Energizing the Class.** Teacher enthusiasm energizes every classroom. The instructor who is excited about the lesson and who is well-prepared inspires students to learn. Engage the class with media such as videos and music. Also, allow students time to meet and greet one another. Invite them to share a brief testimony about their week.

• **Two Teachers in One Class**—Team-teaching is fun! As teachers study and prepare together, iron sharpens iron for creative lessons that never bore. Encourage teachers to study together, and then divide the segments of the lesson. Perhaps one will teach the introduction while the other teaches a section of the text. Encourage them to also become a true team with each contributing throughout the lesson.

• **Remember.** Everyone cannot read or write on the same level. Use different teaching techniques and styles when teaching. How you learn affects how you teach, so be open and willing to learn and teach through various media.

• **Avoid Study in Isolation.** People often "get it" when they are involved with more than talking about the lesson. Why not allow the class to see the connections themselves? Try using a chart to have adult students work in pairs or groups to compare and contrast Bible persons such as David and Solomon or Ruth and Orpah, Naomi's daughters-in-law. To help the students get started, suggest specific categories for comparisons such as lifestyles, families, or public ministry. As class members search the Scriptures, they will learn and remember much more than if you told them about either person.

• **Group Studies.** Have the class form groups, and have each group read the Scripture lesson and a section of the Background for the text. Have each group create a two-minute skit about the Scripture to share with the class. Encourage the groups to use their imaginations and energy. You may want to have at least one "leader" in a group if you have more than two or three reserved people in your class.

• **Volunteers.** Many classes begin with reading the lesson. When class members have studied, this activity is more "bringing minds" together than about the actual lesson. Still, some classes can benefit from dramatic and creative reading of Bible passages at any point in the lesson. When the passage under study lends itself, assign parts to volunteers. This need not be formal—standing up isn't even critical. This strategy works best in passages that have a story such as the conversation between Moses and his father-in-law, Jethro, or Paul confronting the merchants in Thessalonica. Assign one person to each speaking character in the Bible text. Feel free to be creative with giving the class roles as "the crowd." Make sure to assign a narrator who will read the nonspeaking parts. It is fun, it is fast, and it makes for memorable Bible reading.

• **Alternatives.** Select one or two persons from the class to read the Scripture lesson with enthusiasm and drama. Ask a few people to develop a newspaper or magazine headline with a brief story that explains the headlines. Have another group write the headlines and a story that will be used in a cell phone video. (Let the class know that they should bring their cell phones—with video recording—so that most people can share in this activity.)

• **Materials.** You may want to have large sheets of paper, markers, glue or tape, newspapers, and magazines available on a weekly basis for the various activities.

• **Additional Methods.** Write the theme on a large poster board or sheet of paper, and ask each person to write a word or draw a picture that best describes the theme. Read the themes aloud, and discuss any of the pictures before you begin your class discussion or activities. If you have a very large class or time is limited, only select a few words and/or pictures for discussion. You can either lead the discussion or invite members of the class to do so.

• **Web sites.** Connect with us by logging on to urbanministries.com. E-mail us at precepts @urbanministries.com, and send us some of your favorite Teaching Tips for ages 18 and older that you want to share with others. If yours is selected, we will post them under our Teaching Tips sections for Precepts. If you have icebreaker activities, please submit them as well. Your submissions should be no longer than 125 words.

• **Closing.** At the end of the lesson, give your class the assignment of looking for scenes from films or television, advertisements, or parts of songs that either demonstrate the coming week's In Focus story, Lesson in Our Society section, or Make It Happen section. Encourage them to be creative and to come up with an explanation of how their contribution helps make the truth of the lesson come to life.

• **Prayer.** Have a Prayer Request Board for people to write their prayer requests on each Sunday. You may want to make this a weekly activity. Have someone read the prayer requests and let the class decide which prayer requests they will pray for during the week. One Sunday School teacher has his class write their prayer requests on sheets of paper and place them in the middle of the floor once a year. He then shares with the class that he will write them all down in a prayer journal that he keeps and prays over them at least once a week. Be creative and create your own prayer journal or prayer tradition(s) within your class.

Questions Related to the Heritage Profiles:

1. Why are some people chosen over others to be recognized for their achievements?

2. When reading the Heritage Profiles, what contemporary person comes to mind? A family member or friend can be a part of your decision.

3. Have you ever been recognized for a special achievement? How did you feel, and who have you lifted up to receive a special award in your church, community, or family? Why?

4. List three things you believe are important that someone else knows.

5. What similarities do you see between the historical figure and your life? If there are none, share ways the person's life might have made an impact on your life and on future generations.

6. List three characteristics that stand out about the Heritage Profiles that you think are either positive or negative. List three characteristics about your life that you believe are either positive or negative. Compare the lists and write a short paragraph about the similarities and/or differences.

Remember that creative teaching can maximize your students' learning experience.

TABLE OF CONTENTS

Fall Quarter 2017

COVENANT WITH GOD

LESSONS
Unit 1 • Signs of God's Covenants
SEPTEMBER

Unit 2 • Called into Covenant with God
OCTOBER

Unit 3 • An Everlasting Covenant
NOVEMBER

Winter Quarter 2017-2018

FAITH IN ACTION

LESSONS
Unit 1 • The Early Church Proclaims Faith in Christ

Unit 2 • A Living Faith in God
JANUARY

Unit 3 • Self-Controlled, Upright, and Godly Faith
FEBRUARY

2016–2019 Scope and Sequence—Cycle Spread

	FALL	WINTER	SPRING	SUMMER
YEAR ONE 2016–17	**GOD SOVEREIGNTY** **Sovereignty of God** Isaiah Matthew Hebrews Revelation	**CREATION** **Creation: A Divine Cycle** Psalms Luke Galatians	**LOVE** **God Loves Us** Psalms Joel Jonah John Romans Ephesians 1 John	**CALL** **God's Urgent Call** Exodus Judges Isaiah Jeremiah Ezekiel Amos Acts
YEAR TWO 2017–18	**COVENANT** **Covenant with God** Genesis Exodus Numbers 1 Samuel 2 Samuel Nehemiah Jeremiah Ezekiel 1 Corinthians Titus Hebrews	**FAITH** **Faith in Action** Daniel Matthew Acts Ephesians Colossians 1 Timothy James	**WORSHIP** **Acknowledging God** Genesis Exodus Leviticus 2 Chronicles Psalms Luke John 2 Corinthians Hebrews Revelation	**JUSTICE** **Justice in the New Testament** Matthew Luke Romans 2 Corinthians Colossians
YEAR THREE 2018–19	**CREATION** **God's World and God's People** Genesis	**LOVE** **Our Love for God** Exodus Deuteronomy Joshua Psalms Matthew Mark Luke Philippians 2 Thessalonians James 2 John	**CALL** **Discipleship and Mission** Matthew Luke Romans	**COVENANT** **Covenant in God** Ruth 1 Samuel Matthew Luke John Ephesians Hebrews Romans

A Covenant Keeping God

Usually when we see rainbows, it is just a chance for us to take in God's beauty. As a child, we would drink from the water hose and sometimes you could see a small rainbow behind it. Occasionally we would have the chance to see a rainbow that covered the sky after an evening or afternoon of torrential rain. For us it was just another beautiful piece of God's creation.

Then in Sunday School, we learned a deeper meaning for the rainbow. The rainbow is actually a reminder of God's promise to Noah. In Genesis 9, God made a covenant with Noah that Ge would not destroy the earth with water again. The rainbow is a sign of God's covenant. It is a warrior's bow turned upward to heaven instead of down at the earth. After it rains, God communicates that His wrath will no longer to be expressed through a great earth-covering flood.

The rainbow is also a reminder that God's promises remain. The old folks used to say, "If God said it, I believe it and that settles it." God is not a liar. His Word is always true. He never changes. His Word is immutable. So if God makes a promise, He will keep it.

Our reality is that as human,s we cannot keep our word. We can't even say that we are going to do something without saying "the Lord willing." We grow up with our parents and friends many times breaking promises made to us. Our leaders and politicians also continually only make promises to get into office, and have no intention of keeping them. We are very used to people breaking promises.

The one thing this shows us is that we cannot put our trust in the things of this world. The relationships and possessions we invest in are not enduring. In one way or another, they will always let us down.

That's because this world is flawed and sinful. Ever since Adam and Eve disobeyed God's law and sin entered the world, everything has been corrupt, including the promises of others. The fact is that due to our sinful nature, we are all promise breakers and ultimately cannot keep our word outside of Jesus Christ. This is in stark contrast to the holiness and the veracity of God, who cannot break His word.

Despite all of this, many times we trust in the things of this world and the words of humans. We jump at the changes in the stock market and economy. We become bitter at the decisions of public officials. Many times,

the people and conditions of this world hold more sway over us than God and His Word.

This world is temporary; it is not permanent. Our lives are a vapor and we spend a short time on this earth. During that short time, we see different nations rise and fall. Companies boom and then go out of business. Athletes reach their peak and then languish out of the spotlight. When you look at the people who are famous today, you can guarantee that they will not always be so. They will experience their "15 minutes of fame," and then that same notoriety they are experiencing will rest on someone else.

The world is changing at a rapid rate. Moore's Law states that processing speeds or overall processing power will double every two years. We can see this taking place right before our eyes as we see the widespread use of smartphone devices and artificial intelligence. With this kind of rapid technological change, there is no telling what the future holds for us.

In light of all of this change, we must put our trust in God's promises. Only He remains stable and sure. His words never change. We can stand on His promises because He is an eternal covenant-keeping God.

When God makes a promise, you can take it to the bank. All throughout the Bible, beginning with Noah, we see God making covenants with His people. These covenants were constantly broken due to unfaithfulness on the part of humanity. In contrast, the Lord keeps His covenant in spite of our sinfulness.

God is also eternal. Regardless of what is going on in the government or economy, the Lord will remain the same. Politicians may lie. The economy may go up and down. The Lord's Word will always remain. We can always put our faith and hope in Him.

Not only that, but we have a new covenant, sealed with the blood of Christ. Through this new covenant, we have forgiveness of our sins. We have peace and joy and are adopted as the children of God. Through this covenant, we have eternal life in the kingdom.

This covenant gives us peace with our past. Because we have forgiveness of our sins, we don't have to live in guilt and shame. Because of this covenant, there is no need to regret and worry about the past. God has forgiven us of our sins and cast them away from us as far as the East is from the West.

This covenant also gives us joy in our present. Because we are justified in Christ, we have the joy of being God's adopted children. We can rejoice because no matter what happens to us in this life, we are the children of God. Unemployment or racial injustice doesn't change that. God's Word says that no matter what we experience, we can never be separated from His love. That is something that can give you joy no matter what you read on the news.

This new covenant also gives us hope for the future. It is hope that was purchased with Jesus' sacrifice on the Cross. Now, through faith in Him, we have eternal life. We not only have joy in the present but also the promise of joy for all eternity. The trials and tribulations of right now can't outweigh the future joy we will experience as we live in the presence of God forever.

Yes, the world is changing. Our nation is going through all kinds of chaos. Wars and fighting are occurring all over the world as we speak. The boundaries of nations and governments are being rearranged and restructured. As much as the world is changing, we have this new covenant that never changes. It was sealed with the blood of God's own Son. Just like the rainbow that God placed in the sky, we are reminded we have a covenant we can stand on. We can put our trust in this covenant and the covenant-keeping God who made it.

Covenant with God

This quarter considers the major covenants that God makes with people on behalf of the earth and humanity. Beginning with Noah, God promises goodness toward creation. Similar commitments are made with Abram, Phinehas, and Ezekiel. Ultimately, the covenant forms the foundation for the coming Messiah and salvation for the world.

UNIT 1 • SIGNS OF GOD'S COVENANTS

The four lessons in this unit are drawn from Genesis and Ezekiel, celebrating four signs of God's covenant. Promising to renew the cycle of seasons, God creates the rainbow as a permanent reminder of the covenant with every living thing. Circumcision is the sign of the covenant with Abraham and the Sabbath is the sign of the covenant with Israel at Mount Sinai. The last sign is the Spirit-filled heart.

Lesson 1: September 3, 2017
The Rainbow
Genesis 8:20–22, 9:8–17

After tragedy strikes, people have possibilities to seek renewed hope and strength to rebuild their lives. Is there a reliable source humans can turn to for rebuilding and protecting their lives? God used the rainbow to assure Noah that neither humankind nor the earth would ever again be destroyed by water.

Lesson 2: September 10, 2017
Circumcision
Genesis 17:1–14

Humans have an innate desire to support their children and ensure their future. What is required to make this possible? God used circumcision to ratify an everlasting covenant between God and Abram.

Lesson 3: September 17, 2017
Sabbath Observance
Exodus 31:12–18

Multitasking, complex job responsibilities, and diverse family structures and commitments can make people feel overwhelmed. How can one find relief from the tedious and mundane? God commanded Moses and the Israelites to rest on the Sabbath and keep it holy as a sign of their reverence to Him.

Lesson 4: September 24, 2017
Spirit-Filled Heart
Ezekiel 36:22–32

People stubbornly follow their own agendas without regard to the impact of their actions on those they respect and admire. What will motivate these people to change? God will give them new hearts and put a new spirit in their hearts.

UNIT 2 • CALLED INTO COVENANT WITH GOD

Five lessons drawn from Genesis, Exodus, 2 Samuel, and Nehemiah illustrate God's partnership with people who respond and agree to obey His voice. God enters into covenant with Abraham, Moses, and David to work through history, establishing a kingdom that will ultimately bring forth the Messiah. Based on covenant with God, Israel is chosen as His special people.

Lesson 5: October 1, 2017
God's Covenant with Abram
Genesis 15:1–6, 17–21

Desperate from past disappointments and failures, people fear a continued downward spiral of unfulfilled dreams and goals. How can people find hope to reach fulfillment in life? Although childless, Abram based his hope for descendants on the promises of his covenant with the faithful God.

Lesson 6: October 8, 2017
God's Covenant with Israel
Exodus 19:16–25

Because of their human weakness, people need help from beyond themselves. How do people engage a power stronger and different than themselves? In making a covenant with the holy and powerful God, the people of Israel consecrated themselves to stand in His awesome presence.

Lesson 7: October 15, 2017
Obeying God's Law
Exodus 20:18–26

Without obedience to law, people live in chaos, hurting themselves, others, and their environment. Where can people get a law that they will obey? God delivered the commandments to the Israelites while showing divine and holy power that tested them to convince them to obey the laws of the covenant.

Lesson 8: October 22, 2017
God's Covenant with David
2 Samuel 7:1–6, 8–10, 12–16

When entering into relationships with others, people struggle to retain control of their plans and dreams. How can people sacrifice control in order to maintain vital relationships? God's covenant with David is a compromise between the eternal, omnipresent God and the time- and space-bound David by allowing a temple to be built, but beyond David's lifetime.

Lesson 9: October 29, 2017
God's Covenant with the Returned Exiles
Nehemiah 9:32–38, 10:28–29

People find themselves in painful consequences of their own wrongdoing. In the embarrassing angst of suffering for their own wrongs, how can they dare ask for help from others? The people of Israel followed Nehemiah in confessing their wrongs and making a covenant with God to obey the law given through Moses.

UNIT 3 • AN EVERLASTING COVENANT

The four lessons in this unit are drawn from Numbers, 1 Samuel, Jeremiah, Hebrews, and 1 Corinthians and examine the components of the covenant God makes with the priest Phinehas and the divine promise to Israel through the prophet Jeremiah. The unconditional divine promises are to maintain a perpetual priesthood, forgive the unfaithful, and establish a new covenant with God's people. God seals this covenant of pure grace through Christ as mediator and by writing the law in the hearts of His people.

Lesson 10: November 5, 2017
Faithful God, Unfaithful People
Numbers 25:10–13; 1 Samuel 2:30–36

Some people are more faithful to their commitments than others. How do we respond to those who are faithful to their commitments and to those who are not? God rewarded faithful Phinehas and punished Eli's unfaithful children.

Lesson 11: November 12, 2017
Mediator of the New Covenant
Jeremiah 31:27–34

Try as we might, humans often fail in our relationships. How can we restore broken relationships with others? Jeremiah foresaw a time when God would make a new covenant, writing His law on human hearts with the vow to be Israel's God and to make Israel His people.

Lesson 12: November 19, 2017
Mediator of the New Covenant
Hebrews 12:14–15, 18–29

Humans desire to experience a power greater than themselves, but do not always realize that drawing near to such needed power can be an awesome prospect. How can people approach such a power without being consumed? The psalmist affirms that God allows humans to approach the divine; the writer of Hebrews proclaims that Jesus provides the means of boldly approaching the presence of God.

Lesson 13: November 26, 2017
Remembering the Covenant
1 Corinthians 11:23–34

It is often easier to make promises than to keep them. How can we remember to keep the promises we make? Paul exhorted believers to remember these promises through celebrating the Lord's Supper.

3

Teaching Covenant

by Allen Reynolds

Covenant is one of the most important concepts to understand in the Christian faith. The Bible teaches the relationship between God and humanity in terms of covenant. The covenants of the Old Testament are between God and the people of Israel, and the covenant of the New Testament is between Jesus and His disciples and by extension, God and all humanity who receive Jesus as their Savior. The Old Testament covenants are the covenant between God and Noah, God and Abraham, God and Moses (and Israel), and God and David. The two most recognizable covenants in many churches are the covenant with Moses (Mosaic covenant), also known as the "old covenant," and the covenant extended through Jesus called the "new covenant," which is the foundation of Christian faith.

A covenant is more relational than a very strong contract between two parties, although like a contract, it must have a promise and something exchanged in order to make it work properly. Covenants in the ancient world typically required not only an exchange, but also a sign that the exchange occurred. Covenants could be made between two people, two families, or between God and a person or family. The covenant implies a special, exclusive relationship between the two parties. Covenants between God and humans in the world of the Old Testament typically required a blood sacrifice from an animal as a sealing of the covenant. A sign could be given such as building an altar on the spot where the covenant was made.

A covenant typically has four components:
1. A promiser (God in the case of many of the biblical covenants)
2. Something exchanged (sacrifice and promise to obey) and given (promise and benefits)
3. A sign of the agreement (treasured objects, circumcision, blood, etc.)
4. A promisee (receiver of the promise)

A covenant where something is required in exchange to uphold the covenant is called a conditional covenant. An unconditional covenant is where the promiser binds themselves to the covenant's fulfillment, regardless of whether the other party fulfills their covenant obligations.

In teaching and discipling those in the church, we must be very clear on the definition and importance of the concept of covenant as a major theme in the Bible. Without this concept, we are in the dark as to how our relationship with God works.

Many people operate as if they are under the law. They treat their relationship with God as conditional. They live and act as if they are under obligation to perform certain works in order for God to love them and to be in relationship with Him. That's not the covenant we are under. We are operating under the new covenant, a conditional covenant based on the unconditional love of God. It means that God loves us no matter what, we simply receive the covenant by grace through faith and we are motivated to live for Him because of the knowledge of that grace.

Therefore it is imperative in teaching this concept to make sure that students and new believers know the implications of the new covenant. They need to know why it is better than the old covenant. They need to know how each of the covenants are related and whether they are discarded or fulfilled in Christ. It is also important to help them understand the blessings and the benefits of the covenant relationship they have with God through Jesus Christ. It is only through rehearsing these blessings that we can get beyond legalism and into the freedom of living to please God.

As stated, a covenant is like a contract, but it is also very distinct from a contract in at least one significant way. A contract is a promise of goods or services between two parties, but a covenant is the promise of the person and their whole being. This is why covenants in the Bible were serious. They were entered into and understood as a life agreement, with death as the penalty for breaking it. A breach of covenant is like an assault ot the covenant partner. Although seriously entered into and laden with penalties and rewards, contracts do not carry the same weight from a biblical standpoint.

One of the easiest ways to understand covenant is to compare it to marriage. Christian marriage is a covenant between two people that is exclusive and binding, intended for lifelong relationship. When you are married to someone, you should not also be married to someone else. Likewise, God expects exclusive commitment in His covenants that we do not have other gods. Marriage is intended to be a conditional covenant with both people making promises to uphold the marriage even if the other person does not perfectly fulfill his or her promise. The sacrifice or exchange in a marriage is all of me for all of you, all of the husband for all of the wife, submitting to one another mutually, and the two becoming one flesh. In many Western cultures the signs of the marriage covenant are the wedding and the rings as a remembrance. The benefit is lifelong relationship.

Paul says that marriage between believers is supposed to be a reflection of the relationship between Christ and His church. Jesus gave His life for His bride on the Cross and He lives for and in the church still. Likewise, Jesus asks that we, the church, give our lives to be in relationship with and serve Him as His bride. We as Christians are in a covenant relationship with God. Jesus' death, burial, and resurrection are the blessed assurance that our God has brought us into right relationship both in this life and eternity.

Allen Reynolds, M.Div., is the Editor of Adult & Customized Content at UMI.

Faithful God, Unfaithful People

by Michael Roussell

Introduction

The Bible is a record of God's faithfulness to a faithless people. Those of us who are disciples of the Lord Jesus Christ have been blessed beyond measure. The Bible reminds us, however, "For unto whomsoever much is given, of him shall be much required: and to whom men have committed much, of him they will ask the more" (from Luke 12:48).

The good news is that we have been entrusted with the Gospel. Jesus experienced death and separation from the Father, which all unfaithful humanity truly deserves. Our faithful God brought us out of darkness by way of the blood of Jesus and gave us the power to become faithful followers of Him.

Many people in the church, whether due to bad teaching or bad theology, struggle with assurance of salvation. They wonder whether their sin cancels out God's love and promises toward them. To this, we can answer with an unequivocal "No!" In fact, in going back to the Old Testament, Ezekiel substantiates God's faithfulness. The Lord promises to bless even unfaithful people in spite of themselves (Ezekiel 36:22–26).

Israel's Unfaithfulness

In the account of Hosea and Gomer's marriage, we see the record of Gomer's unfaithfulness due to infidelity. Here we find the example of Hosea's provision for a wife who ignored his faithfulness and generosity, ultimately taking for granted his fidelity and goodness to her. Just as Gomer was found unfaithful to Hosea, Israel was found unfaithful to God by worshiping other gods. Israel had put their trust in Baal rather than God.

However, Hosea uses the term "plead" (Hosea 2:2) (Heb. *ryb*, **REEV**), which means to contend or strive physically or with words. The hope is that this plea will result in conviction and that Gomer would change her ways and repent. God's charge against Israel was that they were an adulterous people. Hosea warns the people that a judgment will come if Israel doesn't adhere to the warnings. Nevertheless, the prosperity and blessing they falsely attributed to another god was terminated by God Himself (Hosea 7:14). The Israelites were conquered by Assyria, and their nation became desolate. For the Israelites, this was a sure sign that they were far from God. However this was not the final word, as God ultimately brought about restoration to a repentant and forgiven Israel.

Humanity's Unfaithfulness

Israel's unfaithfulness only mirrors the unfaithfulness of all humanity. This can clearly be seen in the book of Hosea. Israel's characteristics described in Hosea's prophecies are a microcosm of the unfaithfulness of all humanity—in religion, commerce, and politics.

Religion—"And as troops of robbers wait for a man, so the company of priests murder in the way by consent: for they commit lewdness" (Hosea 6:9).

Commerce—"He is a merchant, the balances of deceit are in his hand: he loveth to oppress" (Hosea 12:7).

Politics—"Ephraim feedeth on wind, and followeth after the east wind: he daily increaseth lies and desolation; and they do make a covenant with the Assyrians, and oil is carried into Egypt" (Hosea 12:1).

These different categories of unfaithfulness can still be seen today. Humanity's general trajectory toward unfaithfulness is oftentimes simply recognized as the covenantal definition of sin. From Genesis to Revelation, we have documentation of humanity's unfaithfulness and societal unrighteousness that only the blood of Jesus can wipe away.

Unfaithfulness and the African American Community

In the specific context of the African American community, we can see a people who held on to God through unbearable oppression. Trials and tribulations did not sway or extinguish the faith of those who were wounded every day under the taskmaster's lash and the discrimination of the Jim Crow era. This faith empowered them to press on for justice and overcome barriers. As they sought change and weathered the storms of life, God was central to their quest. The songs and hymns of the Black church buoyed them with joy and hope for a better day. The prophetic preaching of men such as Bishop Henry McNeal Turner and Rev. Martin Luther King Jr. opened up possibilities for those who believed "Trouble Don't Last Always."

Although many factors contribute to the overall negative outcomes experienced by many in the black community, a case can still be made for the lack of authentic faithfulness to God and His word. Soon after gaining civil rights and breaking the chains of segregation, the African American community began a significant drift toward unfaithfulness to God. Massive problems in the inner city and economic upheaval led to a variety of vices and the devastation of once tight-knit, thriving communities. Churches began to be complacent, and many pastors turned to fame and wealth as goals for their ministries. In short, the African American community mirrored Israel in its unfaithfulness. In the same manner as Israel, "they forgot what he had done—the great wonders he had shown them" (Psalm 78:11). In spite of having access to unprecedented prosperity—or maybe because of it—many have turned their back on God or just go through the motions of religion, much like the Israelites in Hosea's day.

Conclusion

Paul tells Timothy and us, "If we endure, we shall also reign with him: if we shall deny him, he also will deny us: if we are faithless, he abideth faithful; for he cannot deny himself" (2 Timothy 2:12–13). In spite of what we do, God has not left us alone. He is no respecter of persons. To see the change that we want to see in our communities, it behooves us to seek God and repent of our ways. He is still a faithful God who wants covenant relationship with a faithful people, no matter what race or ethnicity.

Michael Roussell is an adjunct professor at Trinity International University in Deerfield, IL. He is also the Presiding Bishop of the Chicagoland Ministerial Alliance.

Covenant Faithfulness

by Rabbi Jason Sobel

The idea of covenant, *berit* in Hebrew, forms the foundation of how God operates and interacts with humanity. You can't fully understand God's relationship with believers or salvation history without understanding the concept of covenant. Despite the great spiritual importance and practical significance of covenant for the life of the believer, the concept of covenant is often neglected and misunderstood. Concerning the importance of covenants, Andrew Murray beautifully writes:

"Blessed is the man who truly knows God as his God; who knows what the Covenant promises him; what unwavering confidence of expectation it secures, that all its [covenant's] terms will be fulfilled to him; what a claim and hold it gives him on the Covenant-keeping God Himself. To many a man, who has never thought much of the Covenant, a true and living faith in it would mean the transformation of his whole life. The full knowledge of what God wants to do for him; the assurance that it will be done by an Almighty Power; the being drawn to God Himself in personal surrender, and dependence, and waiting to have it done; all this would make the Covenant the very gate of heaven. May the Holy Spirit give us some vision of its glory." (Andrew Murray, The Two Covenants, 14)

The basic definition of a covenant is a "binding legal relationship between two or more people, nations, or parties." In Jewish Rabbinic thought, a covenant is understood to be "a permanent bond between two parties, symbolizing a friendship so close that they are like a single body and that each is as responsible for each for the other as for himself" (Artscroll Bereshis Commentary, 519–520). A covenant can be understood more broadly defined when between nations as "a treaty, alliance of friendship; between individuals: a pledge or agreement; with obligation between a monarch and subjects: a constitution; between God and man: a covenant accompanied by signs, sacrifices, and a solemn oath that sealed the relationship with promises of blessing for keeping the covenant and cursed for breaking it" (Theological Wordbook of the Old Testament 1:128).

The most common form of covenant in the Ancient Near East was a suzerainty treaty. This type of covenant was entered into between a powerful emperor known as a suzerain, and a vassal, subject, or dependent entity such as a state. These types of covenants legally laid out covenant stipulations, consequences for faithfully keeping or breaking it, witnesses, the duration of the covenant, and how the covenant could be renewed. There was also a religious element to the establishment of any covenant in the Near East, which always included a ritual animal sacrifice (Genesis 15:9), a meal shared between the participants (Genesis 21:27, Exodus 24:11), and covenant signs, an external symbol and reminder of each party's commitment and covenantal obligations.

Looking biblically at the different biblical covenants, there are seven keys we can learn about the nature of covenants in general: 1) biblical covenants are multi-generational and in some cases eternal; 2) covenants are legally binding; 3) covenants are cut, which means that sacrifices were offered as a part of the process of entering into a covenant; 4) covenants can be bi-lateral or unilateral; 5) covenants can be conditional or unconditional; 6) covenants require a means of atonement when broken by one of the parties; and 7) breaking a covenant has severe ramifications. Key biblical covenants that the Lord made include the Noachic covenant (Genesis 8–9), the Abrahamic covenant (Genesis 12, 15, 17), the Sinai covenant (Exodus 19–20), the Davidic covenant (2 Samuel 7), and the new covenant (Jeremiah 31).

The primary covenant that sets the foundations for all the other biblical covenants is the Abrahamic covenant. As part of this covenant, the Lord promised Abraham seed—heirs who inherit and carry forward the blessings and legacy divinely promised to him and Sarah. But when Abraham and his wife became advanced in years, the Lord appeared to Abraham again and promised him "a very great reward," to which he responded, "You have given me no descendants of my own, so one of my servants will be my heir" (Genesis 15:3, NLT). But the Lord spoke to him and said, "You will have a son of your own who will be your heir" (from v. 4). Despite the fact that he and his wife were in their 70s, way past child-bearing years, Abraham believed the Lord without question and knew by faith that Sarah would conceive and bear a son. This absolute belief in the Lord and His promises led God to count "him as righteous because of his faith" (from v. 6).

God then responded by making another promise, "I am the LORD who brought you out of Ur of the Chaldeans to give you this land as your possession" (v. 7). How did Abraham, the father of the faith, respond? He asked the Lord, "How can I be sure that I will actually possess it?" Why did Abraham, this man of great faith, need a sign? How could you believe God without hesitation about the promise of a miraculous son, but then turn around and need a sign about the Promised Land? Did his faith turn to doubt suddenly? Look how the Lord responds: He made covenant with Abraham, known as the *berit bein ha-betarim*, which translates as "covenant between the parts."

What accounts for Abraham's request for a sign and his seeming lack of faith in God's promise to him and his seed to inherit the land? Before the covenant between the parts, Abraham saw his relationship with God as contractual in nature. If he obeyed the Lord, then he and his family would be blessed, but if he disobeyed, then he would lose the blessing. Until this point, Abraham saw God's promise to him as more transactional. Contracts normally place obligations on all parties who enter into them. Both participants must fulfill their contractual obligations, or else face serious consequences including but not limited to the contract becoming null and void.

This was Abraham's concern—he viewed His relationship with God as a contract. What if in the future his seed messed up and sinned, which he knew was inevitable? He must have wondered if this would cause his progeny to forfeit the blessing of inheriting the Promised Land, just like the Amorites and the other Canaanite peoples. For this reason, Abraham needed a sign from God concerning the Land, but not concerning the promise of a child. He was concerned that future generations would not be worthy of the land, and he was right.

He wanted a guarantee from the Lord to assure him and ease his anxiety.

God, who is gracious and compassionate, assuages Abraham's fear in Genesis 15 by helping him understand that their relationship was not transactional or contractual in nature but rather uniquely covenantal: it was based on a special type of covenant, a *berit* in Hebrew. In the Ancient Near East, the most common form of covenant was bilateral. When two parties entered this type of covenant, animals would be sacrificed and cut down the middle into two parts, and both parties would walk between the parts symbolizing that the one who does not keep his end of the covenant agreement would be torn apart like the dead carcasses that they just passed between. It was as if one was saying, "If I break my oath and do not keep the promises made, may what occurred to these animals happen to me."

This common type of covenant was conditional and bilateral, meaning that both parties had to keep the covenantal stipulations or else all commitments would become void. These types of covenantal agreements were contractual in nature, and like the suzerain-vassel treaties of the Ancient Near East, were commonly made between individuals, tribes, and nations. But the type of treaty that God entered into with Abraham as well as David, and with us through the new covenant, was not this type of covenant. These covenants bear many similarities to Near Eastern suzerain treaties, but were significantly different in several key ways.

The type of covenant the Lord entered into with Abraham was different than the norm in that it was a unilateral and unconditional covenant. This is seen by the fact that God put Abraham into a deep sleep before He alone passed through the parts of the covenantal sacrifices (Genesis 15:12–20). The nature of the covenant assured Abraham that God's relationship with him was not contractual or transactional, but an unconditional and eternal covenant. Abraham was asleep and passive at the time this covenant was made, meaning that the Lord is the guarantor. Even when Abraham's children disobeyed and rebelled, they could not permanently forfeit the covenantal promises the Lord made to Abraham.

The covenant between the parts that God made with Abraham is the basis for both the Davidic covenant as well as the new covenant. Paul makes this clear in Galatians: "God gave the promises to Abraham and his child. ... This is what I am trying to say: The agreement God made with Abraham could not be canceled 430 years later when God gave the law to Moses. God would be breaking his promise. For if the inheritance could be received by keeping the law, then it would not be the result of accepting God's promise. But God graciously gave it to Abraham as a promise" (Galatians 3:16–18, NLT).

God's covenant with Israel, the biological descendants of Abraham, which Paul writes of in Romans 9–11, is founded upon the unconditional, unilateral, and eternal nature of the Abrahamic covenant. Paul's theological argument that the church has not replaced Israel is not just a matter of theology, but an essential aspect of understanding God's covenantal faithfulness to all believers.

Some scholars believe that Romans 9–11 is actually a theological rabbit trail, more technically known as an excursus. But Paul's discourse on Israel is central and foundational to the theological case he is making and its practical spiritual application. For this reason, Romans 9–11 is the bridge between Paul's soteriology (doctrine of salvation) in Romans 1–8 and his practical theology in Romans 12–16. In relationship to the great salvation of the Lord, Paul discusses justification by faith, sanctification, and glorification. Then in Romans 8, he lays out his theological understanding of glorification, which culminates in vv. 37–38.

After laying this foundational and breathtaking theological discourse on salvation and glorification, Paul devotes three chapters to speaking about Israel in Romans 9–11. He begins in Romans 9 by writing about Israel's past riches and then discusses the misdirected zeal that led them to reject Jesus as the Messiah (Romans 10), then concludes in Romans 11 by making the case that despite their unbelief, God has not only not rejected Israel but actually has a glorious future in store for them.

God's gracious choice not to reject Israel is central to Paul's entire theological argument in Romans 8:38–39, where he states in connection to the ultimate promise of glorification that "For I am persuaded, that neither death, nor life, nor angels, nor principalities, nor powers, nor things present, nor things to come, Nor height, nor depth, nor any other creature, shall be able to separate us from the love of God, which is in Christ Jesus our Lord."

These few chapters on covenant in Romans are key in establishing our own theology—a beautiful look at God's character in offering salvation, sanctification, and glorification to us all. If the Lord had rejected Israel and the covenant promises He made with Abraham, Isaac, Jacob, and David, how could we be sure that He would not do the same for any believer who sins? If something separated Israel from His promises based on the covenant He made with Abraham, how could we be sure that truly nothing "shall be able to separate us from the love of God, which is in Christ Jesus" (Romans 8:39)? In these chapters, Paul is arguing that because God faithfully kept His covenant with Israel and will ultimately fulfill it, we can be sure He will keep His promises to all believers, whether Gentile or Jewish.

The basis of not rejecting Israel is the covenant the Lord made with the patriarchs (Romans 11:28) as well as gifts and calling of God mentioned at the opening of Romans

9, including the "the covenants, and the giving of the law" (Romans 9:4, KJV). Because God is faithful to Israel, you can be certain that the Lord will be faithful to you! He has demonstrated that nothing will ever separate you from the love that is in Christ Jesus. This could not be said if God had rejected Israel and forsook His covenant with them due to their lack of faithfulness. As part of His promise to Abraham, there will never a time when there is not a faithful remnant of Jewish people who believe. God's covenant with Abraham and his descendants was irrevocable. This is really good news for all followers of Jesus who have entered into the new covenant!

Covenants are part of God's way of operating and relating to us. His relationship with His people never was and never will be contractual or transactional. We are called to imitate the Lord in all His ways, as Rabbi Paul states, "And you should imitate me, just as I imitate Christ" (1 Corinthians 11:1, NLT). If the Lord relates to us on the basis of covenant, shouldn't all of our most important relationships be covenantal in nature?

The church, both universal and local, is meant to be a unified covenant community. Today, however, people don't see it this way. Most Christians, having been influenced by popular secular culture, approach church with a transactional consumer mentality. Too often people change their churches like they change their socks. People simply leave without even talking to the pastor because they take some offense or find something newer and more entertaining somewhere else.

This way of thinking has had really a terrible spiritual effect on the church. It's hard to grow to full maturity if you are not part of a spiritual community where people really know you. It's not enough to just listen to a messages online—every believer needs to be part of a spiritual community where they are learning, worshiping, serving, and doing life with other people who encourage them and provide good counsel when important decisions need to be made. Relationships are like sandpaper for the soul; they are meant to smooth out the rough edges. This happens most safely and effectively in the context of covenantal relationships and community.

The loss of covenantal relationship in the church has also negatively impacted marriage, which God designed to be a covenant between a man and woman. As it says in Genesis 2:24, "a man leaves his father and mother and is joined to his wife, and the two are united into one" (NLT). Today, most people, even believers, treat their marriage relationships as contractual and not covenantal in nature. We treat our spouse as our own personal ISP, Intimate Service Provider. As long as our spouse meets our needs, then everything is fine. But when our spouse fails to consistently meet our needs, divorce is seen as a logical option.

This type of selfish quid pro quo relationship is not what the Lord intended. Marriage is a covenant relationship meant to reflect the relationship between Jesus and the church (Ephesians 5:31–33). Wedding vows are actually a covenantal pledge that we should never enter into lightly. Marriage is a covenantal commitment that we make for richer or for poorer, in sickness and in health, till death do us part. When we have this sort of biblical view of covenant, then we fight for our marriage and do everything we can to honor the commitment and thereby honor the Lord.

Our Lord made clear that God intended marriage to be a lifetime relationship between a man and a woman (Matthew 19:1–10). But Moses permitted divorce because ancient Israelites had hard hearts that led to unacceptable social situations. For the same reason of hard hearts, divorce sometimes becomes inevitable in our day due to abuse, abandonment, neglect, or habitual infidelity. No matter the situation, the Lord would never want any divorced person to live under shame and condemnation. But the biblical understanding of marriage as a covenant demands that we take it very seriously and do all that is within our power to make sure our marriage works.

Quitting is not an option because we find our spouse difficult, no longer attractive, or not perfectly compatible. We should seek to deal with our spouse and all the important relationships in our lives in the same way the Lord reveals Himself to us as "slow to anger and filled with unfailing love and faithfulness. I lavish unfailing love to a thousand generations. I forgive iniquity, rebellion, and sin" (Exodus 34:6–7, NLT).

God will not forget His covenant to us, and neither should we! He is a covenant keeper and always honors His covenantal promises and commitments. Just like the Lord entered into an unconditional, unilateral covenant with Israel through Abraham, He has entered into the same with every follower of Jesus through the new covenant. Every follower of Jesus, no matter what nation they are from, has become a child of Abraham and partakers of the Abrahamic promises as members of the commonwealth of Israel (Ephesians 2:12) through the new covenant that Jesus inaugurated by His death and Resurrection. It is because of the covenant-keeping nature of the Lord that you can be sure He will fulfill His new covenant promise of abundant and eternal life. Seeing church, marriage, and family through the prism of covenant revolutionizes our relationships and demonstrates to the world the type of relationships Jesus died for and desires us to establish.

Discussion questions:
- The Lord demonstrates His character to Abraham and to us through His heart for covenant. How is the covenant God makes with Abraham different than a contract or transaction?
- How should God's covenantal nature transform how we interact with others? What should covenant community look like today?
- What is the significance of Paul's mention of the covenant-keeping nature of God in Romans 9–11, and how does this aspect of God's character impact us?
- How can we be sure God will be faithful in His promises to us?

Sources:
Harris, R. Laird, Gleason L. Archer Jr., and Bruce K. Waltke. *Theological Wordbook of the Old Testament Vol. 2.* Chicago; Moody Press, 1980.
Murray, Andrew. *The Two Covenants: Your Blessing in Christ.* Fort Washington, PA; CLC Publications, 2000.
Zolotowitz, Rabbi Meir. *Bereishis: Genesis/A New Translation with a Commentary Anthologized from Talmudic, Midrashic, and Rabbinic Sources.* New York, NY; Artscroll, 1995.

Rabbi Jason Sobel is a Christian minister, thought leader, storyteller, spiritual guide, and occasional rapper sharing transforming connections about the Messiah and His Jewish roots.

Lewis Latimer

(September 4, 1848–December 11, 1928)

Remember the name Lewis Latimer whenever you use an electric light. Born in 1848 in Chelsea, Massachusetts, Lewis was the youngest of four children. His parents, George and Rebecca, were escaped slaves from Virginia who had run away to gain their freedom. They finally settled in Boston, but their owner came to bring them back to his plantation in Virginia. Local abolitionists raised funds to pay for their freedom, which became a famous case related to the abolition of slavery.

Latimer served in the Union Navy during the Civil War, and in the rank of landsman, he did unskilled labor aboard the ship. After gaining an honorable discharge, Latimer was employed as an office worker with the patent law firm Crosby, Halstead, and Gould. This job would only earn him $3 a week. Soon he learned how to use a set square, ruler, and other tools, which helped him gain a foundation in draftsmanship. When his employer discovered his penchant for sketch drawings, he made Latimer the head draftsman, giving him a weekly salary of $20.

Soon after this, Latimer married Mary Wilson Lewis from Providence, Rhode Island. Eventually, instead of just drawing other people's inventions, Latimer began his own inventions. In 1874, he invented improved toilets for railroad cars. Over time, he became a draftsman at Alexander Graham Bell's patent law firm, and in 1876, Bell employed him to draft the drawings so that the telephone could receive a patent.

Latimer is best known for his invention of a carbon filament used in light bulbs. Although now we use tungsten, at the time Latimer's carbon filaments lasted longer than the paper ones used by Thomas Edison. Along with these inventions, Latimer received patents for a cooling and disinfecting apparatus, a locking rack for hats, coats, umbrellas, and book supports. Latimer was also hired to oversee the installation of electrical street lighting in Montreal, London, New York City, and Philadelphia.

This creative and prolific inventor lived his final years in Flushing, New York, where he taught classes and offered services for soliciting patents. He published a book of poetry before his death in 1928. Latimer was part of the group known as the Edison Pioneers, who said about him: "Broadmindedness, versatility in the accomplishment of things intellectual and cultural, a linguist, a devoted husband and father, all were characteristic of him, and his genial presence will be missed from our gatherings."

Source:
Haskins, Jim. *Outward Dreams: Black Inventors and Their Inventions.* Walker Publishing Co., 1991.

Teaching Tips

Words You Should Know

A. Curse (Genesis 8:21) *qalal* (Heb)—To make despicable, to curse.

B. Perpetual (9:12) *olam* (Heb.)—Eternal, lasting, continuance.

Teacher Preparation

Unifying Principle—Making a Promise. After tragedy strikes, people have possibilities to seek renewed hope and strength to rebuild their lives. Do humans have a reliable source they can turn to for rebuilding and protecting their lives? As an act of benevolence, God used the rainbow to assure Noah that neither humankind nor the earth would ever again be destroyed by water.

A. Read the Bible Background and Devotional Readings.

B. Pray for your students and lesson clarity.

C. Read the lesson Scripture in multiple translations.

O—Open the Lesson

A. Begin the class with prayer.

B. Have the students read the In Focus story.

C. Ask students how events named in the story can weigh on their hearts and how they can view these events from a theological perspective.

D. Have students read the Aim for Change.

P—Present the Scriptures

A. Read the Focal Verses and discuss the Background and The People, Places, and Times sections.

B. Have class share what Scriptures jump out for them and why, with particular emphasis on today's context.

E—Explore the Meaning

A. Use More Light on the Text to help provide more in-depth discussion of the lesson text.

B. Discuss the Lesson in Our Society and Make It Happen sections.

N—Next Steps for Application

A. Summarize the value of God's promises in the midst of turbulent times.

B. End class with a commitment to pray for families, communities, and the nations.

Worship Guide

For the Superintendent and Teacher
Theme: The Rainbow
Song: "I Told the Storm"
Devotional Reading: Isaiah 54:1–10

The Rainbow

Bible Background • GENESIS 8:20–9:17
Printed Text • GENESIS 8:20–22, 9:8–17 | **Devotional Reading • ISAIAH 54:1–10**

—— Aim for Change ——

By the end of this lesson, we will: COMPREHEND the rainbow as a sign of God's grace; APPRECIATE God's ability to renew our lives following difficult times; and WORSHIP God gratefully in light of His continued promises of mercy and grace.

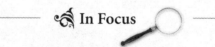

In Focus

More than ten years ago, Hurricane Katrina devastated Troy and Michelle's world. At first, they were just happy to be alive and to be together. They knew things would never be the same again. Troy and Michelle lost their home, had to leave behind all of their possessions, and both lost their jobs as a result of the storm. They couldn't see how their lives would ever be restored. So much good from the past had been washed away in the storm. The couple moved to Houston, and with the help of a church that came to their aid, they slowly regained hope.

Troy and Michelle wondered at times whether they would be whole again, but they held on to the promises of God's Word and believed that they would be restored and receive double for their trouble. The couple remained in constant prayer and made sure to study God's Word to remind them of His faithfulness. At times they couldn't see any immediate change, but they knew that God was there and that He cared for them.

Over the course of time, they were able to rebuild their careers, get a new home, and now have a nine-year-old daughter and an eight-year-old son. Troy and Michelle are careful to give God the glory for their restoration and they teach their children to trust Him.

The way in which we respond to life's ups and downs is the key to not allowing life to control our spirit. How can God's covenant give us hope to rebound after a loss?

—— Keep in Mind ——

"And I will establish my covenant with you, neither shall all flesh be cut off any more by the waters of a flood; neither shall there anymore be a flood to destroy the earth" (Genesis 9:11).

"And I will establish my covenant with you, neither shall all flesh be cut off any more by the waters of a flood; neither shall there anymore be a flood to destroy the earth" (Genesis 9:11).

Focal Verses

KJV **Genesis 8:20** And Noah builded an altar unto the LORD; and took of every clean beast, and of every clean fowl, and offered burnt offerings on the altar.

21 And the LORD smelled a sweet savour; and the LORD said in his heart, I will not again curse the ground any more for man's sake; for the imagination of man's heart is evil from his youth; neither will I again smite any more every thing living, as I have done.

22 While the earth remaineth, seedtime and harvest, and cold and heat, and summer and winter, and day and night shall not cease.

9:8 And God spake unto Noah, and to his sons with him, saying,

9 And I, behold, I establish my covenant with you, and with your seed after you;

10 And with every living creature that is with you, of the fowl, of the cattle, and of every beast of the earth with you; from all that go out of the ark, to every beast of the earth

11 And I will establish my covenant with you, neither shall all flesh be cut off any more by the waters of a flood; neither shall there anymore be a flood to destroy the earth.

12 And God said, This is the token of the covenant which I make between me and you and every living creature that is with you, for perpetual generations:

13 I do set my bow in the cloud, and it shall be for a token of a covenant between me and the earth.

14 And it shall come to pass, when I bring a cloud over the earth, that the bow shall be seen in the cloud:

15 And I will remember my covenant, which is between me and you and every living creature of all flesh; and the waters shall no more become a flood to destroy all flesh.

16 And the bow shall be in the cloud; and I will look upon it, that I may remember the

NLT **Genesis 8:20** Then Noah built an altar to the LORD, and there he sacrificed as burnt offerings the animals and birds that had been approved for that purpose.

21 And the LORD was pleased with the aroma of the sacrifice and said to himself, "I will never again curse the ground because of the human race, even though everything they think or imagine is bent toward evil from childhood. I will never again destroy all living things.

22 As long as the earth remains, there will be planting and harvest, cold and heat, summer and winter, day and night."

9:8 Then God told Noah and his sons,

9 "I hereby confirm my covenant with you and your descendants,

10 and with all the animals that were on the boat with you—the birds, the livestock, and all the wild animals—every living creature on earth.

11 Yes, I am confirming my covenant with you. Never again will floodwaters kill all living creatures; never again will a flood destroy the earth."

12 Then God said, "I am giving you a sign of my covenant with you and with all living creatures, for all generations to come.

13 I have placed my rainbow in the clouds. It is the sign of my covenant with you and with all the earth.

14 When I send clouds over the earth, the rainbow will appear in the clouds,

15 and I will remember my covenant with you and with all living creatures. Never again will the floodwaters destroy all life.

16 When I see the rainbow in the clouds, I will remember the eternal covenant between God and every living creature on earth."

everlasting covenant between God and every living creature of all flesh that is upon the earth.

17 And God said unto Noah, This is the token of the covenant, which I have established between me and all flesh that is upon the earth.

17 Then God said to Noah, "Yes, this rainbow is the sign of the covenant I am confirming with all the creatures on earth."

The People, Places, and Times

Noah A descendant of Seth, born to Adam and Eve after the death of Abel (Genesis 4:25). He was considered a righteous man who lived blameless before God during a wicked and perverse generation. Noah was the father of three sons: Shem, Ham, and Japheth (Genesis 6:9–10). According to the Hebrew account, Noah and his sons were set apart to lead the rebirth of creation.

The Flood. Stories of a flood exist within several ancient cultures to explain this catastrophic event. However, the Jewish version in Genesis 6:9–17 is unique among them in how it focused on the relationship between a monotheistic God and humanity. Although retold against the backdrop of many particular cultures, each story involves the salvation of a blameless man and a woman who were left to lead the re-population of the earth.

How does the fact that the flood story exists in so many cultures inform our telling of the story to those who may not believe?

Background

As the earth's population increased, God saw the fruit of humanity's nature from the fall—it was constantly evil. Humanity's sin and rebellion grieved His heart until it could no longer be tolerated. God declared that His holiness was not going to contend with His creation. However, Noah was counted as blameless before God in this wicked and perverse generation. God warned Noah of the coming wrath

and judgment. He told of the deluge of water that would come to put an end to the depravity. Out of His grace, God instructed Noah to build an ark to save his wife, three sons, and their wives, as well as two animals of each kind, male and female plus animals for sacrifice. Noah did as God commanded and built an ark; God promised that He would make a covenant agreement with Noah because of his obedience and uprightness. When Noah was 600 years old, God fulfilled His prophetic word to destroy the earth by water. Noah, his family, and the animals were set apart by God as survivors.

What does it mean for us to be blameless before God in the 21st century?

At-A-Glance

1. The Perpetual Promise (Genesis 8:20–22)
2. The Promise Sealed (vv. 9:8–13)
3. The Promise Meaning (vv. 14–17)

In Depth

1. The Perpetual Promise (Genesis 8:20–22)

Noah, his family, and the animals were in the ark of safety while the rest of the earth's inhabitants perished. God spoke to Noah directly to let him know that they could safely come out and inhabit the land. In an act of worship for God's protection and provision, Noah built an altar to the Lord and offered a sacrifice of burnt offerings using animals approved by Him. This act of worship was a pleasing delight to God, especially after enduring such wickedness. God's response to this sacrifice also displays His desire to be in intimate fellowship with hearts that are aligned with Him. God makes a promise that He will never curse the ground again because of humanity's inclination to sin.

Further, God promises that once again the earth will continue its seasonal rhythms because of His power, and that as long as it exists, it will continue to produce from the ground, supply cold and heat, change seasons, and continue the cycle of night and day. Humanity is still responsible for the earth's care today and should be wise in using energy resources and seeking sustainable solutions for the health of the environment.

How does God's promise to never destroy the earth with water again give the believer hope?

2. The Promise Sealed (vv. 9:8–13)

God now turns to Noah and makes a personal promise to confirm His covenant through Noah and his sons as well as those who would come after them. God also includes the animals in this promise. As a sign of His covenant agreement between Himself and His creation (which includes humanity, the animals, and the earth) for future generations, God placed a bow in the clouds. The rainbow of colors seen after a rainfall is a symbol of God's continual love and mercy. He continues to keep His promise today that no matter how torrential and destructive storms, hurricanes, or other natural water events might be, they will not destroy the entire earth as happened with the flood. We live in fallen conditions where the earth's natural progression produces events that we cannot fully explain, even with science, but God remains faithful to His covenant. This is how we can maintain hope in the midst of it all.

What can we say to a person who has experienced an act of God that resulted in a loss of loved ones or property?

3. The Promise Meaning (vv. 14–17)

God gives the rainbow and explains that it is a sign of His covenant. He forever seals His promise with the reminder of a rainbow. The rainbow should continue to serve as a reminder for humanity of God's love and good character because He continues to keep His word. God places no further conditions on humanity for the fulfillment of this covenant because it is a promise He made with Himself not to allow His wrath to manifest into destruction with water. The Noahic covenant is regarded as the basis of God's covenant relationship with all of humanity, and subsequent covenants (i.e., Abrahamic, Mosaic, and Davidic) denote His special relationship with Israel. However, the last covenant between God and humanity supersedes them all as Jesus Christ is the fulfillment of these covenants (Hebrews 8:6–13).

How can we remind ourselves of God's good character and His love for us?

Search the Scriptures

1. Do you think the Lord's promise to not destroy the earth with water was a response to Noah's burnt offering? Why or why not (Genesis 8:21–22)?

2. Why was it necessary for God to give Noah and his sons a sign of the covenant (9:12–15)?

Discuss the Meaning

1. How should we see nature's constants (seedtime and harvest, cold and heat, the seasons) in view of God's mercies? Can modern science prove God's reliability?

2. What does it mean to see the rainbow as a symbol of God's character? How has the symbol of the rainbow changed in our world?

Lesson in Our Society

God's Word remains constant; He continues to prove Himself as a covenant-keeping God who loves and cares for His creation. God does not seek to fight with humanity but desires that all come into repentance. Jesus Christ repairs the breach between God and the human race, and because of His blood, we can participate in the last covenant. By faith in the finished work at Calvary's cross, and Jesus' triumphant resurrection, we are able to receive God's Spirit and live in unbroken fellowship with Him.

Noah's display of faith and courage to move on God's command and look for the promise of a new day is reminiscent of how African Americans withstood slavery and segregation until emancipation and the Civil Rights Movement. The African American church was the bedrock of communal hope. We live in perilous times where Satan and humanity's worldly ways cause violence and depravity. When disaster happens—whether a natural or man-made disaster, financial difficulty, death, or any other devastating event—we have hope through our covenant relationship with God.

In what ways can the church use lessons from its role in the Civil Rights Movement to restore communal hope today?

Make It Happen

Christ followers can also be first responders in a time of crisis. It is an opportunity to serve those who are hurting. As you watch the news or are touched personally by some life event:

• Ask God to reveal to you symbols of His hope in today's context.

• Examine how you can remain in faith as you experience a trial, and how you can share that hope with someone who is hurting.

• Look for opportunities to praise God in spite of challenging situations and look to glorify Him in the process.

Follow the Spirit

What God wants me to do:

_____

_____

_____

_____

Remember Your Thoughts

Special insights I have learned:

_____

_____

_____

_____

More Light on the Text
Genesis 8:20–22, 9:8–17

20 And Noah builded an altar unto the LORD; and took of every clean beast, and of every clean fowl, and offered burnt offerings on the altar.

The institution of sacrifice seems to have continued from the time of Cain and Abel. Noah builds an altar to the Lord and makes sacrifices to worship Him and show his thanksgiving for the Lord's protection and care. Noah is careful to sacrifice only clean animals and make whole burnt offerings on the altar as a sign of holiness and devotion.

21 And the LORD smelled a sweet savour; and the LORD said in his heart, I will not again curse the ground any more for man's sake; for the imagination of man's heart is evil from his youth; neither will I again smite any more every thing living, as I have done.

22 While the earth remaineth, seedtime and harvest, and cold and heat, and summer and winter, and day and night shall not cease.

The Lord smelling the savor (Heb. *reach*, **ray-OKH**) of the sacrifices signifies that God is pleased with what Noah has given as a sacrifice. This prompts the Lord to state His promise not to curse the ground because of the sin of humanity. The Lord also acknowledges the sinful nature of humanity and says that He will never again smite every living thing. While the earth remains, the rhythms and patterns of creation would remain in effect. The earth and the environment would no longer have to pay for man's evil.

Genesis 9:8 And God spake unto Noah, and to his sons with him, saying, 9 And I, behold, I establish my covenant with you, and with your seed after you; 10 And with every living creature that is with you, of the fowl, of the cattle, and of every beast of the earth with you; from all that go out of the ark, to every beast of the earth.

Divine sovereignty is in view as God took the initiative and spoke to Noah and his sons. After the destruction of the world by the Flood, Noah became the seminal head of God's new creation because he and his family were the only ones saved from watery death. Possibly to ensure that man would not live in abject fear of Him, God spoke to Noah and made a "covenant" (Heb. *berit*, **ber-EETH**) with him. This is only the second time the word is mentioned in the Bible.

The word is thought to come from a root meaning "to cut." This is supported by the idea of the customary covenantal sacrifice and walking between the divided parts. Other theologians have suggested that "covenant" comes from a root meaning "to eat together or have a banquet." This is also plausible as eating was a common ancient Near Eastern way of establishing friendship. The covenant was a divine ordinance with signs and pledges, much different than our modern-day contracts. It was a binding agreement between two parties, where one party usually had higher status than the other.

Surviving the great Flood, Noah had been through an ordeal. God wanted to assure him that he could now live out his life in peace and rest. God's anger with the world had been appeased, and humanity could now be at peace as well. God's pledge was extended not only to Noah but also to all of his "seed" (Heb. *zera'*, **ZEH-rah**), meaning successive generations. The successive generations would encompass all of humanity as Noah and his family became ancestors of all who live on the earth, even today.

This covenant applies not only to Noah, but the rest of the animal world as well. Note that God includes the cattle (Heb. *behemah*, **beh-hee-MAH**); this word refers to any animal that lives on land, but often has the nuance of a domesticated animal such as various livestock. This is in contrast to every beast (Heb. *chay*, **KHAH-ee**), which generally refers to wild animals. God's covenant includes all creation.

11 And I will establish my covenant with you, neither shall all flesh be cut off any more by the waters of a flood; neither shall there any more be a flood to destroy the earth.

In establishing His covenant with Noah, God made the covenant both universal and unconditional. Noah was not asked to do anything in order for the covenant to remain in force. By including every living creature in the covenant, we are reminded of God's instructions to Adam and Eve to reproduce, multiply, and cover the earth (Genesis 1:28–30). No living thing would be cut off (Heb. *karat*, **ka-ROT**) or exterminated. The word for "cut off" is also assumed to be the root word for "covenant";

in an interesting play on words, this could be interpreted as the Lord saying, "I will cut a covenant with you so that you will not be cut off." Though the earth will one day be destroyed by fire (2 Peter 3:5–7, 10), God here promised that water will never again be the cause for the destruction of all mankind or the earth.

12 And God said, This is the token of the covenant which I make between me and you and every living creature that is with you, for perpetual generations: 13 I do set my bow in the cloud, and it shall be for a token of a covenant between me and the earth.

So that Noah would know that His word is good, God gave a "token" (Heb. *'oth*, **OTH**), meaning a distinguishing mark or miraculous sign—in this case, a sign to remind of a covenant obligation.

This sign is His "bow" (Heb. *qesheth*, **KEH-sheth**). The use of the word "bow" is significant; this use suggests a weapon. As such, this bow is God's bow of war, but here He gives His bow a new use and a new meaning. The bow, or rainbow, will be a reminder to Him of His covenant with Noah and the earth never again to destroy it with water. The arrow that would ordinarily be pointed toward the earth is now pointed toward the heavens, as the bow rests upon the earth's clouds.

This aspect of the narrative bears striking similarities to the Gilgamesh epic, which also tells a tale of cataclysmic flood and the goddess Ishtar basing her oath with the lapis lazuli of her necklace. Additionally, an eleventh-century Assyrian relief portrays a god holding out a hand of blessing and also a bow. These narratives from different Mesopotamian cultures, although differing in the details, show the plausibility of the universal flood account.

14 And it shall come to pass, when I bring a cloud over the earth, that the bow shall be seen in the cloud: 15 And I will remember my covenant, which is between me and you and every living creature of all flesh; and the waters shall no more become a flood to destroy all flesh.

Nothing happens outside of God's permissive will. God brought the cloud and determined that the rainbow would be seen in that cloud. God will see it, but man will be permitted to witness the rainbow as well. Each time we see a rainbow, we should be reminded that God has made a covenant to never again destroy the earth with a great flood. God is faithful and true to His word—a word that remains universal in its application, extending to all flesh, human and non-human. The word "remember" (Heb. *zakar*, **zah-KAR**) should not be taken to imply God's ability to forget, but instead, it has the connotation of caring for someone or being mindful. The Lord will be mindful and care for the whole earth by keeping His covenant and not bringing the flood again.

16 And the bow shall be in the cloud; and I will look upon it, that I may remember the everlasting covenant between God and every living creature of all flesh that is upon the earth. 17 And God said unto Noah, This is the token of the covenant, which I have established between me and all flesh that is upon the earth.

The rainbow usually appears when particles of moisture in a cloud interact with the rays of the sun, usually after a storm. It is comforting to know that the storm of God's wrath that once resulted in a universal Flood will always be quieted when He looks upon His token of peace: the rainbow.

Once more God's covenant is confirmed—the seventh time that God mentions the word "covenant" in this discourse. The number seven oftentimes represents fullness or completion. In the completeness of God's promise, Noah and all mankind can be assured that God is in control and mindful of all that is occurring on the earth. He will not forget.

Sources:
Coffman, James Burton. *Commentary on Genesis.* Abilene, TX: Abilene Christian University Press, 1974.
"Covenant." *The New Unger's Bible Dictionary.* Unger, Merrill, R. K. Harrison, Howard Vos, and Cyril Barber. Chicago: Moody Publishers, 2006.
Dunn, James D. G. and John W. Rogerson. *Commentary on the Bible.* Grand Rapids, MI: Wm. B. Eerdmans Publishing Company, 2003.
Mays, James L., ed. *HarperCollins Bible Commentary.* San Francisco: HarperOne, 1988, 2000.
Walton, John H., Victor H. Matthews, and Mark W. Chavalas. *Bible Background Commentary: Old Testament.* Downers Grove, IL: IVP Academic, 2000.
Zuck, Roy. *The Bible Knowledge Commentary.* Wheaton, IL: Victor Books, 1983.

Say It Correctly

Descendants. di-**SIN**-dents.
Japheth. Jay-feth.

Daily Bible Readings

MONDAY
Noah Found Favor with the Lord
(Genesis 6:1–8)

TUESDAY
People and Creatures Enter the Ark
(Genesis 7:1–10)

WEDNESDAY
People and Creatures Return to the Earth
(Genesis 8:13–19)

THURSDAY
Be Fruitful, Multiply, Fill the Earth
(Genesis 9:1–7)

FRIDAY
Nobody Knows the Day and Hour
(Matthew 24:36–44)

SATURDAY
Under the Rainbow the Angel Speaks
(Revelation 10:1–7)

SUNDAY
The Bow, Sign of God's Promise
(Genesis 8:20–22, 9:8–17)

Notes

_____

_____

_____

_____

Teaching Tips

Words You Should Know

A. Perfect (Genesis 17:1) *tamim* (Heb.)—Whole, complete, sound, upright in conduct, especially toward God.

B. Circumcise (v. 10) *mul* (Heb.)—To cut away, destroy, or to clip.

Teacher Preparation

Unifying Principle—A Sign of Agreement. Humans have an innate desire to support their children and ensure their future. What is required to make this possible? God used circumcision to ratify an everlasting covenant between Himself and Abram in order to make Abram and his descendants prosperous, provided they would walk with God and live blameless lives.

A. Pray that this lesson will help students reflect on God's perpetual promises.

B. Read the Abrahamic narrative to get his backstory (Genesis 12–25).

C. Read the Focal Verses in two or more translations.

O—Open the Lesson

A. Ask students to consider how God has kept His word to Abraham—then and now.

B. Introduce the lesson by reviewing the Aim for Change.

C. Read the In Focus story and discuss how it relates to the lesson title.

P—Present the Scriptures

A. Review the Background and The People, Places, and Times.

B. Have students read the Focal Verses and discuss key points in the text.

E—Explore the Meaning

A. Read and discuss the In Depth section.

B. Have the class answer the Discuss the Meaning questions.

N—Next Steps for Application

A. Review the Lesson in Our Society and Make It Happen section with students.

B. Ask students to share what it means to be branded as a Christ follower.

C. Close the lesson in prayer, asking for the Holy Spirit to enable the church to live with a perfect heart toward God and reflect His love to the world.

Worship Guide

For the Superintendent or Teacher
Theme: Circumcision
Song: "I Give Myself Away"
Devotional Reading: Psalm 105:1–11

Circumcision

Bible Background • GENESIS 17
Printed Text • GENESIS 17:1–14 | Devotional Reading • PSALM 105:1–11

Aim for Change

By the end of this lesson, we will: EXPLORE God's promises to Abraham; APPRAISE the value of outward signs for God's people; and DEVELOP ways to "walk before [God] and be blameless."

In Focus

Alan had been known as a ladies man since high school. All of his friends joked with him that he dated so many women in so little time that he would probably never settle down. Every one of his relationships was fun but short. But then he met Candace. Alan had dated a lot of women, but Candace stood out from them all. Candace was an intelligent, confident, kind-hearted woman who let him know during their first date that she planned to remain celibate until marriage, and that if he wasn't interested in pursuing a committed relationship, he should date someone else. Alan was stunned. He had never experienced a woman being so straightforward with him, and he knew he could not smooth-talk his way into keeping her around as he had with other women.

Alan met up with his good friend John, who was happily married, and shared his feelings. "I've never felt so positive and attracted around a woman," Alan confessed.

John advised that if Alan felt like a relationship with Candace was worth pursuing, he should let go of the "dating around" and keep taking her out. "Who knows, God could have just had you meet your future wife, and if she is, it's definitely worth letting go of the player life," John remarked. Alan heeded John's advice and began to think very seriously about his future.

God desires the very best for us, but obtaining His best requires letting go. What things in your life has God asked you to let go of in order to obtain His best?

Keep in Mind

"This is my covenant, which ye shall keep, between me and you and thy seed after thee; Every man child among you shall be circumcised" (Genesis 17:10).

"This is my covenant, which ye shall keep, between me and you and thy seed after thee; Every man child among you shall be circumcised" (Genesis 17:10).

Focal Verses

KJV **Genesis 17:1** And when Abram was ninety years old and nine, the LORD appeared to Abram, and said unto him, I am the Almighty God; walk before me, and be thou perfect.

2 And I will make my covenant between me and thee, and will multiply thee exceedingly.

3 And Abram fell on his face: and God talked with him, saying,

4 As for me, behold, my covenant is with thee, and thou shalt be a father of many nations.

5 Neither shall thy name any more be called Abram, but thy name shall be Abraham; for a father of many nations have I made thee.

6 And I will make thee exceeding fruitful, and I will make nations of thee, and kings shall come out of thee.

7 And I will establish my covenant between me and thee and thy seed after thee in their generations for an everlasting covenant, to be a God unto thee, and to thy seed after thee.

8 And I will give unto thee, and to thy seed after thee, the land wherein thou art a stranger, all the land of Canaan, for an everlasting possession; and I will be their God.

9 And God said unto Abraham, Thou shalt keep my covenant therefore, thou, and thy seed after thee in their generations.

10 This is my covenant, which ye shall keep, between me and you and thy seed after thee; Every man child among you shall be circumcised.

11 And ye shall circumcise the flesh of your foreskin; and it shall be a token of the covenant betwixt me and you.

12 And he that is eight days old shall be circumcised among you, every man child in your generations, he that is born in the house, or bought with money of any stranger, which is not of thy seed.

NLT **Genesis 17:1** When Abram was ninety-nine years old, the LORD appeared to him and said, "I am El-Shaddai—'God Almighty.' Serve me faithfully and live a blameless life.

2 I will make a covenant with you, by which I will guarantee to give you countless descendants."

3 At this, Abram fell face down on the ground. Then God said to him,

4 "This is my covenant with you: I will make you the father of a multitude of nations!

5 What's more, I am changing your name. It will no longer be Abram. Instead, you will be called Abraham, for you will be the father of many nations.

6 I will make you extremely fruitful. Your descendants will become many nations, and kings will be among them!

7 "I will confirm my covenant with you and your descendants after you, from generation to generation. This is the everlasting covenant: I will always be your God and the God of your descendants after you.

8 And I will give the entire land of Canaan, where you now live as a foreigner, to you and your descendants. It will be their possession forever, and I will be their God."

9 Then God said to Abraham, "Your responsibility is to obey the terms of the covenant. You and all your descendants have this continual responsibility.

10 This is the covenant that you and your descendants must keep: Each male among you must be circumcised.

11 You must cut off the flesh of your foreskin as a sign of the covenant between me and you.

12 From generation to generation, every male child must be circumcised on the eighth day after his birth. This applies not only to

13 He that is born in thy house, and he that is bought with thy money, must needs be circumcised: and my covenant shall be in your flesh for an everlasting covenant.

14 And the uncircumcised man child whose flesh of his foreskin is not circumcised, that soul shall be cut off from his people; he hath broken my covenant.

members of your family but also to the servants born in your household and the foreign-born servants whom you have purchased.

13 All must be circumcised. Your bodies will bear the mark of my everlasting covenant.

14 Any male who fails to be circumcised will be cut off from the covenant family for breaking the covenant."

The People, Places, and Times

Abraham. Abraham was originally from Ur, which was Chaldean territory in modern-day Iraq. He was the son of Terah, who was a descendant of Shem, one of Noah's sons. Noah had declared the Lord God's blessing over Shem who, with his brother, covered Noah when he was naked (Genesis 9:18–26). Later, God would declare an even greater blessing over Abraham.

Almighty God. This is another name ascribed to God's nature and character: El meaning "God," and Shaddai meaning the "Powerful One" or "Mighty One." The term connotes God's majesty as One who is self-sufficient. God's covenant was moral and ethical in character because He was more than able to swear by Himself and honor His word.

What was the relevance of God identifying Himself as "Almighty God" before choosing to reveal the covenant to Abraham?

Background

The Lord God called out Abram, set him apart from his kindred, and promised to bless him. God said He would give Abram land and make him a great nation (Genesis 12:1–3). Abram believed and set out on a journey to follow God's instructions.

Abram and his wife, Sarai, were childless, and in their culture it was to Sarai's shame that she did not bear Abram a son. The word of the Lord came to Abram a second time, and God promised Abram an heir from his own body, assuring Abram that his descendants would be as numerous as the stars (Genesis 15:1–5). Abram believed God, and God determined that it was equal to righteousness (Genesis 15:6).

To reassure Abram, the Lord made a covenant with him and ratified it through the sacrifice of a calf, a female goat, a turtledove, and a young pigeon. Abram split the calf and the female goat and God passed through the sacrificed animals to confirm His oath. Then, God caused Abram to fall into a deep sleep. During this time, He gave Abram a vision of his descendants, declaring to him the land they would possess as a part of this covenant (Genesis 15:9–21).

As time passed and Abram and Sarai experienced more childless years, they thought that this child of promise would come through other means, so they attempted to help God (Genesis 16). However, God's promise to Abram that his descendants would be vast meant that he and Sarai would have their own son. God appeared to Abram again, changed his name to Abraham and Sarai's name to Sarah (Genesis 17:5, 15). Also, God explained to Abraham his responsibility in this covenant: Abraham and every male child of his descendants were to be circumcised (Genesis 17:10–14).

Was God's covenant with Abraham conditional or dependent upon Abraham's covenantal role of circumcision?

At-A-Glance

1. Covenant Renewed (Genesis 17:1–8)
2. Covenant Symbolized (vv. 9–14)

In Depth

1. Covenant Renewed (Genesis 17:1–8)

During this encounter, God appears to Abram to speak His prophetic promise over his life and the lives of his descendants. In the previous chapter, Sarai convinced her husband to have a child through her Egyptian slave, Hagar, because in that culture a female servant could be a second wife. Her children would be the possession of their owner. God comes to Abram when he is ninety-nine and calls him to be fully devoted to the Almighty God. God was calling Abram to serve the one true God only, and He would make a nation through him that would do the same.

In the process, God changes Abram's name, which means "exalted father," to Abraham, meaning "father of many nations." God declares that He will make Abraham exceedingly fruitful, in spite of his mistakes. He declares that kings will come from Abraham's lineage and that He will keep this covenant with Abraham and his descendants forever. God makes a promise to give Abraham's descendants the land of Canaan as their possession and that He would be their God. By faith in Jesus Christ, those included as "Abraham's seed" are extended, and we receive the promise of salvation (Galatians 3:6–9).

Why do you think God decided it was necessary to renew His covenant with Abraham again?

2. Covenant Symbolized (vv. 9–14)

God institutes circumcision as a physical sign to mark that Abraham and his offspring are chosen and set apart from the other pagan cultures as His people. God commanded the generations after Abraham to walk blamelessly before Him by living under His rule and keeping this covenant. Circumcision entails that male children, eight days after birth, have the foreskin cut away as a token of their relationship with God. Moreover, God's command extends to male slaves, either born or purchased from foreigners, who would become a part of their household; they too must also adhere to the covenant.

God contends that anyone who does not comply with cutting away his foreskin is not His and would be cut off from His people. Circumcision is a painful process, but the outward sign of God's promise. Today as an outward sign of inward change, God calls His people to cut away our old nature and trust Him completely as a sign of the new covenant. Abraham believed God, and he was credited with righteousness. When we believe God and receive the gift of salvation through faith in Jesus Christ, taking on His righteousness, we too are counted righteous, set apart, and receive covenant blessings (Romans 4:22–25).

How can one explain the process of a spiritual circumcision of the heart as necessary for salvation?

Search the Scriptures

1. Does God's promise to Abraham apply to believers now in any way? Why or why not (Genesis 17:1–8)?

2. Why would the Lord require those who were foreign born or household servants to be circumcised (vv. 12–14)?

Discuss the Meaning

1. Why do you think God changed Abram's name to Abraham?

2. What was the significance of the physical mark of this covenant?

Lesson in Our Society

God requires those of us who follow Him to cut away sinful activities by presenting our bodies as living sacrifices to Him as our reasonable act of worship (Romans 12:1). The cutting away of our hearts in this context is to live a life that is pleasing to God, obeying His commands to love Him and others. Jesus tells us that these two commandments fulfill the Law and the prophets (Matthew 22:34–40). Like Abraham, we too are marked and are able to inherit God's promise.

Throughout history, and even today, people of African descent are often marginalized and perceived as inferior to those of lighter hues, but God is no respecter of persons, meaning He does not play favorites (cf. Acts 10:34). God has blessed and gifted those of the African Diaspora to succeed against the odds and to make unparalleled contributions toward the advancements of society.

How significant is the National Museum of African American History and Culture in Washington, D.C., in ensuring that our contributions to society are acknowledged and documented for future generations?

Make It Happen

Christianity is not just a religion. It's a relationship. Being a Christian means living differently than the world. A commitment to God in Christ requires sacrifice. Sacrifice is hard, but the reward far exceeds the cost.

• This week, reflect on the symbols of your commitment to your relationship with God and consider what membership in His family means for your life.

• Examine if your faith is reflected in what you value, how you spend your time, your talent, your treasure, and how you treat others.

• Prayerfully list the ways that God has blessed you because of your faith in Jesus Christ and your inheritance of the Abrahamic blessing.

Follow the Spirit

What God wants me to do:

_____

_____

_____

_____

Remember Your Thoughts

Special insights I have learned:

_____

_____

_____

_____

More Light on the Text

Genesis 17:1–14

1 And when Abram was ninety years old and nine, the LORD appeared to Abram, and said unto him, I am the Almighty God; walk before me, and be thou perfect.

This is the fifth time God appears to Abram. The first time, we are told that God commanded him to leave his country, his kindred, and his father's house (Genesis 12:1–3). In this first appearance, the Lord also promised him personal blessings. The second time, God gave him promises concerning his descendants (12:7). The third time, God spoke to him to

31

show him the Promised Land (13:14–17). The fourth time, God encouraged him, promised him an heir, and revealed the vastness and multitudes of his descendants using comparisons with natural phenomena to enable him to comprehend the magnitude of this promise (15:1–5). These past interactions between God and Abram had established a relationship between them. In his interactions with God, Abram had not fully comprehended His personality. All he knew of God was what he received from Him: promises, commands, revelations, and the God-established covenant. Now, when Abram is ninety-nine years old, God declares His mighty power.

Though the Abrahamic covenant is considered to be unilateral, God's proclamation, "I am the Almighty God; walk before me, and be thou perfect," is an exhortation to live in light of the blessings of the covenant. This declaration is God's first step toward revealing His personality to Abram. The word translated "Almighty" is *shaddai* (Heb. **shad-DAH-ee**), meaning "sufficient" or "all-powerful." God assures Abram that He is all-powerful and sufficient for him. This assurance should allay his fears and give him hope that all the promises made to him will be fulfilled. This declaration is meant to make Abram aware that he is dealing with the only true God who is all-powerful and all-sufficient—God with incomparable sovereignty. The word *halak* (Heb. **haw-LAK**) literally means "to go" or "to walk," with reference to the movement made by the feet. In this Scripture, it is used in a figurative sense to refer to personal behavior. Thus, it means to behave oneself. The verb form used here further implies that this behavior is not just a one-time act, but a repetitive action. Abraham should walk—and keep on walking—before God. This conveys the idea of continually living righteously or

responsibly. God is charging Abram to walk uprightly before Him all his days.

Because Abram is from a pagan background (as one who lived in Ur of the Chaldees, which was a center of moon worship), God gives him this charge. Moreover, the Lord had called him away from his kindred and out of his country, and Abram becomes a chosen person through whom God intends to reveal His mighty power. Today, those of us who express faith like Abraham have been called out of the world to live a sanctified life in view of greater hopes—the manifestation of God's glory.

2 And I will make my covenant between me and thee, and will multiply thee exceedingly. 3 And Abram fell on his face: and God talked with him, saying, 4 As for me, behold, my covenant is with thee, and thou shalt be a father of many nations.

God establishes a covenant with Abram. This covenant comprises great personal promises made to Abram. Prior to this time, God had made these promises to him. The word translated "make" is *nathan* (Heb. **naw-TAN**) and means "to give, bestow, grant, or entrust." This is in particular reference to the establishment of a covenant that was originated by God. This covenant is a gift from God to Abram. As mentioned before, this covenant is generally considered to be unilateral since it was first declared by God without any conditions attached. However, verse 1 adds a second element to it, effectively making the covenant bilateral.

Here, we can identify three of the four elements present in a covenant: parties, conditions, and results. God and Abram, certainly, are the parties involved here. Faithful obedience was the condition required by God in this covenant with Abram. The results are the promises to multiply Abram exceedingly and make him a father of many nations.

Abram fell on his face while God talked with him, expressing total submission and a willingness to obey Him. The promise to multiply Abram exceedingly transcends the promise of making him into a great nation (Genesis 12:2). The former promise refers to Abram's seed, through Isaac and Jacob, becoming the Hebrew nation. The latter promise speaks of the nations that were to come out of him, apart from the nation of Israel—peoples, and nations that were to be his descendants through Hagar (16:15) and Keturah (25:1–2). God expresses a willingness to multiply Abram exceedingly, which provokes in Abram a willingness to obey God.

5 Neither shall thy name any more be called Abram, but thy name shall be Abraham; for a father of many nations have I made thee.

Abram means "high father" or "my father is exalted." This meaning is also conveyed in other ancient languages such as Old Babylonian, ancient Egyptian, ancient South Arabic, and Ugaritic. Even in these different languages, the name carried a similar meaning; that is, the name was translated including the word "divine," to render it as "my divine father is exalted." Abraham means "father of a multitude." This new name incorporates God's plan and purpose for Abraham; it points to his destiny, and reflects God's promise for him.

The word translated "father" is *ab* (Heb. **AWB**), which accounts for the first two letters of the names Abram and Abraham. Abram had been accorded the status of a father even while he was a pagan, but the significance of his fatherhood becomes different now that Almighty God is his God. God makes him a father of many nations. This implies a change in his personality and destiny; having been appointed, called, or ordained to be a father of many nations, he has been elevated to a

higher status than that of a "high father" in a pagan context. "Father" also means "founder" and "patriarch." This promise has been fulfilled over the ages. He is the father of the Hebrew nation through the seed of the promise, Isaac. However ,he is also the father of the Ishmaelites, Midianites, Edomites, Shuhites, and many others. His descendants grew into an exceedingly wide circle of peoples, kings, princes, and nations. His fatherhood continues down through a long line of physical descendant progenitors, and also through a "family" that shares his spiritual heritage. All believers who have faith in God are called Abraham's children: "Know ye therefore that they which are of faith, the same are the children of Abraham" (Galatians 3:7).

The change of name indicates an elevation and possibly a rebirth of sorts. It typifies the New Testament experience in which our personalities and appellations or titles change at our rebirth by the Holy Spirit in Christ. We become children of God, for example, saints, the redeemed, kings, and priests.

6 And I will make thee exceeding fruitful, and I will make nations of thee, and kings shall come out of thee.

This is one of the promises God gave to Abraham that is similar to the promise we find in Genesis 12:2. These two promises pertain to nations. While the Genesis 12:2 promise refers to one nation (the nation of Israel) in particular, this Genesis 17:6 promise refers to the other nations of the world. This promise has two referents. First, it refers to Abraham's physical progeny through Ishmael, Zimran, Jokshan, Medan, Midian, Ishbak, and Shuah, who formed various peoples and nations, with their kings. Second, and most importantly, it refers to all believers of all nations who are saved in Jesus Christ. The natural ancestry of Jesus is traced to Abraham (Matthew 1:1–16), and believers are kings and priests unto God (Revelation 5:10); they are coheirs with Christ (Romans 8:17; Galatians 3:29).

7 And I will establish my covenant between me and thee and thy seed after thee in their generations for an everlasting covenant, to be a God unto thee, and to thy seed after thee.

God reveals the extent of His covenant with Abraham. This covenant is established with Abraham, his immediate offspring, and subsequent offspring even unto distant generations. It is intended to be everlasting. The Hebrew word *olam* (Heb. **oh-LOM**) comes from the word for "concealed," thinking of time as though stretching beyond the vanishing point on a horizon, suggesting time out of mind or eternity. This can be translated as a "long duration" or refer strictly to eternal time past or future. Here it is translated as "everlasting," indicating that the covenant would exist continuously upon its inauguration. God's purpose is to have a people descend from Abraham who will perpetuate faith in Him and service to Him—a people to whom He will be God for eternity, who will at no time discontinue their service to Him but take Him as their God permanently. Thus, Abraham was to be the patriarch of a nation made up of God's own people. As the patriarch who acknowledged the true God, Abraham became His first prophet (Genesis 20:7).

The religion of Abraham was supposed to be an expression of faith and obedience to God, characterized by the practice of righteousness, compliance with divinely stipulated laws and ceremonial practices, and recognition of the prophets, priests, and judges as representatives of God. But in the course of time, alien religious beliefs and practices involving other gods arose, claiming to originate from Abraham. The Ishmaelites and Midianites, for instance, introduced major religious elements that became prevalent in the area. Currently, most Arab nations follow Islam—a religion whose founder, Mohammed, also claimed to be greatly influenced by Abraham.

8 And I will give unto thee, and to thy seed after thee, the land wherein thou art a stranger, all the land of Canaan, for an everlasting possession; and I will be their God.

Abraham's nomadic life would be brought to an end by possessing the land where he dwelt as a stranger. God promises to turn the immigrant Abraham into a possessor of a foreign land. The Hebrew word *erets* (**EH-rets**) is translated "land" or "earth"; here it means "country" or "territory." By covenant right, Abraham possesses the Canaanite country, but the twelve tribes of Israel achieved actual possession.

The twelve sons of Jacob eventually became the twelve tribes who settled in the country of the Canaanites, a land flowing with milk and honey. God actually dispossessed the original inhabitants of the land to give it to Abraham's descendants in fulfillment of His covenant. God said it was to be an everlasting possession and therefore meant to be a permanent home for the children of Abraham.

9 And God said unto Abraham, Thou shalt keep my covenant therefore, thou, and thy seed after thee in their generations. 10 This is my covenant, which ye shall keep, between me and you and thy seed after thee; Every man child among you shall be circumcised.

Now God exhorts Abraham to not only keep the covenant himself but also for his seed after him to keep the same covenant. The stipulation is that Abraham would be circumcised as well as those who would come after him as a sign of membership in the covenant community. Circumcision was a widespread practice at the time among many different cultures in the area. What distinguishes the circumcision practice of Abraham and his male descendants is that it is a sign of covenant relationship between them and God Himself.

11 And ye shall circumcise the flesh of your foreskin; and it shall be a token of the covenant betwixt me and you. 12 And he that is eight days old shall be circumcised among you, every man child in your generations, he that is born in the house, or bought with money of any stranger, which is not of thy seed.

Circumcision was a reminder of the covenant between Abraham and God as well as between those descendants of Abraham who were circumcised as well. The command to wait eight days probably stems from the ancient practice of waiting a certain number of days to confirm that the infant will live. Among rabbis, the number seven represents the complete and finite, while eight points toward the miraculous and matters of faith. Therefore, circumcision on the eighth day symbolizes that the child has entered into a community founded on faith.

13 He that is born in thy house, and he that is bought with thy money, must needs be circumcised: and my covenant shall be in your flesh for an everlasting covenant. 14 And the uncircumcised man child whose flesh of his foreskin is not circumcised, that soul shall be cut off from his people; he hath broken my covenant.

Circumcision would not only be required for those who were physical descendants, but also those born in the house or servants bought with Abraham's money. This means that the covenant extended to every male within the nation of Israel. All of the men were to show this sign of belonging to the Lord.

Sources:
Cabal, Ted et. al. *The Apologetics Study Bible.* Holman Christian Standard, Nashville, TN, Holman Bible Publishers, 2007. 29–30.
Cotlar, Yisroel. "Why Wait Eight Days for Circumcision?" Chabad.com. Accessed August 31, 2017. http://www.chabad.org/library/article_cdo/aid/527084/jewish/Why-Wait-Eight-Days-for-the-Circumcision.htm
Van der Mass, Ed M. *Halley's Bible Handbook: Deluxe Edition (25th Edition).* Grand Rapids, MI: Zondervan, 2007. 112-113.
Zodhiates, Spiros. *Key Word Study Bible: King James Version.* Chattanooga, TN: AMG Publishers, 1991. 1626, 1637, 1666.

Say It Correctly

El Shaddai. **EL** sha-**DIE**.
Betwixt. bih-**TWIK**-st.

Daily Bible Readings

MONDAY
Sarah, Mother of Nations
(Genesis 17:15–17)

TUESDAY
Ishmael, Father of a Nation
(Genesis 17:20–22)

WEDNESDAY
All Males of Abraham's Household
Circumcised
(Genesis 17:23–27)

THURSDAY
Circumcision Event Remembered
(Acts 7:1–8)

FRIDAY
God's Promise Realized Through Faith
(Romans 4:13–25)

SATURDAY
Jesus, Mediator of a Better Covenant
(Hebrews 8:1–8)

SUNDAY
God's Covenant with Abraham Reaffirmed
(Genesis 17:1–14)

Notes

_____

_____

_____

_____

Teaching Tips

Words You Should Know

A. Sabbath (Exodus 31:13) *shabbath* (Heb.)—Rest, cease.

B. Holy (v. 14) *qodesh* (Heb.)—Sacredness, consecrated, separateness.

Teacher Preparation

Unifying Principle—Time to Rest and Renew. Multitasking, complex job responsibilities, diverse family structures, and commitments can make people feel overwhelmed. How can one find relief from the fast-paced busyness of everyday life? God commanded Moses and the Israelites to rest on the Sabbath and keep it holy as a sign of their reverence to Him, reflecting that He who created the earth in six days rested on the seventh day.

A. Pray for your class and for wisdom concerning the lesson.

B. Read Exodus 20 and outline the command to remember the Sabbath day.

C. Find pictures from a recent vacation and peaceful, instrumental worship music to bring to class.

O—Open the Lesson

A. After receiving prayer requests, ask a volunteer to open the class with prayer and read the Aim for Change.

B. Have a volunteer read the In Focus story. Discuss the personal, family, and work responsibilities people have every week.

C. Ask the class, "How often during the week do you feel stressed and overwhelmed with things to do? How often do you take the time for rest and renewal during the week?" After they respond, say, "God wants us to rest and be spiritually renewed, so He commanded that we have a Sabbath day."

P—Present the Scriptures

A. Ask for a volunteer to read the Focal Verses.

B. Examine the verses, utilizing Words You Should Know, The People, Places, and Times, Background, the At-A-Glance outline, and More Light on the Text sections.

E—Explore the Meaning

A. Answer the Search the Scriptures questions.

B. Summarize the Discuss the Meaning and Lesson in Our Society.

C. Introduce today's theme.

N—Next Steps for Application

A. Summarize the lesson and encourage students to apply the Make It Happen section to their lives this week.

B. Solicit prayer requests and close in prayer.

Worship Guide

For the Superintendent or Teacher
Theme: Sabbath Observance
Song: "I Come to the Garden Alone"
Devotional Reading: Psalm 92

Sabbath Observance

Bible Background • GENESIS 2:1–3; EXODUS 31:12–18; ISAIAH 56:1–8
Printed Text • EXODUS 31:12–18 | Devotional Reading • PSALM 92

—————— Aim for Change ——————

By the end of this lesson, we will: EXPLORE the Bible's teaching about the Sabbath and its importance; EVALUATE the need to repent for neglecting weekly rest and spiritual renewal; and COMPOSE a thanksgiving to God for the gift of rest and spiritual renewal.

In Focus

Antonio finally relaxed in his own bed after a four-day hospital stay. He had been rushed to the hospital from work after complaining about severe chest pains. The doctors ran many tests and discovered it was an anxiety attack, not a heart attack as they first thought. They told Antonio he must make changes in his life, or it could be a real heart attack next time.

Antonio and his wife, Celestine, had a long talk about what modifications were necessary. Currently, Antonio had a full-time and a part-time job. He also served with three ministries at church. On top of all that, he was the treasurer of his local fraternity chapter. After discussing it with his wife, Antonio felt it was better for him to resign from his part-time job, remove himself from two ministries at church, and let someone else take his position at the fraternity. It was not worth his health to continue with such a stressful schedule.

After Sunday morning worship services, they devoted the other part of the day to relaxing. They did not let anything hinder their plans to rest. Many people thought he was being selfish in his decision, but Celestine and Antonio urged others to rethink how they were living their lives.

How do you make rest a priority in your life? In today's lesson, we will learn how God commanded the Israelites to observe the Sabbath in order to rest and to give honor to Him.

—————— Keep in Mind ——————

"Verily my sabbaths ye shall keep: for it is a sign between me and you throughout your generations that ye may know that I am the LORD that doth sanctify you. Ye shall keep the sabbath therefore; for it is holy unto you" (from Exodus 31:13–14).

"Verily my sabbaths ye shall keep: for it is a sign between me and you throughout your generations that ye may know that I am the LORD that doth sanctify you. Ye shall keep the sabbath therefore; for it is holy unto you" (from Exodus 31:13–14).

Focal Verses

KJV **Exodus 31:12** And the LORD spake unto Moses saying,

13 Speak thou also unto the children of Israel, saying, Verily my sabbaths ye shall keep: for it is a sign between me and you throughout your generations that ye may know that I am the LORD that doth sanctify you.

14 Ye shall keep the sabbath therefore; for it is holy unto you: every one that defileth it shall surely be put to death: for whosoever doeth any work therein, that soul shall be cut off from among his people.

15 Six days may work be done; but in the seventh is the sabbath of rest, holy to the LORD: whosoever doeth any work in the sabbath day, he shall surely be put to death.

16 Wherefore the children of Israel shall keep the Sabbath, to observe the sabbath throughout their generations for a perpetual covenant.

17 It is a sign between me and the children of Israel for ever: for in six days the LORD made heaven and earth, and on the seventh day he rested, and was refreshed.

18 And he gave unto Moses, when he had made an end of communing with him upon Mount Sinai, two tables of testimony, tables of stone, written with the finger of God.

NLT **Exodus 31:12** The LORD then gave these instructions to Moses:

13 "Tell the people of Israel: 'Be careful to keep my Sabbath day, for the Sabbath is a sign of the covenant between me and you from generation to generation. It is given so you may know that I am the LORD, who makes you holy.

14 You must keep the Sabbath day, for it is a holy day for you. Anyone who desecrates it must be put to death; anyone who works on that day will be cut off from the community.

15 You have six days each week for your ordinary work, but the seventh day must be a Sabbath day of complete rest, a holy day dedicated to the LORD. Anyone who works on the Sabbath must be put to death.

16 The people of Israel must keep the Sabbath day by observing it from generation to generation. This is a covenant obligation for all time.

17 It is a permanent sign of my covenant with the people of Israel. For in six days the LORD made heaven and earth, but on the seventh day he stopped working and was refreshed."

18 When the LORD finished speaking with Moses on Mount Sinai, he gave him the two stone tablets inscribed with the terms of the covenant, written by the finger of God.

The People, Places, and Times

Moses. Moses' parents were Amram and Jochebed, who were of the tribe of Levi. In order to save him from death at Pharaoh's order, Moses' mother made a basket, placed him in it, and set it in the Nile River (Exodus 2:1–10). Years later, God called Moses to lead His people out of slavery in Egypt (Exodus 3–4), and his older brother Aaron was made his spokesperson. After Pharaoh's refusal to listen to Moses, God sent ten plagues upon Egypt. Moses led the Hebrews out of Egypt and across the parted Red Sea, but the Egyptians who chased them drowned (12:37–15:20). God provided the Hebrews' daily needs as they traveled through the wilderness. Moses and the people arrived at Mount Sinai, where God gave the Ten Commandments to them, as well as instructions on building a tabernacle as a center of worship.

Israelites. The Israelites were God's chosen people. God had blessed them by delivering them out of slavery. The Passover was instituted to remind them of their exodus from Egypt. God provided manna and quail to feed them during their wilderness journey (16:1–22). At Mount Sinai, the people received the Ten Commandments so they would understand God's holiness and faithfully maintain their covenant relationship (20:1–17). The provisions of God's covenant with Israel are outlined in Exodus 21–24.

What issues could develop among the Israelites that would lead them to violate the Sabbath?

Background

Exodus was written to record the events of Israel's deliverance from Egypt and their development as a nation. It is believed to have been written in the wilderness during Israel's wanderings. The Israelites had been slaves for four hundred years before God sent Moses as a deliverer. Many miracles occurred and are documented in Exodus. This book also contains the Ten Commandments.

Chapters 25–40 focus on building the tabernacle as well as on receiving a covenant. The specific details for constructing the portable tabernacle were given so the Israelites would honor the holiness of God, as this would be His dwelling place among them. God also gave precise instructions for making the priestly garments and consecrating the priests. Today's Focal Verses stress the importance and necessity of keeping the Sabbath as a sign of the covenant relationship between God and His people. The word "sabbath" comes from the Hebrew word meaning "to cease from exertion."

What is the main reason that God commanded the Sabbath to be observed?

At-A-Glance

1. The Sabbath Reinstated (Exodus 31:12–17)
2. Moses Receives the Tablets of Stone (v. 18)

In Depth

1. The Sabbath Reinstated (Exodus 31:12–17)

In verse 13, Moses is told, "You yourself are to speak to the Israelites." God wanted the command on Sabbath observance to come directly from Moses, who was mediator and covenant enforcer at this time during the Israelites history. Moses not only delivered the Law of God but also led the people in obeying it. This included honoring the Sabbath as a sign of God's covenant.

The Sabbath was required in the fourth commandment (20:8–11). This connected it with the rest God took on the seventh day of creation (Genesis 2:2). The Sabbath also is a time to remember what God has done. Any violation of the Sabbath was punishable by death (vv. 14–16), because, for the Israelites, it was not just a self-oriented day of rest, but a time to remember and honor the covenant that God made with them. Most modern-day practicing Jews still observe the Sabbath as a day of rest. The Sabbath day for them is the last day of the week, Saturday. For most Christians, our Sabbath is on the first day of the week, Sunday. This is because it is the day Jesus was resurrected, and as participants in the new covenant, He is our Sabbath rest.

How does the Israelites' observation of Sabbath compare to modern-day Sabbath observations?

2. Moses Receives the Tablets of Stone (v. 18)

The tablets of stone given to Moses were duplicates of the covenant, including the Ten Commandments. Both parties in the covenant received a copy. The copy that belonged to Israel had to be placed in the presence of God in the ark (vv. 25:21–22). These laws helped the nation keep a standard of judgment when people committed specific erroneous behaviors. The command to keep the Sabbath was a part of this law; it was inscribed in stone and contained the firm and faithful words of God for the nation. This is signified by the words "the finger of God."

What changes would have to be made in our society and current legal system if we were strictly governed by the Ten Commandments?

Search the Scriptures

1. Why was the punishment so severe for violating the Sabbath (Exodus 31:14–15)?

2. How is the Sabbath a sign of the covenant between God and the Israelites (v. 17)?

Discuss the Meaning

1. How is it possible for people of faith to both observe and desecrate the Sabbath?

2. How do you define "rest"? What hinders you from regular rest and spiritual renewal?

Lesson in Our Society

Many people have great difficulty taking the time for rest and renewal. Some churches make it hard for us to experience rest, too. Lots of events are scheduled on Saturdays and Sundays, in addition to regular worship services. Churches often feel this is the best available time for most people to participate, which negates the fact that people need to rest. What can be done to help people observe the Sabbath properly?

In the African American context, rest has been especially hard to come by. Many adults work multiple jobs just to make ends meet. Others work non-stop to get ahead in life so they can provide things for their children that they never had a chance to experience. Far from being lazy, as many in our society would choose to believe, we are a hard-working people. At the same time, it would be good for us to heed God's command to rest and trust that He will bless us beyond our own ability and effort.

What support can be given to help people observe the Sabbath properly?

Make It Happen

This week, reevaluate your life by looking at your daily schedule. What effect is your schedule having on you personally, as well as on other members of your family?

• Pray and ask God to forgive you for not taking real time to rest.

• Ask God to guide you in rearranging your schedule to include a Sabbath rest.

• After you make changes, establish boundaries so that others do not violate your Sabbath time.

Follow the Spirit

What God wants me to do:

_____

_____

_____

_____

Remember Your Thoughts

Special insights I have learned:

_____

_____

_____

_____

More Light on the Text

Exodus 31:12–18

12 And the LORD spoke to Moses saying.

This passage begins by establishing Moses as an intermediary. The Lord speaks directly to Moses, who then transmits the information to the Israelites assembled at Mount Sinai. The formula, "And the LORD spoke to Moses saying…" signals the importance of the relationship between God and Moses. The Lord does not speak directly to the people; He speaks to them through Moses.

Throughout the Old Testament in general, and Exodus in particular, the Lord speaks directly to very few individuals. When God does speak directly, it is most often to Moses. Of the 44 occurrences of the Hebrew phrase in Exodus, Moses is the object in all but one instance. Moses has a particularly intimate relationship with the Lord.

13 Speak thou also unto the children of Israel, saying, Verily my sabbaths ye shall keep: for it is a sign between me and you throughout your generations that ye may know that I am the LORD that doth sanctify you.

The Lord instructs the Israelites (through Moses) to keep His Sabbaths exclusively. Some English translations do not consider the particle, 'ak (Heb. **AHK**), which is here translated "verily" and can also be translated "only" or

"nevertheless." This Hebrew word is important here because it sets the Sabbath of the Lord apart from any other sabbath. The Lord encourages the Israelites to acknowledge His Sabbath, perhaps as opposed to a sabbath of another god.

Keeping the Lord's Sabbath serves as an indicator of the special relationship between Him and the Israelites. For the ancient Israelites, disregard for the Sabbath (either by neglect or by violating the restrictions concerning it) is a disregard for the Lord, and a disregard for Him is disregard for the reason and possibility of Israel's existence as a people.

Modern believers can frame the idea of keeping the Sabbath as a way of being reminded of God's presence in their lives. The symbols of the Sabbath and worship—such as specific locations for worship, particular actions, and rituals during worship, and avoiding certain activities on Sabbath days—all work to signal God's presence in the lives of believers.

14 Ye shall keep the sabbath therefore; for it is holy unto you: every one that defileth it shall surely be put to death: for whosoever doeth any work therein, that soul shall be cut off from among his people.

The Lord stresses the importance of keeping the Sabbath by establishing its holy nature and the dire consequences for profaning it. The Hebrew for "holy" used in this verse, qodesh (Heb. **ko-DESH**), may be translated as "apartness" or "sacredness." Throughout the biblical text, qodesh is used to designate places set apart as sacred because of God's presence. This word may also denote objects or even people consecrated as sacred (Leviticus 21:6).

Keeping the Sabbath is presented as holy "unto [the Israelites]." The Sabbath day is not intrinsically holy or sacred, but it is considered holy for the people. Said differently, for those who do not follow the Lord, the Sabbath is not at all special or sacred, but because of their relationship with the Lord, the Sabbath day is holy for the Israelites. This linguistic nuance hearkens to the exclusive covenant relationship between the Israelites and the Lord.

15 Six days may work be done; but in the seventh is the sabbath of rest, holy to the LORD: whosoever doeth any work in the sabbath day, he shall surely be put to death.

Followers of the Lord are not to work on the Sabbath. Working on the Sabbath day of rest will result in death. To careful readers, it might seem extreme to expect a group of ancient, agrarian wanderers not to perform any work at all. After all, the social and topographical conditions would no doubt call for people to, at a minimum, gather water for cleaning and cooking. It seems each case of Sabbath violation is unique. For example, a man found gathering wood on the Sabbath was in violation of the specific ban against kindling a fire on the Sabbath (Exodus 35:3; Numbers 15:32–36). Elsewhere, the people are warned against Sabbath labor even during the busy agricultural seasons (Exodus 34:21), and lifting a burden is forbidden on the Sabbath (Jeremiah 17:21). In any case, the harsh penalties for sabbath violation are indicative of God's holiness and the importance of the Sabbath as a sign of covenant relationship.

In the Old Testament, the thematic treatment of the idea of rest consists of two main strands: the Sabbath rest (from routine labor) and the promise of rest (from wandering/ journeying or from enemy threat) in the land of Canaan. For example, after creating the world, the Lord rests on the seventh day (Genesis 2:2). The Promised Land (Canaan) is positioned as the land of rest for God's people after journeying or warfare (Joshua 1:13). Furthermore, the idea of the land requiring a sabbatical year (Leviticus 25:1–7) also highlights the importance of Sabbath and rest for the ancient Israelites.

The phrase "sabbath of rest" (Heb. *shabbat shabbaton*, **shah-BOT shab-ba-TON**) is affiliated with the Hebrew noun, *shabbat*, which is translated as "a day of rest." The repetition of the word shows that this is not just any sabbath; it's a Sabbath of sabbaths. This follows the Hebrew literary device of repetition to show magnification. A similar phrase is Holy of Holies, also translated as the Most Holy Place. The magnification shows the importance of the day and points toward full obedience in regards to observing it. This magnified phrase *shabbat shabbaton* appears as "sabbath of complete/ solemn rest" for the seventh day (Exodus 32:5; Leviticus 23:3), the annual Day of Atonement (Leviticus 16:31, 23:32), the annual Feast of Trumpets (Leviticus 23:24), and the sabbatical year (Leviticus 25:4).

16 Wherefore the children of Israel shall keep the Sabbath, to observe the sabbath throughout their generations for a perpetual covenant. 17 It is a sign between me and the children of Israel for ever: for in six days the LORD made heaven and earth, and on the seventh day he rested, and was refreshed.

The Lord turns to point out the nature of the covenant relationship that the Israelites' observance of the Sabbath signifies: the covenant is perpetual. The Lord commanded it as a sign of the covenant continuing between the two of them. In many ways, the observance of Sabbath is a response to God's presence in the lives of the Israelites.

The idea of covenant is one of the most important motifs in biblical theology. The Hebrew term *berith* (**beh-REETH**, "covenant") conveys the idea of a solemn commitment guaranteeing promises or obligations undertaken by one or both covenanting parties. While the term applies predominantly to divine–human commitments, it is also used for various agreements between humans (1 Samuel 18:3; 2 Kings 11:17), including marriage (Malachi 2:14), and even in a figurative sense for solemn commitments made with oneself (Job 31:1; Isaiah 28:15). In the Old Testament, prominent covenants with Noah, Abraham, Moses, and David underpin God's relationship with humanity. The rainbow is the sign of the covenant with Noah that God would never again destroy the earth (Genesis 9:11–12). The Abrahamic covenant (Genesis 12:1–3) includes a promise to make Abraham's people into "a great nation," and Exodus 19–24 details the specifics of the Mosaic covenant in which God promises to make Israel "a kingdom of priests, and a holy nation" (Exodus 19:6). Finally, 2 Samuel 7 records the establishment of the Davidic covenant in which God promises that someone from David's lineage would rule forever.

18 And he gave unto Moses, when he had made an end of communing with him upon Mount Sinai, two tables of testimony, tables of stone, written with the finger of God.

This passage concludes with the Lord giving the two stone tablets to Moses, which probably contain the Ten Commandments, and foreshadows the next episode in the narrative, which includes the smashing of the tablets. Additionally, the stone material and the figurative language, "written with the finger of God," both support the long-lasting nature or eternality of the covenant.

Sources:

Life Application Study Bible, New Revised Standard Version. Wheaton, IL: Tyndale House Publishers, Inc., 1989. 94–95, 143.

The NIV Study Bible (Tenth Anniversary Edition). Grand Rapids, MI: Zondervan Publishing House 1995. 131–132

Unger, Merrill F. *Unger's Bible Dictionary*. Chicago, IL: Moody Press. 1985. 939–941.

Unger, Merrill F. *The New Unger's Bible Handbook*. Chicago, IL: Moody Press. 1984. 69–83.

Say It Correctly

Sanctify. **SANK**-tuh-fie.
Perpetual. per-**PEH**-chew-al.

Daily Bible Readings

MONDAY
The Sabbath Commandment
(Exodus 20:8–11)

TUESDAY
Recall God's Deliverance on the Sabbath
(Deuteronomy 5:12–15)

WEDNESDAY
Healing on the Sabbath
(Matthew 12:9–14)

THURSDAY
Teaching on the Sabbath
(Mark 6:1–5)

FRIDAY
Worship on the Sabbath
(Acts 16:11–15)

SATURDAY
A Psalm for the Sabbath
(Psalm 92)

SUNDAY
The Sabbath, Sign of the Covenant
(Exodus 31:12–18)

Teaching Tips

Words You Should Know

A. Profaned (Ezekiel 36:22) *chalal* (Heb.)—To defile, pollute, desecrate.

B. Heart (v. 26) *leb* (Heb.)—Inner man, mind, will.

Teacher Preparation

Unifying Principle—A Change of Heart. People stubbornly follow their own agendas without regard to the impact of their actions on those they respect and admire. What will motivate these people to change? God will give them a new heart and put His Spirit within them.

A. Pray for your class that God would give them changed hearts.

B. Research stories of people whose lives have been radically changed by God. Bring a printed article or a video clip to the class to share with them. You can use resources such as www.iamsecond.com.

O—Open the Lesson

A. Ask a volunteer to open the class with prayer.

B. Have a volunteer read the In Focus story. Discuss the impact ungodly behavior has on personal relationships, family members, and other innocent people.

C. State the Aim For Change.

P—Present the Scriptures

A. Ask for a volunteer to read the Focal Verses.

B. Examine the verses, utilizing Words You Should Know, The People, Places, and Times, Background, the At-A-Glance outline, and More Light on the Text sections.

E—Explore the Meaning

A. Answer the Search the Scriptures questions.

B. Answer questions from the Discuss the Meaning section.

C. Summarize the Lesson in Our Society section and relate it to today's theme.

N—Next Steps for Application

A. Summarize the lesson and encourage students to apply the Make It Happen section to their lives.

B. Remind students to read and meditate on their Daily Bible Readings.

C. Solicit prayer requests and close in prayer.

Worship Guide

For the Superintendent or Teacher
Theme: Spirit-Filled Heart
Song: "O Thou, In Whose Presence"
Devotional Reading: Isaiah 43:14–21

Spirit-Filled Heart

Bible Background • EZEKIEL 36–37; TITUS 3:1–11
Printed Text • EZEKIEL 36:22–32 | Devotional Reading • ISAIAH 43:14–21

Aim for Change

By the end of the lesson, we will: AGREE that a Spirit-filled heart makes a difference in the lives of believers; APPRECIATE the gift of His Spirit; and become RECEPTIVE to the work of God's Spirit in our lives.

In Focus

Tammy Wigington was a very successful bank executive. She had received many awards for her exemplary work. Her office wall was covered with certificates and plaques that Tammy proudly boasted about to everyone. But no one knew her big secret. When Tammy was hired 15 years prior, she had lied about her credentials on her resume. She had not graduated college with a Bachelor's Degree, but an Associate's Degree. Her best friend Tracey, who worked for the bank, did not check her credentials. So Tammy was hired as a bank manager and worked her way up to her current position. However, during the last month, the bank began auditing all the employees' personal files. Tammy was horrified and knew she could be fired.

One day she was notified that she had to attend a meeting about discrepancies in her file. Tammy went to the meeting, and when confronted with their findings of her education, she confessed. After talking with her, they decided not to fire her. After being a successful corporate executive, she would now be demoted to a bank manager until she fulfilled the educational requirements. After she graduated, Tammy could reapply for an executive position. Tammy felt relieved and thanked God for a second chance. She knew she needed a new heart of honesty and humility to succeed in the future.

What causes us to do wrong even when we know the consequences? In today's lesson, we will discover how God's grace can propel us to change.

Keep in Mind

"A new heart also will I give you, and a new spirit will I put within you: and I will take away the stony heart out of your flesh, and I will give you a heart of flesh" (Ezekiel 36:26).

"A new heart also will I give you, and a new spirit will I put within you: and I will take away the stony heart out of your flesh, and I will give you a heart of flesh" (Ezekiel 36:26).

Focal Verses

KJV **Ezekiel 36:22** Therefore say unto the house of Israel, Thus saith the Lord GOD: I do not this for your sakes, O house of Israel, but for mine holy name's sake, which ye have profaned among the heathen whither ye went.

23 And I will sanctify my great name, which was profaned among the heathen, which ye have profaned in the midst of them; and the heathen shall know that I am the LORD saith the Lord GOD, when I shall be sanctified in you before their eyes.

24 For I will take you from among the heathen, and gather you out of all countries, and will bring you into your own land.

25 Then will I sprinkle clean waters upon you, and ye shall be clean: from all your filthiness, and from all your idols, will I cleanse you.

26 A new heart also will I give you, and a new spirit will I put within you: and I will take away the stony heart out of your flesh, and I will give you a heart of flesh.

27 And I will put my spirit within you, and cause you to walk in my statutes, and ye shall keep my judgments, and do them.

28 And ye shall dwell in the land that I gave to your fathers; and ye shall be my people, and I will be your God.

29 I will also save you from all your uncleannesses: and I will call for the corn, and will increase it, and lay no famine upon you.

30 And I will multiply the fruit of the tree, and the increase of the field, that ye shall receive no more reproach of famine among the heathen.

31 Then shall ye remember your own evil ways, and your doings that were not good, and shall loathe yourselves in your own sight for your iniquities and for your abominations.

32 Not for your sakes do I this, saith the Lord GOD, be it known unto you: be ashamed

NLT **Ezekiel 36:22** "Therefore, give the people of Israel this message from the Sovereign LORD: I am bringing you back, but not because you deserve it. I am doing it to protect my holy name, on which you brought shame while you were scattered among the nations.

23 I will show how holy my great name is— the name on which you brought shame among the nations. And when I reveal my holiness through you before their very eyes, says the Sovereign LORD, then the nations will know that I am the LORD.

24 For I will gather you up from all the nations and bring you home again to your land.

25 Then I will sprinkle clean water on you, and you will be clean. Your filth will be washed away, and you will no longer worship idols.

26 And I will give you a new heart, and I will put a new spirit in you. I will take out your stony, stubborn heart and give you a tender, responsive heart.

27 And I will put my Spirit in you so that you will follow my decrees and be careful to obey my regulations.

28 And you will live in Israel, the land I gave your ancestors long ago. You will be my people, and I will be your God.

29 I will cleanse you of your filthy behavior. I will give you good crops of grain, and I will send no more famines on the land.

30 I will give you great harvests from your fruit trees and fields, and never again will the surrounding nations be able to scoff at your land for its famines.

31 Then you will remember your past sins and despise yourselves for all the detestable things you did.

32 But remember, says the Sovereign LORD, I am not doing this because you deserve it.

and confounded for your own ways, O house of Israel.

O my people of Israel, you should be utterly ashamed of all you have done!

The People, Places, and Times

Ezekiel. Ezekiel's name means "God strengthens." He was a priest (Ezekiel 1:3). His wife died the day the siege of Jerusalem began in 588 B.C. (24:1, 15–18). He was a contemporary of Jeremiah, who ministered to the people still in Judah. Ezekiel was deported to Babylon in 597 B.C. with King Jehoiachin. His prophetic ministry among the Babylonian exiles was from 593–571 B.C.

Babylonian Captivity. Nebuchadnezzar conquered Jerusalem and took the captives to Babylon. The three deportations of Israelites to Babylon occurred in roughly 597 B.C., 587 B.C., and 582 B.C. God allowed them to be held by the Babylonians for seventy years. Most of the captives were treated as colonists. The Babylonian exile was brought to a close after the fall of Babylon by Cyrus the Great, who issued a decree at approximately 536 B.C. for the Jews to return and rebuild Jerusalem (Ezra 1:2).

How did Ezekiel's relationship with God affect the reality of being a captive in Babylon?

Background

Ezekiel demonstrated to the people that God had a right to punish them for their sinful behavior and send them into captivity in Babylon (Ezekiel 18:25–29, 33:17–20). He wanted the people to know that God's chastening had a purpose: to correct and prevent the sinful behavior. In the book of Ezekiel, the phrase "then they shall know that I am the Lord" is used seventy times, indicating the purpose of God disciplining His people.

After showing that the people were at fault for their punishment and captivity, Ezekiel promises that God will punish the nations that rejoiced over Israel's fall (Ezekiel 25–32). Eventually, God would restore the Israelites both spiritually and physically (Ezekiel 33–48). God is gracious and compassionate toward His people then and now.

How can the discipline and chastisement of God produce righteous living?

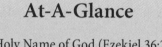

At-A-Glance

1. The Holy Name of God (Ezekiel 36:22–24)
2. The Spiritual Restoration and Physical Restoration (vv. 25–30)
3. The Remembrance and Repentance (vv. 31–32)

In Depth

1. The Holy Name of God (Ezekiel 36:22–24)

God was going to restore the Israelites to protect His holy name. His name is His identity and reputation by which He is known. God's past acts of deliverance sufficiently revealed His true nature. In spite of this, the behavior of the Israelites did not live up to God's holy character. They had profaned His name or made it unholy. This wasn't done secretly; it was done in public "among the nations."

The Israelites did not deserve to be restored or blessed by God. They had shamed God with their evil behavior. But in spite of their sins,

God extended mercy anyway. He revealed His true nature for all the nations to see.

God is merciful, gracious, and compassionate toward us. These are His eternal attributes and they are not predicated on us.

What do we need to modify in our lives in order to better reflect the character of God?

2. The Spiritual Restoration and Physical Restoration (vv. 25–30)

God's first step was to spiritually restore the people. Ezekiel refers to the ritual act of cleansing with water, which was to symbolically purify them (v. 25). The water was mixed with the ashes of a red heifer that did not have a defect or blemish when sacrificed (Numbers 19). Humans could not make themselves clean. Today, the blood of Christ has supreme cleansing power to take away our sin (Hebrews 9:13–14).

The "heart of flesh" represents a pliable, teachable heart versus the "heart of stone," which is hard and stubborn. God promises to give the Israelites a new heart for following Him and infuse His Spirit within them to transform and empower them to submit to His will (vv. 26–27; Psalm 51:7–11). This is needed because on their own, they would always fail to live up to God's standard. The new covenant is promised once again (Jeremiah 31:33–34), and would ultimately be fulfilled in Christ. After the spiritual restoration occurs, God promised to physically restore the Israelites as well. The Israelites would return to their homeland and the land would yield abundant harvests (vv. 28–30).

What is the appropriate way to demonstrate our gratefulness to God for His manifold blessings?

3. The Remembrance and Repentance (vv. 31–32)

After God spiritually and physically restores the Israelites, they will remember their past sins, hate them, and then repent (v. 31). The Lord makes sure that the Israelites know that their goodness is not why He blesses them. God's goodness leads to repentance—in other words, God is God! The blessings that He bestows are not subject to our behavior, but to His identity as God who is gracious and compassionate and full of love for His people. Do we take for granted all the blessings we have been given, not realizing that God's grace is why we have these blessings?

It is easy for us to be proud of our accomplishments and behavior as if they are why we have received so much favor in life. The truth is that no matter how many good deeds we do, we still need God's grace. To think otherwise is an exercise in self-righteousness. This should make us evaluate our lives, repent of wrongdoing, and give thanks to God. He alone is worthy of all honor and glory.

How do we develop a greater sensitivity and receptiveness to the Holy Spirit's nudges toward repentance?

Search the Scriptures

1. Why was God going to act on behalf of Israel (Ezekiel 36:22)?

2. What transformation could be expected when God gave the Israelites a new spirit (v. 27)?

Discuss the Meaning

1. How should we respond to God's grace and mercy toward us?

2. Assess the role confession and repentance have in our spiritual renewal. Is confession more important than repentance, or is it the other way around? Why or why not?

Lesson in Our Society

The world seems to be overrun by people who do evil things. It can make one wonder if people can really change. We do not understand how a heart transformation can occur, but just as God blessed and transformed your life, He can do it for others as well, regardless of their sins. Transformation occurs through the Spirit working on the inside, and eventually, we see it on the outside.

In many African American churches, the culture dictates dressing nicely and being emotionally expressive in services. There is nothing wrong with these things, but we should never judge a person based on their outfit or whether they know how to shout in church. These things do not equate to the inner transformation of the heart, which is what God wants to change and transform.

When you compare your spiritual life now to what it was five years ago, what differences can you identify?

Make It Happen

To have a new heart of flesh is a privilege and a responsibility. With this in mind:

• Repent and thank God for the Spirit that is transforming your life.

• Ask God to make you sensitive to His active work in your life as well as in the life of others.

• List the ways that God has already helped you to make changes in your life.

Follow the Spirit

What God wants me to do:

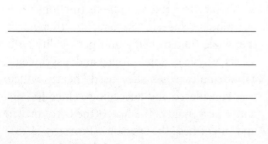

Remember Your Thoughts

Special insights I have learned:

_____

_____

_____

_____

More Light on the Text
Ezekiel 36:22–32

22 Therefore say unto the house of Israel, thus saith the Lord GOD; I do not this for your sakes, O house of Israel, but for mine holy name's sake, which ye have profaned among the heathen, whither ye went.

This passage is the first of three oracles in Ezekiel 36. An oracle is information transmitted from the deity to human beings. An oracle usually either answers important questions or provides a revelation about future events.

In the book of Ezekiel, the problem is that the Israelites have profaned the Lord's name. Furthermore, the Israelites have sullied His name while they were among "the nations to which you came"—the Babylonians who did not follow the Lord. Through the prophetic oracle, the Lord announces preparation to take action in order to protect His name.

23 And I will sanctify my great name, which was profaned among the heathen, which ye have profaned in the midst of them; and the heathen shall know that I am the LORD, saith the Lord GOD, when I shall be sanctified in you before their eyes. 24 For I will take you from among the heathen, and gather you out of all countries, and will bring you into your own land.

The Lord's name and holiness among the *goyim* ("nations") are of utmost concern. The

Hebrew term *goy* (pl, *goyim*, **GOY; goy-EEM**) means a nation, people, or community. In this plural form, it always refers to non-Hebrew peoples. Here, the oracle is most likely referring to the non-Hebrew people whom the Israelites encountered when they were taken into exile. The Israelites had profaned the Lord "in front of company," and therefore have been sent into exile. The exile was intolerable but necessary. The Lord had to take action to ensure that His name's holiness or transcendent power might be vindicated in human history. Specifically, in this oracle, the Lord promises a return of the exiles to their home in the Judean territory.

25 Then will I sprinkle clean water upon you, and ye shall be clean: from all your filthiness, and from all your idols, will I cleanse you.

One way the ancient Israelites reinforced their understanding of themselves as different and set apart from other nations was by establishing boundaries. Throughout the Old Testament, the Israelites mark certain things or activities as "clean" or "unclean." Leviticus 17–26 (the Holiness Code) provides examples of this concern for purity and impurity including religious and cultic cleanliness. Stressing the decree to be holy because Yahweh is holy (Leviticus 19:2, 20:7), these laws contain stipulations regarding illegitimate sacrifice, the proper treatment of blood, prohibitions against a variety of sexual sins, blasphemy, and the role of the priest. These sorts of rules and concerns would have undoubtedly crossed the minds of Ezekiel's audience.

Here, taking center stage are the Hebrew verb *taher* (Heb. **ta-HAIR**), which means "to pronounce clean" or "to purify," and the adjective *tahor* (Heb. **ta-HOR**), which means "clean." The Lord promises to sprinkle clean or pure water on the people. As a result, the people will be clean from all of their uncleanness. Finally, the Lord will purify the people from their idols.

This language hearkens back to the stipulations for holiness and points to a theological hypothesis for the Babylonian exile and the experience of the Judean exiles. For prophets like Ezekiel, one reason for the exile is that the Israelites turned from the Lord and adopted many of the practices of other communities. In so doing, the Israelites defiled themselves or made themselves unclean. As a result, the Lord used the exile to cleanse the people and the land and to restore order. Much of the exilic prophets' concern is identifying what went wrong so that the Israelite community could avoid another catastrophe like an exile in the future. The answer for Ezekiel is attending to ritual and social cleanliness.

26 A new heart also will I give you, and a new spirit will I put within you: and I will take away the stony heart out of your flesh, and I will give you an heart of flesh. 27 And I will put my spirit within you, and cause you to walk in my statutes, and ye shall keep my judgments, and do them.

Building upon the idea that the exilic Israelites have turned away and committed some form of apostasy (the abandonment or renunciation of a religious or political belief), the Lord proposes to correct the situation by changing their heart (Heb. *lev,* **LEB**). Here the word "heart" is used metaphorically to represent the center of something. Note that the ancients did not use detailed psychological vocabulary to make the fine distinctions as in our modern speech. The Israelites thought of the whole human being and personality with all its physical, intellectual, and psychological attributes when they used "heart," which was considered the governing center for the entire personality. The heart (the core) makes and identifies the person (Proverbs 4:23).

Character, personality, will, and mind are modern terms which reflect something of the meaning of "heart" in its biblical usage.

In essence, to change one's heart was to change the will or character. The Lord commits to endow the Israelites with a new will that would be sensitive to Him. In an effort to reclaim the wayward Israelites, the Lord promises to give them a new desire that is an expression of His own spirit. In this way, the covenant relationship might be restored.

The biblical writer paints the Lord as one who is willing to go above and beyond to make things right regardless of who is at fault. This is an encouraging word for modern believers. We serve a God who is willing to extend Himself in order to bring us back into a covenant relationship, even if we have turned away from that relationship.

28 And ye shall dwell in the land that I gave to your fathers; and ye shall be my people, and I will be your God.

Endowed with a new heart and spirit, the Israelites may now benefit from a return to their land. The Lord's promise to return them to the land of their ancestors hearkens back to the Abrahamic Covenant (Genesis 12:1–3), which includes a promise to make Abraham's people into "a great nation" with the promise to bring them into a vast land (Genesis 15:18–21). This is the land that the Israelites inhabited until Nebuchadnezzar seized Jerusalem and deported members of the community to Babylon. The prospect of returning must have held great meaning for the exiles. Beyond leaving their exilic state, returning to "the land that I gave to your fathers" signaled the return to a right relationship with the Lord. The Lord affirms the mending of the covenant relationship with the assurance, "I will be your God."

29 I will also save you from all your uncleannesses: and I will call for the corn,
and will increase it, and lay no famine upon you.

The Lord extends further grace by promising not only to purify the Israelites, but also to protect them from famine. In some ways, these external material changes (plentiful grain in the face of famine) re-inscribe the notion of the inner heart changes made by the Israelites in verse 26. For an agrarian society whose economy is heavily dependent upon crops, animals, and farmland for sustenance, a famine would have dire consequences. If the fields do not produce crops and grain, the people and their animals do not eat. In this way, a famine was synonymous with death.

The Hebrew noun *ra'av* (**rah-AB**) may be translated as "famine" or "hunger." Beyond being physically hungry, this word is also used for a famine of God's Word (Amos 8:11). There is something to be said for being hungry for the Lord. Many modern readers may have experienced situations in which they found themselves in a spiritual famine. In those moments, the urgency of reestablishing and maintaining a relationship with the Lord becomes a life and death situation. God is able to provide divine salvation from the consequences of uncleanness.

30 And I will multiply the fruit of the tree, and the increase of the field, that ye shall receive no more reproach of famine among the heathen. 31 Then shall ye remember your own evil ways, and your doings that were not good, and shall lothe yourselves in your own sight for your iniquities and for your abominations.

These verses extend the idea that the Lord will command nature to produce on behalf of the Israelites now that they have been restored to right relationship. The produce of the land would be responsive to the Lord's command, and the famine associated with judgment earlier in the book would be a thing of the past (Ezekiel 14:21). Additionally, the old ways of the Israelites would be abandoned and forgotten. They would no longer be tempted to turn away from the Lord, but would have an instinctive reaction at the mere remembrance of their former, evil ways. These verses recall Israel's early, sinful history and at the same time warn that this should not be forgotten, but instead be remembered, with real revulsion at the guilt and horror of the past.

32 Not for your sakes do I this, saith the Lord GOD, be it known unto you: be ashamed and confounded for your own ways, O house of Israel.

Returning to the motive outlined in v. 22 ("Not for your sakes do I this"), this verse reiterates that the Israelites' self-promotion and reckless pride associated with their special relationship with the Lord is the central concern of this oracle. The closing imperative ("Be ashamed and confounded") does not call members of its intended audiences to rejoice, but rather to repent.

Responsible discipleship does not lose sight of the fact that we always run the risk of falling short of the conditions of our covenant relationship. We may turn away from the Lord. We may neglect our participation in rituals and customs that reaffirm our relationship to the Lord. We may even align ourselves with things and people that are not godly. And when that happens, the Lord is well within His right to respond in ways that do not bring us joy. As an oracle, however, the words of Ezekiel are meant to serve as a warning. Therefore, for modern readers, this text may serve as a reminder that our relationship with the Lord carries responsibility.

Sources:
Allen, Leslie C. *Ezekiel 20–48*. Grand Rapids, MI: Zondervan, 1990.
Freedman, David Noel, Allen C. Myers, and Astrid B. Beck, eds. *Eerdmans Dictionary of the Bible*. Grand Rapids, MI: W. B. Eerdmans, 2000.
Knohl, Israel. *The Sanctuary of Silence: The Priestly Torah and the Holiness School*. Minneapolis, MN: Fortress, 1995.
Zimmerli, Walther. *Ezekiel 2: A Commentary on the Book of the Prophet Ezekiel, Chapters 25–48*. Minneapolis, MN: Fortress, 1983.

Say It Correctly

Oracle. **OR**-uh-kel.

Daily Bible Readings

MONDAY
A New Covenant of the Heart
(Jeremiah 31:31–34)

TUESDAY
Nations Will Know the Lord
(Ezekiel 36:33–38)

WEDNESDAY
The Lord Will Restore Israel
(Ezekiel 37:11–14)

THURSDAY
Restored as One People
(Ezekiel 37:15–23)

FRIDAY
Making a Covenant of Peace
(Ezekiel 37:24–28)

SATURDAY
Profitable Actions for Everyone
(Titus 3:8–11)

SUNDAY
I Will Restore My Holy Name
(Ezekiel 36:22–32)

Teaching Tips

Words You Should Know

A. Vision (Genesis 15:1) *makhazeh* (Heb.)—A divine revelation while awake providing insight as in a dream.

B. Covenant (v. 18) *berith* (Heb.)—An agreement or understanding between two parties which results in a mutual promise being fulfilled by each.

Teacher Preparation

Unifying Principle—I Will Do This. Due to past disappointments and failures, people fear a continued downward spiral of unfulfilled dreams and goals. How can people find hope to reach fulfillment in life? Although childless, Abram based his hope for descendants on the promises of his covenant with the faithful God.

A. Look up the word "promise." Think about what promises God has fulfilled in your life.

B. Ask yourself what it means to have a covenant with God in today's context.

C. Pray that the Holy Spirit guides you in helping students to experience renewed hope.

O—Open the Lesson

A. Begin the class with prayer.

B. Have students read the In Focus story.

C. Ask the class, "What does it mean to have a covenant with God in today's context?"

D. Have students read the Aim for Change.

P—Present the Scriptures

A. Ask volunteers to read the Focal Verses.

B. Read and discuss the Background section.

C. Use The People, Places, and Times to aid in teaching your lesson.

E—Explore the Meaning

A. Use More Light on the Text to help provide an in-depth discussion of the lesson.

B. Answer the questions in the Discuss the Meaning section.

B. Ask a volunteer to read the Lesson in Our Society and Keep in Mind sections.

N—Next Steps for Application

A. Discuss the Make It Happen section and how to apply it throughout the week.

B. Close class in prayer, thanking God for His covenant with us.

Worship Guide

For the Superintendent or Teacher
Theme: God's Covenant with Abram
Song: "I Just Can't Give Up Now"
Devotional Reading: Psalm 33:1–9

God's Covenant with Abram

Bible Background • GENESIS 15
Printed Text • GENESIS 15:1–6, 17–21 | Devotional Reading • PSALM 33:1–9

—————— Aim for Change ——————

By the end of this lesson, we will: ANALYZE God's promise to Abram; EVALUATE Abram and Sarai's plight by reflecting on times of desperation we have experienced; and CHOOSE methods to bear witness to the hope and fulfillment God has brought to us.

———————— In Focus ————————

Natalie and her husband, Reece, desperately wanted to have children. After waiting the first two years of marriage, they had been trying to get pregnant. Four years later, it still had not happened. They then decided to employ modern medicine and utilize in vitro fertilization, which was expensive. Still they had no success. Natalie felt being childless was possibly their lot in life. "Maybe this is a sign, honey," she told her husband. "God may not have intended for us to have a child of our own." "Don't give up, baby. We just have to believe God and pray. I know we'll be parents, I feel it!" he commented. "We just need to give it time."

Seven months later, Natalie was getting nauseous all of a sudden. Initially she thought it was something she had eaten. However each morning for a week, she got sick. Reece convinced her to go to the doctor, concerned it might be something serious.

After a tense period of waiting, the doctor returned to deliver some important news. "Congratulations, Natalie. You're going to be a mom," the doctor announced. "Excuse me?" she replied. The doctor repeated what she had said. Tears began to stream down Natalie's face as she fully grasped the doctor's words. "Are you okay, Natalie?" the doctor asked, handing her a tissue. Natalie wiped her eyes and said, "Yes, I just can't believe it."

How do you maintain faith in situations where you feel like giving up? In today's lesson, we will learn how God's covenant with Abram encouraged him to keep believing.

—————— Keep in Mind ——————

"In the same day the LORD made a covenant with Abram, saying, Unto thy seed I have given this land, from the river of Egypt, unto the great river, the river Euphrates" (Genesis 15:18).

"In the same day the LORD made a covenant with Abram, saying, Unto thy seed I have given this land, from the river of Egypt, unto the great river, the river Euphrates" (Genesis 15:18).

Focal Verses

KJV **Genesis 15:1** After these things the word of the LORD came unto Abram in a vision, saying, Fear not, Abram: I am thy shield, and thy exceeding great reward.

2 And Abram said, LORD God, what wilt thou give me, seeing I go childless, and the steward of my house is this Eliezer of Damascus?

3 And Abram said, Behold, to me thou hast given no seed: and, lo, one born in my house is mine heir.

4 And, behold, the word of the LORD came unto him, saying, This shall not be thine heir; but he that shall come forth out of thine own bowels shall be thine heir.

5 And he brought him forth abroad, and said, Look now toward heaven, and tell the stars, if thou be able to number them: and he said unto him, So shall thy seed be.

6 And he believed in the LORD; and he counted it to him for righteousness.

17 And it came to pass, that, when the sun went down, and it was dark, behold a smoking furnace, and a burning lamp that passed between those pieces.

18 In the same day the LORD made a covenant with Abram, saying, Unto thy seed have I given this land, from the river of Egypt unto the great river, the river Euphrates:

19 The Kenites, and the Kenizzites, and the Kadmonites,

20 And the Hittites, and the Perizzites, and the Rephaims,

21 And the Amorites, and the Canaanites, and the Girgashites, and the Jebusites.

NLT **Genesis 15:1** Some time later, the LORD spoke to Abram in a vision and said to him, "Do not be afraid, Abram, for I will protect you, and your reward will be great."

2 But Abram replied, "O Sovereign LORD, what good are all your blessings when I don't even have a son? Since you've given me no children, Eliezer of Damascus, a servant in my household, will inherit all my wealth.

3 You have given me no descendants of my own, so one of my servants will be my heir."

4 Then the LORD said to him, "No, your servant will not be your heir, for you will have a son of your own who will be your heir."

5 Then the LORD took Abram outside and said to him, "Look up into the sky and count the stars if you can. That's how many descendants you will have!"

6 And Abram believed the LORD, and the LORD counted him as righteous because of his faith.

17 After the sun went down and darkness fell, Abram saw a smoking firepot and a flaming torch pass between the halves of the carcasses.

18 So the LORD made a covenant with Abram that day and said, "I have given this land to your descendants, all the way from the border of Egypt to the great Euphrates River—

19 the land now occupied by the Kenites, Kenizzites, Kadmonites,

20 Hittites, Perizzites, Rephaites,

21 Amorites, Canaanites, Girgashites, and Jebusites."

The People, Places, and Times

Abram/Abraham. Abram was known as the father of a multitude, the patriarch of the Jewish nation. His story is mostly chronicled in the book of Genesis. Abram was the epitome of a righteous man because of his stalwart faith. Eventually God chose to change Abram's name to Abraham to indicate his destiny as the father of many nations. Abraham's adherence to God's Word allowed him to become a father even in his old age with the birth of Isaac. He was a heroic figure often referenced throughout the Old and New Testaments.

Heir. An heir is someone who is legally entitled to property or family rank as the result of a person's death. In the Old Testament, a father's property was divided among the male children of his legitimate wives. The firstborn son would gain the largest portion due to his rank. One of the eldest's responsibilities would be to take care of his mother, if she was still living. If the a man had no sons, the inheritance went to his daughters, who had to marry within their tribe or risk losing their inheritance. If the man died childless, his property would be divided among his brothers, uncles, or his male servants. The hope in this distribution system was to have the property stay within the family as part of their legacy.

Background

Previously, Abram and his wife, Sarai, had departed Haran because of a severe famine. They decided to go to Egypt. Sarai was beautiful, so the Pharaoh questioned Abram about her. Out of fear that the Pharaoh would kill him to have Sarai, Abram told a half truth and stated that Sarai was his sister instead of his wife. As a result, Sarai was taken to Pharaoh's home. In exchange, Abram received cattle, camels, donkeys, and slaves. The Lord soon stuck Pharaoh's household with plagues because of Abram and Sarai's deceit. Pharaoh asked why Abram lied to him about Sarai. Angry, he sent them both away.

After departing Egypt, Abram rescued his nephew, Lot, from four kings in the region of Sodom and Gomorrah. Lot had lodged near the city of Sodom, and following his arrival, five kings near Jordan were invaded by an

alliance of four kings. When the four kings defeated their enemies, the kings of Sodom and Gomorrah fled, and the four kings seized their property as well. During their invasion, they took Lot and all of his possessions. One of the survivors escaped and informed Abram of the matter. When Abram heard the news about Lot, he assembled over 300 men and attacked them from as far as Hobah to Damascus. He brought back Lot, all of the soldiers' wives, and their goods. Melchizedek, the king of Salem, blessed him for his servitude. When the king of Sodom, however, offered to let Abram keep the possessions, Abram refused. He wanted no one but God to get credit for his wealth.

In spite of his shortcomings, how did Abram demonstrate his faithfulness to God?

At-A-Glance

1. Promise of an Heir (Genesis 15:1–6)
2. Presence of God (v. 17)
3. Promise of Geographic Inheritance (vv. 18–21)

In Depth

1. Promise of an Heir (Genesis 15:1–6)

After all of the events at Sodom and Gomorrah, the Word of the Lord appeared to Abram in a vision. God often revealed His Word to people through visions and dreams. God informed Abram not to be afraid. This command was followed by saying that He would be a shield or protector for him and would reward him for not accepting the soldiers' belongings offered to him by the king of Sodom. Not concerned about earthly riches, Abram desired a child. Abram's reverential response was "Lord," referring to Him as the all-powerful, "You have given me no descendants, so one of my servants will be my heir."

The all-knowing God was aware of Abram's childless plight. In response, He promised Abram that he would have a son of his "own body" who would be his heir. More amazingly, God told Abram that he would have multiple descendants.

God is also aware of our plight as well. When we face impossible situations, not only can God provide for us and work things out, but also He can do "exceedingly abundantly above all we ask or think" (Ephesians 3:20).

Are you facing an impossible situation and depending on God to work things out?

2. Presence of God (v. 17)

The presence of God is often showcased through symbolism throughout the Old Testament. Abram's interaction with God demonstrates His presence through symbolism: a smoking firepot and blazing torch. God showcased Himself by passing between the divided animals. This action was an outward expression of God's covenant with Abram that He would fulfill His promise to him.

Scholars have suggested that the firepot and torch represent several things. Some say they are the Israelites' trials and deliverance; others say the firepot signified the Israelite's affliction and God's Word for the people in Egypt, while the torch represented the Lord's comfort and direction. No matter the opinion, all agree that the symbols represent a manifestation of God's divine presence with Abram. The believer can experience this same presence as a partaker of the Abrahamic blessing.

Do you "see" any symbolism of God's presence in your faith journey?

3. Promise of Geographic Inheritance (vv. 18–21)

God goes into detail about His covenant with Abram. He explains the specifics of the land He would give to Abram's lineage. It would extend from the border of Egypt to the great Euphrates River, a land inhabited by ten different people groups: Kenites, Kenizzites, Kadmonites, Hittites, Perizzites, Rephaites, Amorites, Canaanites, Girgashites, and Jebusites. God outlined what actions He would take on Abram's behalf. He identified the locations and which people would be displaced. All of this occurred to solidify His commitment to Abram and strengthen his faith.

Some might think the child and the land were Abram's prize, but the real prize was God Himself and Abram's communion with Him. The revelation that Abram would have land that his descendants would inherit only bolstered his faith in God. Delay was not denial, but a preparatory pause for the greater portion of the blessing. In the same way, as believers, we may not have the promise of an earthly real estate, but we do have an inheritance to claim when God creates a new heaven and a new earth. That land will be ours to enjoy eternally.

As the heirs of Christ, what inheritance can we anticipate?

Search the Scriptures

1. How could it be perceived that Abram seemed ungrateful to God (Genesis 15:2)?

2. In what ways does God reinforce His covenant to Abram (vv. 17–21)?

Discuss the Meaning

1. What covenant or promise has God made to you? Why can you depend on God to fulfill His promise?

2. Summarize the signs or confirmations God has provided for you as you await His promise in your life.

Lesson in Our Society

We live in a microwave society; we want everything now. This is troublesome because whenever what we desire is delayed or seems impossible, we become disappointed and lose hope. We naturally experience discouragement when people, situations, and circumstances say *no*. That's when faith in God is needed. Many believe that money and other people are the ultimate controllers of our destiny. On the contrary, God can alter lives and change disappointments to delight. Never esteem man's thinking over God's words. Believers live by different standards. God can do what society deems impossible. All He wants is our commitment to His Word.

Over the last few years, we have seen our share of injustices regarding police and the judicial system. Our emotions might urge retaliation, and we might want to take matters into our own hands out of personal desperation. Still, in our spirits, we know that is not how Jesus would respond. How do we hold on to hope and God's promises in the midst of such turmoil?

Look at the life of Jesus. He was innocent of all crimes and was still persecuted. He could have retaliated with a heavenly army, but He chose not to. Jesus suffered so that we may follow His example. Since God is just, we can trust that He will hand out His justice to those who deserve it in its proper season. Our role is to be a positive voice in our community and to do all that we can to peacefully effect change.

How does God's faithfulness to His promises in the past teach us to have hope for the future?

Make It Happen

Like Abram, it is legitimate to voice your concerns to God. His ear is always available to listen to the concerns of His children. What are you believing God for in your life? Have you lost hope because of disappointment, or will you continue to believe?

• Compare and contrast how God's promises were true in biblical times and how they are still true today.

• Consider the importance of legacy and devise ways now that you can be a blessing to future generations.

• Reflect on how you discerned God's promises specifically for you.

Follow the Spirit

What God wants me to do:

_____

_____

_____

_____

Remember Your Thoughts

Special insights I have learned:

_____

_____

_____

_____

More Light on the Text

Genesis 15:1–6, 17–21

1 After these things the word of the LORD came unto Abram in a vision, saying, Fear not, Abram: I am thy shield, and thy exceeding great reward.

Visions and dreams are important ways for God to speak to people in both the Old and New Testaments—God uses visions and dreams to commission prophets (Ezekiel 1:1), instruct about coming offspring (Matthew 1:20–24), and make promises of rewards and warn of punishment (Daniel 2; Revelation 6–7).

God lets Abram know that He is his shield (Heb. *magen*, **mah-GEN**). This type of shield is a small military shield or decorative piece and calls to mind the image of God as not only a protector but also the glory of Abram's house (cf. Psalm 3:3). Abram and his descendants will face many opponents and oppressors, and God promises to be their protector.

The clause, "and thy exceeding great reward" (KJV), assures that God will be both protector and reward. The NLT reads, "and your reward will be great," suggesting that God's reward will exceed expectations. Both are possibilities in the Hebrew language. Whether God Himself is the reward or the provider, the point is that Abram will receive a reward for his faith. Certainly, his relationship with God and the Lord's ongoing protection are rewarded but the passage also promises that Abram's offspring will eventually have land and wealth (vv. 14, 18).

2 And Abram said, LORD God, what wilt thou give me, seeing I go childless, and the steward of my house is this Eliezer of Damascus? 3 And Abram said, Behold, to me thou hast given no seed: and, lo, one born in my house is mine heir.

Abram's response is to ask God what He can possibly give to him as a reward since Abram has no children. There is no one to inherit his household and carry on his name; a man who is not even a blood relation will inherit his household. Abram even uses the Hebrew word for *son* ironically here, calling Eliezer of Damascus literally, "the son ruling my house" (Heb. *ben*, BEN). Offspring, especially male offspring, were a sign of prosperity and security in antiquity. Male children typically inherited the property and carried on the family name. Occasionally daughters could also inherit their parents' property (Joshua 17:3–6), but Abram has neither sons nor daughters. His anguish is clear—he could not consider anything a reward so long as he has no children. The best

he can hope for is to pass his inheritance to a foreigner in his house.

4 And, behold, the word of the LORD came unto him, saying, This shall not be thine heir; but he that shall come forth out of thine own bowels shall be thine heir. 5 And he brought him forth abroad, and said, Look now toward heaven, and tell the stars, if thou be able to number them: and he said unto him, So shall thy seed be.

God responds, saying that the household steward will not inherit Abram's house, but instead, Abram will have a child of his own, who will be his heir. Eliezer of Damascus is called "this one," suggesting that he is closer to Abram because he currently lives in his household, but the actual heir ("that one"), the one yet to be born, is the one who is part of God's promise. What is closest to us is not always what God has in mind, and Abram is reminded of that when he is taken outside of his household ("abroad") and told to count the stars if he can. Again the idea of distance is connected to Abram's offspring and God's promise. His offspring will be as countless as the stars, which are also far removed from his personal household.

6 And he believed in the LORD; and he counted it to him for righteousness.

This verse is central to both Jewish and Christian faiths as it reveals that righteousness is connected to trusting God. Paul cites this verse to remind the churches in Rome and Galatia that faith and trust in God are what matters (Romans 4:3; Galatians 3:6). Paul's point is that it does not matter whether a person is Jewish or Gentile; trust in God is what matters. Abram was considered righteous before the circumcision covenant was established (Genesis 17). Therefore, his trust in God established his relationship with God. The verses that follow detail a faithful person unafraid to question God. Yes, Abram believed God, but he also needed reassurance, so he asked God how he will know that he will inherit the land. God's response is to ask Abram to bring Him sacrifices (v. 9), after which He promises once again that Abram's descendants will inherit the land (vv. 13–16).

17 And it came to pass, that, when the sun went down, and it was dark, behold a smoking furnace, and a burning lamp that passed between those pieces.

During the night, God spoke to Abram in a terrifying dream (v. 12), warning him that his descendants will be oppressed immigrants in a foreign land for 400 years (ten generations). Nevertheless, God will punish the oppressors, Abram's people will leave with great wealth (v. 14), and Abram will live a long life and be buried in peace (v. 15). Not all divine dreams and promises are entirely about peace and prosperity, but God is with His people in the midst of crisis, whether it's childlessness, alienation, or oppression. Now Abram has a vision of a smoking furnace and a burning lamp passing among the pieces of the animal sacrifices. The furnace represents an oven used for baking (Leviticus 2:4), and the burning lamp is God (cf. Exodus 3:2), who passes through the sacrifices while Abram sleeps, indicating His presence with him. The sacrifices are a visual representation of the covenant that will serve as a reminder to Abram and the Israelites who will base their faith and trust in God on this ancestral narrative.

18 In the same day the LORD made a covenant with Abram, saying, Unto thy seed have I given this land, from the river of Egypt unto the great river, the river Euphrates: 19 The Kenites, and the Kenizzites, and the Kadmonites, 20 And the Hittites, and the Perizzites, and the Rephaims, 21 And the Amorites, and the Canaanites, and the Girgashites, and the Jebusites.

The phrase in Hebrew, "made a covenant," is literally to "cut" or "carve" (Heb. *karat*, **kah-ROT**) a covenant. This expression is used both for the covenants God makes with His people and for political agreements between nations and people (Genesis 21:32). The promise God makes to Abram is an official promise that He must keep, with God as Lord and Abram as an obedient servant. Not only will Abram, who has grieved his childlessness, have numerous offspring, but also his descendants will inherit the land from Egypt to the Euphrates. The land promised to Abram is Israel's land at the height of Solomon's reign (1 Kings 4:21).

The relationship of the peoples listed in verses 19–21 is unclear in the Hebrew, as the KJV and other translations indicate. The NLT suggests that these peoples were currently living in the land, but they would not always be there. The Common English Bible suggests that the Israelites will live in the land with these peoples, an accurate description of the situation in Joshua and Judges since the Israelites were not able to drive all the peoples out of the land (Joshua 17:12–13; Judges 1:21–36). This reading is supported by the history of Joshua and Judges, as well as by the Hebrew at the beginning of verse 18.

In this case, God promises a land rich in diversity, with many peoples living together along with the Israelites. Scholar Randall Bailey points out that Genesis frequently talks about the Israelites living among other peoples, who are ancestrally related to the Israelites since all are descendants of Noah (Bailey 111). The apostle Paul's fondness for this chapter may rest not only the fact that circumcision is unnecessary for righteousness, but also that God's promise to Abram includes a family of his own, a secure place to live, and an opportunity to live with people of other families and cultures free from oppression and abounding in prosperity.

Sources:
Bailey, Randall C. "Genesis." *The Peoples' Companion to the Bible.* Edited by Curtiss Paul DeYoung, et al. Minneapolis, MN: Fortress Press, 2010. 111–112.
Brueggemann, Walter. *Genesis. Interpretation 1.* Edited by James Luther Mays, et al. Atlanta: John Knox Press, 1982.
Sarna, Nahum M. *Genesis. The JPS Torah Commentary.* Edited by Nahum Sarna and Chaim Potok. Philadelphia: Jewish Publication Society, 1989.
Wenham, Gordon J. *Genesis 1–15. Word Biblical Commentary 1.* Edited by David A. Hubbard and Glenn W. Barker. Waco, TX: Word Books, 1987.

Say It Correctly

Eliezer. eh-lee-**AY**-zer.
Rephaims. reh-**FEYE**-eems.
Heir. **AIR**.
Euphrates. you-**FRAY**-teez.

Daily Bible Readings

MONDAY
The Lord's Words Become Actions
(Psalm 33:1–9)

TUESDAY
Abram Called and Blessed
(Genesis 12:1–3)

WEDNESDAY
God Promises Abram Land and Descendants
(Genesis 13:14–17)

THURSDAY
Angel Will Lead Conquest of Canaan
(Exodus 23:23–27)

FRIDAY
Promises of Land and Posterity Fulfilled
(1 Kings 4:20–25)

SATURDAY
Abram an Example of Righteous Faith
(Romans 4:1–4)

SUNDAY
Abram Enters into Covenant With God
(Genesis 15:1–6, 17–21)

Notes

Teaching Tips

Words You Should Know

A. Trumpet (Exodus 19:19) *shofar* (Heb.)—A ram's horn used to signal war and peace, celebrations, new moon, new beginnings, danger, and death of a dignitary.

B. Sanctify (v. 22) *qadash* (Heb.)—To remove from common use; to render holy or set apart by means of religious rites.

Teacher Preparation

Unifying Principle—Be Ready. Because of their human weakness, people need help from something outside of themselves. How do people engage a power stronger and different than they are? In making a covenant with the holy and powerful God, the Israelites consecrated themselves to stand in His awesome presence.

A. Read the Bible Background and Devotional Readings.

B. Pray that your students will consecrate themselves.

C. Read the Focal Verses in two or more translations.

O—Open the Lesson

A. Open with prayer and ask God's assistance in teaching today's lesson.

B. Have the students read Aim for Change and the In Focus story.

C. Pose the question, "How many of you have ever had to go to your boss with a difficult question? Did you prepare yourself (e.g., mentally)?"

D. Read the Keep in Mind section and discuss.

P—Present the Scriptures

A. Have volunteers read Focal Verses.

B. Read The People, Places, and Times, Background, and In Depth.

C. Read More Light on the Text and discuss.

E—Explore the Meaning

A. Divide the class into groups and discuss the Lesson in Our Society and Make It Happen sections.

B. Ask students to share the most significant point they learned in the lesson and how they will seek to incorporate it this week.

N—Next Steps for Application

A. Complete the Follow the Spirit and Remember Your Thoughts sections.

B. Close in prayer, thanking God for His presence in class and for continued guidance in our lives.

Worship Guide

For the Superintendent or Teacher
Theme: God's Covenant with Israel
Song: "Create in Me a Clean Heart"
Devotional: Psalm 135:1–9, 19–21

God's Covenant with Israel

Bible Background • EXODUS 19, ISAIAH 60:3
Printed Text • EXODUS 19:16–25 | Devotional Reading • PSALM 135:1–9,19–21

———— Aim for Change ————

By the end of this lesson, we will: EVALUATE ways the Israelites consecrated themselves to receive the Law from a holy, just, and powerful God; ASPIRE to live lives befitting God's obedient servants; and ENGAGE in worship practices reflecting our reverence for God.

———— ✄ In Focus ————

McKay was filled with excitement as she circled through the revolving doors of her new graphics design job. After years of contracting, she desperately wanted to land a full-time job with benefits and paid time off. Now she finally had one! *I can't believe after all these years, I've got a regular job doing something that I love!* She pressed the elevator button to take her to the fifth floor and walked to the Human Resources department.

As she went in, she noticed several other people with a similar gleam on their faces. They undoubtedly must be new hires also. A petite woman with her hair pulled back emerged from one of the offices and announced, "Good morning, everyone!" Her bubbly demeanor confirmed to McKay that this was definitely the right company. "Let me take you to our orientation room. This will be your home for the next week."

McKay was puzzled. She didn't expect an orientation. She thought she'd just be told where to sit.

"We will provide our company's values along with historical information about our company. This will help you understand why this is such a great place to work," the HR associate stated. "We know that you are qualified employees. Now, we want to congratulate you in successfully joining our corporate community. You will love it!" McKay was determined to learn all that she could. She anticipated a bright future in her new job.

How do you handle being introduced to new situations? In today's lesson, we will learn how the Israelites entered their new life as a nation by consecrating themselves to God.

———— Keep in Mind ————

"And Moses brought forth the people out of the camp to meet with God; and they stood at the nether part of the mount" (Exodus 19:17).

"And Moses brought forth the people out of the camp to meet with God; and they stood at the nether part of the mount" (Exodus 19:17).

Focal Verses

KJV **Exodus 19:16** And it came to pass on the third day in the morning, that there were thunders and lightnings, and a thick cloud upon the mount, and the voice of the trumpet exceeding loud; so that all the people that was in the camp trembled.

17 And Moses brought forth the people out of the camp to meet with God; and they stood at the nether part of the mount.

18 And mount Sinai was altogether on a smoke, because the LORD descended upon it in fire: and the smoke thereof ascended as the smoke of a furnace, and the whole mount quaked greatly.

19 And when the voice of the trumpet sounded long, and waxed louder and louder, Moses spake, and God answered him by a voice.

20 And the LORD came down upon mount Sinai, on the top of the mount: and the LORD called Moses up to the top of the mount; and Moses went up.

21 And the LORD said unto Moses, Go down, charge the people, lest they break through unto the LORD to gaze, and many of them perish.

22 And let the priests also, which come near to the LORD, sanctify themselves, lest the LORD break forth upon them.

23 And Moses said unto the LORD, The people cannot come up to mount Sinai: for thou chargedst us, saying, Set bounds about the mount, and sanctify it.

24 And the LORD said unto him, Away, get thee down, and thou shalt come up, thou, and Aaron with thee: but let not the priests and the people break through to come up unto the LORD, lest he break forth upon them.

25 So Moses went down unto the people, and spake unto them.

NLT **Exodus 19:16** On the morning of the third day, thunder roared and lightning flashed, and a dense cloud came down on the mountain. There was a long, loud blast from a ram's horn, and all the people trembled.

17 Moses led them out from the camp to meet with God, and they stood at the foot of the mountain.

18 All of Mount Sinai was covered with smoke because the LORD had descended on it in the form of fire. The smoke billowed into the sky like smoke from a brick kiln, and the whole mountain shook violently.

19 As the blast of the ram's horn grew louder and louder, Moses spoke, and God thundered his reply.

20 The LORD came down on the top of Mount Sinai and called Moses to the top of the mountain. So Moses climbed the mountain.

21 Then the LORD told Moses, "Go back down and warn the people not to break through the boundaries to see the LORD, or they will die.

22 Even the priests who regularly come near to the LORD must purify themselves so that the LORD does not break out and destroy them."

23 "But LORD," Moses protested, "the people cannot come up to Mount Sinai. You already warned us. You told me, 'Mark off a boundary all around the mountain to set it apart as holy.'"

24 But the LORD said, "Go down and bring Aaron back up with you. In the meantime, do not let the priests or the people break through to approach the LORD, or he will break out and destroy them."

25 So Moses went down to the people and told them what the LORD had said.

The People, Places, and Times

Moses. Moses, the Old Testament Hebrew prophet, delivered the Israelites from Egyptian slavery under Pharaoh's rule. His name is derived from the Hebrew root meaning "to take out," since as a baby, he was taken out of the water by Pharaoh's daughter (Exodus 2). Moses was the primary leader and legislator during the Hebrews' time in the wilderness. God gave Moses the Ten Commandments, His covenant with Israel. Moses also acted as interpreter of the Law that established faith and civil traditions, many of which still exist today.

Mount Sinai. This is the mountain where God talked with Moses and gave him the Ten Commandments, also called the Law. This mountain is often paired with Mount Horeb. Scholars believe Horeb is the mountain range, and Mount Sinai is a mountain summit on the ridge. Scholars do not agree on the exact geographic location of Mount Sinai; Jebel Serbel in the central Sinai and Jebel Musa in southern Sinai have been the major contenders. Mount Sinai is viewed as sacred not only in the Jewish tradition, but also for Christians and Muslims as well.

Why was it necessary for God to select sacred places for His people to experience His presence?

Background

Chapter 19 is a pivotal shift in the book of Exodus. It begins with the people of Israel arriving at the wilderness of Sinai. From Mount Sinai, the Lord called Moses and asked him to relay an important message to the people of Israel. He wanted Moses to explain what He had done to the Egyptians and how He had delivered Israel out of their hands. It was for their deliverance, but it was also God's definitive desire to bring the Israelites closer to Him. All they had to do was keep His covenant and He would make them a holy nation, a kingdom of priests.

Subsequently, Moses came down and summoned all of the elders and told the people what the Lord had commanded him. The Israelites agreed to obey all that God commanded. Moses relayed the Israelites' agreement to the Lord. Then, Moses received more instructions. He was to tell the people of Israel that the Lord would come down in the form of a dense cloud so that the people could fully trust the word of Moses.

Before God spoke to them, everyone would need to consecrate themselves—wash their clothes, and stay away from the mountain for three days. Anyone who touched any aspect of the mountain would be stoned to death or shot with arrows. Moses relayed all of the Lord's commands and added that they should abstain from having intimate relations.

What does it mean for us "to consecrate" ourselves before God?

At-A-Glance

1. God's Wondrous Presence
(Exodus 19:16–19)
2. Need for a Mediator (vv. 17, 19–25)

In Depth

1. God's Wondrous Presence (Exodus 19:16–19)

Imagine the grandest special effects in a movie involving a volcano, thunder, and lightning. This would still pale in comparison with the wondrous display God provided at Mount Sinai for the Israelites. On the morning of the third day, following their time of consecration, God displayed Himself through thunder, lightning, a dense cloud, and the sound of a loud trumpet. Mount Sinai was completely enveloped in smoke. The smoke went out as though from a furnace, and the mountain shook.

Thunder, lightning, and smoke have often been associated with God's presence throughout the Old and New Testaments.

For the believer, God's presence signals His power and sovereignty. God is not just at a special designated holy place. He lives within us. This means that our entire lives are consecrated to Him on a daily basis. With this knowledge, we walk in the fear of the Lord. Although we do not witness the same visual spectacle as the Israelites did at the foot of Mount Sinai, still we are in awe of God's presence just the same. And, we fear God, which means that we respect and reverence Him!

How has God demonstrated His power and presence in your life?

2. Need for a Mediator (vv. 17, 19–25)

In these verses, Moses' position as the leader of this movement is reemphasized. It was initially showcased in Egypt with his interactions with Pharaoh. Here he remains as God's choice to be the mediator between Him and the people. In verse 17, Moses leads the people to meet God. In verse 19, Moses converses with God. These actions alone indicate God's favor toward Moses.

In verse 20, God only calls Moses up to the mountain and not the priests. A constant going to and fro from the mountain shows God and Moses exchanging dialogue and continuing their relationship. Yet, if any of the Israelites were to go to the mountain, they would die. Later, God calls Aaron, Moses' brother, to join in the dialogue. God appoints Aaron as Moses' mouthpiece to speak on Moses' behalf.

This should confirm that Moses was the intermediary. He was readying the people for their introduction to God. Moses' encounters with God foreshadow man's need for a mediator, Jesus. God wanted to reinforce the ongoing message that the only way to come into His presence without judgment is through an intermediary assigned by Him. As the Israelites had Moses, we have Jesus—our divine intermediary who goes to the Father on our behalf.

Why are intermediaries important in assessing circumstances in our daily lives?

Search the Scriptures

1. Why do you think God chose to display Himself in multiple forms (Exodus 19:16)? Would you be terrified to "see" God in such a display?

2. Why did God allow Aaron to come up to Mount Sinai but not the rest of the priests or the people (v. 24)?

Discuss the Meaning

1. Why do you think God was seeking to deepen His relationship with the Israelites at Mount Sinai?

2. How does God meet with and talk to His people today?

Lesson in Our Society

As Christians, although we are not of the world, we still can be influenced by it. One of the ways is through a sense of entitlement. This "I am able to do it on my own" mentality can be dangerous. This inward focus on "what I deserve," or "my rights," and "my priority" allows many to believe they don't need anyone else. Self-sufficiency is one of the world's most dangerous fallacies.

The Israelites needed Moses to be the mediator for them because they weren't worthy to be in God's presence, even after consecrating themselves. We need Jesus as our Mediator, because our best righteousness is like filthy rags (Isaiah 64:6). We are never too important to need others, especially God.

Oftentimes, the church can become just a show, but this is not what God intended. We are there to worship the God who has invited us to experience His presence through the New

Covenant. Some of us in the Black community face new challenges. We may have new jobs or new families. Some of us face the challenge of being the only Black person in a certain neighborhood or business.

The good news is that God is there with you. Jesus has already brought you into the presence of the same God who brought Israel into the Promised Land. Don't be afraid of the new situation. Orient yourself around the presence of the Almighty God and He will show you the way forward.

How can we remind ourselves and others that God is present with us in the midst of new challenges?

Make It Happen

As followers of Christ, we are grateful that we have a mediator in Jesus Christ in order to have a relationship with a holy God.

• Spend some time worshiping God and contemplating how holy He is in relation to our sinfulness.

• Write "God" down on a piece of paper and draw a large circle around it. Inside the circle, list what God is responsible for in your life. Then write "Me" on a piece of paper and circle it. In the circle, write what you are responsible for in your life.

• Ask a friend or relative who doesn't know Jesus what comes to mind when they think of being in God's presence.

Follow the Spirit

What God wants me to do:

_____

_____

_____

_____

Remember Your Thoughts

Special insights I have learned:

_____

_____

_____

_____

More Light on the Text

Exodus 19:16–25

16 And it came to pass on the third day in the morning, that there were thunders and lightnings, and a thick cloud upon the mount, and the voice of the trumpet exceeding loud; so that all the people that was in the camp trembled.

Having prepared themselves by staying pure, washing their clothes, and standing at the foot of the mountain, the people experience God's presence as promised in the form of thunder, lightning, a thick cloud, and a very loud trumpet. This causes everyone to tremble. The Hebrew word for "tremble" (*chared*, **khah-RED**) usually has a sense of fear associated with it, so it is more than just a physical shaking from the sights and sounds (see Isaiah 41:5); God's presence evokes fear and trembling. God is at once very noticeable in the forms of loud sounds and lightning, but also enigmatic as a thick cloud covers the mountain.

17 And Moses brought forth the people out of the camp to meet with God; and they stood at the nether part of the mount. 18 And mount Sinai was altogether on a smoke, because the LORD descended upon it in fire: and the smoke thereof ascended as the smoke of a furnace, and the whole mount quaked greatly.

Moses was told that when the horn sounded, the people could go to the mountain (v. 13), and they respond accordingly. Now, the whole mountain is covered in smoke because the Lord has come down to the top of the mountain. God and the people cannot be in too close proximity to one another. The people may not go up the mountain or even touch its border, and God does not descend any farther than the peak. God's presence is once again that of fire and smoke, causing the whole mountain to "quake." This is the same verb that was used in verse 16 concerning the people's response to the thunder, lightning, and cloud. God's presence causes both the people and the mountain itself to tremble.

19 And when the voice of the trumpet sounded long, and waxed louder and louder, Moses spake, and God answered him by a voice.

Sounds keep increasing—the sound of the trumpet, the sound of God's voice. Both "voice" and "thunder" are the same word in Hebrew, which is a general word for a sound (Heb. *qol*, **KOLE**). God shows Himself to the people and commands them through various sounds, including the trumpet, thunder, and His voice. The New Living Translation captures the connection by saying that "God thundered his reply." The trumpet keeps getting louder in order to reveal how powerful God's voice is—louder than even the loudest horn, akin to the sound of thunder.

20 And the LORD came down upon mount Sinai, on the top of the mount: and the LORD called Moses up to the top of the mount; and Moses went up. 21 And the LORD said unto Moses, Go down, charge the people, lest they break through unto the LORD to gaze, and many of them perish. 22 And let the priests also, which come near to the LORD, sanctify themselves, lest the LORD break forth upon them.

The text reminds us that the Lord came down to the top of the mountain and called only Moses to come up. Now God has a command for the people from the top of the mountain. The command is a reiteration of the command God gave Moses to tell the people on the first day—they are not to come close enough to see the Lord. If they do, they will die. The word "breakthrough" (Heb. *haras*, **hah-RAHS**) has the sense of tearing down a structure, in this case, the boundary God has created between the people and His presence (v. 12). Likewise, any priests who approach the Lord must sanctify themselves or the Lord will explode with anger against them. The Hebrew word for "break forth" (*parats*, **pah-RAHTS**) carries a physical image of destruction. The Lord will break out in anger and severely punish (by death) those priests who are not properly set apart for Him.

23 And Moses said unto the LORD, The people cannot come up to mount Sinai: for thou chargedst us, saying, Set bounds about the mount, and sanctify it. 24 And the LORD said unto him, Away, get thee down, and thou shalt come up, thou, and Aaron with thee: but let not the priests and the people break through to come up unto the LORD, lest he break forth upon them.

Moses' response to God's warning of punishment is that the people cannot do what God is warning them against because He has commanded them not to do it. They have already been told to establish a boundary around the mountain and sanctify it (v. 12). "To sanctify" in Hebrew (*qadash*, **kah-DASH**) is always associated with boundaries. To sanctify or consecrate is to set somebody or something apart for a special purpose, whether as a priest or prophet of God or as a burnt offering to Him.

The mountain has been set apart in both a physical and a spiritual sense. God's response is to tell Moses to go back down the mountain and come up with Aaron. None of the priests or the people may cross the boundary, though—only Moses and Aaron or God will explode with anger. Previously the priests were told they must sanctify themselves if they approach God (v. 22), but now they are prohibited from ascending the mountain. Some scholars have proposed that this potential conflict represents different traditions in antiquity, some of which allowed any priest to approach God if properly sanctified, some of which only allowed the high priest to do so. The reason for this seeming conflict in commands regarding the priests is unclear. The most likely answer is that now that Moses is about to ascend the mountain to receive the Ten Commandments, the centerpiece of God's covenant with the Israelites, only Aaron and Moses may ascend the mountain, whereas at other times the priests could approach God (see Exodus 24).

25 So Moses went down unto the people, and spake unto them.

Verse 25 reminds us that throughout the chapter, Moses has been a messenger between God and the people. God does not speak directly to the people not even to the priests, and only at the end of the chapter when God calls Moses back up for the Ten Commandments can Aaron accompany him up the mountain. God's holiness demands fear and honor, and for His people these entail being aware of God's presence and listening to His commands, as well as acknowledging His distinction as the Almighty through a physical distance from God's holy mountain.

Sources:

Durham, John I. *Exodus. Word Biblical Commentary 3*. Edited by David A. Hubbard and Glenn W. Barker. Waco, TX: Word Books, 1987.

Fretheim, Terence E. *Exodus. Interpretation 2*. Edited by James Luther Mays, et al. Atlanta, GA: John Knox Press, 1991.

Pixley, Jorge. "Exodus." *The Peoples' Companion to the Bible*. Edited by Curtiss Paul DeYoung, et al. Minneapolis, MN: Fortress Press, 2010. 112–114.

Propp, William H.C. *Exodus 19–40. Anchor Bible Commentary 2A*. Edited by William Foxwell Albright and David Noel Freedman. New York, NY: Doubleday, 2006.

Sarna, Nahum M. Exodus. *The JPS Torah Commentary*. Edited by Nahum Sarna and Chaim Potok. Philadelphia, PA: Jewish Publication Society, 1989.

Say It Correctly

Sinai. **SIGH**-nigh.
Sanctify. **SANK**-ti-feye.

Daily Bible Readings

MONDAY
You are God's Choice
(Deuteronomy 10:12–22)

TUESDAY
Prepare to Meet Your God
(Exodus 19:9b–15)

WEDNESDAY
The Triumphant Glory of God
(Isaiah 60:1–7)

THURSDAY
House of Israel, Praise the Lord
(Psalm 135:1–9, 19–21)

FRIDAY
Revealed in a New Way
(Luke 9:28–36)

SATURDAY
A Chosen Race, a Holy People
(1 Peter 2:1–10)

SUNDAY
Worship God through Obedience
(Exodus 19:16–25)

Teaching Tips

Words You Should Know

A. Fear (Exodus 20:20) *yare'* (Heb.)—To be afraid; to stand in awe; to show proper honor or reverence.

B. Prove (v. 20) *nasah* (Heb.)—To test.

Teacher Preparation

Unifying Principle—A Covenant is a Serious Thing. Without obedience to law, people live in chaos, hurting themselves, others, and their environment. Where can people get a law that they will obey? God delivered the commandments to the Israelites while showing divine and holy power that tested them to convince them to obey the laws of the covenant.

A. Pray that the Holy Spirit will help your students to honor the contracts and agreements they have made with others.

B. Read Genesis 12:1–3, 15:5, 18, 17:1–16 for background on God's covenant with Abraham.

O—Open the Lesson

A. Open with prayer.

B. Introduce the lesson by reading the Aim for Change statements.

C. Ask a student to read the In Focus story. Then facilitate a brief discussion about it.

P—Present the Scriptures

A. Ask a student to read the Focal Verses.

B. Use The People, Places, and Times, Background, Search the Scriptures, At-A-Glance outline, In Depth, and More Light on the Text sections to clarify the verses.

E—Explore the Meaning

A. Depending on the size of the class, divide the class into groups of four to six students each. Invite them to talk about the Discuss the Meaning, Lesson in Our Society, and Make It Happen sections. Ask each group to select a representative to report their responses.

B. Facilitate a discussion on how the students connect their responses to the Aim for Change and Keep in Mind verse.

N—Next Steps for Application

A. Summarize the lesson.

B. Close with prayer.

Worship Guide

For the Superintendent or Teacher
Theme: Obeying God's Law
Song: "Take My Life and Let It Be"
Devotional Reading: Psalm 119:49–64

Obeying God's Law

Bible Background • EXODUS 20
Printed Text • EXODUS 20:18–26 | Devotional Reading • PSALM 119:49–64

Aim for Change

By the end of this lesson, we will: EXPLORE the divine manifestations and warnings that accompanied the giving of the Ten Commandments; ASPIRE to live in more perfect obedience to God's laws; and SHARE one way to show God that we are serious about obeying His laws.

In Focus

Stephan and Carmella were married right out of school and rented a walk-up apartment near Carmella's parents' brownstone. After four years of hard work and saving what they could, they decided it was time to buy their first home. They found a charming row house in their neighborhood and set off to see the loan officer at the neighborhood bank.

"Banks are imposing, and bankers intimidate me," Stephan told Carmella the morning of their appointment. "Don't worry," Carmella replied, "we are also meeting my uncle who studied law, and he can help us understand the documents and explain our rights and obligations. As for the bank building, those marble columns, high ceilings, and ornate wooden desks are all meant to assure us that the bank is solid, stable, and invested in our community." Excited, yet a bit apprehensive, Stephan held Carmella's hand tightly as they walked through the massive brass and glass doors of the local bank.

On their way back to their apartment, Stephan commented, "I feel so much better. The people at the bank were respectful and were willing to trust us with this loan. Let's pray together right now that God will help us to honor our part in this, and that He will enable us to show that their trust in us is well placed."

Describe a time when someone didn't do their part to honor an agreement. In this lesson, we will find out how the Israelites were called to honor their covenant agreement with God.

Keep in Mind

"In all places where I record my name I will come unto thee, and I will bless thee" (from Exodus 20:24).

"In all places where I record my name I will come unto thee, and I will bless thee" (from Exodus 20:24).

Focal Verses

KJV **Exodus 20:18** And all the people saw the thundering, and the lightnings, and the noise of the trumpet, and the mountain smoking: and when the people saw it, they removed, and stood afar off.

19 And they said unto Moses, Speak thou with us, and we will hear: but let not God speak with us, lest we die.

20 And Moses said unto the people, Fear not: for God is come to prove you, and that his fear may be before your faces, that ye sin not.

21 And the people stood afar off, and Moses drew near unto the thick darkness where God was.

22 And the LORD said unto Moses, Thus thou shalt say unto the children of Israel, Ye have seen that I have talked with you from heaven.

23 Ye shall not make with me gods of silver, neither shall ye make unto you gods of gold.

24 An altar of earth thou shalt make unto me, and shalt sacrifice thereon thy burnt offerings, and they peace offering, they sheep, and thine oxen: In all places where I record my name I will come unto thee, and I will bless thee.

25 And if thou wilt make me an altar of stone, thou shalt not build it of hewn stone: for if thou lift up they tool upon it, thou hast polluted it.

26 Neither shalt thou go up by steps unto mine altar, that thy nakedness be not discovered thereon.

NLT **Exodus 20:18** When the people heard the thunder and the loud blast of the ram's horn, and when they saw the flashes of lightning and the smoke billowing from the mountain, they stood at a distance, trembling with fear.

19 And they said to Moses, "You speak to us, and we will listen. But don't let God speak directly to us, or we will die!"

20 "Don't be afraid," Moses answered them, "for God has come in this way to test you, and so that your fear of him will keep you from sinning!"

21 As the people stood in the distance, Moses approached the dark cloud where God was.

22 And the LORD said to Moses, "Say this to the people of Israel: You saw for yourselves that I spoke to you from heaven.

23 Remember, you must not make any idols of silver or gold to rival me.

24 Build for me an altar made of earth, and offer your sacrifices to me—your burnt offerings and peace offerings, your sheep and goats, and your cattle. Build my altar whenever I cause my name to be remembered, and I will come to you and bless you.

25 If you use stones to build my altar, use only natural, uncut stones. Do not shape the stones with a tool, for that would make the altar unfit for holy use.

26 And do not approach my altar by going up steps. If you do, someone might look up under your clothing and see your nakedness."

The People, Places, and Times

Moses. Moses plays a prominent role in the events of this passage. Born a Hebrew slave, Moses was raised in the home of the Pharaoh. As a young man, he witnessed a fellow Hebrew being unjustly beaten, so he reacted by killing the attacker. So, he had to flee to Midian where he married and raised a family. Some years later, God chose Moses to return to Egypt and lead the Hebrew people out of slavery. In the process, God shaped and molded Moses into His faithful servant who became an outstanding leader of His people.

Mount Sinai. The events of this passage take place at Mount Sinai, often referred to as "the mountain of God." It is believed by some to be located about fifty miles north of the southern tip of the Sinai Peninsula, in an area now controlled by Egypt. On this mountain, Moses met God in the burning bush, and here God called Moses to go to Egypt and lead His people out of slavery (Exodus 3). Many years later, the prophet Elijah would return to this mountain (which is also called Horeb) and hear from God in the gentle whisper of a still, small voice (1 Kings 19:8–13).

How would you evaluate Moses' relationship with God? Did God direct Moses' life in ways that helped Moses mature and become the leader that He needed?

Background

The events of this Scripture take place in the third month after God had led the Israelites out of slavery in Egypt. For nearly three months, a vast multitude of men, women, and children had been slowly moving across formidable deserts. All the miraculous events that God had ordained in Egypt, including the night of the Passover and the parting of the Red Sea, were certainly still fresh in their minds. In the past few months, they had seen the presence of God in the pillar of fire by night and the cloud by day. They had been miraculously fed by the manna and quail. God had provided water when none was to be found. The Israelites were constantly aware of the presence and power of God in their midst. Now they were camped at the foot of Mount Sinai, where God would once again show His mighty power and give the Law to His people through their leader

Moses. Through the process, the people would learn more about God and what He expected of them.

How would you evaluate the importance of the Ten Commandments in the lives of the Israelites, as well as all modern-day believers?

At-A-Glance

1. God Makes His Presence Known (Exodus 20:18)
2. The People Show Reverent Fear (vv. 19–21)
3. God Encourages Proper Worship (vv. 22–26)

In Depth

1. God Makes His Presence Known (Exodus 20:18)

For three months, God had made His presence known through miraculous physical phenomenon such as the pillar of cloud by day and the pillar of fire by night. He led them to stop at Mount Sinai, where He would give His people the Law.

The Israelites' stopping at Mount Sinai mirrors what happens in a believer's life. We worship the Lord and come to know who He is before we are given commands to obey. The Law outlined how they were expected to live as His people in relationship with Him and in relationship with each other. They were expected to fulfill these covenant requirements. This is in line with the commands that Jesus put forth as the first and second greatest commandments for us—to love God and to love people.

It was important for God to make sure His people knew that it was He, Almighty God, the God of their fathers, who was giving the Law. So He used spectacular divine manifestations to cause them to respond in fear and reverence to keep their covenant commitment. He used smoke, thunder, the sound of heavenly trumpets, and lightning. God's manifestation of His presence had the desired effect. The presence of God and the recognized authorship of His commands also causes us to reverence God, receive His words, and obey them.

What has caused you to fear and revere God lately?

2. The People Show Reverent Fear (vv. 19–21)

The people withdrew in fear, knowing that they were truly in the presence of Almighty God. Yet Moses told them, "Fear not, for God is come to prove you" (v. 20). What Moses was telling them was that they should not withdraw from God in terror; God intended to use this experience to instill in them a reverent awe of Him. It was as if God were saying, "I want you to know I really mean business here!" Thus, "fear of the LORD" would prompt His people to want to keep the Law, and never sin.

God also used the divine manifestations to underscore the importance of His commands that He would be their only God, and that they were never to make any idols. After all they had seen, heard, and experienced, it is hard to imagine that any of the Israelites would ever consider following any other god! They had heard His voice and seen His power, yet they had not seen Him in any physical shape or form. But God knows the fragility of human nature, and no matter how many times they experienced God's miracles and presence, they turned to idols. It is the same way with us. We often forget who God is and turn to less-than-satisfactory idols.

What motivates you to modify your behavior and respond to God in obedience?

3. God Encourages Worship (vv. 22–26)

Finally, God gave instructions on the building of altars to be used in worship. While this command seems unusual for us, it was fitting for the culture of the time. From the beginning, God has always desired worship, and at that time worship included sacrifices and burnt offerings. What God wanted to make clear with the commands of verses 24–26 was that the altars were to be temporary and portable. They were not yet in the Promised Land, and their focus was to be on the object of their worship rather than the place of their sacrifice. The stones were to be unhewn, perhaps so that no one would be tempted to carve the stones into some image or idol. And the altars were not to have steps leading up to them, so that their sacrifices would be made in humility and modesty. Again, the focus was then, and is now, on the object of our worship, not on the means, place, or structure.

How and where can we create opportunities to worship God in addition to Saturday and Sunday worship service?

Search the Scriptures

1. Moses says that God appeared in the way He did so that the people would not sin (Exodus 20:20). How does God's presence keep us from sinning?

2. Why did God want them to make an altar of unhewn stone (v. 25)?

Discuss the Meaning

In this Scripture, we learn a lot about God, His power, and His desire for us to live in obedience and fellowship with Him. What can we do to achieve and keep a proper attitude of awe, reverence, fear, and love for Him?

Lesson in Our Society

Places such as banks, courtrooms, and churches are intentionally built to inspire awe, respect, and even proper fear in us. And in those places, we often enter into agreements where we make certain promises and receive certain privileges. The awe, respect, and fear generated by our surroundings, as well as our faith in God, should prompt us to live up to the promises we have made, and joyfully comply with agreements in which we have entered. In this way, we will enjoy more blessings and peace in our relationship with God and with our neighbors.

Some years ago, Tavis Smiley helped to develop a book titled *The Covenant with Black America*. The book outlines strategies for the betterment of the African American community. This book addresses the problem on a structural level, but there also could be a solution to improving the African American community on a personal level. We need to tackle some of the weightier economic, educational, and health issues that plague our communities.

At the same time, we also need to fear God and treat Him with reverence and respect. We need to live up to the agreements we have made in our churches, businesses, and relationships. *How can we prioritize our relationship with God and seek to improve our dealings with others?*

Make It Happen

God's greatness and awesomeness compel us to honor our commitment to Him. Here are some ways we can remember to honor Him and what He has done in our lives:

• Go outdoors and look up at the sky to remind yourself of the greatness of God.

• Bring a special offering in thanksgiving to God.

• Spend time each morning reading God's Word and writing down a Bible verse on a card that you take with you.

Follow the Spirit

What God wants me to do:

_____

_____

_____

_____

Remember Your Thoughts

Special insights I have learned:

_____

_____

_____

_____

More Light on the Text
Exodus 20:18–26

18 And all the people saw the thunderings, and the lightnings, and the noise of the trumpet, and the mountain smoking: and when the people saw it, they removed, and stood afar off.

The people of Israel witnessed the visible and audible manifestation of God's presence on the mountain. Thunder and lightning were typical signs associated with ancient Near Eastern gods of the time, but the difference is that usually these were seen in battle. On this occasion, God revealed Himself to people, which was unheard of in the narratives of the gods at the time.

The Children of Israel are now in the presence of God! Their reaction shows that this manifestation of God's presence was something far from the ordinary. The lightning they see and thunder they hear cause them to be in awe, which is expressed in their removing themselves and standing back from the mountain.

19 And they said unto Moses, Speak thou with us, and we will hear: but let not God speak with us, lest we die. 20 And Moses said unto the people, Fear not: for God is come to prove you, and that his fear may be before your faces, that ye sin not.

They call out to Moses and ask that he would speak to them instead of Yahweh. Their reason is that they could bear to hear Moses' words, but hearing Yahweh made them feel as though they would die.

Moses assures them and tells them not to be afraid. Although they should have a healthy fear of Yahweh—which is respect—Moses encourages the Israelites that they do not have to fear that they will die from hearing God's voice. The purpose of Yahweh's presence on the mountain is to prove (Heb. *nasah*, **nah-SAH**) them. This word is from a root word which means to smell or test by the smell. In this context, it means to ascertain the nature of something, including any faults or imperfections. The Lord wants the people to fear Him in a healthy way so that their lives would be free from sin.

21 And the people stood afar off, and Moses drew near unto the thick darkness where God was. 22 And the Lord said unto Moses, Thus thou shalt say unto the children of Israel, Ye have seen that I have talked with you from heaven.

The people are still described as standing "afar off" as Moses draws near to God. The "thick darkness" is one word in the Hebrew (*'arapel*, **ah-rah-FELL**). It should be distinguished from just the opposite of light. The thick darkness described here is similar to a cloud of smoke, gas, or dust. This could refer to storm clouds which would accompany the

thunder and the lightning mentioned previously. This also aligns with the fact that the mountain was emitting smoke.

The presence of the Almighty was a mystery to most Israelites, but Moses enters into the darkness to hear from God. As he approaches God for the people, Moses acts as mediator. First, he goes to the Lord to hear from Him, then the Lord commands Moses to go to the people and speak to them. Moses is told to let them know that God has spoken to them "from heaven," in order to assure them that the words come from God even though Moses is delivering them.

23 Ye shall not make with me gods of silver, neither shall ye make unto you gods of gold. 24 An altar of earth thou shalt make unto me, and shalt sacrifice thereon thy burnt offerings, and thy peace offerings, thy sheep, and thine oxen: in all places where I record my name I will come unto thee, and I will bless thee.

The Lord again warns against making idols, but the wording is very specific. He warns them not to make any idols "with me," meaning that they could not worship God along with other gods. He wants their exclusive allegiance. Nothing else must share in the worship due to Him.

He also informs Moses that an altar of earth is required in order to make sacrifices to Him. This was most likely intended to foster humility in worship. The Israelites would not be tempted to focus on the monuments they made for worship, but on God alone. Many altars from the region were known to have been constructed of mud bricks, although no Israelite altars of this sort have been found.

25 And if thou wilt make me an altar of stone, thou shalt not build it of hewn stone: for if thou lift up thy tool upon it, thou hast

polluted it. **26 Neither shalt thou go up by steps unto mine altar, that thy nakedness be not discovered thereon.**

These verses warn against two things. First of all, if an altar is made of stone, then it must not be "hewn" stone. No work was to be done to shape or cut it. If any work was done on the altar to cut or shape it, then it would be polluted (Heb. *chalal*, **kha-LOL**). This word means more than just physically dirtying someone or something; it means to defile the sacred character of someone or something, to treat it as common rather than showing the honor it deserves.

The second thing that the Lord commands Moses to tell the people is not go up steps to the altar. This was to ensure modesty among the people. In contrast to the surrounding nations, the Israelites would not go up steps to the altar to expose themselves. Ritual nudity was a common practice for pagan worshipers of the surrounding nations, and God wanted absolute holiness when it came to His people's worship practices.

Sources:
The Holy Bible, King James Version. Zondervan, 1992.
Life Application Study Bible, New Living Translation. Tyndale, 1996.
Enns, Peter. *The NIV Application Commentary, Exodus*. Zondervan, 2000.
Kaiser, Walter C. Jr. *The Expositor's Bible Commentary, Exodus*. Frank Baebelein, gen. ed. Zondervan, 2000.
Strong's Exhaustive Concordance. Thomas Nelson Publishers. 1990.

Daily Bible Readings

MONDAY
People Hear God Speak the Commandments
(Deuteronomy 5:22–27)

TUESDAY
God's Exclusive Claim
(Exodus 20:1–12)

WEDNESDAY
Guide for Human Relationships
(Exodus 20:13–17)

THURSDAY
The Law Finds Fulfillment in Jesus
(Matthew 5:17–20)

FRIDAY
Anger Leads to Murder
(Matthew 5:21–26)

SATURDAY
Lust Leads to Adultery
(Matthew 5:27–32)

SUNDAY
People Hear God's Word from Moses
(Exodus 20:18–26)

Say It Correctly

Hewn. **HEE**-yoon.
Altar. **AL**-ter.

Notes

_____

_____

Teaching Tips

Words You Should Know

A. House (2 Samuel 7:1) *bayith* (Heb.)—A palace, a temple or home that can be seen from afar off; a family, offspring, or dynasty.

B. Tabernacle (v. 6) *mishkan* (Heb.)—Dwelling place, tent.

Teacher Preparation

Unifying Principle—A Much Bigger Plan. When entering into relationships with others, people struggle to give up control of their plans and dreams. How can people sacrifice control in order to maintain vital relationships? God's covenant with David is a compromise between the eternal, omnipresent God and the time-and space-bound David.

A. Pray for your students that they would seek God first before moving forward with any new (or great) ideas.

B. Read the suggested devotional reading, Psalm 89:1–15. Consider how the psalmist praises God for His eternal covenant with David, yet struggles to understand how God will fulfill that covenant in light of the disobedience and subsequent punishment Israel was experiencing at the time.

C. Read Acts 2:22–36. Consider how Jesus is the fulfillment of God's promise to David.

O—Open the Lesson

A. Open with prayer.

B. Introduce the lesson by reading the Aim for Change.

C. Ask a student to read the In Focus story. Then facilitate a brief discussion about it.

P—Present the Scriptures

A. Ask a student to read the Focal Verses.

B. Use The People, Places, and Times, Background, Search the Scriptures, At-A-Glance outline, In Depth, and More Light on the Text to clarify the verses.

E—Explore the Meaning

A. Invite the class to analyze the Discuss the Meaning, Lesson in Our Society, and Make It Happen sections.

B. Facilitate a discussion on how the students connect their responses to the Aim for Change and Keep in Mind verse.

N—Next Steps for Application

A. Summarize the lesson.

B. Close with prayer.

Worship Guide

For the Superintendent and Teacher
Theme: God's Covenant with David
Song: "Great is Thy Faithfulness"
Devotional Reading: Psalm 89:1–15

God's Covenant with David

Bible Background • 2 SAMUEL 7:1–16; PSALM 89; 1 CHRONICLES 22:6–8
Printed Text • 2 SAMUEL 7:1–6, 8–10, 12–16 | Devotional Reading • PSALM 89:1–15

—— Aim for Change ——

By the end of this lesson, we will: ANALYZE David's desire and the Lord's promise; CONFESS our natural human limitations to serve God in a manner that is worthy of the eternal and omnipresent Creator; and APPRECIATE God's blessings and how we don't need to earn them through impressive acts of service.

In Focus

Excitement filled the air as Antwon strode unexpectedly into the business meeting in the basement of the aging inner-city church. Basketball had been Antwon's ticket out of the impoverished neighborhood and his source of considerable wealth. He had come back to his childhood church with a proposal. Concerned that attendance had fallen off and that the church, like the rest of the neighborhood, was in decline, Antwon offered to pay the construction costs of a new church building if a suitable site could be found. Certainly, he figured, a beautiful new facility would bring the people back into the church.

The pastor shook Antwon's hand and said simply, "The Lord sent you to help us, but there's a greater need."

To the faithful few gathered, he asked, "Do we need a new building? Do we need a change of location? Or do we need a change of hearts? The local free medical clinic just moved out of our neighborhood. Will we follow them and move out, too? Or could we maybe bring a free medical clinic into the church? Perhaps we need to return to acts of mercy and service, bringing the needy inside and showing them grace."

Has God ever unexpectedly changed or redirected your plans or dreams? In this lesson, we will see how God changed David's plans and entered into a covenant relationship with him.

—— Keep in Mind ——

"And thine house and thy kingdom shall be established for ever before thee; thy throne shall be established forever" (2 Samuel 7:16).

"And thine house and thy kingdom shall be established for ever before thee; thy throne shall be established forever" (2 Samuel 7:16).

Focal Verses

KJV **2 Samuel 7:1** And it came to pass, when the king sat in his house, and the Lord had given him rest round about from all this enemies;

2 That the king said unto Nathan the prophet, See now, I dwell in an house of cedar, but the ark of God dwelleth within curtains.

3 And Nathan said to the king, Go, do all that is in thine heart; for the Lord is with thee.

4 And it came to pass that night, that the word of the Lord came unto Nathan, saying,

5 Go and tell my servant David, Thus saith the Lord, Shalt thou build me an house for me to dwell in?

6 Whereas I have not dwelt in any house since the time that I brought up the children of Israel out of Egypt, even to this day, but have walked in a tent and in a tabernacle.

8 Now therefore so shalt thou say unto my servant David, Thus saith the Lord of hosts, I took thee from the sheepcote, from following the sheep, to be ruler over my people, over Israel:

9 And I was with thee whithersoever thou wentest, and have cut off all thine enemies out of thy sight, and have made thee a great name, like unto the name of the great men that are in the earth.

10 Moreover I will appoint a place for my people Israel, and will plant them, that they may dwell in a place of their own, and move no more; neither shall the children of wickedness afflict them any more, as beforetime.

12 And when thy days be fulfilled, and thou shalt sleep with thy fathers, I will set up thy seed after thee, which shall proceed out of thy bowels, and I will establish his kingdom.

13 He shall build an house for my name, and I will stablish the throne of his kingdom for ever.

NLT **2 Samuel 7:1** When King David was settled in his palace and the Lord had given him rest from all the surrounding enemies,

2 the king summoned Nathan the prophet. "Look," David said, "I am living in a beautiful cedar palace, but the Ark of God is out there in a tent!"

3 Nathan replied to the king, "Go ahead and do whatever you have in mind, for the Lord is with you."

4 But that same night the Lord said to Nathan,

5 Go and tell my servant David, "This is what the Lord has declared: Are you the one to build a house for me to live in?

6 I have never lived in a house from the day I brought the Israelites out of Egypt until this very day. I have always moved from one place to another with a tent and a Tabernacle as my dwelling.

8 Now go and say to my servant David, "this is what the Lord of Heaven's Armies has declared; I took you from tending sheep in the pasture and selected you to be the leader of my people Israel.

9 I have been with you wherever you have gone, and I have destroyed all your enemies before your eyes. Now I will make your name as famous as anyone who has ever lived on the earth!

10 And I will provide a homeland for my people Israel, planting them in a secure place where they will never be disturbed. Evil nations won't oppress them as they've done in the past.

12 For when you die and are buried with your ancestors, I will raise up one of your descendants, your own offspring, and I will make his kingdom strong.

14 I will be his father, and he shall be my son. If he commit iniquity, I will chasten him with the rod of men, and with the stripes of the children of men:

15 But my mercy shall not depart away from him, as I took it from Saul, whom I put away before thee.

16 And thine house and thy kingdom shall be established for ever before thee; thy throne shall be established forever.

13 He is the one who will build a house—a temple—for my name. And I will secure his royal throne forever.

14 I will be his father, and he will be my son. If he sins, I will correct and discipline him with the rod, like any father would do.

15 But my favor will not be taken from him as I took it from Saul, whom I removed from your sight.

16 Your house and your kingdom will continue before me for all time, and your throne will be secure forever."

The People, Places, and Times

David. King David played a prominent role in Israel's early history. Born in Bethlehem, he worked as a shepherd for his father, Jesse. As a young man, with one smooth stone David killed Goliath, that much-feared giant Philistine warrior whom David called that "uncircumcised Philistine" (1 Samuel 17:26). God said that David was a man after His own heart (1 Samuel 13:14; Acts 13:22). Among David's sons was Solomon, who would succeed David as king and build the Temple in Jerusalem. David was a great man, but not without his faults. He gave in to lust and committed adultery, and then arranged for the murder of his lover's husband. He was at times deceitful and brash. Yet he loved and trusted God. He confessed and repented of his sins (Psalm 51). As promised by God in today's passage, Jesus was a descendant of David (Matthew 1:1).

Nathan. Nathan was King David's friend, confidant, and counselor. He was a prophet sent by God to act as His spokesman to David. Nathan had to confront David with the truth, even when that truth would prove painful for David. Sometimes, as in today's passage, Nathan had to tell David that God did not approve of what he was planning or what he had done. At the same time, Nathan was able to assure David of God's forgiveness of confessed sins. Nathan is a biblical example of something we all need—a true, godly friend and advisor.

How do national leaders normally choose to react to God's Word?

Background

The events described in this Scripture take place in Jerusalem, the then-capital of a strong and united Israel. The year is roughly 1000 BC. Previously, for more than 300 years, Israel had been ruled by judges and advised by various prophets. During that period, Israel faced near constant wars with various Canaanite tribes, including the ruthless Philistines. Those battles continued even under Israel's first king, Saul, and second king, David.

This week's Scripture begins by saying that God had given David rest from all his surrounding enemies (2 Samuel 7:1). Under David's rule, the Philistines, Moabites, and others were finally defeated. This is significant because David was finally able to establish Israel as a formidable power in the region and set up his son, Solomon, to possess all the land that God had promised. David was instrumental in strengthening and uniting Israel, and making it a great and wealthy nation. He captured Jerusalem, moved the Ark of the Covenant there, and built a magnificent palace for himself.

How was David rewarded for his faithfulness to God?

At-A-Glance

1. A Good Idea But Not a God Idea (2 Samuel 7:1–2)
2. When God Says No (vv. 3–6)
3. Greater Plans for You (vv. 8–10, 12–16)

In Depth

1. A Good Idea But Not a God Idea (2 Samuel 7:1–2)

David loved his new home in Jerusalem, just five miles from his birthplace in Bethlehem. Jerusalem was the well-fortified capital of his kingdom. David's palace was enormous, several stories tall, and built of thick hewn limestone, with massive cedar timbers and paneling. The palace was meant to impress—a fitting home for the wealthiest and most powerful king in that area of the world.

David also loved God and had set up the Tabernacle nearby. It was meant to be portable so God would dwell among His people wherever they went. Now, David felt that their wandering days were over. He felt that since he had a permanent home, it was only fitting to build a permanent and more beautiful home for the Ark. It seemed to be a "good idea," but not a "God idea," as we shall see later in the text. Many times, we as believers have good ideas but they're not always ideas sourced and supported by God.

When we have great ideas and formulate wonderful plans, why is it important to consult God first?

2. When God Says No (vv. 3–6)

David had not consulted God on the matter of building a temple. That night, God spoke to Nathan, and told him to relay a message to David: that God gently rejected David's offer to build a temple for Him. God reminds David that He has led and guided him from the role of humble shepherd through many battles to the position of king.

David was king of Israel, but he was still God's servant (vv. 5, 8). Although God does not divulge all of His reasons for not wanting David to build the temple in these verses, David does reveal the real reason in 1 Chronicles 28:2–3. There David says, "It was my desire to build a Temple … but God said to me, 'You must not build a Temple to honor my name, for you are a warrior and have shed much blood'" (NIV).

What happens when the plans we develop conflict with God's will?

3. Greater Plans for You (vv. 8–10, 12–16)

God may have rejected David's plan to build the temple, but He revealed that He had even greater plans for David. In a play on words, God essentially says, "You planned to build a house (permanent dwelling place) for Me, but instead I will build a house (permanent family dynasty) for you." The Hebrew word for "house" is used in both cases, yet the meanings are vastly different, and clear from the context.

God is declaring or making a covenant with David that He is going to do something even more spectacular than anything any person, even a king, could do! He will do something of eternal significance that will impact all of humanity! He is establishing a royal bloodline through David from which kings will come. David's own son, Solomon, would succeed David as king, and be the one to build the Temple.

Little did David know that one of his later descendants would be Jesus Christ of Nazareth,

God's own Son, Savior of all who believe in Him. Jesus is, and forever will be, the ultimate fulfillment of God's covenant with David. Even before Jesus is born, the angel says of Him, "The Lord God shall give unto him the throne of his father David, and … of his Kingdom there shall be no end" (Luke 1:32–33).

How does accepting God's "no" show great faith in His future plans for our lives?

Search the Scriptures

1 What was the Lord's reason for not wanting David to build a temple (2 Samuel 7:5–6)?

2. Why is it unwise to forge ahead with our own ideas without seeking the counsel of God?

Discuss the Meaning

The text says that David "summoned" the prophet Nathan to discuss his idea to build a temple for the Lord (vv. 1–2). At first, Nathan told him to do what he had in mind. Only after Nathan talked it over with God did he go back to tell David that God had rejected his idea. What does this tell us about seeking counsel concerning our future plans?

Lesson in Our Society

We live in an age of reality TV, where we see home makeovers unfolding in 30 minutes and ultra-successful startup businesses that seem to make millions in months. We admire people who seem to instinctively know what to do, and do it quickly. We look up to those who can rally others to fix things, build things, or help make the world a better place. It may seem like those people have good ideas and know how to get things done in mere moments, yet what we don't often see is that the best leaders of churches, businesses, or families have likely spent many hours in consultation with others about their plans before they put them into action.

What would it look like for us not to just say that we are going to pray about something, but to actually sit and wait for God's answers? As African Americans, we are known as a praying people, but are we a *listening* people? What if God wants to give us solutions to the challenges that we face on a day-to-day basis? It's not just enough to have good ideas. It's best to wait on God's idea.

Why is it important to accept constructive criticism of our plans before we act?

Make It Happen

This lesson teaches us that as Christians, we should seek the counsel of Scripture, the advice of a mentor, and spend much time in prayer before we embark on any endeavor. God may reveal that your plan is good, or He might just reveal that He has a different plan.

• Write a letter to God about a dream or plan you have and allow time for God to reveal to you His will.

• Find someone who has seen a vision or dream realized in their life. Talk to them about the roadblocks and obstacles they may have encountered along the way.

• Look up specific promises that God has given us as believers and list all the times that God has fulfilled His promises. Share with a fellow classmate.

Follow the Spirit

What God wants me to do:

_____

_____

_____

_____

Remember Your Thoughts

Special insights I have learned:

_____

_____

_____

_____

More Light on the Text

2 Samuel 7:1–6, 8–10, 12–16

1 And it came to pass, when the king sat in his house, and the LORD had given him rest round about from all this enemies; 2 That the king said unto Nathan the prophet, See now, I dwell in an house of cedar, but the ark of God dwelleth within curtains. 3 And Nathan said to the king, Go, do all that is in thine heart; for the LORD is with thee.

David now sits in the palace that he has built for himself. This is a season where he has rest from all of Israel's enemies. The text makes sure to say that it was not David who had given himself rest, but the Lord. This realization possibly prompts David to think about the splendor of his house, yet God, who made it all possible, did not have a permanent house among His people.

The use of cedar for building temples and palaces was common at the time. Cedar (Heb. *erez*, **EH-rez**) does not contain any knots and does not decay. The material is appropriate for a building intended to house royalty.

4 And it came to pass that night, that the word of the LORD came unto Nathan, saying,

In verse 4, we see the typical prophetic formula, "the word of the LORD [Yahweh] came unto…" This formula occurs some 200 times in the Old Testament, especially in the books of Jeremiah and Ezekiel. The fact that the word came to Nathan at night may suggest that this Word from God came to him in a dream or a vision, which was also typical of how God communicated in these times.

5 Go and tell my servant David, Thus saith the LORD, Shalt thou build me an house for me to dwell in?

This word that Nathan received for David was in response to the previous conversation about David's desire to build a house for God. The word "house" (Heb. *bayith*, **BAH-yith**) has wide applications, most often used for a family dwelling. It is also used, as in this case, to refer to the temple of a deity. David presumed that since he had a house while the Ark of the Covenant resided in a tent, he should build a house for God. In that exchange, Nathan encouraged David, even though Nathan had not yet consulted God.

In verse 4, the Word of the Lord came to Nathan in the form of this corrective. The interesting twist in verse 5 is that although God called David "my servant" (a term used to convey honor), it is followed by God's rhetorical question to Nathan regarding David's plans: "Shalt thou build me an house for me to dwell in?" While this question was about David and his intentions, it was also about God challenging the very notion that He can be contained in a house. The pronoun "thou" (you) is most likely emphatic, indicating the negation concerns the person (David) rather than the action itself (the building of the temple). This implies that God's reason for denying David's plan was not that He did not want a temple built, but that He did not want David to be the one to build it.

6 Whereas I have not dwelt in any house since the time that I brought up the children of Israel out of Egypt, even to this day, but have walked in a tent and in a tabernacle.

God had been always present with His people, so the need for a house, while not outright rejected, was here questioned. God relays that in times past, He walked or traveled with Israel in a tent (Heb. ʾohel, **OH-hel**) or nomad's tent. It was a tabernacle (Heb. *mishkhan*, **mish-KON**), which is a dwelling place but in some instances can refer to a shepherd's hut. Throughout that time, God never said anything about wanting a different place for His presence to reside among Israel.

8 Now therefore so shalt thou say unto my servant David, Thus saith the LORD of hosts, I took thee from the sheepcote, from following the sheep, to be ruler over my people, over Israel. 9 And I was with thee whithersoever thou wentest, and have cut off all thine enemies out of thy sight, and have made thee a great name, like unto the name of the great men that are in the earth. 10 Moreover I will appoint a place for my people Israel, and will plant them, that they may dwell in a place of their own, and move no more; neither shall the children of wickedness afflict them any more, as beforetime.

As God had shown Himself to His people through His chosen leaders, He was now saying to David that his life had been a testimony to God's presence and power. He took him from the sheepcote (Heb. *naveh*, **nah-VEH**) and herding sheep. Sheepcotes are not often spoken of today, but they refer to a pen or covered area where sheep are kept. The Hebrew word has a variety of meanings, including a home for people or a den for animals. In this case, the word is used for the meadow or pasture where David grazed his sheep. God had done much for David; He didn't need David to construct an impressive building in which He would dwell.

God indicated to David that He had given him peace and victory over his enemies. God did this to remind David that He had established him; David should not establish God by building a place for Him to dwell. That God "will appoint a place for my people" (v. 10) references what

God had done and how He had shown Himself to His people by providing a place for them—a place of peace where they could live free from oppression and enemy attack.

12 And when thy days be fulfilled, and thou shalt sleep with thy fathers, I will set up thy seed after thee, which shall proceed out of thy bowels, and I will establish his kingdom. 13 He shall build an house for my name, and I will stablish the throne of his kingdom for ever.

As for a temple, David would not be allowed to build it; that honor would be given to Solomon. Debate surrounds the application and meaning of, "and I will stablish the throne of his kingdom for ever" (from v. 13). Establishing a throne forever could be fulfilled in two ways; it could refer to David and his physical descendants, or to Jesus (as seen in Matthew 1:1). Other references in verse 12 immediately refer to Solomon but also have prophetic implications.

In the early church, this verse was viewed as support for Jesus as the Messiah; God raised up Jesus (Acts 13:23), through His resurrection, as the ruling son of David. Remember that first-generation Christians were taking their cues from Jesus, who claimed that He would destroy and raise up or build a new temple (John 2:19–22). Jesus also claimed to have an eternal throne (Matthew 19:28–29) and an imperishable kingdom (John 18:36). In the final analysis, the key here is God's sovereignty to act and establish not a house of cedar—but a people who were loved by Him, led by Him, and given not just a home, but heritage.

14 I will be his father, and he shall be my son. If he commit iniquity, I will chasten him with the rod of men, and with the stripes of the children of men: 15 But my mercy shall not depart away from him, as I took it from

Saul, whom I put away before thee. 16 And thine house and thy kingdom shall be established for ever before thee:

The reference to the father-son relationship once again presents commentators with a dilemma. To whom was this referring? Was it referring to David and his son, as it was believed that the Davidic king was the son of Yahweh, or referring to Jesus, the Son of God? Use of the term "son" was common in this period to represent at least three concepts: adoption, covenant, and royal grant.

History suggests that the sins of David's descendants would bring punishment and alienation, but would not result in God's withdrawal of His love. In the end, God would establish David's house, kingdom, and throne forever. Therefore, we end up with God being a God of His word, doing what He said He would do. It wasn't about David or his son building a house for God; rather, it was about how God was going to build a "house" for His people through His Son.

Sources:

Anderson, A. A. *2 Samuel. Word Biblical Commentary*. Vol. 11. Nashville, TN: Thomas Nelson Publishers, 1989. 118.

Bergen, Robert D. *1, 2 Samuel. The New American Commentary*. Vol. 7. Nashville, TN: Holman Reference, 1996), 120. 338–340.

Concordia Self-Study Bible: NIV. St. Louis, MO: Concordia Publishing House, 1986.

Walvoord, John F. and Roy B. Zuck, eds. *The Bible Knowledge Commentary: Old Testament*. Wheaton, IL: Chariot Victor Publishing, 1985. 464.

Say It Correctly

Sheepcote. **SHEEP**-coat.
Portent. **POR**-tint.

Daily Bible Readings

MONDAY
Samuel Anoints David King of Israel
(1 Samuel 16:1, 11–13)

TUESDAY
God to Build the House of David
(1 Chronicles 17:9–15)

WEDNESDAY
Resources to Build the Temple
(1 Chronicles 22:2–5)

THURSDAY
David Instructs Solomon
About the Temple
(1 Chronicles 22:6–16)

FRIDAY
Extolling the Majesty of the Lord
(Psalm 89:1–15)

SATURDAY
David, Prepared for Service
(1 Samuel 16:19–23)

SUNDAY
God's Covenant with David
(2 Samuel 7:1–6, 8–10, 12–16)

Notes

Teaching Tips

Words You Should Know

A. Terrible (Nehemiah 9:32) *yare* (Heb.)—To be fearful, dreadful; to cause astonishment and awe.

B. Mercy (v. 32) *chesed* (Heb.)—Goodness, faithfulness, loving compassion and unfailing love toward others.

Teacher Preparation

Unifying Principle—Sign on the Dotted Line. People can face painful consequences because of their own wrongdoing. In the embarrassing angst of suffering for their own wrongs, how can they dare ask for help from others? The people of Israel, hurting from painful losses from the exile for their sins, followed Nehemiah in confessing their wrongs and making a covenant with God to obey the Law given through Moses.

A. Pray that students will be humble enough to ask for help.

B. Study the companion lesson in the *Precepts For Living®* Study Guide thoroughly in advance.

O—Open the Lesson

A. Introduce today's lesson title and Aim for Change.

B. Pray for students to develop a clear understanding of the reality of negative consequences and the necessity of confessing and repenting.

C. Have students read the Keep in Mind verse and In Focus story.

P—Present the Scriptures

A. Give students a few minutes to silently read Nehemiah 9, The People, Places, and Times, and Background.

B. Have students re-read Focal Verses (aloud or silently), encouraging them to keep in mind the information presented in Nehemiah 9, The People, Places, and Times, and Background.

C. Use In Depth content and Search the Scriptures to facilitate discussion on the Focal Verses.

E—Explore the Meaning

A. Have the class explore Discuss the Meaning.

B. Read Lesson in Our Society and have students make observations.

N—Next Steps for Application

A. Briefly review the lesson, highlighting the Keep in Mind verse.

B. Read Make It Happen and re-read the Aim for Change aloud.

C. Pray with students that they will continue to be sensitive to personal sin and repent.

God's Covenant with the Returned Exiles

Bible Background • NEHEMIAH 9–10
Printed Text • NEHEMIAH 9:32–38, 10:28–29 | Devotional Reading • PSALM 103:1–14

— Aim for Change —

By the end of the lesson, we will: SURVEY the prayer recorded in Nehemiah 9 for repentance and covenant affirmation; REPENT of personal and corporate sinful attitudes and actions; and COMMIT to following God's ways in daily life.

In Focus

For years, she sensed God was pursuing her. And for years she had run, determined to live her own way, on her own terms. She never expected this. She never considered the impact that her decisions would have on her young son, Michael.

Michael was only six, so he didn't really comprehend the gravity of how Michelle had been living. This made it easier for Michelle to continue in her sinful ways.

Each time Michelle found herself in trouble, she would pray and ask God to forgive that "mistake" and ask Him to give her just one more chance. Each time, He did. And, each time, she would thank Him for being so gracious, kind and loving. But she had forgotten that God is also just. Until now.

The man she had decided that she "loved," in spite of repeated warnings and pleas from family and friends—both hers and his—was facing time in prison. And he decided to take her down with him. No, she wasn't really involved. But it was his word against hers.

As she faced a court date to determine her fate, she understood that she had been "sorry," but being sorry was not the same as repentance. With true reverence for God, she bowed down to the ground, saying, "Father, forgive me. I turn away from sin and turn toward You."

How do you know if you have truly repented? In this lesson, we will see a picture of what it means to truly repent.

— Keep in Mind —

"Howbeit thou art just in all that is brought upon us; for thou hast done right, but we have done wickedly" (Nehemiah 9:33).

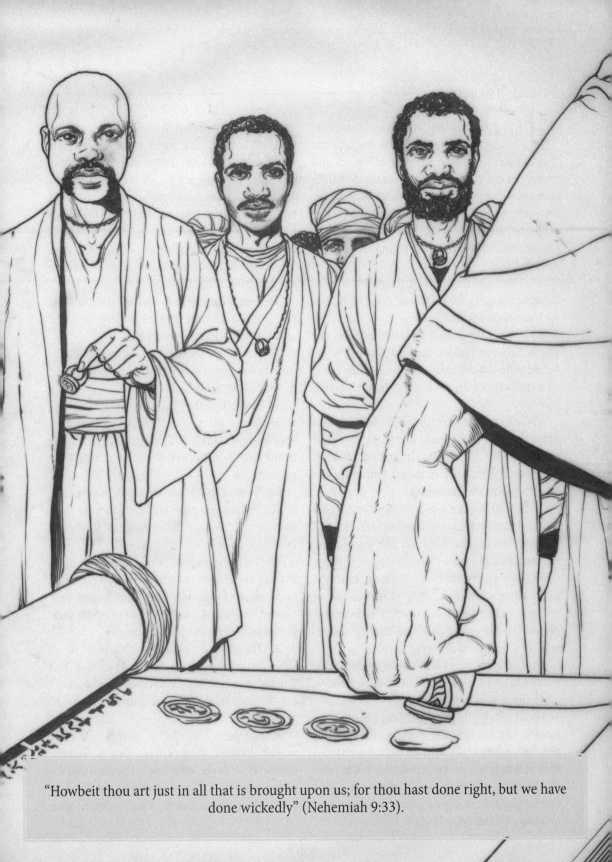

"Howbeit thou art just in all that is brought upon us; for thou hast done right, but we have done wickedly" (Nehemiah 9:33).

Focal Verses

KJV **Nehemiah 9:32** Now therefore, our God, the great, the mighty, and the terrible God, who keepest covenant and mercy, let not all the trouble seem little before thee, that hath come upon us, on our kings, on our princes, and on our priests, and on our prophets, and on our fathers, and on all thy people, since the time of the kings of Assyria unto this day.

33 Howbeit thou art just in all that is brought upon us; for thou hast done right, but we have done wickedly:

34 Neither have our kings, our princes, our priests, nor our fathers, kept thy law, nor hearkened unto thy commandments and thy testimonies, wherewith thou didst testify against them.

35 For they have not served thee in their kingdom, and in thy great goodness that thou gavest them, and in the large and fat land which thou gavest before them, neither turned they from their wicked works.

36 Behold, we are servants this day, and for the land that thou gavest unto our fathers to eat the fruit thereof and the good thereof, behold, we are servants in it:

37 And it yieldeth much increase unto the kings whom thou hast set over us because of our sins: also they have dominion over our bodies, and over our cattle, at their pleasure, and we are in great distress.

38 And because of all this we make a sure covenant, and write it; and our princes, Levites, and priests, seal unto it.

10:28 And the rest of the people, the priests, the Levites, the porters, the singers, the Nethinims, and all they that had separated themselves from the people of the lands unto the law of God, their wives, their sons, and their daughters, every one having knowledge, and having understanding;

NLT **Nehemiah 9:32** "And now, our God, the great and mighty and awesome God, who keeps his covenant of unfailing love, do not let all the hardships we have suffered seem insignificant to you. Great trouble has come upon us and upon our kings and leaders and priests and prophets and ancestors—all of your people—from the days when the kings of Assyria first triumphed over us until now.

33 Every time you punished us you were being just. We have sinned greatly, and you gave us only what we deserved.

34 Our kings, leaders, priests, and ancestors did not obey your Law or listen to the warnings in your commands and laws.

35 Even while they had their own kingdom, they did not serve you, though you showered your goodness on them. You gave them a large, fertile land, but they refused to turn from their wickedness.

36 So now today we are slaves in the land of plenty that you gave our ancestors for their enjoyment! We are slaves here in this good land.

37 The lush produce of this land piles up in the hands of the kings whom you have set over us because of our sins. They have power over us and our livestock. We serve them at their pleasure, and we are in great misery."

38 The people responded, "In view of all this, we are making a solemn promise and putting it in writing. On this sealed document are the names of our leaders and Levites and priests."

10:28 Then the rest of the people—the priests, Levites, gatekeepers, singers, Temple servants, and all who had separated themselves from the pagan people of the land in order to obey the Law of God, together with

29 They clave to their brethren, their nobles, and entered into a curse, and into an oath, to walk in God's law, which was given by Moses the servant of God, and to observe and do all the commandments of the LORD our Lord, and his judgments and his statutes.

their wives, sons, daughters, and all who were old enough to understand—

29 joined their leaders and bound themselves with an oath. They swore a curse on themselves if they failed to obey the Law of God as issued by his servant Moses. They solemnly promised to carefully follow all the commands, regulations, and decrees of the LORD our Lord.

The People, Places, and Times

Nehemiah. The book of Nehemiah is written primarily by Nehemiah (whose name means "Jehovah consoles"), the cupbearer to King Artaxerxes I Longimanus. Some portions are attributed to Ezra, but based on Nehemiah's memoirs, Nehemiah 9 is traditionally considered to be Ezra's prayer. While serving the king, Nehemiah received word about the deplorable condition of Jerusalem, its walls, and its people, years after the Babylonian invasion and exile. He took great risk to present his dilemma to the king, and he created a plan to help rebuild the walls and morale of the people.

King Artaxerxes granted Nehemiah's request to return to Jerusalem, providing him with supplies and armed security. Nehemiah promised to return.

Nehemiah successfully motivated the Jews to rebuild the wall in 52 days, despite threats, intimidation, and abuse. He went on to serve as governor in Jerusalem for 12 years—coming alongside Ezra to spur the people on to confession and repentance.

Nethinims. Written as Nethinims in the King James Version (10:28), other translations refer to them as "temple servants." These servants were tasked with jobs such as carrying wood or gathering water "for the service of the Levites" (Ezra 8:20).

How did the support of the king make a difference for Nehemiah in rebuilding the walls of the city?

Background

For generations, and under multiple kings after David, the Jews continually failed to obey God's commands or heed the warnings of many prophets. They worshiped idols, married heathens, ignored the Law, killed prophets, and more. As God warned through the prophets, He allowed other nations to besiege them, destroy their land, scatter them throughout the earth, and enslave them—Israel first, in 722 BC, by Assyria, then Judah, when Jerusalem was conquered over a number of years ending in 586 BC under Nebuchadnezzar, king of Babylon.

As promised, the Jews remained in exile for 70 years. Then, in 539 BC, Cyrus the Great conquered Babylon and established the Persian Empire. He would eventually decree that the Jews could return to Jerusalem and rebuild. However, the walls would remain in ruins, leaving Jerusalem unfortified and exposed to enemies. Upon inquiring about the state of Jerusalem, and the Jews who had escaped death and survived captivity, Nehemiah writes, "They said to me, 'Things are not going well for those who returned to the province of Judah. They are in great trouble and disgrace. The wall of Jerusalem has been torn down, and the gates have been destroyed by fire'" (Nehemiah 1:3). This motivated him to pray, mourn, and fast, with the results being a national confession of sins, repentance, and rebuilding.

How might we apply the practice of national confession to our own country?

At-A-Glance

1. The Confession (Nehemiah 9:32–38)
2. The Repentance (10:28–29)

In Depth

1. The Confession (Nehemiah 9:32–38)

Two days after the Feast of Tabernacles, the Israelites came together in fasting and mourning wearing sackcloth and ashes (9:1). They separated themselves from all foreigners (failure to do this in previous generations was part of their downfall), "confessed their own sins and the sins of their ancestors" (v. 2), read from the Law, and worshiped God. All of these things had been long neglected over the years.

Nehemiah 9 continues with Ezra's prayer providing a brief history of the Jews and their relationship with God. He contrasts their unfaithfulness and wickedness with God's power, loyalty, mercy, and commitment. They broke their side of the covenant, yet God maintained His. Verses 32–38 continue this contrast, pointing out that they are unworthy of God's attention in comparison to His awesomeness (v. 32).

Ezra confesses that they are sinners, worthy of the calamities that have fallen upon them over the years; their sin was widespread. They are now slaves in their own land. They asked God for deliverance so they could enjoy the land He had promised and granted generations prior.

In our lives today, there are often many things we can enjoy that God promises, but our sin and unfaithfulness keep us from obtaining them. Confession can get us on the right path to pursue God's blessings.

How can repentance and confession of sins change your circumstances?

2. The Repentance (10:28–29)

Nehemiah 10 opens with a list of leaders, priests, and Levites, beginning with Nehemiah, who made a binding agreement with the Lord by placing their seals on the document (similar to today's signatures) indicating their commitment to repent. Other lower dignitaries, such as gatekeepers, singers, and temple servants, followed suit in separating from the outside influences that contributed to their forefathers' disloyalty and wickedness. Not only did they flee from evil influences, they also turned to God and "solemnly promised to carefully follow all the commands, regulations, and decrees of the LORD our Lord" (v. 29). They invoked a curse upon themselves if they failed to keep their oath, which was similar to the original covenant found in Deuteronomy 27–28. Chapter 10 continues with the stipulations of their agreement, including keeping the Sabbath and sabbatical year and avoiding intermarriages. Not only did they confess their sin, they also changed their behavior, which is true repentance.

Why is there a need to rededicate and recommit ourselves to God after a period of separation?

Search the Scriptures

1. Why does Ezra's prayer make only one request (Nehemiah 9:32)?
2. What indicates that this repentance is genuine (v. 38, 10:28–29)?

Discuss the Meaning

Often, we look at the events of the Old Testament as though its principles are antiquated. The God of love, mercy, and forgiveness is also a just God who still hates sin and desires repentance.

What does Nehemiah 9 teach about the character of God? What can we learn about prayer and repentance?

Lesson in Our Society

Repentance seems to be a foreign concept in our society. We often use the term "justice" as it relates to societal woes, but rarely do we take into consideration the role of repentance. We say we want justice when what we often really desire is vengeance.

God is just, not vengeful. For years He extended mercy to a disloyal people. He still does. Repentance brings about the restoration of relationships, and restoration is what our broken families, communities, society, and nation need. This occurs by repenting—turning away from sin and going in the opposite direction toward God.

Many issues in our community require justice. As African Americans, we support movements calling for fair treatment by police officers and demand a halt to the mass incarceration of our youth. These movements also need to be coupled with genuine repentance. We have sinned against God in many ways. Some of our problems stem from destructive forces outside of our community, but we also need to confess the sinful habits in our hearts and homes. A national movement in the African American community of genuine prayer and repentance might result in real change and exponential blessings for our children and grandchildren.

What type of honest discussions are necessary within our congregations that will create opportunities for repentance, forgiveness, and healing?

Make It Happen

This lesson causes us to examine sin—personal and societal. In what areas of your life do you need to confess sin?

• Ask God to reveal any personal sin, and then confess and repent.

• Ask God to reveal the ways that we as a church, society, and nation have strayed away from Him, and then confess and repent.

• Gather some friends and church members and begin to confess and repent together as you pray for God's blessing for your family, church, community, and nation.

Follow the Spirit

What God wants me to do:

_____

_____

_____

_____

Remember Your Thoughts

Special insights I have learned:

_____

_____

_____

_____

More Light on the Text
Nehemiah 9:32–38, 10:28–29

32 Now therefore, our God, the great, the mighty, and the terrible God, who keepest covenant and mercy, let not all the trouble

seem little before thee, that hath come upon us, on our kings, on our princes, and on our priests, and on our prophets, and on our fathers, and on all thy people, since the time of the kings of Assyria unto this day.

The prayer's moving and significant climax brings two unshakable ideas to the forefront: first, that God is the powerful head of His people who disciplines them for their sin; and second, that the human powers, those responsible for Israel's worship and protection, have played a central role in the aggrieving sin that led to this discipline. The people confess that God is utterly powerful, beyond them in every way, and even "terrible" (Heb. *yare*, **yah-REY**) in the sense of inspiring terror and awe by being holy, not cruel or capricious. The word stems from the verb meaning "to fear," but is also related to the word "fearsome." But—and here is the beautiful mystery of biblical religion from first to last—our God, so mighty beyond comprehension, so other and set apart, is also the God "who keepest covenant and mercy," that is, who makes glorious promises and keeps them even when the promises made back to Him are broken.

On this basis alone, the people can beseech God and ask that their history of trouble not "seem little before thee." Their hope is that God will recognize their suffering and repentance, and this will prompt Him to have mercy on them once again. Although their own leaders fail them again and again, the people confess their hope that their King of all kings will never fall short of His promise. And lest they appear to be shifting the blame, the prayer notes that from the first exile ("the time of the kings of Assyria") to today, the guilt lies not only on the leaders but also "on our fathers, and on all thy people."

33 Howbeit thou art just in all that is brought upon us; for thou hast done right,

but we have done wickedly: **34 Neither have our kings, our princes, our priests, nor our fathers, kept thy law, nor hearkened unto thy commandments and thy testimonies, wherewith thou didst testify against them.**

Near the end of the book of Deuteronomy, after the detailed proclamation of God's Law to Israel, the people are commanded to renew the covenant they made at Mount Sinai. When they crossed over the Jordan, they were to hold an unforgettable ceremony (Deuteronomy 27). Half of Israel's tribes would stand on Mt. Gerizim to represent the blessing of God for obedience, and the other half on nearby Mt. Ebal to represent His curse for disobedience. Meanwhile, Moses declares God's curses and blessings before the people.

Before the people enter the Promised Land, the Lord has clearly established the basis upon which they will find the life they seek. They have agreed and bound themselves to the covenant. This is what Ezra refers to when he speaks of "thy testimonies wherewith thou didst testify against them." The word *'eduth* (Heb. **eh-DOOTH**) is the word used for testimony or witness. This word carries the meaning of "warnings," which points to the gravity of the Israelites' sin against the Lord.

Given this history, none of their descendants—including those standing before God this day in a rebuilt Jerusalem—can claim unfair punishment. And so the prayer of confession acknowledges that the people have chosen Mount Ebal. They have chosen the curse. As a result, God has been perfectly just to carry out what He promised, while amazingly merciful in allowing a return for a faithful remnant of the people.

35 For they have not served thee in their kingdom, and in thy great goodness that thou gavest them, and in the large and fat

land which thou gavest before them, neither turned they from their wicked works.

The community's prayer now brings to light another reason God has been perfectly justified in disciplining the people. Not only did they repeatedly and egregiously break their covenantal promises to Him, but they also spurned and misused the generosity with which He lavished good things upon them. The "fat land" of their home (meaning it was rich with resources), the kingdom He gave them when they begged for a king to rule them (see 1 Samuel 8), and all His goodness in delivering them from both want and fear—the result of all these things is that "they have not served thee in their kingdom … neither turned they from their wicked works" (Nehemiah 9:35). This vivid contrast presents an unmistakable picture of God's righteousness and Israel's guilt.

36 Behold, we are servants this day, and for the land that thou gavest unto our fathers to eat the fruit thereof and the good thereof, behold, we are servants in it:

The prayer draws to a close with acknowledgment of a painful irony: that the Israelites, called by God to rule on His behalf over the land of Palestine, have now returned to that land, only to be servants rather than masters, small and insignificant rather than great and filled with blessings. Although this return to Israel was hopeful and merciful, the nation never does gain the former glory it knew under the reigns of David and Solomon. One empire replaces another in ruling over Israel: from Persia to Greece, and from Greece to Rome. Israel will be left to look for a greater King to lead them into the true fulfillment of the Abrahamic promise. Then, because his was a poor family when He was as an infant, and later because He was a suffering servant rather than a victorious warrior, many missed Jesus and still overlook Him to this day.

37 And it yieldeth much increase unto the kings whom thou hast set over us because of our sins: also they have dominion over our bodies, and over our cattle, at their pleasure, and we are in great distress. 38 And because of all this we make a sure covenant, and write it; and our princes, Levites, and priests, seal unto it.

The prayer concludes with a description of the situation of God's people. Because of the people's sins, the land produces a harvest for kings who do not even worship Yahweh. These kings have dominion over the people's bodies and their cattle as well. This is a cause for great distress (Heb. *tsarah*, **tsah-RAH**). The word means "tightness" and therefore this is a very troublesome situation. It is also a word used for a female rival or adversary, as in the way Peninah is described in relation to Hannah in 1 Samuel 1:6.

All of these words are a preface to the signing of a covenant by the princes, Levites, and priests. They all put a seal on this document, a common practice in the ancient world. Most cultures at the time used cylinder seals, but the Hebrews preferred a stamp seal. This tool was a semiprecious stone engraved with a unique mark that signified a person of status or the authority of a particular government.

10:28 And the rest of the people, the priests, the Levites, the porters, the singers, the Nethinims, and all they that had separated themselves from the people of the lands unto the law of God, their wives, their sons, and their daughters, every one having knowledge, and having understanding;

Among the terms of the covenant is their commitment to follow the commandment of the Lord their God according to the Law that Moses gave to them. The commitment starts with their separation from the people of the land—the other nations. One of God's important covenant agreements with Israel is that they should not have any union, neither in marriage nor in fellowship, with the heathen nations as they live in the land which He promised to give to their fathers (Leviticus 20:26; Numbers 23:9; Deuteronomy 7:2–3).

Joshua instructs the people, "That ye come not among these nations, these that remain among you; neither make mention of the name of their gods, nor cause to swear by them, neither serve them, nor bow yourselves unto them" (Joshua 23:7). Evidently, one of Israel's acts of rebellion and disobedience that led them to greater sins, and consequently to experience God's anger and discipline, was their abandonment of this law. As a demonstration of their changed, repentant heart and their resolve to return to their God, they pledged to separate themselves from the heathen nations.

Verse 28 lists the group of people who committed themselves to following the Lord. The list includes "the priests, the Levites, the porters, the singers, the Nethinims, and all they that had separated themselves from the people of the lands." This inclusion shows the total commitment of every level of society. The verb tense "had separated" implies that many of the people had already separated themselves from their foreign wives, as indicated in Ezra 9–10.

29 They clave to their brethren, their nobles, and entered into a curse, and into an oath, to walk in God's law, which was given by Moses the servant of God, and to observe and do all the commandments of the LORD our Lord, and his judgments and his statutes;

Having understood the Law and resolved to change their ways, the people enter into a covenant with one another, including all the nobles and other officials, to obey the Law, observe all the commandments of the Lord, and keep His statutes. The phrase "they clave to

their brethren" means that the people bonded together with their brothers, that is, they were united in their resolution. "They clave" is the Hebrew *chazaq* (**khah-ZAK**), which means to make firm, repair, or cleave. The author describes this covenant by using two synonymous Hebrew nouns: *'alah* (**aw-LAW**) and *shebu'ah* (**sheb-oo-AW**), both meaning "something sworn," e.g., an oath or a curse. The word *'alah* seems to imply that failure to keep the covenant would bring a grievous punishment, while *shebu'ah* implies a promissory oath to live in covenant with the law of the Lord. The use of both synonyms indicates the importance of the covenant and the people's resolve to obey the Law.

The terms of the covenant are detailed in the rest of this chapter. The covenant is summed up in the following statement: "To walk in God's law, which was given by Moses the servant of God, and to observe and do all the commandments of the LORD our Lord, and his judgments and his statutes" (v. 29).

Sources:
Kidner, Derek. *Ezra & Nehemiah: An Introduction and Commentary*. Downers Grove, IL: InterVarsity Press, 1979.
Myers, Allen C., ed. *The Eerdmans Bible Dictionary*. Grand Rapids, MI: William B. Eerdmans Publishing Company, 1996.
The New Interpreter's Bible, Volume Three. Nashville, TN: Abingdon Press, 1999.

Say It Correctly

Nethinims. neth-i-**NIMS**.
Assyria. ah-**SEAR**-ee-ah.

Daily Bible Readings

MONDAY
Israel Gathers for National Confession
(Nehemiah 9:1–5a)

TUESDAY
God: Creator and Covenant Maker
(Nehemiah 9:5b–8)

WEDNESDAY
God Meets Rebellion
with Steadfast Love
(Nehemiah 9:26–31)

THURSDAY
Redeemer of Israel's Iniquities
(Psalm 130)

FRIDAY
Forgive Fellow Believers Repeatedly
(Luke 17:1–4)

SATURDAY
God's Kindness Leads to Repentance
(Romans 2:1–8)

SUNDAY
Confession and Covenant Renewal
(Nehemiah 9:32–38, 10:28–29)

Notes

_____

_____

_____

_____

Teaching Tips

Words You Should Know

A. Zealous (Numbers 25:11) *qana'* (Heb.)—To be jealous of, envious of, or zealous of.

B. Atonement (v. 13) *kaphar* (Heb.)—To cover over, atone for sin; pacify.

Teacher Preparation

Unifying Principle—Unwavering Commitment. Some people are more faithful to their commitments than others. How do we respond to those who are faithful to their commitments and to those who are not? God rewarded faithful Phinehas and punished Eli's unfaithful children, thus proving that He is faithful to the everlasting covenant with His people.

A. Pray that you and your students will be faithful.

B. Study the companion lesson thoroughly in advance.

C. Think about times when you have kept commitments to God and others. What about times when you have failed to keep your commitments? What have been the consequences?

O—Open the Lesson

A. Ask students to identify and describe people they would consider to be faithful. Then, ask about experiences with unfaithful people who fail to keep commitments. Discuss the outcomes of both types of people.

B. Introduce today's lesson title and Aim for Change. Pray for students to fully grasp the seriousness of remaining faithful to God and to honestly examine their own lives.

C. Have students read the Keep in Mind verse and In Focus story.

P—Present the Scriptures

A. Have students read the Focal Verses (aloud or silently).

B. Read and discuss The People, Places, and Times and Background sections.

C. Use In Depth content and Search the Scriptures to facilitate discussion on the Focal Verses.

E—Explore the Meaning

A. Have the class answer the Discuss the Meaning questions.

B. Read Lesson in Our Society and have students make observations.

N—Next Steps for Application

A. Encourage students to apply the Make It Happen section to their lives.

B. Pray with students that they will be able to move forward with a new commitment of serving God and others faithfully.

Worship Guide

For the Superintendent or Teacher
Theme: Faithful God, Unfaithful People
Song: "Trust and Obey"
Devotional Reading: Psalm 44:1–8, 13–19, 26

105

Faithful God, Unfaithful People

Bible Background • NUMBERS 25; 1 SAMUEL 2:27–36
Printed Text • NUMBERS 25:10–13; 1 SAMUEL 2:30–36 | Devotional Reading • PSALM 44:1–8, 13–19, 26

—————— Aim for Change ——————

By the end of the lesson, we will: EVALUATE God's responses to Phinehas in Numbers 25 with Hophni and Phinehas in 1 Samuel 2; REFLECT on the consequences of infidelity to God; and DECIDE to serve God and others faithfully.

———— 🔖 In Focus 🔍 ————

"Do you, Charles, take this woman, Sandra, to have and to hold from this day forward, for better or worse, for richer or poorer, in sickness or in health, to love and to cherish from this day forward until death do you part?"

"I do."

That was sixteen years ago. And he meant it—then.

Then, about six years into it, Charles just couldn't see why he made that commitment. "If I would've known then…" he said. He felt as though he should have stayed single. Life was simpler then. He could make his own decisions, live his own life, and he wasn't so stressed out. Sandra was great, and they had two beautiful little ones. But he just felt too overwhelmed by the responsibility. So, despite godly counsel, advice, praying, begging, and pleading—he left.

Now, ten years later, he has been married (and divorced) twice. Sandra has since remarried a wonderful man that his children adore and call "Daddy." Charles is filled with regret and wants a relationship with his children. But with the passing of time, his children felt the impact of his abandonment and wanted very little to do with him.

What are the rewards and penalties we receive for honoring or dishonoring commitments in our lives? In this lesson, we will examine rewards and penalties for commitments made to God—honored and dishonored.

—————— Keep in Mind ——————

"I will raise me up a faithful priest, that shall do according to that which is in mine heart and in my mind" (from 1 Samuel 2:35).

"I will raise me up a faithful priest, that shall do according to that which is in mine heart and in my mind" (from 1 Samuel 2:35).

Focal Verses

KJV

Numbers 25:10 And the LORD spake unto Moses, saying,

11 Phinehas, the son of Eleazar, the son of Aaron the priest, hath turned my wrath away from the children of Israel, while he was zealous for my sake among them, that I consumed not the children of Israel in my jealousy.

12 Wherefore say, Behold, I give unto him my covenant of peace:

13 And he shall have it, and his seed after him, even the covenant of an everlasting priesthood; because he was zealous for his God, and made an atonement for the children of Israel.

1 Samuel 2:30 Wherefore the LORD God of Israel saith, I said indeed that thy house, and the house of thy father, should walk before me forever: but now the LORD saith, Be it far from me; for them that honour me I will honour, and they that despise me shall be lightly esteemed.

31 Behold, the days come, that I will cut off thine arm, and the arm of thy father's house, that there shall not be an old man in thine house.

32 And thou shalt see an enemy in my habitation, in all the wealth which God shall give Israel: and there shall not be an old man in thine house for ever.

33 And the man of thine, whom I shall not cut off from mine altar, shall be to consume thine eyes, and to grieve thine heart: and all the increase of thine house shall die in the flower of their age.

34 And this shall be a sign unto thee, that shall come upon thy two sons, on Hophni and Phinehas; in one day they shall die both of them.

35 And I will raise me up a faithful priest, that shall do according to that which is in mine heart and in my mind: and I will build him a sure house; and he shall walk before mine anointed forever.

NLT

Numbers 25:10 Then the LORD said to Moses,

11 "Phinehas son of Eleazar and grandson of Aaron the priest has turned my anger away from the Israelites by being as zealous among them as I was. So I stopped destroying all Israel as I had intended to do in my zealous anger.

12 Now tell him that I am making my special covenant of peace with him.

13 In this covenant, I give him and his descendants a permanent right to the priesthood, for in his zeal for me, his God, he purified the people of Israel, making them right with me."

1 Samuel 2:30 "Therefore, the LORD, the God of Israel, says: I promised that your branch of the tribe of Levi would always be my priests. But I will honor those who honor me, and I will despise those who think lightly of me.

31 The time is coming when I will put an end to your family, so it will no longer serve as my priests. All the members of your family will die before their time. None will reach old age.

32 You will watch with envy as I pour out prosperity on the people of Israel. But no members of your family will ever live out their days.

33 The few not cut off from serving at my altar will survive, but only so their eyes can go blind and their hearts break, and their children will die a violent death.

34 And to prove that what I have said will come true, I will cause your two sons, Hophni and Phinehas, to die on the same day!

35 "Then I will raise up a faithful priest who will serve me and do what I desire. I will establish his family, and they will be priests to my anointed kings forever.

36 Then all of your surviving family will bow before him, begging for money and food. 'Please,' they will say, 'give us jobs among the priests so we will have enough to eat.'"

36 And it shall come to pass, that every one that is left in thine house shall come and crouch to him for a piece of silver and a morsel of bread, and shall say, Put me, I pray thee, into one of the priests' offices, that I may eat a piece of bread.

The People, Places, and Times

Phinehas. This lesson features two men named Phinehas, but their lives are starkly different. Phinehas in Numbers 25 was the son of Eleazar and grandson of Aaron, Moses' brother through whom God established the Aaronic priesthood. As Moses tells the judges that they must execute the leaders involved in blatant idolatry (vv. 4–5), the Israelite Zimri brazenly brings a Moabite woman, Cozbi, into the Israelite camp "in the sight of all the congregation of the children of Israel, who were weeping before the door of the tabernacle of the congregation" (v. 6). In righteous anger, Phinehas followed them into the tent and thrust a spear through both of them. This action puts an end to the plague God had sent because of the Israelites' idolatry.

Phinehas of 1 Samuel 2 is one of the two sons of Eli who served as priests. He and his brother, Hophni, are introduced as wicked men who "had no respect for the LORD" (v. 12). They were greedy, deceitful, sexually immoral, and intimidating. A messenger from the Lord confronted Eli with the truth that he did little to correct his sons. Why, he asked, did Eli honor his sons more than God (v. 29)? As a result, they were killed.

Eli. Eli, a high priest of Israel, was from the line of Aaron to whom God promised an everlasting priesthood. He also served as judge of Israel who cared for Samuel as a child after his mother devoted him to Lord (1 Samuel 1:24–28). Scripture indicates that Eli was devoted to God; however, his sons were not. While he addressed his sons' sins, he did not discipline them; they faced no repercussions for their actions (v. 25). As a result, God promises the eventual destruction of his priestly line (see 1 Samuel 2:34; 3:13; 4:16–18).

When we evaluate the lives of the two Phinehases, what can we argue about the influence parents have in the lives of subsequent generations?

Background

One of the Israelites' biggest downfalls was idolatry. On multiple occasions, God commanded them to be faithful to Him by avoiding idol worship (Exodus 20:3–6; Deuteronomy 27:15). In Numbers 25, the Israelites are on the threshold of entering into the Promised Land. A hired prophet named Balaam had unsuccessfully attempted to curse Israel (Numbers 22–24). Since he could not curse them, he found a way to compromise their morals by advising Moabite women to seduce the Israelite men (31:16).

It worked; many men engaged in sexual relations as part of the worship of the Canaanite god, Baal. This unfaithfulness led God to instruct Moses to have the leaders in this sin killed with their bodies put on display (possibly impaled) for all to see. He sent a plague that ultimately kills 24,000 people until Phinehas drives a spear into a man who brought a Moabite woman into his tent.

Over the years, this type of unfaithfulness became a regular occurrence in Israel. By the time of the Judges, Israel was continually trapped in a cycle of sin and repentance. Ultimately, the sons of Eli, the priest, would be punished for not honoring the Lord as had their ancestor, Phinehas.

How would you compare and contrast God's response to obedience versus disobedience?

At-A-Glance

1. The Reward for Faithfulness
(Numbers 25:10–13)
2. The Penalty for Unfaithfulness
(1 Samuel 2:30–36)

In Depth

1. The Reward of Faithfulness (Numbers 25:10–13)

Phinehas' response to the sinfulness of Zimri and Cozbi, though extreme, demonstrated his fierce protectiveness of God's holiness and was in line with the punishment God had already delivered. Priests were set apart for God's service: offering sacrifices, leading in worship, modeling holiness, and representing His people. Phinehas' actions revealed his zeal, courage, faithfulness, and commitment—all essential qualities as a priest. These qualities were in stark contrast to the community's sins.

The reward for his faithfulness was threefold: 1) the plague stopped, 2) the sins of the people were forgiven and they were made right with God, and, 3) the promise that God made to Aaron to have an everlasting priesthood would be carried on through Phinehas' descendants as opposed to any other grandsons. Faithfulness definitely has its rewards in our lives as well.

How will your faithfulness to God affect your children and grandchildren?

2. The Penalty of Unfaithfulness (1 Samuel 2:30–36)

In contrast to Phinehas' faithfulness and reward, we see God's judgment on the sins of Hophni and Phinehas who were enabled by Eli. An unnamed man of God comes to Eli explaining that God is judging his sons' sins and Eli's own indulgence and lack of discipline (1 Samuel 2:27–36). Although God promised that Eli's branch of Levi would always serve as priests, we see that this promise was upon the condition of continued faithfulness.

Hophni and Phinehas took advantage of the priesthood. They took by force the meat offering for themselves before it was consecrated to God. They lay with the women who served at the entrance to the tent of meeting. They were out of control, wicked, and unrepentant. Not only would they die, but generations to come would face additional penalties as repercussions for their sins.

First, Eli's priestly line would be cut off (1 Samuel 2:34; 3:13; 4:16–18). Furthermore, very few men in his family would live to see old age, dying in the prime of their lives. And, those who did survive would be filled with grief, struggling to eat and live, begging for opportunities to serve and to support themselves. Sometimes our unfaithfulness to God not only affects us but also others connected to us as well.

How might your unfaithfulness to God create negative repercussions for your children and grandchildren?

Search the Scriptures

1. Was Phinehas too extreme in his zeal for God? Why or why not (Numbers 25:13)?

2. Compare and contrast God's punishment on Hophni and Phinehas and His blessing on the faithful priest (1 Samuel 2:31–36).

Discuss the Meaning

These two Scriptures illustrate the commitment levels of two types of servants of God—faithful and unfaithful. What do we learn about God, His desires, and the seriousness with which He views sin and faithfulness? How does this inform your level of commitment to Christ? Measure your level of commitment on a scale of 1 to 10. Why did you choose the number you chose?

Lesson in Our Society

We struggle with commitments, particularly if they have no immediate benefit. The variety, ease, and instantness of technology makes "bailing out" less painful. If you find an event better than the one you committed to earlier, it's easy to send a quick text. There's no need to discuss or feel bad. One can even file for a "simple" divorce.

But, there are always consequences. Keeping commitments builds trust, enhances character, and makes people feel loved and valued. Serving God well furthers the Gospel. Failure to keep commitments can do the opposite. Consider people you know who are faithful versus those are not. What do you think about their character? How productive and effective are they? At work? At church? In relationships?

One major area where faithfulness is lacking is in the area of sexual relationships. The statistics bear this out: According to a 2009 report by the U.S. Census Bureau, the divorce rate among Black women is 49% as opposed to 41% for non-Hispanic White women. According to the Centers for Disease Control and Prevention, African Americans are the racial/ethnic group most affected by HIV. These statistics are alarming and a result of unfaithfulness to not

just each other, but especially to God. The consequences affect those directly involved and generations to come. Faithfulness to God—and to one another—promises a lasting foundation for the next generation.

In what areas of your life is God calling you to adopt a deeper level of faithfulness?

Make It Happen

Our commitments display the strength or weakness of our character. Take some time this week to evaluate and re-affirm commitments you have made in your life:

• Make a list of all the commitments you have and evaluate whether you can keep these commitments.

• Practice saying "no" to people's requests. Don't overwhelm yourself with more obligations than you can handle.

• Make a small commitment for a week: something simple like drinking a certain amount of water or exercising for 10 minutes. Successfully practicing small commitments makes us strong enough to keep the more serious ones.

Follow the Spirit

What God wants me to do:

Remember Your Thoughts

Special insights I have learned:

More Light on the Text
Numbers 25:10–13

10 And the LORD spake unto Moses, saying, 11 Phinehas, the son of Eleazar, the son of Aaron the priest, hath turned my wrath away from the children of Israel, while he was zealous for my sake among them, that I consumed not the children of Israel in my jealousy.

In the aftermath of the plague that God used to judge the Israelites, He spotlights Phinehas, the grandson of Aaron. The Israelites were being judged for participating in an idolatrous orgy with the people of Moab. In the midst of this debauchery, the leaders of the people were commanded to execute everyone involved. One offender had brought a Midianite woman to his family to lead them along in this heinous sin. This was enough for Phinehas to thrust a javelin into both the man and the woman and kill them. After this, the plague stopped.

The commendation is given to Phinehas for turning away God's wrath (Heb. *chemah*, **kheh-MAH**) and for being zealous (Heb. *qinah*, **KEE-nah**) for His sake. The words here are very similar; both are related to anger. *Chemah* is derived from the word for warmth and heat and can refer to rage or poison. The word for zealous is taken from a root that means to be made red, and hence the redness of face when excited to anger or jealousy. This word is used in Numbers in reference to a jealous husband who believes his wife has committed adultery (Numbers 5:11–31). This was not just Phinehas' own zeal, but the Hebrew construction of the words is literally "because he acted zealously with my zeal." In other words, Phinehas was acting as one man and with the same mind as God. Due to the intensity of Phinehas' zeal for

God, the Children of Israel were not consumed (Heb. *kalah*, **kha-LAH**), which means to put to an end or destroy. Phinehas' act averted the total destruction of the Israelite nation.

12 Wherefore say, Behold, I give unto him my covenant of peace: 13 And he shall have it, and his seed after him, even the covenant of an everlasting priesthood; because he was zealous for his God, and made an atonement for the children of Israel.

A covenant of peace is offered to Phinehas. This is a covenant that provides assurance to the people receiving it that God is with them for their good. This covenant is for an everlasting priesthood, a perpetual agreement for Phinehas and his descendants to conduct worship in the temple. It was all based on his heart's attitude of "zealousness for his God," through which he made atonement (Heb. *kaphar*, **kha-FAR**) for the Children of Israel. This word means to cover over. The execution of the man and the Midianite woman was considered a ransom to God and an offering that covered over the sin of Israel.

1 Samuel 2:30–36

30 Wherefore the LORD God of Israel saith, I said indeed that thy house, and the house of thy father, should walk before me for ever: but now the LORD saith, Be it far from me; for them that honour me I will honour, and they that despise me shall be lightly esteemed.

An unknown man of God approaches Eli the priest with a message. This unknown man of God is a prophet and delivers the message of God's displeasure with Eli and his household. First, God reiterates the covenant that He made with Eli's ancestor, Phinehas, given to "thy house and the house of thy father." Here the word "house" has to do with the dynasty or family rather than a physical building.

Now, God speaks of judgment on Eli and his descendants. His sons had no regard for the Lord. The Lord then informs Eli that this judgment is because of the lack of honor (Heb. *kabad*, **kha-VAD**) given to Him. This word carries the image of being made heavy. Now the house of Eli would not be honored; instead they will be lightly esteemed (Heb. *qalal*, **ka-LAHL**). This word is the exact opposite of honor. If to be honored is to carry weight or to be heavy, this word means to be thought of lightly or as something small.

31 Behold, the days come, that I will cut off thine arm, and the arm of thy father's house, that there shall not be an old man in thine house. 32 And thou shalt see an enemy in my habitation, in all the wealth which God shall give Israel: and there shall not be an old man in thine house for ever.

God says that He will cut off Eli's arm and the arm of his father's house. The cutting off of the arm is not to be taken literally. The arm is a symbol of strength (Exodus 6:6; 2 Chronicles 32:8). This cutting off will be seen in the fact that there would be no older members of Eli's house still living.

Not only that, but Eli would see an enemy of God's people in His habitation (Heb. *ma'on*, **MAH-own**), which means dwelling place or refuge. Here as well as in other historical texts along with the psalms, it refers to the tabernacle. This prophecy was fulfilled when the Philistines took away the Ark of the Covenant; they would also take away Israel's wealth. Finally, Eli's house would have no elder at all, thus diminishing his clan's power in the Israelite tribal structure.

33 And the man of thine, whom I shall not cut off from mine altar, shall be to consume thine eyes, and to grieve thine heart: and all the increase of thine house shall die in the flower of their age. 34 And this shall be a sign unto thee, that shall come upon thy two sons, on Hophni and Phinehas; in one day they shall die both of them.

The Lord would not cut off all of Eli's descendants. He would keep one remaining descendant to remind Eli of his sin. His heart would be grieved (Heb. *adab*, **ah-DOB**). The word for grief comes from a root that means to pine away and languish. On top of that, every descendant of his would die "in the flower of their age." The Hebrew for the phrase "the flower of their age" is one word, *enosh* (Heb. **ee-NOHSH**); the distinction here is that they will not become old men (Heb. *zaqen*, **ZAH-kin**), as mentioned in previous verses. The KJV renders this "the flower of their age," while other translations suggest that they're dying "like mortals." A few others suggest that they'll die "when they become men." No matter the translation, the judgment on Eli's house would be total and devastating and involve not just Eli as an individual, but all of his descendants as well.

The prophet then gives Eli a sign that would confirm that all of this would happen: both of his sons, Hophni and Phinehas, would die in the same day. This prophecy would come true in 1 Samuel 4:10–11.

35 And I will raise me up a faithful priest, that shall do according to that which is in mine heart and in my mind: and I will build him a sure house; and he shall walk before mine anointed for ever.

The prophecy here of another faithful priest has many different possibilities for fulfillment. The man of God could be talking about Zadok, the priest who would replace Abiathar (1 Kings 2:35; 1 Chronicles 29:22). He could also be talking about Jesus as the great High Priest who fulfills this prophecy to the letter. This prophecy is more than likely speaking of both Zadok and Jesus. Zadok was raised up officially as the priest in line after Abiathar. Jesus is our great High Priest after the order of Melchizedek.

36 And it shall come to pass, that every one that is left in thine house shall come and crouch to him for a piece of silver and a morsel of bread, and shall say, Put me, I pray thee, into one of the priests' offices, that I may eat a piece of bread.

This is the worst of the prophecy and displays how low Eli's house will fall. No one in Eli's house will be respectable; they will have to beg for their livelihood. They will crouch or lower themselves for a piece of silver and ask for a "morsel" (Heb. *kikkar,* **ki-KAR**) of bread, which could refer to a round loaf, or even just a piece (Heb. *pat,* **PAHT**), which was just a mouthful. The house of Eli would not only lose its power and prestige, but it would also be destitute.

Sources:

Kreider, Rose M. and Renee Ellis. "Number, Timing, and Duration of Marriages and Divorces: 2009." *Current Population Reports, P70-125.* U.S. Census Bureau, Washington, D.C., 2011.

Radmacher, Earl D., ed. *Nelson Study Bible, New King James Version.* Nashville, TN: Thomas Nelson Publishers, 1997. 272–273, 454–455.

Ryrie, Charles C. *Ryrie Study Bible, New International Version.* Chicago, IL: Moody Press. 1986. 223, 366–370.

Unger, Merrill F. *The New Unger's Bible Dictionary.* Chicago, IL: Moody Press, 1988.

Walton, John H., Victor H. Matthews, and Mark W. Chavalas. *The IVP Bible Background Commentary: Old Testament.* Downers Grove, IL: InterVarsity Press, 2000. 284.

Walvoord, John F., and Roy B. Zuck, eds. *The Bible Knowledge Commentary: New Testament.* USA: Victor Books, SP Publications, Inc., 1983. 245–246, 434–4.

"HIV Among African Americans. Centers for Disease Control and Prevention." http://www.cdc.gov/hiv/group/racialethnic/africanamericans/

Say It Correctly

Phinehas. fi-**NEE**-us.
Hophni. hof-**NEE**.

Daily Bible Readings

MONDAY
God Always Faithful
(Psalm 44:1–8)

TUESDAY
Performing a Good Service to Jesus
(Matthew 26:6–13)

WEDNESDAY
Serve the Lord and One Another
(Romans 12:9–18)

THURSDAY
Called to Mission Service
(Philemon 8–16)

FRIDAY
Tragic Result of Worshiping Baal of Peor
(Numbers 25:1–9)

SATURDAY
Treating Offerings with Contempt
(1 Samuel 2:12–17)

SUNDAY
Covenant of a Perpetual Priesthood
(Numbers 25:10–13; 1 Samuel 2:30–36)

Teaching Tips

Words You Should Know

A. Inward parts (Jeremiah 31:33) *qereb* (Heb.)—Inner part, center and seat of thought and emotion.

B. Iniquity (v. 34) *avon* (Heb.)—Perversity, depravity, and guilt.

Teacher Preparation

Unifying Principle—Written on the Heart. Try as we might, humans often fail in our relationships. How can we restore broken relationships with others? Jeremiah foresaw a time when God would make a new covenant, writing His Law on human hearts with the vow to be Israel's God and to make Israel His people.

A. Take an assessment of your own relationships. Where has there been a "breaking of a covenant"? How have you worked to rectify and mend that relationship?

B. Pray for students to be open to how God can write a new covenant Law on their hearts.

O—Open the Lesson

A. Invite a student to pray for the class.

B. Direct students to read the In Focus story either as a group or individually.

C. Read Jeremiah 31:27–34 and pray for your time together.

P—Present the Scriptures

A. After reading the Scripture from either the King James Version or New Living Translation, ask a student to read the text from another translation like the Amplified or Message. Pay attention to any keywords or phrases that are highlighted in either translation. You can have several students read a few verses each.

B. Use The People, Places, and Times, Background, Search the Scriptures, At-a-Glance outline, In Depth, and More Light on the Text to explicate the verses.

E—Explore the Meaning

A. Ask the students to answer the question from the Discuss the Meaning section.

B. Breaking the students up into groups, ask them to read the Lesson in Our Society and Make It Happen sections. Ask students to write down the differences God expects from the Israelites after this new covenant is established. Have them share their findings with the larger group.

N—Next Steps for Application

A. Summarize the lesson and encourage students to apply the Make It Happen section.

B. Close the group in prayer.

Worship Guide

For the Superintendent or Teacher
Theme: Promise of a New Covenant
Song: "Standing on the Promises of God"
Devotional Reading: Psalm 87

Promise of a New Covenant

Bible Background • JEREMIAH 31
Printed Text • JEREMIAH 31:27–34 | Devotional Reading • PSALM 87

─────────── **Aim for Change** ───────────

By the end of the lesson, we will: EVALUATE Jeremiah's message about the new covenant; ASSESS how the new covenant makes a difference in our relationship with God; and DECIDE to live in accordance with the law written on our hearts.

─────── **In Focus** ───────

After a decade of marriage, James and his wife Lauren hit some tough times. Experiencing some health challenges and layoffs at work, the couple found themselves frustrated with each other and angry with God. One night, James and Lauren's arguments over finances led Lauren to declare she wanted a divorce. The words stunned both her and James; at the beginning of their marriage, they committed themselves to never utter the word *divorce*. Ten years later, life made it difficult for them to remember the beautiful ways in which God brought them together.

How did our marriage get to this point? James thought to himself. He left the house and decided to clear his head. He couldn't believe those words had come out of her mouth. There were so many problems that they had both faced. To give up on their marriage was definitely not the answer.

The next day, James got up early to pray to God about his marital troubles. After a while, Lauren came into his prayer closet with a piece of paper in her hand. It was their marriage license. "When we got married, we came into covenant with one other—for better or for worst, for richer or for poorer. God dealt with my heart all night and reminded me that we have more to fight for than each other. Please forgive me."

What do you do when you feel like giving up on a commitment you have made? Even when our relationships with each other and God get tough, we can remember the loving covenant God graced us with to keep moving forward.

─────────── **Keep in Mind** ───────────

"Behold, the days come, saith the LORD, that I will make a new covenant with the house of Israel, and with the house of Judah" (Jeremiah 31:31).

116

"Behold, the days come, saith the LORD, that I will make a new covenant with the house of Israel, and with the house of Judah" (Jeremiah 31:31).

Focal Verses

KJV **Jeremiah 31:27** Behold, the days come, saith the LORD, that I will sow the house of Israel and the house of Judah with the seed of man, and with the seed of beast.

28 And it shall come to pass, that like as I have watched over them, to pluck up, and to break down, and to throw down, and to destroy, and to afflict; so will I watch over them, to build, and to plant, saith the LORD.

29 In those days they shall say no more, The fathers have eaten a sour grape, and the children's teeth are set on edge.

30 But every one shall die for his own iniquity: every man that eateth the sour grape, his teeth shall be set on edge.

31 Behold, the days come, saith the LORD, that I will make a new covenant with the house of Israel, and with the house of Judah:

32 Not according to the covenant that I made with their fathers in the day that I took them by the hand to bring them out of the land of Egypt; which my covenant they brake, although I was an husband unto them, saith the LORD:

33 But this shall be the covenant that I will make with the house of Israel; After those days, saith the LORD, I will put my law in their inward parts, and write it in their hearts; and will be their God, and they shall be my people.

34 And they shall teach no more every man his neighbour, and every man his brother, saying, Know the LORD: for they shall all know me, from the least of them unto the greatest of them, saith the LORD: for I will forgive their iniquity, and I will remember their sin no more.

NLT **Jeremiah 31:27** "The day is coming," says the LORD, "when I will greatly increase the human population and the number of animals here in Israel and Judah.

28 In the past I deliberately uprooted and tore down this nation. I overthrew it, destroyed it, and brought disaster upon it. But in the future I will just as deliberately plant it and build it up. I, the LORD, have spoken!

29 "The people will no longer quote this proverb: 'The parents have eaten sour grapes, but their children's mouths pucker at the taste.'

30 All people will die for their own sins— those who eat the sour grapes will be the ones whose mouths will pucker.

31 "The day is coming," says the LORD, "when I will make a new covenant with the people of Israel and Judah.

32 This covenant will not be like the one I made with their ancestors when I took them by the hand and brought them out of the land of Egypt. They broke that covenant, though I loved them as a husband loves his wife," says the LORD.

33 "But this is the new covenant I will make with the people of Israel after those days," says the LORD. "I will put my instructions deep within them, and I will write them on their hearts. I will be their God, and they will be my people.

34 And they will not need to teach their neighbors, nor will they need to teach their relatives, saying, 'You should know the LORD.' For everyone, from the least to the greatest, will know me already," says the LORD. "And I will forgive their wickedness, and I will never again remember their sins."

The People, Places, and Times

Jeremiah. Jeremiah was born into a priestly family and called to be a prophet at a young age. His words were not accepted by the establishment in Judah. Considered one of the most revealing prophets of the Old Testament, Jeremiah's prophetic career prepared the Children of Israel for their imminent exile. His poetic words, graced by God's calling, offered both warning and promise to the Israelites. Jeremiah's words are regarded as an important part of the prophetic calling and trajectory of the Israelites and still resonate as important words for us today.

Pre-Exilic. The book of Jeremiah is a pre-exilic prophetic book, meaning that it was written prior to Israel's exile from the Promised Land. This is important to know as it helps us better understand Jeremiah's role as a prophet. It also helps us understand his prophecy of impending exile and the promise of a new covenant as reflective of the overarching themes of the text. Jeremiah's prophecy speaks into the future, when God's new covenant would restore them to the Promised Land and empower His people to live for Him by writing His laws on their hearts.

How can you experience rejection and persecution for proclaiming God's Word but still be counted as successful?

Background

The book of Jeremiah is prophesying the Israelites' Babylonian capture, period of captivity, and return to the Promised Land. In chapter 31, Jeremiah not only offers them the hope of freedom, but also a new covenant that is more than just following rules; it is covenant that changes the heart. This new covenant, Jeremiah explains, will be with them even when they are absent from one another and serve as a permanent reminder of God's grace and redemptive power.

When facing troubling news, how can we convince others there is hope for the future?

At-A-Glance

1. Payback for Disobedience
(Jeremiah 31:27–30)
2. Restoration Through a New Covenant
(vv. 31–34)

In Depth

1. Payback for Disobedience (Jeremiah 31:27–30)

Jeremiah talks about the days when God will repopulate the land of Israel and Judah. A re-population is needed because their sins will bring about God's judgment and punishment. Their idolatry and injustice will cause them to be conquered by the Babylonians and taken into exile. But after this, He would restore them. Their land would be repopulated and He would not allow them to be afflicted anymore. The Lord watched over them to discipline and afflict them in order for them to repent. In the coming days, when they are brought back from the exile, there will be a different kind of watching; the Lord will watch over them to restore them and help them rebuild their broken nation.

God reminds them of a popular proverb about sour grapes. This proverb was used to explain how children suffered the consequences of their parents' disobedience. The Lord said that this dynamic would no longer be in effect. In the days when He brought Israel back, every person would pay for his or her own sinful ways. This means that He would treat each person's sin individually. A person's sin will be their own responsibility, and they will reap the consequence of their good or bad choices.

When confronted with their sins, what excuses do some people create to justify their wrongdoing?

2. Restoration Through a New Covenant (vv. 31–34)

God's new covenant with Israel was unprecedented. He had made covenants with their ancestors in the past and recalls how the covenant He made with Israel had been broken. This happened in spite of God pursuing and loving them with the same force and intensity as a husband who loves his wife. The Children of Israel and Judah broke this covenant time and time again. By detailing how His people broke the old one, God shows the need for a new covenant.

While covenants with people like Abraham and Noah or even the Children of Israel had power, this covenant was a new development in God's relationship with His people. It required Israel to stop focusing so much on habitually following rules. Verse 32 says the new covenant would not look like "the covenant that I made with their fathers in the day that I took them by the hand to bring them out of the land of Egypt." God is noting that the covenant He had made then required spoon feeding the Israelites, giving one rule after another for them to follow and prove their love toward God. This new covenant, written on the hearts of people, is about a shift in attitude and proximity. God says no matter where you are, no matter what you do, His presence is with you in your heart.

How can our relationship with God be restored so we can develop a new life of faithfulness?

Search the Scriptures

1. In what ways did the Israelites' perpetual disobedience affect their lives (Jeremiah 31:27–30)?

2. How was this covenant vastly different from the covenants God had made with the Israelites in the past (vv. 33–34)?

Discuss the Meaning

Oftentimes we become so legalistic in our worship to God that we forget the ways in which He wants our hearts to be soft and open toward Him. How can we begin to shift our worship of God to less focus on rules and more focus on our hearts and attitude?

Lesson in Our Society

In a world where rules matter, we can easily take a rigid approach to developing our relationship with God. We can begin to tout how much of a "better" Christian we are because we are in line with the rules and regulations of church and society. But when we take this approach, we run the risk of ostracizing and marginalizing people who might be new to the faith or have a different understanding of God. Jeremiah's prophecy was important because it helped shift social and cultural understanding of what it meant to be in obedience to God—obedience in the heart made for outward expressions of obedience.

Many times in our churches, we can mistake the outward expressions and appearances as a measure of what's going on in a person's heart. For example, if someone is dressed nicely in a suit or wears a big "church hat," then we assume that they are in a good place with God. We listen to how a person talks with certain religious tones and assume this is the way a holy person talks. This is not necessarily the case. God is more concerned about what goes on in the heart than these outward expressions.

What examples do you see of people being judged prematurely based on their appearance or background?

Make It Happen

As followers of Christ, we are called to obey God, not just with an outward show, but with the right inner attitude. With this in mind:

• Compile a list of different outward signs of obedience, and next to them, write down the inward heart attitude that they are supposed to convey.

• If there is anyone with whom you need to make amends, call or write a letter in order to reconcile with them.

• Without using a Bible, write out several verses you know by heart, and then write down how God has used them to impact your life.

Follow the Spirit

What God wants me to do:

_____

_____

_____

_____

Remember Your Thoughts

Special insights I have learned:

_____

_____

_____

_____

More Light on the Text

Jeremiah 31:27–34

27 Behold, the days come, saith the lord, that I will sow the house of Israel and the house of Judah with the seed of man, and with the seed of beast.

Jeremiah continues his message from the Lord, relating His promises to the people. Here (vv. 27–34) he quotes the Lord. The exclamation "behold" (often translated as "lo," "see," or "look") tends to add emphasis and assurance to what is being said. Here the Lord says to the people through Jeremiah, "Look!" as if calling them to pay attention to what He is about to tell them. The Lord's promise to the people is that He will repopulate the houses of Israel and Judah with both the "seed of man" and "the seed of beast." The Lord uses an agricultural metaphor of sowing seed to describe how He will replenish the land with people and animals (cf. Hosea 2:23). This metaphor is also used to describe scattering the people from their land (Zechariah 10:9).

28 And it shall come to pass, that like as I have watched over them, to pluck up, and to break down, and to throw down, and to destroy, and to afflict; so will I watch over them, to build, and to plant, saith the LORD.

In verse 28, the Lord assures the people of a total reversal of the calamity that previously befell them (both Israel and Judah) under His watchful eyes. Here, just as in the past when He watched the destruction of the people, the Lord will watch over them to ensure their rebuilding and replanting in their land. In the past, the Lord seemed to supervise the total destruction of the land as described by a number of action verbs—"pluck up … break down … to destroy, and to afflict"—but in the future, He will watch over them "to build, and to plant" them again in the land. The terrible loss of human and animal lives during the invasion of the land and the cities of the past (see Jeremiah 7:20) will be reversed in the future. Old horrors will be replaced with blessings to come.

29 In those days they shall say no more, The fathers have eaten a sour grape, and the

121

children's teeth are set on edge. 30 But every one shall die for his own iniquity: every man that eateth the sour grape, his teeth shall be set on edge.

When all these things come to pass, the people would no longer have reason to complain or criticize God's righteousness and justice, using the common adage "the fathers have eaten a sour grape, and the children's teeth as set on edge," which they used during their suffering and exile. Unlike in the past where the people complained of being punished because of their father's sins, the future will be different (Ezekiel 18:1–4, 20–21). Instead, everyone will be responsible for his or her own acts. No more will the children pay for the sin of their fathers; nor will the fathers bear the brunt of their children's wrongdoing. But anyone who sins will be punished for his or her own iniquity, since every soul belongs to God (Ezekiel 18:4).

31 Behold, the days come, saith the LORD, that I will make a new covenant with the house of Israel, and with the house of Judah: 32 Not according to the covenant that I made with their fathers in the day that I took them by the hand to bring them out of the land of Egypt; which my covenant they brake, although I was an husband unto them, saith the LORD.

The good news of the future is not restricted to improving the people's physical condition. The Lord promises to change His relational condition to His people. The change in relationship will focus on improving His "covenant" (Heb. *berit*, **beh-REET**) with "the house of Israel and with the house of Judah." *Berit* or "covenant" can also be rendered as "an alliance" or a "treaty between two people or a group of people"; it is more binding than a mere agreement between two people. The Hebrew verb used for "to make" a covenant is *karat* (Heb. **kah-ROT**), which in its simplest form means

"to cut." This originally involved cutting of flesh (e.g., animals) and passing through the pieces. The implication of "cutting" a covenant was that whoever broke the covenant would be cut in pieces just like an animal. In some traditions such as the Igbo tribe of Nigeria, people made treaties by making a little cut in each person's finger and squeezing their blood into a cup of wine. The cup is then passed around from which each person drinks. It is strongly believed that whoever broke the covenant would die.

The Lord promises to make a new covenant with the people, which will replace the old one He had made with their forefathers when they left Egypt. The old covenant with Israel after the Exodus from Egypt refers to the Sinai covenant, also known as the Law of Moses. The problem with the old covenant is that the people did not keep it and therefore rendered it ineffective. Hence, the Lord finds it necessary to make a new covenant (see Hebrews 8:6–13).

Different translators have interpreted the phrase "although I was an husband unto them" in a number of ways. The word "husband" comes from the Hebrew word *ba'al* (**bah-AHL**), which can be rendered as a master, one who has dominion, husband, or married spouse. Hence the differences in interpretation, where other translations speak of authority and dominion or a reassertion of authority. The phrase refers to the people breaking the covenant. The word *ba'al* should therefore be interpreted with the idea of a "loving and caring" attitude of a husband towards his wife. The Lord uses the husband and wife metaphor to describe His loving relationship with the Children of Israel (Isaiah 54:5; Hosea 2:16). Therefore, it makes sense to render this part of the verse as "my covenant they brake, although I was an husband unto them."

33 But this shall be the covenant that I will make with the house of Israel; After those days, saith the LORD, I will put my law in their inward parts, and write it in their hearts; and will be their God, and they shall be my people.

The new covenant will not be the same as the old. The two have a number of differences and special features. First, while the old covenant was written on tablets of stone, the new covenant will be written in the heart; the material the covenant is written on and the content are markedly different. The tablets of stone are external, while the law written on the heart is internal (Psalm 37:31). Obedience to this covenant comes from the inside, not the outside.

This Scripture clearly states that the new covenant will not be the same as the old covenant God made with Moses (v. 32). The new covenant is what has been accomplished through Jesus as found in the New Testament (see Hebrews 12:24, 13:20). This promise points beyond the time of Jeremiah and the house of Israel; it points us to the New Testament and the Christian Gospel, fulfilled in Christ Jesus when He confirms: "This cup is the new testament [covenant] in my blood, which is shed for you" (Luke 22:20). This covenant is for all those who will come to God through His Son, Jesus Christ—both Jews and Gentiles. The new covenant will bring about a relational restoration between the Lord and His people, which hitherto had been severed as a result of breaking the old covenant. Now, God says that He "will be their God, and they shall be my people."

34 And they shall teach no more every man his neighbour, and every man his brother, saying, Know the LORD: for they shall all know me, from the least of them unto the greatest of them, saith the LORD: for I will forgive their iniquity, and I will remember their sin no more.

The second special feature in the new covenant is that because the Law would be written in their hearts, the people would have no need to teach others to know God. Until now the priests, scribes, and prophets were the custodians of the Law and so-called mediators of knowledge, but in the new covenant, the Law would be internalized in the hearts of God's people. This divine transformation of human nature will result in the personal knowledge and love of God from the least to the greatest. This means class distinction will be no more, and everyone will have equal opportunity and responsibility to know and love God.

Consequently, their iniquity will be forgiven and their sin remembered no more. Just as forgiveness was incorporated in the old covenant (Leviticus 4:31, 35), forgiveness would become the cornerstone of the relationship. This prophecy is now completely fulfilled in Jesus Christ for all generations. Through Him we have forgiveness and the Holy Spirit dwelling inside us leads us and guides us into all truth (John 14:17, 16:13).

Sources:
Alexander, David, et al. *Eerdman's Handbook to the Bible*. Grand Rapids, MI: Wm. B. Eerdmans Publishing Company, 1994.
Dunn, James D. G. and John W. Rogerson. *Commentary on the Bible*. Grand Rapids, MI: Wm. B. Eerdmans Publishing Company, 2003.
Elwell, Walter A. *Baker Theological Dictionary of the Bible*. Grand Rapids, MI: Baker Book House Company, 1996.
Howley, G.C.D., F.F. Bruce, and H. L. Ellison. *The New Layman's Bible Commentary*. Grand Rapids, MI: Zondervan, 1979.

Say It Correctly

Iniquity. ih-**NICK**-wih-tee.
Captivity. cap-**TIH**-vuh-tee.

Daily Bible Readings

MONDAY
God's Love Brings the People Together
(Jeremiah 31:1–6)

TUESDAY
People with Disabilities Welcome
(Jeremiah 31:7–9)

WEDNESDAY
Israel Celebrates Their Homecoming
(Jeremiah 31:10–14)

THURSDAY
Rachel's Children Come Home
(Jeremiah 31:15–20)

FRIDAY
Covenant Relationship Restored
(Hosea 2:16–20)

SATURDAY
In Remembrance of Me
(Luke 22:14–20)

SUNDAY
Accountability Under the New Covenant
(Jeremiah 31:27–34)

Notes

Teaching Tips

Words You Should Know

A. Intreat (Hebrews 12:19) *paraiteomai* (Gk.)—To beg pardon, avert displeasure, to excuse.

B. Mediator (v. 24) *mesites* (Gk.)—One who intervenes to make or restore peace and friendship or to form a compact or for ratifying a covenant, a medium of communication, arbitrator.

Teacher Preparation

Unifying Principle—The Go-Between. Humans desire to experience a power greater than themselves, but do not always realize that drawing near to such necessary power can be a terrifying prospect. How can people approach such a power without being consumed? In Psalm 66, the psalmist affirms that God allows humans to approach the divine; the writer of Hebrews proclaims that Jesus provides the means needed to boldly approach God's presence.

A. Jesus came to be the Mediator between mankind and God. What is the role of a mediator? Use a dictionary to define the word and a thesaurus to identify synonyms. Write the definition and synonyms down to share with participants in the group.

B. Pray for today's session that hearts would be open and willing to explore the need to draw nearer to God's power and presence.

O—Open the Lesson

A. Invite someone to pray for your time together.

B. Direct students to read the In Focus story either as a group or individually.

C. Discuss the question at the conclusion of the In Focus story.

P—Present the Scriptures

A. Have someone read the Focal Verses.

B. Use The People, Places, and Times, Background, Search the Scriptures, At-A-Glance outline, In Depth, and More Light on the Text to explicate the verses.

E—Explore the Meaning

A. Have students answer the Discuss the Meaning questions.

B. Read the Lesson in Our Society section and discuss the implications for everyday life.

N—Next Steps for Application

A. Encourage the class to apply the suggestions in the Make It Happen section.

B. Close the group in prayer.

Worship Guide

For the Superintendent or Teacher
Theme: Mediator of the New Covenant
Song: "Bow Down and Worship Him"
Devotional Reading: Psalm 66

Mediator of the New Covenant

Bible Background • HEBREWS 12:14–15, 18–29; PSALM 66
Printed Text • HEBREWS 12:14–15, 18–29 | Devotional Reading • PSALM 66

Aim for Change

By the end of the lesson, we will: CONSIDER the meaning of the Bible's teaching that God is "a consuming fire"; REPENT of our lack of holiness; and CELEBRATE Jesus as the Mediator who brings us into God's presence.

In Focus

On the first week of her new job, Sarah's anxiety was through the roof. A relatively shy person, working at one of the city's largest law firms as a paralegal was an exciting yet daunting experience for her. She had no time to slowly ease into the work. The office had been needing someone to fill her role for a month. This had put them behind in many cases, and Sarah's help was very welcome.

Once she settled at the desk, her new boss knocked on her door, bringing her first assignments for the week. She welcomed the new tasks but found herself immediately overwhelmed with the pressure of deadlines, an office phone ringing off the hook, and dozens of emails to answer all at once. Sarah completed her tasks with excellence, but she felt a certain inner anxiety inside.

After an hour of work, Sarah realized she did not take the time to read her daily devotion. This devotion had been a part of her morning routine for years, but with the excitement and anxiousness of starting a new job, she had forgotten this key piece of her day. Quietly Sarah took out her phone, opened the Bible app, and read the devotion for the day. Immediately, a peace came over her. Sarah was able to center herself to take on the tasks before her.

How do you cope during times when you are afraid and overwhelmed? When we take time to seek God, He will always be there to guide us, even when we are afraid and overwhelmed.

Keep in Mind

"Wherefore we receiving a kingdom which cannot be moved, let us have grace, whereby we may serve God acceptably with reverence and godly fear" (Hebrews 12:28).

"Wherefore we receiving a kingdom which cannot be moved, let us have grace, whereby we may serve God acceptably with reverence and godly fear" (Hebrews 12:28).

Focal Verses

KJV **Hebrews 12:14** Follow peace with all men, and holiness, without which no man shall see the Lord:

15 Looking diligently lest any man fail of the grace of God; lest any root of bitterness springing up trouble you, and thereby many be defiled;

18 For ye are not come unto the mount that might be touched, and that burned with fire, nor unto blackness, and darkness, and tempest,

19 And the sound of a trumpet, and the voice of words; which voice they that heard intreated that the word should not be spoken to them any more:

20 (For they could not endure that which was commanded, And if so much as a beast touch the mountain, it shall be stoned, or thrust through with a dart:

21 And so terrible was the sight, that Moses said, I exceedingly fear and quake:)

22 But ye are come unto mount Sion, and unto the city of the living God, the heavenly Jerusalem, and to an innumerable company of angels,

23 To the general assembly and church of the firstborn, which are written in heaven, and to God the Judge of all, and to the spirits of just men made perfect,

24 And to Jesus the mediator of the new covenant, and to the blood of sprinkling, that speaketh better things than that of Abel.

25 See that ye refuse not him that speaketh. For if they escaped not who refused him that spake on earth, much more shall not we escape, if we turn away from him that speaketh from heaven:

26 Whose voice then shook the earth: but now he hath promised, saying, Yet once more I shake not the earth only, but also heaven.

NLT **Hebrews 12:14** Work at living in peace with everyone, and work at living a holy life, for those who are not holy will not see the Lord.

15 Look after each other so that none of you fails to receive the grace of God. Watch out that no poisonous root of bitterness grows up to trouble you, corrupting many.

18 You have not come to a physical mountain, to a place of flaming fire, darkness, gloom, and whirlwind, as the Israelites did at Mount Sinai.

19 For they heard an awesome trumpet blast and a voice so terrible that they begged God to stop speaking.

20 They staggered back under God's command: "If even an animal touches the mountain, it must be stoned to death."

21 Moses himself was so frightened at the sight that he said, "I am terrified and trembling."

22 No, you have come to Mount Zion, to the city of the living God, the heavenly Jerusalem, and to countless thousands of angels in a joyful gathering.

23 You have come to the assembly of God's firstborn children, whose names are written in heaven. You have come to God himself, who is the judge over all things. You have come to the spirits of the righteous ones in heaven who have now been made perfect.

24 You have come to Jesus, the one who mediates the new covenant between God and people, and to the sprinkled blood, which speaks of forgiveness instead of crying out for vengeance like the blood of Abel.

25 Be careful that you do not refuse to listen to the One who is speaking. For if the people of Israel did not escape when they refused to listen to Moses, the earthly messenger, we will

27 And this word, Yet once more, signifieth the removing of those things that are shaken, as of things that are made, that those things which cannot be shaken may remain.

28 Wherefore we receiving a kingdom which cannot be moved, let us have grace, whereby we may serve God acceptably with reverence and godly fear:

29 For our God is a consuming fire.

certainly not escape if we reject the One who speaks to us from heaven!

26 When God spoke from Mount Sinai his voice shook the earth, but now he makes another promise: "Once again I will shake not only the earth but the heavens also."

27 This means that all of creation will be shaken and removed, so that only unshakable things will remain.

28 Since we are receiving a Kingdom that is unshakable, let us be thankful and please God by worshiping him with holy fear and awe.

29 For our God is a devouring fire.

The People, Places, and Times

Hebrews. In Genesis 14:13, Abram (Abraham) is the first person to be called a "Hebrew," and his descendants (through Isaac's line) would go on to be known as "Hebrews" (also called Israelites and Jews). The origin of the term is debated. Some scholars believe it is derived from the name "Eber," one of Abram's ancestors. Still, others hold that it comes from the term "ha ibhri" from *abar* (Heb. **ah-BAR**), which means to "cross over." This could be an allusion to describe Abram and his family "crossing over" the river Euphrates in their journey from Ur to Haran or from Haran to Canaan (Genesis 11:31, 12:4, 5). It is believed that the book of Hebrews was written to a largely Jewish audience who had converted to Christianity some time prior to the writing of the epistle.

Mt. Zion. Synonymous with Jerusalem, but most commonly referred to a specific mountain near Jerusalem, Mt. Zion. It is also regarded as a synonym for the people of God. It later became a term that denoted the church (Hebrews 12:22–23) as well as the heavenly city (Revelation 14:1).

How does the city of Jerusalem help connect us with our faith as Christians?

Background

The book of Hebrews was written to Jewish Christians who were facing great persecution at the time. Many Jewish Christians found it difficult to remain faithful to Christianity, and the author of Hebrews knew this. Much of the language used in Hebrews is reminiscent of traditional/ancient Jewish customs; scholars believe that these references were to help Jewish Christians make connections with the common Jewish traditions of temple worship redemption found in the Old Testament and the new covenantal experiences of Jesus in the New Testament. While the author of the book of Hebrews is unknown, the text begins to frame the work of Jesus Christ as Mediator to new believers who needed reassurance that their lives as Christians were blessed in the midst of persecution for their faith.

In the Scripture, we see the writer exhorting and encouraging his Jewish audience to seek to live a godly life in light of having Christ as Mediator and the same God who visited their ancestors on Mt. Sinai. This should cause them to worship in their daily lives with reverence and fear. This is because they are not at Mt. Sinai, but in the presence of the God who is a consuming fire, and Jesus who is the Mediator of a better covenant.

How can we make use of suffering and persecution to develop our faith and pursue godly living?

At-A-Glance

1. God's Grace (Hebrews 12:14–15)
2. To Fear and Revere God (vv. 18–24)
3. Jesus as Our Mediator (vv. 25–29)

In Depth

1. God's Grace (Hebrews 12:14–15)

The author encourages the Jewish Christians to pursue peace in their personal relationships. This is coupled with holiness, as they are directly linked. This holiness is a necessary prerequisite to seeing God. Both of these exhortations are faintly reminiscent of Jesus' words in the Sermon on the Mount. The call to pursue peace resembles the verse within the Beatitudes that states, "Blessed are the peacemakers: for they shall be called the children of God" (Matthew 5:9). The call to pursue holiness is similar to another beatitude: "Blessed are the pure in heart: for they shall see God" (v. 8). The author of Hebrews makes it clear that these things should remain a priority above all else.

They should watch over their hearts diligently in order to make sure they can partake in God's grace so that the believers do not allow any root of bitterness to grow in their hearts and therefore spread to the other members of the church. The Jewish Christians were to remain vigilant against dysfunction defiling their relationships. To defile these relationships would also defile their worship of and relationship with God.

When we make it our aim to pursue peace, how does it modify our relationships with others?

2. To Fear and Revere God (vv. 18–24)

The ancestors of this New Testament audience had experienced God with much fear and trepidation. Because of this, biblical leaders like Moses had to serve as a mediator between God and mankind. Many of these New Testament readers had heard of the "fire, darkness, [and] gloom" (Hebrews 12:18, NLT) that came with coming into God's divine presence. They had an ever-present terror of approaching God—the fear of death was a real concern for many.

Whenever God made His presence visible on Mt. Sinai, the people were afraid to approach Him. A certain protocol had to be followed when approaching Him. Not following it led to death. This caused the Children of Israel to stay away from the mountain, as the risk was too great. This was a paradox because they desired strongly to seek God, but at the same time, the fear of death often kept people from approaching Him.

What factors explain the reasons people today refrain from approaching and seeking God?

3. Jesus as Our Mediator (vv. 25–29)

Jesus' entry into the world helped eradicate this paradox by making it easier (and safer) for people to communicate with God without the fear of imminent death. Because of Jesus, we do not face the kind of destruction that we deserve because of our sins. Although we do not have to follow certain rules and regulations in approaching Him, God is still holy and will not tolerate sin. That is why a mediator is needed. Only through Jesus alone can we have a relationship with the God who stirred up fear through the threat of physical death. Now the threat of spiritual death is real for those who refuse to listen to His words today.

The once-dreadful fear of encountering the God who is a consuming fire evaporates when we come to Him through Jesus. At the same time, we realize the seriousness of approaching the God who now speaks from heaven, not just the earth as He did on Mt. Sinai. Jesus as Mediator offers us the opportunity to approach the throne of grace with gratefulness and gratitude.

Why is prayer and worship distinguished as the most important ways to approach God?

Search the Scriptures

1. How can we show thanks to God for sending Jesus as our Mediator? How can we leverage our relationship with Jesus to have even greater access to the Father?

2. Consider your relationships with people of authority in your life; how do you manage both reverential respect and genuine positive encounters with them? In what ways do you imagine your ability to successfully manage those relationships reflective in your relationship with God?

Discuss the Meaning

The age-old stories of how the Israelites experienced judgment as a result of their disobedience can possibly misshape our understanding of how much God wants to be in relationship with us. Jesus' sacrifice for us makes it possible for us to commune with God unlike the Children of Israel, who dared not approach God. How has your faith journey been shaped? Do you view God as a tyrant or as your Father in heaven who desires to be in relationship with you?

Lesson in Our Society

With changes in laws and policies in the United States, many Christians find it difficult to express their love for God without fear of persecution. Challenges in freedom of speech and expression of religion under the guise of being "politically correct" leave many Christians feeling tentative about speaking up because of these man-made laws. Take courage! We worship God in spirit and in truth (John 4:24) and find freedom in knowing that our relationship with Jesus creates opportunities to not only worship God, but also to share the gift of salvation with others—freely!

African Americans have a rich history of obeying the law of God over the law of man. This can be clearly seen in the work of the Underground Railroad during slavery and in the Civil Rights Movement. From the fruit of these movements, it is clear that we as Christians are called to obey God rather than man. The African church father, St. Augustine, wrote that an "unjust law is no law at all." It is with this conviction that we worship God in holy reverence and fear, knowing that He is the ultimate authority to whom we will have to answer.

How does the practice of civil disobedience connect with our desire to obey God in standing up against injustices in the world?

Make It Happen

With Jesus as the Mediator of a new and better covenant, we have the freedom to worship God. With this in mind:

• Research countries where believers face persecution and think about the ways they must sacrifice in order to worship God in a hostile environment.

• Create a list of things in your life that need to be abandoned in order to worship a holy God.

• This week, when you pray, spend 15 minutes just worshiping God without asking Him for anything.

Follow the Spirit

What God wants me to do:

_____

_____

_____

_____

Remember Your Thoughts

Special insights I have learned:

_____

_____

_____

_____

More Light on the Text

Hebrews 12:14–15, 18–29

14 Follow peace with all men, and holiness, without which no man shall see the Lord.

The writer of Hebrews encourages his readers to follow peace with everyone, along with holiness. The word for "follow" is *dioko* (Gk. **dee-OH-koh**) and can be used to refer to a pursuit of something in a hostile manner or persecution. Alternatively, it can mean to run swiftly in order to catch a person or thing. Here it figuratively means to press on or run a race swiftly to reach the goal.

This is supported by the following phrase, "without which no man shall see the Lord." This ought to give the believer pause. Continued sanctification is the mark of those who truly believe. Without this following and pressing into peace and holiness, the goal of seeing the Lord will not be reached. This verse does not denigrate faith as the means to a relationship

with God or the promise of eternal life. Far from setting up a works-based salvation, this exhortation from the writer of Hebrews describes the path of those who have faith and encourages us to continue to pursue holiness.

15 Looking diligently lest any man fail of the grace of God; lest any root of bitterness springing up trouble you, and thereby many be defiled.

The believers are then exhorted to look diligently (Gk. *episkopeo*, **eh-pi-sko-PEH-oh**). This word is actually related to the same word used for the work of the elders who look after and care for the church. In the same way, the individual believer needs to look after his or her own soul, to prevent "failing" of the grace of God. The word for "fail" here (Gk. *hystereo*, **hu-ste-REH-oh**) means to "fall short" (cf. Romans 3:23). In other words, it's not talking about falling from a certain level, but not making it to that level in the first place. The consequences of this failure to experience grace could manifest itself in a root of bitterness (Gk. *pikria*, **pee-KREE-ah**), which is metaphorically bitter hatred—a result of not pursuing peace with everyone. Not only is this harmful to the person who has failed to experience God's grace, but also through this bitter hatred many may be defiled. The word for defiled (Gk. *miaino*, **me-AYE-no**) can mean to dye with another color or to stain. Figuratively, it means to contaminate spiritually and morally. This is the end result of a root of bitterness springing up among the people of God. The writer of Hebrews warns believers to be on guard against such a thing happening among them.

18 For ye are not come unto the mount that might be touched, and that burned with fire, nor unto blackness, and darkness, and tempest, 19 And the sound of a trumpet, and the voice of words; which voice they that

heard intreated that the word should not be spoken to them any more: 20 (For they could not endure that which was commanded, And if so much as a beast touch the mountain, it shall be stoned, or thrust through with a dart: 21 And so terrible was the sight, that Moses said, I exceedingly fear and quake).

Beginning from verse 18, the author of Hebrews proceeds to contrast the Jewish and Christian ways by juxtaposing the terrors associated with the giving of the Law on Mt. Sinai with the joys and glory associated with Mt. Zion. Although the description in vv. 18–21 leaves no doubt that the writer has Sinai in mind, he makes no explicit reference to the mountain of revelation. The phenomena listed are all associated with the Sinai event (Deuteronomy 4:11). Elsewhere, they are all linked with the presence of God: "fire" (Judges 13:20), "darkness" (1 Kings 8:12), and "tempest" (Nahum 1:3). The picture strikes terror in the heart. The author warns that great privilege means great responsibility.

The Israelites were terrified by the experience. They responded to a "voice of words" by pleading to receive no further message (v. 19). The writer's statement summarizes Deuteronomy 5:23–27, particularly verse 25, where the people express the fear that they will be consumed by the fire if they continue to listen to God's voice (see Exodus 20:18–19). So they asked to hear God's voice no more. They were overcome with awe and wanted no further part in the wonderful events. The fearfulness of the giving of the Law on Sinai is brought out with reference to one of the commands laid on the people, namely, that neither man nor beast should even touch the mountain under penalty of death (Exodus 19:13). In effect, the command that nothing touch it indicates the holiness and separateness of the mountain. Judgment for anyone who ignores God's holiness is swift and terrible. Hebrews

12:21 is a further indication of the awe of it all. At the time of the giving of the Law, Moses was the leader of the people. He was known as one who had an especially close relationship with God (Exodus 33:11), yet even he was terrified. It was an awe-inspiring occasion, one that affected all the people and terrified even Moses, the man of God.

22 But ye are come unto mount Sion, and unto the city of the living God, the heavenly Jerusalem, and to an innumerable company of angels, 23 To the general assembly and church of the firstborn, which are written in heaven, and to God the Judge of all, and to the spirits of just men made perfect, 24 And to Jesus the mediator of the new covenant, and to the blood of sprinkling, that speaketh better things than that of Abel.

"But" is the strong adversative (Gk. *alla*, **al-LAH**) and introduces a marked contrast; Christians order their lives in accordance with a different revelation. The atmosphere at Mt. Zion is festive. The frightening visual imagery of blazing fire, darkness, and gloom fades before the reality of the city of the living God's heavenly Jerusalem. The destination of the Christian pilgrims is described with various evocative images. First, they have come to Mt. Zion (Hebrews 12:22), which should be understood not as the seat of temporal Israel but as a reference to God's eschatological rule through Christ, just as in Revelation 14:1–5. Second, the same verse states that they have come to the "city of the living God," a city with foundations that the patriarchs looked forward to and one that is eternal (Hebrews 13:14). The book of Revelation also applies this image for God's presence when it speaks of a "holy city" (Revelation 21:2). Third, the verse says they have come to the "heavenly Jerusalem," which is also called "new Jerusalem" (Revelation 3:12).

The city of God is noticeably filled with the life of a more vibrant, dynamic, and powerful sort than on earth. "Innumerable" angels are present as part of the welcoming and celebratory throng (v. 22). Then we have the church of the firstborn. In verse 23, the Greek word *ekklesia* (**ek-klay-SEE-ah**), translated as "church," is taken from the common civic life of the Greeks and normally refers to the official gathering of the leaders or their representatives. The "firstborn" (Gk. *prototokos,* **pro-TOE-toe-koce**) probably refers to all those whom God is leading into glory together with Jesus (Hebrews 2:10). Understood this way, it is synonymous with the later "spirits of just men made perfect" (12:23), or the spirits of righteous people. It is another way of describing the same participants in the true inheritance, which is a participation in God's holiness. The city of God is filled with untold numbers of angels and saints.

The climax is reached in verse 24 with the reference to Jesus, seen here as "the mediator of a new covenant." The author not only affirms the humanity of Jesus and His role as Mediator, but also definitively places Him at God's side—a place that was His from the beginning (Hebrews 1:1–4). Jesus' blood speaks "better things" than that of Abel (12:24); His blood opens up a way into the holiest for people (10:19).

25 See that ye refuse not him that speaketh. For if they escaped not who refused him that spake on earth, much more shall not we escape, if we turn away from him that speaketh from heaven: 26 Whose voice then shook the earth: but now he hath promised, saying, Yet once more I shake not the earth only, but also heaven.

The exposition in Hebrews 12:18–24 abruptly transitions to exhortation in vv. 25–29, and the author, with a sharp change in tone, resumes expressing the urgent concern that characterizes vv. 14–17. Here, the sternness of the warning is justified by the detailing of the privileged status of Christians in vv. 18–24. They have a qualitatively greater responsibility than did Israel to listen attentively to the voice of God. Those who deliberately ignore the end-times revelation of God through His Son and who show contempt for the blessings of the new covenant cannot possibly escape judgment.

The concluding paragraph consists of a sober caution to listen to what God is saying, a concentration of His Word in the form of prophecy, and a final admonition to respond appropriately with gratitude and worship. A tendency toward apathy or complacency is sharply rebuked with the phrase, "Be careful that you do not refuse to listen to the One who is speaking" (12:25, NLT). The form of the statement recalls 3:12, and it connotes a deliberate and culpable refusal to listen to the one speaking. The readers must also be aware that the greater the gift, the greater the responsibility, and the greater the peril involved in its rejection.

The author goes on to recall the solemnity of the events at Sinai (v. 26). Repeatedly, we are told that the earth shook then (Exodus 19:18; Psalm 68:7–8). The writer of Hebrews has already spoken of the awe-inspiring nature of what happened when the Law was given. Now, the reference to the earth shaking brings it all back.

At the same time, it enables the writer to go on to speak of a promise that involved a further shaking recorded in Haggai 2:6. The prophet looked forward to something much grander than Sinai. Then God shook the earth, but Haggai foresaw a day when God would shake "not the earth only, but also heaven" (Hebrews 12:26). This will be no small event, but one of cosmic grandeur. The reference to heaven and earth may be meant to hint at the concept of the new heaven and the new earth (Isaiah 66:22). At any rate, it points to the decisive intervention that God will make at the end of time.

27 And this word, Yet once more, signifieth the removing of those things that are shaken, as of things that are made, that those things which cannot be shaken may remain. 28 Wherefore we receiving a kingdom which cannot be moved, let us have grace, whereby we may serve God acceptably with reverence and godly fear: 29 For our God is a consuming fire.

The writer uses the expression "yet once more" to point out the decisive significance of what he is writing. It has an air of finality. God will make a radical and final change at the decisive time. This physical creation can be shaken, and it is contrasted with what cannot be shaken. These things really matter the things that have the character of permanence. It is God's will for this final differentiation to be made so that only what cannot be shaken will remain.

The ultimate reality of God's sovereignty is evident in verse 28. Believers have received the kingdom of God, which cannot be shaken. The kingdom is something we "receive"; it is not earned or created by believers, but is God's gift. Earthly systems can be shaken and, in due course, will be shaken.

Not so God's kingdom! The author does not simply state that God's kingdom will not be shaken but emphasizes that it *cannot* be shaken. It has a quality found in nothing earthly. It is on the strength of this that the writer gives two exhortations: "let us have grace" and "serve God acceptably." These exhortations could also be understood to mean "let us be thankful," and "let us offer acceptable worship to God." The latter meaning is preferred here. The appropriate response to the gift we have received is gratitude to God and acceptable worship, that is, a manner of life that is pleasing to God. The qualification "with reverence and godly fear" constitutes a sober reminder of God's holy character.

The chapter concludes with an expression apparently taken from Deuteronomy 4:24. The author of Hebrews emphasizes that God is not to be trifled with. It is easy to be so taken up with God's love and compassion that we overlook His implacable opposition to all evil. The wrath of God is not a popular subject today, but it looms large in biblical teaching. Because God is, in fact, a consuming fire, we do best to come to Him on His terms.

Sources:
Keener, Craig S. *The IVP Bible Background Commentary*: New Testament. Downers Grove, IL: InterVarsity Press. 1993
Flemming, Don, ed. *Concise Bible Commentary*. Chattanooga, TN: AMG Publishers, 1994.
Life Application Study Bible, New Living Translation. Wheaton, IL: Tyndale House Publishers, Inc., 2004.

Say It Correctly

Sion. **SI**-yahn.
Innummerable. ih-**NOO**-mer-uh-bl.

Daily Bible Readings

MONDAY
God's Awesome Power
(Psalm 66:1–4)

TUESDAY
Covenant Blessings
(Matthew 5:1–12)

WEDNESDAY
Keep Your Covenant with God
(Deuteronomy 4:21–24)

THURSDAY
Praise God for Answered Prayer
(Psalm 66:16–20)

FRIDAY
Everlasting Single Sacrifice for Sin
(Hebrews 10:11–18)

SATURDAY
Mediator of the New Covenant
(Hebrews 9:11–15)

SUNDAY
Receiving the Unshakable Kingdom
(Hebrews 12:14–15, 18–29)

Notes

_____

_____

_____

_____

Teaching Tips

Words You Should Know

A. Testament (1 Corinthians 11:25) *diatheke* (Gk.)—A compact, a covenant, a disposition or arrangement of any sort.

B. Damnation (v. 29) *krima* (Gk.)—The sentence that a judge decides; the punishment to which one is sentenced.

Teacher Preparation

Unifying Principle—Promises to Remember. It is often easier to make promises than to keep them. How can we remember to keep the promises we make? Paul exhorted believers to remember these promises through celebrating the Lord's Supper in a way that affirms the covenant it embodies.

A. Pray daily for your students to remember and keep their promises.

B. Read the Bible Background in various translations.

C. Read the Devotional Reading and find ways to connect it to the lesson.

O—Open the Lesson

A. Open with prayer.

B. Introduce the lesson by reading the Unifying Principle.

C. Ask a student to read the Aim for Change and the In Focus story. Facilitate a brief discussion on it.

D. Ask students to read the Keep in Mind verse.

P—Present the Scriptures

A. Ask a student to read the Focal Verses.

B. Use The People, Places, and Times, Background, and In Depth sections to clarify the passage.

C. Ask questions from the Search the Scriptures section.

E—Explore the Meaning

A. Ask questions from the Discuss the Meaning section. Have the class engage in a lighthearted debate on the subject.

B. Ask a student read the Lesson in Our Society section.

N—Next Steps for Application

A. Summarize the lesson.

B. Encourage students to apply the Make It Happen suggestions.

C. Close in prayer.

Worship Guide

For the Superintendent or Teacher
Theme: Remembering the Covenant
Song: "I Know It Was the Blood"
Devotional: Colossians 1:9–20

[handwritten: postive - our way Thing]

Remembering the Covenant

Bible Background • 1 CORINTHIANS 11; JUDE 3
Printed Text • 1 CORINTHIANS 11:23–34 | Devotional Reading • COLOSSIANS 1:9–20

Aim for Change

By the end of the lesson, we will: EXPLORE the meaning of the Lord's Supper as a time of covenant remembrance; ASPIRE to partake of the Lord's Supper in a worthy manner as covenant partners with God; and EXPRESS daily through our lifestyles the covenant implications of the Lord's Supper.

In Focus

Mary was rushing to get ready for church after waking up late. She had stayed up all night on the phone gossiping with her friend, Sister Claudine. They talked about almost everyone in the church and in the neighborhood. They might as well have been tabloid reporters. You didn't know what to believe when they got going. Unknown to Mary, her daughter, Jasmine, had been listening the whole time. At first Jasmine was pulled in and delighted to hear the juicy gossip, but then she began to think, *Isn't Mom supposed to be a Christian?* Something didn't add up in Jasmine's mind.

Mary, Jasmine, and her two brothers arrived at church just in time to hear the pastor's sermon. It was on the wisdom of controlling the tongue. As the pastor spoke, Jasmine kept looking at her mother shouting "Amen!" She couldn't believe her mother would agree so strongly and wondered whether she felt any conviction for her conversation the night before. As the rest of the church got up to take communion, Jasmine stayed in her seat. She wondered whether any of this was real. Was this all just for a show? How could her mom take communion after gossiping all night long?

When we take the Lord's Supper, we are remembering the covenant that Christ sealed with His death on the Cross. Was Mary wrong for taking communion? What does it mean to take communion in an unworthy manner?

[handwritten: negetive Thing Not our gway]

Keep in Mind

[handwritten: beat our self down]

"This cup is the new testament in my blood: this do ye, as oft as ye drink it, in remembrance of me" (from 1 Corinthians 11:25).

"This cup is the new testament in my blood: this do ye, as oft as ye drink it, in remembrance of me" (from 1 Corinthians 11:25).

Focal Verses

KJV **1 Corinthians 11:23** For I have received of the Lord that which also I delivered unto you, that the Lord Jesus the same night in which he was betrayed took bread: *stand for*

24 And when he had given thanks, he brake it, and said, Take, eat: this is my body, which is broken for you: this do in remembrance of me.

25 After the same manner also he took the cup, when he had supped, saying, this cup is the new testament in my blood: this do ye, as oft as ye drink it, in remembrance of me. *body*

26 For as often as ye eat this bread, and drink this cup, ye do shew the Lord's death till he come.

27 Wherefore whosoever shall eat this bread, and drink this cup of the Lord, unworthily, shall be guilty of the body and blood of the Lord.

28 But let a man examine himself, and so let him eat of that bread, and drink of that cup.

29 For he that eateth and drinketh unworthily, eateth and drinketh damnation to himself, not discerning the Lord's body.

30 For this cause many are weak and sickly among you, and many sleep.

31 For if we would judge ourselves, we should not be judged.

32 But when we are judged, we are chastened of the Lord, that we should not be condemned with the world.

33 Wherefore, my brethren, when ye come together to eat, tarry one for another.

34 And if any man hunger, let him eat at home; that ye come not together unto condemnation. And the rest will I set in order when I come.

NLT **1 Corinthians 11:23** For I pass on to you what I received from the Lord himself. On the night when he was betrayed, the Lord Jesus took some bread

24 and gave thanks to God for it. Then he broke it in pieces and said, "This is my body, which is given for you. Do this in remembrance of me."

25 In the same way, he took the cup of wine after supper, saying, "This cup is the new covenant between God and his people—an agreement confirmed with my blood. Do this in remembrance of me as often as you drink it."

26 For every time you eat this bread and drink this cup, you are announcing the Lord's death until he comes again.

27 So anyone who eats this bread or drinks this cup of the Lord unworthily is guilty of sinning against the body and blood of the Lord.

28 That is why you should examine yourself before eating the bread and drinking the cup.

29 For if you eat the bread or drink the cup without honoring the body of Christ, you are eating and drinking God's judgment upon yourself.

30 That is why many of you are weak and sick and some have even died.

31 But if we would examine ourselves, we would not be judged by God in this way.

32 Yet when we are judged by the Lord, we are being disciplined so that we will not be condemned along with the world.

33 So, my dear brothers and sisters, when you gather for the Lord's Supper, wait for each other.

34 If you are really hungry, eat at home so you won't bring judgment upon yourselves when you meet together. I'll give you instructions about the other matters after I arrive.

The People, Places, and Times

Wine. A beverage made with fermented grape juice. Noah is believed to have introduced wine after the waters of the Flood subsided (Genesis 9:20–21). People drank mostly water or wine in the ancient world as not much else was available. In the classical and Hellenistic world, wine was mixed with water. To drink wine unmixed was perceived as barbaric in the Greek culture of the time. In the Old Testament, wine was consumed pure and unadulterated. This makes sense when one looks at the warnings to avoid wine and strong drink, as unmixed wine would be very potent (Proverbs 20:1, 23:29–34).

Corinth. The city of Corinth is a port city located on an isthmus that connects mainland Greece with the Peloponnesian peninsula. Its location made Corinth a bustling trade and cultural center. As a result, many religious beliefs were present in Corinth. During the time in which Paul wrote, Corinth was a Roman colony. The ancient city of Corinth, known for its artistry, wealth, and rampant sexual immorality, was destroyed in 146 BC. It was reestablished by Rome in 44 BC. Through revived as a Roman city, Corinth continued to be known for its wanton sexuality.

Why do those who choose to indulge in alcohol, drugs, and sexual immorality denigrate their lives and society?

Background

The Corinthian church had been wrapped up in all kinds of immorality and unethical practices. Although it was a very gifted church in one of the most cosmopolitan cities in the Roman Empire, they were lacking in some basic Christian theology and behavior. In order to help them, Paul wrote the letter that we know as 1 Corinthians, where we see Paul address a list of issues that need to be addressed in the life of the church. This list of issues included celebrity worship of Christian ministers, sexual immorality, eating foods offered to idols, and head coverings for women. Next, he tackles the problem of the Corinthians' lack of love and consideration when taking the Lord's Supper or Communion. Paul has received reports that the Corinthian church has been misrepresenting Christ while taking the Lord's Supper, and he attempts to bring order to what has become a shameful feast.

How does the behavior of the modern-day church compare and contrast to the behavior of the Corinthian church during the Lord's Supper?

At-A-Glance

1. Remembering the Pattern
   (1 Corinthians 11:23–26)
2. Pinpointing the Problem (vv. 27–30)
3. Changing the Practice (vv. 31–34)

In Depth

1. Remembering the Pattern (1 Corinthians 11:23–26)

After letting the Corinthians know that their behavior at the Lord's Supper was unacceptable, Paul proceeds to remind them of the purpose of the meal. He says this tradition was passed on to him, and now he passes this on to the Corinthian church. The meal is not just an arbitrary time for eating and feasting, but a tradition that has been handed down from Jesus to the church.

This tradition was given meaning and significance by Christ Himself on the night that He was betrayed. Jesus took the bread and broke it as a symbol of what His body would go through in agony on the Cross. He would be broken and pierced for the sins of the world. Then He took the cup and passed it around to all the disciples. This cup represented the blood that He would shed, which would provide forgiveness and seal the new covenant that God made with His people. This meal was to be taken in remembrance of Christ and not for self-pleasure. It was a means to show the world that Jesus died and that His sacrifice has made God accessible to all.

What should be our attitude when we participate in the Lord's Supper?

2. Pinpointing the Problem (vv. 27–30)

Now that Paul has reminded them of the reason and sacredness of the Lord's Supper, he pinpoints the problem of the Corinthian church's practice. The rich are participating in an unworthy manner. It is important to note that it was not that they were personally unworthy. Their actions were dishonorable because they did not wait for their poorer brothers before eating. To take the Lord's Supper in an inappropriate manner is serious. Those who do so are guilty of sinning against the body and blood of the Lord—against Christ himself.

Paul reminds the Corinthians that taking the Lord's Supper is a sacred act so they should examine themselves before partaking. This time is to acknowledge the sacredness of the meal as they honor Christ. Keeping this in mind will avoid bringing God's judgment on themselves. Paul underscores this by adding that some have already experienced God's judgment in the form of sickness and even death. This is God's discipline of believers in Corinth who have dishonored Christ by taking the Lord's Supper in an unworthy way.

How often do you choose to take the time to examine yourself before partaking of the Lord's Supper?

3. Changing the Practice (vv. 31–34)

Paul reminded the church at Corinth of the tradition of the Lord's Supper and pointed out the problem of participating unworthily. Now he moves on to changing the way the Corinthians have been practicing the Lord's Supper. If they examined themselves, they would avoid God's judgment. This judgment is not final, but it's a disciplinary action so that God's people wouldn't bring shame to His name. The Corinthians would not be judged like the world. Taking the Lord's Supper inappropriately brought God's discipline down on them, but not necessarily His wrath—this is reserved for those who are not His people.

Paul concludes by specifically calling out the incorrect practice of not waiting for the poorer believers to partake of the Lord's Supper. The rich are not to make a show of feasting and drinking, but to revere and honor Christ by waiting on their fellow brothers and sisters. The meal is not just for satisfying the body; Paul tells the rich to eat at home if they intend to do that. This meal is intended to honor Christ and remember the covenant that He has enacted by His sacrifice on the Cross. If this is not the purpose behind their feasting, then judgment awaits.

How does the Lord's Supper create deeper fellowship with Christ and others?

Search the Scriptures

1. How can believers take the Lord's Supper in an unworthy manner today (1 Corinthians 11:27)?

2. How can we examine ourselves so that we honor God's covenant when we partake of the Lord's Supper or Communion (v. 28)?

Discuss the Meaning

The Lord's Supper, or Communion, can easily become an empty ritual. Some churches practice it once a month, while others practice it weekly, and still other traditions do it on a yearly basis. In your opinion, how frequently should we practice the Lord's Supper in order to keep it from becoming an empty ritual? Explain your answer.

Lesson in Our Society

Taking communion in an unworthy manner isn't the only way that we can dishonor Christ. Ignoring the plight of the poor, holding a grudge, and neglecting or abusing little ones are other ways that we dishonor Christ. Unbelievers aren't the only ones who commit sinful acts; believers themselves can act in ways unbecoming of Christ. To make a mockery of Christ's death before an unbelieving world is to disregard His sacrifice and the agony that He suffered on the Cross. When we sin in front of the world, we bring reproach on His name. Too many scandals have made the world turn from Jesus and look at the church with contempt. Taking communion is not about looking worthy on Sunday; we also need to live our lives in a worthy manner every single day.

Too much is at stake when we fail to honor Christ in our private and public lives. When we choose to blatantly sin, then others conclude that Christ has no power and our faith is meaningless. This is why so many in our communities have turned away from the church and have sought meaning in other things like gangs, drugs, and sex. They conclude that Christianity is just a show. Ultimately, it poorly reflects Jesus.

What things can you do today that will safeguard you against hypocrisy?

Make It Happen

The new covenant given to us through Jesus Christ is worth honoring and remembering. With this in mind:

• List three blessings that the Lord's Supper reminds you of.

• Host a meal in your home and conclude with the Lord's Supper or Communion.

• Memorize 1 Corinthians 11:23–26.

Follow the Spirit

What God wants me to do:

_____

_____

_____

_____

Remember Your Thoughts

Special insights I have learned:

_____

_____

_____

_____

More Light on the Text

1 Corinthians 11:23–34

23 For I have received of the Lord that which also I delivered unto you, that the Lord Jesus the same night in which he was betrayed took bread:

After dealing with the disappointing behavior of the rich in the church at the love feast meal, which preceded the Lord's Supper, Paul reminds them again of the historical background of the Lord's Supper along with the guidelines and conditions. The essential point is that eating the Lord's Supper in an unworthy manner brings consequences. The other point is how to prevent such consequences. Paul starts by first declaring the authenticity of his argument concerning the Lord's Supper and the source for his teaching. As if defending his apostolic authority again (cf. Galatians 1:12, 2:2; Ephesians 3:3), Paul tells them that his teaching is a direct revelation from Christ himself—the same revelation and doctrine that he had already taught them earlier after founding the church. His reminder is now linked to this practice. Since this tradition is being abused, Paul seems compelled to repeat Jesus' actual words in order to remind them of its significance.

Paul says that what he is about to tell is a historical fact. That is, on Jesus' last night with His disciples, He took bread, gave thanks, and gave it to the disciples. He reminds these thoughtless Corinthians of the original setting of the Lord's Supper. The institution of the Lord's Supper took place in the very same night that Jesus was "betrayed" (Gk *paradidomi*, **pah-rah-DEE-doh-me**), which literally means "handed over" to the soldiers. He was given up to the Roman and Jewish authorities (John 18:30; Acts 3:13).

Why is Paul recounting the whole event here? The answer could be that he is following, as one writer points out, the Jewish tradition of the Passover liturgy in which the head of the family recounts the history of past national events in order to remind each participant that he has some continuity in the body of those events. However, the next three verses carry crucial spiritual undertones to the whole situation.

24 And when he had given thanks, he brake it, and said, Take, eat: this is my body, which is broken for you, this do in remembrance of me. 25 After the same manner also he took the cup, when he had supped, saying, This cup is the new testament in my blood: this do ye as oft as ye drink it, in remembrance of me. 26 For as often as ye eat this bread, and drink this cup, ye do shew the Lord's death till he come.

Continuing the narrative, Paul points out that Jesus, after giving thanks, breaks the bread, and offers it to the disciples. In the Gospels, Jesus is shown at various times giving thanks before meals, e.g., during the feeding of the five thousand (John 6:11) and at the Last Supper (Matthew 26:26). Most significant are Christ's words as He gives the bread.

First, "Take, eat: this is my body, which is broken for you." This is in memory of the body of Christ. Just as the bread is broken, Jesus' body was broken for the redemption of sins. As Christians take the bread, we are reminded of the death of Christ, not only as a past event, but also as a present reality. "This do in remembrance of me" serves as the purpose of the institution of the Lord's Supper: that it is a memorial to Christ. It serves as a reminder of the most significant event in history, whereby One died to save the world. It is not a memorial of His life, but of His death (v. 26), which carries redemptive value.

The cup (the wine) in like manner serves the same purpose as the bread, but reminds us of the blood of Christ that was spilled on the Cross. Whether it is wine or juice, the emphasis is on remembering that Jesus' blood was for the cleansing and remission of sins (Matthew 26:28; Ephesians 1:7). The "cup," used figuratively for its contents, is a reference to Jesus' blood that seals the new covenant, which is based on a better promise (Hebrews 8:6, 9:15–22). This replaces the old covenant that God made with Israel. "The new testament in my blood" refers to a new covenant that God made with His people. "Testament" is a translation of the Greek word *diatheke* (**dee-ah-THAY-kay**), which means a contract or covenant.

Paul adds that they should remember Christ as they partake of the cup "as oft as ye drink it," which means that the Lord's Supper ought to be observed as frequently as possible. The Bible does not specify how often; however, the early church observed it either daily (Acts 2:46) or weekly (Acts 20:7). Most churches today practice the Lord's Supper monthly. The real message is that every time we observe the Lord's Supper, we ought to show respect in proclaiming the Lord's death until He returns (v. 26). To "show" (Gk. *kataggello*, **kah-tah-ang-GEH-low**) means to make known openly or to announce abroad. This was a means to announce that His death has made forgiveness and salvation available to all until the time of His Second Coming. The Corinthian church lost sight of this with their greed and selfish behavior and therefore needed to be reminded.

27 Wherefore whosoever shall eat this bread, and drink this cup of the Lord, unworthily, shall be guilty of the body and blood of the Lord. 28 But let a man examine himself, and so let him eat of that bread, and drink of that cup.

After recounting the significance of the Lord's Supper, Paul then warns of the consequences of partaking of the Supper in an unworthy manner as they have exhibited during the meal. Therefore, Paul continues, for the reasons given above (i.e., the significance of the Lord's Supper), that whoever takes it unworthily (Gk. *anaxios*, **ah-nok-SEE-oce**) shall be guilty of sinning against the blood and body of Christ. *Anaxios* means "irreverent" or "disrespectful." The rich Corinthians who did not wait for their brothers and sisters but instead consumed all the food were eating the meal irreverently (v. 21). Paul calls for self-examination before taking the Supper in order to avoid eating in sin. "To examine" (Gk. *dokimazo*, **do-kee-MAD-zo**) is to put to the test. This test concerns our attitude, conduct, behavior toward others, and understanding of the true purpose and nature of the Supper. Paul, in another passage, calls the Corinthians to examine their faith (2 Corinthians 13:5). According to Paul's argument, it is better not to take the Supper at all rather than to take it in an unworthy manner.

29 For he that eateth and drinketh unworthily, eateth and drinketh damnation to himself, not discerning the Lord's body. 30 For this cause many are weak and sickly among you, and many sleep.

Paul now gives the reason for self-examination: "For he that eateth and drinketh unworthily, eateth and drinketh damnation to himself, not discerning the Lord's body." The word "discerning," is the Greek word *diakrino* (**dee-ah-KREE-no**), and speaks of separating, or distinguishing from. By not discerning the Lord's body, Paul speaks of their failure to distinguish between the food of the Lord's Supper and the common food of their private meal or love feast. Alternatively, it may refer to their failure to recognize the Lord's body, that is, reflecting on His death as they eat.

Another interpretation is possible here: "Not discerning the Lord's body" could mean their failure to recognize the distinctive nature of the Church, the body of Christ. This unique nature of the body is demonstrated in the Lord's Supper, symbolized by the common table with one loaf of bread and one cup; they proclaim that through Christ's death, the Church is one body. Failing to recognize the Church in this way, and humiliating the less privileged in the group (vv. 21–22), would incur God's judgment (see Isaiah 1:14–17). Not recognizing the Lord's body is equivalent to making light of the death of Christ, which is for the redemption of the Church, and would also incur God's judgment. Because they have not been respecting the sacrament, this effect is being seen among them—"many become weak and sickly, and some fall asleep" (i.e., die). The Greek verb *koimao* (**koy-MAH-oh**) means to "fall asleep" and sometimes refers to physical sleep (Mark 14:37; Luke 22:45), but often it is a euphemistic figure of speech for dying (John 11:11–14; Acts 7:60).

31 For if we would judge ourselves, we should not be judged. 32 But when we are judged, we are chastened of the Lord, that we should not be condemned with the world.

Paul then gives the purpose of the self-examination: to come to the Lord's table with a pure and clean heart. Paul uses the first person plural, including himself, and gives further reason why we have to examine ourselves before approaching the Lord's Supper table. He says that if the church at Corinth had been self-discerning, the judgment (Gk. *krino*, **KREE-no**) or punishment of verse 30 would not have happened. However, he adds that what they are experiencing presently is God's judgment, which should be understood as fatherly "discipline" (Proverbs 3:11–12; Hebrews 12:5–8). This type of discipline is necessary, Paul seems to say since it will result in repentance so that the believer will not suffer damnation (eternal judgment) as will the rest of the unsaved world (see Revelation 20:12–15). This is related to the thoughts of many rabbis at the time, that the righteous would be disciplined here on earth for the few sins they committed. At the same time, they believed the wicked would be punished for eternity for their many sins.

33 Wherefore, my brethren, when ye come together to eat, tarry one for another. 34 And if any man hunger, let him eat at home; that ye come not together unto damnation. And the rest will I set in order when I come.

Paul goes back to the problem that started the whole theological argument—the meal (vv. 21, 22)—and deals with it in a positive and gentler way. Referring to the Corinthians as brethren, Paul admonishes them to be a caring community, to show concern and respect for every member. One of the practical ways to do this is by being considerate and waiting for others when they gather to feast. He concludes by offering an alternative to avert the Lord's judgment: if anyone wants to eat sumptuously, he or she should do so at home and not at this sacred gathering. This portion is addressed to the wealthy in the Corinthian church; however, it is relevant to any community of believers anywhere and at all times.

Paul closes this section of the letter with a promise to set the rest in order when he visits the Corinthians, which leaves some questions that are hard to answer from the context. What other things he is needing to set in order? Are they matters regarding the relationship between the rich and poor? Or are they other matters that have been reported to him, such as the many issues throughout 1 and 2 Corinthians? These are good questions!

Sources:

Hays, Richard B. *First Corinthians: Interpretation, A Bible Commentary for Teaching and Preaching.* Louisville, KY: John Knox, 1997.

Keener, Craig. *The InterVarsity Press Bible Background Commentary: New Testament.* Downers Grove, IL: InterVarsity Press, 1993.

Prime, Derek. *Opening Up 1 Corinthians. Opening Up Commentary.* Leominster, UK: Day One Publications, 2005.

Utley, Robert James. *Paul's Letters to a Troubled Church: I and II Corinthians.* Study Guide Commentary Series, vol. 6. Marshall, TX: Bible Lessons International, 2002.

Say It Correctly

Damnation. dam-**NAY**-shun.
Chastened. **CHAY**-sind.

Daily Bible Readings

MONDAY
Christ Our Creator, Savior, Peacemaker
(Colossians 1:9–20)

TUESDAY
Mealtime, Foretaste of the Lord's Supper
(1 Corinthians 11:17–22)

WEDNESDAY
Keeping the Faith Entrusted to You
(Jude 1–4, 17–25)

THURSDAY
Preparing to Share the Passover Meal
(Mark 14:12–16)

FRIDAY
Jesus Celebrates with Bread and Cup
(Mark 14:22–25)

SATURDAY
Participating in Spiritual Worship
(Romans 12:1–8)

SUNDAY
Observing the Lord's Supper
(1 Corinthians 11:23–34)

Notes

Faith in Action

The study this quarter explores the twofold nature of faith as belief and action. Selections from Acts show various examples of proclaiming faith in Christ. In the book of Daniel, we see faith in action as sincere, obedient, bold, and strong. The lessons from several epistles show how our actions both as individuals and as communities demonstrate our faith in Christ.

UNIT 1 • THE EARLY CHURCH PROCLAIMS FAITH IN CHRIST

This first section contains five lessons that reveal what the early leaders proclaimed about living our faith in Christ. The Scripture sections in Acts report several examples of social welfare ministry and evangelism in spite of opposition. The lesson in Ephesians teaches about faith that leads to unity in the body of Christ. The Christmas session gives an account of the wise men who faithfully searched for the newborn King of the Jews.

Lesson 1: December 3, 2017
Faith in Jesus
Acts 3:11–21
People who are broken want to be made whole. How and where do they find wholeness? Peter proclaimed that faith in Jesus restores people to wholeness.

Lesson 2: December 10, 2017
Faith to Discern
Acts 13:1–12
Sometimes we are at a loss when unexpected events interfere with our goals. How can we keep our commitments and forge ahead? Empowered by their faith in Jesus, Paul and Barnabas preached and taught about Jesus despite a false prophet's efforts to deter them.

Lesson 3: December 17, 2017
Faith to Persevere
Acts 14:8–11, 19–23
Sometimes the good things we do are blocked by an unexpected obstruction, but we pick up and continue anyway. What gives us the strength to keep going? Even though he was stoned and persecuted, Paul's faith in his message impelled him to continue to proclaim the Good News of God.

Lesson 4: December 24, 2017
Faithful Seekers of the King
Matthew 2:1–12
People often search for the best ways to honor someone they look up to and revere. How can we best honor a special person? The magi traveled a great distance from their own country to Bethlehem in order to give gifts and pay homage to Jesus, the child born King of the Jews.

Lesson 5: December 31, 2017
Faith to Unite
Ephesians 4:1–16
Many people search all their lives for something that will make them feel grounded, whole, and in sync with life. Where can they find that something? Paul told the Ephesians that even though they had many different gifts, their faith in Christ would bring them unity and help them grow together in love.

UNIT 2 • A LIVING FAITH IN GOD

This section has four lessons exploring faith in action from the book of Daniel. These lessons provide models for ways to actively engage in behaviors that demonstrate sincerity, obedience, boldness, and strength of faith.

Lesson 6: January 7, 2018
A Sincere Faith
Daniel 1:8–21

People find themselves confronted by contradictory requirements from different sources of authority. How do we resolve such conflicts? Daniel's active faith, combined with his tact, helped him resolve his conflict and remain obedient to God in terms of dietary requirements.

Lesson 7: January 14, 2018
A Bold Faith
Daniel 3:19–23, 26–28

Sometimes people are challenged to endure great trials and tribulations because of their convictions. How can they face such challenges and remain faithful? Shadrach, Meshach, and Abednego boldly disobeyed the king's command and were delivered from a fiery furnace by the power of God.

Lesson 8: January 21, 2018
A Prayer for an Obedient Faith
Daniel 9:4–8, 15–19

People want release from feelings of shame that can result from past mistakes. Where can they go to find such relief? Daniel prayed to the Lord a prayer of confession, seeking forgiveness, mercy, and strength to obey.

Lesson 9: January 28, 2018
A Strong Faith
Daniel 10:10–19

Sometimes circumstances of life cause us to feel like we can't go on. Where can we find strength to do so? Daniel found strength in prayer and from the angel sent by God to encourage him and answer his prayer.

UNIT 3 • SELF-CONTROLLED, UPRIGHT, AND GODLY FAITH

This third section includes four lessons that look at passages from Acts, James, and 1 Timothy, providing specific examples of faith as both belief and action. James teaches that faith without works is dead. The lesson from 1 Timothy offers instructions about leading others in a life of faith.

Lesson 10: February 4, 2018
Faith Without Works is Dead
James 2:14–26

People know that talk is cheap and actions speak louder than words. How are we to live in this regard? James says that our professions of faith must be matched by accompanying action.

Lesson 11: February 11, 2018
A Disciplined Faith
James 3:1–12

Everyone knows the pain and destruction that result from hurtful words. How do we keep from causing such pain and destruction? James says that we should control our tongue so that only blessings come from it.

Lesson 12: February 18, 2018
Faithful Disciples
Acts 9:36–43

In times of crisis, people look for help. What qualities do they look for in a helper? When Tabitha died, faithful followers of Christ sent for the apostle Peter for help.

Lesson 13: February 25, 2018
Fight the Good Fight of Faith
1 Timothy 6:11–21

We are surrounded by all kinds of advice. What is the best advice to follow? Paul charged Timothy to embrace certain attitudes and actions and avoid others in order to strengthen his faith.

Faith in Action

Evangeline Carey

One church's marquee displayed the mini-sermon, "Know God, Know Peace; No God, No Peace." As the above words indicate, our desperate and segmented world is in need of God's peace; it is anxious and troubled on every hand. Because for so many people, there is no God (the one true God) in their lives, they find themselves with no inner peace. God, then, calls every believer to help our lost fellow man to seek, find, and know Him so that He can perform heart-changing surgery. He calls those who embrace His salvation plan to bring the energy of His unconditional love to our world, so that the power of the Holy Spirit can save the sin-sick soul. He calls us to take His Spirit-empowered Gospel to those who need Him in the wasteland of their life. In fact, He says, "Go ye into all the world, and preach the gospel to every creature. He that believeth and is baptized shall be saved" (from Mark 16:15–16). God desires us to lift up Jesus, His one and only Son—the Lamb without blemish—to potential disciples, and He will draw all men unto Himself (John 12:32). He even anoints and empowers us to carry out His will through His Holy Spirit. Thus every believer should not only be committed to the Truth—Jesus—but also to the people for whom He suffered, bled, died, and rose.

God also mandates us in His complete, revealed Word to love our fellow man. He says, "He that loveth his brother abideth in the light,

and there is none occasion of stumbling in him" (1 John 2:10). God, therefore, calls all believers to take the spiritual blinders off and see both the church and the world through His eyes. He wants believers to see the mental, physical, and spiritual anguish all around us and move out with hands and hearts that bless God and bless others. Therefore in these perilous times, He calls all believers to be godly people. This includes a call to be workers who have a passion for God, who can be a real blessing to Him and others, and who can tell the lost that Jesus Himself is the truth that sets us free from the awful bondage of sin. Hence, God does not want us to be lazy Christians, but to have a twofold commitment to His kingdom-building initiative. He wants us to commit to the truth of His living Word and also to the people to whom He sent His Word.

Christian Role Models

God and the world are in need of Christian role model witnesses to illustrate the character of Christ. Therefore, God needs believers who are in love with Him and will follow Him wholeheartedly. He needs humble people, who are not puffed up with their own importance—who have been delivered by God from any arrogance and pride that might hinder their spiritual mission. He needs believers who will surrender their will to God, be a servant-leader or a follower, and lift up Jesus instead of themselves. He needs workers who will roll up their sleeves and pull their fellow-man out of the sludge of physical and spiritual deprivation and suffering. He tells us, "Hereby perceive we the love of God, because he laid down his life for us: and we ought to lay down our lives for the brethren. But whoso hath this world's good, and seeth his brother have need, and shutteth up his bowels of compassion from him, how dwelleth the love of God in him?" (1 John 3:16–17).

Getting God's Kingdom Perspective

God can and does give us a vision of His kingdom. Phenomenal things are happening with and through Him as we catch the vision and move out to fulfill the call. He tells us His kingdom will consist of "a great multitude, which no man could number, of all nations, and kindreds, and people, and tongues" (Revelation 7:9). They are the ones whose sins are forgiven because they have believed in the Lord Jesus Christ for their salvation.

God Needs Obedient Believers to Work for Him

God needs those who obey His commands to work in His vineyard. Therefore, He needs workers who will go when He says go; do when He says do; speak when He says speak; and be quiet when He says be quiet—stop, listen, and heed. He needs workers who know what it is to stand in the midst of broken dreams, defeat, ruin, confusion, and doubt, and still testify that God is love and He is still at work in their circumstances. He needs workers who know what it is to sink in the mire of bitterness, despair, and self-pity but, through the prayers of other believers, have come out on the other side and can still inspire others with a quiet and confident faith in God's love and care. He needs workers who know what it is to be in constant pain and suffering and still trust the power of

God's deliverance and healing. He needs workers who know what it is to be empty, hurt, lonely, lost, lied to, cheated, and mistreated to live out God's wonderful grace before others so that He can use His unconditional love to draw sincere seekers. He needs ordinary believers to do extraordinary things for Him! God needs us to be committed to Him, obey Him, and press onward to the victory that only He can bring.

Salt, Light, and Grace Moments

I am reminded of two events where believers did not hide their light under a bush but instead illuminated and overshadowed the dark side of human nature. The first one was during 9/11, after the terrorists attacked our shores and wreaked all kinds of havoc and devastation. Some irate American citizens in one large city became vigilantes and decided to storm a mosque in retaliation. However, a group of devout Christians in the same community decided that this was a "salt and light" moment—a time to show unconditional love and God's grace to the Muslim community. Therefore, these believers surrounded the mosque so that the hate mongers could not carry out their sinister plans. They became a light not only to the Muslim community, but also to the world. Onlookers saw the love of Jesus Christ up close and personal from those who are called by His name. This was indeed a witness that could be used to draw not only some of these Muslims, but others around the world to the saving knowledge of Jesus Christ.

Finally, an African American nurse recalled another "grace" moment where she and her physician husband (both devout Christians) were able to witness to a declared racist. This nurse shared how they moved their office into a changing racial neighborhood. One day, a desperate, terminally ill White woman reluctantly came in seeking medical help. She announced to the nurse that she did not like

Black people and used the "n" word. The nurse determined that she would be "salt and light" to this patient. With God's love and strength, she was able to look past this woman's hatred and see her needs. It happened also that the White woman informed her caregivers that she had no money to pay the doctor for her treatment. Still, the African American nurse and doctor found a way to service her and give her free medications.

As this White cancer patient's health became progressively worse and she was no longer able to make office visits for her treatments, the African American nurse went to her home to assist her. At the same time, the doctor and nurse both prayed for the ailing woman's salvation. On some occasions, the nurse and her 4-year-old granddaughter even read Scriptures to her. Finally, on the last day of her life, with the African American nurse by her side, this proclaimed racist accepted Jesus Christ as her personal Savior and went on to be with the Lord. At her memorial service, the White woman's son handed the nurse and her husband full payment for his mother's medical bill.

Through grace extended by believers in a very difficult situation, God saved a needy soul. Needless to say, in both cases, these believers flavored their world with agape (unconditional) love, compassion, and mercy. They became living testimonies—lights in the darkness that overcome evil around them—and showed unbelievers that God is real and His love is alive and well. In fact, God turned the effects of evil into good.

Looking at Our Own Ministries

When we put our ministries on the altar before the living God, He will show us how to love as He does. He will allow us to have His light within us that produces only what is good and true (Ephesians 5:9). We will make the most of every opportunity for doing well in these evil days (v. 16). God will answer people's prayers and meet their requests through us.

God seeks yielded believers who are committed to Christ and His kingdom. The Holy Spirit can stir us to reach out to others with God's love and also give us the spirit of courage to do so. He can give us a passion to pray for others and to help them in their times of need.

Just as we need God, others also need our help to get to God. They need us to help pray them through their crises.

Serving God through Serving Others

God will be glorified when we truly serve Him through serving people that He loves, even though some might be wearing dirty and tattered clothes, hungry, mentally or physically ill, drugged out, drunk, stressed out, disenfranchised, or marginalized. Instead of seeking others to serve us or seeking to bask in the presence of a Holy God all the day long, needy people can be touched by God through us. Our lives can draw them to pray and to seek the Lord. The testimonies of our life can give them hope.

Conclusion

God can do some awesome things through us when we put our ministries in the hand of the Man from Galilee (Jesus) and delight to do His will. He needs lovers of God and mankind. He needs consolers. He needs leaders and followers, who understand brokenness and have the spirit of concern for people. The world is so spiritually poor and needy! Human strength cannot set the captives free; true freedom only comes through the power of an omnipotent God. Can you be counted on to walk in and pour out God's grace—His compassion, forgiveness, love, mercy—and plant the seeds of His Word so that He can bring in the harvest? God has given us the challenge. He has provided the mission, the resources, and strength to get the job done.

Now go bring joy—Christ—to your suffering world, and remember that commitment to truth is empty without commitment to people. That's what it means to put your faith into action.

Evangeline Carey was a staff writer for UMI and had been an adult Sunday School teacher for more than 25 years.

Spiritually Transformative Leadership

Jeanne Porter-King and Samira E. Robinson

Author Fred Smith says in his book *Learning to Lead*, "The right concept of leadership is vital. And without a solid concept of leadership, you have a faulty leadership" (24). As leaders in the service of the Lord, we must have the right concept of what it is we are called to do and why. We must ask ourselves pertinent questions, such as: What is a leader? What assumptions do we make about leadership and the places in which we lead? Transformative leadership provides us with a model of leadership necessary for the twenty-first century.

Many of us grow up believing that leadership is merely about a position—the Sunday School superintendent, the pastor, the usher board president. Transformative leaders realize that spiritual leadership is a process; it's doing God-ordained things to effect change in people's lives. It is a process whereby leaders motivate others to be and do their best, accomplish goals, and realize their divine destiny. For instance, a significant leader in the church is the Sunday School teacher. The Sunday School teacher, who sees him- or herself as a transformative leader, realizes that his or her aim and purpose are to shape, mold, and stimulate thoughts, beliefs, and attitudes about the Lord. He or she must bring forth truth and thus lead his or her students out of the darkness of misinformation. The lesson taught, while universal, holds a unique meaning in each Sunday School class. The teacher sets the tone for the class, and based on the students' level of study, spirituality, and biblical knowledge, influences and impacts youth and adults in positive or not-so-positive ways.

We have followed old models of leadership styles, secular in nature, that have undoubtedly run their course. Often these models reflect a worldly agenda instead of God's purpose. A review of the traditional versus transformative leadership model allows us to compare the purpose and resulting outcomes of each model. Traditional leadership has a history of viewing the leadership roles as a call to dominate or control, and a number of overt and covert methods are used to get what we want. Transformative leaders realize that leadership is a call to service, first to God and then to the people. Secular leadership often focuses on certain techniques and tactics to get a job done. Transformative leadership relies on God's prompting and leading. The secular leadership model emphasizes taking charge, and often the leader takes pride in his or her abilities. The transformative leadership model is activated by one's faith in their position in Christ and God's call in their life. The secular leadership model is often defined by what the world system says is important; the transformative leadership model comes from God's Word and is defined by Him.

Based on the transformative leadership model, church leaders must adopt an approach

that reflects their faith in God and desire to please Him. Church leaders, who desire to be transformative leaders, will have to acclimate themselves to utilizing biblical principles with a revelatory understanding of the needs of today's Sunday School student. The goal must not be to simply get our message to them, but to learn what the message is. In other words, "What is troubling them? What are their goals? What do they want to be when they grow up—spiritually and physically? What gifts has God given them, and what skills do they have?" Transformative leaders must work at knowing the answers to these questions. That is not to say that we have to know every student's personal history and be personally involved with each student. But we should be concerned enough to go beyond the surface, to caring about each person. Then our message will be heard loudly and clearly. The transformative leader is in tune with the heart of God and the heart of the student.

When grasped, these nine spiritual keys to transformative leadership will take you to the next level in your spiritual growth and fulfillment of your purpose as a leader. These nine principles help you function more effectively in your calling to help others:

1. Understand who you are as a person. The transformative leader recognizes whom God has created him or her to be. Leadership is personal. It is about the individual—the unique person whom God has created, not the generic label that society has attempted to construct. The leader is a person first, not a role model. Remember that God blesses people with gifts, not roles or positions. The transformative leader will carry a God-given special mark.

2. Discover and tap into your purpose. God designed each person with a specific purpose in mind. We are His "workmanship" (Ephesians 2:10), or His special creation.

Every new product comes from a manufacturer with instructions. Each person should imagine that he or she is a new product. How would the instructions describing your purpose and function read? What have you been created to do? You are a distinct creation and a model of excellence. What are the unique features, gifts, talents, and abilities with which you have been equipped? Until you can get in touch with this purpose, you will flounder or be less effective as a leader.

3. Determine the proper place for your leadership. Placement is very important to God. God strategically situates His leaders in places to fulfill His purposes in people's lives, such as Esther, Joseph, Paul, and Daniel. He assigns us to work in churches, businesses, service agencies, and elsewhere. Too often, people get frustrated with where they are and fail to see God's workings—that He has strategically placed us. As you pray about placement, ask God where He wants you to offer your gifts and where you can be of the best service for kingdom building.

4. Accept God's preparations for you. Even as Jesus went through extensive preparation for His public ministry, so will every leader go through a preparation phase. Before every harvest comes a season of sowing. Every walk begins with a toddle. In Jesus' preparation, we see isolation and testing—out of which came a clarified purpose. Transformative leaders must accept God's mode of preparation for them. God prepares leaders in His time frame. The leader's preparation includes formal and informal lessons. Every experience, trial, and triumph is a part of the preparation process.

5. Develop a process that is in line with who you are and where God has placed you.

Transformative leaders must make a plan that aligns with their abilities and God's placement. The process refers to the way in which the leader accomplishes his or her goals, tasks, and objectives. The process depends upon the people you lead, the tasks or things that need to be accomplished, and the steps you take to do it based on your leadership style.

6. Utilize the power that you have been given. Transformative leaders must practice using their God-given power. Traditionally, leaders have relied upon power that comes from holding a formal position or title. These leaders operated under the theory, "I get you to do what I want because I'm the boss and I can reward or punish you." Other traditional leaders persuade people using charisma, charm, or personality. God calls for leaders to rely on the dynamic power of the Holy Spirit to guide them, grant wisdom to envision possibilities for their organization or department, and enable them to work with people to get results.

7. Follow the plan that God has laid out for you. Transformative leaders recognize that God has already prepared a plan for them. In Jeremiah 29:11, God told the nation of Israel, "I know the plans I have for you ... They are plans for good and not for disaster, to give you a future and a hope" (NLT). God has laid out plans for nations as well as for individuals. He has the master plan, and the task for the transformative leader is to tap into the Master's plan for their lives and for their organization or group. Transformative leaders do not introduce their own agendas; they go where God says to go and do what He says to do.

8. Love the people God has given you. Transformative leaders do not abandon

those who need them and seek out others with whom they would rather work. The transformative leader resists treating students like needy people and interacts with them as God's entrusted treasures. The transformative leader learns wisely to utilize their team members' gifts. Too often, traditional leaders blame their staffs for their own inadequacies. Worse yet, these leaders perpetually look for people who can produce for them, instead of learning how to cultivate the resources they already have to get a maximum yield.

9. Develop proficiencies that facilitate spiritual transformation. Transformative leaders work to help their spiritual journey through growing their skills. They realize that God works on the inside and that divine purpose starts in the heart of every believer and works its way out. They practice integrity and work on self-improvement, building on their skills and talents.

This transformative leadership model embodies the concept of collaborative leadership, which many organizations and corporations are beginning to use because they now realize that the traditional model has lost its effectiveness. They adopt the new model because they feel the winds of change in society and do not want to be left behind. Corporations and businesses fully intend to be successful in the new millennium. The church, the body of Christ on earth, must not fall behind; rather, we must set the standard for others to follow—especially since the prototype supporting collaborative leadership is spiritual and relational.

People need transformative leadership. In this fast-paced and morally impoverished society, our church and community members need leaders to be dynamic individuals who are willing to accept change and use new ways to reach and teach them. They hunger and thirst for church leaders who are grounded in the Word of God and His divine purpose. It is our challenge, call, and responsibility to become the leaders whom God has ordained—transformative leaders who change lives for the kingdom of God.

Sources:
Learning to Lead–Leadership Books–ChristianityTodayLibrary. com. www.ctlibrary.com/lebooks/theleadershiplibrary/learningtolead.
Smith, Fred. *Learning to Lead*. Sarasota, FL: CTI (Creative Technology of Sarasota, Inc.), 1986. 24.

Jeanne Porter-King is the founder of TransPorter Communications.

Samira E. Robinson is an author and communications consultant.

Every Christian is Called to Mentor

Natasha S. Robinson

In the midst of conversations about personal desires, work and family obligations, and church busyness, Christians sometimes miss the priority to make disciples. Making disciples is the ministry work of all Christ followers and we must not lose sight of it. Mentoring for God's purposes reminds us to make the love of people, and His command to make disciples our first work.

Mentoring is a trusted partnership wherein people share wisdom that fosters spiritual growth and leads to transformation as mentors and mentees grow in their love of Christ, knowledge of self, and love of others.

In short, mentoring by Christians for God's kingdom purposes can be defined as "intentional discipleship." Defining mentoring in these terms affirms that mentoring is the responsibility of all Christians, and reminds us of our primary calling. Although we may receive different spiritual assignments—both formal and informal—along our Christian journey, the call to mentoring is universal. Accepting this responsibility requires our understanding of mentoring for God's kingdom purposes.

Mentoring from the perspective of intentional discipleship means that the words discipleship (biblical) and mentoring (modern) can be used synonymously only when a Christian assumes the responsibility of influence in the life of another for the purpose of loving them well, and drawing mentees into an intimate relationship of following Christ. God uses mentoring to sanctify individuals and transform them into the image of Jesus Christ (Romans 8:29). We make mentoring our priority because Jesus made discipleship His priority (Matthew 28:19–20).

Understanding this responsibility has a tremendous impact on the church, and the good news is that God has not left us alone on this faith journey. The Holy Spirit empowers us to accept the responsibility to mentor in a sacrificial act that glorifies God. When we mentor, we share the message of the whole Gospel, advance God's kingdom mission, challenge disciples to live their lives on purpose, teach them to love well, and equip them for works of righteousness. Mentoring is mutually beneficial and has the same transformative effects on the mentor and mentee. Mentoring in this way is simply an act of obedience.

Christianity is a relational faith, therefore, a "mentor for life" model is communal—encouraging a small group of no more than six mentees. When we mentor for life, we follow the relational mentoring model of Jesus and His twelve apostles. Mentoring is foundational to God's redemptive story because it fulfills the cultural mandate of Genesis 1:28 and the Great Commission of Matthew 28:19–20. From the beginning of His good creation, God said, "It is not good for man to be alone" (from Genesis

2:18, NIV). Therefore, mentoring provides an opportunity for loving companionship. Jesus mentored His disciples with this understanding (John 15:12–15).

"What comes to our minds when we think about God is the most important thing about us." What you think about God shapes your attitude toward Him and other people. This

IMPROVE
SUCCESS
TRAINING
MOTIVATE
WORK
INSPIRE

Mentoring brings God's kingdom agenda into focus, and that is to build a family of worshipers for Himself (Revelation 5:9–12, 7:4–10). When Christians make the commitment to mentor and make disciples, they are embracing the whole Gospel and essentially saying to God, "Thy kingdom come, Thy will be done in earth, as it is in heaven" (Matthew 6:10, KJV).

Jesus taught that the greatest commandment in all eternity is to love God and love other people (Luke 10:25–28). This foundation provides a holistic and progressive framework for mentoring: First, we must know and love God. Secondly, we must affirm our human identity in Christ Jesus. Only then can we learn to love our neighbors. A.W. Tozer writes,

theology has practical application because mentoring includes ethical considerations for how we think and act as ambassadors of Christ on this earth. Mentoring encourages disciples to open their eyes, see the needs of the world, and put their faith into action by responding with compassion and justice: the whole church taking the whole Gospel to the whole world. This is the redemptive work of God.

Assuming a mentoring relationship is a sacred and sacrificial responsibility. It must be approached humbly with the full understanding that the Holy Spirit works to change the hearts of humans. Christian leaders must not attempt to take on that divine responsibility, but rather surrender total transformation to God. Dr. Rick D. Moore writes, "The goal of mentoring … is a difficult thing … indeed it involves an element of the spirit that cannot be packaged, manipulated or controlled." While the Holy Spirit works to change hearts, the human agency of mentoring can facilitate the process of renewing a disciple's mind. The heart and mind are intimately connected; both reveal our love, longing, and the true nature of our will. As a mentor, Christian leaders teach disciples to put off their old self and become new in the attitude of their minds by imitating God and walking in true righteousness and holiness (Ephesians 4:22–24). This is the sacred work of God in which we are called to respond.

Responding rightly to God defines our life purpose. Robert J. Wicks writes, "Perhaps the most critical [puzzle] we face in life is, 'Who am I really?' Through the mentoring relationship, we explore ways to gain sufficient freedom and inner ease to be who we really are so that we, in turn, can be a helping presence to others." In the post-modern society where technology constantly sends false messages, disciples must hold fast to God's truth, finding their identity and purpose in Christ alone. When disciples know and love God and know who they are in Christ Jesus, they can also grow to love their neighbors well.

In conclusion, all Christians are called to mentor, follow Christ's example, and encourage other disciples to live sacrificially for the sake of the Gospel. We must be reminded that our primary sacred calling is being a disciple of Christ (identity), and our primary sacred work (mission/ministry) is making disciples of Christ. All Christians everywhere are called to establish mentoring relationships where disciples can mentor and multiply for God's kingdom. We must be disciples who intentionally make disciples. This is the will of God for us.

Source:

Moore, Rick D. "The Prophet as Mentor: A Crucial Facet of the Biblical Presentations of Moses, Elijah, and Isaiah," Journal of Pentecostal Theology 15, no. 2 (April 1, 2007): 155-172, ATLA Religion Database with ATLASerials, EBSCOhost (accessed July 9, 2012).

Tozer, A.W. *The Knowledge of the Holy*. New York: HarperCollins, 1961. 1.

Wicks, Robert J. *Sharing Wisdom: The Practical Art of Giving and Receiving Mentoring*. New York: The Crossroad Publishing Company, 2000. 115.

Natasha Robinson is the author of "Mentor for Life: Finding Purpose through Intentional Discipleship" and the visionary founder of the nonprofit Leadership Links, Inc. A former Marine Corps Officer, Natasha serves as a Bible teacher, writer, anti-human trafficking advocate, and champion for education.

George Washington Carver

(c. 1864–1943)

The exact details of George Washington Carver's birth are unknown, but the year was thought to be c. 1864 and location near Diamond Grove, Missouri. He died January 5, 1943, in Tuskegee, Alabama.

Carver was the son of a Missouri slave woman owned by Moses Carver. During the Civil War, slave owners found it difficult to hold slaves in such "border states" as Missouri. After the war, all of Moses Carter's slaves disappeared except for George. Frail, sick, and motherless, George returned to his former master's home and was nursed back to health. During his illness, George learned to draw. Later in life, he devoted considerable time to painting flowers, plants, and landscapes. Even when George was told he was no longer a slave, he remained on Moses Carver's plantation until he was about 10 or 12 years old. He eventually left to pursue an education.

By both books and experience, George acquired a fragmentary education while doing whatever work came around in order to subsist. He supported himself by varied occupations, which included general household worker, hotel cook, laundryman, farm laborer, and homesteader. In his late 20s, he managed to obtain a high school education in Minneapolis, Kansas, while working as a farmhand.

After a university in Kansas refused to admit him because he was Black, Carver attended Simpson College in Indianola, Iowa. There, he studied piano and art. He transferred to Iowa State Agricultural College in Ames, Iowa, where he received a bachelor's degree in Agricultural Science in 1894 and a Master of Science degree in 1896.

Carver then joined the faculty of Booker T. Washington's Tuskegee Institute, where he became the Institute's Director of Agricultural Research in 1896. For most of his career, Carver taught and conducted research at the Tuskegee Normal and Industrial Institute (now Tuskegee University) in Tuskegee, Alabama. He helped revolutionize the agricultural economy of the South.

He conducted experiments in soil management and crop production, and directed an experimental farm. Carver found that Alabama's soil was particularly well suited for growing peanuts and sweet potatoes. As a result, he urged Southern farmers to plant peanuts and soybeans, since they could restore nitrogen to the soil while providing the protein so badly needed in the diet of many Southerners. When the state's farmers began

cultivating these crops instead of cotton, they found little demand for them on the market.

Carver set about enlarging the commercial possibilities of the peanut and sweet potato through a long and ingenious program of laboratory research. He ultimately developed 300 derivative products from peanuts—among them cheese, milk, coffee, flour, ink, dyes, plastics, wood stains, soap, linoleum, medicinal oils, and cosmetics—and 118 from sweet potatoes, including flour, vinegar, molasses, rubber, ink, a synthetic rubber, and postage stamp glue. He did work with pecans, soybeans, and other plants as well. Carver changed the face of agriculture in the American South and helped create demand for peanuts and sweet potatoes, establishing them as major American crops.

Teaching Tips

Words You Should Know

A. Marvel (Acts 3:12) *thaumazo* (Gk.)—To admire, have in admiration, marvel, wonder.

B. Power (v. 12) *dunamis* (Gk.)—Power, authority and might.

Teacher Preparation

Unifying Principle—Seeking Wholeness. People who are broken want to be made whole. How and where do they find wholeness? Peter proclaimed that faith in Jesus restores people to wholeness.

A. Pray for clarity and understanding of the lesson.

B. Read the Scriptures in multiple translations.

C. Read the Devotional Reading and reflect on the way it illuminates the printed verses.

O—Open the Lesson

A. Open with prayer, including the Aim for Change.

B. Introduce today's lesson title: "Faith in Jesus."

C. Have your students read the Aim for Change and the Keep in Mind verse together. Discuss the importance of having faith in the name of Jesus and what that looks like or means to them.

D. Tell the students to read the In Focus story silently, and then discuss it.

P—Present the Scriptures

A. Ask for volunteers to read the Focal Verses.

B. Use The People, Places, and Times; Background; Search the Scriptures; the At-A-Glance outline; In Depth; and More Light on the Text to clarify the verses.

E—Explore the Meaning

A. Divide the class into two groups. The first group will discuss what it means to have faith in Jesus' name. The second group will discuss if they've known anyone who has experienced a miracle.

B. Divide the class into groups to talk about the Discuss the Meaning, Lesson in Our Society, and Make It Happen sections. Have the students choose a representative to report their responses.

C. Connect these sections to the Aim for Change and the Keep in Mind verse.

N—Next Steps for Application

A. Summarize the lesson.

B. Ask the students if they have any takeaway thoughts that they would like to share.

C. Close with prayer.

Worship Guide

For the Superintendent or Teacher
Theme: Faith in Jesus
Song: "Anything Can Happen" by Jonathan Nelson
Devotional Reading: Psalm 118:1–14

Faith in Jesus

Bible Background • ACTS 3
Printed Text • ACTS 3:11–21 | Devotional Reading • PSALM 118:1–14

—— Aim for Change ——

By the end of this lesson, we will: EXAMINE the role of Peter's healing miracle in the post-Pentecost time frame; VALUE the need for bold witnessing; and EXERCISE a faith that affirms the identity of Jesus Christ in the twenty-first century.

In Focus

Virginia and her husband Mike had been married for 25 years. After raising four kids, they were now empty nesters and ready to enjoy their retirement. One day, Virginia began to experience pains in her stomach. After going to the doctor, she came back with tears in her eyes, and landed on the bed. Mike followed her into the bedroom and asked what had happened. Virginia shared the bad news: she had cancer, and the doctor had told her it was terminal.

Mike was not a believer and prepared for the worst. Virginia still had faith that God could do the impossible, and she put a call out to everyone in her circle to pray.

At her next doctor's appointment, she sat waiting for her latest test results. The doctor came in with a dumbfounded look on his face. He kept starting to say something, but instead he just kept shaking his head. Finally he informed her that she was cancer-free. She went home and told Mike. Mike couldn't believe it and began weeping for joy. That was the beginning of his newfound faith in Christ.

God does miracles not just for us, but so that others can believe as well. In today's lesson, we will see how a lame man's healing led to Peter preaching the Gospel to those who didn't believe. Have you ever experienced a miraculous healing?

—— Keep in Mind ——

"And his name through faith in his name hath made this man strong, whom ye see and know: yea, the faith which is by him hath given him this perfect soundness in the presence of you all" (Acts 3:16).

"And his name through faith in his name hath made this man strong, whom ye see and know: yea, the faith which is by him hath given him this perfect soundness in the presence of you all" (Acts 3:16).

Focal Verses

KJV **Acts 3:11** And as the lame man which was healed held Peter and John, all the people ran together unto them in the porch that is called Solomon's, greatly wondering.

12 And when Peter saw it, he answered unto the people, Ye men of Israel, why marvel ye at this? or why look ye so earnestly on us, as though by our own power or holiness we had made this man to walk?

13 The God of Abraham, and of Isaac, and of Jacob, the God of our fathers, hath glorified his Son Jesus; whom ye delivered up, and denied him in the presence of Pilate, when he was determined to let him go.

14 But ye denied the Holy One and the Just, and desired a murderer to be granted unto you;

15 And killed the Prince of life, whom God hath raised from the dead; whereof we are witnesses.

16 And his name through faith in his name hath made this man strong, whom ye see and know: yea, the faith which is by him hath given him this perfect soundness in the presence of you all.

17 And now, brethren, I wot that through ignorance ye did it, as did also your rulers.

18 But those things, which God before had shewed by the mouth of all his prophets, that Christ should suffer, he hath so fulfilled.

19 Repent ye therefore, and be converted, that your sins may be blotted out, when the times of refreshing shall come from the presence of the Lord.

20 And he shall send Jesus Christ, which before was preached unto you:

21 Whom the heaven must receive until the times of restitution of all things, which God hath spoken by the mouth of all his holy prophets since the world began.

NLT **Acts 3:11** They all rushed out in amazement to Solomon's Colonnade, where the man was holding tightly to Peter and John.

12 Peter saw his opportunity and addressed the crowd. "People of Israel," he said, "what is so surprising about this? And why stare at us as though we had made this man walk by our own power or godliness?

13 For it is the God of Abraham, Isaac, and Jacob—the God of all our ancestors—who has brought glory to his servant Jesus by doing this. This is the same Jesus whom you handed over and rejected before Pilate, despite Pilate's decision to release him.

14 You rejected this holy, righteous one and instead demanded the release of a murderer.

15 You killed the author of life, but God raised him from the dead. And we are witnesses of this fact!

16 Through faith in the name of Jesus, this man was healed—and you know how crippled he was before. Faith in Jesus' name has healed him before your very eyes.

17 Friends, I realize that what you and your leaders did to Jesus was done in ignorance.

18 But God was fulfilling what all the prophets had foretold about the Messiah—that he must suffer these things.

19 Now repent of your sins and turn to God, so that your sins may be wiped away.

20 Then times of refreshment will come from the presence of the Lord, and he will again send you Jesus, your appointed Messiah.

21 For he must remain in heaven until the time for the final restoration of all things, as God promised long ago through his holy prophets."

The People, Places, and Times

Solomon's Colonnade. This was a porch thought to have been a remnant of the Solomonic temple. It was located on the east side of the Temple and directly above the Kidron valley. This side of the Temple contained the Court of Women and the Beautiful Gate, which gave access to the Court of Israel. On the steps toward this gate, those who were disadvantaged begged for charity.

Peter. Also known as Simon Peter. He was one of the first to follow Jesus after leaving his father's trade as a fishermen. He was a member of the twelve disciples and Jesus' inner circle. Peter was known for being bold and expressive. He also was shown to be weak in his faith by denying Jesus three times. Once Peter was restored and filled with the Holy Spirit, he became a leading figure among the apostles and one of the first to preach to the Gentiles.

Background

On this particular day, Peter and John are on their way to the Temple to pray at "the ninth hour" (Acts 3:1). Their Jewish background had accustomed them to going to prayer at 3 in the afternoon. As they get close to the Temple, they saw a man who had been lame from birth coming every day to the Temple. Peter said, "Look at us!" The lame man would have been expecting money from them. Immediately, Peter took the lame man by the right hand and helped him up. As he did, the man's feet and ankles were instantly healed and strengthened. The lame man jumped up, stood on his feet, and began to walk! Everyone saw him "walking, leaping, and praising God" as he went into the Temple. The text says the people were "filled with wonder and amazement" (v. 10). They were being set up by God to deal with how they view the miracles, signs, and wonders that the apostles were performing in Jesus' name.

At-A-Glance

1. The Meaning of the Miracle (Acts 3:11–13)
2. Miracle of the Preaching (vv. 14–18)
3. Preaching of the Prince of Life (vv. 19–21)

In Depth

1. The Meaning of the Miracle (Acts 3:11–13)

Our verses begin with the people running from Solomon's Colonnade "greatly wondering": here was a man who everyone knew was lame from birth, yet he was completely healed. The people were overwhelmingly astonished and surprised by the power of Jesus being so evident. Yet that is exactly what Peter said in these verses (v. 12). They were surprised because at this point the Jewish people didn't know the power of the Holy Spirit, nor that the power to work miracles in Jesus' name had been passed on to the apostles.

Peter continues to explain the meaning behind the miracle. It was not his power, but the power of the God of Abraham, Isaac, and Jacob—the God of the Jewish ancestors. In other words, this is God's doing through His Servant Jesus Christ, whom the Jewish leaders handed over and rejected before Pilate (v. 13). Peter is seizing the opportunity to tell the reluctant Jews of the real power and purpose of the miracle.

2. Miracle of the Preaching (vv. 14–18)

Next we see Peter attribute this miracle to the power of Jesus. Peter takes advantage of the miracle and begins to preach to the people about Jesus. Peter declares who Jesus is: "the Holy One and the Just" (v. 14). Jesus was blameless. Verse 15 says, "And [you] killed the Prince of life, whom God hath raised from the dead; whereof we are witnesses." Peter reminds them about Jesus Christ—His crucifixion and resurrection. This Gospel is the recurrent theme in Peter's speeches.

Verse 17 says, "I wot (know) that through your ignorance ye did it." Peter seems to make an allowance for this being a sin of ignorance. The people didn't know the true identity of Jesus as the Messiah. In contrast, he supports that Jesus is the true Messiah by the prophecies that He fulfilled. Peter not only explains that Christ died and was raised again, but also shows the sovereignty of God in explaining that it was all a part of His plan. He shows the connection between the miracle and all that the prophets spoke of in the Old Testament.

3. Preaching of the Prince of Life (vv. 19–21)

Peter comes to his sermon's climax and tells the people to repent. He says that they were ignorant, but their rejection of Jesus paved the way for God to use His Servant to save the world. He wasn't only after Israel; He wanted all the nations. This would fulfill God's promise to Abraham, that He would make him to be a blessing and that through him all nations on earth would be blessed (Genesis 12:1–3).

Peter calls the people to repent and turn away from sin so that their sins may be wiped away (Acts 3:19). He wants them to be refreshed by the presence of the Lord until Jesus, the appointed Messiah, returns (v. 20). The Jews were looking for another Messiah, but Jesus is the only Messiah sent by God to save His people from their sins.

Search the Scriptures

1. Why were the people amazed and astonished at the healing of the lame man (Acts 3:11–13)?

2. What would the people's reward be for repenting from their sins (vv. 19–20)?

Discuss the Meaning

There are many modern reports of miraculous healing. What is God's purpose in healing today?

Lesson in Our Society

Every thirteen minutes, someone is diagnosed with some form of cancer. Every year, 1.4 million Americans are diagnosed with diabetes. Add to these other forms of diseases diagnosed every day. If a cure existed for everyone's ailments, regardless of whatever is going on in their body, everyone would take advantage of it. When sickness and infirmity hit our bodies, we are open to trying everything. However, first we must get rid of the myths that crowd out our faith, belief, and trust in Jesus.

We must first debunk the myth of "Maybe Jesus doesn't want to heal me," as well as "Jesus won't heal a sinner like me" and "I do not have enough faith to be healed." These ideas are lies that do not make sense. Is God a healer? As much as we hear about illness and disease, we also hear reports of God healing people through natural and supernatural means. We must also understand that God does not always heal, and human bodies eventually die. Elisha, Paul, David, and many other righteous people in Scripture got sick and did not get healed. Being overcome by illness is not a lack of faith. Yet our faith is in the truth that the same Jesus who healed the lame man is still a healer today, whether or not He heals as we expect it.

Make It Happen

Peter and John bore witness to the person and work of Jesus. How can we do the same thing with our lives?

- Pray and ask God to fill you with boldness and list out those in your life who need to hear the message of Jesus.

- Write out and rehearse your testimony of how Jesus saved you. Keep it to two minutes or less.
- Pray that God would set up divine appointments with others so that you can pray for them and perhaps share your testimony.

Follow the Spirit

What God wants me to do:

_____

_____

_____

_____

Remember Your Thoughts

Special insights I have learned:

_____

_____

_____

_____

More Light on the Text

Acts 3:11–21

11 And as the lame man which was healed held Peter and John, all the people ran together unto them in the porch that is called Solomon's, greatly wondering.

The lame man, now healed, grabbed on to Peter and John and was unwilling to let them get away from him. While he was holding on to the two apostles, the crowd, astonished beyond measure, "ran together unto them in the porch that is called Solomon's." This porch seems to have been a place where the disciples usually gathered together (John 10:23; Acts 5:12).

12 And when Peter saw it, he answered unto the people, Ye men of Israel, why marvel ye at this? or why look ye so earnestly on us, as though by our own power or holiness we had made this man to walk?

Peter seized the opportunity to present the Gospel message. He told the crowd that the man was not healed by any power or piety that he and John possessed. It was not dependent on their claim of personal holiness.

The verb "to walk," used here in a special grammatical construction in the Greek, expresses a purpose or a result. The man did not walk as the result of the apostles' power or devotion. The verse clearly emphasizes that the apostles by themselves could not enable this man to walk.

13 The God of Abraham, and of Isaac, and of Jacob, the God of our fathers, hath glorified his Son Jesus; whom ye delivered up, and denied him in the presence of Pilate, when he was determined to let him go.

In addressing the crowd, Peter chose his words wisely. He wanted not only to gain their attention, but also to show that he identified himself with the nation and hope of Israel. He saw in Jesus a direct continuity with the Old Testament, the fulfillment of the promise to their forefathers. The expression "God of our fathers" is a title of God (Exodus 3:6) intended to emphasize the seriousness of the crime of which the crowd had been guilty. The term is used in contrast with the honor and glorification (Gk. *doxazo*, **dok-SAD-zo**) that God had given to His Son, Jesus.

14 But ye denied the Holy One and the Just, and desired a murderer to be granted unto you.

169

Pilate, the Roman governor, had been willing to release Jesus, but the men of Israel denied Him freedom (Luke 23:22–24). The expression "the Holy One and the Just" is a messianic title for Jesus which is used again in Acts 7:52 and 22:14. The expression is in strong opposition to the word "murderer," used for the person who was released instead of Jesus. These men of Israel had refused to acknowledge Jesus as their divinely appointed King and Savior; instead, they had asked that a condemned murderer, Barabbas, be released (Luke 23:18–19).

15 And killed the Prince of life, whom God hath raised from the dead; whereof we are witnesses.

In so doing, they put the very "Prince of life" to death (an amazing paradox!). The expression "Prince of life" identifies Christ as the source of life and salvation (cf. Acts 5:31). It is also a messianic title for Jesus, meaning that He is the giver of the new life that overcomes death.

Although they killed Him, God restored Jesus to life again. Peter, John, and the apostles had been witnesses to Jesus' resurrection. Here, Peter emphasizes the contrast between the people's treatment of Jesus and the Father's treatment of Him.

16 And his name through faith in his name hath made this man strong, whom ye see and know: yea, the faith which is by him hath given him this perfect soundness in the presence of you all.

In order to explain how the lame man had been healed, Peter referred to the death and resurrection of Christ. The Father had honored Jesus, shown the divine nature of His Son (or Servant), and raised Him from the dead. He also further confirmed Jesus' power by this sign—the healing of the man born crippled—which everyone had seen.

The man had been healed by faith in the power of the name of the exalted Messiah, Jesus. The faith mentioned in this verse could refer to the faith of the man who was healed, as well as the faith of the apostles (cf. v. 5; 1 Corinthians 12:9).

From His place of exaltation, Jesus had endowed His disciples with power to act in His name and perform mighty works just like those He had performed in the days when He still walked among them (John 14:12–14).

17 And now, brethren, I wot that through ignorance ye did it, as did also your rulers. 18 But those things, which God before had shewed by the mouth of all his prophets, that Christ should suffer, he hath so fulfilled.

Peter consoles them by stating that he "wot" that the people acted in ignorance. "Wot" is a word we don't use anymore today that means "know"; the word "wit" comes from the same old verb. The Greek word translated "wot" (Gk. *oida*, **OY-dah**) means to know by reflection or thinking. The writer uses the term here to show that Peter sees beyond the surface of their actions and knows the motivation and context. Not only was the crowd guilty of this ignorant action, but the rulers were as well.

He then goes on to say that this is all according to God's plan. The Greek word (*prokataggello*, **pro-kat-an-GHELL-low**) for "shewed" (modern: shown) means to announce in advance, or to foretell so that everyone knows that this was spoken about beforehand. Through the prophets, God had spoken and said that His Messiah would suffer. These things have now come to pass.

19 Repent ye therefore, and be converted, that your sins may be blotted out, when the times of refreshing shall come from the presence of the Lord. 20 And he shall send Jesus Christ, which before was preached unto you:

Peter now gives instructions for how the crowd should respond: they are to repent (Gk. *metanoeo*, **meh-ta-no-EH-oh**). The idea behind the Greek word is to change one's mind; to repent means to abandon former attitudes, actions, and dispositions and replace them with new ones. This change of mind is accompanied by them being "converted" (Gk. *epistrepho*, **eh-pee-STREH-fo**) which etymologically means to turn back. In this context, it means to turn back or return to God.

As a result, their sins would be blotted out (Gk. *exaleipho*, **ek-sa-LAY-fo**). This word can mean to overlay and cover, or to wipe off. The second meaning is used here; the sins of ignorance in delivering Jesus over to be crucified, as well as any other sins, would be wiped away. The people would also experience the "times of refreshing." The word here for refreshing (Gk. *anapsuxis*, **ah-NOP-sik-sis**) means a cooling or blowing off and also a breathing space; in this context, it means relief. It is unclear whether this refers to the time before the return of the Messiah or the actual time of the Messiah's return. Verse 20 may give insight into the meaning of the previous verse, as Peter says that Jesus would return. This would be necessary relief and seems to be the meaning of the times of refreshing.

21 Whom the heaven must receive until the times of restitution of all things, which God hath spoken by the mouth of all his holy prophets since the world began.

Here Peter speaks of the time in between Christ's ascension and His return. Heaven receives or welcomes Him until the times of restitution (Gk. *apokatastasis*, **ah-po-ka-TA-sta-sees**). The Greek word means to restore someone or something to its previous, satisfactory state. This is a time that Peter asserts the prophets spoke about "since the world began"; this was probably hyperbole or even

a reference to the protoevangelion or pre-gospel of Genesis 3:15. Jews expected that Israel would be restored through Messianic rule (Isaiah 40:9–11; Ezekiel 37:21–28; Amos 9:11–15), but Peter is saying that they can be a part of this time of restoration if they repent and turn to God.

Sources:
Fernando, A. *The NIV Application Commentary on the Book of Acts.* Grand Rapids, MI: Zondervan, 1998.
Hindson, Edward, E., and D.R. Mitchell, eds. *Zondervan King James Version Commentary (New Testament).* Grand Rapids, MI: Zondervan Publishers, 2010.
Keener, C. S. *The IVP Bible Background Commentary (New Testament) 2nd Edition.* Downers Grove, IL: InterVarsity Press Publishers, 2014.
Zodhiates, S. T., and W. Baker. *Hebrew-Greek Key Word Study Bible KJV.* Chattanooga, TN: AMG Publishers, 2008.

Say It Correctly

Colonnade. **KAH**-luh-naid.
Restitution. res-teh-**TOO**-shun.

Daily Bible Readings

MONDAY
Take Refuge in the Lord
(Psalm 118:1–9)

TUESDAY
The Lord, My Strength and Salvation
(Psalm 118:10–14)

WEDNESDAY
A Blessing Promised to All Peoples
(Acts 3:22–26)

THURSDAY
Your Faith Saved You
(Luke 7:44–50)

FRIDAY
Contrasting Responses by Jews and Gentiles
(Acts 13:44–49)

SATURDAY
Crippled Beggar Requests Alms
(Acts 3:1–10)

SUNDAY
Faith in Jesus
(Acts 3:11–21)

Notes

_____

_____

_____

Teaching Tips

Words You Should Know

A. Prophets (Act 13:1) *prophetes* (Gk.)—Foretellers, inspired speakers, interpreters.

B. Ministered (v. 2) *leitourgeo* (Gk.)—To perform religious or charitable functions.

Teacher Preparation

Unifying Principle—Facing Opposition. Sometimes we are at a loss when unexpected events interfere with our goals. How can we keep our commitments and forge ahead? Empowered by their faith in Jesus, Paul and Barnabas preached and taught about Jesus despite a false prophet's efforts to deter them.

A. Pray for lesson clarity and understanding.

B. Read the passage in several translations.

C. Read the companion lesson in the *Precepts For Living®* Study Guide.

O—Open the Lesson

A. Open with prayer, including the Aim to Change.

B. Introduce today's lesson title: "Faith to Discern."

C. Tell the students to read the In Focus story silently, and then discuss it.

P—Present the Scriptures

A. Ask for volunteers to read the Focal Verses aloud.

B. Use The People, Places, and Times; Background; Search the Scriptures; and In Depth sections to clarify the verses.

E—Explore the Meaning

A. Have the students read the Lesson in Our Society section.

B. Divide the class into groups to respond to the Discuss the Meaning and Make It Happen sections. Have the students choose a representative to report their response.

N—Next Steps for Application

A. Summarize the lesson.

B. Ask the students if they have any takeaway thoughts that they would like to share.

C. Close with prayer.

Worship Guide

For the Superintendent or Teacher
Theme: Faith to Discern
Song: "Break Every Chain" by Tasha Cobbs
Devotional Reading: Psalm 146

Faith to Discern

Bible Background • ACTS 13:1–12
Printed Text • ACTS 13:1–12 | Devotional Reading • PSALM 146

——————— Aim for Change ———————

By the end of the lesson, we will: CONTRAST the motives and sources of power of Paul and his companions with those of Elymas; APPRECIATE what it signified for Paul to pronounce blindness on another; and COMMIT to a season of prayer and fasting before embarking on a new ministry.

In Focus

Jeremy didn't know what he was going to do. He had just graduated from college and was feeling torn. He had job offers in two cities. One city was a tech hub and known for all of its great culture and night life. The other city was economically depressed and run down. Jeremy had pursued his degree in computer science mainly for the money, but as he had been on this new journey of following Christ, the money hadn't been that appealing.

The job in the economically depressed area was with a non-profit helping kids learn computer science. He had never thought about his skills actually being used to help others. At the same time, he reasoned he could help others with all the money he would make at the other job. Both choices seemed like reasonable options that God would honor. Jeremy didn't know what to do.

He spoke with his mentor, Paul, who encouraged him to fast and bring the matter to God in prayer. After several days of fasting and worshiping God, Jeremy read Romans 10:14, and the words jumped out at him: "...how can they hear about him unless someone tells them?" (NLT). He realized those were God's words to him personally, and he knew right then that he should accept his call to ministry in the economically depressed area. He didn't know where it would lead, but he knew it was the right choice.

In this lesson, we will look at how Paul and Barnabas heard the voice of the Holy Spirit. How do you discern the next steps God wants you to take?

——————— Keep in Mind ———————

"The Holy Ghost said, Separate me Barnabas and Saul for the work whereunto I have called them" (from Acts 13:2).

"The Holy Ghost said, Separate me Barnabas and Saul for the work whereunto I have called them" (from Acts 13:2).

Focal Verses

KJV **Acts 13:1** Now there were in the church that was at Antioch certain prophets and teachers; as Barnabas, and Simeon that was called Niger, and Lucius of Cyrene, and Manaen, which had been brought up with Herod the tetrarch, and Saul.

2 As they ministered to the Lord, and fasted, the Holy Ghost said, Separate me Barnabas and Saul for the work whereunto I have called them.

3 And when they had fasted and prayed, and laid their hands on them, they sent them away.

4 So they, being sent forth by the Holy Ghost, departed unto Seleucia; and from thence they sailed to Cyprus.

5 And when they were at Salamis, they preached the word of God in the synagogues of the Jews: and they had also John to their minister.

6 And when they had gone through the isle unto Paphos, they found a certain sorcerer, a false prophet, a Jew, whose name was Barjesus:

7 Which was with the deputy of the country, Sergius Paulus, a prudent man; who called for Barnabas and Saul, and desired to hear the word of God.

8 But Elymas the sorcerer (for so is his name by interpretation) withstood them, seeking to turn away the deputy from the faith.

9 Then Saul, (who also is called Paul,) filled with the Holy Ghost, set his eyes on him.

10 And said, O full of all subtilty and all mischief, thou child of the devil, thou enemy of all righteousness, wilt thou not cease to pervert the right ways of the Lord?

11 And now, behold, the hand of the Lord is upon thee, and thou shalt be blind, not seeing the sun for a season. And immediately there fell on him a mist and a darkness; and he went about seeking some to lead him by the hand.

NLT **Acts 13:1** Among the prophets and teachers of the church at Antioch of Syria were Barnabas, Simeon (called "the black man"), Lucius (from Cyrene), Manaen (the childhood companion of King Herod Antipas), and Saul.

2 One day as these men were worshiping the Lord and fasting, the Holy Spirit said, "Appoint Barnabas and Saul for the special work to which I have called them."

3 So after more fasting and prayer, the men laid their hands on them and sent them on their way.

4 So Barnabas and Saul were sent out by the Holy Spirit. They went down to the seaport of Seleucia and then sailed for the island of Cyprus.

5 There, in the town of Salamis, they went to the Jewish synagogues and preached the word of God. John Mark went with them as their assistant.

6 Afterward they traveled from town to town across the entire island until finally they reached Paphos, where they met a Jewish sorcerer, a false prophet named Bar-Jesus.

7 He had attached himself to the governor, Sergius Paulus, who was an intelligent man. The governor invited Barnabas and Saul to visit him, for he wanted to hear the word of God.

8 But Elymas, the sorcerer (as his name means in Greek), interfered and urged the governor to pay no attention to what Barnabas and Saul said. He was trying to keep the governor from believing.

9 Saul, also known as Paul, was filled with the Holy Spirit, and he looked the sorcerer in the eye.

10 Then he said, "You son of the devil, full of every sort of deceit and fraud, and enemy of all that is good! Will you never stop perverting the true ways of the Lord?

12 Then the deputy, when he saw what was done, believed, being astonished at the doctrine of the Lord.

11 Watch now, for the Lord has laid his hand of punishment upon you, and you will be struck blind. You will not see the sunlight for some time." Instantly mist and darkness came over the man's eyes, and he began groping around begging for someone to take his hand and lead him.

12 When the governor saw what had happened, he became a believer, for he was astonished at the teaching about the Lord.

The People, Places, and Times

Antioch (of Syria). The city of Antioch was founded during the period of Seleucid Syria. It was situated on the south bank of the Orontes River. Antioch was a very diverse city and was one of the first places the church was initiated outside of Jerusalem. Antioch is where the followers of the Way were first called Christians.

Cyprus. Cyprus is an island in the Mediterranean Sea, approximately 110 miles long and 50 miles wide. The island's coast is lined with numerous natural harbors. Cyprus' location in the northeastern Mediterranean made it an ideal meeting place for ships from Syria, Asia Minor, Egypt, and Palestine. Barnabas was originally from the island of Cyprus.

Background

The church in Antioch was one of the first churches where Gentiles came to faith in large numbers. Although Peter had previously preached to Gentiles in Joppa, Antioch is where ordinary believers began to preach the Good News to them. As a result, a "great number believed," prompting the church in Jerusalem to send Barnabas to look after the fledgling church and evaluate its work. Barnabas in turn invited Paul to come and teach alongside him at Antioch. Over time, the church grew spiritually and in number.

As they fasted and worshiped, the Holy Spirit spoke, more than likely through one of the prophets or teachers gathered there. The word from God was that Paul and Barnabas should be set apart to be sent to the Gentiles. This was in fulfillment of God's call on Paul's life as detailed in Acts 9:13–16. Here we learn how God instructs Paul and Barnabas as they step out in faith for this special work.

At-A-Glance

1. Summoned by the Holy Spirit (Acts 13:1–3)
2. Sent by the Holy Spirit (vv. 4–8)
3. Saved by the Power of the Spirit (vv. 9–12)

In Depth

1. Summoned by the Holy Spirit (Acts 13:1–3)

In spite of the fact that they had identified prophets and teachers, the church at Antioch sought guidance from the Holy Spirit through prayer and fasting. What an impressive line-up of leaders who would embark upon this journey of fasting, praying, and seeking the Holy Spirit for direction! Paul is listed last, but God has a plan for his life, as we shall see later in the book of Acts.

These five leaders spent time fasting and worshiping to seek the will of God. While they were doing this, the Holy Spirit began to reveal His will. The text says, "Appoint Barnabas and Saul for the special work" He had for them to do. They continued praying and fasting even after they received this word from the Holy Spirit, showing that they were careful to rely on God throughout this new venture. The Antioch leaders laid hands on them. This was a commissioning or sending out of Barnabas and Paul so they would accomplish God's will.

2. Sent by the Holy Spirit (vv. 4–8)

When the Holy Spirit summons, the Spirit also sends. It is safe to say that Barnabas and Paul were on their first missionary journey, but they were not novices (they were in ministry for eight years in Antioch). The church sent them away to do the Lord's work with the Gentiles. They visited several places (vv. 4–6), first Seleucia, and then the island of Cyprus. On Cyprus, they visited Salamis and preached in various synagogues. However, they decided to travel west to Paphos, the location of the Roman colony on the island. There they found a Jewish sorcerer and a false prophet named Elymas, also known as Barjesus. Elymas had attached himself to Sergius Paulus, who was the proconsul (or governor) of the area, who sent for Barnabas and Paul, because he wanted to hear the Word of God.

When Elymas heard Paul and Barnabas' message, he sought to turn Sergius Paulus away from the faith. Elymas was trying to hinder the work of the Lord and actually told Sergius Paulus not to listen to anything they said. He must have felt threatened by the power of God working through their lives and the Gospel message. Their words would have shown that Elymas was a false prophet. Many times when doing God's work, those who are intimidated will try to keep people from hearing because the Word of God has power.

3. Saved by the Power of the Spirit (vv. 9–12)

Paul, full of the Holy Spirit, rebuked Barjesus. The text says he looked him dead in his eye and said, "You son of the devil, full of every sort of deceit and fraud, and enemy of all that is good" (vv. 9–10). Paul was furious at Elymas, and was not going to let him continue to stop the power of the Holy Spirit from ministering to Sergius Paulus. Paul saw that Elymas intended to stop any good thing that God wanted to do; he had no good in him.

Paul declared that Elymas would be blind for a season; he needed to know that he was not in charge or in control. After this, Sergius Paulus believed. He was convinced by the Word of God and the power that backed it up. Since Sergius Paulus was the governor, his voice was very influential on the island as a Gentile believer. Paul and Barnabas might have possibly looked on this as confirmation that God had sent them to proclaim the Gospel to the Gentiles.

Search the Scriptures

1. What are the benefits of entering into a time of corporately seeking God (Acts 13:1–3)?

2. Why was the deputy astonished at the teaching about the Lord (vv. 9–12)?

Discuss the Meaning

Paul and Barnabas relied on the Holy Spirit prior to and during their first missionary journey. What does it mean for you to rely on the Holy Spirit?

Lesson in Our Society

Today, fasting and times of seeking God are not talked about enough. Our churches are filled with those who would like to receive God's power without waiting in His presence. Concerts and fund-raisers seem more appealing than actually seeking God and what He wants. The voice of our favorite preacher is louder in our ears than God's voice. Everyone has his or her own idea, agenda, and plan for living. Fasting especially seems like a relic of a bygone era.

In earlier times, fasting and praying were a regular part of the church's life. Now many are enjoying prosperity and forgetting the God who made us prosperous. In many historic Black churches, fasting and praying were not for special people, but a part of normal Christian life. More than ever, it's essential that we get back to seeking God and worshiping Him just for who He is. Then we can discern what needs to happen in our lives and God can give us direction.

Make It Happen

• Choose a time to fast in the next week and seek God's presence.

• List out three ways God has spoken to you in the past. If you are not sure, discover three ways God has spoken to others.

• Write down how God has used you in the lives of others and reflect on how He wants to use you today.

Follow the Spirit

What God wants me to do:

_____

_____

_____

_____

Remember Your Thoughts

Special insights I have learned:

_____

_____

More Light on the Text

Acts 13:1–12

1 Now there were in the church that was at Antioch certain prophets and teachers; as Barnabas, and Simeon that was called Niger, and Lucius of Cyrene, and Manaen, which had been brought up with Herod the tetrarch, and Saul.

The early church's leadership was diverse. Barnabas was introduced to us earlier in the book of Acts at the end of chapter 4. He was a Levite from the island of Cyprus. Barnabas, whose name means "son of encouragement," convinced the disciples to accept Paul's conversion as genuine. Saul here is the same Paul (v. 9) who would go on to write much of the New Testament, still going by his Hebrew name while among fellow Hebrews.

The word "prophets" refers to "one who, moved by the Spirit of God and hence His organ or spokesman, solemnly declares to men what he has received by inspiration, including future events, and in particular such as relate to the cause and kingdom of God and to human salvation." In other words, these people speak for God Himself and are to represent Him and do as He instructs them.

We hear little about the three other leaders of the Antioch church. Two of the men here are likely from Africa, though we do not know much else about them. Simeon was called Niger, which means "black" in Latin, probably alluding to his dark complexion. Of Lucius, we know only that he was from the city of Cyrene in North Africa. Manaen is Greek for the Hebrew name Menahem, meaning "comforter." In Greek, the word for "brought up with" is *suntrophos* (**SOON-trof-os**) and can be translated as "foster brother," the title given to boys around the same age as the prince who were raised with him in the royal court.

2 As they ministered to the Lord, and fasted, the Holy Ghost said, Separate me Barnabas and Saul for the work whereunto I have called them.

In the Greek, "they ministered" is *leitourgeo* (**lay-toor-GEH-oh**), and in this context refers to prayer, instructing others in the way of salvation, or some other way of working for the Lord. Their ministry was complemented with fasting—either entirely, if the fast lasted only one day, or from customary and choice nourishment, if it continued several days. Therefore, they were found fasting and praying, which made them sensitive to the leading of the Holy Spirit.

In the midst of carrying out their leadership and ministry responsibilities, these men were instructed by the Holy Spirit to appoint Paul and Barnabas to the work to which God had called them. It is worth noting that these men were ministering "to the Lord." They understood to whom their service was to be directed. Subsequently, they ministered to God's people as to the Lord.

3 And when they had fasted and prayed, and laid their hands on them, they sent them away.

Having been instructed by the Spirit to appoint Barnabas and Paul to their work, the leaders at Antioch laid hands on their brothers and sent them away with their blessing. The leaders sent them off as representatives of the entire body; thus, through its leaders, the whole church at Antioch gave its blessings to these two missionaries and sent them to the work.

4 So they, being sent forth by the Holy Ghost, departed unto Seleucia; and from thence they sailed to Cyprus. 5 And when they were at Salamis, they preached the word of God in the synagogues of the Jews: and they had also John to their minister.

Luke, the writer of Acts, tells us here that the Holy Spirit sent Barnabas and Paul forth on their missionary journey. The emphasis, of course, is on the calling of the Spirit to the work of ministry. Ultimately, the Lord calls people into ministry. The church should discern if the call is valid and then commission for service those whose calling is from the Lord.

Having been commissioned, Paul and Barnabas set out for the island of Cyprus, about sixty miles west of the coast of Syria. It is the third largest island in the Mediterranean. Barnabas and Paul most likely chose it as the starting point for their missionary journey because it was close to Antioch, had a large Jewish population, and was familiar territory, being the home of Barnabas. They preached the Word first in the city of Salamis, which was on the east coast of the island. They began in the synagogue, not because their ministry was intended exclusively for Jews, but because this was a good bridge to the Gentile community; here they would encounter Gentiles who were already familiar with and respectful toward God.

John (also known as Mark) was the cousin of Barnabas. He traveled with the two men as an attendant early in the first missionary journey. He would later be the cause of a split between Paul and Barnabas (Acts 15:36–41). Afterward, he would be reconciled to Paul (2 Timothy 4:11).

6 And when they had gone through the isle unto Paphos, they found a certain sorcerer, a false prophet, a Jew, whose name was Barjesus: 7 Which was with the deputy of the country, Sergius Paulus, a prudent man; who called for Barnabas and Saul, and desired to hear the word of God. 8 But

Elymas the sorcerer (for so is his name by interpretation) withstood them, seeking to turn away the deputy from the faith.

Advancing God's purposes is not without its challenges. From Salamis, Paul and Barnabas traveled all the way to the west coast of the island, spreading the Gospel. In the city of Paphos, they encountered the false prophet Barjesus, also called Elymas.

The name "Barjesus" means "son of salvation," which he was not. He was a magician who falsely claimed to be a medium of divine revelation. He had somehow attached himself to the governor at that time, Sergius Paulus. The text tells us that Sergius Paulus was a prudent man (v. 7). "Prudent" in the Greek is *sunetos* (**soo-neh-TOCE**) and means "intelligent, having understanding, wise, learned." Sergius Paulus had either heard about Paul and Barnabas' teaching or had heard them preach the Gospel himself, and so summoned them in order to hear further explanation of the Gospel. Elymas, no doubt afraid of losing the governor's favor, opposed Paul and Barnabas and tried to keep Sergius from believing the Gospel.

9 Then Saul, (who also is called Paul,) filled with the Holy Ghost, set his eyes on him. 10 And said, O full of all subtilty and all mischief, thou child of the devil, thou enemy of all righteousness, wilt thou not cease to pervert the right ways of the Lord? 11 And now, behold, the hand of the Lord is upon thee, and thou shalt be blind, not seeing the sun for a season. And immediately there fell on him a mist and a darkness; and he went about seeking some to lead him by the hand.

Paul "set his eyes" on Elymas (v. 9) and said, "O full of all subtilty and all mischief" (v. 10). "Subtilty," in the Greek, is *dolos* (**DO-los**) and means "craft, deceit, guile." "Mischief" translates the Greek word *rhadiourgia* (**rah-dee-ur-GEE-ah**), which can refer to laziness, but in

this context means fraud or unscrupulousness. Then Paul severely rebuked Elymas for trying to hinder the governor from coming to faith in Christ. The Scripture says that Paul's rebuke was the result of his being filled with the Holy Spirit, as Stephen was when he spoke before the Sanhedrin (Acts 6:10). Indeed, throughout the book of Acts, we hear of the filling of the Spirit as the people of God accomplish the work of ministry.

Paul began with a rebuke centered on the wickedness of Elymas' character. By his attempts to sway the governor from the truth, he had shown that he was not, in fact, a medium of divine revelation, but a son of the devil whose heart was filled with deceit and who never ceased in confusing the way of salvation. He was an enemy of the Gospel of Christ. Thus, because Elymas had attempted to blind the governor to the truth of the Gospel, he would suffer the Lord's judgment of physical blindness for some time. We are not told how long, nor does it seem that Elymas was told either. The results demonstrated that this judgment was from the Lord; Elymas was immediately struck blind and began to fumble about, looking for someone to guide him. What a warning this text is to those who would oppose the Gospel! God does not look lightly on attempts to hinder the spread of His truth. He will respond to those who seek to destroy the work of the Gospel in the lives of those whom He is calling to Himself.

12 Then the deputy, when he saw what was done, believed, being astonished at the doctrine of the Lord.

Elymas had tried to deter the governor from the faith, but the Lord used His judgment on Elymas to bring the governor to faith. The governor was so amazed by what he saw that he believed the teaching of the Lord. Notice that the text does not say that he believed Paul's teaching, because God was using Paul to teach the Word of the Lord. Sergius Paulus believed that what he had been told by Elymas was indeed false, and the message that he heard from Barnabas and Paul was true.

Sources:
Fernando, A. *The NIV Application Commentary on the Book of Acts.* Grand Rapids, MI: Zondervan, 1998.
Hindson, Edward, and D.R. Mitchell, eds. *Zondervan King James Version Commentary (New Testament).* Grand Rapids, MI: Zondervan, 2010.
Keener, C. S. *The IVP Bible Background Commentary (New Testament).* 2nd Edition. Downers Grove, IL: Intervarsity Press, 2014.
MacDonald, William. *Believers Bible Commentary, Old and New Testament.* Nashville, TN: Thomas Nelson Publishers, 1989.
Zodhiates, S. T., and W. Baker. *Hebrew-Greek Key Word Study Bible KJV.* Chattanooga, TN: AMG Publishers, 2008.

Say It Correctly

Manaen. ma-**NA**-in.
Elymas. eh-**LEE**-mahs.
Sergius Paulus. ser-**JEE**-us pah-**LUS**.

Daily Bible Readings

MONDAY
Joshua Discerned as New Leader
(Deuteronomy 31:14–15, 23; 34:9)

TUESDAY
Eli Senses God's Call to Samuel
(1 Samuel 3:1–9)

WEDNESDAY
Test the Spirits
(1 John 4:1–6)

THURSDAY
Blind Man Discerns Jesus as Prophet
(John 9:13–17)

FRIDAY
Paul's Strategy: Jews First, Then Greeks
(Romans 1:8–12, 16–17)

SATURDAY
Door of Faith Opened to Gentiles
(Acts 14:21–28)

SUNDAY
Spirit-filled Leadership Discernment
(Acts 13:1–12)

Notes

_____

_____

_____

_____

Teaching Tips

Words You Should Know

A. Tribulation (Acts 14:22) *thlipsis* (Gk.)—Affliction, oppression.

B. Elders (v. 23) *presbyteros* (Gk.)—Older people; those who presided over the assemblies or churches.

Teacher Preparation

Unifying Principle—Persevering Through Opposition. Sometimes the good things we do are blocked by an unexpected obstruction, but we pick up and go on anyway. What gives us the strength to keep going? Even though he was stoned and persecuted, Paul's faith in his message compelled him to continue to proclaim the Good News of God.

A. Pray that students will be encouraged to persevere through difficult times.

B. Read the verses in two or more translations to gain a better understanding.

C. Research the phrase "Kingdom of God" in the New Testament.

O—Open the Lesson

A. Open with prayer.

B. Introduce today's lesson title.

C. Have the class read the Aim for Change, In Focus story, and Keep in Mind together.

P—Present the Scriptures

A. Have volunteers read the Focal Verses.

B. Use The People, Places, and Times; Background; and At-A-Glance to clarify the Scripture passages.

E—Explore the Meaning

A. Direct the group to read In Depth.

B. Answer the Search the Scripture and Discuss the Meaning questions.

N—Next Steps for Application

A. Summarize the lesson by giving individual class members encouragement, and by prompting the class to find opportunity throughout the week to encourage others.

B. Close with prayer.

Worship Guide

For the Superintendent or Teacher
Theme: Faith to Persevere
Song: "I'm on the Battlefield"
Devotional Reading: 2 Corinthians 1:3–11

Faith to Persevere

Bible Background • ACTS 14; COLOSSIANS 2:6–7
Printed Text • ACTS 14:8–11, 19–23 | Devotional Reading • 2 CORINTHIANS 1:3–11

——————————— Aim for Change ———————————

By the end of the lesson, we will: EVALUATE the nature of the miracle performed at Lystra; CONSIDER the fickleness of the crowd mentality; and PRAY for courage and strength in the face of resistance to the Gospel.

————————  In Focus ————————

John traveled to China every year on business, and always made sure to visit with his friend, Chen. Chen worked in the same industry but was also a local pastor for an underground house church. Each year, Chen told stories of people being saved and delivered, but he also told how careful people had to be when they came to church.

They didn't broadcast their gatherings with flyers or let people know on social media. They had to work in secret or risk severe consequences like imprisonment or even death. The church members had to stagger their arrival, usually over several hours, to keep their meetings secret.

This year, John was excited to meet with Chen. When he arrived at his host company in China, Chen was not a part of their meeting. John inquired about him and learned that Chen had been sentenced to a work camp because the police discovered that he was leading a house church. His wife had been forced to flee to protect herself and their son.

John learned that through it all, Chen continued to preach the Gospel to his cellmates and to the prison guards. He knew that this was part of following Jesus in a country that was hostile to the Gospel. John was deeply saddened that Chen was imprisoned, but he had great admiration for his faith to persevere in the midst of opposition.

God gives us faith to persevere in spite of the opposition that we face. How do you find that faith when you are faced with conflict?

———————— Keep in Mind ————————

"They returned again to Lystra, and to Iconium, and Antioch, confirming the souls of the disciples, and exhorting them to continue in the faith, and that we must through much tribulation enter into the kingdom of God" (Acts 14:21–22).

"They returned again to Lystra, and to Iconium, and Antioch, confirming the souls of the disciples, and exhorting them to continue in the faith, and that we must through much tribulation enter into the kingdom of God" (Acts 14:21–22).

Focal Verses

KJV **Acts 14: 8** And there sat a certain man at Lystra, impotent in his feet, being a cripple from his mother's womb, who never had walked:

9 The same heard Paul speak: who steadfastly beholding him, and perceiving that he had faith to be healed,

10 Said with a loud voice, Stand upright on thy feet. And he leaped and walked.

11 And when the people saw what Paul had done, they lifted up their voices, saying in the speech of Lyconia, The gods are come down to us in the likeness of men.

19 And there came thither certain Jews from Antioch and Iconium, who persuaded the people, and having stoned Paul, drew him out of the city, supposing he had been dead.

20 Howbeit, as the disciples stood round about him, he rose up, and came into the city: and the next day he departed with Barnabas to Derbe.

21 And when they had preached the gospel to that city, and had taught many, they returned again to Lystra, and to Iconium, and Antioch,

22 Confirming the souls of the disciples, and exhorting them to continue in the faith, and that we must through much tribulation enter into the kingdom of God.

23 And when they had ordained them elders in every church, and had prayed with fasting, they commended them to the Lord, on whom they believed.

NLT **Acts 14:8** While they were at Lystra, Paul and Barnabas came upon a man with crippled feet. He had been that way from birth, so he had never walked. He was sitting

9 and listening as Paul preached. Looking straight at him, Paul realized he had faith to be healed.

10 So Paul called to him in a loud voice, "Stand up!" And the man jumped to his feet and started walking.

11 When the crowd saw what Paul had done, they shouted in their local dialect, "These men are gods in human form!"

19 Then some Jews arrived from Antioch and Iconium and won the crowds to their side. They stoned Paul and dragged him out of town, thinking he was dead.

20 But as the believers gathered around him, he got up and went back into the town. The next day he left with Barnabas for Derbe.

21 After preaching the Good News in Derbe and making many disciples, Paul and Barnabas returned to Lystra, Iconium, and Antioch of Pisidia,

22 where they strengthened the believers. They encouraged them to continue in the faith, reminding them that we must suffer many hardships to enter the Kingdom of God.

23 Paul and Barnabas also appointed elders in every church. With prayer and fasting, they turned the elders over to the care of the Lord, in whom they had put their trust.

The People, Places, and Times

Iconium. A city in central Asia Minor. It is home to a lush agricultural production, and because of its location, served as a link between ancient trade routes. Iconium is now the site of the modern-day Turkish city of Konya.

Lystra. A small village and Roman colony eighteen miles southwest of Iconium in modern central Turkey. An inscription dedicating a statue to the Greek gods Zeus and Hermes was discovered there. It was quite possibly the hometown of Timothy (Acts 16:1).

Antioch (of Pisidia). This city is not the same Antioch spoken of in Acts 13:1. It was situated in the area of Pisidia on the Anatolian peninsula. Antioch of Pisidia was located on the southern bank of the Anthios river. The city was believed to have been founded by a Seleucid king or by Seleucius himself. As a Roman colony, the city became a miniature version of Rome, complete with ornate sculptures and architecture.

Background

Jesus tells His disciples, "You shall be my witness in Jerusalem, and in Judea and Samaria, and to the end of the earth" (from Acts 1:8). These words outline the book of Acts and highlight three stages in the church's early development:

• Acts 1–7: The apostles witness to Jews in Jerusalem.

• Acts 8–12: In response to persecution, and through the leading and empowering of the Holy Spirit, Paul and his companions share the message of the kingdom of God (14:22) to the Samaritans in Judea and Samaria.

• Acts 13–28: Paul witnesses to Gentiles as he journeys to the ends of the earth.

The events in today's passage occur during the third stage of the church's early development. The previous chapter recounts Barnabas' return to evangelize in his hometown region, Cyprus. Paul, with holy boldness, confronts the Jewish sorcerer Barjesus and witnesses the governor Sergius Paulus' conversion. Next, they traveled to Iconium, where they witnessed in the synagogue to both Jews and Greeks. They were again met with violent opposition before traveling to Lystra (14:6).

At-A-Glance

1. Kingdom Breakthrough at Lystra
(Acts 14:8–11)
2. Kingdom Opposition is Normal (vv. 19–23)

In Depth

1. Kingdom Breakthrough at Lystra (Acts 14:8–11)

Paul and Barnabas fled Antioch for Lystra in continued obedience to God. As the church grew beyond Jerusalem, God confirmed His presence by repeating the same miracle twice: once in Jerusalem (Acts 3:2–12) and again in Lystra. God used both Peter and Paul to heal men who were lame from birth, and they gave honor to Him rather than accept recognition for themselves.

The crowd initially responds with wonder and awe, assuming these wonder workers to be gods (Acts 14:11). They could only comprehend this concept in terms that they understood. Paul and Barnabas would need to explain how the man was healed through the power of Jesus and not pagan gods. While a miraculous healing is a kingdom breakthrough, we also can see that misunderstanding can become a barrier to people entering the kingdom of God.

2. Kingdom Opposition is Normal (vv. 19–23)

After Jews arrived from Antioch and Iconium, the story takes a drastic turn. These Jews had forced Paul and Barnabas to leave those cities. They now persuade the crowd to stone Paul to death. The crowd believed they had killed Paul, so they dragged his body outside the town.

In this time of pain and suffering, Paul had two sources of comfort. The first was the presence of the "Father of mercies and the God of all comfort" (2 Corinthians 1:3). His second source of comfort was the caring presence of the disciples in Lystra who gathered around him until he was able to get up, leave the city, and go to Derbe.

After Derbe, Paul returns to Lystra, Iconium, and Antioch, coming full circle to strengthen the believers and exhort them to remain true to the faith. Some of these believers had earlier gathered around him after his stoning. Now they receive encouragement from him and are exhorted to hold fast to the faith despite hardship. Paul lets them know that persecution and hardship are part of the normal Christian life.

Search the Scriptures

1. Is there ever a time when we should avoid persecution (Acts 14:22)?

2. Why is tribulation required to enter the kingdom of God (v. 22)?

Discuss the Meaning

In Paul and Barnabas' story today they endured persecution by the power of God. How does recognizing God's presence help us persevere in our faith, especially as we face opposition?

Lesson in Our Society

Beyond the borders of the United States, Christians are dying in record numbers. These modern-day martyrs face beheadings on television, abductions from school, indefinite imprisonment without trial, and countless other atrocities. According to the Center for the Study of Global Christianity, approximately 100,000 Christians were killed each year from 2000 to 2010, including almost 1,000 in 2016 in Nigeria alone. The reality that more believers have died for Christ in the 20th and 21st centuries than in all previous centuries combined lends itself to meditation on a phrase in an old hymn: *Should I be carried to the sky on flowery*

beds of ease, while others fought to win the prize and sailed through bloody seas?

In America, to date, we have not experienced this type of persecution for our faith. However, with every personal interaction, our Christian witness is on the line and our loves, fears, and values are tested. The African American church knows suffering from the rich tradition of the Civil Rights Movement—a campaign that was grounded in the faith. Today, standing boldly is complicated by social pressure to compromise and fit in, but God can strengthen His people to remain fully committed to Jesus.

Make It Happen

• Go to www.persecution.com to learn more about the prayer needs of the persecuted church around the world.

• Commit to praying for believers living in a dangerous or hostile area.

• Make your commitment to Jesus known to family or friends who might be hostile to the message of the Gospel.

Follow the Spirit

What God wants me to do:

_____

_____

_____

Remember Your Thoughts

Special insights I have learned:

_____

_____

_____

More Light on the Text

Acts 14:8–11, 19–23

14:8 And there sat a certain man at Lystra, impotent in his feet, being a cripple from his mother's womb, who never had walked:

In the first century AD, all of the Anatolian Peninsula (modern central Turkey and the area in which Lystra was located) was controlled by the Roman Empire. Rome made Lystra a colony in 6 BC, and the city was incorporated into Galatia at a later date. During Paul's time, the city was known as a key location for learning. The population consisted of Roman soldiers, Greeks and Jews (Acts 16:1, 3), and native Lycaonians (14:11). Paul and Barnabas visited the city several times (in AD 48 and 51) and it was where Paul met Timothy (16:1).

In the ancient world, disability was considered a divine punishment from the gods; it was believed that a person was disabled because either they or their parents had done something wrong or sinned. The belief that disability implied punishment for wrongdoing was extremely stigmatizing. The healings that Jesus and the apostles perform radically denounce this widespread notion. Jesus directly explains to His disciples that rather than a sign of sin, disabilities are an opportunity for God to be glorified (John 9:3).

9 The same heard Paul speak: who stedfastly beholding him, and perceiving that he had faith to be healed, 10 Said with a loud voice, Stand upright on thy feet. And he leaped and walked.

Usually, healing is authorized "in the name of Jesus" in Acts, and typically does not originate solely with the apostles. For example, Peter's healing of a crippled man is done "in the name of Jesus Christ" (3:6). However, here Paul's healing omits this statement. In this verse, the man's faith in the God Paul preached causes his healing. Paul's actions are similar to that of Jesus in the Gospels (cf. Mark 2:1–12; John 5:1–9).

11 And when the people saw what Paul had done, they lifted up their voices, saying in the speech of Lycaonia, The gods are come down to us in the likeness of men.

The people who were prepared to worship Paul and Barnabas as gods were not Greeks or Romans, but native Lycaonians, made evident by the phrase "in the speech of Lycaonia." The local elites and educated people of the land spoke Greek (which was the common language of the Roman Empire) as well as Latin.

The people, upon seeing Paul's healing ability, believed that he and Barnabas were the gods of their belief system incarnated in human form. Archaeological evidence indicates that Hermes and Zeus were the patron gods of this city. Later, the Scripture (v. 12) states that this is who the people believe them to be.

19 And there came thither certain Jews from Antioch and Iconium, who persuaded the people, and having stoned Paul, drew him out of the city, supposing he had been dead.

The New Testament refers to two cities named Antioch—one in Syria and one located in Pisidia (in Asia Minor). Both cities are named after the Seleucid ruler Antiochus IV, a ruthless king who controlled Syria from 175–164 BC. In Antioch of Syria, a vital Jewish disaporan community flourished and Paul began his ministry, also stopping in Antioch of Pisidia.

Stoning was the form of capital punishment prescribed in the Torah. Typically, the act took place outside the walls of the city (Leviticus 24:23; Numbers 15:35–36; 1 Kings 21:13). The witnesses to the offense cast the first stones, and the rest of the people followed (Deuteronomy 17:7); all this was done to purge evil from the community (22:21). A death penalty—often by the act of stoning—was required for a person found guilty of various offenses, including idolatry, prophesying in the name of a foreign god, divination, blasphemy, and adultery.

20 Howbeit, as the disciples stood round about him, he rose up, and came into the city: and the next day he departed with Barnabas to Derbe. 21 And when they had preached the gospel to that city, and had taught many, they returned again to Lystra, and to Iconium, and Antioch, 22 Confirming the souls of the disciples, and exhorting them to continue in the faith, and that we must through much tribulation enter into the kingdom of God. 23 And when they had ordained them elders in every church, and had prayed with fasting, they commended them to the Lord, on whom they believed.

Derbe was located in the south of Galatia, a Roman province established in 25 BC, not far from Iconium.

"The Good News" is synonymous with the Gospel. Christians often understand the term to imply the Good News of Jesus Christ, and in this verse, Paul and Barnabas are obviously preaching the Gospel of Jesus. The term "good news" (Gk. *euangelion*), however, was a term that also had significance with the Roman emperor, Augustus, who regularly applied the term to his decrees. The term was appropriated by the Christian community and applied to the humble, non-elite Jesus. This countered the Roman imperial structure because only the emperor could spread the good news. The appropriation of imperial attributes, like spreading good news, to a subject of the Empire, like Jesus, would have been considered resistant to the Roman Empire. According to Roman state religion, only the emperor was considered a son of god.

In addition, the Jewish community would not have welcomed Paul's telling of the Good

News of Jesus because this belief conflicted with their religious beliefs. It is important to note that the early Christians were still a part of the Jewish synagogue, and thus were considered Jews. Their presence in the synagogues would have caused dissension among the group as they developed their understanding that Jesus was the Messiah, the Son of God.

Sources:

Foxe, John., Berry, W. Grinton., ed. *Foxe's Book of Martyrs.* Grand Rapids, MI: Baker Book House Company, 1998.

Hefley, James & Marti. *By Their Blood: Christian Martyrs of the Twentieth Century.* Grand Rapids, MI: Baker Book House Company. Reprint,1996.

Mandryk, Jason. *Operation World: The Definitive Prayer Guide to Every Nation, 7th Edition.* Colorado Springs, CO: Biblica Publishing, 2010. xxiii.

Marshall, I. Howard. *The Acts of the Apostles: An Introduction and Commentary.* Grand Rapids, MI: William B. Eerdmans Publishing Company, Reprint 1980.

Carter, Warren. *The Roman Empire and the New Testament: An Essential Guide.* Nashville: Abingdon Press, 2006, 83-100.

Say It Correctly

Lystra. **LIE**-strah.
Iconium. ahy-**KOH**-nee-uhm.
Pisidia. pi-**SID**-ee-uh.

Daily Bible Readings

MONDAY
Rejoicing While Struggling and Suffering
(Colossians 1:24–2:5)

TUESDAY
Both Jews and Gentiles Called to Repent
(Acts 17:22–33)

WEDNESDAY
Believing and Suffering in Christ
(Philippians 1:27–30)

THURSDAY
Suffering So Others May Be Saved
(2 Timothy 2:1–10)

FRIDAY
Consolation When Afflicted
(2 Corinthians 1:3–11)

SATURDAY
Speaking Boldly, Forced to Flee
(Acts 14:1–7)

SUNDAY
Proclaiming Christ Faithfully Despite Angry
Opposition
(Acts 14:8–11, 19–23)

Notes

_____

_____

_____

_____

Teaching Tips

Words You Should Know

A. Worship (Matthew 2:2) *proskyneo* (Gk.)—To pay homage to a dignitary.

B. Wise men (2:1) *magos* (Gk.)—Babylonian, Chaldean, Persian, and Median name for astrologers, priests, seers, etc.

Teacher Preparation

Unifying Principle—Giving Gifts of Honor. People often search for the best ways to honor someone they look up to and revere. How can we best honor a special person? The magi traveled a great distance from their own country to Bethlehem in order to give gifts and pay homage to Jesus, the Child born the King of the Jews.

A. Pray that students will have a fresh appreciation of the birth of Jesus.

B. Pay special attention to the Background and be prepared for questions about the relevance of tradition to living out a life of faith.

C. Prepare yourself by reading the Devotional Readings.

O—Open the Lesson

A. Open with prayer, including the Aim for Change.

B. Ask students to list people or positions that are respected and ways that we attempt to honor them. Ask how does this list inform our worship of Jesus?

C. Have the students read the In Focus story and discuss.

P—Present the Scriptures

A. Have volunteers read the Focal Verses.

B. Ask students to discuss the difference between following rules, rituals, and ceremony and worshiping Jesus.

E—Explore the Meaning

A. Direct the class to read and discuss The People, Places, and Times; Background; and In Depth sections.

B. Divide the class into groups to read and discuss Search the Scriptures and Discuss the Meaning. Have someone report group answers to the class.

N—Next Steps for Application

A. Summarize the lesson by connecting Lesson in Our Society and Make It Happen to the Keep in Mind verse.

B. Close with prayer.

Worship Guide

For the Superintendent or Teacher
Theme: Faithful Seekers of the King
Song: "O, Come All Ye Faithful"
Devotional Reading: Isaiah 49:1–7

Faithful Seekers of the King

Bible Background • MATTHEW 2:1–12
Printed Text • MATTHEW 2:1–12 | Devotional Reading • ISAIAH 49:1–7

—————— Aim for Change ——————

By the end of the lesson, we will: CONTRAST the role and motives of the magi with the role and motives of King Herod; APPRECIATE the magi's deep commitment to honor Jesus; and COMMIT to honor God on a daily basis by spending time in His presence.

In Focus

Craig huddled over his office computer. He had "married" this job eight years ago, sacrificing early mornings, late nights, and family time, even taking work home over the weekends. Consequently, Craig missed church services often and neglected time for praying and reading the Bible. One day at work, he read an email announcement: Carla, one of his mentees, had received the promotion for which he had worked so tirelessly.

Torrents of humiliation, anger, resentment, and jealousy obstructed his thoughts and suctioned all the air out of his lungs, constricting his chest. Mouth gaping open, he battled for that first breath, and then the next, before pushing back from his desk and standing to consider his options.

Enough is enough, he decided. He had given more than his share to this job. Bleary eyes scorned the recognition certificates lining his wall. He yearned to rip them off their carefully arranged perches.

Surprisingly, an idea trickled across his mind. What if he put as much energy and effort into honoring Christ as he put into his job? Before he had become such a workaholic, Craig had put Christ first in his life. Craig looked up to heaven and sighed. It was time to use his life to honor Jesus and not for self-promotion.

In this lesson, we learn how the wise men sought to honor Jesus. How do you make it a priority to honor God in your daily life?

—————— Keep in Mind ——————

"And when they were come into the house, they saw the young child with Mary his mother, and fell down, and worshipped him: and when they had opened their treasures, they presented unto him gifts; gold, and frankincense, and myrrh" (Matthew 2:11).

"And when they were come into the house, they saw the young child with Mary his mother, and fell down, and worshipped him: and when they had opened their treasures, they presented unto him gifts; gold, and frankincense, and myrrh" (Matthew 2:11).

Focal Verses

KJV **Matthew 2:1** Now when Jesus was born in Bethlehem of Judaea in the days of Herod the king, behold, there came wise men from the east to Jerusalem,

2 Saying, Where is he that is born King of the Jews? for we have seen his star in the east, and are come to worship him.

3 When Herod the king had heard these things, he was troubled, and all Jerusalem with him.

4 And when he had gathered all the chief priests and scribes of the people together, he demanded of them where Christ should be born.

5 And they said unto him, In Bethlehem of Judaea: for thus it is written by the prophet,

6 And thou Bethlehem, in the land of Judah, art not the least among the princes of Judah: for out of thee shall come a Governor, that shall rule my people Israel.

7 Then Herod, when he had privily called the wise men, enquired of them diligently what time the star appeared.

8 And he sent them to Bethlehem, and said, Go and search diligently for the young child; and when ye have found him, bring me word again, that I may come and worship him also.

9 When they had heard the king, they departed; and, lo, the star, which they saw in the east, went before them, till it came and stood over where the young child was.

10 When they saw the star, they rejoiced with exceeding great joy.

11 And when they were come into the house, they saw the young child with Mary his mother, and fell down, and worshipped him: and when they had opened their treasures, they presented unto him gifts; gold, and frankincense, and myrrh.

NLT **Matthew 2:1** Jesus was born in Bethlehem in Judea, during the reign of King Herod. About that time some wise men from eastern lands arrived in Jerusalem, asking,

2 "Where is the newborn king of the Jews? We saw his star as it rose, and we have come to worship him."

3 King Herod was deeply disturbed when he heard this, as was everyone in Jerusalem.

4 He called a meeting of the leading priests and teachers of religious law and asked, "Where is the Messiah supposed to be born?"

5 "In Bethlehem in Judea," they said, "for this is what the prophet wrote:

6 'And you, O Bethlehem in the land of Judah, are not least among the ruling cities of Judah, for a ruler will come from you who will be the shepherd for my people Israel.'"

7 Then Herod called for a private meeting with the wise men, and he learned from them the time when the star first appeared.

8 Then he told them, "Go to Bethlehem and search carefully for the child. And when you find him, come back and tell me so that I can go and worship him, too!"

9 After this interview the wise men went their way. And the star they had seen in the east guided them to Bethlehem. It went ahead of them and stopped over the place where the child was.

10 When they saw the star, they were filled with joy!

11 They entered the house and saw the child with his mother, Mary, and they bowed down and worshiped him. Then they opened their treasure chests and gave him gifts of gold, frankincense, and myrrh.

12 When it was time to leave, they returned to their own country by another route, for God

12 And being warned of God in a dream that they should not return to Herod, they departed into their own country another way.

had warned them in a dream not to return to Herod.

The People, Places, and Times

Herod the Great. His father was an Edomite, and his mother was an Arabian. The Romans made Herod king of Judea in 40 BC. He was a merciless tyrant with a penchant for building projects, such as rebuilding the second Temple in Jerusalem. Herod hoped his projects would gain him favor with the Jews. However, he used taxes to fund his construction and placed an economic burden on the people of Judea. Additionally, Herod was brutally violent. He is reputed to have killed his wife, brother-in-law, mother-in-law, two of his sons, and a large number of rabbis, in addition to the biblical account of ordering the massacre of all boys from the area in and around Bethlehem who were age two and younger (Matthew 2:16).

Bethlehem. The name means "house of bread" or "granary" and is mentioned five times in Matthew. The town, which is also where David was born, is located five miles south of Jerusalem. As Israel's most popular king, the town of his birth became a royal city. Hundreds of years before Christ, the prophet Micah accurately prophesied that Bethlehem would be the birthplace of the Messiah (Micah 5:2).

How do you give honor to God when facing oppression or injustice from those in power?

Background

God's incarnation is an event that split history. Previous to His coming to live with us, all history looked forward to the Messiah's coming. The significance of His presence here on earth is reflected by the division within the Gregorian calendar. Human history has been categorized in relation to His birth. Dates and events prior His coming ("Before Christ" or BC) are referenced differently than events occurring after His coming (in the year of our Lord, Anno Domini, AD).

This event was celebrated not only by shepherds and angels, but also by wise men from the East. Although Matthew does not state how many wise men followed the star, tradition assigned three travelers to the three gifts, tying their pilgrimage to Psalm 72:10, and declaring the travelers to be kings.

How can we modify the secular celebration of Christmas to incorporate its spiritual significance?

At-A-Glance

1. Required Preparation (Matthew 2:1)
2. Change of Focus (vv. 2–8)
3. Changes of Posture (vv. 9–11)
4. A Different Direction (vv. 4, 12)

In Depth

1. Required Preparation (Matthew 2:1)

The announcement of Christ's birth comes from astrologers from the East (Matthew 2:1). These travelers noticed an unusual, distinctive light in the sky. Understanding its meaning, they were compelled to find and pay homage to a newborn, foreign king. They were Gentiles, experts in astrology, interpreters of dreams, and magicians on a pilgrimage to honor the "one who has been born king." It is important to note that astrology then was very similar to astrology today.

Preparation included bringing gifts and offerings. These actions remind us that we cannot honor God with empty hands or empty hearts. Honoring our King requires us to come prepared to worship with praise and thanksgiving (Psalm 100), a tithe (1 Corinthians 16:2), or a repentant heart (Mark 1:15).

What are you prepared to sacrifice this Christmas season in honor of what God has done on your behalf?

2. Change of Focus (vv. 2–8)

Unlike the wise men whose eyes were trained upward, Herod's eyes were focused on himself and all he could lose to this rival new king. So, he was disturbed when he heard the news. Feeling threatened, he offered lip service, rather than heart service to the Great One the star represented.

The travelers left the comforts of home and obediently followed the star so that they could worship the King of the Jews. In contrast, Herod's home was geographically closer to Bethlehem. However, blind ambition kept Herod chained in Jerusalem, tied to an earthly throne. With the wrong motivation, Herod asked the priests and scribes questions about where the Christ was to be born. But worshiping the King was not his goal.

Why is it hard to choose between focusing on the things of God or focusing on self?

3. Changes of Posture (vv. 9–11)

When the travelers found Jesus, they were overjoyed and came bowing, reflecting the attitude of their heart with the posture of their bodies. Additionally, like the woman with the alabaster box (Matthew 26:7), they also brought gifts that reflected their best and their full commitment—gold, frankincense, and myrrh. These gifts are often said to symbolize different aspects of Jesus' person and work. The gold is said to symbolize His kingship; frankincense worship; and myrrh, a spice used for embalming, His death on the Cross.

Is kneeling or lifting hands in worship a form of honoring God?

4. A Different Direction (vv. 4, 12)

News of the strangers visiting the King probably spread throughout Jerusalem. Furthermore, the scribes and priests understood that the prophecy referred to the birth of their Messiah. From King Herod's inquiry, the scribes and priests could have surmised that Micah's prophecy had been fulfilled. But, unlike the wise men, the religious leaders did not travel from Jerusalem to Bethlehem.

The wise men changed direction twice. Their first change in direction was their travel to Bethlehem. Their second directional change was leaving Bethlehem to return home rather than returning to tell Herod about the King, as Herod had commanded. Throughout their journey, the wise men saw, heard, and lived through the daily changes integral to following and knowing God's leading. Their journey remains a legacy for all who truly yearn to worship God.

Do you recall a time when God rearranged your plans and you willingly followed the new direction?

Search the Scriptures

1. How might a high social position lead to a negative idea about God (Matthew 2:3)?

2. Joy is often associated with the Christmas season (Matthew 2:10; Luke 2:10). How is following Jesus the same as pursuing joy?

Discuss the Meaning

The celebration of Christ's birth is unusual because we are the ones who receive the gifts (Matthew 2:11–12). How can we redirect the celebration to refocus on our King?

Lesson in Our Society

Traditions are customs that tie us to the past and frame our understanding of the present. Celebrating Christmas is a church tradition. Negro spirituals such as "Go Tell it on the Mountain," "Mary Had a Baby," and "The Virgin Mary Had a Baby Boy" provide insight into how enslaved African Americans may have responded to the Christian celebration. They welcomed and worshiped King Jesus who "came down from the glorious kingdom." Despite financial, social, and many other challenges, Christmas remained a time for reconnecting with family and celebrating at church.

Focusing attention on the Christ of Christmas is challenging, often made more difficult by the busyness of the season, which distracts rather than prepares for Bible reflection or worship. Like the travelers from the East, we are to look up, recognize His shining light, and follow where the Bible leads.

What church or family traditions help you celebrate Jesus' birth during the Christmas season?

Make It Happen

• Make an appointment on your calendar to worship Jesus.

• Prepare gifts for others in church, such as a word of encouragement or an act of service.

• Volunteer your time to serve those who are less fortunate during this holiday season as an act of worship to the King.

Follow the Spirit

What God wants me to do:

_____

_____

_____

_____

Remember Your Thoughts

Special insights I have learned:

_____

_____

_____

_____

More Light on the Text
Matthew 2:1–12

1 Now when Jesus was born in Bethlehem of Judaea in the days of Herod the king, behold, there came wise men from the east to Jerusalem.

Matthew sets the stage in this introductory verse by identifying Bethlehem as the place and the time as the days of Herod the King. The Greek word *de* translated "now" is used primarily to inform the reader of the continuing conversation about Jesus, which began in chapter 1. In a sense, the writer seems to be preparing the reader for more surprises. The first chapter began with a statement of genealogy and Joseph's vision of an angel. Chapter 2 continues by explaining the events that followed.

"In the days of Herod" refers to the time period when Herod and his sons ruled over a section of Judea (Matthew 2:1–3). Herod the Great was the ruler in power when Jesus was born. He felt threatened by Jesus' birth and tried to kill Him. Herod had three sons who also ruled after his death: Herod Archelaus, Herod Philip, and Herod Antipas, who beheaded John the Baptist and condemned Jesus to die. The entire Herod family, including Herod the Great, was wicked and murderous (see Luke 13:31–32; 23:6–12; Acts 4:27).

By all accounts, this period was marked by political subjugation, religious interference, and conflict within the territories of Israel.

According to scholars, Rome gave Herod the title "King of the Jews." He was a psychologically troubled man who was so suspicious and paranoid that he executed one of his wives and two of his sons.

The wise men (Gk. *magos*, **MAH-GOS**) were men of rank who more than likely had wealth in abundance; they were considered by some scholars to be kings. Origin, the third century theologian, identified three wise men, probably because of the three gifts.

2 Saying, Where is he that is born King of the Jews? For we have seen his star in the east, and are come to worship him.

These wise men were usually knowledgeable in astrological analysis. We now know that African people were familiar with the constellations, and with that knowledge came the ability to interpret the effect of what was happening in the solar systems. The Dogon and Ibos people of West Africa exemplify such knowledge among African peoples. Of course, the ancient Egyptians knew the movement of heavenly bodies as well. Scholars debate whether these wise men came from Babylon, Persia, or Arabia, as the term "East" could mean any of these locations. Herodotus uses the term for a class of priests in Persia.

Upon finding this new King, the wise men would worship and pay homage to Him. They asked a question that changed the mindset of many throughout history and brought the people of God out of their sleepwalking. No longer would the people of Israel and their pretend king be able to avoid the divine interrogative. By asking this question, these wise ones were forcing Herod and his court to think about the promise of the everlasting God.

Imagine, they were foreigners, yet were the first to understand that the Messiah had come—they had seen His star! Not only did they see the sign, but they also came to worship.

Remember, these men were deeply learned, and not many things gave them a sense of awe. With all of their learning and wealth, they still came to worship. The word "worship" is the Greek word *proskuneo* (**proce-koo-NEH-oh**), meaning "to kiss the hand and prostrate oneself in homage." They came to give reverence and to adore this newborn King.

3 When Herod the king had heard these things, he was troubled, and all Jerusalem with him.

Given the reputation of these keepers of secrets, Herod, who perceived himself to be the foundation of power and sovereignty in Judah, heard this news and was troubled. The implication is that the news of a king of Israelite descent had been born to replace the mean, destructive ruler from Idumea.

The word translated "was troubled" is from the Greek word *tarasso* (**ta-ra-SO**), which means to "stir or to agitate." Simply stated, Herod was angry. This man who had worked so hard to be accepted by the people of Israel now realized there was a threat to his usurped title.

4 And when he had gathered all the chief priests and scribes of the people together, he demanded of them where Christ should be born.

In this verse, we see Herod's strategy for dealing with his troubled heart. First, he called the very people who were guardians of the promise—the chief priests. Note that they were not the high priests. The idea here is that he gathered them together as God would have gathered them. They convened, however, not in response to what God was doing, but to be entertained in Herod's company.

5 And they said unto him, In Bethlehem of Judaea: for thus it is written by the prophet,

We find Matthew using his signature phrase: "thus it is written." The Israelites always looked at what God spoke through the prophets to determine what was happening in the present. This passage states "the prophet," yet has no name attached to it. For the Israelites, the prophet's identity was not important because the prophet simply acted as a foreteller. What is important to remember is that they saw the Scripture as being inspired by God. To them, these things were not mere poetic revelings, but divine insight into the future.

6 And thou Bethlehem, in the land of Judah, art not the least among the princes of Judah: for out of thee shall come a Governor, that shall rule my people Israel.

Verse 6 is a paraphrase of Micah 5:2. This prophecy gave the religious leaders and the people hope that the promises made to their ancestors, via the prophets, would be fulfilled. Bethlehem (which means "house of bread") was the birthplace of their beloved king of Israel, David, who was the monarchical ancestor of the Messiah. The promise is made specifically to include the Israelites who were a part of Judah.

This verse features a correlation to the story of the anointing of David as king. The Greek word *elachistos* (**eh-LACK-see-toce**) is translated "least"; it is the superlative form of the word *elachus,* which means "short." It also means least in terms of size, quantity, or dignity. Recall that David, who was considered the "least," was appointed king, and this event took place in Bethlehem (1 Samuel 16). Even the prophet was misled by David's size. Here the prophet is emphatic: "thou Bethlehem … art not the least."

Implicit is the understanding that people might have considered Bethlehem to be of no consequence, just as David's father considered him to be of no consequence. Yet, in God's eyes, neither David nor Bethlehem were by any means "the least." Economically, Bethlehem did not have the power to rival Jerusalem or Bethel. Yet God was about to do something great with it. Just as God looked beyond David's stature and anointed him king, so it will be with the city of Christ's birth.

The passage states that something substantial—someone of importance—was going to come out of this city. Someone considered to be a nobody would emerge as a chief among leaders. Verse 6 also describes what the leader will do. The Greek word used here for "rule" is *poimaino* (**poy-MY-no**), which means "to tend as a shepherd and to feed the sheep." His work is directed to all people, not just to the people of Bethlehem.

7 Then Herod, when he had privily called the wise men, enquired of them diligently what time the star appeared.

Having discovered that this King would be born among a people he thought inferior, Herod called the wise men privately, to ask them when the Child was to be born. The verb phrase "enquired … diligently" is translated from the Greek word *akriboo* (**ah-kree-BOH-oh**), meaning that he wanted the wise men to provide the exact or specific time of the star's appearance.

8 And he sent them to Bethlehem, and said, Go and search diligently for the young child; and when ye have found him, bring me word again, that I may come and worship him also.

This verse demonstrates Herod's pretension and deception. He is attempting to use these men of wisdom to lead him to the Christ child. He let them depart for the purpose of accomplishing an objective different from what he states. Again, they are to search for the child "diligently," which is the adverbial form of the verb from the previous verse (Gk. *akribos*, **ah-kree-BOCE**). This highlights the determination of those who seek to undermine the work of God.

9 When they had heard the king, they departed; and, lo, the star, which they saw in the east, went before them, till it came and stood over where the young child was.

The wise men did follow a number of the king's suggestions. They did indeed traverse the land. They removed themselves from Herod's presence. They did not stop their journey; they kept on walking in the light of the star.

An important word here is the Greek word *proago* (**pro-AH-go**), which is translated as "go before." The star is now seen as a princely messenger leading an audience into the presence of a powerful king. They were preceded by this divine messenger, which announced to them the place where God, in meekness, now lays.

Similarly, the light of God's Word will lead us until we come to the time and place that He intends for us. The light of God's presence will lead us to fulfill His purpose in our lives.

10 When they saw the star, they rejoiced with exceeding great joy.

Here we read the wise men's response. As you recall, when they were talking with Herod, the star was hidden from their sight. In verse 10, "they saw the star." The word "saw" denotes a sense of realization. This second sight affirmed the experience they had back in their home town. Their knowledge was now confirmed by seeing the star. We are told that they "rejoiced with exceeding great joy."

11 And when they were come into the house, they saw the young child with Mary his mother, and fell down, and worshiped him: and when they had opened their

treasures, they presented unto him gifts; gold, and frankincense, and myrrh.

The magi came from the east, and the star guided them to the exact location in Bethlehem. They brought three gifts: gold, for Jesus as king; sweet-smelling frankincense, for burning in worship and prayer for Jesus the divine; and the embalming spice myrrh, for Jesus the crucified Savior.

Much has been made of the symbolism of the gifts. Gold was a sign of wealth representing the king's or queen's ability to provide for his or her subjects. It was also used for religious ornamentation. The word "frankincense" (Gk. *libanos*, **LEE-bah-NOCE**) is taken from the Hebrew *lebonah*, which refers to the incense tree, as well as to incense itself. Myrrh (Gk. *smurna*, **sm-EARN-ah**) was an ointment used for burial in many African traditions. The perfumed or scented oil is still used in many parts of Africa and Asia today.

These wise ones had saved their treasures so they would able to give. In fact, the word "treasure" (Gk. *thesauros*, **theh-sow-ROCE**) could also mean a deposit of wealth. We are told that they offered gifts to Him. The word for "gifts" is *doron* (Gk. **doe-ROAN**), which refers to "a present," but can specifically imply the sense of making a sacrifice.

12 And being warned of God in a dream that they should not return to Herod, they departed into their own country another way.

This verse deals with divine intervention to save the wise men from serving as instruments for carrying out Herod's work. We are told that the Lord appeared and spoke to them in a dream (Gk. *onar*, **OH-nar**), which means an utterance similar to what occurred in oracles. In a sense, it means after they had seen the Lord, they could not bear to think of Herod and his request. The word translated "warned" (Gk.

chrematizo, **kray-mah-TEED-zo**) means that they were called or admonished. God revealed something to them. For the first time in all of these conversations and in their long journey, God speaks to the wise ones. This dream was so authoritative that they did not return to Herod. Instead, they went back to their homeland another way.

Sources:
Blainey, Geoffrey. *A Short History of Christianity.* Lamham, MD: First Rowman & Littlefield, 2014.
Comay, Joan, and Ronald Brownrigg. *Who's Who in the Bible.* Vol. 1. New York: Bonanza Books, 1980.
Chadwick, Owen. *A History of Christianity.* New York: St. Martin's Press, 1995.
Edwards, David L. *Christianity: The First Two Thousand Years.* Maryknoll, NY: Orbus Books, 1997.
France, R. T. *The Gospel According To Matthew: An Introduction and Commentary.* Grand Rapids, MI: Eerdmans Publishing, 1985.
Latourette, Kenneth Scott. *History of Christianity.* New York: Harper Brothers Publishers, 1953.
Morris, Leon. *The Gospel According to Matthew.* Grand Rapids, MI: Eerdmans Publishing, 1992.
Tasker, R.V.G., ed. *The Gospel According to St. Matthew: An Introduction and Commentary.* Grand Rapids, MI: Eerdmans Publishing, 1977.

Say It Correctly

Herod. **HEH**-rud.
Judea. joo-**DAY**-uh.

Daily Bible Readings

MONDAY
God Saves Moses
(Exodus 1:22–2:10)

TUESDAY
Light to the Nations
(Isaiah 42:1–9)

WEDNESDAY
A Peaceful Ruler from Bethlehem
(Micah 5:1–5)

THURSDAY
Faithful to God's Plan
(Matthew 1:18–25)

FRIDAY
Escape for Family; Massacre of Infants
(Matthew 2:13–18)

SATURDAY
Holy Family Settles in Nazareth
(Matthew 2:19–23)

SUNDAY
Wise Men Seek, Then Worship Jesus
(Matthew 2:1–12)

Notes

_____

_____

_____

_____

Teaching Tips

Words You Should Know

A. Calling (Ephesians 4:4) *klesis* (Gk.)—The invitation to experience special privilege and responsibility.

B. Perfecting (v. 12) *katarismos* (Gk.)—To make complete, furnish, equip, or prepare.

Teacher Preparation

Unifying Principle—United We Stand. Many people search all their lives for something that will make them feel grounded, whole, and in sync with life. Where can they find that something? Paul told the Ephesians that even though they had many different gifts, their faith in Christ would bring them unity and help them grow together in love.

A. Pray for unity in your church, ministry, or school.

B. Read the passage in several translations.

C. Read the companion lesson in the *Precepts For Living*® Study Guide.

O—Open the Lesson

A. Ask one of the students to open with prayer.

B. Introduce the lesson, highlighting the Keep in Mind Verse.

C. Inform the class they are all uniquely gifted, and set a tone of excitement for the session.

P—Present the Scriptures

A. Ask volunteers to read the Focal Verses.

B. Discuss The People, Places, and Times, Background, and In Depth sections.

E—Explore the Meaning

A. Answer the questions from the Search the Scriptures and Discuss the Meaning sections.

B. Read the Lesson in Our Society section.

N—Next Steps for Application

A. Encourage the class to apply the Make It Happen section.

B. Ask for a volunteer to close in prayer.

Worship Guide

For the Superintendent or Teacher
Theme: Faith to Unite
Song: "Love Lifted Me"
Devotional Reading: Psalm 68:1–6, 15–20, 32–35

Faith to Unite

Bible Background • EPHESIANS 4
Printed Text • EPHESIANS 4:1–16 | Devotional Reading • PSALM 68:1–6, 15–20, 32–35

—————— Aim for Change ——————

By the end of this lessons, we will: AGREE that our identity in Christ is foundational to Christian unity; VALUE the diversity of spiritual giftedness in the church; and COMMIT to exercising spiritual gifts according to Scripture.

In Focus

Junior was the oldest of three sons. He loved soccer and was a math whiz. The middle son loved basketball and reading, and the youngest was a star pitcher who also excelled on the debate team. The three were often in competition with each other trying to prove who was strongest, smartest, and the best.

Tension ruled the household as each son vied for his father's approval. Because of the constant arguments, family gatherings were never fun.

At a family reunion, emotions erupted. When photos of the three sons flashed on the screen, the brothers started to make fun of one another with harsh, embarrassing put-downs.

Their dad had enough! He asked his sons to excuse themselves and they went into the hall for a heart-to-heart talk. "Listen, this competition between the three of you is way out of hand. Pride is the problem here, and there's a serious lack of respect for one another. Yes, you all are different, but different doesn't mean better or worse. It just means different."

The boys stood silently, looking down at their shoes. Their dad continued, "Boys, I'm so embarrassed. Your mother is, too. We're family! We're here to support one another. Each of you has gifts and talents. It's not about what you do, but who you are."

His father put his arms around his sons. "Let's huddle," Dad said. "We're a team—it could be soccer, basketball, or baseball, doesn't matter! We're a team. We're in this together."

Each one of us has been given unique gifts by God. How important is it to support, respect, and value one another?

—————— Keep in Mind ——————

"I therefore, the prisoner of the Lord, beseech you that ye walk worthy of the vocation wherewith ye are called, With all lowliness and meekness, with longsuffering, forbearing one another in love; Endeavouring to keep the unity of the Spirit in the bond of peace" (Ephesians 4:1–3).

"I therefore, the prisoner of the Lord, beseech you that ye walk worthy of the vocation wherewith ye are called, With all lowliness and meekness, with longsuffering, forbearing one another in love; Endeavouring to keep the unity of the Spirit in the bond of peace" (Ephesians 4:1–3).

Focal Verses

KJV **Ephesians 4:1** I therefore, the prisoner of the Lord, beseech you that ye walk worthy of the vocation wherewith ye are called,

2 With all lowliness and meekness, with longsuffering, forbearing one another in love;

3 Endeavoring to keep the unity of the Spirit in the bond of peace.

4 There is one body, and one Spirit, even as ye are called in one hope of your calling;

5 One Lord, one faith, one baptism,

6 One God and Father of all, who is above all, and through all, and in you all.

7 But unto every one of us is given grace according to the measure of the gift of Christ.

8 Wherefore he saith, When he ascended up on high, he led captivity captive, and gave gifts unto men.

9 (Now that he ascended, what is it but that he also descended first into the lower parts of the earth?

10 He that descended is the same also that ascended up far above all heavens, that he might fill all things.)

11 And he gave some, apostles; and some, prophets; and some, evangelists; and some, pastors and teachers;

12 For the perfecting of the saints, for the work of the ministry, for the edifying of the body of Christ:

13 Till we all come in the unity of the faith, and of the knowledge of the Son of God, unto a perfect man, unto the measure of the stature of the fulness of Christ:

14 That we henceforth be no more children, tossed to and fro, and carried about with every wind of doctrine, by the sleight of men, and cunning craftiness, whereby they lie in wait to deceive;

NLT **Ephesians 4:1** Therefore I, a prisoner for serving the Lord, beg you to lead a life worthy of your calling, for you have been called by God.

2 Always be humble and gentle. Be patient with each other, making allowance for each other's faults because of your love.

3 Make every effort to keep yourselves united in the Spirit, binding yourselves together with peace.

4 For there is one body and one Spirit, just as you have been called to one glorious hope for the future.

5 There is one Lord, one faith, one baptism,

6 one God and Father of all, who is over all, in all, and living through all.

7 However, he has given each one of us a special gift through the generosity of Christ.

8 That is why the Scriptures say, "When he ascended to the heights, he led a crowd of captives and gave gifts to his people."

9 Notice that it says "he ascended." This clearly means that Christ also descended to our lowly world.

10 And the same one who descended is the one who ascended higher than all the heavens, so that he might fill the entire universe with himself.

11 Now these are the gifts Christ gave to the church: the apostles, the prophets, the evangelists, and the pastors and teachers.

12 Their responsibility is to equip God's people to do his work and build up the church, the body of Christ.

13 This will continue until we all come to such unity in our faith and knowledge of God's Son that we will be mature in the Lord, measuring up to the full and complete standard of Christ.

14 Then we will no longer be immature like children. We won't be tossed and blown about

15 But speaking the truth in love, may grow up into him in all things, which is the head, even Christ:

16 From whom the whole body fitly joined together and compacted by that which every joint supplieth, according to the effectual working in the measure of every part, maketh increase of the body unto the edifying of itself in love.

by every wind of new teaching. We will not be influenced when people try to trick us with lies so clever they sound like the truth.

15 Instead, we will speak the truth in love, growing in every way more and more like Christ, who is the head of his body, the church.

16 He makes the whole body fit together perfectly. As each part does its own special work, it helps the other parts grow, so that the whole body is healthy and growing and full of love.

The People, Places, and Times

Paul. A well-educated Roman citizen, Paul's birth name was Saul. He was a Pharisee who persecuted Christians as proof of his zeal for the Jewish faith and way of life. On such a mission on the road to Damascus, he had a remarkable encounter with Jesus. Shortly after, he learned of his call from God to take His "name before the Gentiles, and kings, and the children of Israel" (Acts 9:15). As an apostle, Paul's life exemplified one of great sacrifice and persecution. He wrote about his experiences in hopes of drawing people to Christ and to strengthen and mature believers.

Ephesians. The church of Ephesus was first started by Paul. He visited the city at the end of his second missionary journey (Acts 18:18–21). Then he returned on his third missionary journey and taught there for approximately two years (Acts 19:1–41). So many people turned from worshiping the Greek goddess Artemis that a riot was started by the silversmiths who created her idols. Paul wrote an epistle to the church, now known as the book of Ephesians. In the letter, Paul does not address a specific problem. Many have speculated that the church at Ephesus, while not absent of problems, was a healthy New Testament church.

If the apostle Paul were to write to your church today, would he consider it a healthy church? Why or why not?

Background

Paul writes to the Ephesians while under house arrest. His testimony about Christ had taken him all the way to Rome, where he waited to go on trial before Caesar. During this time, he sent a letter to the Ephesians explaining great mysteries of the faith and specifically the mystery of the church. While the first part of the letter is a theological explanation (1:1–3:21), the latter part of the letter is a practical exhortation or encouragement (4:1–6:24).

In today's verses, Paul begins with the encouragement of unity in diversity. The imagery of the "body of Christ" is powerful because it calls all believers to rise above their individual circumstances and backgrounds to focus on Christ. The challenge, of course, is functioning as a unified body when people are so different. While the task of unity has not become any easier over time, the need for it is as urgent now as when Christ first called His believers to be one, just as He and the Father are one (John 17:21).

What contemporary issue(s) causes the greatest divide in the church?

207

At-A-Glance

1. One Calling (Ephesians 4:1–3)
2. One Hope (vv. 4–10)
3. One Church (vv. 11–16)

into which all believers are united by the Holy Spirit, according to Jesus' own promise (Acts 1:8). The one hope of our calling, which comes from our one Lord, is exercised in one faith, and is expressed within one baptism.

How does love of God and others support unity amongst believers?

In Depth

1. One Calling (Ephesians 4:1–3)

Paul describes himself as a prisoner of the Lord, yet this is in contrast to his actual pedigree as a Pharisee and a "Hebrew of Hebrews" (Philippians 3:4–5). Although Paul had every right to retain his stature within the Jewish community, he prefers instead to be identified by his calling to advance the Gospel of Christ through great suffering (Acts 9:1–20).

Paul's instruction to answer the call with "lowliness and meekness, forbearing one another in love" helps us focus on God's intentions for us; when we put aside our own desires and ideas, we can put our attention where it belongs. Paul makes it clear that just as he has been called to be a prisoner of the Gospel, so too must everyone else cast aside their worldly possessions and enter a similar state of servitude to answer the call of Christ.

How does division in our churches hinder our witness for Christ?

2. One Hope (vv. 4–10)

Hope expresses expectation. It is not a conditional statement, which allows room for chance or human failure to factor in; instead, it is an assurance as we focus our attention on things to come. All believers have this hope— Jesus is coming again! We will be united eternally with Christ, so let's be in unity now. The resurrection hope is for all believers no matter their ethnic background or social class.

When Paul speaks about "one body and one Spirit," he refers to the body of Christ,

3. One Church (vv. 11–16)

Paul acknowledges that apostleship, prophecy, evangelism, and even pastoring and teaching the flock of God are all God's gifts, which He gives to whomever He chooses. These gifts are not to cause division, but rather to equip or train believers. The word "equip" evokes a doctor who sets a bone during surgery; with the gifts in operation, the church will not be out of joint. Whether the gift is to pastor, teach, or preach, the goal is the same.

Most importantly, the church is the body of Christ. We are all called and encouraged to occupy our proper place and exercise the gifts uniquely given to us by God. The body is "fitly joined together," which implies again that nothing is out of joint. The gifts assure completeness (v. 16). The goal for the body—the saints—is that we mature into the knowledge of the Son of God.

With all of the gifts operating as they should, the church will be vibrant and effective with everything it needs to guard against false teaching. Believers will not be confused and deceived by the "sleight of men" and "cunning craftiness" (v. 16). The diverse gifts were given to guarantee that the church matures and grows in love, just like a healthy body.

How do the diverse gifts of the church complement each other to fulfill our holy mission?

Search the Scriptures

1. How should we respond when people attempt to justify alternate routes to God, or alternative religions (Ephesians 4:4–5)?

2. How do you know if you have been "called" for a particular work of ministry (vv. 11–12)?

Discuss the Meaning

1. What does it mean to "walk worthy" of the vocation to which we are called?

2. How can imperfect people attempt to "walk worthy" in this way? What do we have at our disposal that makes such a walk possible?

Lesson in Our Society

Our world has made a church out of celebrity and a god out of money. How can we aspire to financial success and stability without lapsing into idolatrous behavior? The simplest answer is to remain committed to seeking God for all that we need. Some may encourage a more extreme avoidance of popular culture or social interaction, but that would deny others the chance to see Christ at work in us. We should, therefore, be confident in knowing what we believe, establish healthy boundaries, and keep our trust firmly in God.

How is unity developed and maintained among the body of believers?

Make It Happen

• Take time to discover your spiritual gifts and ask for opportunities to serve.

• Encourage three brothers and sisters in Christ. Give them a call or send an encouraging text.

• Pray for the leaders of the church that they would be faithful in their task of "equipping the saints for the work of the ministry."

Follow the Spirit

What God wants me to do:

_____

_____

Remember Your Thoughts

Special insights I have learned:

_____

_____

_____

_____

More Light on the Text

Ephesians 4:1–16

1 I therefore, the prisoner of the Lord, beseech you that ye walk worthy of the vocation wherewith ye are called.

Using an emphatic first person pronoun "I" (Gk. *ego,* **EH-go**), Paul begins his appeal by reintroducing himself, as in 3:1, as the prisoner of the Lord. This probably is to assert his apostolic authority. The use of the conjunction "therefore" adds the emphatic nature of the *ego.* The phrase can then be reworded as, "Therefore (i.e., in view of the things God has done through history), I myself, a prisoner of the Lord appeal to you." The phrase "the prisoner of the Lord" probably means that Paul was both a prisoner of Jesus in loyal and loving obedience as an apostle, and a prisoner for Christ because he was under arrest and in custody.

"To walk" (Gk. *peripateo,* **pair-ee-pa-TEH-oh**) is an idiomatic way of saying "to lead a life, conduct oneself, or behave" (2:2). Paul urges them to conduct their lives in such manner that would match their calling, i.e., their commitment in Christ. Since the Christian life is a response to God's call and willing obedience to Him, life is lived moment by moment and day by day in a way that demonstrates true commitment.

2 With all lowliness and meekness, with longsuffering, forbearing one another in love.

Paul gives five characteristics of such a life: lowliness, meekness, longsuffering (patience), mutual forbearance, and love. The unity of the church, Paul seems to imply, starts with individuals. Earlier, Paul prays to God that "Christ may dwell in (our) hearts by faith, that (we may be) rooted and grounded in love" (Ephesians 3:17); love, he implies, is the soil in which we must grow and the foundation in which we must build a unified church.

To maintain unity in the church, we should walk in lowliness (Gk. *tapeinophrosune*, **ta-pay-no-fro-SOO-nay**)—a debasing quality and unacceptable virtue especially among the Greek world, and even today. The word is better translated "lowliness of mind," a state of mind that prioritizes others' worth and value over the self. The same mind was in Christ—He emptied Himself and took the form of a servant even unto death (Philippians 2:3–8). We are also expected to walk in meekness (Gk. *praotes*, **prah-OH-tees**) or gentleness. Meekness is strength under control—a gentle nature that does not want to fight or impose upon others. It defers to those who might harm you, which is related to the next virtue. We are also called to be long-suffering (Gk. *makrothumia*, **ma-crow-thew-ME-ah**) which means patience or endurance, i.e., not seeking revenge or being aggravated by others. This is a virtue God shows to us through Christ. Forbearing one another (Gk. *anechomai*, **ah-NEH-kho-my**) has the idea of putting up with, or enduring and bearing with, someone's mistakes or attitude. It speaks of being tolerant toward others and having a mutual understanding.

3 Endeavoring to keep the unity of the Spirit in the bond of peace.

Paul identifies the nature of the church's unity as the unity of the Spirit. He urges the Church to endeavor (Gk. *spoudazo*, **spoo-DOD-zo**) to keep the unity of the Spirit in the bond of peace. The word *spoudazo*, translated in different ways in the New Testament (e.g., "diligent," Titus 3:12; "study," 2 Timothy 2:15; "do diligence," 2 Timothy 4:9), means "to spare no effort" or leave no stone unturned in order to preserve the unity of the Spirit. In other words, we should do our utmost to preserve the Spirit's unity.

Paul could mean one of two things when he refers to "the unity of the Spirit." First, some translate it to mean the Christian's spiritual harmony, using the small letter "s" for spirit (also meaning "heart" or "soul"). The idea then is that Christian unity is in the heart; it does not lie in one set of thoughts, nor in one form and mode of worship, but in one heart and one mind. The second, and more accepted meaning, is the unity which the Spirit creates or gives, starting in the individual hearts of its members. Preserving this unity therefore depends on both individual and corporate efforts of all members of the body of Christ, and begins with the attitudes in our hearts.

4 There is one body, and one Spirit, even as ye are called in one hope of your calling; 5 One Lord, one faith, one baptism, 6 One God and Father of all, who is above all, and through all, and in you all.

In these three verses, Paul declares implicitly that the unity of the church arises from the unity of the Godhead, making deliberate reference to the Trinity. First, the church is one body because there is one Spirit by which it was created. Earlier, in Ephesians 1:23, Paul calls the church the body of Christ, comprised of both Jews and Gentiles. The unity of this body is due to the work of the Holy Spirit, who also indwells the body. One Spirit unifies and works through the body, which is the church.

This cluster of phrases describes the greatness and magnitude of this one God whom all Christians have in common as Father. The God, whom the Jews acclaim as "One" in opposition to the Gentiles' many gods, is now the Father of all. This Father God is "above all" (i.e., over all things). This refers to the sovereign, supreme, and transcendent nature of God. He is "through all," which probably speaks of active participation in the activities of His creation—human lives in particular. He is "in you all" with particular reference to the church at Ephesus, which is comprised of the Jewish and Gentile believers, and it also refers indeed to the universal church.

7 But unto every one of us is given grace according to the measure of the gift of Christ. 8 Wherefore he saith, When he ascended up on high, he led captivity captive, and gave gifts unto men.

Paul begins the section with the conjunction "but," which suggests that in spite of the unity (oneness in the body), each member has room for individuality as well, which is evident in the giving of gifts. Each one of us, Paul says, "is given grace according to the measure of the gift of Christ." The word for "grace" (Gk. *charis,* **KHAR-eese**) used here is the same grace by which sinners receive forgiveness (2:5, 8); they both are God's favor to those who don't deserve it. The difference is that God's favor comes in different forms at different times in a believer's walk—sometimes as forgiveness of sins, other times as the gift that Christ is pleased to give.

The sentence "When he ascended up on high, he led captivity captive, and gave gifts unto men" refers to Christ's ascension to the right hand of the Father as conqueror over death, defeating Satan and his agents. Jesus liberated those who were bound and took them like captives into heaven; they are secure. From there He gives gifts to the church, which might refer to the bestowing of gifts by the Holy Spirit.

9 (Now that he ascended, what is it but that he also descended first into the lower parts of the earth? 10 He that descended is the same also that ascended up far above all heavens, that he might fill all things.)

As an aside, Paul offers support and elaboration of Christ's ascension (vv. 9–10). Here, Paul argues—by pointing to the death and resurrection of Christ—that for Christ to ascend into heaven, He must have descended and snatched the keys of death, hell, and the grave. Paul alluded to the same idea earlier in the letter (1:20–22), and explains this further in his letter to the Philippians (2:6–10, where he talks about how Christ humbled Himself to die on the Cross but was then resurrected and exalted above every created thing).

Paul insists that the One who descended is the same who ascended far above everything else, that He might fill all things (v. 10). The phrase "fill all things" (Gk. *pleroo,* **pleh-ROH-oh**) means "to accomplish" or "fulfill" all things. It seems to speak about completing His mission. The purpose of His ascension into heaven is then to free Him to accomplish fully the purpose for which He descended. One of those purposes is the distribution of gifts to the church by the Holy Spirit.

11 And he gave some, apostles; and some, prophets; and some, evangelists; and some, pastors and teachers; 12 For the perfecting of the saints, for the work of the ministry, for the edifying of the body of Christ:

Here, Paul lists five administrative offices given to the church: apostles, prophets, evangelists, pastors, and teachers. The word "apostle" is used in three ways in the New

Testament. First, it simply means "the ones sent" (John 13:16). In this case, it applies to every individual Christian, for we are all sent as ambassadors of Christ to proclaim Him to the world. Second, there were apostles of the church (2 Corinthians 8:23), who were sent out by the church as messengers and missionaries. Third, a small group had a special designation as apostles, consisting of the Twelve (including Matthias), Paul, and James the brother of Jesus. They were eyewitnesses to the risen Lord, chosen and authorized by Christ (Acts 1:21, 22; 10:40–41; 1 Corinthians 9:1; 15:8–9). The second designation is probably the sense in which Paul uses the word here.

The next gift is the prophets with special ability from God to give guidance to the Christian community and declare His will (e.g., Acts 13:1–4). Next are the evangelists, preachers, or those who proclaim the Gospel (e.g., Philip, Acts 21:8; and Timothy, 2 Timothy 4:5). Then we have the pastors or shepherds, who are also teachers who give instructions. Some argue that pastors and teachers are two names for the same ministry, but they can be two separate ministries since we have some Christian teachers who are not pastors. However, all five relate to one form of teaching or the other, and they are set in the church to fulfill certain purposes and functions. These functions are twofold: to equip ("perfecting") the saints for the work of ministry, and to build up ("edifying") the body of Christ.

The word translated "perfecting" is the Greek word *katartismos* (**kah-tar-tees-mahs**), which means "to equip, to prepare, or to make ready." Therefore, the function of apostles, prophets, evangelists, pastors, and teachers is to prepare God's people for the work of ministry or service. The same word for ministry is used when Christ said that He came to serve rather than to be served (Mark 10:45), and for Peter's mother-in-law serving the physical needs of her visitors (Mark 1:31). These various teachers are endowed with the grace of God to prepare people to work within the church community.

The second function of the people endowed with special gifts is to edify or build up the body of Christ. The word used here in the King James Version, "edifying" (Gk. *oikodome*, **oy-ko-do-MEH**), has an architectural undertone. It means building a house, but is used figuratively here to refer to building up the members of the body of Christ.

13 Till we all come in the unity of the faith, and of the knowledge of the Son of God, unto a perfect man, unto the measure of the stature of the fulness of Christ: 14 That we henceforth be no more children, tossed to and fro, and carried about with every wind of doctrine, by the sleight of men, and cunning craftiness, whereby they lie in wait to deceive.

While the major twofold function and purpose of the gifts are to equip God's people for the work of the ministry and to build up the body, the ultimate goal is threefold. Here, the word "unity" modifies both faith and knowledge. We are to continue to grow until we attain a complete unity of the faith (cf. v. 3, unity of the Spirit). Paul speaks of Jews and Gentiles being knit together in the belief of the Gospel of Christ (v. 5). The ministry of all members will also help the church grow to the full knowledge of Jesus. The apostle has already mentioned our knowledge of God (1:17); now the focus is on the knowledge of Christ. The aspiration of all Christians should be to attain this unity, which is based on our mutual understanding of who Christ is.

The full faith and knowledge of the Son of God leads to maturity and being "perfect." "Perfect" (Gk. *teleios*, **TEH-lay-oce**) here refers to that which has reached the age of maturity or adulthood, rather than moral perfection. Although some interpret this as individual maturity in Christ, which is also a New Testament concept, the maturity here refers to the whole body of Christ. This maturity or perfection is measured "unto the measure of the stature of the fulness of Christ," i.e. according to Christ's standards. In verse 7, Christ is the measure of God's grace. Here, He is the measure or the yardstick of all maturity.

Paul uses the picture of a boat in a rough sea being tossed to and fro by the waves and "carried about by every wind of doctrine." Some people cannot make up their mind, but often change from one opinion to another, according to the last teaching they heard, or books they read, or information they received. There is no stability in their thoughts. Such people are easy prey to those who wish to deceive them.

"Sleight" is a word we don't use today except in the phrase "sleight of hand"; it means cunning and slyness. The Greek word it translates, *kubeia* (**koo-BAY-ah**), literally means "dice playing" and is used metaphorically here to describe the deception, trickery, and manipulation of unscrupulous people who take advantage of people's ignorance.

15 But speaking the truth in love, may grow up into him in all things, which is the head, even Christ.

Paul moves from the mark of immaturity, which is doctrinal instability, to the qualities of mature Christianity, which will promote unity and peace within the body. These qualities are seemingly a rare combination: truth and love. We can communicate the truth so that unity can be maintained, Paul says, by speaking the truth in love. This statement also carries the idea that we should speak with truthfulness and genuineness to one another as opposed to insincerity and cunning behavior, aiming to deceive others for our own selfish gain.

16 From whom the whole body fitly joined together and compacted by that which every joint supplieth, according to the effectual working in the measure of every part, maketh increase of the body unto the edifying of itself in love.

Paul then employs biological metaphors, using the human anatomy, to describe the church's relationship with Christ. Paul compares the natural body and Christ's mystical body, the church. As the body has many component parts which are joined fittingly together by different ligaments to the head, and each part works corporately with other parts, so it is with the church. Love is the important trait that controls the functionality of all parts of the church body in relation to one another (vv. 2, 15–16, 5:2).

Sources:
LaTourette, Kenneth Scott. *A History of Christianity: Volume I: Beginnings to 1500.* San Francisco, CA: Harper Collins Publishers, 1975.
Danker, Frederick William. *A Greek-English Lexicon of the New Testament & Other Early Christian Literature, 3rd Ed.* Chicago, IL: the University of Chicago Press, 2000.

Say It Correctly

Endeavoring. in-**DEV**-or-ing.
Effectual. ef-fek-**CHOO**-ul.

Daily Bible Readings

MONDAY
Live the New Life in Christ
(Ephesians 4:17–24)

TUESDAY
Live as Imitators of God
(Ephesians 4:25–5:2)

WEDNESDAY
Disciplined Living in Christ
(Colossians 3:1–11)

THURSDAY
Leadership Gifts in the Church
(1 Corinthians 12:27–31)

FRIDAY
Accept the Gifts of Weaker Members
(1 Corinthians 12:12–13, 22–26)

SATURDAY
Experience the Unity of Spirit
(1 Peter 3:8–12)

SUNDAY
Seek the Common Life from Above
(Ephesians 4:1–16)

Notes

_____

_____

_____

_____

Teaching Tips

Words You Should Know

A. Defile (Daniel 1:8) *ga'al* (Heb.)—To pollute, desecrate, stain.

B. Countenance (vv. 13, 15) *mar'eh* (Heb.)—Sight, appearance.

Teacher Preparation

Unifying Principle—Living Your Convictions. People find themselves confronted by contradictory requirements from different sources of authority. How do we resolve such conflicts? Daniel's active faith combined with his tact helped him resolve his conflict and remain obedient to God in terms of dietary requirements.

A. Pray that students will stand up for their convictions.

B. Read the Scripture in at least two translations.

C. Read the companion lesson in the *Precepts For Living®* Study Guide.

O—Open the Lesson

A. Ask a student to read the Devotional Reading (Psalm 56) for the class.

B. Pray for the class.

C. Have the class read the In Focus story.

P—Present the Scriptures

A. Have the class read the Focal Verses.

B. Have the class read The People, Places, and Times; Background; and In Depth sections.

E—Explore the Meaning

A. Answer the questions in the Search the Scriptures and Discuss the Meaning sections.

B. Read the Lesson in Our Society section.

N—Next Steps for Application

A. Encourage the students to apply the Make It Happen section in the coming week.

B. Have someone pray to close out the class.

Worship Guide

For the Superintendent or Teacher
Theme: A Sincere Faith
Song: "Lord, You Are Welcome In This Place"
Devotional Reading: Psalm 56

A Sincere Faith

Bible Background • DANIEL 1
Printed Text • DANIEL 1:8–21 | Devotional Reading • PSALM 56

—— Aim for Change ——

By the end of the lesson, we will: ANALYZE the choice that Daniel and his friends faced and that choice's outcome; ASPIRE to have the faith of Daniel when confronted with contradictory directives from authorities; and IDENTIFY similar situations that call for the exercise of faith.

—— In Focus ——

Taylor had been working at her new company a little over a month, and she had just been invited by her co-workers out to lunch. While at lunch her co-worker Tina asked if she was doing anything for the weekend. She had not been out in a while, and replied that she did not have plans yet. Tina asked if she would like to go to a party in a what Taylor knew was a neighborhood known for drug dealing.

Tina said, "Most of us who work here hang out around there together, and it would be cool to have you join us." Two of the other co-workers at the table nodded in agreement.

Taylor thought about it for a second. She remembered her cousin almost overdosing at a party in that same neighborhood. She knew that God had not called her to be involved in that kind of environment.

"No, I think I'll pass. I'm not really into the party scene like that. But let me pay for lunch today, I appreciate you all inviting me."

Sometimes God places us in situations where our faith will be tested. Have you ever been tempted to compromise the standards of your faith to be accepted by others?

—— Keep in Mind ——

"But Daniel purposed in his heart that he would not defile himself with the portion of the king's meat, nor with the wine which he drank" (from Daniel 1:8).

"But Daniel purposed in his heart that he would not defile himself with the portion of the king's meat, nor with the wine which he drank" (from Daniel 1:8).

Focal Verses

KJV **Daniel 1:8** But Daniel purposed in his heart that he would not defile himself with the portion of the king's meat, nor with the wine which he drank: therefore he requested of the prince of the eunuchs that he might not defile himself.

9 Now God had brought Daniel into favour and tender love with the prince of the eunuchs.

10 And the prince of the eunuchs said unto Daniel, I fear my lord the king, who hath appointed your meat and your drink: for why should he see your faces worse liking than the children which are of your sort? then shall ye make me endanger my head to the king.

11 Then said Daniel to Melzar, whom the prince of the eunuchs had set over Daniel, Hananiah, Mishael, and Azariah,

12 Prove thy servants, I beseech thee, ten days; and let them give us pulse to eat, and water to drink.

13 Then let our countenances be looked upon before thee, and the countenance of the children that eat of the portion of the king's meat: and as thou seest, deal with thy servants.

14 So he consented to them in this matter, and proved them ten days.

15 And at the end of ten days their countenances appeared fairer and fatter in flesh than all the children which did eat the portion of the king's meat.

16 Thus Melzar took away the portion of their meat, and the wine that they should drink; and gave them pulse.

17 As for these four children, God gave them knowledge and skill in all learning and wisdom: and Daniel had understanding in all visions and dreams.

18 Now at the end of the days that the king had said he should bring them in, then the prince of the eunuchs brought them in before Nebuchadnezzar.

NLT **Daniel 1:8** But Daniel was determined not to defile himself by eating the food and wine given to them by the king. He asked the chief of staff for permission not to eat these unacceptable foods.

9 Now God had given the chief of staff both respect and affection for Daniel.

10 But he responded, "I am afraid of my lord the king, who has ordered that you eat this food and wine. If you become pale and thin compared to the other youths your age, I am afraid the king will have me beheaded."

11 Daniel spoke with the attendant who had been appointed by the chief of staff to look after Daniel, Hananiah, Mishael, and Azariah.

12 "Please test us for ten days on a diet of vegetables and water," Daniel said.

13 "At the end of the ten days, see how we look compared to the other young men who are eating the king's food. Then make your decision in light of what you see."

14 The attendant agreed to Daniel's suggestion and tested them for ten days.

15 At the end of the ten days, Daniel and his three friends looked healthier and better nourished than the young men who had been eating the food assigned by the king.

16 So after that, the attendant fed them only vegetables instead of the food and wine provided for the others.

17 God gave these four young men an unusual aptitude for understanding every aspect of literature and wisdom. And God gave Daniel the special ability to interpret the meanings of visions and dreams.

18 When the training period ordered by the king was completed, the chief of staff brought all the young men to King Nebuchadnezzar.

19 The king talked with them, and no one impressed him as much as Daniel, Hananiah,

19 And the king communed with them; and among them all was found none like Daniel, Hananiah, Mishael, and Azariah: therefore stood they before the king.

20 And in all matters of wisdom and understanding, that the king enquired of them, he found them ten times better than all the magicians and astrologers that were in all his realm.

21 And Daniel continued even unto the first year of king Cyrus.

Mishael, and Azariah. So they entered the royal service.

20 Whenever the king consulted them in any matter requiring wisdom and balanced judgment, he found them ten times more capable than any of the magicians and enchanters in his entire kingdom.

21 Daniel remained in the royal service until the first year of the reign of King Cyrus.

The People, Places, and Times

Pulse. In the Hebrew language, this includes everything that is grown from sown seed—not only vegetables, but also fruit, legumes, grains, and bread. It was very similar to a healthy vegetarian diet. This type of food was eaten in a partial fast, excluding meat, dairy, and other delicacies. Eating pulse was not a condemnation of meat eating in general, but regarded by the participant as a way to humble themselves before God.

Eunuch. A eunuch was usually a man who was castrated. These men were guardians of the women of the court, chosen because they could not harm them sexually. Eunuchs were also placed in charge of other court offices because they were single-minded; they were not distracted by sexual desires or family responsibilities. In the ancient world, eunuchs were considered remarkable for their faithfulness to their masters. Eunuchs were common in the royal courts of the Jews, Persians, Babylonians, Romans, and Greeks. In the Law, it was forbidden for eunuchs to be a part of public worship (Deuteronomy 23:1). Elsewhere in the New Testament, Jesus commends those who have figuratively made themselves eunuchs for the kingdom of God (Matthew 19:12).

Why is obedience to God's Word important in developing and strengthening our faith?

Background

The book of Daniel opens with the statement that God delivered His people into captivity. Other prophets issued warnings of this captivity, and Daniel experiences and keeps a journal of this exile firsthand. While captivity is never the ideal, God's promise not to leave or forsake His people is evident in these writings. Although Daniel's companions would be memorialized by their Babylonian names (Shadrach, Meshach, and Abednego), Daniel retained his identity and reputation throughout history for the courageous stand he took for God. Mishael, Azariah, and Hananiah were also faithful. They chose to be thrown into a fiery furnace rather than bow down to the king's golden idol.

What does it mean to be faithful?

At-A-Glance

1. Purpose Over Pressure (Daniel 1:8–14)
2. Faith Over Fear (vv. 15–16)
3. Testimony After the Test (vv. 17–21)

In Depth

1. Purpose Over Pressure (Daniel 1:8–14)

Daniel maintained an important element of his identity. His purpose in refusing to eat the particular food that the king had provided was much less about ingesting food, and more about maintaining faithfulness to God's Law (Leviticus 17:7–16). While Daniel was in the king's control, he had to obey certain rules, but he still maintained control over his own body.

This type of commitment should also reside within us and resonate with our family, friends, neighbors, and co-workers. More than a simple protest, Daniel asked permission to follow an alternate diet, and also offered a test run so that they could be monitored and protected from others who might be jealous of their special treatment. Often our purposes can be thwarted by pressure from our peers and the powers that be.

Devising a plan of action might be the best tool to employ, considering that temptations and threats will indeed come. Daniel's purpose to obey God was exemplified by his statement of refusal, and his willingness to operate under certain conditions that would satisfy both sides.

When we face temptations to compromise or disobey God, what should we do to resist?

2. Faith Over Fear (vv. 15–16)

Daniel asked to be fed a vegetarian diet in order to avoid eating meat sacrificed to idols, and to avoid other trappings of Gentile royalty that might have compromised his dietary restrictions. We may at times be questioned as to why we refrain from certain activities even though they can seem harmless and pose no visible threat.

As Daniel and his companions ate a diet of pulse (vegetables), rather than consume the king's meat and drink, others expected them to wither away. However, as they feasted on vegetables and stood on their faith in God, they were blessed with even healthier appearances than all those in the royal household.

Likewise, our faith should literally show in our lives, because God's presence is impossible to ignore. Their patience and calmness in this high pressured situation helped them operate less out of fear and more through faith in God. They were confident that they would not only survive, but thrive in God's care.

How can our faith support us in triumphing over our fears?

3. Testimony After the Test (vv. 17–21)

Despite Daniel's youth, and the fact that he was a captive, he honored God in all that he did. Moreover, he did not plot to escape his captivity or otherwise thwart Nebuchadnezzar's schemes. By staying where God had placed him, Daniel and his friends were able to be witnesses of God's power simply by being obedient. Their peaceful resistance to the meal requirement was balanced by their willingness to serve and answer to the king.

Their physical appearance astounded those around them, especially when accompanied by the God-given gifts of discernment and prophecy. Daniel and his friends' testimony was not in their ability to pray for and receive an immediate release from captivity, but rather a demonstration of how God kept them, elevated them, and ultimately made them victorious in a treacherous situation. In time, Daniel and his friends would be tested further by the pagan king, but they continued to be faithful to their God.

What are the benefits of choosing to obey God and remain faithful?

Search the Scriptures

1. How did Daniel phrase his request to make it seem more favorable to the attendant (Daniel 1:13)?

2. How was God working in the lives of Daniel and his friends while they were in captivity (vv. 9, 17)?

Discuss the Meaning

1. How can we be sure that we are able to defend our faith?

2. What are some of the "Nebuchadnezzars" that we face today?

Lesson in Our Society

Those whom society designates as role models are not guaranteed to be examples worth following. Our culture celebrates celebrity for the sake of fame and seems to worship money at any cost, regardless of the true price in terms of morals and decency. How then can we demonstrate principles and cherish faith in God when the very opposite is what receives all of the attention?

The church must be willing to speak the truth, identify both the good and the questionable, and try every spirit against the Spirit of God. A simple act of discernment can prevent disaster and may well save a soul.

If you evaluate your personal life, do you demonstrate the characteristics of a positive role model?

Make It Happen

• Write out a list of positive Christian role models who exhibit a life of conviction and character.

• Choose to fast from specific foods this week, e.g., meat or sweets.

• Pray that God would give you convictions that come from Him and not your other authority figures.

Follow the Spirit

What God wants me to do:

_____

Remember Your Thoughts

Special insights I have learned:

_____

_____

_____

More Light on the Text
Daniel 1:8–21

8 But Daniel purposed in his heart that he would not defile himself with the portion of the king's meat, nor with the wine which he drank: therefore he requested of the prince of the eunuchs that he might not defile himself.

Following the defeat of Judah, Daniel and his friends (Hananiah, Mishael, and Azariah) were among the young men taken into exile in Babylon. Going into captivity meant that the people of Judah would be subjected to the traditions and practices of Babylon, a pagan nation. Daniel 1 records that these young men were given new Babylonian names. Each of their Hebrew names contained a name for the true God ("el," meaning "God," or "iah," an abbreviation for Yahweh). Each Babylonian name contained the name of a pagan deity. The deportation of these young men fulfilled the warning Isaiah had given King Hezekiah in 2 Kings 20:17–18.

It was forbidden by the Law of Moses for God's people to eat certain foods or participate in pagan rituals and practices. To do so was to be "defiled" (Heb. *ga'al*, **gah-AL**), or declared ceremonially unclean for worship. As a captive, Daniel was subject to Babylonian law, but he loved God and decided firmly to remain loyal to worshiping Him. Daniel refused to let anything defile his heart. One way to remain ceremonially pure was to refuse to eat the "king's meat" (Heb. *pathbag melek*, **path-BAG MEH-lek**). This meat was probably first offered to idols, and Daniel and his friends were determined to avoid the sin of idolatry, which was the very reason that Judah was now in captivity. Also, God's Law prohibited the consumption of meat from certain kinds of "unclean" animals (Genesis 9:3–4; Leviticus 7:26–27, 11:3–8, 26–39).

Daniel also refused drink the king's wine. The word used for "which he drank" in verse 8 and "that they should drink" in verse 16 is *mishteh* (**meesh-TEH**), a Hebrew term meaning "feast" or "banquet." Its use in this context could be understood to communicate that daily meals in the king's household were feasts, especially when compared to the type and quantity of food and drink most people were able to obtain on a regular basis. Drunkenness has always been regarded as both a moral failure (Deuteronomy 21:20; Ephesians 5:18) and an ill-advised lapse of self-control (Proverbs 20:1, 23:20–21).

9 Now God had brought Daniel into favour and tender love with the prince of the eunuchs.

The word for "favour" (Heb. *chesed*, **KHEH-sed**) means "goodness" or "kindness." It is often translated "loving-kindness" in the Old Testament to describe God's gracious acts to preserve and redeem His people. In a few other places in the Old Testament, *chesed* is used together with *racham* (Heb. **RAH-kham**, here "tender love") to form an expression that

describes God's feelings toward His children (see Psalm 103:4; Hosea 2:19; Jeremiah 16:5).

God gave Daniel such favor with the "prince of the eunuchs." Although we typically think about this story as concerning Daniel's courage to stand up for his convictions, this passage actually points out God's faithfulness. Daniel and his friends were experiencing the consequences of Judah's disobedience. By causing the eunuch to be sympathetic toward Daniel, God was acting in faithfulness to His promise and honoring the prayers of the righteous from ages past.

10 And the prince of the eunuchs said unto Daniel, I fear my lord the king, who hath appointed your meat and your drink: for why should he see your faces worse liking than the children which are of your sort? then shall ye make me endanger my head to the king.

The chief eunuch believed that changing the diet of those under his care would be directly disobeying the king's orders. This was no trivial matter, because the king had absolute power! During the chief eunuch's service, he had no doubt seen what happened to people who dared to contradict the king.

The verb translated "worse liking" (Heb. *za'af*, **zah-AF**) literally means "to fret, be sad, or out of humor." The only other place this form occurs in the Old Testament refers to a dejected facial expression (Genesis 40:6). The chief eunuch's concern was that Daniel's health would suffer in comparison to the health of the other young men who would remain on the king's diet.

The phrase "endanger my head" could be translated more literally "make me guilty." The chief eunuch could have been an extremely conscientious man who really didn't want to act on his own initiative without authorization from his superior, or he might simply have been intimidated by the thought of capital punishment. The latter seems most likely, given the conspicuous use of the word "head." In this text, the eunuch believed that giving in to Daniel would be putting his "head" (in English we might say "neck") on the line.

11 Then said Daniel to Melzar, whom the prince of the eunuchs had set over Daniel, Hananiah, Mishael, and Azariah, 12 Prove thy servants, I beseech thee, ten days; and let them give us pulse to eat, and water to drink.

The chief eunuch did not deny Daniel's request outright, but indicated that he was not comfortable with the proposition. Daniel then made his request to the steward assigned to him. Melzar was a Babylonian title, perhaps meaning "guardian." Modern English translations interpret the word as a title, not a name. Regardless of whether Melzar was actually his name, he was obviously charged with caring for Daniel and his friends.

Daniel asked Melzar to "prove" (Heb. *nasah*, **nah-SAH**) or perform a test to see how well Daniel and his comrades would survive on a diet that was more fitting for them. The phrase "I beseech thee" tells us that Daniel had intensified his request. Some English versions use the word "please" to convey the mood of Daniel's request (NLT). He was appealing to Melzar's high opinion of him, and he did so in a respectful and courteous manner.

Daniel asked for "pulse" (Heb. *zeroa'*, **zay-RO-ah**), which means "that which is sown" and refers to vegetables. He wanted a diet of only vegetables. While Daniel's concern appears religious and not motivated by health purposes, it is still notable to realize that few people—probably only the king and members of the nobility—would have owned enough land to produce meat for consumption on a regular basis. Meat was a luxury. The average person may have eaten meat as little as once

or twice per year, and primarily on special religious observances.

13 Then let our countenances be looked upon before thee, and the countenance of the children that eat of the portion of the king's meat: and as thou seest, deal with thy servants.

Daniel likely asked for the ten-day test as a way to acknowledge the eunuchs' concerns. By our thinking, ten days on an alternate diet would neither be long enough for their appearance to suffer nor show significant improvement. But Daniel's faith was in God, and in ten days he knew that God would make the difference and give them favor. If the Lord wanted him to stand for righteousness by abstaining from the king's food, God would direct the heart of the men who had the power to make it possible for him. Daniel could only have faith to believe that God would reveal Himself in the midst of the test, proving to all that He was God Almighty.

14 So he consented to them in this matter, and proved them ten days. 15 And at the end of ten days their countenances appeared fairer and fatter in flesh than all the children which did eat the portion of the king's meat.

At the end of the test, Daniel and his friends looked better than the children who had eaten from the king's table. The term "appeared" is a Hebrew word, *ra'ah* (**rah-AH**), which means to look intently or inspect. The test of ten days ended with a close inspection of the progress made by Daniel, Hananiah, Mishael, and Azariah.

Their countenances were "fairer" (Heb. *tov*, **TOVE**), a common Old Testament word normally translated "good." Some English translations render it "better" (ESV, NASB). The word "fatter" (Heb. *bari'*, **bah-REE**) seems to imply that they had not wasted away, but instead fared well, looking more stout and healthy than their counterparts. In the ancient Near East, girth was a sign of wealth. The common people worked too hard and had too little food available to gain weight. In the ancient world, like underdeveloped regions today, food was scarce and fitness was threatened by malnourishment. If Daniel and the others gained weight, God did it!

16 Thus Melzar took away the portion of their meat, and the wine that they should drink; and gave them pulse.

Up to this point, the text has only indicated that vegetables and water were added to Daniel's supply of food. No doubt the king's meat was delivered daily even if it wasn't eaten. Now Melzar took away the meat and wine. He took action to completely fulfill Daniel's wish.

17 As for these four children, God gave them knowledge and skill in all learning and wisdom: and Daniel had understanding in all visions and dreams.

Daniel, Shadrach, Meshach, and Abednego received both "knowledge" (Heb. *madda‘*, **mad-DAH**)—also translated "science" (Daniel 1:4) and "thought" (Ecclesiastes 10:20)—and "skill" in abundance. The word here for "skill" (Heb. *sakal*, **sah-KAL**) comes from a verb that means "to be prudent." Other English translations render this word "intelligence" (NASB). Their knowledge and skill came in learning and wisdom. "Learning" (Heb. *sefer*, **SEH-fer**) literally means "writing" or "book."

"Wisdom" (Heb. *chokmah*, **khoak-MAH**) is a common word in the Old Testament with a variety of possible connotations, including skill or aptitude, experience, good sense, shrewdness, intellectual capacity, and godly insight. These Hebrew words used for "knowledge," "skill," "learning," "wisdom," and "understanding" are the exact words used in Daniel 1:3–4

when Nebuchadnezzar outlined his goals for the young captives. God gave Daniel and his friends exactly what the king was looking for when he established their training program. Daniel was also especially blessed with the ability to understand visions and dreams—an indication that God was truly with him and would speak through him (see Numbers 12:6), as he did in several instances recorded in this book (see 2:19, 7:1, 8:1).

18 Now at the end of the days that the king had said he should bring them in, then the prince of the eunuchs brought them in before Nebuchadnezzar.

The eunuchs honored Daniel's dietary wishes. The moment of truth, however, came when Daniel and his friends were to stand before the king. After three years of first-class education and accommodations (see 1:4), would the Hebrew youth measure up to the king's expectations? Their future—perhaps even their lives and the lives of the men who cared for and trained Daniel and his friends—were dependent on the outcome.

19 And the king communed with them; and among them all was found none like Daniel, Hananiah, Mishael, and Azariah: therefore stood they before the king.

The king likely interrogated the young men, either individually or in groups, to discern the depth of their understanding. Daniel, Hananiah, Mishael, and Azariah stood head and shoulders above the rest of the captives.

While these four young men distinguished themselves before Nebuchadnezzar, they also distinguished themselves before God through their courage and faithfulness to God's commands. Many other Jewish youth were enrolled in the same program of education and leadership development. But only these four—certainly a minority—are recorded to have maintained steadfast loyalty to their God.

The phrase "stood before the king" is a literal rendering of the Hebrew. The words are the same ones used in verse 5, which indicates these young men would be working for the king. Some English versions translate the phrase "entered the royal service" (NLT). The conversation with the king was a combination of a final exam and job interview.

We see here a principle of privilege coupled with responsibility. God entrusted Daniel and his friends with great gifts, but those gifts came with an obligation. God called them to stand with courage and conviction repeatedly throughout the time of their service. The king, as the rest of the book shows, was a demanding and unjust man at times. God gives good gifts, but not necessarily to make our lives easier or more comfortable. He frequently calls His most gifted servants to exercise great courage and count any present happiness as loss for the sake of advancing His eternal kingdom.

20 And in all matters of wisdom and understanding, that the king enquired of them, he found them ten times better than all the magicians and astrologers that were in all his realm. 21 And Daniel continued even unto the first year of king Cyrus.

Daniel and his three friends were wiser than all their peers and outdid even the king's diviners. "The magicians and astrologers" refers to those who sought secret knowledge through communication with the spirit world. The diviners believed these spirits to be gods or the spirits of deceased people. It was common in the ancient world for rulers to consult experts in the occult.

The Scriptures do not allow the practice of divination by God's people. Rather, we are to listen to those through whom He has chosen to speak (Deuteronomy 18:10–15). God calls His people to live in faith, trusting that whatever He ordains is right and that He will tell us what we need to know at the right time. The Bible is our guide.

We later learn that Daniel was actually appointed chief of the magicians and wise men because Nebuchadnezzar realized that Daniel was filled with the Spirit of God, and that he was actually correct in his interpretations and predictions, unlike the king's magicians (Daniel 2:24, 5:11). Of course, Daniel disavowed the techniques and beliefs of the pagan magicians entirely. He explains that only God can reveal mysteries, and men can only have access to divine knowledge when God chooses to reveal Himself (Daniel 2:27–30).

Daniel, Hananiah, Mishael, and Azariah (Shadrach, Meshach, Abednego) were "rising stars" in Babylon after their interview with the king. At the time of their exile, no one would have predicted their ascent to the upper echelons of Babylonian government in the next three years. After all, they were basically prisoners of war. But God called them to act courageously, and He honored their faithfulness by using them to leave a powerful and lasting testimony of the one true, living God. By sticking to their convictions, they experienced the power of God in incredible ways.

Sources:

Adeyemo, Tokunboh, ed. "Daniel." *Africa Bible Commentary*. Grand Rapids, MI: Zondervan, 2006. 989–1012.

LaCocque, André. "Daniel." *Global Bible Commentary*. Edited by Daniel Patte, et al. Nashville, TN: Abingdon Press, 2004. 2653–261.

Lai, Barbara M. Leung. "Daniel." *The People's Companion to the Bible*. Edited by Curtiss Paul DeYoung, et al. Minneapolis, MN: Fortress Press, 2010. 162–63.

Newsom, Carol A. *Daniel: A Commentary*. Old Testament Library. Edited by William P. Brown, Carol A. Newsom, and Brent A. Strawn. Louisville, KY: Westminster John Knox Press, 2014.

Say It Correctly

Hananiah. hah-nah-**NIGH**-ah.
Mishael. **MEE**-shah-el.
Azariah. As-uh-**RYE**-uh.

Daily Bible Readings

MONDAY
In God I Put My Trust
(Psalm 56)

TUESDAY
The Lord God Defeats Baal
(1 Kings 18:30–39)

WEDNESDAY
Faithful Living in Another Land
(Jeremiah 29:4–9)

THURSDAY
Always Live as Salt and Light
(Matthew 5:13–16)

FRIDAY
Be Faithful When Tested
(Revelation 2:8–11)

SATURDAY
Training Plan for the Captives
(Daniel 1:3–7)

SUNDAY
Stand by Your Principles
(Daniel 1:8–21)

Notes

_____

_____

_____

_____

Teaching Tips

Words You Should Know

A. Visage (Daniel 3:19) *'anaf* (Aram.)—Face.

B. Worship (v. 28) *segid* (Aram.)—Pay honor, do homage.

Teacher Preparation

Unifying Principle—No Matter the Cost. Sometimes people are challenged to endure great trials and tribulations because of their convictions. How can they face such challenges and remain faithful? Shadrach, Meshach, and Abednego boldly disobeyed the king's command, faced life-threatening consequences and were delivered from a fiery furnace by the power of God.

A. Pray for your students to have courage during trials.

B. Read Daniel 1–3 in at least two translations to understand the full context of the passage.

C. Note possible discussion topics as you are studying and preparing for your lesson.

O—Open the Lesson

A. Pray for lesson clarity, participation, and open dialogue.

B. Introduce the lesson title.

C. Have participants read the Aim for Change and Keep in Mind verse together, and discuss.

D. Read the In Focus story to the class.

P—Present the Scriptures

A. Have participants read the Focal Verses silently.

B. Use The People, Places, and Times and Background sections to clarify the verses.

C. Pay close attention to the In Depth section as it may shape the Explore the Meaning discussions.

E—Explore the Meaning

A. Depending on the class size, break into groups and complete Discuss the Meaning. Have students select a representative to report their responses.

B. Bring the entire class back together and begin a discussion using the Lesson in Our Society section.

N—Next Steps for Application

A. Have students consider the Make It Happen exercise independently.

B. Summarize key points of the lesson.

C. Close with prayer.

Worship Guide

For the Superintendent or Teacher
Theme: A Bold Faith
Song: "Lord, Help Me to Hold Out"
Devotional Reading: Romans 12:9–21

227

A Bold Faith

Bible Background • DANIEL 3
Printed Text • DANIEL 3:19–23, 26–28 | Devotional Reading • ROMANS 12:9–21

Aim for Change

By the end of this lesson we will: EXPLORE the connection between the faith of Shadrach, Meshach, and Abednego and their deliverance from the fiery furnace; VALUE their faith commitment; and IDENTIFY situations that call for faith during persecution.

In Focus

Just two years ago, Danielle's father came to visit her for the weekend. When he returned home on Monday, he went to the doctor and was told that he had cancer. That same day, Danielle's entire department was laid off and she found herself without a job. If that wasn't enough, the house she was supposed to close on the following Friday fell through as well.

It seemed as if Danielle was going through a Job experience where all she had to depend on was faith in God. Because her father was sick and she was no longer employed, flying back and forth to take care of him quickly depleted her savings. She was barely able to pay for her living expenses.

One day, an acquaintance approached her and said she knew Danielle was going through a rough time and how she might have a possible solution to her money problems. She explained that she received checks from different people, and if Danielle would deposit them into her account and cash them, her friend would give her a portion of each one.

She showed Danielle a check for $5,700. This whole arrangement seemed suspicious to Danielle and more than likely illegal. Even though it took her a moment to get the words out, she refused. Although she was struggling financially and didn't have a place to live, Danielle believed God would provide, so she remained faithful.

Today's lesson is about standing firm in convictions. Describe a time when you had to stand firm in your convictions in the midst of a situation filled with pressure.

Keep in Mind

"Blessed be the God of Shadrach, Meshach, and Abednego, who hath sent his angel, and delivered his servants that trusted in him, and have changed the king's word, and yielded their bodies, that they might not serve nor worship any god, except their own God" (from Daniel 3:28).

"Blessed be the God of Shadrach, Meshach, and Abednego, who hath sent his angel, and delivered his servants that trusted in him, and have changed the king's word, and yielded their bodies, that they might not serve nor worship any god, except their own God" (from Daniel 3:28).

Focal Verses

KJV **Daniel 3:19** Then was Nebuchadnezzar full of fury, and the form of his visage was changed against Shadrach, Meshach, and Abednego: therefore he spake, and commanded that they should heat the furnace one seven times more than it was wont to be heated.

20 And he commanded the most mighty men that were in his army to bind Shadrach, Meshach, and Abednego, and to cast them into the burning fiery furnace.

21 Then these men were bound in their coats, their hosen, and their hats, and their other garments, and were cast into the midst of the burning fiery furnace.

22 Therefore because the king's commandment was urgent, and the furnace exceeding hot, the flames of the fire slew those men that took up Shadrach, Meshach, and Abednego.

23 And these three men, Shadrach, Meshach, and Abednego, fell down bound into the midst of the burning fiery furnace.

26 Then Nebuchadnezzar came near to the mouth of the burning fiery furnace, and spake, and said, Shadrach, Meshach, and Abednego, ye servants of the most high God, come forth, and come hither. Then Shadrach, Meshach, and Abednego, came forth of the midst of the fire.

27 And the princes, governors, and captains, and the king's counsellors, being gathered together, saw these men, upon whose bodies the fire had no power, nor was an hair of their head singed, neither were their coats changed, nor the smell of fire had passed on them.

28 Then Nebuchadnezzar spake, and said, Blessed be the God of Shadrach, Meshach, and Abednego, who hath sent his angel, and delivered his servants that trusted in him, and have changed the king's word, and yielded their

NLT **Daniel 3:19** Nebuchadnezzar was so furious with Shadrach, Meshach, and Abednego that his face became distorted with rage. He commanded that the furnace be heated seven times hotter than usual.

20 Then he ordered some of the strongest men of his army to bind Shadrach, Meshach, and Abednego and throw them into the blazing furnace.

21 So they tied them up and threw them into the furnace, fully dressed in their pants, turbans, robes, and other garments.

22 And because the king, in his anger, had demanded such a hot fire in the furnace, the flames killed the soldiers as they threw the three men in.

23 So Shadrach, Meshach, and Abednego, securely tied, fell into the roaring flames.

26 Then Nebuchadnezzar came as close as he could to the door of the flaming furnace and shouted: "Shadrach, Meshach, and Abednego, servants of the Most High God, come out! Come here!" So Shadrach, Meshach, and Abednego stepped out of the fire.

27 Then the high officers, officials, governors, and advisers crowded around them and saw that the fire had not touched them. Not a hair on their heads was singed, and their clothing was not scorched. They didn't even smell of smoke!

28 Then Nebuchadnezzar said, "Praise to the God of Shadrach, Meshach, and Abednego! He sent his angel to rescue his servants who trusted in him. They defied the king's command and were willing to die rather than serve or worship any god except their own God.

bodies, that they might not serve nor worship any god, except their own God.

The People, Places, and Times

Chaldean. The chronology of the Chaldeans is anything but straightforward. Initially, Chaldea referred only to a region at the head of the Persian Gulf that is south of Babylonia. During the eighth century BC, the tribes in this region were united and rose to power over Babylon. Over the course of approximately 100 years, and with the subsequent rise of Nebuchadnezzar's father, the Chaldean's strength continuously increased. Although the Chaldeans are presented as an opposing force to the Hebrews in the biblical text, they were held in high regard among many foreign nations. They were known for their study habits and dedication to doing good. Eventually, Greek historians began to use the term "Chaldean" to refer to Babylonian priests and wise men, which is how it became synonymous for Babylonia in the Scriptures.

Nebuchadnezzar. Nebuchadnezzar was a Chaldean king who ruled Babylonia from approximately 605 to 562 BC. His name is a plea to the son of the Babylonian deity of wisdom, Marduk, and means "O god Nabu preserve my firstborn son." Nebuchadnezzar destroyed Solomon's Temple, also known as the first Temple. He captured Jerusalem and exiled the people. Nebuchadnezzar is mentioned often in the Old Testament and he had many notable acts during his reign. In addition to his conquest of Jerusalem, Nebuchadnezzar was the first Babylonian king to rule Egypt when he defeated Pharaoh Necho. He is also credited for building the Hanging Gardens (one of the Seven Wonders of the Ancient World).

How can God use world leaders to execute His plans in dealing with sinful people?

Background

This passage is part of a significant section of Daniel that is written in Aramaic (2:4–7:28), with the remaining portions written in the usual Old Testament language of Hebrew (1:1–2:4, 8:1–12:13). The Aramaic section spans both the historical (Daniel 1–6) and visionary (7–12) parts of Daniel, making the book highly representative of the typical life of an exile or refugee, such as Daniel, who must know more than one language to survive.

Today's section follows the rise of Daniel and his companions in the king's court after several miraculous events (1:18–20, 2:24–49). Now, some of the Chaldeans (those from southern Babylonia, near the Persian Gulf) accuse Shadrach, Meschach, and Abednego of transgressing the royal decree by not bowing down and worshiping the gold statue the king had created (3:1–12). The king follows the Chaldeans' suggestion and prepares the fiery furnace to punish the three Jews for not obeying the decree.

How are the lives of Daniel and his friends similar to our lives as believers in the 21st century?

At-A-Glance

1. Turn Up the Heat (Daniel 3:19–21)
2. Falling in the Fire (vv. 22–23)
3. Out of the Fiery Furnace (vv. 26–28)

In Depth

1. Turn Up the Heat (Daniel 3:19–21)

In the most figurative sense of the word, Nebuchadnezzar was "heated." Known for his emotionalism and anger, he was so upset when Shadrach, Meshach, and Abednego refused to bow down to the golden idol that his facial expression immediately changed and he made an impulsive decision to throw the young men into the furnace.

The furnace was most likely a lime furnace, which had a tall chimney on top for smoke and a window or opening on the bottom for inserting fuel. People could be thrown in at the top, which would be extra hot because of the rising air and smoke—so hot that the guards would die.

The king summoned the strongest guards to bind the three Hebrew boys, and decided the furnace should be seven times hotter. Many times, there is an expectation that faith, integrity, and truth will vindicate us, but sometimes being on the side of justice turns up the fire and increases the level of discomfort in our lives.

How should we prepare for persecution when we stand up against the injustices of the world?

2. Falling in the Fire (vv. 22–23)

The text sets up the next scene and displays the intensity of the fire by making it clear that it was perfect for human execution. The guards who threw Shadrach, Meshach, and Abednego into the fire were themselves killed by the intensity of the heat.

But the three Hebrew boys fell down into the furnace in the middle of the flames. This was the first miracle. They survived!

Read verses 24-25 in your Bible. The king saw something unusual. The boys were alive and walking in the furnace. But, he also saw something else. There was a fourth man walking in the flames; some commentators say that He was the preincarnate Christ, Jesus before His incarnation, and others interpret the fourth man as an angel.

Have you ever escaped a very trying situation because you stood for God?

3. Out of the Fiery Furnace (vv. 26–28)

The king calls to Shadrach, Meshach, and Abednego and addresses them as servants of the Most High God. He tells them to come out of the furnace.

After intense persecution, the three are vindicated for their faithfulness to the God of Israel. In the presence of the entire court, including the officials that condemned them, the king acknowledges what is apparent—the Hebrew men sustained the fire unharmed. They didn't even smell like smoke. King Nebuchadnezzar blesses the God of Shadrach, Meshach, and Abednego.

This entire account is known as the "fiery furnace" in the Christian tradition. It serves as an example of unwavering faith and God's saving power. What encouragement to obey God rather than man!

How do you explain to others that God's presence has been manifested in your life?

Search the Scriptures

1. What was Nebuchadnezzar's response to the Hebres boys' refusal (Daniel 3:19)?

2. To whom did Nebuchadnezzar give honor for delivering the Hebrew boys, and why was this so significant (v. 28)?

Discuss the Meaning

Considering the situation of the three Hebrew boys, does it require more faith to trust in a miracle, or to do what is right without a miracle guaranteed? How does it feel to know that God will sometimes allow us to face the fire?

Lesson in Our Society

Today's lesson is about faith in action and conviction. In many cases, we are called to stand firm in our convictions when we face external pressure from society. Rev. Dr. Martin Luther King Jr. and other leaders who joined him in nonviolent protest also faced the same challenge. They had to stand strong even when hosed, attacked by dogs, and beaten with billy clubs. They knew they were standing up for right and that God would deliver them one way or another. Many paid the ultimate price for freedom with their lives.

Make It Happen

Idolatry does not present itself today as a sixty-cubit gold statue, but many false gods seek priority in our lives.

- List things that appear as "must dos" and "must haves."
- Based on how you spend your time and money, what is your main focus?
- Do you need to make changes to ensure you are faithful to God?

Follow the Spirit

What God wants me to do:

_____

_____

_____

_____

Remember Your Thoughts

Special insights I have learned:

_____

_____

More Light on the Text

Daniel 3:19–23, 26–28

19 Then was Nebuchadnezzar full of fury, and the form of his visage was changed against Shadrach, Meshach, and Abednego: therefore he spake, and commanded that they should heat the furnace one seven times more than it was wont to be heated. 20 And he commanded the most mighty men that were in his army to bind Shadrach, Meshach, and Abednego, and to cast them into the burning fiery furnace.

The king had been informed that the three Jews whom he appointed to the administration of Babylon had not bowed down and worshiped the king's statue (2:48–49, 3:12). The king called Shadrach, Meshach, and Abednego and gave them one more chance to bow down to the statue and worship his idol (v. 15). They refused, telling the king that their God will save them from the furnace (v. 17).

The king was so enraged that he ordered the furnace be heated to seven times its usual temperature. Words for heat prevail in this section, not only regarding the furnace, though this is the most frequent reference. The word for the king's anger is also the Aramaic word for heat (Aram. *khema'*, **khe-MAH**, poison, heat, wrath). The king is so angry his face is heated with wrath and he makes the heat seven times hotter. The king has his strongest warriors bind the Jews and cast them into the burning fiery furnace.

This expression "burning fiery furnace" is repeated eight times in this passage, intensifying the heat of the furnace with two words for fire. In English, such an expression would be called redundant, but in Aramaic the repetition of two synonyms—*yeqad* (**yeh-KOD**, burning) and *nur* (**NOOR**, fiery)—intensifies their effect. The punishment could not be any worse. As a result, the Jews' faith could not be any stronger, nor God's salvation of them any more glorious.

21 Then these men were bound in their coats, their hosen, and their hats, and their other garments, and were cast into the midst of the burning fiery furnace.

The narrative takes care to inform us that Shadrach, Meshach, and Abednego were cast into the furnace in all of their clothing. The purpose of mentioning the clothing here is to emphasize God's saving power later when the men exit the furnace unscathed; not even a hair on their heads nor their garments was singed (v. 27). The narrative also repeats the binding of the men three times: when they are cast into the furnace, when the king asks if his command has been fulfilled (v. 24), and when the king sees the men in the furnace unbound (v. 25).

22 Therefore because the king's commandment was urgent, and the furnace exceeding hot, the flame of the fire slew those men that took up Shadrach, Meshach, and Abednego. 23 And these three men, Shadrach, Meshach, and Abednego, fell down bound into the midst of the burning fiery furnace.

The text tells us that the king's command was "urgent." In Aramaic, this word can also mean "harsh" (*khatsaf*, **khat-SAF**). In fact, the king's order was so harsh, and the furnace was so hot, that the warriors who threw the Jews into the furnace were killed by the fire. This part of the event calls to mind scurrying and haste, where a master commands his servants so forcefully that they get harmed because they are so afraid that they cannot think of being cautious.

This passage is a reminder of how dangerous human power can become when an individual or group is allowed such power and is permitted to make decisions based on anger and hatred, whether related to religious faith, race, or other ways of differentiating one person or group from another. The king's warriors are killed just getting close to the furnace, so we know how hot the furnace really is, and now the three Jews have been thrown into the burning fiery furnace.

26 Then Nebuchadnezzar came near to the mouth of the burning fiery furnace, and spake, and said, Shadrach, Meshach, and Abednego, ye servants of the most high God, come forth, and come hither. Then Shadrach, Meshach, and Abednego, came forth of the midst of the fire. 27 And the princes, governors, and captains, and the king's counsellors, being gathered together, saw these men, upon whose bodies the fire had no power, nor was an hair of their head singed, neither were their coats changed, nor the smell of fire had passed on them.

Despite being thrown into the furnace that killed even those who came near it, when the king calls the three Jews to come out, they do so! The king recognized that the God these Jews said would save them (vv. 16–17) is the "most high God."

To add to the miraculous nature of the event, when the men exit the furnace, the governors and other leaders look at them and realize that they have not been harmed in the least—not a hair on their heads nor any part of their clothing has been singed. They do not even smell like the fire. It is as though a barrier protected them while they were inside the furnace. Only the most high God would be able to perform such a miracle.

28 Then Nebuchadnezzar spake, and said, Blessed be the God of Shadrach, Meshach, and Abednego, who hath sent his angel, and delivered his servants that trusted in him, and have changed the king's word, and yielded their bodies, that they might not serve nor worship any god, except their own God.

Nebuchadnezzar responds to the miracle by blessing Shadrach, Meshach, and Abednego's God, recognizing that the fourth person in the furnace (vv. 22–25) was an "angel" (Aram. *mal'ak*, **mall-AHK**, angel, messenger). The king is so changed by the event that he praises the Jews for disobeying his command! In this case, these faithful servants have been saved from death by giving up their bodies, not their faith.

Most of us may not be placed in a position of having to die for our faith. But will we live for our faith? Will we present our bodies as living sacrifices, holy, and acceptable to God (Romans 12:1–2)?

Sources:
Beaulieu, Paul-Alain. "The Babylonian Background of the Motif of the Fiery Furnace in Daniel 3." *Journal of Biblical Literature* Vol. 128, No. 2 (2009). 273–290.
Campbell, Donald K. *Daniel: Decoder of Dreams*. Wheaton, IL: Victor Book, 1977. 8.
Daniel, Sharon Pace. *Smyth & Helwys Bible Commentary*. Macon, GA: Smyth & Helwys Publishing, 2008. 52.
"Furnace." *Easton's Bible Dictionary*. 3rd ed., London: T. Nelson & Sons, 1897.
Goldingay, John E. *Word Biblical Commentary*, Vol. 30. Dallas, TX: Word Books, 1989. 69–76.
Johns, Robert. *The Visions of Daniel the Hebrew Prophet*. Bloomington, IN: WestBow Press, 2012. 22–26.

Say It Correctly

Shadrach. **SHAD**-rak.
Meshach. **MEE**-shak.
Abednego. ah-**BED**-neh-go.
Aramaic. air-uh-**MAY**-ik.

Daily Bible Readings

MONDAY
We Must Speak about Jesus
(Acts 4:13–22)

TUESDAY
We Must Obey God, Not People
(Acts 5:27–32)

WEDNESDAY
Prayer, Fasting, and a Bold Move
(Esther 4:5–17)

THURSDAY
All Ordered to Worship the Image
(Daniel 3:1–12)

FRIDAY
We Will Not Serve Babylonian Gods
(Daniel 3:13–18)

SATURDAY
King Astonished at Jews' Survival
(Daniel 3:24–25)

SUNDAY
God Delivers from the Fiery Furnace
(Daniel 3:19–23, 26–28)

Teaching Tips

Words You Should Know

A. Righteousness (Daniel 9:7) *tsedaqah* (Heb.)—Acting according to God's standard conviction.

B. Trespass (v. 7) *ma'al* (Heb.)—Unfaithfulness, transgression.

Teacher Preparation

Unifying Principle—A Cry for Help. People want release from feelings of shame that may result from past mistakes. Where can they go to find such relief? Daniel prayed to the Lord a prayer of confession, seeking forgiveness, mercy, and strength to obey.

A. Think about prayers you have prayed and how those prayers and the concept of prayer affect your life.

B. Pray for your preparation and individuals who will attend.

C. Complete the *Precepts For Living®* Study Guide to better understand Daniel's prayer.

O—Open the Lesson

A. Introduce the lesson title.

B. Have students read the Aim for Change and Keep in Mind sections silently.

C. Ask for a volunteer to read In Focus and then discuss as a class.

P—Present the Scriptures

A. Ask participants to follow along as you read the Focal Verses aloud.

B. Utilize The People, Places, and Times; Background; Search the Scriptures; At-A-Glance; In Depth; and More Light on the Text as you see fit to provide clarity and possible talking points for discussions.

E—Explore the Meaning

A. Divide the class into groups to complete the Lesson in Our Society. Come back together and discuss as a class.

B. Have participants complete Discuss the Meaning individually. Ask for a few volunteers to share their responses.

N—Next Steps for Application

A. Instruct participants to complete Make It Happen as an individual. Do not ask them to share answers; the exercise is for personal reflection.

B. Ask each student to share one take-away idea they may have from the lesson.

C. Close in prayer.

Worship Guide

For the Superintendent or Teacher
Theme: A Prayer for an Obedient Faith
Song: "Sweet Hour of Prayer"
Devotional Reading: Psalm 130

A Prayer for an Obedient Faith

Bible Background • DANIEL 9:1–19
Printed Text • DANIEL 9:4–8, 15–19 | Devotional Reading • PSALM 130

—————————— **Aim for Change** ——————————

By the end of this lesson we will: VALIDATE Daniel's prayer of confession; RELATE to the need for Daniel's type of prayer today; and PRAY as Daniel prayed.

——————— 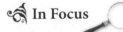 In Focus ———————

Tina was a young mother. She worked hard and was intentional about being the best mom possible for her children. Tina was committed to providing nutritious meals and limiting unhealthy snacks and excessive sugar. She read to her children frequently, tempered consistent discipline with overwhelming love, and sacrificed to send her toddlers to the best preschool she could afford.

One Thursday, Tina went to pick her children up from school and discovered her four-year-old was sitting in isolation. She was in disbelief when the teacher explained that her daughter got upset after losing a game and pushed another child out of his seat. As a result, the other child fell and hit his head. Tina was disappointed with her daughter's behavior, but she also felt a personal sense of guilt and shame.

Tina understood that even well-behaved children acted out from time to time. She talked to her daughter about pushing and took away her favorite toy, but for some reason she just couldn't sleep that night. She began to pray for her daughter and poured out her heart before the Lord. The next morning, Tina arrived at her daughter's school early and waited for the other child's parent to arrive. Tina apologized to the parent and the small child for her daughter's behavior and instantly felt better.

In today's lesson, we will examine the role of confession and intercessory prayer. When have you seen God move powerfully in answer to intercessory prayer?

——————————— **Keep in Mind** ———————————

"O Lord, hear; O Lord, forgive; O Lord, hearken and do; defer not, for thine own sake, O my God: for thy city and thy people are called by thy name" (Daniel 9:19).

"O Lord, hear; O Lord, forgive; O Lord, hearken and do; defer not, for thine own sake, O my God: for thy city and thy people are called by thy name" (Daniel 9:19).

Focal Verses

KJV **Daniel 9:4** And I prayed unto the LORD my God, and made my confession, and said, O Lord, the great and dreadful God, keeping the covenant and mercy to them that love him, and to them that keep his commandments;

5 We have sinned, and have committed iniquity, and have done wickedly, and have rebelled, even by departing from thy precepts and from thy judgments:

6 Neither have we hearkened unto thy servants the prophets, which spake in thy name to our kings, our princes, and our fathers, and to all the people of the land.

7 O LORD, righteousness belongeth unto thee, but unto us confusion of faces, as at this day; to the men of Judah, and to the inhabitants of Jerusalem, and unto all Israel, that are near, and that are far off, through all the countries whither thou hast driven them, because of their trespass that they have trespassed against thee.

8 O Lord, to us belongeth confusion of face, to our kings, to our princes, and to our fathers, because we have sinned against thee.

15 And now, O Lord our God, that hast brought thy people forth out of the land of Egypt with a mighty hand, and hast gotten thee renown, as at this day; we have sinned, we have done wickedly.

16 O LORD, according to all thy righteousness, I beseech thee, let thine anger and thy fury be turned away from thy city Jerusalem, thy holy mountain: because for our sins, and for the iniquities of our fathers, Jerusalem and thy people are become a reproach to all that are about us.

17 Now therefore, O our God, hear the prayer of thy servant, and his supplications, and cause thy face to shine upon thy sanctuary that is desolate, for the Lord's sake.

NLT **Daniel 9:4** I prayed to the LORD my God and confessed: "O Lord, you are a great and awesome God! You always fulfill your covenant and keep your promises of unfailing love to those who love you and obey your commands.

5 But we have sinned and done wrong. We have rebelled against you and scorned your commands and regulations.

6 We have refused to listen to your servants the prophets, who spoke on your authority to our kings and princes and ancestors and to all the people of the land.

7 Lord, you are in the right; but as you see, our faces are covered with shame. This is true of all of us, including the people of Judah and Jerusalem and all Israel, scattered near and far, wherever you have driven us because of our disloyalty to you.

8 O LORD, we and our kings, princes, and ancestors are covered with shame because we have sinned against you.

15 O Lord our God, you brought lasting honor to your name by rescuing your people from Egypt in a great display of power. But we have sinned and are full of wickedness.

16 In view of all your faithful mercies, Lord, please turn your furious anger away from your city Jerusalem, your holy mountain. All the neighboring nations mock Jerusalem and your people because of our sins and the sins of our ancestors.

17 O our God, hear your servant's prayer! Listen as I plead. For your own sake, Lord, smile again on your desolate sanctuary.

18 O my God, lean down and listen to me. Open your eyes and see our despair. See how your city—the city that bears your name—lies in ruins. We make this plea, not because we deserve help, but because of your mercy.

18 O my God, incline thine ear, and hear; open thine eyes, and behold our desolations, and the city which is called by thy name: for we do not present our supplications before thee for our righteousnesses, but for thy great mercies.

19 O Lord, hear; O Lord, forgive; O Lord, hearken and do; defer not, for thine own sake, O my God: for thy city and thy people are called by thy name.

19 O Lord, hear. O Lord, forgive. O Lord, listen and act! For your own sake, do not delay, O my God, for your people and your city bear your name."

The People, Places, and Times

Israel and Judah. Israel is a term that takes on different meanings progressively throughout the Bible. Jacob's name was changed to Israel after he wrestled with an angel all night. Israel means, "he strives with God" (Genesis 32:28, 35:10). The collective name of the twelve tribes that were his descendants was also called Israel. Depending on the period, the name "Israel" also refers to the entire nation (the entire twelve tribes), or solely to the Northern Kingdom.

The Southern Kingdom became known as Judah. The book of Joshua details how the land of Canaan was divided among the descendants of Jacob, also known as the twelve tribes, one of which was Judah. This tribe—along with the tribe of Benjamin—became the Kingdom of Judah centuries later when the Northern tribes rejected Solomon's son as king. Judah was located in the southern part of the Israelites' territory.

Babylonian Captivity. This is the period in biblical history when the people of Judah were defeated and taken away by the powerful nation of Babylonia. Following a yearlong siege, the capital city of Jerusalem and the Temple were destroyed in 587 BC. The actual deportation of the people of Judah took place in three waves, with the last occurring in 582 BC. The Bible implies that the captives were resettled in a single area, which allowed them to continue to practice their religion and culture.

What significance does your place of birth have on your life and the image people create about you?

Background

Daniel means "God is my judge," which is consistent with the actions and visions that unfold throughout the book. The book's purpose is to strengthen and encourage the Jews who were under pressure to compromise or abandon their religion. The book includes Daniel's account of his time in the king's court and his visions. Chapters one through six present God's interventions in a variety of circumstances—interpreting dreams, rescuing the Hebrew boys from the fiery furnace, writing on the banquet wall, and delivering Daniel in a den of lions.

Chapters seven through twelve are considered apocalyptic; they contain revelations about destruction or the end of time. Daniel is complicated because he presents faithfulness and allegiance even while in exile or living in luxury (depending on how you look at it). He foresees further doom for the Israelites, only to end with a message of hope and the Messianic promise. Daniel is an example that God's people can live in a hostile environment and still remain faithful to God.

In what way might you be under pressure and need to be strengthened or encouraged?

At-A-Glance

1. A Word Went Out (Daniel 9:4)
2. Communal Confession (vv. 5–8)
3. Please, God (vv. 15–19)

In Depth

1. A Word Went Out (Daniel 9:4)

The entire book of Daniel is a testament to individual faith, and this prayer is a continuation of that faith. Daniel's prayer is ultimately rooted in the belief that God will remain faithful to the Children of Israel because of the covenant. Daniel's prayer was not a simple statement of, "Sorry, Lord. I did it." Instead, Daniel poured out his heart before God. He first acknowledged God's right to exact punishment for the sins committed against Him. Then he confessed for himself and his people. In addition, Daniel confessed to God, who was a covenant keeper and a giver of mercy. Through their entire period of sin and judgment, God had never failed His people. No matter how many times they forgot God, He had never forgotten them.

When you pray, do you believe by faith that God will answer?

2. Communal Confession (vv. 5–8)

Verses five and six are a confession of Israel's misdeeds and sinful nature. Repentance requires acknowledgment and confession. Daniel presents the nation's sins to God. The Hebrew people had openly rebelled against God and incurred His wrath. They disobeyed His Law and wandered from His precepts. They had willfully refused to yield to God's servants, the prophets who had spoken on His behalf.

He names them individually, but there is no indication that Daniel himself engaged in any of these sins. Although he resided in Jerusalem prior to exile, Daniel prayed for all of Israel, both the Northern and Southern kingdoms, who were divided during this time (v. 7). He recognizes that the entire nation is judged by God.

Why is it good to confess our sins and pray for our nation?

3. Please, God (vv. 15–19)

Daniel's supplication is a true example of intercessory prayer. He pleaded with God to spare the nation. The foundation of his request was not rooted in what the people deserved, but in God's forgiveness. It was in his service to God that Daniel appealed to God to hear his petition and supplications. He begged the Lord three times in three different ways to listen (vv. 17–19). Daniel asked the Lord not only to listen, but also to act. Immediately following the prayer, God responded. The vision Daniel received was not one of hope, but a sign that God was present, listening, and responding. Daniel's prayers and supplications are marvelous examples of how we are to take our petitions to God. We must not blame Him or others. We must come before God acknowledging our own sins and plead for forgiveness, because the failure is not in Him, but in us.

When was the last time you dedicated quality time for praying to God?

Search the Scriptures

1. In addition to praying to God, what else did Daniel say he did (Daniel 9:4)?

2. Why were the Israelites far off in various countries (v. 7)?

Discuss the Meaning

The structure of Daniel's prayer consisted of two parts: confession and supplication.

Confession means admitting and agreeing with God that sin is sin. Supplication is making a request or appeal. How did Daniel utilize each of these elements in his communication with God? How do confession and supplication work together when we pray?

Lesson in Our Society

Modern culture has taught us to approach almost everything from an individual perspective, while the Bible overwhelmingly supports a communal outlook and interconnectedness. This is very similar to the African worldview of *ubuntu*. Instead of Decartes' cogito ergo sum ("I think therefore I am"), *ubuntu* says, "I am what I am because of who we all are." This kind of communal outlook was with our ancestors from the very beginning.

Consider the following questions in light of the biblical and African communal outlook. In multiple ways, do communities (whether ethnic, geographic, religious, countries, etc.) sin and suffer together? If so, is communal repentance needed today? Ultimately, we are responsible for the actions of the community.

If we view our world as God does, what would we conclude is needed for our nation?

Make It Happen

Crying out to God in intercessory prayer is one of the most effective ways to act in faith.

• Make a list of people/communities that need your intercession.

• Think about the last time you cried out to God.

• Write down how you felt afterward.

Follow the Spirit

What God wants me to do:

_____

_____

Remember Your Thoughts

Special insights I have learned:

_____

_____

_____

_____

More Light on the Text
Daniel 9:4–8, 15–19

4 And I prayed unto the LORD my God, and made my confession, and said, O Lord, the great and dreadful God, keeping the covenant and mercy to them that love him, and to them that keep his commandments;

On the outside Daniel was covered in sackcloth and ashes—symbols of his sorrowful spirit. On the inside, he was truly repentant and sought God's mercy as one of many who had transgressed God's Law. Daniel called upon Jehovah Elohim. The word used for "Lord" in this case is the Hebrew word *Yahweh*, the national name for God which declares Jehovah to be the self-existent and eternal God. This word recognizes that God is the Creator of all things and that by Him all things exist. Jehovah is self-existent—He has always been and was not created—and all-powerful.

This righteous man acknowledged his own need for God's forgiveness for his transgressions of God's laws. The Hebrew term for "confession," *yadah* (**yah-DAH**), means "to show oneself as guilty."

Daniel acknowledged that the sin of his people was his sin. He did not attempt to say that the deeds prophesied by Jeremiah were committed by a previous generation. He did not put himself above other Hebrews by reminding God of how he personally had been faithful all the days of his captivity. He had refused the king's food, denied the unjust laws forbidding prayer, and faced the lions' den; however, Daniel knew that those showed God's power, not his own righteousness. God had delivered, and Daniel was humbled by His mercy.

Again Daniel addressed God as "Lord, the great and dreadful." In Hebrew, "great" is *gadol* (**gah-DOLE**), which means "large in magnitude and extent." With this word, Daniel admitted that the God of Judah is larger than Judah itself. God's power and majesty extend far beyond the boundaries of the holy city, Jerusalem. There in Persia, the capital city of a foreign land, God's power was felt. Furthermore, Daniel called God "dreadful" (Heb. *yare'*, **yah-RAY**), which means to inspire or cause fear and awe. God is to be held in awe and revered by all people. His might is so great that He must be given the honor due His name. God had kept the covenant with Israel through their exile, His faithfulness endured even though Israel was unfaithful.

Daniel's own life had shown that God was faithful. As Daniel tried to serve Him in a strange land, he found that God was present. Daniel was not alone in this. The Hebrew boys who had been thrown into the furnace were witnesses as well. But Daniel's confession of God's merciful grace goes beyond even those few. God's faithfulness had been demonstrated to their fathers—from Adam to Noah, from Abraham to Jacob, through the judges and the prophets, God had been faithful.

5 We have sinned, and have committed iniquity, and have done wickedly, and have rebelled, even by departing from thy precepts and from thy judgments: 6 Neither have we hearkened unto thy servants the prophets, which spake in thy name to our kings, our princes, and our fathers, and to all the people of the land.

Daniel confessed that the Children of Israel were covenant breakers. Through their own fault, God had punished them by allowing them to go into bondage to the Babylonians. Because of their sin, the punishment had continued upon their children for multiple generations. In all of this, God was blameless. He had been merciful toward them. The Hebrew people could blame no one but themselves and could turn to no one but the Lord.

In addition, all the captive Israelites had committed "iniquity" (Heb. *'avah*, **ah-VAH**), which is closely related to words meaning twist, distort, and pervert. They had perverted God's Law and had done wrong before Him. They had twisted His edicts and failed to follow His will in His way. To further show how they did not follow God's directives, Daniel said that the people "have done wickedly." This phrase in Hebrew is *rasha'* (**rah-SHAH**), and it means "to condemn as guilty" and "to act wickedly," referring to their unethical and irreligious acts. Daniel has no doubt in his mind that God was just in condemning the idolatry and unfaithfulness of His people.

The Hebrew word *shama'* (**shah-MAH**), translated "hearkened," means that the people had not heard or been obedient to God's Word. To *shama'* means to listen with the intention of obeying, to pay strict attention to what is said, and then to yield to the will of the one who gives direction. Daniel knew that as the people and nation walked in sin, they broke their covenant relationship with a Holy God. They had refused to listen and obey God or hear God's prophets. These spokesmen had warned them again and again that departing from His precepts and judgments would kindle the hot anger of Almighty God and He would punish them. They had no excuse for their disobedience because the prophets spoke to their kings, princes, forefathers, and all the people of the land.

But the people and their leaders failed to listen; they would not hear nor heed. Consequently, they had to suffer the consequences of their disobedience—captivity again! Their history had revealed God's deliverance from Egypt, but their actions had caused them to be placed under the thumb of oppressors while their places of worship and their homes were destroyed and their children were led away to other lands.

7 O Lord, righteousness belongeth unto thee, but unto us confusion of faces, as at this day; to the men of Judah, and to the inhabitants of Jerusalem, and unto all Israel, that are near, and that are far off, through all the countries whither thou hast driven them, because of their trespass that they have trespassed against thee. 8 O Lord, to us belongeth confusion of face, to our kings, to our princes, and to our fathers, because we have sinned against thee.

Daniel again acknowledged God as his Lord. He recognized the righteous attributes of the God he served. Daniel admitted to God that He was right in His punishment of Israel. He had dealt righteously with His people. They, on the other hand, were the possessors of "confusion" (Heb. *boshet,* **BO-shet**), or in modern wording "shame." Because of Israel's disobedience, their faces were covered with shame, while God's glory is righteous.

Daniel also confessed that the people of Judah, Jerusalem, and all Israel, scattered far and near, were to bear the shame of being in captivity. Daniel knew they were scattered because of their own disobedience in breaking of God's covenant. God would not tolerate their disloyalty. Neither did God merit their unfaithfulness to Him; He had been too good to the Israelites.

15 And now, O Lord our God, that hast brought thy people forth out of the land of Egypt with a mighty hand, and hast gotten thee renown, as at this day; we have sinned, we have done wickedly. 16 O LORD, according to all thy righteousness, I beseech thee, let thine anger and thy fury be turned away from thy city Jerusalem, thy holy mountain: because for our sins, and for the iniquities of our fathers, Jerusalem and thy people are become a reproach to all that are about us.

Daniel continues to pray and mentions the act of God bringing Israel from Egyptian bondage. He also speaks of God's renown (Heb. *shem,* **SHAYM**), which means "name" but in this context refers to His name and the fame that accompanies it. In contrast to God's deliverance and renown among the nations, Daniel speaks of the people's sinfulness. Because of the people's sins, Jerusalem and the people of Israel have become a reproach (Heb. *cherpah,* **KER-pa**), which means a taunt or scorn of an enemy. In this sense, the stigma and shame of such taunts rest on Israel.

17 Now therefore, O our God, hear the prayer of thy servant, and his supplications, and cause thy face to shine upon thy sanctuary that is desolate, for the Lord's sake.

Here Daniel pleads with God as he cries out to the Lord because of his deep concern for the nation and the city of Jerusalem. Here is where God had placed His sanctuary! Daniel reminded Elohim that Israel was His special possession. The nation was God's chosen people, elected by Him to be representatives of His power and glory to the rest of the world. God had ordained them to be an example of His power to other nations.

Daniel also pleaded with God to hear his prayer, the prayer of His servant. The phrase "of thy servant" means bondsman or slave in Hebrew. Daniel again acknowledged that he was a servant who served as a prophet or spokesman of the Most High God. Daniel was interceding from the position of a servant of God.

Daniel asked the Lord, for His own sake, to smile again on His Temple. The Temple at Jerusalem had been foreshadowed by the tabernacle in the wilderness; it had been promised to David, then built by Solomon. The Temple was destroyed in the destruction of Jerusalem and then sat desolate, a mockery to the power of God. The word used for "sanctuary" is the Hebrew word *miqdash* (**meek-DOSH**), which refers to the sacred or holy place of worship. In essence, Daniel asked God to restore His holy Temple in Jerusalem, His "sacred place," so that all people would know His name and His power.

18 O my God, incline thine ear, and hear; open thine eyes, and behold our desolations, and the city which is called by thy name: for we do not present our supplications before thee for our righteousnesses, but for thy great mercies.

Daniel asked God to do three things: to "incline" (Heb. *natah*, **nah-TAH**) His ear, to "open" (Heb. *paqakh*, **pah-KAKH**) His eyes, and to "behold" (Heb. *ra'ah*, **rah-AH**) the desolation. Daniel asked Almighty God to extend or stretch His ear to hear his petitions for the people and the nation. He begged God to open His eyes so He could be vigilant. He wanted God to fully observe and care for the pressing situation of His chosen people, to see their wretchedness, and to see Jerusalem in ruin.

Since Daniel was the intercessor for the Israelites, he told God that he and the people were not asking because they deserved His help. In fact, Daniel and the nation knew they deserved God's wrath and punishment. But Daniel asked God for help because He is merciful. Daniel acknowledged that God is a God of great compassion. Even though God judges sin, He still shows mercy to those who love Him and are faithful to Him.

19 O Lord, hear; O Lord, forgive; O Lord, hearken and do; defer not, for thine own sake, O my God: for thy city and thy people are called by thy name.

Finally Daniel, in making intercession for the Israelites and the nation, begged God to forgive the people and the nation. The Hebrew word for "forgive" is *salakh* (**saw-LAKH**), which comes from a root word meaning of lightness or lifting up. Daniel asked God to pardon the people individually and the nation collectively for their sin. Daniel came in prayer to his God with a broken and contrite heart and a repentant spirit. He did not come before God trying to make excuses or to place blame. Daniel knew that the omniscient and omnipresent God knew the full extent of their transgressions and disobedience; therefore, Daniel wanted God to hear his pleas and act on their behalf.

Daniel wanted God to make things right, to put things back together again. He wanted God to put Jerusalem and the Temple back in order. The urgency of Daniel's prayer is that he asked God not to defer (Heb. *'achar*, **ah-KHAR**) or delay this work. Daniel wanted God to answer his prayer quickly. He realized that the seventy years prophesied by Jeremiah were almost up, and he knew that the sins of the people were still counted against them.

It was not, however, for selfish reasons that Daniel wanted God's swift reconciliation. He wanted God to set things right "for thine own sake, O my God." In other words, since the Children of Israel were God's own special possessions, Daniel reminded God that His mercy was needed for His own glory, for the restoration of Jerusalem and the Temple, for the return of the city and the people called by God's name. Once more Daniel reminded God that the Israelites were elected by Him; they were His chosen people. Daniel presents a wonderful example of intercession. He recognized God's response was rooted in God's mercy because Israel had sinned against God while God always remains faithful.

Sources:

Achtemeier, Paul J., ed. *HarperCollins Bible Dictionary*. San Francisco, CA: Harper San Francisco, 1996. 449, 549–550.

Goldingay, John E. *Word Biblical Commentary*, Vol. 30. Dallas, TX: Word Books, 1989.

Johns, Robert. *The Visions of Daniel the Hebrew Prophet*. Bloomington, IN: WestBow Press, 2012. 54–56.

Pace, Sharon. *Smyth & Helwys Bible Commentary: Daniel*. Macon, GA: Smyth & Helwys Publishing, 2008. 12, 27–28.

Say It Correctly

Hearkened. **HAR**-kend.
Desolate. **DEH**-so-let.

Daily Bible Readings

MONDAY
Plea for God's Forgiveness and Mercy
(Nehemiah 1:4–11)

TUESDAY
Disobedience Results in Israel's Downfall
(Jeremiah 25:8–14)

WEDNESDAY
A Renewed Call to Repentance
(Joel 1:13–20)

THURSDAY
Seeking Answers Through Prayer
and Supplication
(Daniel 9:1–3)

FRIDAY
Prayer of Confession for Israel's Sins
(Daniel 9:9–14)

SATURDAY
Receiving Answers to Prayer and Confession
(Daniel 9:20–24)

SUNDAY
Daniel's Prayer of Confession
and Supplication
(Daniel 9:4–8, 15–19)

Notes

_____

_____

_____

Teaching Tips

Words You Should Know

A. Beloved (Daniel 10:11) *khemdah* (Heb.)—Most desirable, highly esteemed, lovely, delightful, most admired, delight, desire, pleasant, precious.

B. Strength (v. 16) *khazaq* (Heb.)—Bind, seize, to be strong, courageous, cure, help, and repair, fortify.

Teacher Preparation

Unifying Principle—Strength When You Need It Most. Sometimes circumstances cause us to feel like we can't go on. Where can we find strength to do so? Daniel found strength in prayer and from the angel sent by God to encourage him and answer his prayer.

A. Pray for each of the students, calling them by name and interceding for specific circumstances in their life.

B. Reading through the Bible lesson in at least two translations and use the companion lesson in the *Precepts For Living®* Study Guide.

O—Open the Lesson

A. Open the class with prayer.

B. Have a volunteer read the Lesson Title, Aim for Change, and the Keep in Mind verse.

C. Ask the class to read the In Focus story, and then discuss.

P—Present the Scriptures

A. Go around the room and have each student read a Scripture from the Focal Verses.

B. Ask for volunteers to read The People, Places, and Times; Background; and In Depth sections and discuss.

E—Explore the Meaning

A. Answer the question from the Discuss the Meaning section.

B. Ask for a volunteer to read the Lesson in Our Society section.

N—Next Steps for Application

A. Encourage the class to apply the Make It Happen Section.

B. Close with prayer.

Worship Guide

For the Superintendent or Teacher
Theme: A Strong Faith
Song: "Great is Thy Faithfulness"
Devotional Reading: Revelation 1:9–18

A Strong Faith

Bible Background • DANIEL 10–11
Printed Text • DANIEL 10:10–19 | Devotional Reading • REVELATION 1:9–18

Aim for Change

By the end of this lesson we will: ANALYZE the account of Daniel's visit by an angel; VISUALIZE Daniel's state of mind during the angelic visit; and EXPRESS gratitude that God's people always receive from God exactly what they need at the time.

In Focus

Ellen buried her face in her hands. Today she didn't care if her makeup smeared or if she looked crazy as she sat in the car. She spent an hour reading her Bible, studying the words and cross-references, singing and worshiping before the Lord, but it all seemed useless. She had just come back from inquiring about a job at the local community college as a receptionist.

Ellen had been job hunting for a long time now. She never thought she would be in this place. It seemed like it would be easy to get hired somewhere else after she was laid off. *How long, Lord?* She sobbed. *I thought I'd have a job already but I keep coming up with nothing. It's been months and I've gone through job sites and asked all my friends for referrals. Nobody has even given me an interview.*

The knock on her window startled her. "You alright, honey?" Her elderly neighbor from across the street peered into the car. "Anytime you want to come over and have prayer with me about anything, I'm always home." Ellen looked up at the woman, tears still streaming down her face. Ellen began to smile. "God, thank You! You sent her right on time. You haven't forgot about me after all."

Sometimes the answers to our prayers are delayed but not denied, and God will send the right encouragement at just the right time. Have you ever received encouragement from God to continue praying for something after a long period of silence?

Keep in Mind

"And said, O man greatly beloved, fear not: peace be unto thee, be strong, yea, be strong. And when he had spoken unto me, I was strengthened, and said, Let my lord speak; for thou hast strengthened me" (Daniel 10:19).

"And said, O man greatly beloved, fear not: peace be unto thee, be strong, yea, be strong. And when he had spoken unto me, I was strengthened, and said, Let my lord speak; for thou hast strengthened me" (Daniel 10:19).

Focal Verses

KJV **Daniel 10:10** And, behold, an hand touched me, which set me upon my knees and upon the palms of my hands.

11 And he said unto me, O Daniel, a man greatly beloved, understand the words that I speak unto thee, and stand upright: for unto thee am I now sent. And when he had spoken this word unto me, I stood trembling.

12 Then said he unto me, Fear not, Daniel: for from the first day that thou didst set thine heart to understand, and to chasten thyself before thy God, thy words were heard, and I am come for thy words.

13 But the prince of the kingdom of Persia withstood me one and twenty days: but, lo, Michael, one of the chief princes, came to help me; and I remained there with the kings of Persia.

14 Now I am come to make thee understand what shall befall thy people in the latter days: for yet the vision is for many days.

15 And when he had spoken such words unto me, I set my face toward the ground, and I became dumb.

16 And, behold, one like the similitude of the sons of men touched my lips: then I opened my mouth, and spake, and said unto him that stood before me, O my lord, by the vision my sorrows are turned upon me, and I have retained no strength.

17 For how can the servant of this my lord talk with this my lord? for as for me, straightway there remained no strength in me, neither is there breath left in me.

18 Then there came again and touched me one like the appearance of a man, and he strengthened me,

19 And said, O man greatly beloved, fear not: peace be unto thee, be strong, yea, be strong. And when he had spoken unto me, I

NLT **Daniel 10:10** Just then a hand touched me and lifted me, still trembling, to my hands and knees.

11 And the man said to me, "Daniel, you are very precious to God, so listen carefully to what I have to say to you. Stand up, for I have been sent to you." When he said this to me, I stood up, still trembling.

12 Then he said, "Don't be afraid, Daniel. Since the first day you began to pray for understanding and to humble yourself before your God, your request has been heard in heaven. I have come in answer to your prayer.

13 But for twenty-one days the spirit prince of the kingdom of Persia blocked my way. Then Michael, one of the archangels came to help me, and I left him there with the spirit prince of the kingdom of Persia.

14 Now I am here to explain what will happen to your people in the future, for this vision concerns a time yet to come."

15 While he was speaking to me, I looked down at the ground, unable to say a word.

16 Then the one who looked like a man touched my lips, and I opened my mouth and began to speak. I said to the one standing in front of me, "I am filled with anguish because of the vision I have seen, my lord, and I am very weak.

17 How can someone like me, your servant, talk to you, my lord? My strength is gone, and I can hardly breathe."

18 Then the one who looked like a man touched me again, and I felt my strength returning.

19 "Don't be afraid," he said, "for you are very precious to God. Peace! Be encouraged! Be strong!" As he spoke these words to me, I suddenly felt stronger and said to him, "Please speak to me, my lord, for you have strengthened me."

was strengthened, and said, Let my lord speak; for thou hast strengthened me.

The People, Places, and Times

Prince of the kingdom of Persia. A demonic influence and/or entity that had power over the affairs of the kings of Medo-Persia. The prince commissioned spiritual forces to oppose the Israelite remnant by attempting to stop the Temple rebuilding in Jerusalem. This angel of darkness represented the Persian world power, to which Israel was then subject. This is the reason Daniel's prayer was hindered.

Michael. An angel of God, Michael was a messenger sent to battle the prince of the kingdom of Persia on Daniel's behalf. In several passages of Scripture, Michael is associated with battles between good angels and evil angels (Jude 9; Revelation 12:7).

Background

Daniel had fasted and prayed to God, asking Him to forgive his people because they had sinned and caused Jerusalem to be destroyed (Daniel 9). God responded by sending Gabriel to give Daniel understanding and a vision regarding the end of Jerusalem's destruction (9:20–27). Now, Daniel fasts again and prays for three weeks regarding Jerusalem's destruction and his people's sins. God sends a messenger to give him understanding and a vision, this time concerning things that will happen during the Persian and Greek empires (Daniel 10).

This section is part of a series of apocalyptic visions (Daniel 7–12) that God gives Daniel in order for him to understand what is going to happen on the grand political scale in the future. In the final vision, Daniel is responding to the historical crisis in Jerusalem that has prevented the rebuilding of the Temple according to God's promised time line (Daniel 10–13). Although Cyrus of Persia allowed Jewish deportees, such as Ezra, to return to Jerusalem and rebuild the city and Temple, for a time the work was stopped until the years of Darius (Ezra 1:1–4, 4:1–5).

During this time, Daniel fasts and prays for God's people and the future of the holy city. Throughout, it is clear that Daniel's close relationship to God and his humility, fasting, and prayer are what prompt God to reveal His plans to Daniel (Daniel 9:22–23).

At-A-Glance

1. Strengthened to Stand (Daniel 10:10–11)
2. Strengthened After a Battle (vv. 12–14)
3. Strengthened for the Revelation (vv. 15–19)

In Depth

1. Strengthened to Stand (Daniel 10:10–11)

Daniel encountered a vision after three weeks of fasting. The appearance of an incredible-looking angel caused Daniel to recognize his sinfulness in the presence of such holiness. The experience humbled him, and he passed out and slumped to the ground when the angel began to speak (Daniel 10:7–9).

The angel touched Daniel to strengthen him; he needed to be attentive to receive God's message. The angel's touch gave Daniel enough fortitude to climb to his hands and knees. The angel referred to Daniel as "greatly beloved" by the Lord, who wanted him to hear and understand His message. So Daniel stood to his feet, still trembling.

Daniel was to record the future three hundred years in advance. God also revealed to Daniel end-time events pertaining to the coming Antichrist (Daniel 11–12).

2. Strengthened After a Battle (vv. 12–14)

The angelic messenger told Daniel not to fear, but to compose himself. In order to listen to the heavenly communication, Daniel's mind needed to be free from terror. The first day he humbled himself and started to pray, God heard his petition, provided an answer, and sent it to him. However, satanic forces interfered and kept Daniel from receiving the message for three weeks.

The evil, demonic, angelic force hindered God's response to Daniel. He is identified as the "prince of the kingdom of Persia"—a fallen angel who was given authority by Satan to watch over the affairs of the Medo-Persian Empire. Rank, hierarchy, and organization exist in both the heavenly and demonic angelic realm (Ephesians 1:21, 6:12; Colossians 1:16, 2:15).

Michael, one of God's chief angels, came to assist the angelic messenger for Daniel. This angel is known for battle in the heavens between good and evil. Note that this angelic being is certainly not Christ, because Jesus never needed help to overcome any satanic force.

The conquest in the heavens ended. God's angel overcame the demonic forces, and now Daniel can receive His message. Daniel's prayers were neither fruitless nor in vain; he's now ready to hear the weighty prophecies in the following chapters, which cover important future events.

3. Strengthened for the Revelation (vv. 15–19)

Daniel, feeling unworthy, got weak once again and prostrated himself on the ground. He was unable to speak. The angel touched his lips, restored his speech, and filled his heart with boldness. Daniel recognized the angel as one sent from God. He asked the angel how he could talk, since he had lost his breath and his strength. Once again, the angelic being lifted him up. Some scholars identify the angel as Gabriel. While the angel's identity is uncertain, we know that Daniel needed strength to receive the explanation of the vision.

Search the Scriptures

1. Why did Daniel not receive an answer for twenty-one days (Daniel 10:12–13)?

2. How did the angel strengthen Daniel (vv. 18–19)?

Discuss the Meaning

Even mature Christians experience situations that make them wonder where God is, and why He is silent during difficult times. Why do you think God allows us to go through those types of experiences?

Lesson in Our Society

Statistics reveal that believers struggle with issues just like unbelievers. Divorce, porn addiction, and depression are just a few of the challenges Christians experience, just like their non-Christian neighbors. The angel strengthening Daniel stands as a good example of how God will come along and fortify His children. He knows our public and private conflicts. Be patient and wait on God; He knows the right time to intervene.

Make It Happen

• Encourage someone you know who's been going through a trial this week. Let her or him know that God hasn't given up; He has not forgotten.

• Breathe fresh life into a prayer that you may have stopped praying due to lack of perseverance or doubt.

• Find someone to pray with during this week.

Follow the Spirit

What God wants me to do:

_____

_____

_____

_____

Remember Your Thoughts

Special insights I have learned:

_____

_____

_____

_____

More Light on the Text

Daniel 10:10–19

10 And, behold, an hand touched me, which set me upon my knees and upon the palms of my hands. 11 And he said unto me, O Daniel, a man greatly beloved, understand the words that I speak unto thee, and stand upright: for unto thee am I now sent. And when he had spoken this word unto me, I stood trembling.

After three weeks of fasting and prayer, on the twenty-fourth day, Daniel sees a vision. Many interpret this as Gabriel appearing again to Daniel, but the text does not specify here, so it could be another messenger of God (Daniel 8:16, 9:21). Other people are with Daniel, but

they do not see the vision. The vision is so powerful, though, that it knocks Daniel to the ground and even causes the others to run away in terror (v. 7).

Daniel tells us that a hand touched him and set him on his hands and knees, telling him to stand up. It is not clear whether the hand belongs to the man in the vision. In Hebrew, the word for "hand" also means "power" or "strength" (*yad*, **YAHD**), so it could refer to God's hand or power lifting Daniel up (see Ezekiel 3:14, 22). In any case, given that this man is a messenger of God, it is ultimately God's power lifting Daniel up. In contrast to Ezekiel's vision (Ezekiel 2:2), Daniel can only get to his hands and knees, indicating a more powerful experience.

The man calls Daniel "greatly beloved" (Heb. *khemdah*, **khem-DAH**), meaning "pleasant, wanted or desired, precious as a jewel." The angel stresses that Daniel is important to God and tells him to understand the words about to be spoken. Daniel has to stand up.

The text emphasizes standing because the command "stand up" and the word translated "upright" in the KJV both come from the Hebrew root meaning to stand (*'amad*, **ah-MAHD**). The idea is that Daniel should be in a ready position to receive and understand the vision. Then Daniel stood up, but he was trembling. His instinct in the presence of this powerful experience with a divine messenger is to faint—lose strength and fall down (see vv. 8, 17; Ezekiel 1:28–2:2).

12 Then said he unto me, Fear not, Daniel: for from the first day that thou didst set thine heart to understand, and to chasten thyself before thy God, thy words were heard, and I am come for thy words.

The messenger tells Daniel not to be afraid. God has heard Daniel's words from the first day he began fasting and praying in order to humble himself before God and gain understanding. The word for "chasten thyself" (Heb. 'anah, **ah-NAH**) means to submit yourself, but it also came to mean ritual fasting in later Hebrew texts like Ezra, Daniel, and the Dead Sea Scrolls. Refraining from eating and drinking makes a person physically weak. This was often accompanied by putting ashes on the head and sitting on the ground in mourning and prayer.

Daniel did this for three weeks. God gives understanding to the humble and to those who are truly ready to understand the situation, no matter how dire.

13 But the prince of the kingdom of Persia withstood me one and twenty days: but, lo, Michael, one of the chief princes, came to help me; and I remained there with the kings of Persia. 14 Now I am come to make thee understand what shall befall thy people in the latter days: for yet the vision is for many days.

The messenger reveals a heavenly conflict between the Lord's messenger and a supernatural Persian messenger who prevented him from coming to Daniel for twenty-one days. God heard Daniel's prayer immediately and responded, but enemy powers prevailed for a time until Michael came to help him.

Michael is one of God's chief angels and is mentioned in other heavenly battles (Revelation 12:7). "And I remained there with the kings of Persia" refers to the twenty-one days that the messenger was detained among the Persian angels, emphasizing that this was a political battle between supernatural beings of Persia and the supernatural beings assigned by God. The Persian angels were strong, just as the Persian Empire was strong, and the messenger had to fight evil resistance just as Daniel and the Jews must resist the Persian Empire. Then

God sent extra help, and the messenger was finally able to come to Daniel.

God's purpose is to help Daniel understand what will happen to his people through another vision (Daniel 11:2). The somewhat cryptic English phrase "for yet the vision is for many days" means that there is another vision for those future days regarding Daniel's people. He received visions in chapters 7–9, which were also about political events, but Daniel still really needs to understand the fate of Jerusalem. Now, God answers Daniel's prayers regarding Jerusalem with a new vision, which he will need help understanding.

We can only imagine how overwhelmed Daniel must have been. He was receiving visions about political realms and their evil deeds, and ultimate destruction as a result. All the while, he was reading the Hebrew prophets, and when he came to Jeremiah's prophecies about Jerusalem's destruction by the Babylonians (Jeremiah 52), a fate he himself saw when he was exiled to Babylon (Daniel 1), he was stricken with grief concerning his people and the city of God. He fasted and prayed, and finally he would receive an answer from God.

15 And when he had spoken such words unto me, I set my face toward the ground, and I became dumb. 16 And, behold, one like the similitude of the sons of men touched my lips: then I opened my mouth, and spake, and said unto him that stood before me, O my lord, by the vision my sorrows are turned upon me, and I have retained no strength. 17 For how can the servant of this my lord talk with this my lord? for as for me, straightway there remained no strength in me, neither is there breath left in me.

Every time this messenger speaks, Daniel falls down and loses strength. The first time (v. 9), he was knocked unconscious by the speech, and even this time he is dumbstruck. The "one like the similitude of the sons of men" probably refers to angelic beings (see 7:13). To touch a person's lips in a heavenly vision has symbolic meaning. In the vision of Isaiah's call, the angelic seraphim touch his lips with burning coal in order to purify his speech to be God's prophet (Isaiah 6:6–7).

Daniel immediately loses strength when the messenger appears or speaks. The question "For how can the servant of this my lord talk with this my lord?" emphasizes Daniel's humble position. As a servant of God, he is merely a servant of God's messenger, who is in a more authoritative position than Daniel, so how can Daniel speak to this lordly divine messenger? Daniel has no strength or breath to do so.

18 Then there came again and touched me one like the appearance of a man, and he strengthened me, 19 And said, O man greatly beloved, fear not: peace be unto thee, be strong, yea, be strong. And when he had spoken unto me, I was strengthened, and said, Let my lord speak; for thou hast strengthened me.

Daniel has lost all strength, but as soon as he is touched by the messenger, he is strengthened. In visions, to say that somebody has the appearance of a man or a son of man indicates that there is something distinct about the being. The person seeing the vision recognizes that this is no mere human, but somehow a being that looks like a human. The messenger seems familiar, but he is from the heavenly realm.

The messenger again reminds Daniel that he is precious and tells him not to be afraid but be at peace, and twice encourages him to be strong. Daniel's strength is a key part of this passage. He made himself physically weak through fasting (vv. 2–3), then loses strength when the messenger appears or

speaks (vv. 8, 17). The messenger keeps helping him, encouraging him as God's beloved (vv. 11, 19), lifting him up (v. 10), and telling him to be strong (v. 18).

It only takes a word from the messenger for Daniel to be strengthened. He is ready to hear God's word. The messenger responds by telling Daniel that after the vision, he will have to leave to fight the leader of Persia, and then the leader of Greece will come, predicting the future fall of the Persian Empire to Alexander the Great (vv. 20–21). This seems to suggest a correlation between heavenly and earthly warfare.

Amid crisis, Daniel turns to God's Word (9:2), as well as fasting and prayer for understanding and strength. God responds with a helper to strengthen Daniel and give him understanding.

Sources:
Adeyemo, Tokunboh. "Daniel." *Africa Bible Commentary*. Grand Rapids, MI: Zondervan, 2006. 989–1012.
LaCocque, André. "Daniel." *Global Bible Commentary*. Nashville, TN: Abingdon Press, 2004. 2653–2261.
Lai, Barbara M. Leung. "Daniel." *The Peoples' Companion to the Bible*. Minneapolis, MN: Fortress Press, 2010. 162–163.
Newsom, Carol A. *Daniel: A Commentary*. Old Testament Library. Louisville, KY: Westminster John Knox Press, 2014.
Smith-Christopher. Daniel L. "The Book of Daniel." *New Interpreter's Bible*, Vol. 7. Nashville, TN: Abingdon Press, 1996. 19–152.

Say It Correctly

Chasten. **CHAY**-sun.
Similitude. sih-**MIL**-uh-tude.

Daily Bible Readings

MONDAY
A Vision Sends Jacob to Egypt
(Genesis 46:1–7)

TUESDAY
Joshua, Be Strong and Courageous
(Joshua 1:1–9)

WEDNESDAY
Ezekiel Called to Speak to Israel
(Ezekiel 1:26–2:7)

THURSDAY
Paul Called to Macedonia in a Vision
(Acts 16:6–10)

FRIDAY
Daniel Sees a Vision
(Daniel 10:1–9)

SATURDAY
Time of the End
(Daniel 12:8–13)

SUNDAY
Be Strong and Courageous
(Daniel 10:10–19)

Notes

Teaching Tips

Words You Should Know

A. Faith (James 2:14) *pistis* (Gk.)—Persuasion, credence, moral conviction, truth itself, assurance, belief.

B. Works (v. 14) *ergon* (Gk.)—Toil as in an effort or occupation; act, deed, doing, labor.

Teacher Preparation

Unifying Principle—Actions Speak Louder Than Words. People know that talk is cheap and that actions speak louder than words. How should we live in this regard? James says that our professions of faith must be matched by accompanying action.

A. Pray that students will grasp the importance demonstrating their faith through action.

B. Read the Bible Background and Devotional Readings. Read the Focus Verses in several translations.

C. Assign two or three students ahead of time to prepare a short skit of the In Focus story.

O—Open the Lesson

A. Open with prayer and introduce the lesson title.

B. Have the class read together the Keep in Mind verse.

C. Have the appointed volunteers act out the In Focus skit. Allow time for reactions.

P—Present the Scriptures

A. Ask for volunteers to read the Focal Verses.

B. Divide into pairs and have each group go over The People, Places, and Times; Background; and the In Depth sections.

E—Explore the Meaning

A. Answer the questions in Search the Scriptures.

B. Read the Discuss the Meaning, Lesson in Our Society, and Make It Happen sections.

C. Discuss the quote from D.L. Moody. Challenge the class to use insights discovered from the lesson.

N—Next Steps for Application

A. Save enough time for silence and prayer. Challenge students to prayerfully ask the Holy Spirit to help them understand the difference between dead works and real faith.

B. Encourage the class to spend the rest of the week thinking and praying about how to put this lesson into practice.

C. Close in prayer.

Worship Guide

For the Superintendent or Teacher
Theme: Faith Without Works is Dead
Song: "Give Me a Clean Heart"
Devotional Reading: Psalm 143

Faith Without Works is Dead

Bible Background • JAMES 2:14–26
Printed Text • JAMES 2:14–26 | Devotional Reading • PSALM 143

Aim for Change

By the end of the lesson we will: AGREE with the teachings of James regarding the relationship between faith and works; REPENT for those times when our words were not supported by corresponding actions; and REVERE God with actions that match our faith expressions.

In Focus

Today was the first day that Pastor Jackson would be introduced as the new pastor. He decided to test his new congregation to assess their spiritual growth.

He dressed as a homeless man and walked around the church. Only three people said hello. He asked for money to buy food. Everyone refused. The "homeless" man greeted others, but they returned cold, icy stares.

It was time for the announcement! As the congregation clapped with excitement, they scowled at the homeless man who was walking toward the front of the church. When he stood in the pulpit, he told them the Scripture lesson was from Matthew 25:35.

Pastor Jackson told his congregation how he felt about what he'd just experienced. Some began to cry. Nearly everyone felt a sense of shame, especially Deacon Jones. The congregation couldn't stop thinking about their lack of compassion and outreach. Homeless people were a common sight all around their parish, but they were ignored and neglected. So much religious busyness took priority.

Deacon Jones met with Pastor Jackson and launched a food pantry ministry. They didn't have to work hard to sign up volunteers. Members in the entire church found a way to become personally involved.

In today's lesson, we will learn what it means to have an authentic and genuine faith. In what ways has God called you to put your faith into action?

Keep in Mind

"Even so faith, if it hath not works, is dead, being alone" (James 2:17).

"Even so faith, if it hath not works, is dead, being alone" (James 2:17).

Focal Verses

KJV **James 2:14** What doth it profit, my brethren, though a man say he hath faith, and have not works? can faith save him?

15 If a brother or sister be naked, and destitute of daily food,

16 And one of you say unto them, Depart in peace, be ye warmed and filled; notwithstanding ye give them not those things which are needful to the body; what doth it profit?

17 Even so faith, if it hath not works, is dead, being alone.

18 Yea, a man may say, Thou hast faith, and I have works: shew me thy faith without thy works, and I will shew thee my faith by my works.

19 Thou believest that there is one God; thou doest well: the devils also believe, and tremble.

20 But wilt thou know, O vain man, that faith without works is dead?

21 Was not Abraham our father justified by works, when he had offered Isaac his son upon the altar?

22 Seest thou how faith wrought with his works, and by works was faith made perfect?

23 And the scripture was fulfilled which saith, Abraham believed God, and it was imputed unto him for righteousness: and he was called the Friend of God.

24 Ye see then how that by works a man is justified, and not by faith only.

25 Likewise also was not Rahab the harlot justified by works, when she had received the messengers, and had sent them out another way?

26 For as the body without the spirit is dead, so faith without works is dead also.

NLT **James 2:14** What good is it, dear brothers and sisters, if you say you have faith but don't show it by your actions? Can that kind of faith save anyone?

15 Suppose you see a brother or sister, who has no food or clothing,

16 and you say, "Good-bye and have a good day; stay warm and eat well"—but then you don't give that person any food or clothing. What good does that do?

17 So you see, faith by itself isn't enough. Unless it produces good deeds, it is dead and useless.

18 Now someone may argue, "Some people have faith; others have good deeds." But I say, "How can you show me your faith if you don't have good deeds? I will show you my faith by my good deeds."

19 You say you have faith, for you believe that there is one God. Good for you! Even the demons believe this, and they tremble in terror.

20 How foolish! Can't you see that faith without good deeds is useless?

21 Don't you remember that our ancestor Abraham was shown to be right with God by his actions when he offered his son Isaac on the altar?

22 You see, his faith and his actions worked together. His actions made his faith complete.

23 And so it happened just as the Scriptures say: "Abraham believed God, and God counted him as righteous because of his faith." He was even called the friend of God.

24 So you see, we are shown to be right with God by what we do, not by faith alone.

25 Rahab the prostitute is another example. She was shown to be right with God by her actions when she hid those messengers and sent them safely away by a different road.

26 Just as the body is dead without breath, so also faith is dead without good works.

The People, Places, and Times

Abraham. Abraham was the son of Terah. He was from Ur of the Chaldees in what is modern-day Iraq. God spoke to Abraham and called him to go to an unknown land, promising to bless him and make him into a great nation (Genesis 12:1–4). Abraham obeyed, demonstrating great faith in God. He is considered the father of faith (Hebrews 11:8) and the patriarch of three major world religions (Judaism, Christianity, Islam).

Rahab. Rahab was a prostitute who lived in Jericho. She was visited by two spies who were hiding from the Canaanite inhabitants of the city. In return for her protection, the two Israelite spies promised to spare her and her family during the city's conquest (Joshua 2:14). She was to place a scarlet thread outside of her window to indicate her allegiance to Israel (v. 18). Rahab is in the lineage of Christ (Matthew 1:5) and mentioned in Hebrews 11 in the "Hall of Faith."

Background

The book of James is one of the earliest letters. It was written by James, the half-brother of Jesus Christ, between AD 48 and 62. Tradition holds that James did not become a believer until he saw Christ after the Resurrection. James is now the leader of the church in Jerusalem during a time of major transition (Acts 12:17, 15:13). Severe persecution following the stoning of Stephen scattered Jewish Christians throughout the Mediterranean world. James wrote to encourage his fellow believers during this extremely difficult time.

At-A-Glance

1. Dead Works (James 2:14–17)
2. Profession Without Possession (vv. 18–20)
3. The Body Without the Spirit (vv. 20–26)

In Depth

1. Dead Works (James 2:14–17)

James explains that people can claim to have faith, but if they do not accompany their words by action, that faith is worth nothing. Even Jesus warned that only those who do the Father's will would enter the kingdom of heaven, not those who say, "Lord, Lord!" (Matthew 7:21).

Similarly, James underscores the relationship between faith and works. Works, or being good and doing good deeds, cannot earn salvation; faith or believing in Jesus is the only way to eternal life (Ephesians 2:8–9). Once a person is saved—truly saved—change occurs and good works, or actions, result. The evidence of salvation is an obedient lifestyle conforming with God's Word. James gives the example of a brother or sister who needs food and shelter in verses 15–16. He argued it is no good to say, "I'm praying that you'll be warm and get something to eat!" and then walk away without providing what that brother or sister needs—it's empty words. James uses a rhetorical question to underscore that a person who truly cares will do something to help.

Having faith is the heart of James' practical letter. If a person shows no evidence of a changed lifestyle, James says that faith, no matter how loudly expressed, is dead and worthless (James 2:17). True faith always results in a transformed life. As the old folks used to sing, "The things I used to do, I don't do no more."

2. Profession Without Possession (vv. 18–20)

James shows the shallowness of profession without possession. He compares and contrasts a person who says they have faith but no works or evidence to a person who says that the evidence of their faith is demonstrated in their lifestyle.

In verse 19, the Lord's brother shares insight about the demonic world. He says in essence, that it's great that a person believes there is one God, but demons also believe that Jesus is who He says He is. And (to the shame of some so-called believers) at least the demons tremble at the very thought. But do demons believe to the extent of changing? Of course not! So what good is their belief?

James calls such thinking "foolish" in verse 20. He urges believers to examine themselves thoroughly and not be fooled about eternal life. Unfortunately, some Christians will miss heaven by 18 inches—the space between the head and the heart. Intellectual agreement with the Bible, knowing Scripture, going to church, singing in the choir, or serving on the deacon board is not enough. Heart transformation that produces a changed life is what matters.

3. The Body Without the Spirit (vv. 21–26)

James uses Abraham's willingness to offer his son Isaac as another example of faith. Abraham had waited many years to have a son. In fact, he was one hundred years old and his wife, Sarah, was ninety (Genesis 17:17). But God promised Abraham that he and Sarah would have a son. Isaac was that promise fulfilled.

Then God told Abraham to sacrifice his son as a burnt offering (Genesis 22:2). In the morning, Abraham got up, took Isaac, and headed up the mountain. He made an altar, placed his son on the altar, and lifted his hand to kill his son. God stopped him and instead provided a ram in the bush (22:13).

Why was Abraham so willing to obey God? He was convinced that God had a larger plan that he could not see, because God had promised that Abraham would be the father of many nations (Genesis 17:5–6). That's faith in action.

Is Abraham too righteous to use as a comparison? How about Rahab? In verse 25, James swings the pendulum to the other extreme to demonstrate that a harlot demonstrated faith in action when she hid the spies (Joshua 2:1).

Without the spirit or breath, the body has no life. It is dead, writes James in summary (v. 26). So, too, is verbal assent—nice words like "Praise the Lord"—without the corresponding action of a changed life.

Search the Scriptures

1. Why is faith without works dead (James 2:17)?

2. What is the role of works in relation to faith (v. 22)?

Discuss the Meaning

D.L. Moody said, "Every Bible should be bound in shoe leather." True faith walks itself out in the believer's daily life. How can we ensure that our faith affects our daily life?

Lesson in Our Society

Too many of us live undisciplined lives. Romans 12:1–2 provides the formula for us to cultivate authentic faith. Because of all that God has done for us, we should willingly present Him our lives as a sacrificial offering. "Here I am, Lord. Make me the person You want me to be."

Transformation, the process of changing from a caterpillar to a butterfly, will only result when our minds are renewed. Studying God's Word—and applying what we learn in our daily lives—will produce the kind of faith James intends.

Make It Happen

• Do a self-evaluation. If someone accused you of being a Christian, is there enough evidence to convict you?

• Become part of a small-group Bible study so you will be accountable to others, and they will be accountable to you.

• Consider sponsoring a child through an organization such as Compassion International at www.compassion.com. Or encourage your church to start a foster care program (visit www.covenantsforkids.info).

Follow the Spirit

What God wants me to do:

_____

_____

_____

_____

Remember Your Thoughts

Special insights I have learned:

_____

_____

_____

_____

More Light on the Text

James 2:14–26

14 What doth it profit, my brethren, though a man say he hath faith, and have not works? Can faith save him?

It may be helpful to note that the literary construction of this part of the book of James is one of a proposition supported by arguments and then summarized with conclusions. The proposition opens with a pair of rhetorical questions, the first of which basically says, "Suppose a man says he has faith but not works." This is quite different from James wording it, "Suppose a man has faith." To actually have faith versus saying you have faith are two entirely different things. Today, the second rhetorical question would be worded, "This kind of faith—claimed faith without works—can't save him, can it?" Of course, the correct answer is no, as James will demonstrate.

15 If a brother or sister be naked, and destitute of daily food, 16 And one of you say unto them, Depart in peace, be ye warmed and filled; notwithstanding ye give them not those things which are needful to the body; what doth it profit? 17 Even so faith, if it hath not works, is dead, being alone.

The proposition continues with a hypothetical example, employing hyperbole with a "naked" (Gk. *gumnos*, **goom-NOCE**) brother or sister, indicating someone in dire straits or desperate need, rather than an actual complete lack of clothing. This is reinforced with the supporting phrase "destitute of daily food." The word "destitute" (Gk. *leipo*, **LYE-po**) also means to lag or be left behind. This destitute brother or sister has been left behind in terms of financial provision and life's necessities.

The common phrase "depart in peace" means, in essence, "Go get what you need somewhere else, from someone else—but know that I care," or the popular "go and be filled." More modern similar responses might be "God helps those who help themselves," or the even colder, "You got yourself into this mess, so you can get yourself out of it." Such words come from a faith that is dead (Gk. *nekros*, **neck-ROCE**), which is the plain sense of the word. James was not pulling punches.

"What doth it profit?" James asked. In other words, "What good is a dead faith?" A dead faith is devoid of corresponding actions. The actions do not save you, but they are evidence that the faith you possess is alive. Genuine faith is a gift from God (Ephesians 2:8), and works are a natural expression of such faith. Faith and works are two sides of the same coin.

18 Yea, a man may say, Thou hast faith, and I have works: shew me thy faith without thy works, and I will shew thee my faith by my works. 19 Thou believest that there is one God; thou doest well: the devils also believe, and tremble. 20 But wilt thou know, O vain man, that faith without works is dead?

Having stated his proposition with rhetorical and hypothetical questions that provoke an obvious answer, James next argues his case via a fictional debater. Person A has faith without deeds; Person B has faith with deeds. From Person A, James asked for evidence of the faith he claimed to possess, reminding him that even demons can make such claims. At the thought of God, demons would even "tremble" (Gk. *phrisso*, **FREE-so**), a word bringing to mind the idea of shuddering and one's hair standing on end. However, for Person B, the evidence of faith speaks for itself—the deeds are the evidence.

21 Was not Abraham our father justified by works, when he had offered Isaac his son upon the altar? 22 Seest thou how faith wrought with his works, and by works was faith made perfect? 23 And the scripture was fulfilled which saith, Abraham believed God, and it was imputed unto him for righteousness: and he was called the Friend of God.

It would be both normal and expected for any Jew talking about faith to mention Abraham. James explains that God called Abraham righteous because of his faith. Here, James revisits the familiar details of Abraham's "works"—offering Isaac on the altar by faith—actively trusting God, even if it meant cooperating with God when it seemed to go against His own promise.

James was saying that Abraham's obedient "work" was a tangible act of faith—putting Isaac on the altar and being willing to sacrifice even the son of promise at God's command. God reckoned Abraham's faith as righteous in the seemingly impossible covenant promise of countless generations born to an elderly couple (Genesis 15:6). He was justified (Gk. *dikaioo*, **dee-keye-OH-oh**), or declared to be righteous. Abraham had faith, and God made a covenant with him because of it. Then Abraham proved his faith with the "work" of obeying God and being willing to sacrifice Isaac.

24 Ye see then how that by works a man is justified, and not by faith only.

Having made his proposition with questions, illustrations, an example, and having presented an argument from the Old Testament, James makes an early conclusion before making yet another argument from the Old Testament. This statement, which too many have pulled out of the context of his carefully constructed presentation, has caused problems and confusion through the centuries. Such approaches to interpreting Scripture are simply poor hermeneutics. Earlier, James made a parallel argument, which also must remain within the context of his epistle, regarding being a hearer of the Word versus being a doer (1:22–25).

25 Likewise also was not Rahab the harlot justified by works, when she had received

the messengers, and had sent them out another way?

James next appeals to an opposite type of character from the Old Testament for the second part of the argument section of his presentation. Some might feel like they cannot relate to the head of the Jewish nation, the national shining star, Abraham. However, perhaps an example from the opposite side of society would be closer to home or at least more relatable.

This unlikely pair shared both differences and similarities. One was Hebrew, the other Gentile; one was called by God, the other originally destined for destruction; one was a man, the other a woman; one was the father of faith, the other a lowly prostitute; one went through a long-term process of interacting with God and proving his faith; the other only had hearsay to guide her quick thinking.

For similarities, both were foreigners, both showed hospitality to strangers (Genesis 18:1–5; Joshua 2:1), and both became ancestors of Jesus (Matthew 1:2, 5). Rahab took her place in history next to Abraham because she had faith in God and acted on her faith—a simple but profound lesson that is completely transcultural for all believers.

26 For as the body without the spirit is dead, so faith without works is dead also.

James puts the conclusion on his argument by stating a clear and evident illustration of his point. Faith with works constitutes a living faith. Absent of works, faith is a cold and lifeless body. It is not genuine faith. Works do not save, but they are evidence that faith is alive.

Sources:
Burdick, Donald W. "James." *The Expositor's Bible Commentary with the New International Version: Hebrews, James, 1, 2 Peter, 1, 2, 3 John, Jude, Revelation,* Vol. 12. Grand Rapids, MI: Zondervan, 1981. 181–185.
Draper, Charles W., Chad Brand, and Archie England, eds. *Holman Illustrated Bible Dictionary.* Grand Rapids, MI: Holman Reference, 2003.
Kistemaker, Simon J. *James and I–III John.* New Testament Commentary. Grand Rapids, MI: Baker Publishing Group, 1986. 87–102.
Martin, R. A. and John H. Elliott. *James, 1–2 Peter, Jude.* Augsburg Commentary on the New Testament. Minneapolis, MN: Fortress Press, 1982. 28–36.
Myers, Allen C., John W. Simpson, Philip A. Frank, Timothy P. Jenney, and Ralph W. Vunderink, eds. *The Eerdmans Bible Dictionary.* Grand Rapids, MI: Wm. B. Eerdmans Publishing Company, 1996.

Say It Correctly

Destitute. **DES**-te-toot.
Imputed. im-**PYUT**-ed.
Rahab. **RAY**-hab.

Daily Bible Readings

MONDAY
Fulfilling the Law
(James 2:8–13)

TUESDAY
The Royal Law
(Leviticus 19:13–18)

WEDNESDAY
Teach Me to Do Your Will
(Psalm 143)

THURSDAY
Justified by Faith
(Romans 3:21–31)

FRIDAY
Christ Lives in Me
(Galatians 2:15–21)

SATURDAY
Spirit Comes Through Faith, Not Law
(Galatians 3:6–14)

SUNDAY
Faith Without Works is Dead
(James 2:14–26)

Teaching Tips

Words You Should Know

A. Masters (James 3:1) *didaskalos* (Gk.)—Teachers.

B. Governor (v. 4) *euthuno* (Gk.)—That which steers or directs; steersman.

Teacher Preparation

Unifying Principle—Taming the Tongue. Everyone knows the pain and destruction that results from hurtful words. How do we keep from causing such distress? James says that we should control our tongue so that only blessings come from it.

A. Pray for your students, that they will watch their words.

B. Read the passage in various translations.

C. Find media examples of leaders using language that either blesses or curses others for discussion.

O—Open the Lesson

A. Ask a volunteer to lead the class in prayer.

B. Introduce the subject of today's lesson and have the students read the Keep in Mind verse.

C. Ask a volunteer to read the In Focus story.

P—Present the Scriptures

A. Ask for volunteers to read the Focal Verses.

B. Read and discuss The People, Places, and Times; Background; and In Depth sections to clarify the meaning of the verses.

E—Explore the Meaning

A. Have the class answer questions from the Search the Scriptures and Discuss the Meaning sections.

B. Have the class read the Lesson in Our Society section.

N—Next Steps for Application

A. Read the Make It Happen section and discuss ways the students can apply it to their lives.

B. Close with prayer, asking God to help the students use the power of their words in ways that heal and don't hurt.

Worship Guide

For the Superintendent or Teacher
Theme: A Disciplined Faith
Song: "Speak to My Heart" by Donnie McClurkin
Devotional Reading: Psalm 34:1–14

A Disciplined Faith

Bible Background • JAMES 3:1–12
Printed Text • JAMES 3:1–12 | Devotional Reading • PSALM 34:1–14

Aim for Change

By the end of the lesson, we will: AGREE with James' analogies regarding the use of the tongue; VALUE the ability to exercise control over the tongue; and PRAY for God's help to speak in ways that result in blessings.

In Focus

Ramon and Yvette were attending their first city council meeting since becoming naturalized U.S. citizens. The school board budget was on the agenda, and as new residents of the city, they were excited to help make decisions affecting the education of their three children. But because of a substantial shortfall in city revenues, the council was proposing not only to close some of the schools, but also to curtail some city services.

Council president Mr. Williams opened the meeting by confirming the city's dire financial plight. He remarked that "all these immigrants are causing the budget strain. I wish all these new people had never come here."

Mr. Williams was also the Chairman of the Deacon Board at his church, and noting that many of the new residents had settled in the neighborhood where his church was located, he said, "Even though these people come to church, they don't contribute much." As a result, he said the church was also having financial problems.

Becoming extremely upset, Ramon and Yvette felt they were being held responsible for the city's financial problems. They too, wished that they had never come.

Words have the power to hurt or heal. What we say reflects who we are in the Lord. How do you show God's love and wisdom when you hold your tongue?

Keep in Mind

"But the tongue can no man tame; it is an unruly evil, full of deadly poison" (James 3:8).

"But the tongue can no man tame; it is an unruly evil, full of deadly poison" (James 3:8).

Focal Verses

KJV **James 3:1** My brethren, be not many masters, knowing that we shall receive the greater condemnation.

2 For in many things we offend all. If any man offend not in word, the same is a perfect man, and able also to bridle the whole body.

3 Behold, we put bits in the horses' mouths, that they may obey us; and we turn about their whole body.

4 Behold also the ships, which though they be so great, and are driven of fierce winds, yet are they turned about with a very small helm, whithersoever the governor listeth.

5 Even so the tongue is a little member, and boasteth great things. Behold, how great a matter a little fire kindleth!

6 And the tongue is a fire, a world of iniquity: so is the tongue among our members, that it defileth the whole body, and setteth on fire the course of nature; and it is set on fire of hell.

7 For every kind of beasts, and of birds, and of serpents, and of things in the sea, is tamed, and hath been tamed of mankind:

8 But the tongue can no man tame; it is an unruly evil, full of deadly poison.

9 Therewith bless we God, even the Father; and therewith curse we men, which are made after the similitude of God.

10 Out of the same mouth proceedeth blessing and cursing. My brethren, these things ought not so to be.

11 Doth a fountain send forth at the same place sweet water and bitter?

12 Can the fig tree, my brethren, bear olive berries? either a vine, figs? so can no fountain both yield salt water and fresh.

NLT **James 3:1** Dear brothers and sisters, not many of you should become teachers in the church, for we who teach will be judged more strictly.

2 Indeed, we all make many mistakes. For if we could control our tongues, we would be perfect and could also control ourselves in every other way.

3 We can make a large horse go wherever we want by means of a small bit in its mouth.

4 And a small rudder makes a huge ship turn wherever the pilot chooses to go, even though the winds are strong.

5 In the same way, the tongue is a small thing that makes grand speeches. But a tiny spark can set a great forest on fire.

6 And among all the parts of the body, the tongue is a flame of fire. It is a whole world of wickedness, corrupting your entire body. It can set your whole life on fire, for it is set on fire by hell itself.

7 People can tame all kinds of animals, birds, reptiles, and fish,

8 but no one can tame the tongue. It is restless and evil, full of deadly poison.

9 Sometimes it praises our Lord and Father, and sometimes it curses those who have been made in the image of God.

10 And so blessing and cursing come pouring out of the same mouth. Surely, my brothers and sisters, this is not right!

11 Does a spring of water bubble out with both fresh water and bitter water?

12 Does a fig tree produce olives, or a grapevine produce figs? No, and you can't draw fresh water from a salty spring.

The People, Places, and Times

James. The New Testament identifies five men named James. Although there is no general consensus among scholars, the author of this letter is believed to be James, the younger half-brother of Jesus. Although James did not accept Jesus as the Messiah until after the Resurrection, he became a leader in the church at Jerusalem at a time when persecution of Jewish believers was increasing, thus scattering Christians throughout the Roman Empire. This forced many of the displaced Jewish Christians to settle in nations of unbelievers. Most scholars believe that the book of James was written between AD 48 and 62, before the Jerusalem Council (Acts 15), making it possibly the first New Testament book to be written.

Hell. For those in the Jewish context, hell was a real place and considered the final abode of the wicked. In the New Testament, the word for hell is Gehenna. This was the name of a garbage dump outside of the city in the Valley of Hinnom where garbage and dead animals were taken out of the city and burned.

What would cause James to write to Jewish believers concerning the wise use of the tongue?

Background

In the first century, Jewish culture was rich in oral traditions, much of which was advanced by itinerant religious teachers who frequently traveled to provide instruction on how to live a godly life. Unfortunately, a number of these instructors were false prophets who spoke more in their own interests than to present the Good News of Jesus Christ. The early Christians were confronted with the challenges of false teachings from those who claimed to represent the Word of the Lord.

Consequently, James teaches Jewish Christians how to live practically in the way of Jesus. This includes the area of controlling the tongue. James' world was bombarded with speech, both good and bad. His writings emphasized that what came out of the mouth was a reflection of what was in the heart, and he used examples from everyday life in the ancient Near East. James preached against using contradictory speech. Controlling the tongue was important to a fulfilled life in Christ.

How can our words give others a personal distaste for God?

At-A-Glance

1. Sobering Warnings (James 3:1–2)
2. Sobering Challenges (vv. 3–6)
3. Sobering Realities (vv. 7–8)
4. Sobering Contradictions (vv. 9–12)

In Depth

1. Sobering Warnings (James 3:1–2)

This sobering warning is aimed at those who would teach the Word of the Lord. Teachers are in a position to inform and misinform others. James cautions that this highly valued and respected position should not be taken lightly.

James warns those who aspire to teach, informing them they would receive harsher judgment and greater condemnation. James is certainly aware of the power teachers hold in shaping the spiritual lives of others. He warns teachers to examine their motives and not be self-serving. Teachers are tasked with stronger speech ethics as a way of achieving the maturity needed to keep the "whole body" in check.

Why do teachers need to select their words carefully and weigh the affect of their words on those they lead?

2. Sobering Challenges (vv. 3–6)

James demonstrates the challenges of taming the tongue using images of things that affected Jewish life and survival. Horses were a common form of land transportation, but wild horses had to be tamed in order to use them. James describes the tongue similarly. Using a bit, a skillful rider can control the horse's every move. An experienced captain will successfully guide a ship of any size by controlling the rudder. Particularly if a ship is experiencing severe sea conditions, mastery of the rudder makes the difference between death and deliverance.

James challenged believers to control their speech to avoid self-destruction. Describing the tongue as a fire, James cautions against allowing Satan to use the tongue to "setteth on fire the course of nature." The tongue has the power to ignite the fire of hell.

How can we learn to control and modify the words that come out of our mouths?

3. Sobering Realities (vv. 7–8)

James issues another startling revelation. Animals can be tamed, but the tongue cannot. Trained animals were known to be an amazing sight in the first century Greco-Roman culture. However, James says the skills do not exist that can tame the tongue.

His shocking comparisons continue. Since the Fall of humanity, snakes have been considered repulsive and deadly. James similarly characterizes the untamed tongue. James' description recalls David's prayer to be delivered from evil men who "have sharpened their tongues like a serpent; adders' poison is under their lips" (Psalm 140:3). James issues this sobering reality—words kill. Without God, James warned, believers would not only destroy other Christians, but also be consumed by the deadly poison that resides within the power of the tongue.

What are some examples of how your words can produce negative impacts on someone's life?

4. Sobering Contradictions (vv. 9–12)

The contradictions James describes are reflective of our human nature. James addresses these double-minded, double-talking contradictions by using the example of believers who speak out of both sides of their mouths—blessing God, yet cursing people. God is consistent, and Christian speech must consistently reflect the heart of God. Words from the mouth speak the content of the heart.

James says blessings can neither come from a heart filled with venom, nor can curses come from a heart of love. In much the same way that olives cannot come from a fig tree nor can a spring produce both fresh and salt water, James punctuates the need for believers to think, say, and do those things that reflect who they are in Christ. The reality of the heart will flow through the consistency of ethical speech.

When people irritate you, how difficult is it to stop and pray before speaking?

Search the Scriptures

1. What does James say humans have the ability to tame (James 3:7)?

2. What action does James describe as wrong (v. 10)?

Discuss the Meaning

In these verses, James points out the dangers of an unbridled tongue. How has the wisdom of restraining one's speech in a difficult situation made a difference in the outcome?

Lesson in Our Society

The U.S. Constitution guarantees certain freedoms, among them speech. As such, we live in a society where people feel free to say anything, to anybody, at any time, and in any place. Especially if what is said has the guise of truth, people feel justified in not holding their tongue for any reason, no matter who is hurt or offended. Even our politicians and leaders can lack integrity in their speech through demeaning words and half-truths. Not only that, but through social media we now have the ability to spread venomous words to the masses.

What you have to say might be important, but just as important is what you don't say. Proverbs 18:21 points out that "death and life are in the power of the tongue." How will you use that power—as a sword or a shield? The ability to control the tongue demonstrates spiritual growth and maturity. When we allow our words to be guided by God's wisdom, the tongue will be used not as a curse in destroying His people, but as a blessing which builds them up.

How can our words be used to build up others in the body of Christ and formulate more loving relationships?

Make It Happen

• Use the "4-Way Test" developed by Rotary International as a guide for how to direct your speech. Ask: "Is it the truth? Is it fair to all concerned? Will it build good will and better friendships? Will it be beneficial to all concerned?"

• Make a point to encourage someone every day this week as a way to counter negative speech.

• Spend a day in silence as a way to discipline the tongue.

Follow the Spirit

What God wants me to do:

_____

_____

_____

_____

Remember Your Thoughts

Special insights I have learned:

_____

_____

_____

_____

More Light on the Text

1 My brethren, be not many masters, knowing that we shall receive the greater condemnation.

The Greek word *didaskaloi* (**did-AS-kal-oy**), translated in the King James Version as "masters," also means "teachers." The teachers in this context were Jewish men, including the author, James, with expert training in the Scripture. As such, they were authority figures held in high esteem. Some people wanted to become teachers to attain higher social status. However, those trained in the Scripture were also charged with imparting to the community how to live according to God's will, so they were held to a higher standard. If they led the believers astray, they would be judged more harshly than others.

2 For in many things we offend all. If any man offend not in word, the same is a perfect man, and able also to bridle the whole body.

The Greek word for "offend" is *ptaio* (**PTIE-oh**) and means to stumble. James acknowledges that as human beings, we too often get tripped up and do or say things we don't intend. But the person who has the ability to guard his or her speech achieves perfection in disciplining his or her entire body.

The Greek word for "perfect" (*teleios*, **TEH-lee-oce**), when referring to human beings, does not mean without sin. Rather, it symbolizes the attainment of a virtue in a moral sense.

272

For example, we often hear that "patience is a virtue." Anyone who has worked with children knows that they can test patience, but a person who can deal with them without complaining or losing control of his or her temper is considered perfect in this sense.

A bridle is a harness that fits over a horse's head. It has a bit that fits into the horse's mouth and reins that guide the animal in the direction it should go. Figuratively, to "bridle" one's speech means to show restraint.

3 Behold, we put bits in the horses' mouths, that they may obey us; and we turn about their whole body.

Horses were a common mode of transportation in the first century. Roman soldiers also used them in battles. People who ride horses use a bridle to control or guide the horse's movement. The horse responds to the tugging on the bit in its mouth by turning its whole body in the direction its rider wants it to go. Likewise, when we demonstrate the ability to control our speech, we display the discipline to govern other members of our body and guide them in the direction they should go.

4 Behold also the ships, which though they be so great, and are driven of fierce winds, yet are they turned about with a very small helm, whithersoever the governor listeth.

James furthers his argument on the importance of selecting teachers who have mastered the ability to guard their speech (and therefore their whole bodies) by using the example of a ship at sea being steered by something as small as a rudder. The Greek verb *metago* (**meh-TAH-go**) means to guide, turn about, or direct. Similar to the horse, a large ship, which needs the power of strong winds in order to move it, is able to be steered by such a small thing as the rudder.

5 Even so the tongue is a little member, and boasteth great things. Behold, how great a matter a little fire kindleth!

James finally gets to the heart of his sermon: something as small as the tongue can wield great power for good or evil. The forest fire metaphor is a good example of how a single spark can start a fire that can quickly burn out of control. If the right person is in control of speech, then he or she can guide others in the right way to go. Likewise, a single word by a person with no self-control can do damage that can take months or even years to repair.

6 And the tongue is a fire, a world of iniquity: so is the tongue among our members, that it defileth the whole body, and setteth on fire the course of nature; and it is set on fire of hell.

James returned again to the metaphor of the tongue represented by the teacher within the community whose speech could bring good or evil to bear. This verse is obscure and many scholars have found it difficult to interpret. The world of first-century Rome was far removed from our contemporary society, and many of the metaphors and images used in ancient writings such as the Bible are unfamiliar to today's readers.

The Greek word for "iniquity," also translated unrighteousness, is *adikia* (**ah-dee-KEE-ah**) and means a deed violating law and justice, as in an unfair judge. A biased judge who hands down an unjust ruling negatively impacts the individual, his or her family, and the whole community. Likewise the tongue, with its potential for sin, represents a smaller version of the potential for all of humanity to sin.

7 For every kind of beasts, and of birds, and of serpents, and of things in the sea, is tamed, and hath been tamed of mankind.

James likens the tongue to a living being. However, in contrast to all the creatures of the land and sea, which human beings are capable of restraining, people appear to be incapable of taming their tongue.

8 But the tongue can no man tame; it is an unruly evil, full of deadly poison.

We might believe that James exaggerated the power of the tongue by comparing it to fires raging out of control. However, he took very seriously the power of someone in the authoritative position of a teacher to do great harm if he or she does not have the ability to control his or her speech.

James refers to the tongue as "an unruly evil." In the Greco-Roman context of the first century, the word "evil" (Gk. *kakon*, **kah-CONE**) meant to be foul or rotten down to the bone. It was an inward decay, like a cancer developing and spreading through one's body. Anyone who has ever been the victim of slander knows how lies left unchallenged can destroy careers and lives.

9 Therewith bless we God, even the Father; and therewith curse we men, which are made after the similitude of God.

The very same tongue we use to bless God can also be used to curse others. The Greek word for "bless," *eulogeo* (**ew-low-GEH-oh**), is from the same root as the English word "eulogy" and means to speak well. To bless someone is to speak well of them or praise them. In contrast, "to curse" (Gk. *kataraomai*, **kah-tah-RAH-oh-my**) someone means to doom or call down evil upon him or her. As creatures made in the image and likeness of God, we should have only good words for one another.

10 Out of the same mouth proceedeth blessing and cursing. My brethren, these things ought not so to be.

The Greek word for "mouth," *stoma* (**STO-ma**), refers both to a physical opening and also to speech, especially eloquent speech. It can also mean the edge of a sword. Metaphorically, the tongue can be a sharp sword cutting down people with insults and imprecations, or it can offer words of praise that lift up people. The notion that both virtuous and vile speech can come from the same source was anathema to James.

11 Doth a fountain send forth at the same place sweet water and bitter?

Fresh or living (Gk. *glukus*, **GLOO-koos**, literally "sweet") water is from a new or previously unused source. Bitter or brackish water is fresh water mixed with salt water, such as in river estuaries in Louisiana. Living water is uncontaminated and refreshing; you wouldn't want to drink from brackish water that has not been treated to remove the saltiness.

Those of us who grew up in urban areas have probably never encountered brackish water. However, people from rural areas likely learned as children not to drink such water. James rhetorically asked whether fresh and brackish water can come from the same source, knowing that his audience, who had come in contact with both types, would answer no.

12 Can the fig tree, my brethren, bear olive berries? Either a vine, figs? So can no fountain both yield salt water and fresh.

Being an effective preacher requires delivering a message using illustrations your audience is familiar with. James did a commendable job demonstrating his point using metaphors, images, and illustrations from the world around his audience, such as the modes of travel and the methods of husbandry.

Anyone who has ever cultivated or produced crops for food knows that a fig tree cannot yield olives any more than a grapevine can produce figs. This would be an aberration of nature. The fig tree can only produce figs and the olive tree only olives, as is their nature. Likewise, salt water cannot yield sweet (fresh) water. James was making the point that a person with an evil disposition is not likely to be virtuous, as it is not in them to do so.

Sources:
Bauer, Walter, William F. Arndt, F. Wilbur Gingrich, and Frederick Danker, eds. *A Greek-English Lexicon of the New Testament and Other Early Christian Literature, Second Edition.* Chicago, IL: University of Chicago Press, 1979.
Coogan, Michael D. *The Oxford History of the Biblical World.* New York: Oxford University Press Inc., 2001.
Danker, F.W., ed. *A Greek-English Lexicon of the New Testament and Other Early Christian Literature, 3rd Edition.* Chicago, IL: The University of Chicago Press, 2001.
Davids, Peter H. *The Epistle of James. The New International Greek Testament Commentary.* Grand Rapids, MI: Wm. B. Eerdmans Publishing Company, 1982.
Life Application Study Bible. Grand Rapids, MI: Zondervan and Tyndale House Publishers, Inc. 2011.
The New Interpreter's Study Bible. Nashville, TN: Abingdon Press, 2003.
Ryken, L, J. Wilhoit, and T. Longman III, eds. *Dictionary of Biblical Imagery.* Downers Grove, IL: InterVarsity Press, 1998.

Say It Correctly

Similitude. sih-**MIL**-ih-tude.
Eulogeo. ew-low-**GEH**-oh.

Daily Bible Readings

MONDAY
People Live by God's Word
(Deuteronomy 8:1–3)

TUESDAY
Set a Guard over My Mouth
(Psalm 141:1–4)

WEDNESDAY
Judged by Your Words
(Matthew 12:33–37)

THURSDAY
From the Heart the Mouth Speaks
(Luke 6:43–45)

FRIDAY
Infants and Babies Speak
(Matthew 21:14–16)

SATURDAY
Say Only "Yes" or "No
(Matthew 5:33–37)

SUNDAY
Control Your Tongue
(James 3:1–12)

Notes

Teaching Tips

Words You Should Know

A. Almsdeed (Acts 9:36) *eleos* (Gk.)—Mercy, pity, spiritual alms.

B. Chamber (v. 39) *hyperoon* (Gk.)—Highest part of the house; the upper room or story where women usually resided.

Teacher Preparation

Unifying Principle—Looking for Help. In times of crisis, people look for help. What qualities do they look for in someone who can help? When Tabitha died, faithful followers of Christ sent for the apostle Peter for help.

A. Pray that you and your students will be faithful followers who are able to help others.

B. Read the passage in various translations.

C. Meditate on the devotional reading: 1 Peter 1:3–9, 4:7–11.

O—Open the Lesson

A. Open with prayer and pray for students who may have recently lost loved ones.

B. Introduce the subject of today's lesson and have the students read the Aim for Change.

C. Read the In Focus story and discuss ways of helping others, particularly in times of grief.

D. Ask students to share experiences of ways they have encountered miracles.

P—Present the Scriptures

A. Ask for volunteers to read the Focal Verses.

B. Read and discuss The People, Places, and Times; Background; and In Depth sections.

C. Use a map of ancient Palestine to explain Peter's route during his mission of preaching and healing.

E—Explore the Meaning

A. Answer questions from the Search the Scriptures and Discuss the Meaning sections.

B. Have the students read and discuss ways 1 Peter 1:3–9 supports the lesson theme of faith and prayer.

C. Ask for a volunteer to read the Lesson in Our Society section.

N—Next Steps for Application

A. Encourage the students to apply the Make It Happen section.

B. Close with prayer that the participants would adopt the faith of those who sent for Peter.

Worship Guide

For the Superintendent or Teacher
Theme: Faithful Disciples
Song: "The Solid Rock"
Devotional Reading: 1 Peter 1:3–9, 4:7–11

Faithful Disciples

Bible Background • ACTS 9:36–43
Printed Text • ACTS 9:36–43 | Devotional Reading • 1 PETER 1:3–9, 4:7–11

—— Aim for Change ——

By the end of this lesson, we will: AGREE on key elements of active faith in the account of Tabitha's resurrection; RELATE to the feelings of loss and the faith of those who sent for Peter after Tabitha died; and ADOPT the faith of those who sent for Peter.

 In Focus

Darrell and Kisha had been excited about the birth of their new baby girl. When the day arrived, Darrell was in the delivery room to witness the birth of his daughter. Kisha's parents were also on hand to welcome their new grandbaby.

Tragedy struck one month later as baby Aiesha died of congenital heart failure. A few days later, Darrell's parents came from out of town to console the bereaved couple, accompanied by the Williamses, a couple whom neither Kisha nor Darrell knew.

Darrell's parents said that when the Williamses found out about baby Aiesha, they wanted to come. The Williamses explained, "We, too, lost our baby when she was only three months old. We thought it would help you to know that others understand the pain you are feeling. It helped us with our healing, and we pray that our being here will help you." Darrell and Kisha thanked them both for coming and said they appreciated their help and support.

During times of crisis, it might be difficult to help others see how God's grace works in even the most difficult circumstances. How will you make a difference for someone who is suffering from loss?

—— Keep in Mind ——

"But Peter put them all forth, and kneeled down, and prayed; and turning him to the body said, Tabitha, arise. And she opened her eyes: and when she saw Peter, she sat up" (Acts 9:40).

"But Peter put them all forth, and kneeled down, and prayed; and turning him to the body said, Tabitha, arise. And she opened her eyes: and when she saw Peter, she sat up" (Acts 9:40).

Focal Verses

KJV **Acts 9:36** Now there was at Joppa a certain disciple named Tabitha, which by interpretation is called Dorcas: this woman was full of good works and almsdeeds which she did.

37 And it came to pass in those days, that she was sick, and died: whom when they had washed, they laid her in an upper chamber.

38 And forasmuch as Lydda was nigh to Joppa, and the disciples had heard that Peter was there, they sent unto him two men, desiring him that he would not delay to come to them.

39 Then Peter arose and went with them. When he was come, they brought him into the upper chamber: and all the widows stood by him weeping, and shewing the coats and garments which Dorcas made, while she was with them.

40 But Peter put them all forth, and kneeled down, and prayed; and turning him to the body said, Tabitha, arise. And she opened her eyes: and when she saw Peter, she sat up.

41 And he gave her his hand, and lifted her up, and when he had called the saints and widows, presented her alive.

42 And it was known throughout all Joppa; and many believed in the Lord.

43 And it came to pass, that he tarried many days in Joppa with one Simon a tanner.

NLT **Acts 9:36** There was a believer in Joppa named Tabitha (which in Greek is Dorcas). She was always doing kind things for others and helping the poor.

37 About this time she became ill and died. Her body was washed for burial and laid in an upstairs room.

38 But the believers had heard that Peter was nearby at Lydda, so they sent two men to beg him, "Please come as soon as possible!"

39 So Peter returned with them; and as soon as he arrived, they took him to the upstairs room. The room was filled with widows who were weeping and showing him the coats and other clothes Dorcas had made for them.

40 But Peter asked them all to leave the room; then he knelt and prayed. Turning to the body he said, "Get up, Tabitha." And she opened her eyes! When she saw Peter, she sat up!

41 He gave her his hand and helped her up. Then he called in the widows and all the believers, and he presented her to them alive.

42 The news spread through the whole town, and many believed in the Lord.

43 And Peter stayed a long time in Joppa, living with Simon, a tanner of hides.

The People, Places, and Times

Simon Peter. One of Jesus' initial twelve disciples, Simon Peter was positioned by Jesus as a leader among them. Jesus included him in His "inner circle" along with John and James. Jesus characterized him as a rock (thus the name Peter), yet he denied Christ three times during Jesus' trial. After the Resurrection, Jesus countered Peter's denial when He asked Peter three times, "Do you love Me?" Peter experienced tremendous persecution and understood loss and suffering firsthand.

Tabitha (Dorcas). An important person in Joppa, she is identified as a disciple (Acts 9:36). Her value in the community comes from her "almsdeeds" (good works and acts of charity).

The widows who gathered to mourn her were among the first to see her restored to life.

Joppa. An important port city in Palestine, overlooking the Mediterranean Sea. Solomon used cedars from Lebanon, which had been floated into Joppa's harbor, for use in the construction of the Temple (2 Chronicles 2:16). The prophet Jonah commenced his ill-fated trip from the port of Joppa (Jonah 1:3).

Whom can you point out in your community that is making an impact on the lives of others because of their good works?

Background

The book of Acts shows how the church fulfills Christ's mandate to go into all the world and preach the Gospel. Through persecution, the church spirals from Judea, Jerusalem, and Samaria to all of the earth. As the church grows, Gentile believers are welcomed into the faith. Peter, one of the apostles, plays a leading role in spreading the Gospel.

While preaching and healing, Peter traveled to the town of Lydda (near Joppa) and meets Aeneas, a bedridden paralytic man. Peter tells him that the power of the Lord has healed him, and to get up and make his bed (Acts 9:32–34). When Tabitha dies, disciples send two men to bring Peter immediately to the bedside of the woman described as "full of good works and almsdeeds" (Acts 9:36).

How did the Holy Spirit change Peter's life and ministry?

At-A-Glance

1. A Miracle is Needed (Acts 9:36–38)
2. Expect a Miracle (vv. 39–40)
3. A Miracle Occurs (vv. 41–43)

In Depth

1. A Miracle is Needed (Acts 9:36–38)

Tabitha was an important woman in the community at Joppa. The fact that she was known by both Hebrew and Greek names suggests that she made a significant impact on a number of cultural and societal levels in the Judeo-Christian community, as well as in the Greco-Roman world. When she becomes ill and dies, the disciples in Joppa recognize that a miracle is needed, and send for the miracle worker—Peter, the man who had called on the power of the Lord to heal a paralytic, and it was done. Peter was at the town of Lydda; Tabitha was approximately fourteen miles away from a miracle.

Why did the believers in Joppa decide to seek Peter instead of praying for her themselves?

2. Expect a Miracle (vv. 39–40)

When Tabitha died, her body was washed, prepared, and displayed in accordance with the standard traditions practiced by both Jews and Gentiles. When Peter arrived, the widows were deeply mourning the loss of their sister. They made sure Peter understood her kindness and usefulness by showing him their clothing, since Tabitha was known for making robes and other clothing for the poor. They likely expected Peter to perform a miracle for the life of this good and generous woman.

This expectation is evidenced by the disciples sending for Peter to come immediately. The text doesn't say, but perhaps that urgency was based on the fact that Jews at the time believed the soul passed into the realm of the dead (Sheol) on the third day after death. Peter had performed a miracle in Lydda; they had reason to hope for a miracle in Joppa.

When we pray, can we predict whether or not God will respond to our prayers of faith the same way as before?

3. A Miracle Occurs (vv. 41–43)

When the residents of Joppa saw that Tabitha had been restored to life, many believed in the Lord. Miracles occur for this purpose. The residents of Joppa may have grieved the initial loss of their beloved Tabitha, but God's actions through Peter not only returned earthy life, but also secured eternal life for those who believed as a result.

What miraculous act of power did God perform through Jesus that should cause everyone to decide to believe in Him?

Search the Scriptures

1. What does Peter do when he arrives at the place Tabitha had been laid (Acts 9:40)?

2. What happens after Tabitha is restored to life (v. 42)?

Discuss the Meaning

Mourning the loss of loved ones is an important and natural part of the healing process. Believers must have faith in God, even in times of great sorrow and suffering. Peter's prayers restored Tabitha's life. How do prayers to a faithful God bring life and renewal, even in the midst of death and grieving?

Lesson in Our Society

When well-known philanthropists die, much of the grieving and remembrances focus on the void that will follow. It is no wonder that people weep and mourn when someone with values and commitment to others dies—it impacts every life that they touched.

We all know someone who has passed away yet their impact still lives on. Notable figures such as Martin Luther King Jr. and Nelson Mandela come to mind. Even those in our family and local communities have a similar impact.

Death and grief can often leave the spirit bitter and empty, but the power of faith in God will result in hope for all who believe. There is life after death. Through faithful works, our impact continues after death, and we are also assured of eternal life. Jesus embodied this assurance—the miracle that believers can expect.

When someone dies, how does our faith provide encouragement and hope to others?

Make It Happen

• Call, visit, or send cards to those who have lost loved ones.

• Build up your faith through prayer and reading the stories of healing in the Bible.

• Honor those who have had a great impact in the community even after they've passed away.

Follow the Spirit

What God wants me to do:

_____

_____

_____

_____

Remember Your Thoughts

Special insights I have learned:

_____

_____

_____

_____

More Light on the Text

Acts 9:36–43

36 Now there was at Joppa a certain disciple named Tabitha, which by interpretation is called Dorcas: this woman was full of good works and almsdeeds which she did.

In this Scripture, the power of Christ is again demonstrated through the apostle Peter. Joppa was not far from Lydda, about fourteen miles away on the Mediterranean coast. Luke, the author of Acts, introduces us at great length to this woman Tabitha, or Dorcas (the Aramaic and Greek words, respectively, for "gazelle").

Luke is drawing on a rich Jewish tradition, one in which a life characterized by these virtues was highly valued when he refers to Tabitha's "good works" and "almsdeeds." The Greek word for "almsdeeds" (*eleemosune*, **eh-lee-ah-mo-SOO-nay**, usually translated simply "alms") is related to the word for mercy or pity. Christianity, a religion that arose out of Judaism, does not disown this value but keeps it, provided that such works and almsdeeds are not seen as gaining salvation for the person who performs them.

In the New Testament, this sort of person has typically demonstrated by his or her good works how much he or she is waiting for the kingdom of God to come (see also the centurion, Matthew 8:1–12). Luke's point is not to show that Tabitha somehow deserved to be raised from the dead because of her good life; rather, he is showing that wherever the kingdom of God spreads, it brings not only power for miracles, but also power for changed lives. We can assume that Tabitha had already been favored by God, as demonstrated by her life of works done in worship of Him.

37 And it came to pass in those days, that she was sick, and died: whom when they had washed, they laid her in an upper chamber.

Tabitha's death came at just the time God intended—that He might display His power through it. We are told that "they" (probably Tabitha's family and friends) washed her body, but rather than burying it, they laid it in the upper chamber. By mentioning this, Luke intends his readers to recall the Old Testament accounts in which the dead were placed in upper rooms, with the specific hope of their being healed by the prophet Elijah or Elisha (1 Kings 17:19; 2 Kings 4:10, 21). These disciples were full of hope, even in the midst of their mourning. In the arrival of the apostle Peter, their hope will find joyful realization.

38 And forasmuch as Lydda was nigh to Joppa, and the disciples had heard that Peter was there, they sent unto him two men, desiring him that he would not delay to come to them.

No doubt the disciples had heard of the miracle that occurred not far away, in the life of Aeneas. Such an event would have rippled throughout the surrounding countryside. This delegation of disciples did not seek Peter because he was some kind of unique faith healer, but because he was an apostle—an eyewitness to the majesty of Christ. So greatly did they care about Tabitha, that they insisted Peter come without delay (Gk. *okneo*, **oak-NEH-oh**, to hesitate or be slow).

39 Then Peter arose and went with them. When he was come, they brought him into the upper chamber: and all the widows stood by him weeping, and shewing the coats and garments which Dorcas made, while she was with them.

Peter's quick response showed the disciples' faithfulness and rightness in seeking him. Here the story begins to resemble the account in which Jesus was called upon to heal a sick girl, who died while He was on the way (Mark

5:35–43). This similarity is no accident. Luke is showing that Jesus had given His authority to the apostles to carry out His mission. Where the apostles are, there the power of Jesus is also.

Although we cannot be sure, it seems likely that the widows, who were present at Tabitha's side, were actually wearing the coats and garments they showed Peter. The Greek words here for coats (*chiton*, **khite-ON**) and garments (*himation*, **he-MA-tee-on**) usually refer to different articles of clothing. The *chiton* is a simple tunic worn next to the skin, either as an undergarment or a simple dress. The *himation* was a larger outer garment, worn as a cloak often for warmth.

Tabitha was skilled and caring enough to provide both kinds of garments for the needy. The point of showing these to Peter would be to show that Tabitha had followed the Jewish tradition of kindness to widows (Exodus 22:21–22; Deuteronomy 24:17–21). Whether or not they were wearing the garments, the presence of these widows and their great grief at Tabitha's death show us for certain how kind Tabitha had been to those in need.

40 But Peter put them all forth, and kneeled down, and prayed; and turning him to the body said, Tabitha, arise. And she opened her eyes: and when she saw Peter, she sat up.

Like his master, Jesus (Mark 5:40), Peter told all the people to leave the room. He then accessed the two sources of power that Jesus had given to His apostles and His church: prayer and His words. Again, Peter did not possess it in his own strength or by some sort of magic. His prayer would have been an expression of absolute dependence upon Jesus for any power.

Speakers of Aramaic would have recognized that Peter's words to Tabitha—"Get up, Tabitha"—were almost identical to the words Jesus spoke: *Talitha, koumi* ("little girl, get up";

Mark 5:41, NLT). Luke shows us, by means of this similarity, that Jesus' words will be powerful and effective in the life of His disciples. As a result of prayer and Jesus' words, the disciples' hopes are realized, the power of God is once again shown forth, and Peter's identity—as a vessel of Christ's glory—is confirmed anew.

41 And he gave her his hand, and lifted her up, and when he had called the saints and widows, presented her alive.

The main new piece of information given to us in this verse is the detail of Peter presenting Tabitha alive to the saints and widows. Once again, Peter reflected Jesus in the way he carried out this miracle. Like Jesus, when He raised the widow's son (Luke 7:15), Peter gave attention to those grieving, not just to the one raised from the dead. Like Jesus, Peter presented the dead-and-now-living person to those who loved her.

By this, Luke shows us again that the purpose of miracles extends well beyond those immediately healed or raised. The disciples had been faithful in seeking the true Source of power and grace in their grief, and their faithfulness was honored by God.

42 And it was known throughout all Joppa; and many believed in the Lord.

Just as Aeneas in Lydda, this miracle brought about the conversion of many in the surrounding area. The miracle had once again reached its fullest purpose: producing faith. Unlike the religious leaders and others who resisted Jesus despite seeing His miracles (John 12:37), those favored by God see His miracles and believe.

This verse focuses on their faith, which was an equally important part of conversion. In this pairing, we see the biblical truth that faith and repentance are two sides of the same coin. When the Holy Spirit enlightens a person to see the glory of God in Christ, that person turns from sin to believing on Christ, trusting in His person and work for salvation.

43 And it came to pass,that he tarried many days in Joppa with one Simon a tanner.

The apostles were not just itinerant miracle workers; they were pastors at heart. Like Paul, who stayed and suffered long with those to whom he ministered, Peter now stayed in the region in which the healings had taken place in order to ground these disciples, both new and old, in the realities of the Gospel of Christ.

Finally, Luke adds a seemingly insignificant but ultimately powerful detail: that Peter stayed with a tanner. Since tanning was ceremonially defiling (because of constant contact with dead animals) in the Jewish mindset, tanning was an unclean occupation. How could a good Jew like Peter stay in the house of a ceremonially unclean man? Luke is setting the stage for the vision that Peter will experience in chapter 10—a vision that will show him beyond a doubt that God intends for the Gentiles to be included in the body of Christ. Peter's lodging with a tanner foreshadowed this world-changing event and the coming of the Gentiles full-force into the church. In these accounts, Luke has shown that (1) Peter is indeed an apostle blessed with the power of Christ, and that (2) Jesus calls Gentiles and Jews alike to Himself.

Sources:
Coogan, Michael D. *The Oxford History of the Biblical World*. New York: Oxford University Press Inc., 2001.
Danker, F.W. *A Greek-English Lexicon of the New Testament and Other Early Christian Literature*. 3rd Ed. Chicago, IL: The University of Chicago Press, 2001.
Harrelson, Walter J. *The New Interpreter's Study Bible*. Nashville, TN: Abingdon Press, 2003.
Ryken, L., J. Wilhoit, T. Longman III, eds. *Dictionary of Biblical Imagery*. Downers Grove, IL: InterVarsity Press, 1998.

Say It Correctly

Joppa. **JAH**-puh.
Dorcas. **DOOR**-kuss.

Daily Bible Readings

MONDAY
Widow's Son Restored to Life
(1 Kings 17:17–24)

TUESDAY
Jesus Raises Widow's Son
(Luke 7:11–17)

WEDNESDAY
Care for Widows and Orphans
(James 1:22–27)

THURSDAY
Peter's Healing Ministry
(Acts 5:12–16)

FRIDAY
Philip's Preaching Ministry
(Acts 8:4–8)

SATURDAY
Aeneas Healed, Residents Turn to God
(Acts 9:32–35)

SUNDAY
Calling the Church to Active Service
(Acts 9:36–43)

Teaching Tips

Words You Should Know

A. Faith (1 Timothy 6:12) *pistis* (Gk.)—Firm persuasion.

B. Science (v. 20) *gnosis* (Gk.)—Knowledge.

Teacher Preparation

Unifying Principle—Be Strong. We are surrounded by all kinds of advice. What is the best advice to follow? Paul charged Timothy to embrace certain attitudes and actions, and avoid others in order to strengthen his faith.

A. Pray for your students and lesson clarity.

B. Read through all of 1 and 2 Timothy in one sitting to get a good sense of the kind of person Timothy was.

C. Pay special attention to 1 Timothy 1:18–19, 4:14 and 2 Timothy 1:6–7, as these shed light on Timothy's personality and calling.

O—Open the Lesson

A. Open with prayer, including the Aim for Change.

B. Introduce today's lesson title.

P—Present the Scriptures

A. Solicit volunteers to read the Focal Verses.

B. Read and discuss The People, Places, and Times; Background; and In Depth sections.

E—Explore the Meaning

A. Have the class answer the questions in the Search the Scriptures and Discuss the Meaning sections.

B. Ask a volunteer to read the Lesson in Our Society section and discuss.

N—Next Steps for Application

A. Encourage the class to apply the Make It Happen section.

B. Close with prayer.

Worship Guide

For the Superintendent or Teacher
Theme: Fight the Good Fight of Faith
Song: "It Is Well"
Devotional Reading: 1 Thessalonians 2:17–3:10

Fight the Good Fight of Faith

Bible Background • 1 TIMOTHY 6:11–21
Printed Text • 1 TIMOTHY 6:11–21 | Devotional Reading • 1 THESSALONIANS 2:17–3:10

—————— Aim for Change ——————

By the end of this lesson we will: EXPLORE the attitudes and actions Paul charged Timothy to embrace and avoid; VALUE personally the attitudes and actions Paul charged Timothy to embrace; and IDENTIFY personal actions and attitudes that need to be changed and commit to doing so.

———————— ✦ In Focus ————————

Alan professed to be a Christian and specifically sought to date women in the church. However, Alan's walk was very different from his talk. He always pursued a sexual relationship with women, and when he met one who obeyed the Word of God by living sexually pure, he would immediately end the relationship.

One day, Alan met Tracy, a beautiful young lady who loved the Lord. Alan really liked Tracy and told her that he could handle dating by her standards. After much prayer and conversation with others who knew Alan, Tracy decided that she would end the relationship because she did not feel that his intentions were genuine. Alan was devastated, and for the first time in his adult life, he turned to the Lord, sincerely asking for Jesus to come into his heart and change his life. Allowing some time to pass, rather than pursing a romantic relationship with Tracy, Alan sought to truly be her friend and brother in Christ.

Being a Christian requires a real commitment to godly living. In today's lesson, Paul encourages Timothy to fight the good fight of faith. When did you make a real commitment to godly living?

—————— Keep in Mind ——————

"Fight the good fight of faith, lay hold on eternal life, whereunto thou art also called, and hast professed a good profession before many witnesses" (1 Timothy 6:12, KJV).

"Fight the good fight of faith, lay hold on eternal life, whereunto thou art also called, and hast professed a good profession before many witnesses" (1 Timothy 6:12, KJV).

Focal Verses

KJV **1 Timothy 6:11** But thou, O man of God, flee these things; and follow after righteousness, godliness, faith, love, patience, meekness.

12 Fight the good fight of faith, lay hold on eternal life, whereunto thou art also called, and hast professed a good profession before many witnesses.

13 I give thee charge in the sight of God, who quickeneth all things, and before Christ Jesus, who before Pontius Pilate witnessed a good confession;

14 That thou keep this commandment without spot, unrebukable, until the appearing of our Lord Jesus Christ:

15 Which in his times he shall shew, who is the blessed and only Potentate, the King of kings, and Lord of lords;

16 Who only hath immortality, dwelling in the light which no man can approach unto; whom no man hath seen, nor can see: to whom be honour and power everlasting. Amen.

17 Charge them that are rich in this world, that they be not highminded, nor trust in uncertain riches, but in the living God, who giveth us richly all things to enjoy;

18 That they do good, that they be rich in good works, ready to distribute, willing to communicate;

19 Laying up in store for themselves a good foundation against the time to come, that they may lay hold on eternal life.

20 O Timothy, keep that which is committed to thy trust, avoiding profane and vain babblings, and oppositions of science falsely so called:

21 Which some professing have erred concerning the faith. Grace be with thee. Amen.

NLT **1 Timothy 6:11** But you, Timothy, are a man of God; so run from all these evil things. Pursue righteousness and a godly life, along with faith, love, perseverance, and gentleness.

12 Fight the good fight for the true faith. Hold tightly to the eternal life to which God has called you, which you have declared so well before many witnesses.

13 And I charge you before God, who gives life to all, and before Christ Jesus, who gave a good testimony before Pontius Pilate,

14 that you obey this command without wavering. Then no one can find fault with you from now until our Lord Jesus Christ comes again.

15 For, at just the right time Christ will be revealed from heaven by the blessed and only almighty God, the King of all kings and Lord of all lords.

16 He alone can never die, and he lives in light so brilliant that no human can approach him. No human eye has ever seen him, nor ever will. All honor and power to him forever! Amen.

17 Teach those who are rich in this world not to be proud and not to trust in their money, which is so unreliable. Their trust should be in God, who richly gives us all we need for our enjoyment.

18 Tell them to use their money to do good. They should be rich in good works and generous to those in need, always being ready to share with others.

19 By doing this they will be storing up their treasure as a good foundation for the future so that they may experience true life.

20 Timothy, guard what God has entrusted to you. Avoid godless, foolish discussions with those who oppose you with their so-called knowledge.

21 Some people have wandered from the faith by following such foolishness. May God's grace be with you all.

The People, Places, and Times

Timothy. Timothy met the apostle Paul during Paul's second missionary journey (Acts 16:1–5). His faith in God was largely due to the example of his mother and grandmother (2 Timothy 1:5). He was assigned the responsibility of preaching, teaching, and leading the church in Ephesus (1 Timothy 1:3–5). It is commonly believed that Timothy was a young man—probably under 30 years of age—when he was charged with leading the Ephesian church.

Ephesus. Ephesus was a thriving port city during the first century AD. It was located along the Cayster River next to the Aegean Sea with a population of nearly 500,000 people. It was mostly revered for their unique image of the goddess Artemis (Roman: Diana) housed in a great temple, one of the seven wonders of the ancient world. The city had a large Jewish population, and Paul spent two years ministering and sharing the Gospel with all who were willing to listen (Acts 19:8–10). This was a tough place to minister, though, and Paul faced many obstacles. The main challenges he confronted included variations of Christian doctrine circulating in the region (Acts 19:1–7), hostile unbelieving Jews (vv. 8–9), occult activity (vv. 18–19), and riotous crowds (vv. 29–31).

Background

The book of 1 Timothy can rightly be divided into two intersecting themes: right faith and right action. Timothy's main mission in Ephesus was to stop certain people from teaching false doctrine (1 Timothy 1:3–4). Some people believed that they had superior knowledge and thus a superior faith. This type of faith had little to do with living righteously in everyday life. The false teachers were spreading this message throughout the churches. There is little doubt that Timothy would have preferred to be elsewhere, as this assignment was a daunting task for a young man of his age. To ensure success, Timothy needed to serve the Lord in the power of the Spirit and remember the example Paul had left him.

At-A-Glance

1. Right Faith and Right Action
(1 Timothy 6:11–16)
2. Instructions for the Rich (vv. 17–19)
3. Guarding the Deposit of Faith (vv. 20–21)

In Depth

1. Right Faith and Right Action (1 Timothy 6:11–16)

Biblically speaking, faith never refers to one's opinion, as the word is popularly used today. Rather, the basic meaning refers to a firm persuasion. A more precise understanding of its use in 1 Timothy involves trusting someone and placing confidence in what they say. With this in mind, Timothy was encouraged to stand firm in faith. He was to avoid the teachings and negative attitudes propagated by the false teachers, and instead embrace the sound teachings and godly virtues Paul taught (v. 11).

This was sure to be a difficult task, and therefore, Timothy needed to "fight the good fight of faith" in order to succeed (v. 12). This phrase was originally used in reference to athletes in ancient Greece and here conveys the idea that Timothy's assignment would require agonizing effort. This is because Timothy would have to explain his actions to God at the time of Jesus' return (v. 14). However, Timothy need not fear anything, since God has all power, including power over life and death (vv. 15–16). He was fully equipped for the task.

2. Instructions for the Rich (vv. 17–19)

The problems in the Ephesian church were multifaceted. All of them, however, stemmed from some wrong attitude and doctrine. Just as Timothy had to correct and rebuke the false teachers, so he also had to rebuke and correct those who had misguided beliefs about money (vv. 17–19). Timothy was warned of the dangers of embracing this version of prosperity and was commanded to flee from it (vv. 10–11). He was to instruct the wealthy to trust in God instead of money and to invest in the life to come (vv. 18–19).

3. Guarding the Deposit of Faith (vv. 20–21)

The phrase "that which is committed to thy trust" (v. 20) appears a total of three times in 1 and 2 Timothy (1 Timothy 6:20; 2 Timothy 1:13–14), and refers to the truth of the Gospel. Sound doctrine, faith, and truth are repeated themes throughout these epistles, and the church was created to promote and defend them all (1 Timothy 3:15). Some in the Ephesian church believed they had superior knowledge to that of Timothy's, but Paul calls their knowledge false (v. 20). The KJV's use of the word "science" here does not convey the modern meaning, but could be translated more generally as "knowledge"; Paul is not anti-science, but wants Timothy to avoid false doctrine. Timothy had to guard the Gospel and

persist in its truths no matter how inconvenient it became to do so. The reward was sure to be great.

Search the Scriptures

1. Why was it essential for Timothy to successfully guard what was entrusted to him (1 Timothy 6:20)?

2. Why did Paul repeatedly remind Timothy of his calling (v. 12)?

Discuss the Meaning

Many Christians greatly misunderstand what faith actually is. Many view it as something that exists solely between themselves and God with little to no public expression and objective content. What kind of faith does 1 Timothy describe?

Lesson in Our Society

We live in exciting times. Many African American pastors are seeking additional resources and sharing teachings to help their congregations take advantage of the wealth of information and opportunities available in their communities. They are also teaching to keep true to faith in Jesus Christ in a complex world. This is not just for the sake of head knowledge. We need leaders who can encourage us to stay on course when it comes to aligning our faith with action. We need leaders who can not only recite Greek and Hebrew, but also make the Word practical in our lives. This will give us a vibrant faith that can transform our lives and communities.

Make It Happen

• Decide to mentor a new believer in living out their faith. If you are a new believer, seek out a mentor to help you live out your faith.

• List out the ways that you have incorporated your faith into your everyday life.

• Create a spiritual genealogy chart and track how your faith has been handed down to you.

Follow the Spirit

What God wants me to do:

_____

_____

_____

_____

Remember Your Thoughts

Special insights I have learned:

_____

_____

_____

_____

More Light on the Text

1 Timothy 6:11–21

11 But thou, O man of God, flee these things; and follow after righteousness, godliness, faith, love, patience, meekness.

The verse begins with a call to Timothy to be completely different from the men Paul has just talked about in the preceding verses and, instead, to be a "man of God." The designation "man of God" (Gk. *anthropos tou theou*, **AN-throw-poce too theh-OO**) occurs only twice in the New Testament (the other is in 2 Timothy 3:17), but is used with some frequency in the Septuagint, the Greek translation of the Old Testament, with the Hebrew *ish elohim* (**EESH eh-low-HEEM**) to refer to men

such as Moses, Samuel, David, Elijah, Elisha, and other leaders, including some who remain anonymous.

In its usage here, it is not certain whether Paul intends to use the phrase in the specific or general way. Perhaps Paul uses the phrase in a transitional sense uniquely appropriate to the situation of the church at Crete, as signified by what he says about the "man of God" here and in 2 Timothy 3:17. If this is the case, it would apply to every Christian, although its immediate application is to Timothy. Understood this way, the phrase suggests one who was uniquely a "man of God," but it is applied here to one who is both a spiritual leader and at the same time an example to all believers of what each one should be as a "man of God" (cf. 1 Timothy 4:12).

Paul's instruction to Timothy is threefold, and both negative and positive. First, Paul commands Timothy to flee "these things," a reference to the list of sins that he enumerated in the preceding verses, particularly verse 10, where Paul zeros in on the love of money, which he identified as the root of all kinds of evil. The Greek word for flee here is *pheugo* (**FEW-go**), from which the English word "fugitive" is derived. Timothy must not only run; he must flee, connoting a sense of utter desperation. Timothy must not entertain those sins for a moment. They are not to be touched with the proverbial ten-foot pole. Timothy, like Christians today, must do his utmost to get as far away as he possibly can from someone or something leading him to these things. He should not be attracted to the blessings that they offer, nor the financial gain they promise.

Second, Paul does not only command Timothy to flee; he must go in a certain direction—following after virtues such as righteousness, godliness, faith, love, patience, and meekness. The phrase "follow after" translates the Greek word *dioko* (**dee-OH-ko**), which literally means to pursue and is used predominantly in the New Testament—particularly by Paul—either in the sense of persecuting someone, or in the sense of "following zealously after" or "pursuing" Christian virtues, as here (see Romans 14:19; 1 Corinthians 14:1; 1 Thessalonians 5:15; 2 Timothy 2:22).

12 Fight the good fight of faith, lay hold on eternal life, whereunto thou art also called, and hast professed a good profession before many witnesses.

Here Paul continues with his third exhortation to Timothy: "Fight the good fight of faith," a phrase nearly identical to Paul's personal statement in a later letter to Timothy (2 Timothy 4:7). The verb *agonizomai* (Gk. **ah-go-NID-zo-my**), from which the word "agonize" is derived, and the noun *agon* (Gk. **AH-gon**) are both used to denote a fight, struggle, or contest. It is not certain whether Paul has an athletic or military metaphor in mind here. What is clear is that the phrase conveys the basic idea of "struggle": Paul wants Timothy to be willing to suffer for the Gospel, to struggle in its service, and to do so when he is opposed. It is a hard struggle, but it will all seem worthwhile when Timothy sees it in the light of eternity, so he must "lay hold of ... eternal life." The present imperative form of this verb suggests that this struggle is continuous and never-ending. Paul considers it a good fight both because it is engaged in for God and the Gospel, and also because it is inherent to the Gospel making its way in an evil world.

Paul goes on to give the reason for the exhortation by reminding Timothy that he first entered into it when he "professed a good profession before many witnesses." This is describing the day that he first confessed his sin to God and trusted in Christ. So Paul reminds Timothy of that historical moment when he made this confession before so many witnesses, who would have been able to testify to it and thus to Timothy's public commitment, to which Paul now calls him.

The idea presented here is of Timothy taking hold of the truth and living it out in the context of the struggle he is involved in at Ephesus. The battle for the Good News is a battle that involves people's eternal destiny, and Timothy has got to keep that perspective. The leaders who had strayed had been seduced by money, prestige, and power. They had lost sight of this eternal dimension, but Timothy has to be different.

13 I give thee charge in the sight of God, who quickeneth all things, and before Christ Jesus, who before Pontius Pilate witnessed a good confession.

Paul now gives Timothy a charge (Gk. *parangello,* **pah-ron-geh-LO**), or commands him with authority to do something. In ancient times, a charge for someone to do something with the gods as witnesses was a serious matter. A command of this type was binding for those so charged. Paul thus charges Timothy in the sight of God "who quickeneth all things." "Quickeneth" is an old English word used to translate the Greek word *zoopoieo* (**zoo-oh-poy-EH-oh**), which simply means to make alive.

Paul takes the God who gives life to all things as a witness. He also includes Christ Jesus as a witness and also as an example of someone who witnessed (Gk. *martureo*, **mar-too-REH-oh**), or who spoke a good confession. This would be to encourage Timothy to follow Jesus' moral example in bearing witness to the faith and sound doctrine.

14 That thou keep this commandment without spot, unrebukable, until the

appearing of our Lord Jesus Christ: 15 Which in his times he shall shew, who is the blessed and only Potentate, the King of kings, and Lord of lords.

Timothy is told to keep not just one commandment, but the sound doctrine and instructions that Paul lays out in this letter. This is to be obeyed, preserved, and guarded, which is the meaning of keep (Gk. *tereo*, **tay-REH-oh**). It must be free from any corruption and "without spot" (Gk. *aspilos*, **AS-pee-LOHS**) or free from guilt. Paul here may be pointing toward the requirements of Old Testament sacrifices to be unblemished and free from defect.

This command must be kept until the appearing (Gk. *epiphaneia*, **eh-pee-FAH-nay-ah**) of Jesus. The word "appearing" means the event of something becoming visible, usually a deity. Timothy is to keep the sound doctrine given to him until the return of Jesus Christ. "Which in his times" can also be translated as "at the proper time." It could be that the early church was getting settled with the idea that Jesus' return was not imminent as they first believed. It is Jesus "who is the blessed and only Potentate," or sovereign ruler. These words were very radical in the time of Imperial Rome and could have been taken for treason.

16 Who only hath immortality, dwelling in the light which no man can approach unto; whom no man hath seen, nor can see: to whom be honour and power everlasting. Amen.

Paul concludes this praise for God with describing the qualities of Jesus that separate Him from being just an ordinary man but God Himself. Jesus alone has immortality. "Immortal" was a title for God in Hellenistic Judaism, and here Paul adds the qualifier that Jesus alone has immortality. Jesus also dwells in light that no human can approach and also that no man can see Him. This is an allusion to

God's statement that "no man can see me and live" (Exodus 33:20). Jesus carries these same attributes, and in concluding this praise section, Paul also cements sound doctrine and the fundamentals of the faith. Jesus is God.

17 Charge them that are rich in this world, that they be not highminded, nor trust in uncertain riches, but in the living God, who giveth us richly all things to enjoy; 18 That they do good, that they be rich in good works, ready to distribute, willing to communicate.

Although he tells Timothy to shun the pursuit of riches, Paul gives Timothy instructions for the rich. They should not be high-minded (Gk. *hupselophroneo*, **hoop-seh-low-fro-NEH-oh**), that is, haughty. The word carries the connotation of one who is marked not only by arrogance but also a contempt for those they view as not reaching their status. They also are not to trust in "uncertain riches." This brings to mind Proverbs 23:4–5, where the writer exhorts his audience not to labor after riches that will take wings and fly.

Instead of being proud and haughty and trusting in wealth, the rich are to trust in God, "who giveth us richly" everything we need. The word for "giveth" (Gk. *parecho*, **pah-REH-kho**) in this context means to give what is necessary and useful. God provides what is necessary and useful to us, not necessarily luxuries. Timothy must lead the rich to "do good" and "be rich in good works." Judaism stressed that riches, far from being evil, were a responsibility for those who were given them. Their duty is to be "ready to distribute" (Gk. *eumetadotos*, **ew-meh-TA-doe-toce**) or be generous without hesitation. They must be willing to "communicate" (Gk. *koinonikos*, **koy-no-nee-KOCE**). This word is related to *koinonia* (Gk. **koy-no-NEE-ah**), which is the word we use for communion or participating in fellowship. *Koinonikos* then carries with it the idea of giving as a form of participating or sharing with others.

19 Laying up in store for themselves a good foundation against the time to come, that they may lay hold on eternal life. 20 O Timothy, keep that which is committed to thy trust, avoiding profane and vain babblings, and oppositions of science falsely so called: 21 Which some professing have erred concerning the faith. Grace be with thee. Amen.

The idea of laying up treasure in heaven is not new to Judaism and is taught by Jesus in the Sermon on the Mount (Matthew 6:19–20). Those who give to help others' needs will be free to pursue eternal life.

Lastly, Paul reiterates that Timothy keep the sound doctrine that has been committed to his trust. This involves avoiding profane (Gk. *bebelos*, **BEH-bay-loce)** or pointless babbling and oppositions (Gk. *antithesis*, **an-TEA-thee-seese**) or contradictions of what the false teachers were calling "science" (Gk. *gnosis*, **GNO-seese**). Because of the use of the word *gnosis*, many speculate that these false teachers were involved in "gnostic" heresy. This could have been the case, as many philosophers were said to impart knowledge. This falsely-called knowledge can lead people to err from the faith.

Sources:
Knight, George W. *The Pastoral Epistles: A Commentary on the Greek Text, New International Greek Testament Commentary.* Grand Rapids, MI: W.B. Eerdmans; Paternoster Press, 1992.
Mounce, William D. *Pastoral Epistles.* Vol. 46. Word Biblical Commentary. Dallas, TX: Word, Incorporated, 2000.
Saarinen, Risto. *The Pastoral Epistles with Philemon and Jude.* Grand Rapids, MI: Brazos Press, 2008.
Staton, Knofel. *Timothy-Philemon: Unlocking the Scriptures for You.* Standard Bible Studies. Cincinnati, OH: Standard, 1988.
Wall, Robert W. *1 & 2 Timothy and Titus.* The Two Horizons New Testament Commentary. Grand Rapids, MI: Eerdmans, 2012.

Say It Correctly

Potentate. **PO**-ten-tate.
Aegean. uh-**GEE**-an.
Gnostic. **NOSS**-tic.

Daily Bible Readings

MONDAY
Timothy Joins Paul's Team
(Acts 16:1–5)

TUESDAY
Timothy, an Active Teacher with Paul
(1 Corinthians 4:14–21)

WEDNESDAY
Epaphroditus, Paul's Coworker and Minister
(Philippians 2:25–30)

THURSDAY
Timothy, Paul's Envoy to the Churches
(1 Thessalonians 3:1–10)

FRIDAY
Teach the Sound Words of Christ
(1 Timothy 6:2–8)

SATURDAY
Love of Money, Root of Many Evils
(1 Timothy 6:9–10)

SUNDAY
The Good Fight of Faith
(1 Timothy 6:11–21)

Acknowledging God

This quarter focuses on ways God's people have acknowledged the greatness of their God. The quarter begins with guidance for following Him. Then, with Easter, the quarter turns to ways Jesus provided a channel for giving God glory and honor. The quarter concludes with a look at times when the Hebrew people sang praises to God.

UNIT 1 • FOLLOW IN MY WAYS

This section provides four Scripture sessions, drawn from Genesis and 2 Chronicles, showing how Abraham and Solomon acknowledged God by following His guidance.

Lesson 1: March 4, 2018
The Lord Will Provide
Genesis 22:1–3, 6–14

People are reluctant to make challenging personal sacrifices for fear of losing everything. How can they learn to offer difficult sacrifices even in the face of fear? By being willing to offer his son, Abraham learned to trust God, who provided everything he needed.

Lesson 2: March 11, 2018
There is No God Like You
2 Chronicles 6:12–21

People want to know that others will keep their word. How can they respond to a fulfilled promise? At the Temple dedication, Solomon thanked the Lord for keeping God's promise.

Lesson 3: March 18, 2018
The People Gave Thanks to God
2 Chronicles 7:1–9

People often celebrate what seems important to them. How can their celebrations become a form of worship? As they dedicated the Temple, Solomon and the people worshiped the Lord by bowing on their knees, making burnt offerings, playing music, and praying.

Lesson 4: March 25, 2018
Keep My Statutes and Ordinances
2 Chronicles 7:12–22

Living a just and merciful life requires people to sacrifice their own desires and thoughts. What are consequences for not choosing to be just and merciful? God told Solomon that if he did not follow the statutes and ordinances given to him by the Lord, then calamity would come upon the people and the Temple would be abandoned.

UNIT 2 • ALL GLORY AND HONOR

This section has five lessons. The Scripture sessions from Luke and John deal with how Jesus' resurrection opened the way to honor God. The visions in Revelation praise God with majestic symbolism.

Lesson 5: April 1, 2018 (Easter)
He Has Risen
Luke 24:1–12, 30–35

People often question the promises of their leaders. How can they come to have assurance in the midst of doubt? In the breaking of bread and making Himself known to His disciples, the risen Christ kept His promises.

Lesson 6: April 8, 2018
The Risen Lord Appears
John 21:1–14

Sometimes life seems humdrum and unproductive. Where can people recognize purpose and direction for their lives? When the disciples followed guidance given by a man on the shore, they recognized that Jesus had given the directions and they joined Him in fellowship.

Lesson 7: April 15, 2018
Follow Me
John 21:15–25

People are sometimes reluctant to show love and care for others. How can they be encouraged to show compassion for others? Jesus calls Peter and all disciples to show their love for Him by taking care of His sheep.

Lesson 8: April 22, 2018
The Lord God the Almighty
Revelation 4:1–6, 8–11

People wonder to whom they should give ultimate allegiance. Who deserves to be worshiped and praised? The book of Revelation teaches that God alone is worthy of all praise, wonder, and awe.

Lesson 9: April 29, 2018
Blessing, Glory, Honor Forever
Revelation 5:6–14

People find it difficult to find a source of allegiance that is permanent and lasting. What type of response do they give when they find this lasting allegiance? Revelation speaks of joyful praise and eternal worship of God.

UNIT 3 • GIVE PRAISE TO GOD

This final section has four lessons that emphasize the people's response by bringing offerings and dedicating their lives to God's work found in Exodus, Leviticus, and 2 Corinthians. The unit concludes with one lesson drawn from Psalms and Hebrews that rejoices in God's reconciling action on behalf of the people.

Lesson 10: May 6, 2018
Giving from a Generous Heart
Exodus 35:20–29; 2 Corinthians 9:6–8

People want to live lives of gratitude. How can they express their thankfulness properly? God welcomes the offerings of those who give with generous and cheerful hearts.

Lesson 11: May 13, 2018
Bringing First Fruits
Leviticus 23:9–14, 22

In a culture of scarcity, people acquire and hoard the best they can afford. How can they live less fearfully and more joyfully during difficult economic times? God called His people to worship Him with the first and best of their lives.

Lesson 12: May 20, 2018
Remembering with Joy
Leviticus 25:1–12

People hold a sense of entitlement when it comes to their wealth, possessions, and land. How can they be freed from their possessions possessing them? God called the covenant people to active, responsible, and joyful stewardship of all He had given them.

Lesson 13: May 27, 2018
Rejoicing in Restoration
Psalm 34:1–10; Hebrews 2:17–18

People want relief from their fears and brokenness. Where does such hope come from? Hopes for restoration are found through God's gift of Jesus Christ and His sacrifice.

The Rightful Object of Our Worship

Everyone worships someone or something. The essential question in life is not whether I will worship something, but who or what do I worship? Many would like to believe that they do not worship anything. They would rather exist in a secular universe devoid of God and talk of worship. The fact is even those who would like to dismiss worship as something primitive often worship themselves or their ideas. There is an innate desire in us as human beings for someone or something to be our ultimate allegiance and the primary motivating factor of our lives. When you look around at the daily lives of those around you, we can easily observe what holds their ultimate allegiance. You can tell by the way they treat their possessions or relationships. You can tell by the way they relate to their jobs and their recreational activities. We are all worshiping something.

These objects of worship are never worth our time and attention. We worship them and receive nothing in return. We experience their fragility and futility. There is an emptiness that comes with worshiping things that are not worthy of our worship. It is the inevitable result of idolatry. Idolatry is worshiping anything that is not God, placing our proper desire for worship onto an object unworthy of worship. As Christ-followers, we have the Son of God Himself as an object of worship. He is the rightful object of worship because of His person, purpose, and position.

His Person

Jesus is the sinless Son of God. He is the second Person of the Trinity. All of the attributes of God the Father can be attributed to Jesus. He is faithful. He is loving. He is holy. He is sovereign. In fact Jesus said Himself that if you have seen Him, you have seen the Father. He is the image of the invisible God. Many people want to see God. They desire to know exactly what God is like. What pleases Him and what displeases Him? In Jesus, we get our answer to that question. Jesus is also a man. He is the Word made flesh that came down to dwell among us. In Jesus we see the perfect man. The life of Jesus shows us the life that we were created for. When we examine the Gospels, we are struck by the way Jesus handled different situations. Through it all, His humanity and His deity shine through. One of the reasons Jesus is our rightful object of worship is who He is.

His Purpose

The Apostle John stated that "the Son of God came to destroy the works of the devil" (1 John 3:8, NLT). Jesus came to earth with a grand purpose. It was planned before the foundation of the world that Jesus would atone for the sins of humanity. He came to model the life we are to live as humans, but that wasn't all. He also came to remove the barrier to living that life: sin. As the sinless Son of God, Jesus came to be a sacrifice for the world. Instead of coming

to rule as a king, He died as a criminal for a greater purpose. This purpose and plan was to give His blood for the forgiveness of our sins so that nothing could stand in the way of our having a relationship with God the Father. Sin made us distant enemies, but Jesus' work on the Cross made us sons and daughters. He is the rightful object of worship because He gave us a right relationship with the Father.

His Position

Jesus died, but that was not the end of the story. Three days later, He rose again. With a new resurrected body, Jesus had conquered death and was given all authority in heaven and in earth. For forty days He stayed with the disciples, teaching them about the kingdom of God, and then He ascended into heaven to be with His Father. Now He sits at the right hand of God as our advocate. Paul says that "now he is far above any ruler or authority or power or leader or anything else—not only in this world but also in the world to come. God has put all things under the authority of Christ and has made him head over all things for the benefit of the church" (Ephesians 1:21–22, NLT). Christ is the ruler of the universe. There is nothing that exists that is not under His authority. He is the King of kings and the Lord of lords. He has

no rivals or competitors. There is no one that He can be compared to. This is why He is the rightful object of worship.

As we look at our lives, let us examine whether we are worshiping the idols of this world or the rightful object of worship: Jesus Christ. Let's take a close look at our financial budgets and the way we spend our time. Let's reflect on what makes us angry, happy, or sad. Sometimes there is a clue hidden in our emotions on what truly holds our allegiance. The Westminster Confession states that "the chief end of man is to glorify God and enjoy him forever." Is this your main goal in life? We were created to worship, and it is not a matter of whether we worship or not, but who will be our object of worship. This world gives worship to things that are not worthy of worship. The followers of Christ have Jesus Christ as our object of worship. Because of His person, purpose, and position, we can give Him all of our money, time, and effort. It is through Him that we can fulfill the first and greatest commandment to love God with all our heart, soul, and might. This is the right response toward the rightful object of our worship.

Surrender, the Best Teacher of Worship

by Beverly Moore

Acts of worship such as praise, thanksgiving, and giving are valuable and required expressions of our love and appreciation for God. However, at the heart of worship is our ability to be vulnerable by placing our complete trust in our God whom we cannot see. As Christian educators, we are instruments of God used in the spiritual formation of His people. We are charged with helping others cultivate an intimate relationship with God through the transforming study and application of His Word. Worship is a lifestyle, one that must be taught with repetition and modeling. To use worship as a teaching tool requires the ability to be transparent with your students. Students are able to relate to teachers who can be real about their struggles yet show them how they are able to overcome them through surrendering to God. This is ultimately an act of worship.

I am reminded of Moses, whom God used as His instrument to deliver His people out of bondage in Egypt after years of captivity. Throughout the Pentateuch, we see Moses in his humanity relate to God and the people he was called to serve. God uses Moses to lead His people because of the intimate relationship he developed with God through his surrendered life. The relationship Moses had with God could only be cultivated through continual dependence, fidelity, and surrender to His will. Moses could not teach the Children of Israel how to worship God without having seen Him

proved in his own life. Indeed Moses had plenty of object lessons in knowing not just God's acts, but also His ways (Psalm 103:7). And so it is with us in today's context as Christian educators: pastors, ministers, and teachers alike, our lives often become object lessons where we too are called upon to surrender all to Jesus. It is in these experiences that we obtain the best lessons to pass on to others.

In the book of Deuteronomy, Moses prepares the Children of Israel to take possession of the Promised Land. That generation survived the wilderness through God's sustaining power and goodness. Moses, as God's mouthpiece, was tasked with reiterating His laws, commandments, and ordinances to the Children of Israel, and instilling in them specific directions for how to worship. God was very clear: He did not want the people, whom He had chosen and called out from among the other nations of the world as His treasured possession, to copy the pagan worship practices (Deuteronomy 12:1–5, 29–32). Through Moses, God established what was acceptable worship to Him and shared with Israel the blessings of obedience to His commands. Most notably, God instructed the Children of Israel: "And thou shalt love the LORD thy God with all thine heart, and with all thy soul, and with all thy might. And these words, which I command thee this day, shall be in thine heart" (Deuteronomy 6:5–6). This passage of Scripture is included in what is known

in the Jewish culture as the Shema, which in Hebrew is the first word of the commandment and means to "listen" or "hear." Even today, faithful Jews still recite the Shema as an expression of their devotion to God, and it is a good practice for us as Christians to call to mind and live out these words from the Shema. Loving God with all our heart, soul, and might is to surrender to Him in every area of our lives.

To use worship as a teaching tool is to usher people into the presence of God by aiding their understanding of what it means to live in unbroken fellowship with Him. Living in unbroken fellowship with God in response to His goodness and redemptive work through Jesus Christ means that we live our lives as modeled by our Lord, who showed us how to be one with the Father (John 17:21–23). Worship is a lifestyle, so we should see every

aspect of our lives as worship to the Lord. We can be accustomed to compartmentalizing our lives—church lives versus the rest of our social lives—but true worship recognizes God in everything that we do. As the theologian and statesman Abraham Kuyper has said, "There is not a square inch in the whole domain of our human existence over which Christ, who is Sovereign over all, does not cry: 'Mine!'" In these words is a challenge for us to surrender on a daily basis.

We can also use worship as a means of showing people how to deal with life's adverse situations. In these times worship is not automatic, and a conscious decision to believe God over circumstances is needed. Through worship, we are able to draw strength from the presence and power of God and His Word. As Christian educators, we are directly responsible for equipping the saints in how to count it as joy when they experience hardships (James 1:2). Martin Luther said the very highest worship of God is that we trust Him: "God cannot be worshiped unless you ascribe to Him the glory of truthfulness and all goodness which is due to Him." We are central as influencers for God to instruct and facilitate students in learning how to redirect negative circumstances, especially those thoughts born through spiritual attacks. By living a life surrendered to God, our reasonable act of worship (Romans 12:1), we entrust our lives to the One who is sovereign. In other words, we teach our students through the Word of God how to respond differently when they are hit with life's blows, sure in knowing that God is good and trustworthy when circumstances are not.

Finally, our worship teaches students who God is, to know His character, and to be personally affirmed because of His acceptance. Jesus, our Master teacher, shows us through His life and ministry how we are to reflect the knowledge of God's character. Jesus said, "He that speaketh of himself seeketh his own glory: but he that seeketh his glory that sent him, the same is true, and no unrighteousness is in him" (John 7:18). Jesus was affirmed by His relationship with His Father and did not seek the glory of man (John 5:30, 41). When He met the woman at the well, He noted that "true worshippers shall worship the Father in spirit and in truth: for the Father seeketh such to worship him" (from John 4:23). At the heart of God's character is the knowledge that His intentions and motives are always pure, good, and in our best interest. We are affirmed in our place in Him by knowing that we are accepted as one of His beloved, chosen in Him before the foundation of the world (Ephesians 1:4–6). With that said, we wear the brand of Jesus by receiving our identity in Him. We know who we are and whose we are, and because we place our trust in His goodness and faithfulness, total surrender is not burdensome. Our lives are hidden in Christ in God (Colossians 3:3). We are able to teach students how to base their identity on who they are in Christ, not the labels of the world, nor the past, nor the present whether good or bad. Bruce Wilkerson said in his book *The Seven Laws of the Learner*: "Application must ultimately lead the students from studying the Bible to obeying the Lord … Christianity is not a set of facts but relationship with a living Person Jesus Christ" (160). As teachers, our function in the body of Christ is to cultivate true worship of God, which is more than just a mere performance of religious ritual, but a surrender of our hearts and lives to the King of the universe, Jesus Christ.

Sources:
Luther, Martin. "On the Freedom of a Christian." *Luther's Works*, vol. 31. Philadelphia: Fortress Press, 1957. 350, 353.
Wilkerson, Bruce. *The Seven Laws of the Learner: How to Teach Almost Anything to Practically Anyone!* Sisters, OR: Multnomah Publishers, 1992. 160.

Beverly Moore is a Bible Teacher and Independent Church Marketing Communications Consultant.

The Last Seder: Not Just the Last Supper

by Rabbi Jason Sobel

Jesus died during Passover, which is why He is called the Passover Lamb. Before His death, He dined with His disciples in what is known as the Last Supper—but the Last Supper was actually the Last Seder. Jesus was observing Passover by having a traditional dinner called a Seder with His closest friends.

The most famous illustration of the Last Supper is a painting by Leonardo da Vinci in which Jesus and His very western European-looking disciples are gathered around a table with glasses of wine, loaves of fluffy white bread, and fish. Since Passover is a Jewish holiday also known as the Feast of Unleavened Bread, da Vinci was way off in his depiction— there's no way leavened loaves and fish sat on Jesus' table. He and His disciples would have been eating the large, flat cracker called *matzah* in honor of this holiday. Why? The answer is in the backstory of Passover.

Passed Over

The Jews had been plagued by the Egyptians and trapped in slavery for 400 years. God heard the cries of their hearts, and selected Moses as His man to set them free. Pharaoh proved unwilling to let his slaves go and cause an economic downturn, so God plagued the Egyptians in ten different ways, the tenth plague being the death of the firstborn son in all the Egyptians' households.

Pharaoh relented and finally let the Children of Israel go free. But shortly after releasing them, he changed his mind, mounting his horses and chariots to chase them down. Israel seemed to be in a precarious situation with the Red Sea on one side and the advancing army of Pharaoh on the other side, but God can make a way where there seems to be none. He brought them through on dry ground as He parted the Red Sea and then drowned their enemies in it, leading to great deliverance for the Children of Israel. Passover celebrates this supernatural act of redemption that the Lord wrought for His covenant people.

Discussion Question

There are many significant connections between events in the Old and New Testament. How does knowing that Jesus died on Passover enrich your perspective of His gift to us on the Cross?

The Roots of the Passover Celebration

The Israelites are given specific instructions for how to celebrate Passover:

"These are the appointed feasts of *ADONAI*, holy convocations which you are to proclaim in their appointed season. During the first month, on the fourteenth day of the month in the evening, is *ADONAI's* Passover. On the fifteenth day of the same month is the Feast of *Matzot* to *ADONAI*. For seven days you are to eat *matzah*. On the first day you are to have a holy convocation and you should do no regular work. Instead you are to present an offering made by fire to *ADONAI* for seven days. On the seventh day is a holy convocation, when you are to do no regular work." (Leviticus 23:4–8, TLV)

Passover, or *Pesach* in Hebrew, literally means to "skip over," referring to the angel of death who skipped or passed over the Jewish households marked by the lambs' blood on their doorways. When Pharaoh finally cried uncle and the Jews were free to go, God instructed them to hit the road in haste, so they baked their bread quickly, not allowing it to rise, which is why unleavened bread, *matzah*, is eaten throughout this holiday.

Central to the celebration of Passover is the Seder meal, which is usually eaten at home with friends and family. *Seder* in Hebrew literally means "order" and refers to the order of Passover service, which is centered around telling the story of the Exodus from Egypt, eating *matzah* and bitter herbs, and drinking four cups of grape juice or wine. A key aspect of the Passover was the offering of the Passover lamb, but since the destruction the Jerusalem Temple in AD 70, the Passover offering has ceased. The biblical source for the primary elements for the Passover are found in Exodus:

They are to eat the meat that night, roasted over a fire. With *matzot* and bitter herbs they are to eat it. ... During the first month in the evening of the fourteenth day of the month, you are to eat *matzot*, until the evening of the twenty-first day of the month. For seven days no *hametz* is to be found in your houses, for whoever eats *hametz*, that soul will be cut off from the congregation of Israel, whether he is an outsider or one who is born in the land. You are to eat no *hametz*; in all your houses you are to eat *matzot*. (Exodus 12:8, 18–20, TLV)

Do you see why the dinner rolls and fish on da Vinci's table don't accurately portray the Last Supper/Seder of our Lord?

Loving-Kindness is the Foundation

In Jewish thought, the world stands on three pillars: the Word of God (Torah), divine service (worship), and deeds of loving-kindness. Having established these three, Jewish thought asks, "Of which of those three will we experience the coming of the Messiah? We will experience it through exercising loving-kindness." For this reason, we are called to take the freedom encountered at Passover and use it as fuel in our fight against the modern injustices around us.

The celebration of Passover begins with inviting the poor and needy into our homes. Some actually have the tradition of opening the front door and yelling into the streets, "Whoever is poor, whoever is in need, come in and eat with us." The Passover story is not just meant to be retelling historical fact. It is meant to change our lives and impact the way we live, for we are instructed, "You must not mistreat or oppress foreigners in any way. Remember, you yourselves were once foreigners in the land of Egypt" (Exodus 22:21, NLT).

We cannot forget where we come from—our past needs to affect us in the present. How can we celebrate Passover, known as "the time of our freedom," and close our eyes to the oppression and slavery in our world today? We see dreadful examples of hate, exploitation, and even genocide in parts of Africa and the Middle East. The Passover story reminds us of past redemption so we can help repair and transform the world in the present by joining hands to fight modern-day injustice, oppression, and slavery. It beckons us not just to identify with the oppressed but calls us to be like Moses, living as prophetic voices that speak to the modern Pharaohs of our world saying, "Let my people go!" God's people should demonstrate the goodness, power, and loving-kindness of the Lord by fighting the plagues of hatred, racism, poverty, injustice, slavery, and genocide.

Everyone who sits at the Passover table is supposed to see themselves as if they were the ones who actually came forth out the land of Egypt. Every generation has an obligation to tell the story of Israel's salvation and liberation. When we eat the *matzah*, known as the bread of affliction, and the bitter herbs that remind us of how the Egyptians embittered our lives with harsh labor, we can't help but remember and fight for those who are experiencing this reality today.

Discussion Question

God frees us from our captivity to give us a testimony of His love that will impact the world. Discuss how He might want to use your story of personal deliverance to reveal Himself to others or tangibly meet the needs of those around you.

Messiah in the Passover

What we know today as the Lord's Supper was instituted at a Passover Seder, which Jesus celebrated with His disciples:

When the hour came, *Yeshua* reclined at table, and the emissaries with Him. And He said to them, "I have eagerly desired to eat this Passover with you before I suffer. For I tell you, I will never eat it again until it is fulfilled in the kingdom of God." (Luke 22:14–16, TLV)

All of the central elements of the Passover Seder contain hints pointing to our Messiah Jesus. In fact, you miss out on the full meaning of both communion and Easter if you don't understand them within the context of Passover. Let's take a deeper look.

The Messianic Meaning of the Matzah

Matzah bread has almost a corrugated look, with holes like dotted lines running vertically alongside rows of browned pockets of dough that form peaks and valleys. The bread represents the centuries of slavery in Egypt endured by the Jews, with the brown stripes running the length of the bread recalling the lashings of the slave drivers upon our enslaved ancestors. *Matzah* is also known as the bread of freedom and healing, a reminder of when God redeemed the Jews from Egypt with a "powerful arm" (from Exodus 6:6, NLT).

We can also see Jesus represented in the *matzah*. Isaiah describes the messianic Suffering Servant:

Surely He has borne our griefs and carried our pains. Yet we esteemed Him stricken, struck by God, and afflicted. But He was pierced because of our transgressions… The chastisement for our *shalom* was upon Him, and by His stripes we are healed. (from Isaiah 53:4–5, TLV)

Jesus' personal "bread of affliction" was the weight of our sins. The *matzah*'s holes stand for His piercings. The brown stripes represent His stripes by which we are healed from bondage to sin and our own "Egypts," the personal prisons that confine and limit us from being who God wants us to be and doing what He has destined for us.

The *matzah* is broken during the fourth step in the Seder called *yachatz*, meaning "to break." During the Last Seder, *matzah* was the bread Jesus lifted, broke, and "gave it to the disciples, saying, 'Take this and eat it, for this is my body'" (from Matthew 26:26, NLT). Communion is looked upon as a mini-Passover each time we partake.

Did you ever think there was such deep meaning in so thin a cracker?

The Four Cups

The Passover Seder is centered around all drinking four cups of wine or grape. Each cup has deep spiritual significance and symbolizes the four distinct promises God made to the Jewish people in Exodus 6:6–7.

The first cup is known as the cup of sanctification. Jesus began His Seder by reciting the blessing over this first cup. We read this: "Then he took a cup of wine and gave thanks to God for it. Then he said, 'Take this and share it among yourselves'" (Luke 22:17). We respond to the cup of sanctification by crying out, "God, make us holy. Set us apart for Your plans and holy purposes for our lives."

The second cup is commonly referred to as the cup of plagues, by which we remember that God did not just redeem, but He redeemed us with great signs and great wonders. We remember that God, through Moses, turned water into blood, and that the Messiah's first miracle turned water into wine because He is greater than Moses.

The third cup is the cup of redemption, which reminds us of the blood of the Passover lamb put on the doorposts of the house. At the Passover Seder, Jesus also blessed this third cup and gave it to His disciples. He said, "This is the blood, which I poured out for you for the remission of sins for the inauguration of the new covenant" (Matthew 26:28, author's paraphrase). Just like the blood on the doorposts of the house spared Israel from the plague of the death of the firstborn, in the same way, those who belong to Jesus have been bought by the blood of the Lamb. We do not have to experience the wrath of God and His judgment because Jesus died as the ultimate Passover Lamb! Whenever we partake of the Lord's Supper, we are drinking symbolically and spiritually partaking of the third cup.

The fourth cup is the cup of acceptance—for God said, "I will claim you as my own people" (from Exodus 6:7, NLT)—and of thanksgiving, because we say it over the psalms of praise known as *hallel*. This cup looks to the future, to the coming of the kingdom. It was over the fourth cup that Jesus said, "I will never again drink of the fruit of the vine, until that day when I drink it anew in the kingdom of God" (from Mark 14:25, TLV). With this cup, we acknowledge and give thanks for our acceptance as children of the King, knowing His position, power, and authority as the Messiah.

Discussion Question

Now that you know the background of Passover and why it is significant to us as believers, discuss the symbols we use to celebrate it, from the *matzah* bread to the four cups we consume. How do these customs enhance and add meaning to the celebration of Passover?

Yeshua as the Greater Moses

There has never been another prophet in Israel like Moses, whom the LORD knew face to face. The LORD sent him to perform all the miraculous signs and wonders in the land of Egypt against Pharaoh, and all his servants, and his entire land. (Deuteronomy 34:10–11, NLT)

Deuteronomy 34 says two things that made Moses unique: God spoke to him face-to-face, and he performed unique signs and wonders when he delivered Israel out of Egypt. One of the ways that God spoke to Moses was through the burning bush. The book of Hebrews tells us that it was not an ordinary bush—it was a thorn bush. Why did God reveal Himself to

Moses in a thorn bush? Thorns represent affliction, suffering, and pain.

Through the symbol of the thorn bush, God is saying, "I have seen your pain. I have seen your suffering. I have seen what has been happening to you for all of these hundreds of years, and I identify with you. I understand what you have been through, and it breaks My heart." Compassion moved Him to redeem His people, causing Moses to tell Israel that God had remembered their prayers, and He cared for them.

What encircled the head of the King of kings when He hung on the Cross? An intertwining of thorns served as His crown, which also signifies the Fall (Genesis 3:18). Jesus took the affliction for the sin of man, absorbing all the pain and suffering meant for us and undoing the curse of creation. He took the fall for the Fall. He allowed Himself to be put upon a tree (the Cross) to restore what had been taken from the tree.

Moses' unique relationship with God is also demonstrated by the fact that he could enter into God's holy presence on a regular basis, unlike regular members of the Israelite congregation. When Jesus, the unique Son of God, died upon the Cross, the curtain separating the Holy of Holies was torn in two, allowing all to enter and ending the separation between God and man.

Another correlation between Moses and Jesus is the ninth plague. There were three days of darkness over Egypt. When Jesus hung on the Cross, there were three hours of darkness between the sixth and ninth hour. The tenth plague was the death of the firstborn son in all the Egyptian households. The angel passed over the houses of the Jews, which were marked by the lambs' blood. Jesus is God's firstborn Son, and His blood, the blood of the Lamb, allows us to pass over from death to eternal life!

Moses' first miracle when he was delivering the Jews from Egypt was to turn the water of the Nile into blood. Jesus' first public miracle at the start of His ministry of redemption was to turn the water into wine, a wine so fine that the master of ceremonies commented that the best was saved for last. Jesus, as the greater Moses, came not to bring death, but life: "I am come that they might have life, and that they might have it more abundantly" (from John 10:10, KJV). Jesus, the greater Moses, the Passover Lamb, delivers us into the Promised Land of eternal life in God!

Discussion Question

Recount the prophetic similarities between Moses and Yeshua. How did Moses serve as a prototype for the Passover Lamb?

Living in Light of the Passover

All of us, like Israel, must go through the process of coming out of our own "Egypt," a tight space or a place of confinement and restriction that seeks to box us in. The Pharaohs in your life want to see you locked in a box of self-limitation that robs you of our true identity and destiny. Don't let your outer or inner Pharaohs win, and don't let your Egypts define you! You were created for freedom and destiny. You have incredible power, purpose, and potential through faith in Jesus, your Passover Lamb, and the might of the Holy Spirit who dwells in all those who believe.

Source:
Scripture taken from the *Messianic Jewish Family Bible*, Tree of Life Version. Copyright © 2015 by the Messianic Jewish Family Bible Society. Used by permission of the Messianic Jewish Family Bible Society.

Rabbi Jason Sobel is a Christian minister, thought leader, storyteller, spiritual guide, and occasional rapper sharing transforming connections about the Messiah and His Jewish roots.

Frederick Douglass

(c. 1818–1895)

Frederick Douglass was born a slave but rose to be a confidant and advisor to the President of the United States. Douglass fought for the abolition of slavery and championed the cause of freedom, both as an orator and as a writer. He wrote several autobiographies that detail the suffering that slaves endured. When people heard him speak or read his writings, they could hardly believe such eloquence came from a former slave.

Frederick Douglass was born around 1818. As a young child, Frederick became the slave of Thomas Auld and his wife, Sophia. He often heard Sophia Auld reading aloud from the Bible, and one day he asked her to teach him how to read. She began teaching him and was delighted with the quickness with which he learned. But when Thomas Auld discovered that she was teaching him to read, he made his wife stop. He told her that reading would make Frederick unfit for slavery, but Frederick learned to read despite his master's attempts to stop him.

At 13 years of age, Douglass became interested in religion. He heard a preacher say that "all men, great and small, bond and free, were sinners in the sight of God; that they were by nature rebels against his government; and that they must repent of their sins and be reconciled to God through Christ" (Douglass, 90). Frederick felt a great burden lift from his heart as he accepted Jesus. This left him with a great hunger to pray and to read the Bible. He spent much time praying and studying God's Word with an elderly Black Christian man, but the Aulds soon forbade him to spend any more time with him.

Frederick was frequently moved from one slavery situation to another. At age 16 he spent one year with a "slave breaker." When this man tried to whip Frederick for a second time, Frederick defended himself fiercely. He learned that passivity in such a situation only made matters worse. The man never tried to whip Frederick again.

After that year, he was sent to a man who was easier on his slaves, but Frederick only desired freedom all the more. While holding an illegal Sunday School class with four young men, Frederick began to plan an escape with his students. Their plot was discovered, and Frederick ended up in jail.

After spending time in jail, Frederick was mercifully sent back to the Aulds in Baltimore. There, he was hired out in the shipbuilding business as a caulker. Every penny that he earned was turned over to Thomas Auld. Once he spent the weekend at a camp meeting hoping to earn some extra money, but that, too, was taken away from him.

This injustice burned within him because he knew that the full amount rightfully belonged to him. At this point, he made hasty plans to escape to freedom. Dressed as a sailor, with borrowed papers that confirmed his occupation, Douglas boarded a train. He was very nervous about being discovered, but he made it to Wilmington, where he boarded a steamboat for Philadelphia and then took the train to New York. His wife-to-be, a free Black from Baltimore, met him in New York, and there they were married.

Frederick soon discovered that New York was not as safe as he had thought. A White abolitionist directed him to New Bedford, where he was able to work and support both himself and his wife. It was hard labor, but he was thankful to be working for himself.

When Douglass became known to the abolitionists, they asked him to tell his story so that people could hear of the horrors of slavery. He told his story and denounced slavery with such brilliant rhetoric that people could hardly believe he had ever been a slave. Still, Frederick realized that by giving the details, he was in danger of being snatched back into slavery. So abolitionist friends took him to England, where for two years he spoke for the cause and remained free. Finally, two friends paid his old slave master for his freedom, and he was able to come back to the United States to continue his fight for the abolition of slavery. Upon returning, he wrote for abolitionist newspapers and eventually started his own paper, the *North Star*.

When the Civil War finally came, Douglass approached Abraham Lincoln about recruiting Blacks to join the fight. He advocated that the "black iron hand" (Douglass, 336) be joined to the White in this fight. Later, he again spoke with Abraham Lincoln about the fact that Black soldiers were being paid only half as much as White soldiers. In addition, he let the president know that Black soldiers should also be allowed to rise to the rank of officer.

Douglass lived well beyond the Civil War. He continued fighting for equal rights for Blacks. He also fought for voting rights, women's rights, and temperance. He was appointed by President Harrison as Consul General in Haiti. Douglass died in 1895.

Teaching Tips

Words You Should Know

A. Test (Genesis 22:1) *nasa* (Heb.)—Try, i.e., attempt to learn the true nature of something.

B. Provide (v. 14) *ra'ah* (Heb.)—Give aid or support by making available whatever supplies are needed, as an extension of appearing on the scene of a situation.

Teacher Preparation

Unifying Principle—A Test of Trust. People are reluctant to make challenging personal sacrifices for fear of losing everything. How can they learn to offer difficult sacrifices even in the face of fear? By being willing to offer his son, Abraham trusted God, who provided everything he needed.

A. Pray that students will be faithful in tests that prove their faith.

B. Read and research Genesis 22 in various Bible resources (e.g., commentary, journal articles).

C. Complete the companion lesson in the *Precepts For Living*® Study Guide.

O—Open the Lesson

A. Open with prayer, including the Aim for Change.

B. Introduce today's lesson title.

C. Ask the class to read the In Focus story silently by themselves or with someone else (being careful not to disturb others), then discuss it.

P—Present the Scriptures

A. Have volunteers read the Focal Verses.

B. Use The People, Places, and Times; Background; Search the Scriptures; At-A-Glance outline; In Depth; and More Light on the Text sections.

E—Explore the Meaning

A. Split the class in half to answer the Discuss the Meaning section.

B. Have a volunteer read the Lesson in Our Society section.

N—Next Steps for Application

A. Summarize the lesson.

B. For a lively discussion, invite students to ask—and to answer—questions.

C. Close with prayer.

Worship Guide

For the Superintendent or Teacher
Theme: The Lord Will Provide
Song: Gave It All
Devotional Reading: Psalm 20

The Lord Will Provide

Bible Background • GENESIS 22
Printed Text • GENESIS 22: 1–3, 6–14 | Devotional Reading • PSALM 20

—————— Aim for Change ——————

By the end of the lesson we will: EXPLORE God's call to radical personal sacrifice; APPRECIATE the difficulty of following His directives; and EMULATE those who make extreme personal sacrifices for God.

————— In Focus —————

It had always been difficult for Janet to build new relationships. As a young woman, Janet worked to build friendships with a group of young ladies and formed a deep meaningful community—they understood her, loved her, rebuked her when necessary, and challenged her spiritually. So Janet did not understand why God was leading her to move to another state for school, away from her bona fide friends and everything else that was familiar to her. Janet was torn; she had made a commitment to follow God wherever He might lead, but this time around, the sacrifice seemed much greater than what she could afford.

Janet desperately missed home. She had decided to obey God's plan for this season of her life, despite reservations about relocating. Surrounded by people from different cultures and backgrounds, she felt alone in this big city. But as time progressed, Janet began to hope in the possibilities of building new relationships.

Karen was one person she was growing closer to; they had a few classes together and attended the same church. Janet was amazed at how many things they had in common. Gradually, Janet could see God working in her situation, providing her with opportunities to build new friendships.

As disciples, we are called to obey God in every circumstance, even when following His instructions is uncomfortable for us. How can we prepare ourselves for a life of sacrifice in the kingdom of God?

—————— Keep in Mind ——————

"And Abraham said, My son, God will provide himself a lamb for a burnt offering: so they went both of them together" (Genesis 22:8).

"And Abraham said, My son, God will provide himself a lamb for a burnt offering: so they went both of them together" (Genesis 22:8).

Focal Verses

KJV **Genesis 22:1** And it came to pass after these things, that God did tempt Abraham, and said unto him, Abraham: and he said, Behold, here I am.

2 And he said, Take now thy son, thine only son Isaac, whom thou lovest, and get thee into the land of Moriah; and offer him there for a burnt offering upon one of the mountains which I will tell thee of.

3 And Abraham rose up early in the morning, and saddled his ass, and took two of his young men with him, and Isaac his son, and clave the wood for the burnt offering, and rose up, and went unto the place of which God had told him.

6 Abraham took the wood of the burnt offering and laid it on Isaac his son, and he took in his hand the fire and the knife. So the two of them walked on together.

7 And Isaac spake unto Abraham his father, and said, My father: and he said, Here am I, my son. And he said, Behold the fire and the wood: but where is the lamb for a burnt offering?

8 And Abraham said, My son, God will provide himself a lamb for a burnt offering: so they went both of them together.

9 And they came to the place which God had told him of; and Abraham built an altar there, and laid the wood in order, and bound Isaac his son, and laid him on the altar upon the wood.

10 And Abraham stretched forth his hand, and took the knife to slay his son.

11 And the angel of the Lord called unto him out of heaven, and said, Abraham, Abraham: and he said, Here am I.

12 And he said, Lay not thine hand upon the lad, neither do thou any thing unto him: for now I know that thou fearest God, seeing thou hast not withheld thy son, thine only son from me.

NLT **Genesis 22:1** Some time later, God tested Abraham's faith. "Abraham!" God called. "Yes," he replied. "Here I am."

2 "Take your son, your only son—yes, Isaac, whom you love so much—and go to the land of Moriah. Go and sacrifice him as a burnt offering on one of the mountains, which I will show you."

3 The next morning Abraham got up early. He saddled his donkey and took two of his servants with him, along with his son, Isaac. Then he chopped wood for a fire for a burnt offering and set out for the place God had told him about.

6 So Abraham placed the wood for the burnt offering on Isaac's shoulders, while he himself carried the fire and the knife. As the two of them walked on together,

7 Isaac turned to Abraham and said, "Father?" "Yes, my son?" Abraham replied. "We have the fire and the wood," the boy said, "but where is the sheep for the burnt offering?"

8 "God will provide a sheep for the burnt offering, my son," Abraham answered. And they both walked on together.

9 When they arrived at the place where God had told him to go, Abraham built an altar and arranged the wood on it. Then he tied his son, Isaac, and laid him on the altar on top of the wood.

10 And Abraham picked up the knife to kill his son as a sacrifice.

11 At that moment the angel of the Lord called to him from heaven, "Abraham! Abraham!" "Yes," Abraham replied. "Here I am!"

12 "Don't lay a hand on the boy!" the angel said. "Do not hurt him in any way, for now I know that you truly fear God. You have not

13 And Abraham lifted up his eyes, and looked, and behold behind him a ram caught in a thicket by his horns: and Abraham went and took the ram, and offered him up for a burnt offering in the stead of his son.

14 And Abraham called the name of that place Jehovahjireh: as it is said to this day, In the mount of the LORD it shall be seen.

withheld from me even your son, your only son."

13 Then Abraham looked up and saw a ram caught by its horns in a thicket. So he took the ram and sacrificed it as a burnt offering in place of his son.

14 Abraham named the place Yahweh-Yireh (which means "the Lord will provide"). To this day, people still use that name as a proverb: "On the mountain of the LORD it will be provided."

The People, Places, and Times

Mount Moriah. The place where Abraham went to sacrifice Isaac was Mount Moriah, the same place where Solomon would later erect the first temple (2 Chronicles 3:1). The text helps us understand general geographical details regarding where Abraham built the altar. From Beersheba, the journey took two full days. On the third day, the mountain range came into sight (v. 4), which suggests that the place was a little farther north than Jerusalem. It must have been physically exhausting, but more emotionally exhausting for Abraham as he tried to reconcile God's promise to establish an everlasting covenant with Isaac with the request to offer up Isaac as a sacrifice.

Burnt offering. The first mention of burnt offerings occurs in Genesis 8:20 and thus long antedated the tabernacle system. Burnt offerings were God's requirement that provided a temporary covering of sins foreshadowing the perfect and complete sacrifice of Jesus Christ (Leviticus 5:10). The "burnt offering" was fully consumed, producing an aroma that pleased the Lord (Genesis 8:21; Leviticus 1:9). It was understood to be an integral aspect of worship to the Lord, as Abraham states on his way to offer the sacrifice: "I and the lad will go yonder and worship" (Genesis 22:5). That Abraham

was commanded to offer Isaac as a burnt offering was unusual and foreshadows God's sacrifice of His only begotten Son (John 3:16).

What in your life would be considered a burnt offering?

Background

Finally, Abraham and Sarah were beginning to experience the fulfillment of God's covenantal promise with the birth of their son, Isaac (Genesis 12:1, 21:1–3). The name Isaac literally means "laughter." When Isaac was born, Sarah said, "God hath made me to laugh, so that all that hear will laugh with me." His name highlights the tension in Sarah's response to God's promise concerning the gift of a descendant, which seemed impossible at the time. Sarah had previously laughed at God in mockery, which reflected her lack of trust. Now, she joins with Abraham in laughter with faith and gratitude.

After twenty-four years of waiting, Isaac arrived! He was God's promise fulfilled. Abraham and Sarah were confident that their God could make the impossible possible.

What promises of God have you waited on to be fulfilled which proved to be a test of your faith?

At-A-Glance

1. The Test of Abraham's Obedience
(Genesis 22:1–3)
2. The Devotion of Abraham's Obedience
(vv. 6–10)
3. The Blessing of Abraham's Obedience
(vv. 11–14)

In Depth

1. The Test of Abraham's Obedience (Genesis 22:1–3)

Abraham entered into a God-orchestrated test where he was instructed to offer Isaac as a sacrifice. That God tests His people is not exceptional; it is a means of revealing obedience (e.g., Exodus 15:25, 16:4; Judges 2:22). For Abraham, this test was the culmination of a journey that started in Genesis 12:1.

The command to sacrifice Isaac appeared to place Abraham at risk of losing the son of promise through whom God would give Abraham descendants. Abraham had reluctantly sent away Ishmael, his son through Hagar (Genesis 21:8–21). The descriptors used in reference to Isaac as the son whom he loves indicates that this request was extremely costly to Abraham. He was to kill the child that he had believed in God for all these years. Nevertheless, in immediate obedience, he got up "early in the morning" to obey (v. 2).

Does it take more time for you to obey God's commands when there is personal sacrifice involved?

2. The Devotion of Abraham's Obedience (vv. 6–10)

Abraham was convinced that God would be able to resurrect Isaac from the dead, even from the ashes of a burnt offering (Hebrews 11:19). As the two traveled together, Isaac raised a question about the lamb that was to be sacrificed. Something was not right! He was old enough to have sensibly observed sacrifices by his father in the past, and he knew what was required.

Abraham answered in a manner that seemed vague, although it captured his sincere willingness to obey whatever God instructed. God would be the provider, since He was the one who had issued the command. At the designated spot, Abraham prepares the altar. His obedience is showcased by his attention to follow the exact details of preparing an offering.

How do our actions correlate to our faith and trust in God?

3. The Blessing of Abraham's Obedience (vv. 11–14)

As Abraham lifted his hand with the knife and was about to kill Isaac, the angel of the LORD intervened. Abraham was told to "lay not thine hand upon the lad"—a very different command than God's first instruction. To say that Abraham probably felt relieved is an understatement.

Abraham feared God. He demonstrated that he respected and revered God. How? He did not withhold his son—the only son through whom God would fulfill His promise. Abraham's faith, made complete by passing this test, had significant ramifications on his generation as well as the generations after him (James 2:22).

How can our sacrifice and obedience create greater blessings for us and others?

Search the Scriptures

1. Why did God put Abraham's faith to the test (Genesis 22:1)? Was this the only way God would know whether Abraham's faith was genuine (v. 12)?

2. Was the test ultimately for God's sake or for Abraham's?

Discuss the Meaning

Abraham passed the test! He believed that God would fulfill His promise no matter what the circumstance. If God had to raise Isaac from the ashes, Abraham was confident that he would. Active faith requires obedience even when we don't know the outcome. Daily we must count the cost associated with following God and determine for ourselves whether He is deserving of our trust and total obedience.

How does our love for others compare to our love for God? What did Abraham's willingness to sacrifice Isaac say about his worship of God?

Lesson in Our Society

Children, money, careers, material possessions, friends, and even our role in the church are sometimes valued more than we value God. What or whom do we worship? Placing God's blessings in perspective will help us avoid dethroning God from the center of our lives. For Abraham, a relationship with God had immense worth and value above anyone or anything else. God was the object of his worship, and that truth was demonstrated in how Abraham lived.

How do we sacrifice personal desire to love others and bring God glory?

Make It Happen

Make a list of things you could give up if God asked you to do so. Consider what's not on the list. Are these things more important to you than your relationship with God?

Talk to God about the treasures in your life or whatever consumes your time to the extent that it pushes you away from Him, such as television, social media, the phone, or certain people. Think about the different needs of people around you and decide on a practical way to meet one of those needs. Then go, and for the sake of your God, be a blessing to others.

Follow the Spirit

What God wants me to do:

_____

_____

_____

_____

Remember Your Thoughts

Special insights I have learned:

_____

_____

_____

_____

More Light on the Text

Genesis 22:1–3, 6–14

1 And it came to pass after these things, that God did tempt Abraham, and said unto him, Abraham: and he said, Behold, here I am.

In Jewish tradition, this chapter is referred to as the Aqedah, which means "the binding," which speaks to Abraham's test. The idea of being tested is rarely a pleasant one. However, when God is the tester, the test promotes good over evil (James 1:13). Instead of "tempt" (Heb. *nasah*, **nah-SAH**), here most modern translations have "test," giving a clearer picture of what God is doing. Such a test serves a dual purpose: revealing where one's allegiance lies as well as unveiling aspects of the divine character and Person. In Abraham's case, it revealed that he feared the Lord (v. 12). Many other times throughout Scripture, God tests His people to see their faith and obedience (Deuteronomy 8:2; Judges 2:22; 2 Chronicles 32:31).

Abraham's response to God's call was, "Here I am" (Heb. *hinneh*, **hee-NAY**), a familiar response to God in other places in Scripture (Exodus 3:4; 1 Samuel 3:4; Isaiah 6:8). By this response, Abraham not only answered God but also voiced his availability and willingness to do as instructed.

2 And he said, Take now thy son, thine only son Isaac, whom thou lovest, and get thee into the land of Moriah; and offer him there for a burnt offering upon one of the mountains which I will tell thee of.

This account includes many christological overtones. The father-son relationship between Abraham and Isaac is reminiscent of the heavenly Father-Son relationship. Some scholars suggest that the Hebrew word *yakhid* (**ya-KHEED**), here translated "only," should be understood in the sense of "uniqueness" (since Isaac was technically not Abraham's only son); both Isaac and Jesus are unique sons of promise. It is translated with the word *agapetos* (Gk. **ah-ga-peh-TOCE**), "beloved" in the Septuagint. This is the same word used for Jesus at His transfiguration (Matthew 17:5). Both Isaac and Jesus were beloved sons. The identity of the son is described with extremely emotive language: "thy son, thine only son Isaac, whom thou lovest" (v. 2). There could be no doubt concerning Abraham's affection for his son and the tremendous loss that this would be to him.

3 And Abraham rose up early in the morning, and saddled his ass, and took two of his young men with him, and Isaac his son, and clave the wood for the burnt offering, and rose up, and went unto the place of which God had told him.

We are not told whether Sarah knew what Abraham was about to do. Perhaps he left early before she had the opportunity to find out and oppose his carrying out God's instruction. In any event, Abraham immediately responds in obedience, unlike previous rebuttals to God, suggesting Eliezer (15:2) or Ishmael (17:18, 21:11) as substitutes through which the promise was fulfilled. As he prepares for the journey ahead, Abraham packs the essential wood necessary for building the altar, which demonstrated his resolve to carry out divine directive.

6 Abraham took the wood of the burnt offering and laid it on Isaac his son, and he took in his hand the fire and the knife. So the two of them walked on together.

Commentators suggest symbolism in Abraham's action. The wood is transferred from the beast and laid on Isaac, the new burden bearer as well as the sacrificial lamb. Abraham, as the offerer, is said to be carrying the fire and knife. The use of the reflexive "himself" or "in his (own) hands" significantly emphasizes his deep-seated commitment to accomplishing the task.

7 And Isaac spake unto Abraham his father, and said, My father: and he said, Here am I, my son. And he said, Behold the fire and the wood: but where is the lamb for a burnt offering? 8 And Abraham said, My son, God will provide himself a lamb for a burnt offering: so they went both of them together.

These verses build the tension of the narrative. Isaac, who had been silent all this time, speaks up. He understood what was about to take place but noticed that the sacrificial sheep was missing. Animal sacrifices were instituted by God from the very beginning. Cain and Abel brought sacrifices to the Lord (Genesis 4:3–4). These sacrifices were pre-Tabernacle and served the purpose of pointing toward the ultimate sacrifice: the Lamb of God that would take away "the sin of the world" (John 1:29).

Abraham's response to Isaac's question, "God will provide himself a lamb for a burnt offering," implies much about Abraham's faith, God's ultimate plan for salvation, and Abraham's convictions concerning God's person. The Hebrew *ra'ah* (**ra-AH**), which is translated as "will provide," generally denotes the act of seeing with one's own eyes. Essentially, Abraham was insinuating that God would see the current situation and make available what was best.

For Abraham, Isaac was the lamb God was providing. The translation of the verb in the future tense must not be understood as merely referring to what God does in the future. In Abraham's faith journey, God had provided in the past and in the present, and He would in the future as well.

Additionally, commentators view Abraham's answer as typologically important, linking the discourse to Jesus as a lamb specifically provided (John 1:29; 1 Corinthians 5:7). Jesus would be God's provision to permanently deal with sin in the world making it possible for mankind to be reconciled back to God.

9 And they came to the place which God had told him of; and Abraham built an altar there, and laid the wood in order, and bound Isaac his son, and laid him on the altar upon the wood. 10 And Abraham stretched forth his hand, and took the knife to slay his son.

The fact that Isaac allows Abraham to tie him to the altar is noteworthy. Isaac's exact age is not revealed in the text, but he was certainly old enough to run away or overpower his father. Despite this, he was still a willing sacrifice. Another allusion to Jesus can be derived from Isaac's posture toward being sacrificed. Jesus, too, was the willing sacrifice who "opened not his mouth: he is brought as a lamb to the slaughter" (from Isaiah 53:7).

11 And the angel of the Lord called unto him out of heaven, and said, Abraham, Abraham: and he said, Here am I. 12 And he said, Lay not thine hand upon the lad, neither do thou any thing unto him: for now I know that thou fearest God, seeing thou hast not withheld thy son, thine only son from me.

Abraham had completed the test; the storyline reverses the threat to the boy. While Isaac was not killed, it was clear that Abraham had every intention of doing so. Abraham's obedience had been revealed through the process, resulting in commendation as one who truly feared God. This fear of God describes Abraham's obedience and trust motivated by his love of God above all else (Deuteronomy 10:12–13).

13 And Abraham lifted up his eyes, and looked, and behold behind him a ram caught in a thicket by his horns: and Abraham went and took the ram, and offered him up for a burnt offering in the stead of his son. 14 And Abraham called the name of that place Jehovahjireh: as it is said to this day, In the mount of the LORD it shall be seen.

Again, the keyword "provide" (Heb. *ra'ah*, ra-AH) is used when Abraham spots the ram ("looked," v. 13) and when he names the sacred site ("jireh," v. 14). The ram caught in the thicket became a substitute sacrifice in place of Isaac. Though Isaac is delivered, Abraham was not deterred from what he had come to the mountain to do. Together with his son, they worshiped God in that place.

Sources:
Edersheim, A. *Bible History: Old Testament.* Vol. 1. Grand Rapids, MI: William B. Eerdmans Publishing Company, 1975. 101.
Guzik, David. "Study Guide for Genesis 22." https://www. blueletterbible.org/comm/guzik_david/studyguide_gen/ gen_22.cfm
Mathews, K.A. "Genesis 11:27–50:26." Vol. 1B. *The Moody Bible Commentary.* Michael Rydelnik and Michael G. Vanlaningham, eds. Nashville, TN: Broadman & Holman Publishers, 2014. 284.

Swanson, J. *Dictionary of Biblical Languages with Semantic Domains: Hebrew (Old Testament)*. Electronic ed. Oak Harbor, WA: Logos Research Systems, Inc., 1997.

VanGemeren, W., ed. *New International Dictionary of Old Testament Theology and Exegesis*. Vol. 3. Grand Rapids, MI: Zondervan Publishing House, 1997. 1009.

Say It Correctly

Moriah. more-**EYE**-uh.
Antedated. an-tuh-**DATE**-ed.

Daily Bible Readings

MONDAY
Don't Forget the Lord's Provisions
(Deuteronomy 8:11–20)

TUESDAY
Jesus Tested in the Wilderness
(Matthew 4:1–11)

WEDNESDAY
Angel Confirms Direction for Jesus
(Luke 22:39–46)

THURSDAY
Prayer for Help in Time of Crisis
(Psalm 20)

FRIDAY
Family Lineage of Abraham Preserved
(Hebrews 11:17–22)

SATURDAY
God Blesses Abraham for Obedience
(Genesis 22:15–19)

SUNDAY
God Provides the Sacrificial Ram
(Genesis 22:1–3, 6–14)

Notes

Teaching Tips

Words You Should Know

A. Keeping (2 Chronicles 6:14) *shamar* (Heb.)—To pay careful attention; to cause a state or condition to remain.

B. Covenant (v. 14) *berit* (Heb.)—Treaty, compact, i.e., an agreement between two parties; a promise.

Teacher Preparation

Unifying Principle—Promises Kept. People want to know that others will keep their word. How can they respond to a fulfilled promise? At the Temple dedication, Solomon thanked God for keeping His promise.

A. Pray that your students will have thankful hearts.

B. Read 2 Chronicles 6 in various translations.

C. Complete the companion lesson in the *Precepts For Living*® Study Guide.

O—Open the Lesson

A. Open with prayer, including the Aim for Change.

B. Introduce today's lesson title.

C. Have your students read the Aim for Change and Keep in Mind verse together.

P—Present the Scriptures

A. Have volunteers read the Focal Verses.

B. Read and discuss The People, Places, and Times; Background; Search the Scriptures; At-A-Glance outline; In Depth; and More Light on the Text to clarify the sections.

E—Explore the Meaning

A. Have the class answer the Search the Scriptures and Discuss the Meaning questions.

B. Have a volunteer read the Lesson in Our Society section.

N—Next Steps for Application

A. Ask students to discuss ways that God has kept His promises to them.

B. Also encourage students who may be disappointed in God to explain why. Ask the class to listen patiently, quietly, and prayerfully.

C. Encourage the class to apply the Make It Happen section.

Worship Guide

For the Superintendent or Teacher
Theme: There is No God Like You
Song: "There is None Like You"
Devotional Reading: Psalm 132

There is No God Like You

Bible Background • 2 CHRONICLES 6:1–21
Printed Text • 2 CHRONICLES 6:12–21 | Devotional Reading • PSALM 132

Aim for Change

By the end of this lesson, we will: VALIDATE God's promise to perpetually provide Jerusalem a Davidic king; AFFIRM the faithfulness of God and the Christian conviction that Jesus is that Davidic heir; and CONTINUE a prayer life that affirms and trusts God's promises.

In Focus

Brian had enough. This was the last time he was going to depend on Marcus to help him out with doing different jobs. Marcus was Brian's protégé as well as an excellent craftsman, but he was almost never on time, even though he promised not to be late. Marcus' tardiness was negatively affecting the timeline for completing projects. Brian had confronted Marcus about his tardiness multiple times, but nothing much had changed.

Marcus did not understand why his pay was late this month. Brian knew this was his main source of income for rent and other bills. Furthermore, they had previously agreed that he would be paid on the last Friday of every month. Marcus approached Brian and voiced his frustration. How could Brian not pay him as planned? Brian revealed that he had deliberately withheld Marcus' check in order to teach him what it means to keep his word. Finally, Marcus understood and connected Brian's lesson to his tardiness. He would be at work on time from now on.

We all are called to live in a covenantal relationship with God. In today's lesson, we will examine how God keeps His promises to us and how we also must keep our promises to Him by the way in which we live. Have you ever noticed how often God keeps His promises in your life?

Keep in Mind

"Thou which hast kept with thy servant David my father that which thou hast promised him; and spakest with thy mouth, and hast fulfilled it with thine hand, as it is this day" (2 Chronicles 6:15).

"Thou which hast kept with thy servant David my father that which thou hast promised him; and spakest with thy mouth, and hast fulfilled it with thine hand, as it is this day" (2 Chronicles 6:15).

Focal Verses

KJV **2 Chronicles 6:12** And he stood before the altar of the LORD in the presence of all the congregation of Israel, and spread forth his hands:

13 For Solomon had made a brasen scaffold of five cubits long, and five cubits broad, and three cubits high, and had set it in the midst of the court: and upon it he stood, and kneeled down upon his knees before all the congregation of Israel, and spread forth his hands toward heaven.

14 And said, O LORD God of Israel, there is no God like thee in the heaven, nor in the earth; which keepest covenant, and shewest mercy unto thy servants, that walk before thee with all their hearts:

15 Thou which hast kept with thy servant David my father that which thou hast promised him; and spakest with thy mouth, and hast fulfilled it with thine hand, as it is this day.

16 Now therefore, O LORD God of Israel, keep with thy servant David my father that which thou hast promised him, saying, There shall not fail thee a man in my sight to sit upon the throne of Israel; yet so that thy children take heed to their way to walk in my law, as thou hast walked before me.

17 Now then, O LORD God of Israel, let thy word be verified, which thou hast spoken unto thy servant David.

18 But will God in very deed dwell with men on the earth? behold, heaven and the heaven of heavens cannot contain thee; how much less this house which I have built!

19 Have respect therefore to the prayer of thy servant, and to his supplication, O LORD my God, to hearken unto the cry and the prayer which thy servant prayeth before thee:

20 That thine eyes may be open upon this house day and night, upon the place whereof thou hast said that thou wouldest put thy name

NLT **2 Chronicles 6:12** Then Solomon stood before the altar of the LORD in front of the entire community of Israel, and he lifted his hands in prayer.

13 Now Solomon had made a bronze platform 7 1/2 feet long, 7 1/2 feet wide, and 4 1/2 feet high and had placed it at the center of the Temple's outer courtyard. He stood on the platform, and then he knelt in front of the entire community of Israel and lifted his hands toward heaven.

14 He prayed, "O LORD, God of Israel, there is no God like you in all of heaven and earth. You keep your covenant and show unfailing love to all who walk before you in wholehearted devotion.

15 You have kept your promise to your servant David, my father. You made that promise with your own mouth, and with your own hands you have fulfilled it today.

16 And now, O LORD, God of Israel, carry out the additional promise you made to your servant David, my father. For you said to him, 'If your descendants guard their behavior and faithfully follow my Law as you have done, one of them will always sit on the throne of Israel.'

17 Now, O LORD, God of Israel, fulfill this promise to your servant David.

18 But will God really live on earth among people? Why, even the highest heavens cannot contain you. How much less this Temple I have built!

19 Nevertheless, listen to my prayer and my plea, O LORD my God. Hear the cry and the prayer that your servant is making to you.

20 May you watch over this Temple day and night, this place where you have said you would put your name. May you always hear the prayers I make toward this place.

21 May you hear the humble and earnest requests from me and your people Israel when there; to hearken unto the prayer which thy servant prayeth toward this place.

21 Hearken therefore unto the supplications of thy servant, and of thy people Israel, which they shall make toward this place: hear thou from thy dwelling place, even from heaven; and when thou hearest, forgive.

we pray toward this place. Yes, hear us from heaven where you live, and when you hear, forgive.

The People, Places, and Times

The Temple. King David's desire was to build a temple for God (1 Chronicles 28:2). However, God rejected David's plan because he had "shed much blood upon the earth in [God's] sight." The task was charged to his son, Solomon, who began construction after his father's death (1 Chronicles 28:6; 1 Kings 5:3).

The Temple would be a memorial for Israel where they would turn their hearts toward God. As the resting place for the Ark of the Covenant, it provided a permanent place for the Lord instead of the tent of dwelling. For Solomon and the people, the Temple symbolized the presence of God.

Davidic Covenant. In the Davidic covenant between God and David, God promises David that He will establish a royal dynasty from the seed of David—a kingdom that would endure forever (2 Samuel 7:5–16; 1 Chronicles 17:11–14; 2 Chronicles 6:16). Solomon's building of the Temple was a realization of covenantal terms, which were culminated in the birth and return of Jesus Christ (Luke 1:31–33; Matthew 1:1).

What type of covenants do we create and enter into today?

Background

The people of Israel, who had wandered in the desert 40 years, were now completely settled in the Promised Land. They had recently transitioned from a period when judges ruled to a new stage of governance where they had a king to rule over them like other nations. However, the king was not to be as other kings. Yahweh was still very much the King, which meant that Israel was still very much a theocratic nation—one governed by God.

Although David could not build the Temple, he prepared everything that his son would need. He gave Solomon the building plans, gold and silver, including gold and silver lampstands, gold and silver tables, forks, bowls, gold for the altar, gold for the chariots and gold for the cherubim, plus bronze, iron, wood, onyx stones, precious stones, and marble (1 Chronicles 28:11–18, 29:1–2).

Still, Solomon lacked one major ingredient—the right man with the skill to build the Temple (2 Chronicles 2:7). Solomon wrote to Hiram, King of Tyre, who responded that he would send his master craftsman Huram, who was skilled to work in gold and silver, bronze and iron, stone and wood (1 Kings 7:14; 2 Chronicles 2:13–14).

Construction for the Temple began in the fourth year of Solomon's reign, and completing the Temple took seven years. Solomon spared no expense in his efforts to produce something wonderful and great (2 Chronicles 2:9). He employed the services of Phoenician craftsmen as well as other skilled workers from the community, which included immigrants.

With the Temple completed and furnished, Solomon gathers all of the people to bless them

(2 Chronicles 6:3). He offers a magnificent prayer of dedication saying, "For he is good; for his mercy endureth forever" (2 Chronicles 7:3).

How would you rate the importance your church building has in the lives of the people of God?

At-A-Glance

1. Solomon's Posture for Prayer
   (2 Chronicles 6:12–13)
2. Solomon's Adoration in Prayer (vv. 14–15)
3. Solomon's Petition in Prayer (vv. 16–21)

In Depth

1. Solomon's Posture for Prayer (2 Chronicles 6:12–13)

The dedication of the Temple was an historic occasion for all of Israel. Solomon prayed on a bronze altar kneeling with his hands spread toward heaven, which was a common gesture of prayer (Exodus 9:33; Ezra 9:5; Job 11:13). Solomon's posture reflected his humility and submission to God.

What are some of the typical postures people choose to take during prayer?

2. Solomon's Adoration in Prayer (vv. 14–15)

The prayer begins with adoration and praise for God. Solomon points to God's transcendent uniqueness: "there is no God like thee in the heaven, nor in the earth." Solomon acknowledged God as covenant-keeping and loving. God had proven to keep His promises to His people. With the Temple completed, an important aspect of the promise to David was now realized.

Solomon recognized the responsibility of the people in their relationship with the bilateral covenant. God was keeping His promise to them because of His love for them. In the same

manner, the people were to keep the covenant by continuing to live in obedience to God, which would reflect their love for Him.

Why do we consider expressing adoration and praise towards God important during prayer?

3. Solomon's Petition in Prayer (vv. 16–21)

As Solomon prays, he transitions from praise and adoration to supplication. He makes three main requests:

(1) "keep ... that which thou hast promised him"—Solomon prayed that God would keep His promise to his father, David. This did not express doubt—Solomon was already seeing the promise fulfilled—but rather, it was a reminder to God that He had promised David a perpetual kingdom. David's heirs would sit on the throne of Israel, foreshadowing Jesus, the son of David.

(2) "have respect ... to the prayer of thy servant"—Solomon petitioned God to respect his prayer. This was an invitation for God to always be at the very center of everything, actively working in their affairs.

(3) "Hearken ... and when thou hearest, forgive"—Solomon's final request is that God will hear from His dwelling place, and forgive. This humble supplication acknowledges the people's tendency to sin. He presents several scenarios and pleads with God to hear from heaven and forgive.

How do the elements of Solomon's prayer compare and/or contrast to the Lord's Prayer (Matthew 6:9–13)?

Search the Scriptures

1. What does it mean to "walk in my law" (2 Chronicles 6:16)?

2. Is there anything we might learn from Solomon's posture in prayer (v. 13)?

Discuss the Meaning

God always keeps His promises. Unfortunately, the same cannot be said of us. We are prone to break our promises to God, ourselves, and others. What does keeping our word say about integrity? Discuss the impact of kept or broken promises in one's personal life and the life of the larger community. What can we do to help us keep our promises?

Lesson in Our Society

Many people are guilty of not keeping their promises. They make commitments to themselves and others and then abandon them when they no longer want to abide by the terms. Fathers and mothers abandon their children; wives and husbands divorce one another and go their separate ways; resolutions to eat better and exercise are broken daily; and church members promise to volunteer but are too busy to serve as they should.

Broken promises are not without their consequences, which include pain, hurt, disappointment, and distrust. In what ways have people not kept their word in your life? In what ways have you not kept your word to others? For Solomon, God had proven to be a keeper of His word, and the people of Israel were encouraged to do the same in order to experience covenant blessings.

How can a deeper prayer life support us in being more faithful to our promises?

Make It Happen

As believers, we are spiritual leaders to a world that is lost. We should exemplify Christ by how we walk or live daily. Three ways to do this are:

(1) Keep our promises—List one promise that you've made and are determined to keep.

(2) Maintain an active prayer life—Commit to pray daily. Invite neighbors, co-workers, friends, and church members to pray with you.

(3) Be accountable—Keep a journal about this lesson and write down what God is saying to you.

Follow the Spirit

What God wants me to do:

_____

_____

_____

_____

Remember Your Thoughts

Special insights I have learned:

_____

_____

_____

_____

More Light on the Text

2 Chronicles 6:12–21

12 And he stood before the altar of the LORD in the presence of all the congregation of Israel, and spread forth his hands: 13 For Solomon had made a brasen scaffold of five cubits long, and five cubits broad, and three cubits high, and had set it in the midst of the court: and upon it he stood, and kneeled down upon his knees before all the congregation of Israel, and spread forth his hands toward heaven.

A parallel account occurs in 1 Kings 8:22–61. Both versions are similar; however, v. 13 lacks the parallel account. At first, Solomon stood before the altar, then he knelt with hands raised. Solomon's posture is not only positioned for prayer before God but also before the whole congregation. By his public actions as king (as well as building the Temple), Solomon communicated the prominence and position of prayer to God.

14 And said, O LORD God of Israel, there is no God like thee in the heaven, nor in the earth; which keepest covenant, and shewest mercy unto thy servants, that walk before thee with all their hearts: 15 Thou which hast kept with thy servant David my father that which thou hast promised him; and spakest with thy mouth, and hast fulfilled it with thine hand, as it is this day.

Direct speech in a narrative is always noteworthy. Solomon's prayer of dedication is said to be one of the most beautiful passages in the Bible. His proclamation that "there is no God like thee" must be seen not only as an absolute truth based on his relationship with God, but also as an indictment on the surrounding nations who worshiped pagan gods. There really was no God like Yahweh, and the God of Israel was the only God in the heaven and in the earth.

This praise is followed by three important theological words: "keep," "covenant," and "mercy." The verb *shamar* (**sha-MAR**) means to keep, but could also be translated here as "observe" or "guard" or even "to be a watchman." In the sentence, *shamar* highlights an attribute inherent to divine nature. God is and will always be the kind of God who keeps covenant (*berit*, **beh-REET**) and mercy. Steadfast love, or "mercy" here (*khesed*, **KHEH-sed**), is the emblematic quality of the covenant relationship, a quality of God (Psalm 136; Jeremiah 9:24), and required of His covenant partners. This was evident in the establishment of the Davidic dynasty—the promise made to David through Nathan. Of course, a basic condition was that David's descendants would walk in

obedience as outlined in the Torah, the divine commandments and teachings that were given to Moses.

16 Now therefore, O LORD God of Israel, keep with thy servant David my father that which thou hast promised him, saying, There shall not fail thee a man in my sight to sit upon the throne of Israel; yet so that thy children take heed to their way to walk in my law, as thou hast walked before me. 17 Now then, O LORD God of Israel, let thy word be verified, which thou hast spoken unto thy servant David.

In these verses, Solomon makes direct reference to the covenantal provision made with David. In it, the terms governing both parties are highlighted. God would establish the Davidic throne forever. Jesus was the fulfillment of that. And the people were expected to "take heed to their way" and live according to divine standards.

The Hebrew word translated "take heed" is the same *shamar* used to show how God keeps His side of the covenant. The people of Israel are to be just as devoted to keeping the covenant as God is. In so doing, they are to "walk" (Heb. *halak*, **ha-LOCK**) in His law. This is a very common word in the Old Testament and can refer to physical walking or to the manner in which a life is lived. David gave his people an example of how to walk as he "walked" (same Hebrew) before God. This points to the heavy burden of role modeling and accountability for pastors and leaders.

18 But will God in very deed dwell with men on the earth? Behold, heaven and the heaven of heavens cannot contain thee; how much less this house which I have built!

In verse 18, Solomon realized a theological truth that David might not have fully realized: God could not be contained in any building or structure. The prophet Isaiah later comments in a vision that just the train of God's robe fills the Temple grounds (Isaiah 6:1). The point of the Temple was not to house the deity, but to provide a special place to remember His name. It was a point of connection between Earth and God's heavenly abode. The Temple was a physical structure where the people could offer sacrifices and pray. However, God's presence was not to be reduced to or confined to the Temple. He is transcendent, which means above all. Solomon uses the term "heaven of heavens" which is the Hebrew way of doubling to show a superlative, like the Holy of Holies. Heaven of heavens refers to another heaven above the normal heaven; it might mean the place where God and His angels live, as opposed to heaven, which is basically the sky and space where the sun, moon, and stars are. Alternately, Solomon could just be describing the poetic awe of God's majesty.

19 Have respect therefore to the prayer of thy servant, and to his supplication, O LORD my God, to hearken unto the cry and the prayer which thy servant prayeth before thee: 20 That thine eyes may be open upon this house day and night, upon the place whereof thou hast said that thou wouldest put thy name there; to hearken unto the prayer which thy servant prayeth toward this place. 21 Hearken therefore unto the supplications of thy servant, and of thy people Israel, which they shall make toward this place: hear thou from thy dwelling place, even from heaven; and when thou hearest, forgive.

Solomon asked God to incline His ear toward the king and the people when they prayed from the Temple. The overall tone of what he prays reflects his awareness of his sinfulness—and that of the nation—before the God of Israel who is gracious. Since the Temple

would be the place where sacrifices are offered, Israel would need God's acceptance of those sacrifices and His forgiveness of their sins. He ends the prayer with a request for God to forgive (Heb. *salakh*, **sah-LOCK**).

The concept of forgiveness of sins is central to Judeo-Christian theology. Throughout the Old Testament, God is the only person ever seen as the subject of the verb *salakh*; only God grants forgiveness. In order to be forgiven, first the perpetrator must confess his or her wrongdoing, make atonement, and ask for forgiveness. Once these steps are completed, God is full of graciousness and mercy and He will forgive, bringing us back into community with Himself and with fellow believers, and restoring us to blessing.

Sources:
Edersheim, A. *Bible History: Old Testament.* Vol. 5. Grand Rapids, MI: William B. Eerdmans Publishing Company, 1975. 86.
Spence-Jones, H. D. M., ed. *2 Chronicles.* New York: Funk & Wagnalls Company, 1909. 63.
Thompson, J. A. *1, 2 Chronicles.* Vol. 9. Nashville, TN: Broadman & Holman Publishers, 1994. 228.
VanGemeren, W., ed. *New International Dictionary of Old Testament Theology and Exegesis.* Grand Rapids, MI: Zondervan Publishing House, 1997.

Say It Correctly

Brasen. **BRAY**-zin.
Bilateral. bye-**LAT**-er-ull.
Davidic. dah-**VIH**-dic.

Daily Bible Readings

MONDAY
God Selects the Family of David
(Psalm 132:8–12)

TUESDAY
God Chooses to Dwell in Zion
(Psalm 132:13–18)

WEDNESDAY
Jesus, Heir of David's Throne
(Acts 2:29–36)

THURSDAY
Solomon Completes the Temple
(2 Chronicles 6:1–11)

FRIDAY
Foreigners Welcome in God's Temple
(2 Chronicles 6:28–33)

SATURDAY
Prayers of Repentance During Captivity
(2 Chronicles 6:36–40)

SUNDAY
Solomon's Prayer of Dedication
(2 Chronicles 6:12–21)

Notes

_____

_____

_____

_____

Teaching Tips

Words You Should Know

A. Glory (2 Chronicles 7:1) *kabod* (Heb.)—Splendor; refers to the "weighty" presence of a highly desired object.

B. Worshiped (v. 3) *shachah* (Heb.)—To bow down or prostrate oneself before a superior entity, such as God.

Teacher Preparation

Unifying Principle—Finding Inspiration. People often celebrate what seems important to them. How can their celebrations become a form of worship? As they dedicated the Temple, Solomon and the people worshiped the Lord by bowing on their knees, making burnt offerings, playing music, and praying.

A. Pray that students would celebrate God.

B. Complete Lesson 3 in the *Precepts For Living*® Personal Study Guide.

C. Be prepared to discuss ways of planning non-religious celebrations (birthdays, showers, picnics) that honor God.

O—Open the Lesson

A. Open with prayer. Remember to invite the Holy Spirit to lead your Bible study.

B. Read Aim for Change and the Keep in Mind verse in unison.

C. Have your class read the In Focus story silently. Invite discussion.

D. Invite class members to share ways in which they worship/show reverence to God. Discuss how fasting from food or other types of abstinence can serve as forms of worship.

P—Present the Scriptures

A. Ask for a volunteer to read the Focal Verses.

B. Ask for volunteers to read The People, Places, and Times, Background, and In Depth sections. Encourage discussion.

E—Explore the Meaning

A. Discuss the Search the Scriptures and Discuss the Meaning sections.

B. Have a volunteer read the Lesson in Our Society section.

N—Next Steps for Application

A. Encourage students to apply the Make It Happen section.

B. Close in prayer.

Worship Guide

For the Superintendent or Teacher
Theme: The People Gave Thanks to God
Song: "Great is Thy Faithfulness"
Devotional Reading: Psalm 138

The People Gave Thanks to God

Bible Background • 2 CHRONICLES 7:1–11
Printed Text • 2 CHRONICLES 7:1–9 | Devotional Reading • PSALM 138

Aim for Change

By the end of this lesson, we will: AGREE with being thankful and worship God; ASPIRE to worship Him in both simple and grand ways; and PLAN a celebratory worship service to celebrate God's promises.

In Focus

It was her 40th birthday, and friends and family surprised Charlene with a birthday party. Food, laughter, and plenty of stories kept the party fun. At the end of the evening, Charlene's mom hugged her. She said, "Sweetheart, I know it hasn't been easy. I see the sadness in your eyes. It's been five years since Stephen died in Afghanistan. God will fill your void and bless you with someone to share your life." Charlene and her mom hugged as tears ran down their cheeks.

Charlene said, "Sometimes I feel so tired and lost."

Charlene's mom whispered, "Let's pray right now. Dear God, thank You for Your strength and comfort right now. Thank You for blessing Charlene, who has a heart to love and follow You. Encourage her heart. Thank You for hearing and answering prayers. In Jesus' name, we pray. Amen. Trust God, Charlene. He is able to handle your fears and sadness."

Several weeks later, Charlene's friend Alyssa called. She said, "My brother Eric just moved back to town. I would love for the two of you to meet. Can you come over to my house Saturday afternoon around 2:00? We're having a family get-together to welcome him home!"

This lesson will demonstrate how God responds with approval to our faithful prayers and worship. How do you show your thankfulness to God?

Keep in Mind

"And when all the children of Israel saw how the fire came down, and the glory of the LORD upon the house, they bowed themselves with their faces to the ground upon the pavement, and worshipped, and praised the LORD, saying, For he is good; for his mercy endureth for ever" (2 Chronicles 7:3).

"And when all the children of Israel saw how the fire came down, and the glory of the LORD upon the house, they bowed themselves with their faces to the ground upon the pavement, and worshipped, and praised the LORD, saying, For he is good; for his mercy endureth for ever" (2 Chronicles 7:3).

Focal Verses

KJV **2 Chronicles 7:1** Now when Solomon had made an end of praying, the fire came down from heaven, and consumed the burnt offering and the sacrifices; and the glory of the LORD filled the house.

2 And the priests could not enter into the house of the LORD, because the glory of the LORD had filled the LORD's house.

3 And when all the children of Israel saw how the fire came down, and the glory of the LORD upon the house, they bowed themselves with their faces to the ground upon the pavement, and worshipped, and praised the LORD, saying, For he is good; for his mercy endureth for ever.

4 Then the king and all the people offered sacrifices before the LORD.

5 And king Solomon offered a sacrifice of twenty and two thousand oxen, and an hundred and twenty thousand sheep: so the king and all the people dedicated the house of God.

6 And the priests waited on their offices: the Levites also with instruments of musick of the LORD, which David the king had made to praise the LORD, because his mercy endureth for ever, when David praised by their ministry; and the priests sounded trumpets before them, and all Israel stood.

7 Moreover Solomon hallowed the middle of the court that was before the house of the LORD: for there he offered burnt offerings, and the fat of the peace offerings, because the brasen altar which Solomon had made was not able to receive the burnt offerings, and the meat offerings, and the fat.

8 Also at the same time Solomon kept the feast seven days, and all Israel with him, a very great congregation, from the entering in of Hamath unto the river of Egypt.

NLT **2 Chronicles 7:1** When Solomon finished praying, fire flashed down from heaven and burned up the burnt offerings and sacrifices, and the glorious presence of the LORD filled the Temple.

2 The priests could not enter the Temple of the LORD because the glorious presence of the LORD filled it.

3 When all the people of Israel saw the fire coming down and the glorious presence of the LORD filling the Temple, they fell face down on the ground and worshiped and praised the LORD, saying, "He is good! His faithful love endures forever!"

4 Then the king and all the people offered sacrifices to the LORD.

5 King Solomon offered a sacrifice of 22,000 cattle and 120,000 sheep and goats. And so the king and all the people dedicated the Temple of God.

6 The priests took their assigned positions, and so did the Levites who were singing, "His faithful love endures forever!" They accompanied the singing with music from the instruments King David had made for praising the LORD. Across from the Levites, the priests blew the trumpets, while all Israel stood.

7 Solomon then consecrated the central area of the courtyard in front of the LORD's Temple. He offered burnt offerings and the fat of peace offerings there, because the bronze altar he had built could not hold all the burnt offerings, grain offerings, and sacrificial fat.

8 For the next seven days Solomon and all Israel celebrated the Festival of Shelters. A large congregation had gathered from as far away as Lebo-hamath in the north and the Brook of Egypt in the south.

9 On the eighth day they had a closing ceremony, for they had celebrated the dedication

9 And in the eighth day they made a solemn assembly: for they kept the dedication of the altar seven days, and the feast seven days. of the altar for seven days and the Festival of Shelters for seven days.

The People, Places, and Times

King Solomon. Solomon, son of David, became the third king of Israel. He was responsible for building Israel to its largest territorial borders as well as guiding the young nation to its most significant economic prosperity. Early in his reign, King Solomon was faithful to God. One night at a place called Gibeon (where the Tabernacle was located), God appeared to King Solomon in a dream and offered to grant him anything he asked for. King Solomon asked God for wisdom, which he was granted along with great wealth and honor.

King Solomon was the wisest man of his day. He understood botany and zoology and was a great writer (1 Kings 4:33). He is credited with writing three thousand proverbs, one thousand songs (v. 32), two psalms (Psalm 72, 127), and the books of Proverbs, Ecclesiastes, and Song of Solomon (Proverbs 1:1; Ecclesiastes 1:1).

The Temple. Commonly referred to as Solomon's Temple, it is one of the king's most notable accomplishments. The Temple was built in 949 BC in Jerusalem and was completed in seven years by the best craftsmen and with the finest materials (1 Kings 5:6, 6:2–38). Here, God's name was remembered, and this holy place would become the center of sacrifice, worship, and spiritual strength for the Jewish people of that time.

Do you set aside a space or time to be holy to God where you can spend intentional time with Him?

Background

While King Solomon was given the honor of building and dedicating the Temple, his father, King David, first conceived the idea of building a spectacular house for God (2 Samuel 7:2). Although God did not grant King David permission to build the Temple, King David designed the Temple, gathered building materials, designated its caretakers, and planned the worship services (1 Chronicles 22–26), as Solomon was still young and inexperienced.

The Temple was divided into three sections: (1) a porch, or portico, was the entrance into the temple; (2) the Holy Place, or "main hall," contained the ten golden candlesticks (1 Kings 7:49), twelve tables with twelve loaves of shewbread, and the incense altar; (3) and the Most Holy Place, or inner sanctuary, is where the Ark of the Covenant and God's presence resided.

During the days of annual Temple worship, only high priests were allowed to enter the Most Holy Place to be in God's presence. There they prayed and made atoning sacrifices for themselves and for the entire nation on the Day of Atonement. Solomon's Temple was destroyed in 586 BC when the Babylonians destroyed Jerusalem and captured the Jewish people.

The innermost sanctuary of the Temple, representing God's presence, which was once reserved only for high priests, was symbolically made accessible to all believers by Jesus' atoning death on the Cross. The Temple veil was torn in half, top to bottom (Matthew 27:51; Mark 15:38; Luke 23:45). We can now enter into God's presence at any time or place.

Do you recall a time when answers to prayers were not immediate but you still choose to trust God?

In Depth

1. God's Glory Fills the Temple (2 Chronicles 7:1–2)

King Solomon has completed the prayer he began in the previous chapter (2 Chronicles 6:12–42). As a sign of divine approval for the built Temple, and also for Solomon's prayer, God sent fire down from heaven to consume the sacrifice that Solomon had placed on the altar (2 Chronicles 7:1).

While we no longer present animal sacrifices to God, we are to present ourselves as living sacrifices (Romans 12:1). Our bodies are now the temple which God fills with His glorious presence (2 Corinthians 6:16). As we present our lives to God, He will fill us with His Spirit so that we manifest the attributes of His presence (Galatians 5:18–26).

When God answers our prayers, how does it produce greater faith?

2. The People Worship God (v. 3)

When the people saw that God's presence had filled the Temple, they bowed down and worshiped Him. They shouted praises, "For he is good; for his mercy endureth for ever." Here we are shown the perfect response to God's presence—worship!

Worship takes on many forms in believers' lives. In the physical sense, worship may include standing, kneeling, bowing down, or lifting hands in reverence. In a deeper sense, worship is living in obedience to God's Word. When God's presence has consumed us, our hearts will be in a continual state of worship and we will be willing to obey Him in every area of our lives.

How has disobedience to God produced negative consequences in your life as well as others?

3. Sacrifice and Celebrations (vv. 4–9)

A "great congregation" gathered to celebrate the dedication of the Temple. Many people brought sacrifices, and Solomon himself provided 22,000 cattle and 120,000 sheep and goats. The bronze altar could not fit so many sacrifices, so King Solomon had to consecrate the courtyard to be used for sacrificial offerings.

God's faithfulness to us is endless and unparalleled. He does not judge us by the size of our offerings, but the motivation of our hearts. Our most significant worship comes from heartfelt obedience, which pleases the Lord (Psalm 51:16–17; Micah 6:6–8). Give from your heart and God will always be honored by your gift.

How can pride hinder our reconciliation with God and others?

Search the Scriptures

1. How did God respond to King Solomon's prayer (2 Chronicles 7:1)?

2. How did the people respond to the presence of God (v. 3)?

Discuss the Meaning

This lesson teaches us that God faithfully answers prayer, that we should dedicate and regard our bodies as His temple, and that the correct response to God's presence in our lives is worship. How will you respond to His constant faithfulness and presence in your life?

Lesson in Our Society

We are constantly bombarded by disturbing news, whether it's about health, finances, relationships, violence, or terrorism. Often, situations appear unresolvable when we rely only on ourselves or the efforts of those around us. We may even feel we have reason to fear or distrust our politicians or law enforcement officials.

In the African American community, we face poverty, fatherlessness, and violence among and against our citizens. But God has not forgotten or turned His back on our communities. He has promised never to forsake us. But have we, as believers, forsaken Him? Are there more folks in the clubs on Saturday night than in the church on Sunday morning?

We must continue to find our inspiration and hope by adhering to and leaning on God's promises. As believers, we are bound together by our deeply rooted faith in Christ, and only by sharing and celebrating His love for us will we improve our communities and bring peace to our world.

What steps can we take to facilitate healing in our communities as we support those experiencing human rights violations?

Make It Happen

• Pray each day for your community, nation, and world.

• Choose at least one person and pray for them daily this week.

• Organize a celebration at your church specifically designed to encourage and share God's love with those who live in the surrounding neighborhood.

Follow the Spirit

What God wants me to do:

_____

_____

Remember Your Thoughts

Special insights I have learned:

_____

_____

_____

_____

More Light on the Text

2 Chronicles 7:1–9

1 Now when Solomon had made an end of praying, the fire came down from heaven, and consumed the burnt offering and the sacrifices; and the glory of the LORD filled the house. 2 And the priests could not enter into the house of the LORD, because the glory of the LORD had filled the LORD's house.

God is pleased with Solomon's prayer and supplication and responds positively by consuming the offering and sacrifices with fire from heaven. Divine fire has appeared at other important moments in Israel's history, such as during the times of Moses (Leviticus 9:23–24), David (1 Chronicles 21:26), and Elijah (1 Kings 18:36–38). The fire here signifies that Solomon has successfully completed building the Temple to God's specifications, and this new Temple is His dwelling place and the approved place of worship and sacrifice.

God consecrates, or sets apart for holy use, His house by filling it with His glory, just as He once did the Tabernacle in Moses' time (Exodus 40:34). The Hebrew word for "glory" in these verses is *chabod* (**kah-VODE**), literally meaning "weight." God is a heavyweight when it comes to His beauty, splendor, honor, majesty, and renown!

The Lord's glory is so intense that the priests were unable to enter into the Temple. This appears to repeat the event described when the Ark was first brought into the Temple—the cloud, the glory of the Lord, filled the Temple so much so that the priests could not continue ministering (2 Chronicles 5:13–14).

3 And when all the children of Israel saw how the fire came down, and the glory of the LORD upon the house, they bowed themselves with their faces to the ground upon the pavement, and worshipped, and praised the LORD, saying, For he is good; for his mercy endureth for ever.

The glory of God's presence evokes worship and praise. To worship is to show honor, reverence, and adoration to God. Worship expresses itself verbally in praise. Some Bible translations use the word "thank" rather than "praise." The Hebrew word here translated "praise" is *yadah* (**yah-dah**), meaning to worship with extended hands, to praise, or to give thanks.

Praise and thanksgiving are closely related. To praise God is to express admiration or approval for Him simply for being who He is, and to thank God is to express gratitude for what He has done.

God is both good and merciful. That He is good means that He is the source of everything that makes life possible and worthwhile, and that He is merciful means that God is faithful in His love toward us.

Perhaps a better synonym for the word "mercy" in verse 3 is the word "commitment." The Hebrew word is *chesed* (**CHEH-sed**), which the NLT translates as "faithful love." God's intrinsic goodness and mercy are qualities that evoke praise. His demonstration of goodness and mercy to us gives us concrete reasons to thank Him. The refrain "For he is good; for his mercy endureth for ever" is echoed in Psalm 106, 118, and 136.

4 Then the king and all the people offered sacrifices before the LORD. 5 And king Solomon offered a sacrifice of twenty and two thousand oxen, and an hundred and twenty thousand sheep: so the king and all the people dedicated the house of God. 6 And the priests waited on their offices: the Levites also with instruments of musick of the LORD, which David the king had made to praise the LORD, because his mercy endureth for ever, when David praised by their ministry; and the priests sounded trumpets before them, and all Israel stood. 7 Moreover Solomon hallowed the middle of the court that was before the house of the LORD: for there he offered burnt offerings, and the fat of the peace offerings, because the brasen altar which Solomon had made was not able to receive the burnt offerings, and the meat offerings, and the fat.

The people respond to the Lord's goodness and mercy in word and deed. Not only do they praise God with their mouths, they also offer Him tangible sacrifices. They offer thousands of animals to the Lord—a lot of bloodshed!

The abundance of sacrifices gives us some insight into the magnitude of the Lord's goodness and mercy. A generous God deserves unending praise, thanksgiving, and sacrifice. So many sacrifices are offered to Him that a special area in front of the Temple was consecrated to receive all of the sacrifices. Several days of rejoicing followed.

This passage mentions David throughout. In the dedication, the Levites even used musical instruments that King David had made and played (v. 6). Even though God did not allow David to build the Temple, he still played an important part in setting the stage for its construction and this resultant celebration.

8 Also at the same time Solomon kept the feast seven days, and all Israel with him, a very great congregation, from the entering in of Hamath unto the river of Egypt. 9 And in the eighth day they made a solemn assembly: for they kept the dedication of the altar seven days, and the feast seven days.

The festival truly is a kingdom-wide celebration. The people come from as far away as northern Africa to celebrate, represented by the river of Egypt. The "entering in of Hamath" (KJV), also called the city of Lebo-Hamath (NLT), is located in Lebanon, north of Israel. The people praise the Lord with instruments and songs and the celebration lasts for two weeks. The normal seven days of the Feast of Tabernacles is extended for this special occasion.

Sources:
Douglas, J.D., & Tenney, M.C. *Zondervan Illustrated Bible Dictionary.* Grand Rapids, MI: Zondervan, 1987.
Tuell, S.S. *Interpretation: A Bible Commentary for Teaching and Preaching: First and Second Chronicles.* Louisville, KY: John Knox Press, 2001.

Say It Correctly

Portico. por-ti-**KO**.
Hamath. **HAH**-mahth.

Daily Bible Readings

MONDAY
God Listens to Obedient Worshipers
(John 9:24–38)

TUESDAY
An International Worship Service
(Isaiah 19:19–25)

WEDNESDAY
Hezekiah Arranges a Worship Service
(2 Chronicles 29:25–30)

THURSDAY
Deliverance from Many Troubles
(Psalm 107:1–9)

FRIDAY
Healed and Forgiven
(Psalm 107:17–22)

SATURDAY
Assembly Attendees Blessed by Solomon
(1 Kings 8:54–61)

SUNDAY
Solomon Dedicates the Temple
(2 Chronicles 7:1–9)

Notes

_____

_____

_____

_____

Teaching Tips

Words You Should Know

A. Prayer (2 Chronicles 7:12) *tephillah* (Heb.)—Intercession or supplication made on behalf of a person or a situation.

B. Humble (v. 14) *kana'* (Heb.)—To subdue oneself in repentance, especially before God.

Teacher Preparation

Unifying Principle—Get It Together. Living a just and merciful life requires people to sacrifice their own desires and thoughts. What are the consequences for not choosing to be just and merciful? God told Solomon that if he did not follow the Lord's statutes and ordinances, then calamity would come upon the people and the Temple would be abandoned.

A. Seek deeper understanding of the meaning of the lesson by studying the Background Scripture and Devotional Reading in several different translations.

B. Complete Lesson 4 in the *Precepts For Living*® Personal Study Guide.

C. Be prepared to give an example of how God blessed you as a result of your obedience to Him.

O—Open the Lesson

A. Open with prayer. Remember to invite the Holy Spirit to lead your Bible study.

B. Read Aim for Change and the Keep in Mind verse.

C. Have your class read the In Focus story silently. Invite discussion.

P—Present the Scriptures

A. Have a volunteer read the Focal Verses.

B. Discuss the verses in light of Words You Should Know; The People, Places, and Times; Background; and In Depth sections.

E—Explore the Meaning

A. Answer and discuss the Search the Scripture questions.

B. Ask for volunteers to read Discuss the Meaning, Lesson in Our Society, and Make it Happen sections. Encourage discussion.

N—Next Steps for Application

A. Review the "H-P-S-R" (humble-pray-seek-repent) strategy of 2 Chronicles 7:14.

B. Ask students to prepare to give an account next week of how they utilized this strategy during the upcoming week.

C. Close in prayer.

Worship Guide

For the Superintendent or Teacher
Theme: Keep My Statutes and Ordinances
Song: "I Will Come and Bow Down"
Devotional Reading: Isaiah 58:6–12

Keep My Statutes and Ordinances

Bible Background • 2 CHRONICLES 7:12–22
Printed Text • 2 CHRONICLES 7:12–22 | Devotional Reading • ISAIAH 58:6–12

—————— Aim for Change ——————

By the end of this lesson, we will: EXAMINE the harsh consequences of disobedience to God; REPENT of present-day idolatry and other behaviors that separate us from God; and COMMIT to lives of obedient worship.

——————— In Focus ———————

One Saturday morning, Karen and her fifteen-year-old daughter, Jessica, awakened to learn that a tragedy had occurred overnight in a nearby community. Apparently a man with a gun walked into a restaurant and began to shoot people eating there. Every channel on the television reported this horrible story. Jessica had already seen it on Facebook before she came downstairs.

The look on Jessica's face as she watched the news broke her mother's heart. Karen could see from Jessica's expression that she was very saddened and couldn't understand why horrible things like this seemed to keep happening. When Jessica finally spoke she said, "Mama, when you were a kid, did awful stuff like this happen?" Karen thought for a minute before she answered and replied, "Honey, this world has always been filled with tragedies that break our hearts. When I was a girl, if Mama or Grandma heard some bad news, they would get on the phone and start praying with folks. If something really bad happened, we would go down to the church and the adults would pray together for hours." Karen took Jessica's hands and they prayed together, asking God to comfort the families who had lost or injured loved ones, to help the families to forgive the person responsible, and to show everyone the cure for this plague of violence in their community.

God continues to respond to those who earnestly seek Him and are willing to obey His commands. What is your plan for seeking God on a regular basis?

——————— Keep in Mind ———————

"If my people, which are called by my name, shall humble themselves, and pray, and seek my face, and turn from their wicked ways; then will I hear from heaven, and will forgive their sin, and will heal their land" (2 Chronicles 7:14).

"If my people, which are called by my name, shall humble themselves, and pray, and seek my face, and turn from their wicked ways; then will I hear from heaven, and will forgive their sin, and will heal their land" (2 Chronicles 7:14).

Focal Verses

KJV **2 Chronicles 7:12** And the LORD appeared to Solomon by night, and said unto him, I have heard thy prayer, and have chosen this place to myself for an house of sacrifice.

13 If I shut up heaven that there be no rain, or if I command the locusts to devour the land, or if I send pestilence among my people;

14 If my people, which are called by my name, shall humble themselves, and pray, and seek my face, and turn from their wicked ways; then will I hear from heaven, and will forgive their sin, and will heal their land.

15 Now mine eyes shall be open, and mine ears attent unto the prayer that is made in this place.

16 For now have I chosen and sanctified this house, that my name may be there for ever: and mine eyes and mine heart shall be there perpetually.

17 And as for thee, if thou wilt walk before me, as David thy father walked, and do according to all that I have commanded thee, and shalt observe my statutes and my judgments;

18 Then will I stablish the throne of thy kingdom, according as I have covenanted with David thy father, saying, There shall not fail thee a man to be ruler in Israel.

19 But if ye turn away, and forsake my statutes and my commandments, which I have set before you, and shall go and serve other gods, and worship them;

20 Then will I pluck them up by the roots out of my land which I have given them; and this house, which I have sanctified for my name, will I cast out of my sight, and will make it to be a proverb and a byword among all nations.

21 And this house, which is high, shall be an astonishment to every one that passeth by it; so that he shall say, Why hath the LORD done thus unto this land, and unto this house?

NLT **2 Chronicles 7:12** Then one night the LORD appeared to Solomon and said, "I have heard your prayer and have chosen this Temple as the place for making sacrifices.

13 At times I might shut up the heavens so that no rain falls, or command grasshoppers to devour your crops, or send plagues among you.

14 Then if my people who are called by my name will humble themselves and pray and seek my face and turn from their wicked ways, I will hear from heaven and will forgive their sins and restore their land.

15 My eyes will be open and my ears attentive to every prayer made in this place.

16 For I have chosen this Temple and set it apart to be holy—a place where my name will be honored forever. I will always watch over it, for it is dear to my heart.

17 As for you, if you faithfully follow me as David your father did, obeying all my commands, decrees, and regulations,

18 Then I will establish the throne of your dynasty. For I made this covenant with your father, David, when I said, 'One of your descendants will always rule over Israel.'

19 But if you or your descendants abandon me and disobey the decrees and commands I have given you, and if you serve and worship other gods,

20 Then I will uproot the people from this land that I have given them. I will reject this Temple that I have made holy to honor my name. I will make it an object of mockery and ridicule among the nations.

21 And though this Temple is impressive now, all who pass by will be appalled. They will ask, 'Why did the LORD do such terrible things to this land and to this Temple?'

22 And the answer will be, 'Because his people abandoned the LORD, the God of their

22 And it shall be answered, Because they forsook the LORD God of their fathers, which brought them forth out of the land of Egypt, and laid hold on other gods, and worshipped them, and served them: therefore hath he brought all this evil upon them.

ancestors, who brought them out of Egypt, and they worshiped other gods instead and bowed down to them. That is why he has brought all these disasters on them.'"

The People, Places, and Times

Locusts and Pestilence. When our Bible was written, locusts had significance beyond simply being insects. They were often thought of as a judgment sent from God (Exodus 10:4). They symbolized God's displeasure and punishment because they were capable of destroying large areas of vegetation and depleting necessary food sources. Pestilence was thought to represent God's judgment on Israel for her lack of obedience or for rebellion against God (1 Kings 8:37; Jeremiah 14:12; Ezekiel 5:12).

Rainfall. Rainfall is most abundant in Israel during the spring, known as the "latter rains," and during the fall, known as the "former rains." The greatest amount of rain falls between November and February. Abundant rainfall at the proper time was thought to be a blessing from God for obedience (Deuteronomy 28:12); conversely, lack of rain was considered to be punishment for disobedience (vv. 23–24). King Solomon prayed to God not only for protection against their enemies, but also protection against pestilence, sickness, and drought (2 Chronicles 6:26–28).

Can we conclude that God still sends or allows famines, pestilence, and sickness as judgment upon the earth? Why or why not?

Background

The books of 1 and 2 Chronicles were written to the Jews returning from the Babylonian exile, as a record of Israel's spiritual history. The same events are also recorded in 2 Samuel and 1 and 2 Kings, but the perspective of Chronicles

is predominantly spiritual, while the other accounts are more political. The significance of the different perspectives lies in the fact that the author, who was probably a priest, was more concerned with retelling the events that would encourage the newly freed exiles to stay close to God and avoid repeating the sins of the past.

In 2 Chronicles 6, during the dedication of the first Temple, Solomon prays to God on behalf of the people of Israel. Solomon begins his prayer by reminding God that he is David's son and that God has promised to be faithful to David. This is reminiscent of how we pray to God in Jesus' name. We depend on the righteousness granted to us by our faith in Jesus when we appeal to God in prayer, just as Solomon depended upon God's promise of faithfulness to David.

In his prayer, Solomon asked God to honor every prayer made in or toward the Temple. He specifically asks God to forgive everyone who will repent and return to Him (2 Chronicles 6:21–24). Solomon knew poor rainfall, agricultural pestilence, and sickness were punishments for the people's sins. God answers Solomon in 2 Chronicles 7:12–22.

Do you recall a time when answers to prayers were not immediate but you still chose to trust God?

At-A-Glance

1. God Appears to Solomon
   (2 Chronicles 7:12)
2. The Judgment (v. 13)
3. The Cure (vv. 14–22)

In Depth

1. God Appears to Solomon (2 Chronicles 7:12)

The Lord appeared to Solomon as He had done in the past at Gibeon (2 Chronicles 1:3–10). God assured Solomon that He had heard his prayer and would honor it. The house that Solomon had built had been approved by God, and He would place His name there.

Placing a name tag or stamp on something implies ownership. Through Christ, God has placed His name on each of us. We belong to Christ; we are called by His name (Christians). As we will see, wearing the stamp on the outside is not enough; God requires our complete dedication to Him, inside and out.

When God answers our prayers, how does it produce greater faith?

2. The Judgment (v. 13)

In verse 13, God refers to specific conditions that Solomon had mentioned in his prayer (2 Chronicles 6). These particular conditions, when they occurred, were thought to be punishments for disobedience to God. God lets Solomon know that He was attentive to the specific details of his prayer by mentioning drought, locusts, and pestilence, just as Solomon had.

As believers, we have every right to expect God to answer our prayers specifically and to address our needs in detail (1 Peter 3:12; Philippians 4:6–7, 19). As with Solomon, God expects our continued obedience to Him.

How has disobedience to God produced negative consequences in your life as well as others?

3. The Cure (vv. 14–22)

While God's plan was to answer Solomon's prayer and those of the people, a specific formula needed to be followed in order for God to remove His judgment and forgive their sins. This formula, "H-P-S-R," is spelled out in verse 14 (humble, pray, seek, repent).

In God's answer to Solomon, He tells him that if the people commit sin, leading to judgment, they would need to take specific steps to return to God's favor. First, they would need to humble themselves, which not only means to physically bow before God, but also admit their wrongdoing. They would then need to pray for His mercy, seek and worship Him and Him alone, and turn from their wrongdoing. Only then would God answer their prayers and heal their land.

Thinking of God's blessings as "conditional" is not an easy pill to swallow. However, 2 Chronicles 7:14 is clearly an "if-then" statement made by God. This applies to His people today as well. If we expect to experience the abundance of God's blessings, we must first humble ourselves and confess that we need Him in every area of our lives. We must admit we are helpless without Him and be unwilling to place anything above Him. We cannot let our pride or fear of social pressure stand in the way of crying out to God when we need Him most.

Is there a time when being prideful hindered your reconciliation with God and others?

Search the Scriptures

1. Why did God mention rain, locusts, and pestilence (2 Chronicles 7:13)?

2. Why did God say He would bring judgment upon His people (vv. 19–20)?

Discuss the Meaning

True repentance begins with humility. God shows us His formula for repentance in this week's lesson. How might we more accurately reflect our complete dependence upon God? How are we showing that we are still willing to accept His guidance?

Lesson in Our Society

Solomon must have been highly pleased to learn that God approved of the Temple he built for Him and that He heard his prayer. Even while He was pleased with Solomon, God spelled out His plan for repentance. As believers, we are righteous in God's eyes by our faith in Jesus. However, we too must be reminded that God still expects us to obey Him. God is willing to heal our land if we invite Him back into our circumstances, pray for His mercy, get rid of any idols that we have placed above Him, and collectively turn from our disobedience.

There is no substitute for obedience, and we must remain steadfast when God's statutes are being aggressively challenged on every level. In many African American communities, citizens are treated brutally by law enforcement officials. While it sounds impossible and even ludicrous to suggest, obedience to God requires us to forgive any type of wrongdoing. God will never ask us to do anything that His grace will not facilitate. However, it is up to us not to allow anger or bitterness to take root in our hearts. Surrender every emotion to God, commit to forgiveness, and He will heal your heart.

How can we facilitate healing and resist bitterness and help others do the same in the midst of mistreatment?

Make It Happen

• Identify one area of known disobedience in your life, ask God's forgiveness, and repent.

• Reach out to a person with whom you've been angry or upset with recently and smooth things over.

• Ask God to show you hidden or subtle areas of disobedience in your life and pray for the wisdom and the will to correct them.

Follow the Spirit

What God wants me to do:

_____

_____

_____

_____

Remember Your Thoughts

Special insights I have learned:

_____

_____

_____

_____

More Light on the Text

2 Chronicles 7:12–22

12 And the LORD appeared to Solomon by night, and said unto him, I have heard thy prayer, and have chosen this place to myself for an house of sacrifice.

Here God appears to Solomon a second time. The parallel text for this vision is 1 Kings 9:1–9, and the first appearance is described in 1 Kings 3:5–9. This second appearance is in the form of a dream or nighttime vision. During this encounter, God tells Solomon that He accepts the Temple as His dwelling place and the new place of sacrifice. Just as God has confirmed His endorsement of the new Temple publicly through fire (2 Chronicles 7:1–7), He now privately confirms to Solomon that He has heard the prayer of dedication offered by His servant (2 Chronicles 6:12–42).

13 If I shut up heaven that there be no rain, or if I command the locusts to devour the land, or if I send pestilence among my people; 14 If my people, which are called by my name, shall humble themselves, and pray, and seek my face, and turn from their wicked ways; then will I hear from heaven, and will forgive their sin, and will heal their land.

These verses describe the cause and effect relationship between obedience and God's blessing, and apply specifically to His covenantal people, who at the time possess the Promised Land. First, God warns against sinfulness and apathy and encourages humility and repentance (vv. 14–15). Verse 14 is probably the most famous verse in 1 and 2 Chronicles; however, these verses should not be applied uncritically to modern times. God is warning Solomon and the people about what will happen to them (and to the land) if they do not repent. Yet, even though the immediate context of these verses refers to Israel, we can be assured that God responds to humble prayer in every age (2 Chronicles 6:32–33).

The warning for God's people to humble themselves and "turn from" (Heb. *shuv*, **SHOOVE**) their evil ways contains an important lesson about repentance. It involves both turning away from sin and turning to God. God's response to His people is forgiveness and healing.

15 Now mine eyes shall be open, and mine ears attent unto the prayer that is made in this place. 16 For now have I chosen and sanctified this house, that my name may be there for ever: and mine eyes and mine heart shall be there perpetually.

In these verses, God affirms His real presence in the Temple. He has chosen and sanctified the house. To "choose" translates from the Hebrew word *bakhar* (**bah-KHAR**), which holds the idea of testing something and

selecting it for being the best. It can also be translated "to love." To "sanctify" or "consecrate" translates from the Hebrew word *qadash* (**kah-DOSH**), literally meaning "to set apart." God's eyes, ears, heart, and name are attached to this holy place. The reference to the Temple as a dwelling place for the name of God is first found in Deuteronomy 12:11. These verses (like other Bible passages) use anthropomorphisms, which means attributing human characteristics to God. God is Spirit and does not have literal eyes, ears, etc., but anthropomorphic language helps the hearer of God's declarations or reader of the text appreciate that God is personal. He relates to human beings in ways that we can understand. God is intimately connected to His people.

17 And as for thee, if thou wilt walk before me, as David thy father walked, and do according to all that I have commanded thee, and shalt observe my statutes and my judgments; 18 Then will I stablish the throne of thy kingdom, according as I have covenanted with David thy father, saying, There shall not fail thee a man to be ruler in Israel.

These verses are a warning to Solomon himself to walk with the Lord. The perpetuity of his kingdom is contingent upon his obedience. If Solomon or his descendants should turn away from God, then negative consequences will result. One would think that a man with as much wisdom as Solomon would have heeded God's words. Unfortunately, Solomon did not continue in the wisdom and knowledge that he had received.

19 But if ye turn away, and forsake my statutes and my commandments, which I have set before you, and shall go and serve other gods, and worship them; 20 Then will I pluck them up by the roots out of my land which I have given them; and this house,

which I have sanctified for my name, will I cast out of my sight, and will make it to be a proverb and a byword among all nations. 21 And this house, which is high, shall be an astonishment to every one that passeth by it; so that he shall say, Why hath the LORD done thus unto this land, and unto this house? 22 And it shall be answered, Because they forsook the LORD God of their fathers, which brought them forth out of the land of Egypt, and laid hold on other gods, and worshipped them, and served them: therefore hath he brought all this evil upon them.

These verses are a warning to Israel collectively to keep God's commandments and forsake idolatry. The result of disobedience will be exile, ridicule, and destruction. The word used for "serve" in verse 19 is *'abad* (**ah-VOD**), from the same root as the Hebrew word for servant or slave. God warns them against becoming slaves to other gods. "Byword" (*sheninah*, **shuh-nee-NAH**) is always used in conjunction with "proverb" (*mashal*, **mah-SHOL**) and other words of warning and derision. Its root speaks of the sharp, cutting sting a byword has on its recipient. A proverb is used here in the regular sense, as a wise, moral saying uttered to teach a lesson. Israel's downfall would be a lesson, a morality tale, to the rest of the nations of what happens when one disobeys God. Obedience to God leads to prosperity; disobedience leads to calamity. Since God is merciful, heartfelt repentance leads to forgiveness, healing, and restoration.

Sources:
Douglas, J.D., & Tenney, M.C. *Zondervan Illustrated Bible Dictionary.* Grand Rapids, MI: Zondervan, 1987.
Tuell, S.S. *Interpretation: A Bible Commentary for Teaching and Preaching: First and Second Chronicles.* Louisville, KY: John Knox Press, 2001.
Wiersbe, W.W. *The Wiersbe Bible Commentary.* Colorado Springs, CO: David C. Cook, 2007.
Wilcock, M.J. *The Message of Chronicles.* The Bible Speaks Today. Downers Grove, IL: InterVarsity Press, 1987.

Say It Correctly

Pestilence. pe-sti-**LEN(T)S.**
Perpetually. per-**PE**-choo-uh-lee.

Daily Bible Readings

MONDAY
God Wants Activists Who Fast
(Isaiah 58:6–12)

TUESDAY
Reconciliation Makes Gift-Giving Just
(Matthew 5:21–26)

WEDNESDAY
Treat Others Fairly with Compassion
(Exodus 22:21–29)

THURSDAY
Life is the Best Choice
(Deuteronomy 30:15–20)

FRIDAY
Faithful Walking: Key to Solomon's Rule
(1 Kings 9:1–5)

SATURDAY
Dangerous Results of Unfaithful Actions
(1 Kings 9:6–9)

SUNDAY
Results of Solomon's Decisions and Actions
(2 Chronicles 7:12–22)

Teaching Tips

Words You Should Know

A. Sepulchre (Luke 24:1) *mnema* (Gk.)—A grave; a small compartment carved out of rock or built with stone in which a dead person is buried.

B. Perplexed (v. 4) *diaporeo* (Gk.)—To be confused, puzzled, or filled with uncertainty.

Teacher Preparation

Unifying Principle—A Promise Kept. People often question the promises of their leaders. How can they come to have assurance in the midst of doubt? In the breaking of bread and making Himself known to His disciples, the risen Christ kept His promises.

A. Pray for pastors and leaders to lead with integrity.

B. Read Luke 24 in at least two translations.

C. Complete the companion lesson in the *Precepts For Living®* Personal Study Guide.

O—Open the Lesson

A. Open with prayer.

B. Read Aim for Change and the Keep in Mind verse together. Discuss.

C. Invite the class to read the In Focus story silently, then discuss it.

P—Present the Scriptures

A. Have volunteers read or summarize the Focal Verses.

B. Use The People, Places, and Times; Background; Search the Scriptures; At-A-Glance; In Depth; and More Light on the Text to clarify the verses.

C. Share with the class a time you were unable to keep a promise and how you felt about disappointing yourself or others.

E—Explore the Meaning

A. Divide the class into groups to talk about the Discuss the Meaning, Lesson in Our Society, and Make It Happen sections. Tell the students to select a representative to report their responses.

B. Connect these sections to the Aim for Change and the Keep in Mind verse.

N—Next Steps for Application

A. Summarize the lesson.

B. Write some takeaway principles under the Follow the Spirit or Remember Your Thoughts section.

C. Close with prayer.

Worship Guide

For the Superintendent and the Teacher
Theme: He Has Risen
Song: "Because He Lives"
Devotional Reading: Luke 24:36–49

He Has Risen

Bible Background • LUKE 24:1–35
Printed Text • LUKE 24:1–12, 30–35 | Devotional Reading • LUKE 24:36–49

——— Aim for Change ———

By the end of the lesson, we will: DECIDE that the account of the Resurrection binds us to Christ and to one another; VALUE the promise that Christ is with us as we celebrate communion; and REJOICE in the knowledge of Christ's resurrection and presence among us.

In Focus

"If you've seen this 73-year-old man, please contact your local police station," the television newscaster pleaded. Amanda couldn't believe that her father's picture was staring back at her from the television screen. Three days ago, he had left for Lou's Barber Shop, promising that he'd be right back. Even then, Amanda had doubted his words.

Over the past few months, Amanda's dad's memory had been deteriorating. While the former attorney still knew his way around his hometown, other previously familiar communities were starting to pose a challenge. But before Amanda could say, "Dad, let me take you," he had driven down the driveway.

Seated on the sofa surrounded by relatives, Amanda allowed her tears to flow. She said a quiet prayer and at that moment, she felt an overwhelming sense of peace. It was almost as if Christ Himself had come into the room and touched her on the shoulder to let her know everything was going to be all right.

Just then, the phone rang and Uncle Carlos answered it. "Amanda! Amanda! They found your dad!" he screamed. "He drove inside the abandoned warehouse near Lou's and he's been there ever since. A security guard found him an hour ago. He's fine! He's alive!" Amanda ran from the house, praising God and shouting, "Dad's alive! He's alive!"

The joy of learning that someone we love is well and we will see them again turns sorrow into rejoicing. How can you experience the reality of Christ's resurrection today?

——— Keep in Mind ———

"The Lord is risen indeed" (from Luke 24:34).

"The Lord is risen indeed" (from Luke 24:34).

Focal Verses

KJV **Luke 24:1** Now upon the first day of the week, very early in the morning, they came unto the sepulchre, bringing the spices which they had prepared, and certain others with them.

2 And they found the stone rolled away from the sepulchre.

3 And they entered in, and found not the body of the Lord Jesus.

4 And it came to pass, as they were much perplexed thereabout, behold, two men stood by them in shining garments:

5 And as they were afraid, and bowed down their faces to the earth, they said unto them, Why seek ye the living among the dead?

6 He is not here, but is risen: remember how he spake unto you when he was yet in Galilee,

7 Saying, The Son of man must be delivered into the hands of sinful men, and be crucified, and the third day rise again.

8 And they remembered his words,

9 And returned from the sepulchre, and told all these things unto the eleven, and to all the rest.

10 It was Mary Magdalene, and Joanna, and Mary the mother of James, and other women that were with them, which told these things unto the apostles.

11 And their words seemed to them as idle tales, and they believed them not.

12 Then arose Peter, and ran unto the sepulchre; and stooping down, he beheld the linen clothes laid by themselves, and departed, wondering in himself at that which was come to pass.

30 And it came to pass, as he sat at meat with them, he took bread, and blessed it, and brake, and gave to them.

31 And their eyes were opened, and they knew him; and he vanished out of their sight.

NLT **Luke 24:1** But very early on Sunday morning the women went to the tomb, taking the spices they had prepared.

2 They found that the stone had been rolled away from the entrance.

3 So they went in, but they didn't find the body of the Lord Jesus.

4 As they stood there puzzled, two men suddenly appeared to them, clothed in dazzling robes.

5 The women were terrified and bowed with their faces to the ground. Then the men asked, "Why are you looking among the dead for someone who is alive?

6 He isn't here! He is risen from the dead! Remember what he told you back in Galilee,

7 that the Son of Man must be betrayed into the hands of sinful men and be crucified, and that he would rise again on the third day."

8 Then they remembered that he had said this.

9 So they rushed back from the tomb to tell his eleven disciples—and everyone else—what had happened.

10 It was Mary Magdalene, Joanna, Mary the mother of James, and several other women who told the apostles what had happened.

11 But the story sounded like nonsense to the men, so they didn't believe it.

12 However, Peter jumped up and ran to the tomb to look. Stooping, he peered in and saw the empty linen wrappings; then he went home again, wondering what had happened.

30 As they sat down to eat, he took the bread and blessed it. Then he broke it and gave it to them.

31 Suddenly, their eyes were opened, and they recognized him. And at that moment he disappeared!

32 And they said one to another, Did not our heart burn within us, while he talked with us by the way, and while he opened to us the scriptures?

33 And they rose up the same hour, and returned to Jerusalem, and found the eleven gathered together, and them that were with them,

34 Saying, The Lord is risen indeed, and hath appeared to Simon.

35 And they told what things were done in the way, and how he was known of them in breaking of bread.

32 They said to each other, "Didn't our hearts burn within us as he talked with us on the road and explained the Scriptures to us?"

33 And within the hour they were on their way back to Jerusalem. There they found the eleven disciples and the others who had gathered with them,

34 who said, "The Lord has really risen! He appeared to Peter."

35 Then the two from Emmaus told their story of how Jesus had appeared to them as they were walking along the road, and how they had recognized him as he was breaking the bread.

The People, Places, and Times

Passover. The Jewish festival of Passover, related to the Feast of Unleavened Bread, was taking place during the time of Christ's crucifixion, death, burial, and resurrection. Passover, a time of remembrance and thanksgiving, commemorates God's miraculous deliverance of the Children of Israel from bondage in Egypt (Exodus 12). The firstborn sons of the people of Israel were "passed over" or spared from death by killing a lamb without blemish and placing its blood on the doorposts of their houses.

Preparation for Burial. Jewish custom at the time of Christ's death called for a dead body to be prepared for burial within a day. This requirement might have been established because of sanitation problems and fear of religious defilement from touching a decaying body (Numbers 9:10–14). The bodies of the dead were washed and wrapped in a shroud filled with sweet-smelling spices. Relatives often added more spices several days later to mask the increasing odor. Once the body was decomposed, the dried bones were placed in a stone chest called an ossuary.

How do modern-day burial rituals compare and/or contrast to the burial rituals of Jesus' time?

Background

In the beginning, God made a promise to humanity (Genesis 3:15). Adam's sin had brought death to humanity and God promised that He would send someone whose death would restore eternal life (Romans 5:12–21). As His plan of redemption started its journey through history, God continually provided glimpses into how the promise would unfold. Zechariah 11:12–13 says that this redeemer would be betrayed for 30 pieces of silver; Isaiah 53:5–12 tells us that He would be a sacrifice for sin and crucified with criminals; Psalm 16:10 revealed that He would be resurrected from the dead; and Psalm 68:18 pointed to His ascension into heaven.

Old Testament writers recorded more than 300 promises or prophecies concerning God's plan to restore a righteous relationship with His creation. As Jesus walked with His disciples, He shared many of these promises with them, but they didn't fully understand His words. His miracles made them think that Jesus could be the promised Messiah, but witnessing His agonizing death on the Cross caused many of them to lose hope.

On a walk to the city of Emmaus, two of Jesus' disciples were discussing what they had heard earlier that day—that Jesus had been resurrected from the dead. They asked each other about how this could have happened. Jesus, a compassionate teacher, joined their journey and discussion. Referencing the Old Testament Scriptures, He explained the events that puzzled them. In the intimacy of a meal, these disciples realized that the person who had been foretold in Scripture was now breaking bread with them. Their hope returned. Jesus was alive. God's promise had been fulfilled.

How can a personal encounter with God create transformation in our lives?

At-A-Glance

1. Breaking Free from Death (Luke 24:1–10)
2. Breaking Through Unbelief (vv. 11–12)
3. Breaking Bread (vv. 30–35)

In Depth

1. Breaking Free from Death (Luke 24:1–10)

The women who went to anoint Jesus' body with fragrant spices probably thought that their greatest challenge would be removing the stone that blocked access to the chamber where His body had been placed. When they arrived, however, the stone had already been removed, and to their bewilderment, Jesus' body was missing.

The only possible answer, they concluded, was that someone had taken His body. But angels who were at Jesus' tomb offered the explanation. Jesus had risen, just as He had promised!

This puzzling news was also good news, and the women, who were the first ones to tell it, ran to inform the disciples. Throughout His life and in His death and resurrection, Jesus irrefutably proves that He is the promised Messiah.

Why do we sometimes assume the worst reason for something happening instead of hoping the best?

2. Breaking Through Unbelief (vv. 11–12)

"Too good to be true" is perhaps what the disciples said when the women reported that Jesus was alive. Some of the disciples had witnessed His trial, others His crucifixion, and they all knew the finality of death.

After a short while, Peter, wanting to investigate for himself, ran to the burial place and entered the tomb. Just as the women had said, the grave clothes were there, but Jesus' body was not. Perplexed, Peter walked away, trying to imagine all the possible scenarios that could have caused the disappearance of Jesus' body. The idea that Jesus had actually risen from the dead was still too amazing to believe. God often invites us to trust His word before we understand the way in which He will fulfill it.

How can we convince others to develop a greater trust in the promises of God?

3. Breaking Bread (vv. 30–35)

The account advances to a different setting a little while later. Two disciples invited a "stranger" into their home for a meal. They had met this traveler on their walk to Emmaus, a city about seven miles from Jerusalem. This stranger wanted to know why they were sad and inquired about the topic of their conversation as He walked with them.

The two disciples were surprised by the question. As far as they were concerned, everyone was talking about the events that had happened in Jerusalem over the past few days. They told the stranger that many people had thought that a man named Jesus was the promised deliverer of Israel, but His crucifixion had dashed their hopes. Then they told the stranger that a recent report was circulating that Jesus was alive. That news caused even more questions.

At that point, the stranger explained the Scriptures to them to show that it had been prophesied that the promised deliverer would suffer many hardships, including death. By now, they arrived at the village and were heading inside the home. But they were so intrigued with the conversation that they wanted to hear more from Him. So naturally, they extended hospitality to this lone traveler by inviting the stranger into their home for a meal.

Once inside, the stranger took the bread, blessed it, and broke it. In that moment, the eyes of the two disciples were opened. They realized that the very One of whom the Scriptures spoke was seated at the table with them. Jesus was the promised deliverer!

Overtaken with this realization, the disciples hurried back to Jerusalem to tell the other disciples that they had seen the risen Christ. Imagine their amazement. When we experience the reality of Christ's resurrection, we too are to go tell it on the mountains, over the hills and everywhere! Jesus is risen!

How can fellowship with others help us develop fresh insight into the nature and ways of God?

Search the Scriptures

1. The angels asked the women, "Why do you seek the living among the dead?" Where have you expected to find God, but didn't (Luke 24:5)?

2. Two disciples walking along a road didn't expect to meet Jesus, but did. Where has Jesus unexpectedly shown up in your life (v. 32)?

Discuss the Meaning

Without Christ's death, burial, and resurrection, humanity would have remained in bondage to sin (1 Corinthians 15:16–17). People who lack the life-changing knowledge of a risen Savior find themselves either living lives of hopelessness or still waiting for the promised deliverer.

How might we do a better job of teaching from Scripture that Jesus is not a dead historical figure but a living Lord and Savior?

Lesson in Our Society

The disappointments of life can sometimes cause believers to lose hope in the promises of God. Nothing short of a miracle will help them find a job when the economy is down, restore a marriage shattered by betrayal or indifference, find healing when the doctors have given up, or pay debts that have kept them in bondage for decades. Desperate prayers seem to have gone unanswered, and God's presence no longer appears to be in the places where they used to find Him.

The Good News of Easter—Resurrection Sunday—is not fancy clothes or a new hat. It is not just the tradition some people have. The Good News of the Easter account is the truth that Jesus will find us, join us in our journey, and show us that His plan for us is still good, even in the most difficult moments of our lives.

What do you need God to resurrect in your community? What do you need God to resurrect in your life?

Make It Happen

• Write in your journal about the ways the Resurrection has personally changed your life.

• Search the Scriptures and meditate on the prophecies concerning the Resurrection.

• Make it your goal to explain your hope in the Resurrection to at least one person in the next five days.

Follow the Spirit

What God wants me to do:

_____

_____

_____

_____

Remember Your Thoughts

Special insights I have learned:

_____

_____

_____

_____

More Light on the Text

Luke 24: 1–12, 30–35

1 Now upon the first day of the week, very early in the morning, they came unto the sepulchre, bringing the spices which they had prepared, and certain others with them.

The previouus chapter Luke 23 ended at the lowest point of human history. Thanks be to God, Luke's account, along with the other Gospel records, does not end with those unthinkable words about the Son of God: that He "gave up the ghost."

Instead, Luke immediately begins to offer hope that prepares us for the glorious resurrection account. First, Luke tells us about a Roman centurion who, unlike his mocking counterparts whom we encountered in the last chapter, saw Jesus' death with the eyes of faith. He said, "Certainly this was a righteous man." Luke also shows us that many who witnessed the Crucifixion were filled with so much horror and regret that they "smote their breasts" at what they had just seen.

Another faithful light, shining in the darkness of Luke 23, is Joseph of Arimathea. He was a member of the council who had condemned Jesus, but he had not agreed to the condemnation. Luke tells us that Joseph asked Pilate for Jesus' body and sought to bury Him with the honor He deserved. Finally, Luke once again focuses on the faithful women followers of Christ, telling us first that these women had followed Him from Galilee (23:49). And, they followed Joseph to the tomb, prepared spices to lovingly anoint Jesus' body, and then further demonstrated their obedience to God by resting on the Sabbath. This brings us to the Resurrection account as Luke begins it here.

2 And they found the stone rolled away from the sepulchre. 3 And they entered in, and found not the body of the Lord Jesus.

Luke is a master storyteller. He details that the women prepared spices to bring to the tomb, and now he sets up only one possible expectation: They would find a dead body inside when they returned! Only if we truly strive to put ourselves in the account to feel what they felt—instead of yawning because we know how the story ends—will we begin to experience even a shadow of the wonder, fear, confusion, and excitement the women felt at the tomb.

Jesus' words to them during His life assured that He would die and then rise on the third day. But the rest of this passage shows that they had not understood what He meant. Instead, they were totally confused about what their eyes were seeing. Luke inserts here a little detail with enormous significance.

Rather than simply talking about the "body of Jesus," he refers to Him as "the Lord Jesus." Such an appellation probably does not surprise us, but it would have been a very strange way to speak about a man who had just suffered the shameful death of a criminal.

4 And it came to pass, as they were much perplexed thereabout, behold, two men stood by them in shining garments:

When they couldn't find the body, the women were "much perplexed" (Gk. *diaporeo*, **dee-ah-pour-EH-oh**). This word only appears in the New Testament in Luke's writings, and it means to be completely at a loss about what to think. The next time that people were this confused was the extraordinary event at Pentecost (Acts 2:12), and later, Peter's vision of unclean animals to eat (Acts 10:17). The women at the tomb could not fathom the new thing that God was doing on Resurrection morning.

Though the women had been told that this would take place (vv. 6–8), God sent His Word to them in their confusion. It came in this case through divine messengers, probably angels (v. 23), bringing God's merciful message to His people. The Greek word meaning "behold" (*idou*, **ee-DOO**) draws attention to something happening suddenly and often surprisingly.

While these women still had their minds on earthly explanations of Jesus' disappeared body, the angels represented a shocking and glorious appearance from heaven. Their "shining garments" added a source of fear as the women's reaction in the next verse makes clear. The message, however, ultimately would not bring fear and trepidation, but overwhelming joy and relief.

5 And as they were afraid, and bowed down their faces to the earth, they said unto them, Why seek ye the living among the dead?

This terrified reaction to an angelic appearance seems universal in the Bible, as Luke shows by recording the reactions of Zechariah (Luke 1:12) and Mary (v. 29). While the angels' message was ultimately joyous and merciful, their initial question matched their fearsome demeanor in its sternness: "Why seek ye the living among the dead?"

This mild rebuke calls to mind what Jesus had to say to the Sadducees who did not believe in the resurrection (Luke 20:38): "For He is not a God of the dead, but of the living." Indeed, despite the fact that most Jews at the time (Sadducees aside) believed in the resurrection in theory, not even Jesus' most faithful disciples believed He would rise from the cruel death of Calvary.

6 He is not here, but is risen: remember how he spake unto you when he was yet in Galilee.

Here is the incontrovertible proof of the resurrection—the empty tomb. The angels announced the joyful news with the simple words, "He is not here." They also introduced the problem that has troubled, and continues to trouble, those who deny the truth of the bodily resurrection. Where did the body go? Did the Romans take it? Did the Jewish leaders hide Him?

Neither group would have wanted to have anyone believe that Jesus had risen from the dead, so they simply would have produced the body! Obviously they did not possess it—nor did anyone else. These faithful women were about to be reminded by the angels about a truth that the church continues to proclaim every Easter: "He is not here; He is risen!"

7 Saying, The Son of man must be delivered into the hands of sinful men, and be crucified, and the third day rise again.

The angelic reminder calls to mind two warnings that Jesus gave to His disciples. In Luke 9:22, just after Peter confessed Jesus' true identity, the Savior says: "The Son of man must suffer many things, and be rejected of the elders and chief priests and scribes, and be slain, and be raised the third day."

Later, just before the disciples' argument about who was the greatest, Luke again reports Jesus' prediction of His suffering, though this time without the specific resurrection promise: "Let these sayings sink down into your ears: for the Son of man shall be delivered into the hands of men" (v. 44). From this passage, it is clear enough that none of the disciples had ears of faith, such that Jesus' promise about His great work of death and resurrection could "sink down into their ears." Were we alive at that time, would we have believed?

8 And they remembered his words.

With their memory restored by the angelic presence, the women are now ready to explain the empty tomb in terms of the Gospel message of the Resurrection. The empty tomb, the presence of angels, the angels' words in and of themselves could not have erased the sorrow from their hearts. Only His words could change and cheer!

9 And returned from the sepulchre, and told all these things unto the eleven, and to all the rest.

The scriptural pattern is that those transformed by the Word and work of Christ go forth and tell others of His kindness and glory. These women adhered to that glorious tradition, except that they were... women!

Their first witness was to the rest of the disciples to share the news. Those who received the women's message were all of "the eleven." Eight times Luke referred to the core of the disciples as "the twelve," but here in chapter 24,

Luke speaks of the "eleven"; Judas Iscariot, who betrayed the Lord Jesus, had hung himself.

The women spoke to the remaining eleven. Speaking to all the rest is a reference to the many other disciples who were present.

10 It was Mary Magdalene and Joanna, and Mary the mother of James, and other women that were with them, which told these things unto the apostles.

Luke now identifies the women who had gone to the tomb and beheld the angelic vision and the absence of Jesus' body from the tomb. We might wonder, why mention their names now and not earlier in chapter 24 or in chapter 23, when they were first spoken of as preparing spices to anoint Jesus' dead body?

The answer probably has to do with the importance of eyewitness testimony in the Bible. The Bible consistently shows that an account of the truth must be established and verified on the testimony of "two or three witnesses" (Deuteronomy 17:6; Matthew 18:16). Luke produces three witnesses here.

Also, it would have been important that these witnesses were trustworthy, because what they were reporting would have been astonishing and unbelievable. To this end, Luke mentions two women whom he commended for their ministry to and support of Jesus—Mary Magdalene and Joanna (Luke 8:1–3). By adding "Mary the mother of James," Luke not only introduces a third witness, but also mentions that she is a relative of one of the apostles. She was trusted because of her relationship to James.

11 And their words seemed to them as idle tales, and they believed them not.

Despite the women's excitement, the apostles refused to believe their testimony. In fact, to the apostles, it seemed as if the women told "idle tales," a phrase that translates the Greek word *leros* (**LAY-ros**). Simply put, the apostles thought these women were babbling nonsense or were insane.

Why did they fail to receive the message? Throughout the book of Luke, these men had consistently shown a failure to understand Jesus' mission. They simply could not grasp the picture of a Messiah who would suffer and die for His people. Even the fact that the women claimed angels had confirmed Jesus' message did not change the apostles' minds. They probably assumed the women were hallucinating in their great grief over Jesus' death.

But another factor probably weighed in as well. This culture distrusted female testimony. In the first century, women were not regarded as authoritative or held in any significant value. Perhaps these apostles were deeply tainted by cultural prejudice as they listened to the women's eyewitness testimony. That Luke includes the women's testimony supports that his Gospel is that of the marginalized.

12 Then arose Peter, and ran unto the sepulchre; and stooping down, he beheld the linen clothes laid by themselves, and departed, wondering in himself at that which was come to pass.

Peter went to verify the story for himself. Like the women, he entered all the way into the tomb. Luke makes it clear that no one who witnessed the empty tomb could have possibly been mistaken about Jesus' absence. Jesus, unmistakably, was not there! Peter's reaction was not quite the same as the women's. He left "wondering in himself at that which was come to pass," which suggests that Peter was puzzled because the linen clothes were neatly laying on the side.

The word for "wondering" (Gk. *thaumazo*, **thow-MOD-zo**) means not so much doubting as just marveling in amazement. The event is too amazing to sink in right away, so

that you might exclaim, "Unbelievable!" The Resurrection is filled with hope, longing, the graciousness of God, and also with hesitation and unbelief from those who followed Christ.

30 And it came to pass, as he sat at meat with them, he took bread, and blessed it, and brake, and gave to them.

While on the Emmaus Road, the disciples fail to recognize Jesus. Even His explanation from the Scripture and verbal rebuke could not help them. For this reason, once they got indoors and were about to eat, Jesus took the responsibility of sharing the bread, usually taken by the host, not the guest.

It's possible that Jesus chose to break bread as a reminder of His previous act of doing so (Luke 22:19), and in this way, He confirmed His identity. It could also be that when Jesus was handing the bread to them, they saw the scars from the nails in His hands.

31 And their eyes were opened, and they knew him; and he vanished out of their sight.

Their eyes were opened as Jesus broke the bread with them. The truthfulness of the women's or Peter's testimony was now beyond a shadow of doubt. However, they did not enjoy His presence for long because He quickly disappeared from their sight.

This disappearance does not make Jesus' resurrected body immaterial. Had it been so, He could not have eaten with them. Furthermore, the record of Jesus' different appearances and sudden disappearances testifies that it was supernatural and might be a characteristic of the resurrected body.

32 And they said one to another, Did not our heart burn within us, while he talked with us by the way, and while he opened to us the scriptures?

Now that the disciples have recognized Him, they analyze their journey with a stranger who talked to them. Their hearts burned within them because Jesus had explained and made plain the Scriptures.

Jesus probably referred to the prophecies and symbols of the Old Testament that related to His life and ministry as He taught the two disciples. The breaking of bread was the climax of the lesson to the surprise of His incredulous disciples.

33 And they rose up the same hour, and returned to Jerusalem, and found the eleven gathered together, and them that were with them.

Whatever their reason for coming back to Emmaus, it became less important in comparison to their encounter with the risen Christ. They could not keep the news to themselves. They returned to Jerusalem to share the Good News with the remaining eleven apostles where they were gathered.

34 Saying, The Lord is risen indeed, and hath appeared to Simon. 35 And they told what things were done in the way, and how he was known of them in breaking of bread.

The two disciples came back and testified saying, "The Lord is risen indeed, and hath appeared to Simon (Peter)." The disciples now recognize Jesus for who He claimed to be: the Christ, the Messiah. In overcoming death, Jesus proves to be the Lord of lords and the King of kings.

The two disciples reported their own encounter with Jesus with particular emphasis on the breaking of bread. That Jesus is risen indeed is an expression of victory and hope then, and now!

Sources:
Black, Mark C. *The College Press NIV Commentary: Luke.* Joplin, MO: College Press Publishing, 1996.
Craddock, Fred B. *Interpretation: A Bible Commentary for Teaching and Preaching (Luke).* Louisville, KY: John Knox Press, 1990. 279-288.
Morris, Leon. *Tyndale New Testament Commentaries: Luke.* Grand Rapids, MI: Wm. B. Eerdmans, 1986.

Say It Correctly

Magdalene. mag-**DUH**-len.
Sepulchre. se-**PUL**-kur.

Daily Bible Readings

MONDAY
Jesus Foretells His Suffering and Death
(Mark 8:31–9:1)

TUESDAY
Do This in Remembrance of Me
(1 Corinthians 11:23–26)

WEDNESDAY
First Examine Yourselves, Then Eat
(1 Corinthians 11:27–34)

THURSDAY
Wash One Another's Feet
(John 13:1–5, 12–17)

FRIDAY
Women First Witnesses to Empty Tomb
(Luke 24:22–24)

SATURDAY
Jesus Meets Disciples on Emmaus Road
(Luke 24:13–21)

SUNDAY
Jesus Lives Again
(Luke 24:1–12, 30–35)

Teaching Tips

Words You Should Know

A. Girt (John 21:7) *diazonnumi* (Gk.)—To secure, fasten, or hold together by encompassing or tying with a belt, strap, or material.

B. Cubit (v. 8) *pechus* (Gk.)—An ancient unit of measurement based on the length of an arm, approximately 18 inches.

C. Durst (v. 12) *tolmao* (Gk.)—To have courage or boldness, to dare someone to perform a task.

Teacher Preparation

Unifying Principle—What is This Love? Sometimes life seems humdrum and unproductive. Where can people recognize purpose and direction for their lives? When the disciples followed guidance given by a man on the shore, they recognized it was Jesus who had given the directions and they joined Him in fellowship.

A. Pray for your students and lesson clarity.

B. Read John 21:1–14 in several translations.

C. Complete the companion lesson in the *Precepts For Living®* Personal Study Guide.

O—Open the Lesson

A. Open with prayer, including the Aim for Change.

B. Introduce today's lesson title.

C. Have students read the Aim for Change and Keep in Mind verse together. Discuss.

D. Tell the class to read the In Focus story silently, then discuss it.

P—Present the Scriptures

A. Have volunteers read or summarize the Focal Verses.

B. Use The People, Places, and Times; Background; In Depth; and More Light on the Text sections to clarify the verses.

E—Explore the Meaning

A. Divide the class into groups to analyze the Discuss the Meaning, Lesson in Our Society, and Make It Happen sections. Tell the students to select a representative to share their thoughts with the class.

B. Connect these sections to the Aim for Change and the Keep in Mind verse.

N—Next Steps for Application

A. Write some take-away principles under the Follow the Spirit or Remember Your Thoughts section.

B. Close with prayer.

C. Provide refreshments and invite students to a time of fellowship after the class.

Worship Guide

For the Superintendent or Teacher
Theme: The Risen Lord Appears
Song: "I Want to Be a Follower of Christ"
Devotional Reading: Psalm 19:7–10,
119:105–112

The Risen Lord Appears

Bible Background • JOHN 21:1–14
Printed Text • JOHN 21:1–14 | Devotional Reading • PSALM 19:7–10, 119:105–112

——— Aim for Change ———

By the end of this lesson, we will: SUMMARIZE the account of the risen Christ's appearance to seven disciples on the shore of the Sea of Galilee; AFFIRM the symbolic and real presence of Christ in our communal meal; and PRACTICE the presence of Christ by eating together often.

——— 🔍 In Focus ———

"I've been studying all night and I still don't understand how to work these problems," Jamal told his sister. "I can't face Mom if I fail this class and lose my scholarship. I can't afford to come back to State for another semester; I need to graduate now!" Sarah knew how much her big brother wanted to succeed and help Mom by graduating. She also knew how much he wanted that accounting job their neighbor, Mr. Harrison, had promised him if he finished college this spring. With Jamal's help, his mother would finally be able to purchase a home, a dream she was starting to believe would never come true. Sarah suggested that they go and get some food at Jamal's favorite restaurant. At first he refused, but then he decided it would be good to get a break and let his mind rest.

As Jamal and Sarah ate, he remembered all of the moments she had brought him there before. When he faced trouble, he would come to that restaurant and Sarah would often pray for him there. When he looked at the familiar setting, he remembered God had met him there and brought him through hard times before.

"Sarah, could you pray for me?" Jamal asked.

"Of course, God is here and ready to listen to us as we pray," Sarah responded.

Sometimes when we are in familiar places, we have memories of God's work in our past and realize He is meeting us right where we are as He has in the past. Do you have a moment when a memory reminded you of God's present nearness in your life?

——— Keep in Mind ———

"Jesus saith unto them, Come and dine. And none of the disciples durst ask him, Who art thou? knowing that it was the Lord" (John 21:12).

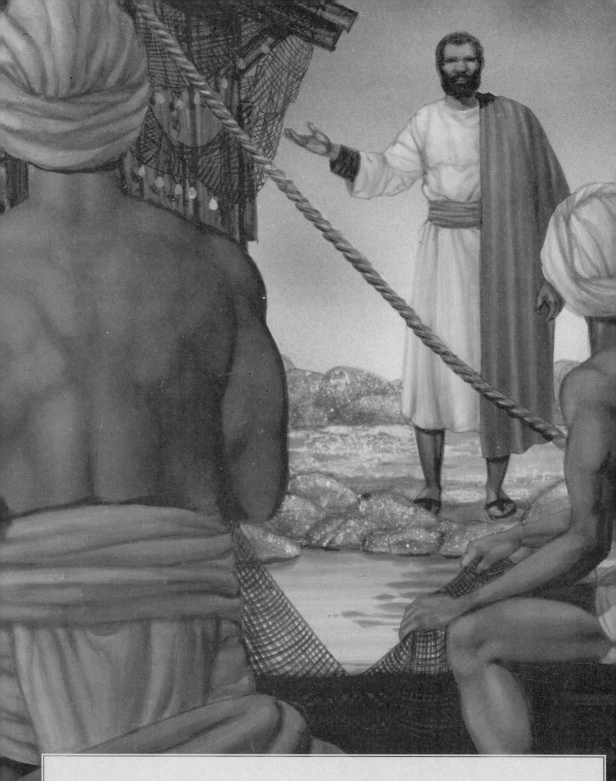

"Jesus saith unto them, Come and dine. And none of the disciples durst ask him, Who art thou? knowing that it was the Lord" (John 21:12).

Focal Verses

KJV **John 21:1** After these things Jesus shewed himself again to the disciples at the sea of Tiberias; and on this wise shewed he himself.

2 There were together Simon Peter, and Thomas called Didymus, and Nathanael of Cana in Galilee, and the sons of Zebedee, and two other of his disciples.

3 Simon Peter saith unto them, I go a fishing. They say unto him, We also go with thee. They went forth, and entered into a ship immediately; and that night they caught nothing.

4 But when the morning was now come, Jesus stood on the shore: but the disciples knew not that it was Jesus.

5 Then Jesus saith unto them, Children, have ye any meat? They answered him, No.

6 And he said unto them, Cast the net on the right side of the ship, and ye shall find. They cast therefore, and now they were not able to draw it for the multitude of fishes.

7 Therefore that disciple whom Jesus loved saith unto Peter, It is the Lord. Now when Simon Peter heard that it was the Lord, he girt his fisher's coat unto him, (for he was naked,) and did cast himself into the sea.

8 And the other disciples came in a little ship; (for they were not far from land, but as it were two hundred cubits,) dragging the net with fishes.

9 As soon then as they were come to land, they saw a fire of coals there, and fish laid thereon, and bread.

10 Jesus saith unto them, Bring of the fish which ye have now caught.

11 Simon Peter went up, and drew the net to land full of great fishes, an hundred and fifty and three: and for all there were so many, yet was not the net broken.

NLT **John 21:1** Later, Jesus appeared again to the disciples beside the Sea of Galilee. This is how it happened.

2 Several of the disciples were there— Simon Peter, Thomas (nicknamed the Twin), Nathanael from Cana in Galilee, the sons of Zebedee, and two other disciples.

3 Simon Peter said, "I'm going fishing." "We'll come, too," they all said. So they went out in the boat, but they caught nothing all night.

4 At dawn Jesus was standing on the beach, but the disciples couldn't see who he was.

5 He called out, "Fellows, have you caught any fish?" "No," they replied.

6 Then he said, "Throw out your net on the right-hand side of the boat, and you'll get some!" So they did, and they couldn't haul in the net because there were so many fish in it.

7 Then the disciple Jesus loved said to Peter, "It's the Lord!" When Simon Peter heard that it was the Lord, he put on his tunic (for he had stripped for work), jumped into the water, and headed to shore.

8 The others stayed with the boat and pulled the loaded net to the shore, for they were only about a hundred yards from shore.

9 When they got there, they found breakfast waiting for them—fish cooking over a charcoal fire, and some bread.

10 "Bring some of the fish you've just caught," Jesus said.

11 So Simon Peter went aboard and dragged the net to the shore. There were 153 large fish, and yet the net hadn't torn.

12 "Now come and have some breakfast!" Jesus said. None of the disciples dared to ask him, "Who are you?" They knew it was the Lord.

13 Then Jesus served them the bread and the fish.

12 Jesus saith unto them, Come and dine. And none of the disciples durst ask him, Who art thou? knowing that it was the Lord.

13 Jesus then cometh, and taketh bread, and giveth them, and fish likewise.

14 This is now the third time that Jesus shewed himself to his disciples, after that he was risen from the dead.

14 This was the third time Jesus had appeared to his disciples since he had been raised from the dead.

The People, Places, and Times

Fishing in the first century. Several fishing methods were in use during the time of Christ. They included casting a net, dragging a net, and using a hook and line. A person would cast a net, making it fall flat on the surface of the water, and enclose a school of fish, which were then pulled to shore. Dragging nets were long and supported by floating devices. They were spread on the lake at night and hauled in by boat during the morning. A baited hook was used along the shore. Since biblical times, fishing has been important to the economic life of Israel.

Galilee. The region of Galilee is a cool, lush area of fertile plains and hills. Jesus was raised in Nazareth of Galilee, and most of His ministry occurred around the Sea of Galilee, including the Sermon on the Mount and His Transfiguration. Jesus walked on the waters of the Sea of Galilee and shared many parables near its shores. More than twenty of His miracles happened in Galilee. Nazareth, a small town in Galilee, was the hometown of Jesus' mother, Mary. During the time of Christ, Nazareth was held in disregard. The prevailing thought was no one of any worth could come from such an insignificant town.

Sons of Zebedee. Two of Jesus' disciples, James and John, were the sons of a Galilean fisherman named Zebedee. Their mother was Salome, who served Jesus when He ministered in Galilee and was present at His crucifixion. The father and sons were mending nets when Jesus called the two brothers to follow him. John wrote the Gospel of John, three epistles and the book of Revelation. James was also one of three disciples to see Jesus' Transfiguration.

What have you left behind for the sake of following Christ?

Background

After His resurrection, Jesus appeared numerous times to His disciples and followers, providing them with convincing proof that He was risen indeed. Several of these appearances happened in Jerusalem (John 20:10–17, 19–23, 26–29; Matthew 28:9–10; Luke 24:13–27, 33–34, 50–51) and two occurred in Galilee—meeting the disciples at the Sea of Galilee (John 21) and gathering with followers on a mountain (Matthew 28:16). Scripture also records that Jesus appeared to James (1 Corinthians 15:7) and to Paul on the road to Damascus (Acts 9:1–9). Often Jesus was not recognized immediately by His disciples when He appeared to them. His words and actions caused them to know Him. The historical fact of Jesus' resurrection is core to Christian belief. Jesus was condemned to death because He claimed to be the Son of God (Matthew 26:63–65). By rising from the dead, He gave irrefutable proof that He was who He said He was. By the same power that raised Jesus from the dead, the disciples went on to perform miracles (Acts 2:43) and preached that salvation and remission of sin were available because of Jesus' resurrection (Luke 24:47).

How can a personal encounter with God create a transformation in our lives?

At-A-Glance

1. Doing What You Know (John 21:1–3)
2. Doing What Jesus Says (vv. 4–6)
3. Experiencing Unimaginable Results (vv. 7–14)

In Depth

1. Doing What You Know (John 21:1–3)

The women who went to Jesus' tomb met an angel who told them to go and report to Jesus' disciples that He has risen and they should meet Him in Galilee (Matthew 28:5). Galilee was in the northern part of Israel, and several of Jesus' disciples lived and worked there. Though they had followed the instructions to go to Galilee, they didn't know what to do next. Peter decided to go fishing and the others joined him. A long night on the waters went unrewarded—often the result of an occupation like fishing.

Waiting for God's next direction is a challenging spiritual discipline for many people; it goes against the natural inclination to make things happen.

What do you do when you are waiting to hear from God? How do you remain patient?

2. Doing What Jesus Says (vv. 4–6)

Jesus showed up on the shore and inquired whether the disciples had caught any food. They responded no, and Jesus told them to cast their nets to the right side of the boat. After their night at sea, it would have been reasonable for the disciples to be too tired to try again, or question the direction of a stranger on shore, but they followed Jesus' words and were rewarded with a large quantity of fish.

When we stay open to instruction and the wisdom of God, we often experience the blessing that follows obedience.

How can we convince others to develop a greater trust in the promises of God?

3. Experiencing Unimaginable Results (vv. 7–14)

This miraculous catch caused John to remember another time a man had told them to cast down their nets. John exclaimed to the other disciples that the man on shore was Jesus (Luke 5:1–11). Upon hearing this news, Peter couldn't wait for the boat to return to shore; he grabbed his clothes, jumped in the water, and swam to meet Jesus. As the others came to shore, they saw that Jesus had prepared bread and fish for them to eat. Often considered an impetuous person, Peter gets to Jesus as quickly as he can. He realizes that Jesus is now waiting on them, and Peter doesn't want to miss this opportunity to be in His transforming presence.

Jesus, always caring and compassionate toward His people, invited His disciples to a meal with Him when they arrived on shore. The long night of unrewarded struggle was over; the invitation was to dine on what Jesus offered. This was time to sit and renew their relationship with Christ. In sharing this meal and fellowship around the campfire, the disciples didn't have to ask who was present with them; they knew without a doubt He was their Lord and Savior, Jesus Christ. The risen Christ looks for opportunities to express His love; He is a very present help to those experiencing failure, loss, or disillusionment.

How can fellowship with others help us develop fresh revelations about God?

Search the Scriptures

1. Compare and contrast the events of Luke 5:1–11 with today's lesson (John 21:1–14).

2. Why didn't the disciples recognize Jesus when they first saw Him on the shore (v. 4)?

Discuss the Meaning

Following the lead of Peter, the disciples decide to go fishing, but their efforts were in vain. Why would Jesus come to His disciples at their moment of failure to prepare a meal and fellowship with them?

Lesson in Our Society

In the 1992 Olympics, Derek Redmond was favored to win the 400-meter semifinals until a pulled hamstring caused him to collapse on the Barcelona track. Determined to continue, Redmond started to limp his way to the finish line. His father, seeing his son's struggle, came out of the stands, broke through security, and helped him complete the race. Few people remember who won this race, but no one has forgotten the love of this father when his son experienced failure.

Many of us have a friend or relative who has experienced a setback or stumbled along the way. As African Americans, we need to follow the example of Derek Redmond's father and come alongside those who experience injustice, navigate a new life stage, or are stuck in poverty. Coming alongside those who have had a setback is one way to help keep relationships, families, and communities intact.

What are some ways you can come alongside and support people in your life?

Make It Happen

• Name some ways to support someone who has stumbled on the road of life.

• Make a point to acknowledge Jesus' presence during your mealtimes.

• Write in your journal about the ways you have experienced Jesus' presence during times of discouragement and disappointment.

Follow the Spirit

What God wants me to do:

_____

_____

_____

_____

Remember Your Thoughts

Special insights I have learned:

_____

_____

_____

_____

More Light on the Text
John 21:1–14

1 After these things Jesus shewed himself again to the disciples at the sea of Tiberias; and on this wise shewed he himself. 2 There were together Simon Peter, and Thomas called Didymus, and Nathanael of Cana in Galilee, and the sons of Zebedee, and two other of his disciples.

Prior to His crucifixion, Jesus had told His disciples that after He was risen, He would proceed to Galilee, where they were to meet him (Matthew 26:38; Mark 14:28). Although the other Gospel accounts also refer to Christ's post-resurrection appearance there, only John provides the details of the scene at the Sea of Tiberias, also known as the Sea of Galilee, where Jesus showed (Gk. *phaneroo*, **fah-neh-ROH-oh**, "made manifest, revealed") Himself to the disciples. A fishing scene provides the occasion for Jesus to reveal Himself. Here we have the longest account of a post-resurrection appearance in Galilee. "After these things"

365

refers not only to 20:30–31 but to the preceding accounts of Jesus' appearances. John introduces the scene by the expression, "and on this wise shewed he himself," which literally translated is "he revealed or manifested himself in this manner." The expression implies that Jesus certainly was alive, even if His disciples or followers had not seen Him. For John, Christ's revelation is a concrete reality of heaven upon earth.

3 Simon Peter saith unto them, I go a fishing. They say unto him, We also go with thee. They went forth, and entered into a ship immediately; and that night they caught nothing. 4 But when the morning was now come, Jesus stood on the shore: but the disciples knew not that it was Jesus.

In spite of the fact that these disciples had seen and talked with their risen Lord on two different occasions, they were still sheep without a shepherd. The disciples were still in an uncertain mood between the resurrection and ascension. Although the gloom of Good Friday had given way to the joy of Easter morning, it was still not clear to them what they were to do. Were they to remain idle? It was only natural for the disciples to go back to what they knew how to do—their previous occupation. So Peter's announcement of a fishing expedition, "I go a fishing," was received with much enthusiasm. The disciples labored all night, the best time for fishing, but caught nothing. Their best efforts with the nets throughout the peak fishing hours of the night brought them no success, no doubt baffling these experienced fishermen. If night was a time of failure when nothing could be done, the antidote must be light. Hence it is probably not just a matter of style for John to note that in the morning, when there was light, Jesus stood on the shore. He was unrecognizable. The word John uses is *eido* (Gk. **AY-doe**), which is more literally "to

see" and also means "to know." Therefore, the disciples' lack of recognition might have been due either to the dimness of the morning or the extraordinary nature of His appearance. What is important to note is that Jesus always revealed Himself only as He willed in keeping with the needs of His followers.

5 Then Jesus saith unto them, Children, have ye any meat? They answered him, No. 6 And he said unto them, Cast the net on the right side of the ship, and ye shall find. They cast therefore, and now they were not able to draw it for the multitude of fishes. 7 Therefore that disciple whom Jesus loved saith unto Peter, It is the Lord. Now when Simon Peter heard that it was the Lord, he girt his fisher's coat unto him, (for he was naked,) and did cast himself into the sea.

In verses 5 and 6, Jesus initiates a conversation with the disciples with a question: "Children, have ye any meat?" They answered with a monosyllable "No" (Gk. *ou*, **OO**), something that shows their disappointment. The disciples appear to not be inclined to delve into the details of their unproductive night. Jesus then gave the unsuspecting disciples a specific instruction on where to cast the net. His sovereignty and supernatural knowledge, which have been seen frequently in the earlier chapters of John's Gospel, reappear in His command to them to cast the net to the right side of the ship. Their compliance brings about the miraculous haul of a huge number of fish. This might well be meant to recall scriptural prophecy. In other words, strange as the advice from this "stranger" might have been, these experienced fishermen obeyed. In obedience to Jesus' command, they caught a big haul of fish. Obedience to God often yields positive results even when His command seems not to make sense.

In verse 7, John continues to use his regular manner of designating himself: "that disciple whom Jesus loved." John recognizes Jesus more quickly than the rest, and his first thought is to tell Peter. Using the mass of fish, Jesus had made His presence known, and Peter abandons everything, boat as well as fish, and runs straight to Jesus in his familiar impetuousness. John remains in the boat with the rest.

Only an eyewitness could mention the detail about Peter not wearing the coat. The disciples had worked "naked," which, however, does not mean stripped of all clothing, as some suppose. Peter was only without a coat, not without clothes altogether.

8 And the other disciples came in a little ship; (for they were not far from land, but as it were two hundred cubits,) dragging the net with fishes. 9 As soon then as they were come to land, they saw a fire of coals there, and fish laid thereon, and bread.

The rest of the crew came ashore with the boat. Evidently the disciples still found the net full of fish to be too heavy to haul on board, so they simply dragged it along. Even with Peter in the boat, these seven men did not have the strength to haul up the net; with Peter removed, they were less able to do so. They thus simply dragged the net to shore. The weight indicated hints at the size of the fish. The disciples come to the shore with their enormous bounty. The astounding manifestations of this early morning hour are by no means ended with the catch of fish. As soon as they came to land, they saw a fire of coals there, with a fish laid on top of them and bread nearby. The surprise of the disciples is marked by the present tense, "they see"—namely, that here on the shore a charcoal fire has been laid, and the coals are still glowing. And a fish has been laid on these coals, lying there roasting. Bread is there, too, to go with the fish, the same word as that used in 6:9 and 11. Everything is ready for a meal!

10 Jesus saith unto them, Bring of the fish which ye have now caught. 11 Simon Peter went up, and drew the net to land full of great fishes, an hundred and fifty and three: and for all there were so many, yet was not the net broken.

Peter at once—again first to act—enters the boat, and then draws the net up after him onto the land. Whether the number of fish caught has some significance is unclear; it might be just a detail of how carefully the disciples counted their haul. We should take care not to create or force some hidden meaning in the biblical text.

This miraculous catch has some significant differences from the circumstances of the draw of fishes at the beginning of the Lord's ministry (Luke 5:1–10). Augustine, an early church father, draws them out very well; he says the one was the symbol of the church at present, the other of the church perfected. In the one we have good and bad, in the other good only; there Christ also is on the water, here He is on the land; there the draw is left in the boats, here it is landed on the beach; there the nets are let down as it might be, here in a special part; there the nets are rending, here they are not broken; there the boats are on the point of sinking with their load, here they are not laden; there the fish are not numbered, here the number is exactly given. It seems impossible not to acknowledge that there is a spiritual meaning in these variations of the two narratives which consistently converge to distinct ends.

12 Jesus saith unto them, Come and dine. And none of the disciples durst ask him, Who art thou? knowing that it was the Lord. 13 Jesus then cometh, and taketh bread, and giveth them, and fish likewise. 14 This is now the third time that Jesus shewed himself to his disciples, after that he was risen from the dead.

One curious feature of verse 12 is its statement that the disciples did not dare to ask the name of their host, because they knew it was the Lord. This is a characteristic feature of the Resurrection appearances in the Gospels. It is related to, yet different from, the experience of the Emmaus disciples, who did not know the identity of the Lord until He broke the bread; here the disciples know the Lord as He invites them, before participating in the meal, yet they have a peculiar uneasiness toward Him, which we presume must have disappeared during the meal. A feeling of respectful fear prevents the disciples from approaching their mysterious Lord. But Jesus broke the ice as He now distributes bread and fish among the disciples to eat. For even though He, as the risen Lord, does not Himself participate in the meal, the sense is that table fellowship between the risen Jesus and the disciples is now established.

It is important to note that in 6:11, "Jesus took the loaves, and ... distributed them ...; so also the fish"; here "Jesus ... took the bread and gave it to them, and in the same way the fish." Both scenes carry overtones of the church's eucharistic meal. Jesus has empowered the disciples for their mission of fishing, enabling them to make their catch, and He now provides nourishment for them in their task.

Sources:

Borchert, Gerald L. *John 12–21*. The New American Commentary. Vol. 25B. Nashville, TN: Broadman & Holman Publishers, 2002.

Carson, D. A. *The Gospel According to John*. The Pillar New Testament Commentary. Grand Rapids, MI: InterVarsity Press, 1991.

Dongell, Joseph. *John: A Bible Commentary in the Wesleyan Tradition*. Indianapolis, IN: Wesleyan Publishing House, 1997.

Lincoln, Andrew T. *The Gospel According to Saint John*. Black's New Testament Commentary. London: Continuum, 2005.

Daily Bible Readings

MONDAY
The Reasons for the Resurrection
(Luke 24:36–49)

TUESDAY
Paul—Witness to the Resurrected Christ
(1 Corinthians 15:1–8)

WEDNESDAY
Scriptures Equip Disciples for Good Work
(2 Timothy 3:14–17)

THURSDAY
Ethiopian Eunuch Hears the Good News
(Acts 8:26–35)

FRIDAY
Lead My People and Follow Me
(John 21:15–23)

SATURDAY
John's Testimony to Jesus is True
(John 20:30–31, 21:24–25)

SUNDAY
Jesus Serves Breakfast to the Disciples
(John 21:1–14)

Say It Correctly

Galilee. **GAL**-ih-lee.
Tiberias. tie-**BEER**-ih-us.

Teaching Tips

Words You Should Know

A. Love (John 21:15–17) *agapao* and *phileo* (Gk.)—*Agapao*: unconditional love; *phileo*: friendship love.

B. Know (vv. 15–17) *oida* and *ginosko* (Gk.)—*Oida*: being aware of something by observation; *ginosko*: to be intimately familiar.

Teacher Preparation

Unifying Principle—Feeding Time. People are sometimes reluctant to show love and care for others. How can they be encouraged to show compassion for others? Jesus calls Peter and all disciples to show their love for Him by taking care of His sheep.

A. Pray that your students will help someone this week.

B. Read through the lesson and Background Scriptures.

O—Open the Lesson

A. Open with prayer.

B. Have the students read Aim for Change, Focal Verses, and Keep in Mind verse.

C. Ask the class to read the In Focus story silently; then discuss it.

P—Present the Scriptures

A. Divide the class into three groups.

B. Group A will review Discuss the Meaning; Group B will review Lesson in Our Society; Group C will review Make It Happen.

C. Connect these sections to the Aim for Change and Keep in Mind verse.

E—Explore the Meaning

A. Invite a representative from Group A to share with the rest of the class what they have learned from the Discuss the Meaning section.

B. Have a volunteer from Group B read the Lesson in Our Society and discuss.

C. Have a member of Group C discuss the Make It Happen section.

N—Next Steps for Application

A. Summarize the lesson.

B. Close in prayer.

Worship Guide

For the Superintendent or Teacher
Theme: Follow Me
Song: "I Have Decided to Follow Jesus"
Devotional Reading: Matthew 10:5–15

Follow Me

Bible Background • JOHN 21:15–25
Printed Text • JOHN 21:15–25 | Devotional Reading • MATTHEW 10:5–15

Aim for Change

By the end of this lesson, we will: ANALYZE Jesus' questions and Peter's responses to "follow Me"; AFFIRM the restoration of Peter after his threefold denial of Jesus; and OBEY Jesus' commands to "feed My lambs," "tend My sheep," and "feed My sheep."

In Focus

James had been waiting for this moment for a long time. In about two hours, he would finally marry his high school sweetheart, Sheila. James loved Sheila and could not wait to marry her. Right before the wedding, the pastor came to visit with James and Sheila separately. He wanted to calm their nerves and remind them to enjoy this day.

While the pastor needed some time to fill out the marriage license, James took the opportunity to go over the vows that he would soon commit to Sheila. James read them to himself and thought about the reality of each one of them. "To have and to hold from this day forward, for better or for worse, for richer or for poorer, in sickness and in health, to love and to cherish…"

As James began to think over each and every commitment in his vows, he started to cry—not tears of sorrow, but tears of delight. James finally realized that he would have the opportunity to demonstrate his love for his wife throughout his entire life.

This was more than infatuation. They were about to embark on a commitment that would require their whole being. It would be a life of sacrifice, but it was also a life that would be rewarded with joy. As he thought about his bride-to-be, he now fully understood the commitment that he was making. And he was excited to begin.

Just as in marriage, real discipleship requires commitment. Have you made the commitment to follow Christ every moment of every day?

Keep in Mind

"Jesus saith to Simon Peter, Simon, son of Jonas, lovest thou me more than these? He saith unto him, Yea, Lord; thou knowest that I love thee. He saith unto him, Feed my lambs" (John 21:15, KJV).

"Jesus saith to Simon Peter, Simon, son of Jonas, lovest thou me more than these? He saith unto him, Yea, Lord; thou knowest that I love thee. He saith unto him, Feed my lambs" (John 21:15, KJV).

Focal Verses

KJV **John 21:15** So when they had dined, Jesus saith to Simon Peter, Simon, son of Jonas, lovest thou me more than these? He saith unto him, Yea, Lord; thou knowest that I love thee. He saith unto him, Feed my lambs.

16 He saith to him again the second time, Simon, son of Jonas, lovest thou me? He saith unto him, Yea, Lord; thou knowest that I love thee. He saith unto him, Feed my sheep.

17 He saith unto him the third time, Simon, son of Jonas, lovest thou me? Peter was grieved because he said unto him the third time, Lovest thou me? And he said unto him, Lord, thou knowest all things; thou knowest that I love thee. Jesus saith unto him, Feed my sheep.

18 Verily, verily, I say unto thee, When thou wast young, thou girdest thyself, and walkedst whither thou wouldest: but when thou shalt be old, thou shalt stretch forth thy hands, and another shall gird thee, and carry thee whither thou wouldest not.

19 This spake he, signifying by what death he should glorify God. And when he had spoken this, he saith unto him, Follow me.

20 Then Peter, turning about, seeth the disciple whom Jesus loved following; which also leaned on his breast at supper, and said, Lord, which is he that betrayeth thee?

21 Peter seeing him saith to Jesus, Lord, and what shall this man do?

22 Jesus saith unto him, If I will that he tarry till I come, what is that to thee? follow thou me.

23 Then went this saying abroad among the brethren, that that disciple should not die: yet Jesus said not unto him, He shall not die; but, If I will that he tarry till I come, what is that to thee?

24 This is the disciple which testifieth of these things, and wrote these things: and we know that his testimony is true.

NLT **John 21:15** After breakfast Jesus asked Simon Peter, "Simon son of John, do you love me more than these?" "Yes, Lord," Peter replied, "you know I love you." "Then feed my lambs," Jesus told him.

16 Jesus repeated the question: "Simon son of John, do you love me?" "Yes, Lord," Peter said, "you know I love you." "Then take care of my sheep," Jesus said.

17 A third time he asked him, "Simon son of John, do you love me?" Peter was hurt that Jesus asked the question a third time. He said, "Lord, you know everything. You know that I love you." Jesus said, "Then feed my sheep.

18 "I tell you the truth, when you were young, you were able to do as you liked; you dressed yourself and went wherever you wanted to go. But when you are old, you will stretch out your hands, and others will dress you and take you where you don't want to go."

19 Jesus said this to let him know by what kind of death he would glorify God. Then Jesus told him, "Follow me."

20 Peter turned around and saw behind them the disciple Jesus loved—the one who had leaned over to Jesus during supper and asked, "Lord, who will betray you?"

21 Peter asked Jesus, "What about him, Lord?"

22 Jesus replied, "If I want him to remain alive until I return, what is that to you? As for you, follow me."

23 So the rumor spread among the community of believers that this disciple wouldn't die. But that isn't what Jesus said at all. He only said, "If I want him to remain alive until I return, what is that to you?"

24 This disciple is the one who testifies to these events and has recorded them here. And we know that his account of these things is accurate.

25 And there are also many other things which Jesus did, the which, if they should be written every one, I suppose that even the world itself could not contain the books that should be written. Amen.

25 Jesus also did many other things. If they were all written down, I suppose the whole world could not contain the books that would be written.

The People, Places, and Times

Peter. Peter, among the first to be called by Jesus as a disciple and to recognize Him as Messiah, was a prominent apostle in the early church. Originally named Simon, Jesus changed his name to Cephas or Peter, which means "rock" (John 1:42). While some scholars characterize Peter as impetuous because of his quick comments and responses throughout Jesus' ministry, others view him as a spokesperson for the disciples. Peter might have had the courage to say what the other disciples were thinking.

The book of John. John's presentation of Jesus is unique and distinct from that of the Synoptic Gospels. Synoptic means "seeing together" or "similar." Matthew, Mark, and Luke are synoptic; each highlights the same events in Jesus' earthly ministry. John's Gospel begins differently; he presents Jesus Christ as the God who was in the beginning (John 1:1), the Word made flesh (1:14). John foreshadows the rejection of Jesus by His own people (1:11) and the sacrificial role of Jesus as the Lamb of God (1:26).

John's Gospel also ends differently. In John 21, he does not mention the ascension of Jesus nor the Great Commission, but he does report the dramatic commissioning of Peter.

How would you categorize Peter's relationship with Jesus prior to His post-resurrection appearances?

Background

The conclusion of the Gospel of John contains two distinct sections. The first section deals with Peter's reinstatement, while the second section deals with confidence that John provides. Jesus has risen from the dead but not ascended to the Father. He appeared to His disciples several times (John 20:15, 20:26–29, 21:5–23), and now on this last occasion, Jesus places Peter in a shepherd role over His flock.

After Jesus' resurrection, Peter and a few of his fishing partners were at the Sea of Tiberias. Three whirlwind years of Jesus' ministry had ended. He was crucified and risen, and no longer walked with them daily. Without a vision for his future, Peter decides to go back to the work he did before meeting Jesus—he announces that he is going fishing, which seems like a good idea to everyone (John 21:3). But after fishing all night, they caught nothing.

The next morning, someone calls to them from the shore asking if they caught any fish. Peter answers no, and the stranger suggests throwing the net on the other side of the boat. Since a person standing on the shore could often see the schools of fish, Peter obliged. The catch was enormous—153 in fact (probably counted by Peter himself)! John exclaims, "It's the Lord!" and Peter jumps into the water and swims ashore (21:7). The disciples enjoy fish and bread prepared by Jesus Himself.

Do you think reconciliation is possible between those who have betrayed one another? Why or why not?

At-A-Glance

1. Commissioning (John 21:15–17)
2. Consequences (vv. 18–22)
3. Clarity and Confidence (vv. 23–25)

In Depth

1. Commissioning (John 21:15–17)

Before Jesus commissions Peter for service, He must first reinstate him. Peter's three denials of Jesus (John 18:15–27) are canceled by his three confessions of love for Jesus. After Peter's confession comes a command to care for the flock. Peter will have to put his faith into action.

In this section, two different words are used for love, though this does not necessarily mean that Peter loved God less; it is simply John's writing style. John uses two different Greek words for "know," two different Greek words for "feed," and two different words to refer to the flock (i.e., lambs and sheep), as well as two different words for love. While John may use all these words interchangeably, they still communicate the same message: Jesus is restoring Peter to leadership and wants him to demonstrate his love by taking care of His flock.

Do you love Jesus enough to commit your life to serving Him wherever you go or do? Why or why not?

2. Consequences (vv. 18–22)

Following Jesus is not easy. Immediately after commissioning Peter to take care of His flock, Jesus tells him the ultimate consequences that await him. Peter is informed that following Him will cost Peter his life (vv. 18–19). Church history tells us that Roman Emperor Nero crucified Peter, who felt unworthy to die like Jesus and requested that his cross be turned upside down. Peter's death is bittersweet—bitter because he would be crucified, but sweet because his death would glorify God.

Soon after Jesus commands Peter to follow Him, he begins to ask about the other disciple, John (v. 20). Since Peter is known for getting distracted (Matthew 14:29–31), Jesus is there to remind Peter to focus on his mission and tells him again to follow Him (v. 22).

Why is it difficult to prepare for the sacrifice necessary in following God?

3. Clarity and Confidence (vv. 23–25)

John provides both clarity and confidence for readers. He concludes his book by clearing up a rumor about himself (v. 23), that John would not die until Christ returned; this was not what Jesus said. This is important because if John did not clear up this rumor, some might not have not believed the Gospel after he died. John concludes by telling his readers that all that Jesus did is not written in this book (cf. John 20:30–31).

What is the most important message John wants us to consider and believe about Jesus?

Search the Scriptures

1. How might Peter have felt when Jesus asked him a third time, "Do you love me" (John 21:17)?

2. Do you love Jesus more than you love your job or vocation? How are you serving Him?

Discuss the Meaning

1. After Jesus reinstates Peter, He tells him to take care of His church. Why is it so hard for Christians to forgive and reinstate fellow believers and church leaders?

2. Peter's death glorified God. Knowing this, how can we as Christians have greater confidence when facing adversity?

Lesson in Our Society

Restore means to mend, similar to setting in place a dislocated member of the spiritual body. Restoration returns people back to their original purpose or position. The African American church has a longstanding record in the ministry of restoration. Whether restoring America's values of justice and equality or even restoring civil rights to people of color, the church has always been on the front lines of this battle.

Whenever discrimination exists, there also is a need for restoration. Discrimination makes things unfair and unequal, whereas restoration forces things to be fair and equal. Where there is personal sin, restoration begins with repentance and forgiveness.

While the ministry of restoration is challenging, it is also necessary because of our faith in Jesus. We must always remember that Jesus had to restore us, and as His people, our mission should be rooted in restoring others.

Who in your life is in need of the ministry of restoration?

Make It Happen

• Ask the Holy Spirit to enable you to restore a broken relationship (friendship, family member, church member, or co-worker).

• Write out a list of things that God has restored to you (i.e., relationships, opportunities, children).

• Meditate on the Keep in Mind verse. Answer the question, "What will it mean for me to feed Jesus' lambs?"

Follow the Spirit

What God wants me to do:

_____

_____

_____

Remember Your Thoughts

Special insights I have learned:

_____

_____

_____

_____

More Light on the Text
John 21:15–25

15 So when they had dined, Jesus saith to Simon Peter, Simon, son of Jonas, lovest thou me more than these? He saith unto him, Yea, Lord; thou knowest that I love thee. He saith unto him, Feed my lambs. 16 He saith to him again the second time, Simon, son of Jonas, lovest thou me? He saith unto him, Yea, Lord; thou knowest that I love thee. He saith unto him, Feed my sheep. 17 He saith unto him the third time, Simon, son of Jonas, lovest thou me? Peter was grieved because he said unto him the third time, Lovest thou me? And he said unto him, Lord, thou knowest all things; thou knowest that I love thee. Jesus saith unto him, Feed my sheep.

According to John, Jesus has now appeared to the disciples for the third time after His resurrection (21:14). He presided over the meal after the catch of fish. After dining, Jesus now turns His attention to Peter. Remember that at the time of the crucifixion, Peter had denied Christ publicly on three occasions. These verses tell of Peter's public restoration.

Jesus asks Peter probing questions. His first question probes Peter to the depth of his being: "Lovest thou me more than these?" An important question is what "these" refers to. First,

Jesus could have been asking Peter whether he loved Christ over the other disciples. Second, Christ could have been asking whether Peter loved Him more than the other disciples did (cf. Mark 14:29, Luke 22:33, John 13:37). Third, Jesus could be inquiring whether Peter loved Him more than his boats and fish (his profession). Perhaps the question's ambiguity is not only intentional, but also suggests the need for full consecration. Jesus intended to make clear a general exclusion of everything that would interfere with Peter's love for Him. With the memory of his recent failure of denying Christ before his death, Peter could not appeal to his record, instead appealing to the Lord's knowledge.

But that is not the end of the matter. Three times Jesus asks the same question (vv. 15–17). It has been noted that Jesus used the Greek word *agapao* (**ah-gah-PAH-oh**), while Peter responds with *phileo* (**fee-LEH-oh**), two different words that translate "love." The former conveys a divine type of love, and the latter means "the feeling of natural love." Most modern commentators agree that John uses the two Greek verbs for love here synonymously, so nothing should be read into the words' different nuances. The rest of Jesus and Peter's conversation is also filled with synonyms. In v. 15, Jesus tells Peter, "Feed (Gk. *bosko*, **BOSS-ko**) my lambs (Gk. *arnion*, **ar-NEE-on**)." But His repeat of the question in v. 16 is, "Feed (Gk. *poimaino*, **poy-MY-no**) my sheep (Gk. *probaton*, **PRO-ba-tone**)." *Bosko* is used more often with pigs, and *poimaino* more often with sheep, but both mean to feed or graze an animal. While *arnion* is usually translated as "lamb" (i.e. a young sheep), in the Greek translation of the Old Testament, the yearling lamb used as a Passover sacrifice is called *probaton* (Exodus 12:4–5).

Jesus asks the third time with a slight modification, using the same word for love that Peter does. Again, Jesus instructs Peter, "Feed my sheep." Peter was grieved (v. 17), not necessarily because Jesus has changed verbs, but because this was the third time the same question had been asked. As Peter had disowned Jesus three times, so Christ requires this elementary yet profound confession three times. Peter's response has no trace of self-righteousness. He can only appeal to the fact that the Lord knows everything, and therefore knows his heart. And that is enough. To avert any doubt that Peter is fully restored to future service, Jesus again commands, "Feed my lambs." In this episode, Jesus makes clear that love is the only adequate basis for service and that those who are commissioned (20:21) have a God-given command to tend, feed, and give watchful care to the sheep.

18 Verily, verily, I say unto thee, When thou wast young, thou girdest thyself, and walkedst whither thou wouldest: but when thou shalt be old, thou shalt stretch forth thy hands, and another shall gird thee, and carry thee whither thou wouldest not. 19 This spake he, signifying by what death he should glorify God. And when he had spoken this, he saith unto him, Follow me.

Jesus continued His conversation with Peter after his rehabilitation and reinstatement. Before Jesus' crucifixion, Peter had stoutly maintained his willingness to die for his Lord. But Jesus had declared his inability to follow and instead predicted his denial (John 13:36–45). Now the Lord predicts Peter's future.

Jesus informs Peter that he must suffer martyrdom as an aspect of his discipleship. Although the word "follow" should be understood literally, the phrase "stretch forth thy hands" is generally agreed to be a reference to crucifixion. That meant that Peter was obliged to "follow" Jesus, even to the point of crucifixion. In this way he would also glorify God, not in the theological impact and significance of

Jesus' death, but as a faithful disciple willing to follow his Master to death (cf. 1 Peter 4:16).

20 Then Peter, turning about, seeth the disciple whom Jesus loved following; which also leaned on his breast at supper, and said, Lord, which is he that betrayeth thee? 21 Peter seeing him saith to Jesus, Lord, and what shall this man do? 22 Jesus saith unto him, If I will that he tarry till I come, what is that to thee? follow thou me. 23 Then went this saying abroad among the brethren, that that disciple should not die: yet Jesus said not unto him, He shall not die; but, If I will that he tarry till I come, what is that to thee?

Turning around and seeing John, the disciple whom Jesus loved, Peter asked a troubling question: "What shall this man do?" It's a very human and natural question to ask "What about someone else?" We tend to focus on comparisons and see how we compare to others, to try to understand our position. This is not the way it works with God, who is concerned about us personally. Of course, He is concerned about our community, our brothers and sisters, our friends, the world. But these can stand in the way of our confronting our own individual responsibilities before God. Our concern for others can actually sidetrack us from facing His personal demands on us. Peter faced this problem in this verse, and Jesus was prepared to focus him on his personal calling.

This conversation between Jesus and Peter resulted in a rumor among early brethren in the Christian faith: that Jesus said John would not die until His return. The fact that John was the last surviving disciple gave strength to this false notion. The evangelist is anxious to make perfectly clear that Jesus had not spoken as matter of fact, but rather in hyperbole, that is, exaggerated language, to make a point to Peter.

24 This is the disciple which testifieth of these things, and wrote these things: and we know that his testimony is true. 25 And there are also many other things which Jesus did, the which, if they should be written every one, I suppose that even the world itself could not contain the books that should be written. Amen.

In concluding his writing, John explains that he was the unnamed disciple referred to in several previous passages. John gave solemn testimony to the truth of what he wrote. His testimony is true. He adds that it was impossible for him or anyone else to write the whole truth about Jesus. Christ did many other things, and it would be impossible to write them all. John ends the book by letting us know that there is much more about Jesus than we know.

Sources:
Borchert, Gerald L. John 12–21, vol. 25B, *The New American Commentary*. Nashville: Broadman & Holman Publishers, 2002.
Brownrigg, R., Comay, J. *Who's Who in the Bible: Two Volumes in One*. New York: Bonanza Books, 1980.
Carson, D.A. *The Gospel according to John, The Pillar New Testament Commentary*. Leicester, England; Grand Rapids, MI: InterVarsity Press; W.B. Eerdmans, 1991.
Dongell, Joseph. *John: A Bible Commentary in the Wesleyan Tradition*. Indianapolis, IN: Wesleyan Publishing House, 1997
Lincoln, Andrew T. *The Gospel According to Saint John, Black's New Testament Commentary*. London: Continuum, 2005.
Tenney, M.C., Douglas, J.D. *Zondervan Illustrated Bible Dictionary*. Grand Rapids, MI: Zondervan, 1987.
Tolbert, L. *Teaching Like Jesus: A Practical Guide to Christian Education in Your Church*. Grand Rapids, MI: Zondervan, 2000.
Vine, W. E., Unger, M. F., and White, W. eds. *Vine's Expository Dictionary of Biblical Words*. Nashville: Thomas Nelson, 1985.

Say It Correctly

Girdest. **GUR**-dist.
Signifying. sig-nuh-**FI**-ying.

Daily Bible Readings

MONDAY
Peter Denies Jesus Three Times
(John 18:15–18, 25–27)

TUESDAY
Thomas Moves from Doubt to Faith
(John 20:24–28)

WEDNESDAY
Go Proclaim the Good News
(Matthew 10:5–15)

THURSDAY
As Laborers, Go into the Harvest
(Matthew 9:35–38)

FRIDAY
Other Sheep Will Listen to Me
(John 10:11–18)

SATURDAY
Lose Your Life for My Sake
(Matthew 10:34–39)

SUNDAY
Follow Me and Feed My Sheep
(John 21:15–25)

Notes

_____

_____

_____

_____

Teaching Tips

Words You Should Know

A. Shew (Revelation 4:1) *deixo* (Gk.)—To point to something and thus draw attention to it.

B. Throne (v. 2) *thronos* (Gk.)—Symbolical expression of God's sovereign majesty.

Teacher Preparation

Unifying Principle—Give Honor to Whom It is Due. People wonder to whom they should give ultimate allegiance. Who deserves to be worshiped and praised? Revelation teaches that God alone is worthy of all praise, wonder, and awe.

A. Pray that your students worship time will be enriched.

B. Pray that the church as a whole will place worship of the Lord above all else.

C. Memorize the Keep in Mind verse.

O—Open the Lesson

A. Ask one of the students to open with prayer.

B. Invite everyone to read aloud the Aim for Change and the Keep in Mind verse.

C. Ask a student to read the In Focus story aloud.

P—Present the Scriptures

A. Ask the students to read the Focal Verses.

B. Use The People, Places, and Times; Background; and In Depth sections to clarify the biblical text.

E—Explore the Meaning

A. Split the class in half to answer the Discuss the Meaning section.

B. Have a volunteer read the Lesson in Our Society section.

N—Next Steps for Application

A. Encourage the class to apply the Make It Happen section to their lives.

B. Close in prayer.

Worship Guide

For the Superintendent or Teacher
Theme: The Lord God the Almighty
Song: "Glory to Glory to Glory" by Fred Hammond
Devotional Reading: Revelation 19:1–8

The Lord God the Almighty

Bible Background • REVELATION 4
Printed Text • REVELATION 4:1–6, 8–11 | Devotional Reading • REVELATION 19:1–8

—————— Aim for Change ——————

By the end of the lesson, we will: RESEARCH the significance of the symbolism of the heavenly worship in Revelation; LONG for the time when God will be worshiped in eternity; and WORSHIP and give praise to our awesome, fearsome God.

——————— In Focus ———————

Jamie began to cry as she walked onto the stage. At the graduation ceremony, she was overwhelmed by all the love and praise she heard from the crowd. As they announced her name, she walked over to receive her degree in Literature. Her mind began to reflect on all of the tests, papers, late nights, and early mornings she had endured in order to be here. Regardless of all of those obstacles, Jamie successfully graduated. She had mastered many subjects from sciences to literature, and was on her way to being a teacher as she had always dreamed. She had done so well in her classes that she was graduating with the highest honors available. Not only that, she had helped the education department secure grant money for continuing research in effectively teaching across cultures. She had achieved far beyond what others expected from her in her small town, and even exceeded her own expectations. More importantly she had gained a sense of self-confidence while in college. She knew who she was and who God created her to be.

As she walked across the stage, she heard cheers from the crowds, but one voice stood out in particular. The voice said, "That's my baby! That's my baby!" As Jamie smiled, she continued to hear the voice say, "You did it, baby. You deserve it."

Jamie receives praise for who she is and for her accomplishments, yet God is infinitely more worthy of praise than any human because of who He is and for what He has done. What are some things you have to praise God for this week?

—————— Keep in Mind ——————

"Thou art worthy, O Lord, to receive glory and honour and power: for thou hast created all things, and for thy pleasure they are and were created" (Revelation 4:11, KJV).

"Thou art worthy, O Lord, to receive glory and honour and power: for thou hast created all things, and for thy pleasure they are and were created" (Revelation 4:11, KJV).

Focal Verses

KJV **Revelation 4:1** After this I looked, and, behold, a door was opened in heaven: and the first voice which I heard was as it were of a trumpet talking with me; which said, Come up hither, and I will shew thee things which must be hereafter.

2 And immediately I was in the spirit: and, behold, a throne was set in heaven, and one sat on the throne.

3 And he that sat was to look upon like a jasper and a sardine stone: and there was a rainbow round about the throne, in sight like unto an emerald.

4 And round about the throne were four and twenty seats: and upon the seats I saw four and twenty elders sitting, clothed in white raiment; and they had on their heads crowns of gold.

5 And out of the throne proceeded lightnings and thunderings and voices: and there were seven lamps of fire burning before the throne, which are the seven Spirits of God.

6 And before the throne there was a sea of glass like unto crystal: and in the midst of the throne, and round about the throne, were four beasts full of eyes before and behind.

8 And the four beasts had each of them six wings about him; and they were full of eyes within: and they rest not day and night, saying, Holy, holy, holy, LORD God Almighty, which was, and is, and is to come.

9 And when those beasts give glory and honour and thanks to him that sat on the throne, who liveth for ever and ever,

10 The four and twenty elders fall down before him that sat on the throne, and worship him that liveth for ever and ever, and cast their crowns before the throne, saying,

11 Thou art worthy, O Lord, to receive glory and honour and power: for thou hast created all things, and for thy pleasure they are and were created.

NLT **Revelation 4:1** Then as I looked, I saw a door standing open in heaven, and the same voice I had heard before spoke to me like a trumpet blast. The voice said, "Come up here, and I will show you what must happen after this."

2 And instantly I was in the Spirit, and I saw a throne in heaven and someone sitting on it.

3 The one sitting on the throne was as brilliant as gemstones—like jasper and carnelian. And the glow of an emerald circled his throne like a rainbow.

4 Twenty-four thrones surrounded him, and twenty-four elders sat on them. They were all clothed in white and had gold crowns on their heads.

5 From the throne came flashes of lightning and the rumble of thunder. And in front of the throne were seven torches with burning flames. This is the sevenfold Spirit of God.

6 In front of the throne was a shiny sea of glass, sparkling like crystal. In the center and around the throne were four living beings, each covered with eyes, front and back.

8 Each of these living beings had six wings, and their wings were covered all over with eyes, inside and out. Day after day and night after night they keep on saying, "Holy, holy, holy is the Lord God, the Almighty—the one who always was, who is, and who is still to come."

9 Whenever the living beings give glory and honor and thanks to the one sitting on the throne (the one who lives forever and ever),

10 the twenty-four elders fall down and worship the one sitting on the throne (the one who lives forever and ever). And they lay their crowns before the throne and say,

11 "You are worthy, O Lord our God, to receive glory and honor and power. For you created all things, and they exist because you created what you pleased."

The People, Places, and Times

Patmos. John writes the book of Revelation while in prison on the island of Patmos, a rocky volcanic island in the Aegean sea. Just as other Christians were being persecuted for their faith (Revelation 2:2–3, 9–10, 13), John is being persecuted for his faith by being exiled to this island (Revelation 1:9).

John. Since the book was written in the mid AD 90s, John is now advanced in age. Faithful for many years, he has suffered greatly, and now he is all alone to live out the rest of his life in exile. To his surprise, Jesus shows up; He does not give a word of encouragement, but rather work to do. Even though John is an old man, he still has purpose that God will use.

How can persecution for our faith produce beneficial outcomes?

Background

This text includes symbolism referencing the Old Testament Scriptures, including Daniel 7, Isaiah 6, and Ezekiel 1. All of these prophets were not only privileged to witness this vision of God on His throne, but also were obligated to tell others what they had witnessed. Similarly, John is now privileged to see this great vision of God on His throne, and also obligated to share his vision.

John's vision of the throne room can also be seen as God's heavenly Temple. It is similar to the pattern of the earthly Temple in at least four ways. The Holy of Holies (from Solomon's Temple) and God's throne room both represent His actual presence. The earthly Temple had seven candlesticks; John's vision contains seven lamps of fire. Cherubim are depicted around the mercy seat of the Temple; here, four living creatures are around the throne. Fourth,

the priests were charged to lead the community into worship (sacrifices, atonement, etc.), while the elders lead worship to God. While there will be no physical temple in heaven (Revelation 21:22), the function the Temple served will still exist.

Why is it essential to develop a discipline of continually worshiping and praising God?

At-A-Glance

1. Invitation to the Throne Room
(Revelation 4:1–3)
2. The Throne Room (vv. 4–6)
3. Worship in the Throne Room (vv. 8–11)

In Depth

1. Invitation to the Throne Room (Revelation 4:1–3)

While John and other believers are being persecuted for their faith, Jesus appears to him—not to reward John for his faithful discipleship, but instead because Jesus has work for him to do. In this chapter, God uses John to witness the throne room in heaven. What John sees is highly symbolic, and many parts of the Scripture refer to Old Testament passages.

John sees God seated on His throne. The throne is symbolic of two ideas: God's sovereignty and His majesty. His sovereignty informs us that God is in control. What a comfort to believers being persecuted for their faith! While a king sits on the throne on earth, God is seated on His throne in heaven. Additionally, God's throne also shows us His majesty. John uses three rare and honorable stones in antiquity to describe the beauty he sees.

What circumstances can cause us to doubt God's sovereignty in the world?

2. The Throne Room (vv. 4–6)

Surrounded by the throne of God are twenty-four lesser thrones, where the elders are seated. While many commentators disagree about who the elders are, more important is their presence and function. Their presence represents those who have been faithful and have overcome (Revelation 3:21). Their function is to worship God by prostrating themselves and offering their crowns (i.e., their glory) to Him. While God is seated on His throne, John sees lightning and hears thunder. Similarly, when Moses went up the mountain to meet God in Exodus 19:16, he heard thunder, lightning, and the voice of a trumpet. These sounds and sights represent the manifest presence of God.

John witnesses a heavenly worship service. The elders portray humanity, while the living creatures portray creation. While God is seated on His throne in majesty and power, all humanity and all creation will worship Him.

Why can we predict total victory over our present circumstances based on the presence of the elders in the throne room?

3. Worship in the Throne Room (vv. 8–11)

The proper response of being in God's presence is worship. Our English word "worship" comes from two Old English words: "worth-ship." In other words, worship has to do with something being worth or worthy of the praise. Here the passage tells two reasons why God is worthy of praise—because of who God is (4:8) and for His accomplishment of creation (4:11).

In the throne room, the living creatures and the elders offer hymns to God. The four living creatures give God glory simply for being Him when they say, "Holy, holy, holy." Holy is the best way to describe God. Here, His holiness describes how He is totally separated from anything in creation. In other words, nothing in all creation comes close to God. In contrast, the elders praise God for what He has done. They recognize and confess that God is the Creator of all things, thus giving Him His due praise.

Why is God ranked above all and worthy of praise and honor?

Search the Scriptures

1. List four similarities between the earthly Temple (Solomon's Temple) and the throne of God.

2. What are two reasons that God is worthy of praise (vv. 8, 11)?

Discuss the Meaning

1. The four living creatures and the twenty-four elders continuously give God praise. What prevents us from worshiping Him?

2. God on the throne represents His power and control. When faced with injustice or persecution, how can believers remind themselves that God is in control?

Lesson in Our Society

In the 20th century, W.E.B. Du Bois suggested that African Americans have double consciousness—self-perception and also perception by others. In other words, African Americans must be aware of themselves—their achievements, their history, their reality—but also the perception of the dominant culture around them. At times, it can be quite a struggle to see oneself through the lens of White America while knowing that lens is somewhat distorted and not truly representative.

This might be particularly useful for African American Christians living in the 21st century. Even though time has changed, the principle has not. We live in a world filled with sin that manifests itself in violence, immorality, injustice, discrimination, racism, and sexism. We live in a world that hates good and loves evil.

However, as Christians, we also live with the reality that God is in control. Though injustice and inequity are real, so is God, and He is just and fair. So even though we live in this world, we live for another world: the kingdom of God. This is why we pray, "Your kingdom come, Your will be done." It reminds us that this earth is temporary. We are sojourners, strangers, and pilgrims on a journey to the new heaven and the new earth, where God's ethics of love and justice rules.

How can our trust in God be developed during times of persecution?

Make It Happen

• Write yourself a letter that testifies of the character of God based on the reasons for worshiping Him.

• Examine the beauty and complexity of God's creation (i.e., grass, flowers, birds, sun, trees). What does creation tell you about the Creator?

• Start every day with an affirmation about the character of God, e.g., "He is good" (Psalm 136:1). Remind yourself this truth before trouble comes.

Follow the Spirit

What God wants me to do:

_____

_____

_____

_____

Remember Your Thoughts

Special insights I have learned:

_____

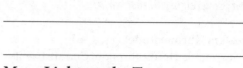

_____

_____

_____

More Light on the Text

Revelation 4:1–6, 8–11

1 After this I looked, and, behold, a door was opened in heaven: and the first voice which I heard was as it were of a trumpet talking with me; which said, Come up hither, and I will shew thee things which must be hereafter. 2 And immediately I was in the spirit: and, behold, a throne was set in heaven, and one sat on the throne.

The opening phrase "after this" signals a transition and conclusion of the seven prophetic messages to the seven churches that the resurrected Jesus spoke to John. The word *idou* (Gk. **ee-DOO**), translated "behold," draws attention to what follows: a door in heaven and a voice that sounded like a trumpet. Most commentators suggest that when a heavenly trumpet is sounded, it is time to listen, because God is about to speak (Revelation 1:10; Exodus 19:16). And speak He does! God commanded John to come up and be shown great things that had yet to come.

When the revelation began, John says he was in the Spirit (1:10). Here, there appears to be a connection between John being "in the Spirit" and being in heaven. Unbridled communion with God is always a working of the Spirit (Galatians 5:25). No earthly invocation is adequate to tantalize God to invite us into His presence. No church program is so appealing to Him that He is compelled to show Himself. The church enters into His presence; He does not enter into ours. The invitation comes from Him alone. We enter His presence boldly, not because of what we do, rather because of what He has done (Hebrews 4:14–16).

John saw a throne set in heaven, and the One who sat on it. This throne, the place of absolute authority and power, is the focus of this section, and Jesus declared that heaven is God's throne (Matthew 5:34).

If heaven is God's throne and John saw a throne set in heaven, then heaven is filled with the presence of God. The word "set" (Gk. *kei-mai*, **KAY-my**) implies more than what occupies time and space. In this passage, the term refers to something that has continuity and purpose.

When God's throne and the One sitting on the throne are the subject, all thoughts must be directed to who He is, what He has done, and why we have been granted the privilege to be in His presence. When God is the focus of praise and adoration, nothing else, however majestic, really matters. All sights and sounds become nothing more than distractions unless they also are focused on Him. John was in God's presence, and He cannot be denied.

3 And he that sat was to look upon like a jasper and a sardine stone: and there was a rainbow round about the throne, in sight like unto an emerald.

God the Father sits on the throne. The question—or rather dilemma—for John then is describing the incomprehensible and indescribable. John does not even try. He does not describe God in anthropomorphic terms, but instead portrays the Lord's splendor and glory by using the imagery of precious stones: jasper, sardine, and emerald. The stones here are a part of the fuller list of gems describing the new Jerusalem (Revelation 21:11, 18–21). The rainbow is a sign of covenant between God and humanity, made with Noah after the Flood (Genesis 9:8–17). This scene prepares the reader for the visions that follow. God's judgment will be tempered with mercy.

Many scholars discuss which contemporary gemstones might be similar to the stones John describes, and what they could represent. Some suggest the jasper was a diamond, the sardine stone was red, and the emerald as today was green. The jasper and sardine were the first and last stones on the breastplate of the high priest (Exodus 28:17, 20), so these stones could represent God's holiness and wrath. On the other hand, the rainbow is evidence of God's completed work of grace and salvation. In His presence, there are no imperfections and no tasks left undone.

4 And round about the throne were four and twenty seats: and upon the seats I saw four and twenty elders sitting, clothed in white raiment; and they had on their heads crowns of gold.

Scholarly discussion of the meaning of the thrones and the elders seated on them varies widely. Some scholars argue that the elders' thrones symbolize the thrones the redeemed will share in God's authority. Some believe the twenty-four elders represent angels who have significant responsibilities, while others believe the elders represent the redeemed of the Lord, because they are sitting, clothed in white, and their heads are crowned with gold. The twenty-four elders have been thought to refer to the twelve tribes in the Old Testament and the twelve apostles of the New Testament. It is most probable, however, that these elders are the redeemed or represent the redeemed, for they clearly pay homage to the Master by offering praise on behalf of the saints (Revelation 5:8–10). What is most important is not who the elders are, but rather what they are doing: sitting down in the presence of the Lord God.

John records is that the elders are sitting rather than voicing praise. Maybe they are so emotionally consumed and so in awe of God that their silence is the only form of praise they can give. Sometimes in His presence, the best thing to do is just to be mesmerized because He just is. John does not end his description of the elders with what they were doing, but what they were wearing—white garments.

John says the elders "were clothed," which in Greek is in the perfect passive tense. The perfect tense conveys action completed in the past with ongoing effects. The passive suggests the elders had nothing to do with clothing themselves. They were as little children clothed by the caring hand of a loving parent. The elders' presence in heaven was all God's doing.

The elders also wore crowns (Gk. *stephanos*, **STEH-fon-oce**) on their heads. These crowns were not *diadema*, the crown of kings. Some suggest the crowns represent the authority of the saints, but the Scripture's overwhelming testimony is that the crowns are given to the victorious (2 Timothy 4:8; Revelation 3:11). They testify of what God has done, not what the redeemed have done. As on Earth, a crown's value comes from the position of the one who bestows the crown. John envisions these elders as having only one responsibility—to point to God's immeasurable, incomprehensible grace.

5 And out of the throne proceeded lightnings and thunderings and voices: and there were seven lamps of fire burning before the throne, which are the seven Spirits of God. 6 And before the throne there was a sea of glass like unto crystal: and in the midst of the throne, and round about the throne, were four beasts full of eyes before and behind.

8 And the four beasts had each of them six wings about him; and they were full of eyes within: and they rest not day and night, saying, Holy, holy, holy, Lord God Almighty, which was, and is, and is to come.

John has clearly stated that the focus of the heavenly beings is the complete, unadulterated adoration of God. In fact, everything in heaven focuses on God. All of creation has but one purpose: to glorify Him.

Most would agree that the thunder and lightning convey the awesome presence of God. The seven Spirits refer to the perfection and fullness of God as evidenced in the work of the Holy Spirit (see Isaiah 11:2). The sea of glass might be a representation of the Old Testament laver (called a sea), where the high priest had to wash prior to ministering before the Lord (2 Chronicles 4:6).

The four beasts possibly represent the cherubim or seraphim. Each had six wings like the seraphim—two wings to cover their eyes, two to cover their feet, and two to fly and do the bidding of God (Isaiah 6:2). The wings of the living creatures suggest swiftness to carry out God's will. The four living creatures and the twenty-four elders cry day and night, "Holy, holy, holy, Lord God Almighty, which was, and is, and is to come." The only other instance where "holy, holy, holy" is used is in Isaiah's vision of the throne of God (Isaiah 6:3).

The conclusion the angels declare in that passage is that the whole Earth is full of His glory, and so it is in heaven. The praise of the living creatures is directed to the attributes of God—which are central to John's vision of God both here and through the entire book—His holiness, power, and eternity.

9 And when those beasts give glory and honour and thanks to him that sat on the throne, who liveth forever and ever, 10 The four and twenty elders fall down before him that sat on the throne, and worship him that liveth forever and ever, and cast their crowns before the throne, saying, 11 Thou art worthy, O Lord, to receive glory and honor and power: for thou hast created all things, and for thy pleasure they are and were created.

As the elders testify to the living beasts' worship, they can do nothing but fall down before Him, give back the crowns they had been given, and declare His praises. It does not matter where the praise comes from or who gives it. When God is praised, the honorable response is that everyone else in the room also worship because He is "worthy" (Gk. *axios*, **AX-ee-os**). God supremely deserves to receive the glory, honor, and power given to Him.

Through John, the Spirit of the Lord says to the church that the reasons the redeemed are to offer continual, unbridled praise to God are: (1) all things were created by Him, and (2) all things were created for His pleasure. God has one design for us: to glorify Him. God is complete in every way. He is self-sufficient, because the whole world and everything in it is His (Psalm 50:12). Yet, God created us anyway; we are the unnecessary necessity, made in God's image to glorify Him.

Too often, God's people hold back their praise. Life is chaotic, and problems can be persistent. However, God is on the throne. All things are created by His will and for His pleasure. Praise and thank Him for what He has done, praise and adore Him for who He is, and praise and honor Him because He didn't have to do it. Hallelujah to the Lamb!

Sources:
Aune, David E. *Word Biblical Commentary: Revelation 1–5*. Dallas, TX: Word Books, 1997.
Kittel, G., Bromiley, G. W., & Friedrich, G. (Eds.). (1964–). *Theological Dictionary of the New Testament*. Electronic ed., Vol. 2. Grand Rapids, MI: Eerdmans, 1964. 25.
Mangina, Joseph L. *Revelation: Brazos Theological Commentary on the Bible*. Grand Rapids, MI: Brazos Press, 2010.
Mounce, Robert H. *The Book of Revelation: New International Commentary on the New Testament*. Revised ed. Grand Rapids, MI: Eerdmans, 1998.
Osborne, Grant R. *Revelation: Baker Exegetical Commentary on the New Testament*. Grand Rapids, MI: Baker Academic, 2002.

Say It Correctly

Sardine. sar-**DEEN.**
Carnelian. car-**NEE**-lee-en.

Daily Bible Readings

MONDAY
God Promises Mercy to All People
(Genesis 9:8–17)

TUESDAY
Job's Pain Determined in Heavenly Court
(Job 1:6–12)

WEDNESDAY
Moses Summoned by God
(Exodus 19:20–25)

THURSDAY
Jesus, Our Example on the Throne
(Hebrews 12:1–6)

FRIDAY
Vision of Four Living Creatures
(Ezekiel 1:5–14)

SATURDAY
Elders Worship and Praise God Together
(Revelation 19:1–8)

SUNDAY
Heavenly Worship
(Revelation 4:1–6, 8–11)

Teaching Tips

Words You Should Know

A. Odour (Revelation 5:8) *thumiama* (Gk.)—Incense.

B. Redeem (v. 9) *agorazo* (Gk.)—To purchase.

Teacher Preparation

Unifying Principle—A World of Joy. People find it difficult to find a source of allegiance that is permanent and lasting. What type of response do they give when they find this lasting allegiance? Revelation speaks of joyful praise and eternal worship of God.

A. Pray that your students enter into joyful praise!

B. Read Revelation 5 twice to understand the context.

C. Think about one person, besides God, whom you believe is most deserving of your honor and respect. Be prepared to share with your students.

O—Open the Lesson

A. Open with prayer.

B. Introduce today's lesson title and Aim For Change.

C. Read the In Focus Story and share with your students why the person you've chosen to speak about deserves your respect and honor.

P—Present the Scriptures

A. Solicit volunteers to read the Focal Verses.

B. Use The People, Places, and Times; Background; Search the Scriptures; At-A-Glance outline; In Depth; and More Light on the Text to clarify the verses.

E—Explore the Meaning

A. Have the class answer the Discuss the Meaning and read the Lesson in Our Society sections.

B. Encourage the students to apply the Make It Happen section.

N—Next Steps for Application

A. Summarize the lesson.

B. Close with prayer.

Worship Guide

For the Superintendent or Teacher
Theme: Blessing, Glory, Honor Forever
Song: "Worthy is the Lamb"
Devotional Reading: Philippians 2:1–11

Blessing, Glory, Honor Forever

Bible Background • REVELATION 5:6–14
Printed Text • REVELATION 5:6–14 | Devotional Reading • PHILIPPIANS 2:1–11

Aim for Change

By the end of this lesson, we will: ANALYZE the symbols of the heavenly worship of the Lamb; REFLECT on the significance of the whole world worshiping the Lamb who was slain; and CELEBRATE with joy the faithfulness of God.

 In Focus

Jesse was always very fond of his uncle, Tony. He thought so highly of him because he knew what Tony had given up in order to make sure that Jesse's life was headed in the right direction. Tony's sister had abandoned Jesse, her son, when he was just eight years old, so Tony took him in and raised him all by himself.

Tony was on the fast track as a star salesman for his company, but he switched to another role so he wouldn't have to travel as much. He didn't flinch when it came to taking care of Jesse, and he knew that it was not only a responsibility but also a privilege to take care of and mold this young life.

Jesse might have been young, but he sure wasn't dumb. He knew very well that Tony had given up many luxuries in life to provide him with a richer and more meaningful experience. In what seemed like a fraction of a second, Jesse went from merely existing to living. Because of Tony's great sacrifice, Jesse determined in his heart to show his gratitude through acts of kindness until the end of their days on earth.

Today we will learn why Jesus is worthy of all praise, honor, and glory forever. Who in your life, besides God, is worthy of honor and respect?

Keep in Mind

"Saying with a loud voice, Worthy is the Lamb that was slain to receive power, and riches, and wisdom, and strength, and honour, and glory, and blessing" (Revelation 5:12, KJV).

"Saying with a loud voice, Worthy is the Lamb that was slain to receive power, and riches, and wisdom, and strength, and honour, and glory, and blessing" (Revelation 5:12, KJV).

Focal Verses

KJV **Revelation 5:6** And I beheld, and, lo, in the midst of the throne and of the four beasts, and in the midst of the elders, stood a Lamb as it had been slain, having seven horns and seven eyes, which are the seven Spirits of God sent forth into all the earth.

7 And he came and took the book out of the right hand of him that sat upon the throne.

8 And when he had taken the book, the four beasts and four and twenty elders fell down before the Lamb, having every one of them harps, and golden vials full of odours, which are the prayers of saints.

9 And they sung a new song, saying, Thou art worthy to take the book, and to open the seals thereof: for thou wast slain, and hast redeemed us to God by thy blood out of every kindred, and tongue, and people, and nation;

10 And hast made us unto our God kings and priests: and we shall reign on the earth.

11 And I beheld, and I heard the voice of many angels round about the throne and the beasts and the elders: and the number of them was ten thousand times ten thousand, and thousands of thousands;

12 Saying with a loud voice, Worthy is the Lamb that was slain to receive power, and riches, and wisdom, and strength, and honour, and glory, and blessing.

13 And every creature which is in heaven, and on the earth, and under the earth, and such as are in the sea, and all that are in them, heard I saying, Blessing, and honour, and glory, and power, be unto him that sitteth upon the throne, and unto the Lamb for ever and ever.

14 And the four beasts said, Amen. And the four and twenty elders fell down and worshipped him that liveth for ever and ever.

NLT **Revelation 5:6** Then I saw a Lamb that looked as if it had been slaughtered, but it was now standing between the throne and the four living beings and among the twenty-four elders. He had seven horns and seven eyes, which represent the sevenfold Spirit of God that is sent out into every part of the earth.

7 He stepped forward and took the scroll from the right hand of the one sitting on the throne.

8 And when he took the scroll, the four living beings and the twenty-four elders fell down before the Lamb. Each one had a harp, and they held gold bowls filled with incense, which are the prayers of God's people.

9 And they sang a new song with these words: "You are worthy to take the scroll and break its seals and open it. For you were slaughtered, and your blood has ransomed people for God from every tribe and language and people and nation.

10 And you have caused them to become a Kingdom of priests for our God. And they will reign on the earth."

11 Then I looked again, and I heard the voices of thousands and millions of angels around the throne and of the living beings and the elders.

12 And they sang in a mighty chorus: "Worthy is the Lamb who was slaughtered— to receive power and riches and wisdom and strength and honor and glory and blessing."

13 And then I heard every creature in heaven and on earth and under the earth and in the sea. They sang: "Blessing and honor and glory and power belong to the one sitting on the throne and to the Lamb forever and ever."

14 And the four living beings said, "Amen!" And the twenty-four elders fell down and worshiped the Lamb.

The People, Places, and Times

John. The author of Revelation simply identifies himself as John (Revelation 1:9). Some have suggested that someone other than the Apostle John, namely some John also known as "the Elder," might have written the book, but this is highly unlikely for at least three reasons. First, the traditional view held by many of the earliest church fathers identifies the Apostle John as the author. Second, the author of Revelation says he was exiled to Patmos as a punishment for his witness of Jesus, and this fits with the traditional view which says the Apostle John spent his latter days in exile on this very island. And third, the author seemed to be well acquainted with the seven churches he was writing to and was writing from the vantage point of one who had been divinely authorized to write (Revelation 1:19; 2–3).

This would make the most sense if the one writing was in fact an apostle of Jesus Christ. For these reasons, then, the traditional view of authorship is probably the correct one.

Patmos. Patmos is an very small island in the middle of the Aegean Sea. To the west of Patmos lay Greece and to the east, Asia Minor, now called Turkey. It was here that the Apostle John wrote this end-times book (Revelation 1:9).

How does isolation help us to encounter God in different ways?

Background

Persecution was nothing new to the Christian church. In fact, early church history holds that all the apostles were martyred with the exception of John. Jesus predicted the twelve disciples would experience persecution (Matthew 10:18; John 16:33). Though John was never martyred for his faith in Jesus, he was banished to the isle of Patmos because of it. He was exiled during the reign of either emperor Nero (AD 54–68) or Domitian (AD 81–96), the latter being the more traditional view. If this is correct, then the most likely date for the writing of Revelation is in the AD 90s.

The recipients of the book of Revelation were the seven churches of Asia Minor (Revelation 1:19–20), a region today known as Turkey. The occasion for this letter was the Lord's command for John to write about what he had seen, what was presently taking place, and what lay ahead (Revelation 1:19).

Chapters two and three give us a glimpse into the state of the churches John was addressing. The issues they were contending with were not entirely different from many of the issues with which churches struggle today. Among the list of sins plaguing these churches were false teachers, a loss of passion for God, occult activity, sexual immorality, idolatry, and greed (Revelation 2–3).

Fortunately, many churches were doing good things as well, and John was careful to encourage them to continue. The overall purpose of Revelation was to encourage the seven churches to remember that God is in control of the affairs of the world. He will punish evil doers but reward the saints with new and eternal blessings.

What are some of the eternal rewards you most anticipate receiving in heaven?

At-A-Glance

1. The Powerful Lamb (Revelation 5:6–7)
2. The Worthy Lamb (vv. 8–14)

In Depth

1. The Powerful Lamb (Revelation 5:6–7)

John saw what others were not permitted to see. It is unclear whether this heavenly experience was some sort of vision, or whether John was miraculously transported to heaven. Whatever the case, it was made possible through the work of the Holy Spirit (Revelation 4:1–2).

In heaven was a scroll containing God's plan for the world and His holy people, yet no one in heaven or on earth was found worthy to open it except the Lion from the tribe of Judah, the Root of David (Revelation 5:1–5). The word "lion" in verse 5 references Christ, and signifies power and rulership (Genesis 49:8–10).

Although one of the elders identifies Christ as "the Lion of the tribe of Judah," He appears before John's eyes as a lamb as if it had been slain (vv. 5–6). The contrasting descriptions evoke powerful imageries. Rulership (lion) and servanthood (lamb) are wrapped up in the single person of Jesus Christ.

But that's not all. John reveals more of what he saw as he describes three qualities of Christ that can only be attributed to God—sovereignty, omniscience, and omnipresence. The number seven has long been understood to signify perfection in the Bible, and the word horn is used repeatedly in Revelation to refer to authority (Revelation 13:1, 17:12).

The "seven horns" in chapter 5 represent perfect authority (sovereignty), and the "seven eyes" and "seven Spirits of God" represent perfect insight (omniscience) and perfect presence (omnipresence), respectively. We learn from vv. 5–6 that Christ is the God-man depicted as a powerful lamb standing before the throne of God.

What is the significance of Christ being depicted as a lamb in comparison to its use during Old Testament times?

2. The Worthy Lamb (vv. 8–14)

A worship scene in heaven fills vv. 8–14. The identity of the elders is unclear, though they may refer to human beings—the twelve apostles and the twelve tribes of Israel (Revelation 21:12–13)—or possibly the angels described in Ezekiel chapters one and ten. Most important

is what the elders and four living creatures are doing: worshiping Christ!

Three components of worship are found right in these verses. They made music with a harp, sang a new song to Christ, and offered prayers unto him (vv. 8–10). The evidence of prayer is concealed somewhat in the King James Version translation as "odour," a word that more closely means "incense." The incense burned in a worship festival that symbolized and joined the people's prayers. As the smoke from the incense and pleasant aroma rose up to heaven, so, too, people's prayers rose up to heaven.

The Lamb is said to be worthy because He has "redeemed" men and women from every people group on the planet (v. 9). The Greek verb translated as "redeemed" here is elsewhere translated "purchased." Their song declares the Lamb to be worthy because He purchased with His own blood every man, woman, boy, and girl from an evil plantation owner—sin—and then Jesus set them free!

Not only will the redeemed worship and praise Christ, but so will all the angels in heaven (v. 11). All of creation sings a new song because God has done something new. He came to earth as the God-man to shed His blood to redeem mankind, and for this, He is worthy to be praised (Revelation 5:9–14).

Why is it sometimes difficult for believers of various races, cultures, and languages to assemble and worship God as one body?

Search the Scriptures

1. What do the lion and lamb represent in reference to the description of Jesus (vv. 5–6)?

2. How are prayers like incense? Does this image encourage you to pray (vv. 8–10)?

Discuss the Meaning

Jesus is worthy because He is both Creator and servant, God and sacrificial lamb. Since the Creator of the universe came to serve the whole population of humanity rather than just a segment of it, what does this say to us about racial reconciliation (Revelation 5:9)?

Lesson in Our Society

We sometimes miss opportunities to celebrate the Lamb with others because of cultural differences. The impact of Jesus' sacrificial death, however, was universal in scope. Millions of people around the globe offer praises to the Lamb on a daily basis. Jesus purchased all believers through His blood and made them into one new man (Ephesians 2:15). The truth is, Christians all over the world are singing the same new song regardless of the color of their skin, level of wealth, or social status.

What can be done to adapt racial and cultural sensitivity and awareness amongst individuals and congregations?

Make It Happen

• Visit a church with people from a different ethnic background than yours.

• Write in your journal about the things that were similar and the things that were different.

• Memorize phrases believers use to praise God in other languages.

Follow the Spirit

What God wants me to do:

_____

_____

_____

_____

Remember Your Thoughts

Special insights I have learned:

_____

_____

_____

_____

More Light on the Text
Revelation 5:6–14

6 And I beheld, and, lo, in the midst of the throne and of the four beasts, and in the midst of the elders, stood a Lamb as it had been slain, having seven horns and seven eyes, which are the seven Spirits of God sent forth into all the earth.

As John turned to see the Lion of Judah (Revelation 5:5), he instead saw a Lamb that looked slaughtered yet stood tall. The Lamb was unique in appearance, having seven horns and seven eyes. Traditionally, the former suggested power and the latter represented knowledge or wisdom. The image of the slaughtered Lamb would have reminded John and his hearers of the Passover lamb of the Exodus and of Isaiah 53:7, which described the Suffering Servant as a lamb led to the slaughter. That the lamb was standing probably refers to Christ's resurrection.

The symbolism adds an apocalyptic element in its connection to the ministry of the "seven Spirits." This phrase is mentioned four times in the book of Revelation (1:4, 3:1, 4:5, 5:6). However, the full end-times identity or purpose of the "seven Spirits" remains unclear. Common speculation is that the seven Spirits reference seven angelic spirits, a symbolism of completeness, or a recollection of the work of the Holy Spirit (Isaiah 11:2). The latter may have the most weight, since the word used for

"Spirit" is *pneuma* (Gk. **puh-NEW-ma**), which many times refers to the Holy Spirit.

7 And he came and took the book out of the right hand of him that sat upon the throne.

Heaven's throne is a primary fixture of symbolism throughout the book of Revelation. It shows God's power to rule (4:8) and His character to be worshiped (4:10, 5:13). Here is where God reveals His sovereign authority to prevail (22:3). Jesus was slain for our sins; only He is worthy to bring people into His kingdom.

The book or scroll that the Lamb takes is unusual because it has writing on the front and back (5:1). Symbolically, this meant that whatever is written on it is expansive—as if it is more than the book can contain. What is written in it remains unclear, but what is apparent is the Lamb takes this without any resistance from "the right hand of him that sat upon the throne."

By noting what happened before and after this moment, we can appreciate how God the Father, the Son, and the Spirit are all present with one another. The Lamb is in the center of the throne (v. 6), then approaches someone on the throne (v. 7). This means that the Lamb occupies the same space and position as the Father but remains distinct (John 10:30). The Spirit likewise demonstrates that the three Persons of the Godhead coexist as One while remaining distinct for a specific role, purpose, ministry, or revelation.

8 And when he had taken the book, the four beasts and four and twenty elders fell down before the Lamb, having every one of them harps, and golden vials full of odours, which are the prayers of saints.

As John watches, Jesus, the slain Lamb, takes the book out of God's hand, and immediately the scene erupts into singing. The four living creatures (beasts) and twenty-four elders fall down before Him in worship. They praise the Lamb for having the authority to take the book from the One on the throne and the ability to carry out God's plan of salvation.

9 And they sung a new song, saying, Thou art worthy to take the book, and to open the seals thereof: for thou wast slain, and hast redeemed us to God by thy blood out of every kindred, and tongue, and people, and nation.

The previous hymn of praise in the heavenly court scene that John saw is offered to God as Creator (4:11). Now, as a mark of Christ's investiture or official ceremony, the four living creatures and twenty-four elders sing praise to Christ as the Redeemer. Christ's sacrifice created the means of redemption that makes it possible for all people in all generations from all nations to worship Him. The Lamb can open the seal as both God and mediator.

10 And hast made us unto our God kings and priests: and we shall reign on the earth.

Anyone who receives the offer of salvation and a new identity through Jesus Christ becomes part of His family. Because He is the king, we become royal in a heavenly sense. Our destiny to reign with Him is not through our own merit but because of His grace. Our capacity to be a royal priesthood is only because we no longer need any mediator except Jesus Himself (2 Timothy 2:12; 1 Peter 2:9).

11 And I beheld, and I heard the voice of many angels round about the throne and the beasts and the elders: and the number of them was ten thousand times ten thousand, and thousands of thousands.

In Revelation 4:9–10, the living beings inspired the elders to worship because of God's authority. The elders and angels both give praise to God. Such a cycle reveals that humanity and heaven are meant to work together and ultimately merge, especially when it comes to seeing and appreciating the different aspects of whom God is. The angels are too numerous to count; the Greek word *myrias* (**moo-re-AS**) can mean the definite number 10,000, but often (especially when doubled as here) it refers to an uncountable multitude.

12 Saying with a loud voice, Worthy is the Lamb that was slain to receive power, and riches, and wisdom, and strength, and honour, and glory, and blessing.

The angels spoke with a loud voice singing a chorus of praise together. While they don't know what it means to be redeemed like the elders do, they can with honesty declare Christ's worthiness. The fact that there are seven specific praises recalls the rabbinic tradition of the number seven symbolizing perfection. Here, the Lamb is worthy to receive power, riches, wisdom, strength, honor, glory, and blessing. A later similar sevenfold list of praise includes blessing, glory, wisdom, thanksgiving, honor, power, and might (7:12).

The word here for power (Gk. *dunamis*, **DOO-nah-mees**) is different from the word for power in verse 13 (Gk. *kratos*, **KRA-toce**). *Dunamis* refers to a person's ability to perform a task; this power comes from a wealth of riches or armies. The word can also be used to refer to a miracle that particularly showed God's power. *Kratos* speaks more to a person's physical strength and can also be translated "dominion," to emphasize one's power over others. It is similar to the word for strength in verse 12, *ischus* (Gk. **ees-KHOOS**), which also refers to physical strength and forcefulness.

While the heavenly chorus does use these distinct words with individual nuances, the words also add to one another to give a grand vision of God. Riches and *ischus* add to one's

dunamis. Honor adds to one's glory. Any one of these words of praise could be considered a blessing. The effect of listing all these synonyms is to overwhelm the worshiper with how completely worthy Jesus is of receiving every good thing.

13 And every creature which is in heaven, and on the earth, and under the earth, and such as are in the sea, and all that are in them, heard I saying, Blessing, and honour, and glory, and power, be unto him that sitteth upon the throne, and unto the Lamb for ever and ever. 14 And the four beasts said, Amen. And the four and twenty elders fell down and worshipped him that liveth for ever and ever.

In many ways, the book of Revelation is a book of restoration. There's no mistake that every area of creation is mentioned here, be it angels from the inner realm of heaven or the creatures who live in the deepest parts of the earth or sea. It's as if, for a moment in time and eternity, everything and everyone recognizes the Lord for who He is, while at the same time realizing He is beyond understanding. God's great power is visible even now (Romans 1), but in that moment it will be a universal shout of praise. The four beasts confirm the praises of the people and the twenty-four elders lead in worshiping the eternal God.

Sources:
Earle, Ralph. *Word Meanings in the New Testament*. Grand Rapids, MI: Hendrickson Publishers, 1986. 460–461.
Elwell, Walter A., and Robert W. Yarbrough. *Encountering the New Testament: A Historical and Theological Survey*. Grand Rapids, MI: Baker Books, 1998. 376–382.
Sproul, R. C., and Robert D. Wolgemuth. *What's in the Bible: A One-Volume Guidebook to God's Word*. Nashville, TN: W Publishing Group, 2000. 355–358.
Wiersbe, Warren W. *The Bible Exposition Commentary*. Vol. 2. Wheaton, IL: Victor Books, 1989. 584–586.

Say It Correctly

Vials. **VAI**-uls.
Kindred. **KIN**-drid.

Daily Bible Readings

MONDAY
Rejoice! Your Salvation is in Christ
(1 Peter 1:3–9)

TUESDAY
All Subject to God Through Christ
(1 Corinthians 15:20–28)

WEDNESDAY
Sanctified by Lambs Sacrificed Daily
(Exodus 29:38–46)

THURSDAY
Christ, Our Suffering, and Salvation
(Romans 8:31–39)

FRIDAY
Eat the Scroll, Speak My Words
(Ezekiel 2:8–3:11)

SATURDAY
Only One Can Open the Scroll
(Revelation 5:1–5)

SUNDAY
All Creatures Worship the Lamb
(Revelation 5:6–14)

Notes

Teaching Tips

Words You Should Know

A. Sow (2 Corinthians 9:6) *speiro* (Gk.)—To scatter seed.

B. Grudgingly (v. 7) *lupe* (Gk.)—Sorrow, pain.

Teacher Preparation

Unifying Principle—When Calamity Comes. People want to live lives of gratitude. How can they express their thankfulness properly? God welcomes the offerings of those who give with generous and cheerful hearts.

A. Review your church's doctrine on giving and stewardship.

B. Read over the Focal Verses and the lesson several times.

C. Pray that the lesson and discussion will be transformative.

O—Open the Lesson

A. Begin with asking a volunteer to pray.

B. Invite initial thoughts and feelings about the sensitive topic of giving.

C. Give an overview of the lesson, emphasizing the Aim for Change and Keep in Mind verse.

D. Have a volunteer read In Focus, then briefly discuss it.

P—Present the Scriptures

A. Ask the class to read silently over the Focal Verses.

B. Read the Key Verse aloud.

C. Read and discuss The People, Places and Times; Background; In Depth; and Search the Scriptures.

E—Explore the Meaning

A. Ask volunteers to discuss their favorite piece of clothing or jewelry, and ask them what it would take for them to give away this favorite valuable item.

B. Connect the time of sharing to the Scripture in Exodus 35; talk about how the Israelites willingly gave their best to build a tabernacle for God.

C. Have discussion about the obstacles that impede our desire to give our best back to God.

N—Next Steps for Application

A. Encourage the class to apply the Make It Happen section.

B. Close in prayer.

Worship Guide

For the Superintendent or Teacher
Theme: Giving from a Generous Heart
Song: "I Surrender"
Devotional Reading: Psalm 112

Giving from a Generous Heart

Bible Background • EXODUS 25:1–7, 35:4–29; LEVITICUS 27:30–33; 2 CORINTHIANS 9:6–8
Printed Text • EXODUS 35:20–29; 2 CORINTHIANS 9:6–8 | **Devotional Reading** • PSALM 112

—————————— Aim for Change ——————————

By the end of this lesson we will VALUE the account of Israel's offering to build and furnish the Tabernacle; APPRECIATE the call to cheerful and generous giving to God; and EMBRACE cheerful and generous giving as a Christian way of life.

—————————— ✑ In Focus ——————————

Money had been tight for months, and it was getting even tighter. Very aware of the situation, Jermaine began to feel the pressure mounting. His family—a wife and two daughters under ten—were depending on him, leaning on him, looking to him. But Jermaine had not been working for two months now, and he was not getting strong leads for prospective jobs.

As the major breadwinner, Jermaine started wondering how he would soon meet their financial demands. *How will I pay the mortgage? How will I take care of the car note? How will we have enough food? How will the utility bills be covered? How?*

As a regular tither, Jermaine had not failed to set aside a tenth of his profits as a gift back to God. He had given out of obedience to God, as taught by the church and seen in Scripture. True, sometimes it had been a struggle, but he had done it nevertheless.

Burdened down by his current situation, Jermaine knelt to pray. He remembered God's promise to those who tithe. He didn't know how God would meet his current needs, but he remembered that He had always provided in the past. As Jermaine got up from praying, he recalled the promise of 2 Corinthians 9:6—God will bountifully bless those who have given bountifully.

In our lesson today, we will study God's expectations for financial stewardship. What motivates you to give generously and cheerfully?

—————————— Keep in Mind ——————————

"He which soweth sparingly shall reap also sparingly; and he which soweth bountifully shall reap also bountifully" (from 2 Corinthians 9:6).

"He which soweth sparingly shall reap also sparingly; and he which soweth bountifully shall reap also bountifully" (from 2 Corinthians 9:6).

Focal Verses

KJV **Exodus 35:20** And all the congregation of the children of Israel departed from the presence of Moses.

21 And they came, every one whose heart stirred him up, and every one whom his spirit made willing, and they brought the LORD's offering to the work of the tabernacle of the congregation, and for all his service, and for the holy garments.

22 And they came, both men and women, as many as were willing hearted, and brought bracelets, and earrings, and rings, and tablets, all jewels of gold: and every man that offered an offering of gold unto the LORD.

23 And every man, with whom was found blue, and purple, and scarlet, and fine linen, and goats' hair, and red skins of rams, and badgers' skins, brought them.

24 Every one that did offer an offering of silver and brass brought the LORD's offering: and every man, with whom was found shittim wood for any work of the service, brought it.

25 And all the women that were wise hearted did spin with their hands, and brought that which they had spun, both of blue, and of purple, and of scarlet, and of fine linen.

26 And all the women whose heart stirred them up in wisdom spun goats' hair.

27 And the rulers brought onyx stones, and stones to be set, for the ephod, and for the breastplate;

28 And spice, and oil for the light, and for the anointing oil, and for the sweet incense.

29 The children of Israel brought a willing offering unto the LORD, every man and woman, whose heart made them willing to bring for all manner of work, which the LORD had commanded to be made by the hand of Moses.

2 Corinthians 9:6 But this I say, He which soweth sparingly shall reap also sparingly; and

NLT **Exodus 35:20** So the whole community of Israel left Moses and returned to their tents.

21 All whose hearts were stirred and whose spirits were moved came and brought their sacred offerings to the LORD. They brought all the materials needed for the Tabernacle, for the performance of its rituals, and for the sacred garments.

22 Both men and women came, all whose hearts were willing. They brought to the LORD their offerings of gold—brooches, earrings, rings from their fingers, and necklaces. They presented gold objects of every kind as a special offering to the LORD.

23 All those who owned the following items willingly brought them: blue, purple, and scarlet thread; fine linen and goat hair for cloth; and tanned ram skins and fine goatskin leather.

24 And all who had silver and bronze objects gave them as a sacred offering to the LORD. And those who had acacia wood brought it for use in the project.

25 All the women who were skilled in sewing and spinning prepared blue, purple, and scarlet thread, and fine linen cloth.

26 All the women who were willing used their skills to spin the goat hair into yarn.

27 The leaders brought onyx stones and the special gemstones to be set in the ephod and the priest's chestpiece.

28 They also brought spices and olive oil for the light, the anointing oil, and the fragrant incense.

29 So the people of Israel—every man and woman who was eager to help in the work the LORD had given them through Moses—brought their gifts and gave them freely to the LORD.

2 Corinthians 9:6 Remember this—a farmer who plants only a few seeds will get a he which soweth bountifully shall reap also bountifully.

7 Every man according as he purposeth in his heart, so let him give; not grudgingly, or of necessity: for God loveth a cheerful giver.

8 And God is able to make all grace abound toward you; that ye, always having all sufficiency in all things, may abound to every good work:

small crop. But the one who plants generously will get a generous crop.

7 You must each decide in your heart how much to give. And don't give reluctantly or in response to pressure. "For God loves a person who gives cheerfully."

8 And God will generously provide all you need. Then you will always have everything you need and plenty left over to share with others.

The People, Places, and Times

Corinthian Church. The Apostle Paul's letter is written to a young church that in many ways is just learning to embody a distinctly Christian identity in the bustling city of Corinth, a place with a culture considered ungodly. Similar to any major American metropolis, Corinth boasted of its wealth, its entertainment, and its well-known name in the region. But while it was attractive for anyone looking for a good time, it could also lure Christians from obeying God. Paul urgently writes to address the discord in the church and explains how they should behave in the larger society.

Collection for Jerusalem. The key verse of this lesson refers to the Corinthians' willingness to contribute to a collection that Paul was gathering from predominantly Gentile churches to take to Jewish Christians at Jerusalem (2 Corinthians 9:6). This is not the first occasion that Paul brings up the importance of contributions; he mentions this in four epistles.

Paul is taking up this collection so that: 1) the gift would be an offering of gratitude on part of the Gentile Christians for receiving their religious heritage from their Jewish brothers and sisters in the faith; 2) the gift would benefit the poor among the Christians in Jerusalem (Acts 11:29–30, Romans 15:25–27); and 3) the

gift would establish credibility for Paul's ministry to the Gentiles among Jewish Christians who looked unfavorably on Paul's mission to the Gentile audiences.

When we collect offerings for the needs of others, how does it point toward our love of Christ?

Background

Between Paul penning the letter of 1 Corinthians to discuss several issues facing the Corinthian church and the letter of 2 Corinthians, he receives correspondence from the church that is not very encouraging. Evidently, some Corinthian Christians did not like Paul's harsh tone, while others questioned the credibility of his apostleship and authority.

Although Paul initially planned to visit the Corinthian church, their response urges him to write again from a distance. Paul certainly writes to address more issues. But what is just as important in 2 Corinthians is for him to ensure that the relationship between him and the church is in good standing (7:8–9).

Much of the contents in 2 Corinthians is Paul's defense of himself and an explanation for his previous harsh tone. All of this sets the table for Paul to discuss the central (and often controversial) topic in the key verses: giving.

Paul writes to the Corinthian church in chapter 9 to return to a subject that he has previously addressed (1 Corinthians 16:1–4; 2

Corinthians 8). He reminds the church about its previous commitment to contribute to the collection for the church in Jerusalem. Paul has previously explained a theology of giving earlier in his correspondence, but feels it necessary to circle back to and reinforce what he has said.

Scholars debate Paul's reasons for collecting an offering for the Christians in Jerusalem. Most agree that Paul is also trying to establish credibility among them because of their unfavorable outlook on his outreach to Gentile Christians. If the offering was small, this would reflect negatively on Paul and his mission to the Gentiles. On the contrary, a large offering would demonstrate evidence of Paul's success in ministry.

As citizens of the prosperous city of Corinth, reason leads us to believe that the Corinthians had enough financial means to contribute significantly to the collection. The question Paul puts before them is, will they?

How often do we suspect personal motives behind leaders asking for money which affects our attitude about giving?

At-A-Glance

1. The Freewill Offering (Exodus 35:20–29)
2. Examine the Seeds You Sow (2 Corinthians 9:6)
3. Examine Your Motive and God's Giving (vv. 7–8)

In Depth

1. The Freewill Offering (Exodus 35:20–29)

Here, the Israelites are faced with a decision of how to respond to Moses' instructions in the previous verses of chapter 35. Previously, Moses tells the Israelites that God expects them to build a tabernacle for Him to dwell and that it is the Israelite camp's responsibility to gather their personal materials to build it. A key part of Moses' statement, however, is that he says God is not forcing them to collect and offer their items, but allowing them to decide freely if and how they would give.

This is what is meant when Moses says, "Take ye from among you an offering unto the Lord: whosoever is of a willing heart, let him bring it, an offering of the Lord; gold, and silver, and brass" (from Exodus 35:5). The responses in vv. 20–29 are a stunning response to the freedom God gives them. Verse 29 sums up the responses, saying that they gave freely, even their most valuable possessions, to the Lord.

How can we differentiate between faithful people who are givers versus generous people who are givers?

2. Examine the Seeds You Sow (2 Corinthians 9:6)

The wisdom presented in this verse was not novel. Commentators suggest the concept circulated throughout antiquity, with the Old Testament presenting it in Proverbs 11:24. But the significance is extremely important for Paul's purpose of motivating the church to give. He adds impetus behind this statement by reminding the church that their lives will benefit because of their gifts to the Jerusalem church. He is not asking them to give beyond their means, but instead encourages sharing since spiritual blessings will result.

What benefits can we anticipate by freely giving tithes and offerings?

3. Examine Your Motive and God's Giving (vv. 7–8)

In this verse, Paul takes a slightly different approach to giving than in verse 6. Paul has already stated that he expects the church to give bountifully. But what seems to be just as important—if not more—is their attitude or emotion toward giving; they should give "cheerfully."

The description of the attitude toward giving should be understood in light of the words surrounding it: "For God loves a person who gives cheerfully." God's love toward a person seems to be expressed by the verse that follows: "And God will generously provide all you need." The word "and" is key here; it indicates that God's action is connected to and conditional on the previous statement.

In other words, it is not enough for the church to give because they think will reap benefits. They must make sure that their hearts and attitudes are right when they give if they want to receive God's blessings and provisions.

The purpose of verse 8 is closely connected to vv. 6–7. While the Corinthians can look forward to reaping God's provisions if they sow with the right attitude, the purpose of their reaping is not merely for selfish reasons. God does not bless with abundance for personal wealth and satisfaction. God blesses so that the church will continue helping others by meeting their needs, just as He has met and continues to meet the Corinthian church's needs.

How does giving out of obligation compare and/or contrast to giving freely and cheerfully of your resources?

Search the Scriptures

1. How does the Israelites' willingness to give influence our attitude about giving (Exodus 35:29)?

2. How would you evaluate your own giving in response to 2 Corinthians 9:7?

Discuss the Meaning

One of the challenges of the Corinthian church was to give an offering to a church with whom they did not have a daily relationship. Nevertheless, they are expected to give. What should motivate Christians to give even when distance or another factor separates us from the persons impacted by our gifts? Does how well we know the individual or community affect how we give to them? Should it?

Lesson in Our Society

In African American history is a rich legacy of sacrifices made to help one another. Sharing food with neighbors, helping to raise someone else's child, or caring for the elderly were the norm. If a person needed help, they knew they could turn to the church.

In the opening story, Jermaine is in crisis. He had faithfully tithed, but now he needs help. This is where the body of believers is needed. This is where our commitment to Christ is assessed. Giving to others, especially those within the church, shows the world that we are not out for ourselves but for the good of all.

What needs in your community could be met by the financial giving of church members?

Make It Happen

• Commit to tithing to your local church.

• Help a family that may be in temporary need.

• Record your expenses for a week and identify ways to redirect some funds to help others.

Follow the Spirit

What God wants me to do:

_____

_____

_____

_____

Remember Your Thoughts

Special insights I have learned:

_____

_____

_____

_____

More Light on the Text

Exodus 35:20–29

20 And all the congregation of the children of Israel departed from the presence of Moses.

After Moses gathers the community together and gives them a set of instructions about how to build the Tabernacle, the people leave his presence. He has given them a list of things needed for the Tabernacle to be completed according to God's design and pattern. They are ready and willing to get the work done.

21 And they came, every one whose heart stirred him up, and every one whom his spirit made willing, and they brought the Lord's offering to the work of the tabernacle of the congregation, and for all his service, and for the holy garments.

The text describes people who gave their offering as those whose heart stirred (Heb. *nasa'*, **nah-SAH**) or lifted them up. The people were moved in their hearts and not just by blind legalism to Moses' instruction; this was not a grudging task. Their spirits were made willing (Heb. *nadab*, **nah-DAV**) or had been impelled. The sense here is that their spirit urged them to give their offering.

22 And they came, both men and women, as many as were willing hearted, and brought bracelets, and earrings, and rings,

and tablets, all jewels of gold: and every man that offered an offering of gold unto the Lord.

Both men and women gave the offering—an equal opportunity to participate in the Lord's work. This offering was open to all whose hearts were willing. The word for willing is *nadib* (Heb. **NAH-deev**) and describes those who spontaneously and readily contribute. This word is also used for a prince or noble, since they are supposed to generously give gifts to their subjects.

The offerings are listed according to the material with the highest value, so all of the gold is listed first. Only jewelry is mentioned, not gold ore from a mine. The Israelites would have had this jewelry from the time they were in Egypt with the surplus of goods the Egyptians had given them at the time of their deliverance (Exodus 12:35–36). The word for tablet (Heb. *kumaz*, **koo-MAHZ**) is likely better translated "necklaces," referring to necklaces made of gold beads, since a golden tablet does not fit with the description of jewelry listed.

23 And every man, with whom was found blue, and purple, and scarlet, and fine linen, and goats' hair, and red skins of rams, and badgers' skins, brought them.

Blue, purple, and scarlet fabric were highly prized in the ancient world as the ingredients (fluid from sea mollusks, for example) were rare and more than likely imported. This made these fabrics very expensive and mostly used for the clothing of the rich and powerful, not commoners. These are listed in descending order according to their value and the desirability of the colors.

Linen was made from beating flax. This meant that the most amount of work had gone into this fabric as opposed to coarser linen. This was another example of valuable material being used to furnish the tabernacle.

The use of skins of badgers (Heb. *takhash*, **tah-KHOSH**) has been debated among scholars. The word is related to the Egyptian word for leather and the Arabic word for dolphin. This has led some to conclude that the word rendered as badger skin should actually be dolphin skin.

24 Every one that did offer an offering of silver and brass brought the Lord's offering: and every man, with whom was found shittim wood for any work of the service, brought it.

Next silver and brass are brought as an offering. These are much less valuable than gold although they do hold some value. Shittim (Heb. *shittah*, **shee-TAH**) or acacia wood is plentiful in Egypt, Arabia, and Ethiopia. This wood was used for the structure of the tabernacle and is known as a very resilient and hard wood. This was good, durable material.

25 And all the women that were wise hearted did spin with their hands, and brought that which they had spun, both of blue, and of purple, and of scarlet, and of fine linen. 26 And all the women whose heart stirred them up in wisdom spun goats' hair.

The text now includes the women with the particular skill of spinning—a very delicate task. If done improperly, the fabric might not be as strong or last as long as it should. These women focused on spinning the large amount of goats' hair needed to cover the Tabernacle.

27 And the rulers brought onyx stones, and stones to be set, for the ephod, and for the breastplate; 28 And spice, and oil for the light, and for the anointing oil, and for the sweet incense.

Next were the onyx stones and other gems needed for the priest's ephod and breastplate.

Scholars debate about whether the onyx was lapus lazuli or another stone, but agree that this stone was probably black with milky white lines. The ephod was a garment that the high priest used to discern God's will for Israel, and the stones might have been used in some mysterious way for this purpose.

Spices and oil were used for the lampstand as well as for anointing oil and incense. These items were also highly valued, especially the ingredients for the incense.

29 The children of Israel brought a willing offering unto the Lord, every man and woman, whose heart made them willing to bring for all manner of work, which the Lord had commanded to be made by the hand of Moses.

The writer reiterates the people's willingness. They brought a willing offering because their hearts made them willing. Their hearts were moved to worship, not only by God's command. This was a genuine freewill offering.

2 Corinthians 9:6–8

6 But this I say, He which soweth sparingly shall reap also sparingly; and he which soweth bountifully shall reap also bountifully.

In this verse, Paul uses a metaphor to explain the importance of giving. The scantier the seeds sown, the scantier the harvest. The word used for bountifully is *eulogia* (Gk. **ew-low-GEE-ah**), which means a blessing or present given to advance the receiver's well-being. Generous giving is a means of blessing the givers and recipients as well.

God is glorified when giving comes from the heart. But He doesn't expect anyone to be manipulated to give what they don't have (i.e., go into debt, make foolish pledges, or give their rent money and hope for the best). It's about proportion and attitude; the poor widow in

Mark gave more than everybody else (Mark 12:41–44).

It is not wise to withhold seeds and expect to get a good harvest. He who trusts in riches falls. He who waters is also watered. Whoever sows will reap.

7 Every man according as he purposeth in his heart, so let him give; not grudgingly, or of necessity: for God loveth a cheerful giver.

The true measure of Christian giving is the freedom of the heart. Giving should be without complaint, like Ananias and his wife Sapphira (Acts 5). They tried to cheat God when they sold their field, withheld some of the money, and lied about it. They were struck dead! Intent is what counts.

Sharing willingly to help brothers and sisters in Christ meet their basic needs is what Paul encourages. Givers must be cheerful (Gk. *hilaros,* **hee-la-ROCE**), a word related to our English word "hilarious." It is used to describe someone who is happy and gracious. We not only need to be willing to give, we also need to be happy while giving.

8 And God is able to make all grace abound toward you; that ye, always having all sufficiency in all things, may abound to every good work.

God is able to take care of us. His grace—giving what we don't deserve or cannot earn—is enough. The word for sufficiency (Gk. *autarkeia,* **aw-TAR-kee-ah**) is a word that philosophers use to describe contentment in any circumstance. For Paul, it is the contentment of knowing that God has supplied everything that is needed to obey Him and to do good while on earth.

Sources:
Achtemeier, Paul J., Joel B. Green, and Marianne Meye Thompson. *Introducing the New Testament: Its Literature and Theology.* Grand Rapids, MI: William B. Eerdmans Publishing Company, 2001.

Attridge, Harold W., ed. *The HarperCollins Study Bible,* Revised Edition. San Francisco, CA: HarperCollins Publishers, 2006.
Blount, Brian K., ed. *True to Our Native Land: An African American New Testament Commentary.* Minneapolis, MN: Fortress Press, 2007. 307–332.
Mounce, William D. *Mounce's Complete Expository Dictionary of Old and New Testament Words.* Grand Rapids, MI: 2006.
Samply, J. Paul. *The New Interpreters Bible,* "The Second Letter to the Corinthians." Nashville, TN: Abingdon Press, 2000. 129–135.

Say It Correctly

Onyx. **AH**-nyks.
Ephod. **EH**-fud.

Daily Bible Readings

MONDAY
Give as Your Heart Prompts You
(Exodus 25:1–9)

TUESDAY
Give Alms Quietly
(Matthew 6:1–4)

WEDNESDAY
Gather Together Your Bountiful Gift
(2 Corinthians 9:1–5)

THURSDAY
All Tithes are Holy
(Leviticus 27:30–33)

FRIDAY
Blessings of the Righteous
(Psalm 112)

SATURDAY
Gifts for the Tabernacle
(Exodus 35:10–19)

SUNDAY
Give Cheerfully and Generously
(Exodus 35:20–29; 2 Corinthians 9:6–8)

Teaching Tips

Words You Should Know

A. Accepted (Leviticus 23:11) *rason* (Heb.)—Pleasure, favor, will; used to describe a sacrifice that is acceptable to God.

B. Statute (v. 14) *huqqa* (Heb.)—Ordinance, regulation, decree, especially one of God.

Teacher Preparation

Unifying Principle—Reasons to Give. In a culture of scarcity, people acquire and hoard the best they can afford. How can they live less fearfully and more joyfully during difficult economic times? God called His people to worship with the first and best of their lives.

A. Read over the lesson and Scriptures at least twice.

B. Pray for the class and notice anyone in need.

C. Fill a basket with bags of grain or bread to use as a visual aid.

D. Prepare a stack of note cards and pencils.

O—Open the Lesson

A. Ask for a volunteer to pray.

B. Give an overview of the lesson and highlight the topic.

C. Read and discuss In Focus.

P—Present the Scriptures

A. Ask the class to read silently over the Focal Verses.

B. Read the Key Verse aloud.

C. Read and discuss The People, Places and Times; Background; In Depth; and Search the Scriptures sections.

E—Explore the Meaning

A. Answer the Discuss the Meaning questions and have someone read the Lesson in Our Society section.

B. Explain that the visual aid is symbolic for the first fruits of Israel. Have the participants use the note cards to jot down one way they could improve giving their first fruits to God, or sharing their fruits with others; collect and share these aloud.

N—Next Steps for Application

A. Read Make It Happen together.

B. Reiterate the suggestion of the exercise in Make It Happen.

C. Commit to praying for the hopes listed on the group's notecards.

Worship Guide

For the Superintendent or Teacher
Theme: Bringing First Fruits
Song: "More Than Anything"
Devotional Reading: Ephesians 4:25–5:2

Bringing First Fruits

Bible Background • LEVITICUS 2:14, 23:9–22
Printed Text • LEVITICUS 23:9–14, 22 | Devotional Reading • EPHESIANS 4:25–5:2

—— Aim for Change ——

By the end of this lesson, we will: EXPLORE the biblical call for offering the first fruits; AVOID giving God leftovers; and COMMIT to give God the first and best in everything we offer.

————— In Focus —————

Regina was fresh out of college, and favor was coming her way. She had been blessed with a lucrative, entry-level job, and she was more than excited to receive that first paycheck. She had already been eying that new purse in the mall and those designer shoes in the window of the boutique next to her corporate office downtown. She had her eyes on jewelry, too!

Her excitement was building, and she wanted to share it with her mother. "Mom, I can't wait," she texted. "I'm going to go straight over to that store and grab that bag after I deposit my check."

Her mother, who had tried to instill a love for God in Regina from an early age, did not hesitate in her response. "No, you won't," she texted back. "You will be writing out your tithe check and putting it in your current purse to take with you to church on Sunday."

Regina recalled memories with her mom at church over the years. Mom had regularly given Regina money to place in the offering plate to help her develop the habit of giving back to God. *Oh, it was so easy when it was really my mom's money I was giving. This giving thing is harder than I expected. I just want to keep my hard-earned money*, she thought.

In today's lesson, we will explore how gratitude is shown through setting aside an offering for God. Besides money, what can you set aside as an offering to God?

—————— Keep in Mind ——————

"Speak unto the children of Israel, and say unto them, When ye be come into the land which I give unto you, and shall reap the harvest thereof, then ye shall bring a sheaf of the firstfruits of your harvest unto the priest" (Leviticus 23:10).

"Speak unto the children of Israel, and say unto them, When ye be come into the land which I give unto you, and shall reap the harvest thereof, then ye shall bring a sheaf of the firstfruits of your harvest unto the priest" (Leviticus 23:10).

Focal Verses

KJV **Leviticus 23:9** And the LORD spake unto Moses, saying,

10 Speak unto the children of Israel, and say unto them, When ye be come into the land which I give unto you, and shall reap the harvest thereof, then ye shall bring a sheaf of the firstfruits of your harvest unto the priest:

11 And he shall wave the sheaf before the LORD, to be accepted for you: on the morrow after the sabbath the priest shall wave it.

12 And ye shall offer that day when ye wave the sheaf an he lamb without blemish of the first year for a burnt offering unto the LORD.

13 And the meat offering thereof shall be two tenth deals of fine flour mingled with oil, an offering made by fire unto the LORD for a sweet savour: and the drink offering thereof shall be of wine, the fourth part of an hin.

14 And ye shall eat neither bread, nor parched corn, nor green ears, until the self-same day that ye have brought an offering unto your God: it shall be a statute for ever throughout your generations in all your dwellings.

22 And when ye reap the harvest of your land, thou shalt not make clean riddance of the corners of thy field when thou reapest, neither shalt thou gather any gleaning of thy harvest: thou shalt leave them unto the poor, and to the stranger: I am the LORD your God.

NLT **Leviticus 23:9** Then the LORD said to Moses,

10 "Give the following instructions to the people of Israel. When you enter the land I am giving you and you harvest its first crops, bring the priest a bundle of grain from the first cutting of your grain harvest.

11 On the day after the Sabbath, the priest will lift it up before the LORD so it may be accepted on your behalf.

12 On that same day you must sacrifice a one-year-old male lamb with no defects as a burnt offering to the LORD.

13 With it you must present a grain offering consisting of four quarts of choice flour moistened with olive oil. It will be a special gift, a pleasing aroma to the LORD. You must also offer one quart of wine as a liquid offering.

14 Do not eat any bread or roasted grain or fresh kernels on that day until you bring this offering to your God. This is a permanent law for you, and it must be observed from generation to generation wherever you live.

22 "When you harvest the crops of your land, do not harvest the grain along the edges of your fields, and do not pick up what the harvesters drop. Leave it for the poor and the foreigners living among you. I am the LORD your God."

The People, Places, and Times

Observation of Firstfruits. This Jewish celebration was linked to the observance of the Passover and the Festival of Harvest, another important time of observance for the Jewish people. The observation served as a reminder to the Israelites that the harvest they had belonged to God and was a result of God's goodness. Whereas Old Testament scholars have had some debate about the initiation of the Passover and the Festival of Unleavened Bread, the significance of these observances is traced back to God's provision of the people during their Exodus from Egypt (see Exodus 12:1–14:6). Likewise the offering of firstfruits was an opportunity to show thanks for God's provision by giving the first of the harvest back to God as an offering.

Harvest. The Passover, the Festival of Unleavened Bread, and the Festival of Harvest were annual Jewish observances that occurred during the spring harvest of barley grain. As an agricultural people dependent on crops, they had expectation and anticipation for a new harvest each spring. Scholars suggest that at each harvest, new crop would be prepared to be stored for the year while old crop from the previous harvest would be discarded, a significant occasion. To set aside time to commemorate God's past and present provisions by taking specific actions with the crop only increased the significance given to the harvest.

What celebrations or special occasions have been selected to be observed by your family and/or church to commemorate God's blessings and provisions for His people?

Background

Leviticus details the laws God gave to the Israelites. While some might sound foreign to modern ears, following them had a great amount of importance for the Israelites then.

Laws provided guidance for daily living, intended to maintain Israel's identity as God's people. The word "covenant" is key here. God and Israel had formed a covenant relationship tracing back to the days of Abraham, Isaac, and Jacob, and now with Moses and Israel. This covenant had terms, and certain laws were instituted to keep the relationship with God in right standing.

The setting of the book is post-exodus from Egypt and pre-entrance into the land that God had promised their ancestors. The Israelites are journeying there, and as they journey toward the destiny God has determined, He prepares them for life in the new land.

Preparation for this new life in Canaan included ensuring that the Israelites did not forget about God or diverge from their identity as His chosen vessels to bless the earth.

Therefore, God directs them to follow very specific rituals and laws, ranging in degree of importance and of type. For example, laws cover making proper sacrifices, maintaining individual and community purity, and keeping the community holy as God is holy. One of these rituals is found in today's passage in Leviticus 23.

Why are laws important in creating balance, order, and unity in society?

At-A-Glance

1. God Provides for Israel (Leviticus 23:9–10)
2. Israel's Offering Back to God (vv. 11–14)
3. God Provides Through Israel (v. 22)

In Depth

1. God Provides for Israel (Leviticus 23:9–10)

This section opens with God speaking through His mediator, Moses, to the Israelites, as God has done throughout their journey out of Egypt and toward the Promised Land. While the last part of verse 10 is God's instruction to Israel, the first half of the verse describes His goodness to Israel. In this way, the covenant relationship between God and Israel is on display; God will fulfill His covenant, which He had confirmed to Moses (Exodus 34).

Two important statements made in the second half of verse 10 cannot be overstated. In this short phrase, "When ye be come into the land which I give unto you, and shall reap the harvest thereof," God confirms that (1) He is indeed leading this nomadic people to a land; (2) this land will be Israel's to inhabit and cultivate; and (3) God will bless them with a fruitful harvest. These words assure that God will continue to bless Israel.

When God promises to provide sustenance as well as additional blessings for us, do we have a tendency to develop into arrogant or grateful people? Why or why not?

2. Israel's Offering Back to God (vv. 11–14)

This section depicts the responsibility God gives the people after they enter the land and begin reaping its benefits. Before doing anything else with the harvest, they must turn their attention toward God. By bringing the first of the harvest to the priest who submits it to God as an offering, Israel symbolizes that they have not forgotten that God freed them from Egypt, sustained them through the wilderness, provided the land of Canaan, and brought forth the harvest's abundance. By submitting their very first crop, they emphasize not fulfilling their personal or communal hunger, but honoring the Lord.

The last statement in this passage indicates the permanence of this ritual. God did not ask Israel to do this once, but to make it a practice that would endure "forever throughout your generations in all your dwellings" (v. 14). Recognition and acknowledgment of God's provision and blessings throughout Israel's history would be an annual ritual at the spring harvest.

If everything we own comes from God, why is it so difficult for us to decide to give our first and best offering to Him?

3. God Provides Through Israel (v. 22)

This passage displays the deep compassion God has for the "least of these," the people on the margins who had uncertainty about their next meal. "The poor" and "the stranger" are people who also should receive God's steadfast love and provision (the narrative of Ruth tells of harvesters who put into practice God's demand; see Ruth 2).

The Israelites are required to embody the same love God has for the poor and foreigners in society, not to ignore them or hoard their crops. This passage also indicates that God has not provided only enough for Israel, but more than enough so that Israel can be a blessing to others. God has chosen to give provisions to Israel so that He can give to others through them.

What causes us to hesitate and assess people before giving to the poor and needy who approach us seeking assistance?

Search the Scriptures

1. What might be the significance of giving God the first crops, as opposed to the second or third (Leviticus 23:10)?

2. What does the permanence of this ritual mean for the future of Israel (Leviticus 23:14)?

Discuss the Meaning

Agricultural labor is not easy work, and there is no guarantee that labor would result in an abundant crop. A first crop brings excitement, but a second or third crop might not come. What feelings, thoughts, or concerns might Israel have needed to overcome to arrive at a point where they would willingly give their first crops to God?

Lesson in Our Society

Our everyday needs can sometimes become obstacles for expressing gratitude to God for His blessings and provisions in our lives. How often do we let paying the bills, buying necessities, and splurging a bit on ourselves take priority over thanking God for our finances and giving cheerfully back to Him through tithes or generous and sacrificial offerings? God's demands for the Israelites are what He also expects from all His children. As provider of all that we have, God is pleased when we consciously remember His provisions and gratefully display our gratitude in giving. He is especially pleased when we teach our children and family to do the same.

If we consider the attitudes of our congregations during the offerings, what are we teaching our younger generations about giving to God?

Make It Happen

• Copy and post verses in a prominent place as a reminder to give to God first.

• Create a list of ten things that are valuable to you and commit to giving one of those things away as an act of worship.

• Write in your journal about how it feels to give away something that is valuable to you as an offering to God.

Follow the Spirit

What God wants me to do:

_____

_____

_____

_____

Remember Your Thoughts

Special insights I have learned:

_____

_____

_____

_____

More Light on the Text

Leviticus 23:9–14, 22

In Leviticus 23, God sets regulations for the major festivals and feasts for the Israelites.

After stipulating the rules for the Sabbath and the Passover, God tells Moses about this observation of the first fruits. This is different from the Feast of the First Fruits, which God details next (Leviticus 23:15–21). The other holidays detailed in this chapter are the Feast of Trumpets, the Day of Atonement, and the Feast of Booths.

The Israelites celebrated three pilgrimage festivals yearly. While some commentators designate all three festivals as agricultural because they follow the agricultural season, the Festival of Unleavened Bread is a historical commemoration of their freedom from slavery in Egypt (in addition to coinciding with the barley harvest). The two agricultural pilgrimage festivals are the Feast of the First Fruits and the Feast of Ingathering. The Feast of the First Fruits at the beginning of the wheat harvest was held fifty days after Passover, also known as Pentecost and the Feast of Weeks. The Feast of Ingathering at the beginning of the grape harvest was also called the Festival of Booths.

While the Passover was the first day of the Feast of Unleavened Bread, the waving of the sheaf took place at the end of the feast. This springtime celebration was in the month Aviv (later called Nisan, contemporary March-April), the month Israel left Egypt. Therefore, it carried a sense of gratitude and memorial. This was a time for the Israelites to remember their deliverance from their former state of slavery in Egypt. As a first fruits offering, the time also symbolized an assurance of a good harvest. It is likely no mistake that this celebration would later coincide with the day of Resurrection. Jesus' resurrection as first fruit among the dead is an assurance of our resurrection (1 Corinthians 15:20).

9 And the LORD spake unto Moses, saying.

The Lord (Heb. *Yahweh*, **YAH-weh**) had brought the Children of Israel out of the land of Egypt under the leadership of Moses. After three months of journey in the desert, they arrived at Sinai (Exodus 19:1–2), where the Lord spoke directly to them in a fearful and solemn manner. They therefore requested that Moses should speak to them on behalf of the Lord so they will not perish (Exodus 20:18–19). From then on, Moses listened to God and conveyed His message to the rest of the people.

10 Speak unto the children of Israel, and say unto them, when ye be come into the land which I give unto you, and shall reap the harvest thereof, then ye shall bring a sheaf of the first fruits of your harvest unto the priest.

Once the people arrive in the land, the Lord deserves their honor and gratitude through the fruits of their labor. The word for "first fruits" (Heb. *re'shit*, **ray-SHEET**) describes the crop that ripens first, but also that which is best, chief, and foremost. The Lord deserves the first place in the life of His people and the finest things of our belongings, and He expects nothing less than the best from us.

In bringing the first fruits to the Lord, the Israelites were expressing their gratitude to Him for His faithfulness, but also their faith in His continued provision. With this small offering of a single sheaf of barley, they recognize that all of their future harvest is also from God. Each year, the Israelites would remind themselves of God's power and favor for giving them a good harvest as well as His faithfulness to give them a harvest in the future.

11 And he shall wave the sheaf before the LORD, to be accepted for you: on the morrow after the sabbath the priest shall wave it.

The gesture symbolizes a presentation to God. The acceptance of the offering is connected to the place it was waved. It should be waved "before the LORD" which means in the house of God (Exodus 23:19).

"On the morrow after the Sabbath" could mean Sunday, if the Sabbath it refers to is the regular seventh day, or it could mean the fifteenth of Nisan if it refers to the Passover Sabbath. Most commentators, however, favor the later Sunday as the day for this offering. This understanding works well with Leviticus 23:15, which counts 50 days after this wave offering to the Feast of First Fruits.

12 And ye shall offer that day when ye wave the sheaf an he lamb without blemish of the first year for a burnt offering unto the LORD.

The day the sheaf is waved, a male yearling lamb without blemish is offered as a burnt offering. Most offerings to the Lord demanded an unblemished animal (Exodus 12:5; Leviticus 1:10, 22:21). The Lord deserves honor and we have to give Him the most precious offering (Malachi 1:8). Following this sacrificial language, the New Testament presents Jesus as the Lamb of God who takes away the sin of the world (John 1:29), and as a Lamb without blemish and without spot (1 Peter 1:19).

A burnt offering (Heb. *olah*, **oh-LAW**) is an offering that is burnt completely to ashes on the altar. It cannot be eaten, neither by the priest nor by the donor. A burnt offering atones for the worshiper's sins and restores fellowship between a sinner and a holy God. Some take it as a symbol of total consecration to the Lord.

13 And the meat offering thereof shall be two tenth deals of fine flour mingled with oil, an offering made by fire unto the LORD for a sweet savor: and the drink offering thereof shall be of wine, the fourth part of an hin.

The King James translates *minchah* (Heb. **min-KHAH**) as "meat offering," but it actually refers to an offering of grain. It was made of the best wheat flour mixed with oil and salt, but honey and yeast were prohibited. A portion of the dough was burnt on the altar and the rest was for the priest to eat.

"Two tenth deals" of flour is about four pounds or fourteen cups. This offering is a sign of dedication to God. The "sweet savor," or soothing aroma, often represents the people's prayers raising favorably to God.

A drink offering (Heb. *nesek*, **NEH-sek**), or libation, is a liquid offering (usually wine) that is actually not ingested at all, but poured out. This particular drink offering measures to the fourth part of an hin, or about 1.5 liters, and was poured at the base of the altar. Note how the drink offering, the burnt offering, and most of the grain offering are all devoted to the altar, given to God and not consumed by the people. As they offer food and drink that they could have enjoyed themselves, they demonstrate their faith in God.

14 And ye shall eat neither bread, nor parched corn, nor green ears, until the self-same day that ye have brought an offering unto your God: it shall be a statute forever throughout your generations in all your dwellings.

Unless the sheaf is waved and all the accompanying offerings are made, no one could eat from harvested barley. Once the Israelites settle in the land, the most important thing for them to remember is that the whole land is God's, and so they cannot enjoy the harvest without first giving God a portion.

This regulation and the entire law had to be passed down throughout the generations (Exodus 12:24). "In all your dwellings" deals with the application of this law throughout the entire land in which the Israelites would live.

22 And when ye reap the harvest of your land, thou shalt not make clean riddance of the corners of thy field when thou reapest, neither shalt thou gather any gleaning of thy harvest: thou shalt leave them unto the poor, and to the stranger: I am the LORD your God.

After making it clear that the Lord has to be first in the life of the people demonstrated by the waving of the first sheaf, verse 22 addresses how neighbors are treated, particularly the deprived. Jesus summarized the Law as loving God with all our heart, mind, soul, and strength, and our neighbor as ourselves (Matthew 22:37–39). God therefore urges the people to remember the poor and the stranger by leaving some crops for them to glean. Ruth and her mother-in-law took advantage of this law in the field of Boaz when they returned from Moab(Ruth 2:1–3).

Sources:

Botterweck, J.G. *Theological Dictionary of the Old Testament*, vol. 2. Grand Rapids, MI: William B. Eerdmans, 1977.

Harris, L.R. Leviticus. In F.E. Gabelein, *The Expositor's Bible Commentary* vol. 2. Grand Rapids, MI: Zondervan, 1990. 501–654.

Harrison, R.K. *Tyndale Old Testament Commentaries*. Edited by D.J. Wiseman, Downers Grove, IL: InterVarsity Press, 1980.

Hartley, J.E. *Word Biblical Commentary: Leviticus*. Dallas: Word Books, 1992.

Levine, B.A. *The Jews Publication Society: Leviticus*. Edited by N. M. Sarna. Philadelphia: The Jews Publication Society, 1989.

Say It Correctly

Hin. **HIN.**
Riddance. ri-**DEN(T)S.**

Daily Bible Readings

MONDAY
Honor God with Your First Fruits
(Proverbs 3:1–10)

TUESDAY
Martyrs, First Fruits for God
(Revelation 14:1–5)

WEDNESDAY
Gifts, a Pleasing Sacrifice to God
(Philippians 4:15–20)

THURSDAY
Preparing Grain Offerings
(Leviticus 2:1–10, 14)

FRIDAY
Acceptable Offerings are Without Blemish
(Leviticus 22:17–20)

SATURDAY
Observing the Sabbaths and the Festivals
(Leviticus 23:1–8)

SUNDAY
Present Your Fruits to God First
(Leviticus 23:9–14, 22)

Notes

_____

_____

_____

_____

Teaching Tips

Words You Should Know

A. Jubilee (Leviticus 25:10–12) *yobel* (Gk.)—Ram's horn, trumpet, jubilee year.

B. Hallow (v. 10) *qadash* (Heb.)—To dedicate, make sacred or holy.

Teacher Preparation

Unifying Principle—A Wake-up Call. People hold a sense of entitlement when it comes to their wealth, possessions, and land. How can they be freed from their possessions possessing them? God called the covenant people to active, responsible, and joyful stewardship of all God had given them.

A. Read the Bible Background and Devotional Readings.

B. Pray that you are an example to your students.

C. Read the Lesson Scripture in multiple translations.

D. Secure a Monopoly board for the Make It Happen activity.

O—Open the Lesson

A. Open with prayer and ask God's assistance in today's lesson.

B. Have the students read the Aim for Change silently.

C. Read the Keep In Mind verse and discuss.

P—Present the Scriptures

A. Have volunteers read the Focal Verses.

B. Read The People, Places, and Times; Background; In Depth; and More Light on the Text sections and discuss.

E—Explore the Meaning

A. Discuss the Lesson in Our Society and Make It Happen sections.

B. Ask students to share the most significant point they learned in the lesson and how they will seek to incorporate it this week.

N—Next Steps for Application

A. Complete the Follow the Spirit and Remember Your Thoughts sections.

B. Close in prayer, thanking God for His presence in class and continued guidance in our lives.

Worship Guide

For the Superintendent or Teacher
Theme: Remembering with Joy
Song: "Blessed" by Fred Hammond
Devotional Reading: Psalm 50:1–15

Remembering with Joy

Bible Background • LEVITICUS 25
Printed Text • LEVITICUS 25:1–12 | Devotional Reading • PSALM 50:1–5

Aim for Change

By the end of the lesson, we will: EVALUATE the implications for land ownership in Israel in the year of Jubilee; ASPIRE to reflecting biblical values in giving; and DESIGN a plan for faithful sharing of personal wealth.

 In Focus

Justin couldn't believe what he was seeing. All of his five senses were overwhelmed. He had never seen poverty like this before. As he walked through the different makeshift shacks and huts in the slums, his heart began to break. The children that approached him were smiling, yet they barely had clothes to wear. His mission trip was showing him a side of the world that he had only seen on TV.

As he walked into the house of one of the leaders, they began a conversation. The leader's name was hard to pronounce, so most of the mission team just called him Jay. Jay began to explain the situation to them: "The way we gauge whether we had a good or bad day is how many meals we have eaten. Some people have just a breakfast kind of day or just a breakfast and dinner kind of day. When you have three whole meals that is something worth celebrating."

"Wow," Justin said. Jay continued, "Our land is filled with abundant resources to provide everything we need to live. It breaks our hearts and pains our stomachs, to see the very food we labor to produce is taken away and shipped off to other countries because of trade regulations. Laziness isn't keeping us in poverty, it's greed and injustice." Justin shook his head. Right then Justin committed to doing what he could to help those who did not have enough.

Life is not about hoarding and accumulating goods for our own personal gain. What can we do to make sure everyone has enough?

Keep in Mind

"And you shall hallow the fiftieth year and you shall proclaim liberty throughout the land to all its inhabitants. It shall be a jubilee for you: you shall return, every one of you, to your property and every one of you to your family" (Leviticus 25:10).

"And you shall hallow the fiftieth year and you shall proclaim liberty throughout the land to all its inhabitants. It shall be a jubilee for you: you shall return, every one of you, to your property and every one of you to your family" (Leviticus 25:10).

Focal Verses

KJV **Leviticus 25:1** And the LORD spake unto Moses in mount Sinai, saying,

2 Speak unto the children of Israel, and say unto them, When ye come into the land which I give you, then shall the land keep a sabbath unto the LORD.

3 Six years thou shalt sow thy field, and six years thou shalt prune thy vineyard, and gather in the fruit thereof;

4 But in the seventh year shall be a sabbath of rest unto the land, a sabbath for the LORD: thou shalt neither sow thy field, nor prune thy vineyard.

5 That which groweth of its own accord of thy harvest thou shalt not reap, neither gather the grapes of thy vine undressed: for it is a year of rest unto the land.

6 And the sabbath of the land shall be meat for you; for thee, and for thy servant, and for thy maid, and for thy hired servant, and for thy stranger that sojourneth with thee.

7 And for thy cattle, and for the beast that are in thy land, shall all the increase thereof be meat.

8 And thou shalt number seven sabbaths of years unto thee, seven times seven years; and the space of the seven sabbaths of years shall be unto thee forty and nine years.

9 Then shalt thou cause the trumpet of the jubile to sound on the tenth day of the seventh month, in the day of atonement shall ye make the trumpet sound throughout all your land.

10 And ye shall hallow the fiftieth year, and proclaim liberty throughout all the land unto all the inhabitants thereof: it shall be a jubile unto you; and ye shall return every man unto his possession, and ye shall return every man unto his family.

11 A jubile shall that fiftieth year be unto you: ye shall not sow, neither reap that which

NLT **Leviticus 25:1** While Moses was on Mount Sinai, the LORD said to him,

2 "Give the following instructions to the people of Israel. When you have entered the land I am giving you, the land itself must observe a Sabbath rest before the LORD every seventh year.

3 For six years you may plant your fields and prune your vineyards and harvest your crops,

4 but during the seventh year the land must have a Sabbath year of complete rest. It is the LORD's Sabbath. Do not plant your fields or prune your vineyards during that year.

5 And don't store away the crops that grow on their own or gather the grapes from your unpruned vines. The land must have a year of complete rest.

6 But you may eat whatever the land produces on its own during its Sabbath. This applies to you, your male and female servants, your hired workers, and the temporary residents who live with you.

7 Your livestock and the wild animals in your land will also be allowed to eat what the land produces.

8 "In addition, you must count off seven Sabbath years, seven sets of seven years, adding up to forty-nine years in all.

9 Then on the Day of Atonement in the fiftieth year, blow the ram's horn loud and long throughout the land.

10 Set this year apart as holy, a time to proclaim freedom throughout the land for all who live there. It will be a jubilee year for you, when each of you may return to the land that belonged to your ancestors and return to your own clan.

11 This fiftieth year will be a jubilee for you. During that year you must not plant your fields or store away any of the crops that grow groweth of itself in it, nor gather the grapes in it of thy vine undressed.

12 For it is the jubilee; it shall be holy unto you: ye shall eat the increase thereof out of the field.

on their own, and don't gather the grapes from your unpruned vines.

12 It will be a jubilee year for you, and you must keep it holy. But you may eat whatever the land produces on its own.

The People, Places, and Times

Day of Atonement. The Day of Atonement is considered the most important holiday in the Jewish calendar. Usually celebrated in mid-September or mid-October, this holiday was the day that the high priest went beyond the veil in the Temple to atone for the sins of Israel. The high priest would take the blood of a young bull and sprinkle it over the mercy seat, which was on top of the Ark of the Covenant. There he would confess the sins of the nation. On this day, the Children of Israel were required to "afflict their souls," which is believed to mean fasting (Leviticus 23:27, 29, 32).

Trumpet. This instrument was usually created out of a ram's horn. Moses also commissioned straight metal trumpets as well (Numbers 10:10). These trumpets were not musical instruments, but were used to signal a proclamation or warning to the people. Their use was mostly for announcing public events such as war, a call to worship, or even claims to kingship (Judges 3:27; Isaiah 27:13; 1 Kings 1:34).

Why do you think the Day of Atonement (Yom Kippur) is considered the most important holiday in the Jewish calendar?

Background

Leviticus is a book filled with laws that governed how the Israelites, and particularly the priests, were to approach God. It is about holiness and how an unholy people could have a relationship with a holy God. These laws included instructions for how to offer sacrifices

and also for how to remain ritually clean in various circumstances.

The book also contained laws concerning the required feasts and holy days in the Israelite community. Leviticus 25 speaks of one of these holy days: the Year of Jubilee. In the Year of Jubilee, giving the land rest and freeing others from bondage is not only good, it is also a requirement for communal holiness. In God's eyes, we must take care of the land and our brothers and sisters.

Do you think the abundance of laws turns people off from reading the book of Leviticus? Why or why not?

At-A-Glance

1. Give the Land Rest (Leviticus 25:1–5)
2. Let God Provide for You (vv. 6–7)
3. Proclaim Liberty (vv. 8–12)

In Depth

1. Give the Land Rest (Leviticus 25:1–5)

Moses is speaking to the people of Israel regarding the command for them not only to personally take a Sabbath, but also grant the land a time of rest as well. For six years, the Israelites are to work the land, and on the seventh year, the land is supposed to have rest, without sowing or plowing, nor pruning or gathering of the harvest. The land is supposed to lie still.

This rest was to happen for a whole year. This Sabbath rest for the land was a display of the reality of the Israelites' position as stewards of the land and not its owners. God gave them the land as a gift, and therefore they were charged to take care of it. Christians are to have this perspective in every area of life; we are stewards and do not own anything. This should cause us to pause and remember the God who is the source of all of our gifts.

Since most of us do not have an agricultural lifestyle, how can we practice this command of allowing the land to take a sabbath?

2. Let God Provide for You (vv. 6–7)

While the previous verses state that no gathering was supposed to happen, many commentators have reflected that organized agricultural practice is in view. Otherwise, the allowances of vv. 6–7 contradict what the Israelites are commanded to abstain from in vv. 4–5. What Moses is saying to the Israelites is that they are to abstain from organized agricultural production and only eat from the fields what is necessary for sustaining their lives.

These verses are a reminder that God has provided everything necessary for us. Our task is not to slave and grind constantly in order to live. Many of our endeavors are driven by selfish ambition and greed. God provides for all of His children and we are to enjoy and remember that He, not we, sustains life.

Would it be hard to obey the command to cease from work?

3. Proclaim Liberty (vv. 8–12)

The Israelites are to not only give the land rest, but also proclaim liberty to the enslaved. After seven Sabbaths of years (49 years), they were to blow the trumpet on the Day of Atonement and signal an emancipation of all slaves and the return of property taken as payment for debt. This Year of Jubilee would have the same instructions regarding the land as other Sabbath years—no organized

agricultural labor was to take place, but the people would eat from the uncultivated increase to sustain life.

No record of biblical history indicates that the Israelites actually practiced the Year of Jubilee. In fact, the prophet Jeremiah says that punishment from God came to Israel because they failed to give the land rest. The command to practice a Sabbath of Sabbaths highlights the importance that God places on the common good as opposed to the selfish pursuit of individual gain.

Do you believe it would be beneficial to have a national program to free people from debt? Why or why not?

Search the Scriptures

1. What implication is there for us today that God set aside every seven years to give the land rest (Leviticus 25:4)?

2. Since the Israelites were only allowed to eat what the field produced on its own during the Year of Jubilee, what does this say about their reliance on God (v. 12)?

Discuss the Meaning

1. In light of the instructions to the Israelites regarding the Year of Jubilee, what would God's Jubilee include in our time?

2. What can we learn about God's desire for our relationship with Him, others, and our property and employees from the institution of a Jubilee Year?

Lesson in Our Society

Economic equality and care for the earth are very controversial topics. As African Americans, these issues are very important to our history and our present. As descendants of slaves, we have been overlooked when it comes to a collective share in our country's wealth. Many have advocated for reparations to no avail. At the same time, our standard of living is higher than most of the world's just by virtue of living in the United States. Additionally, our country exploits other communities globally for resources and labor in order to provide luxuries to satisfy our greed.

Both of these problems can be solved through the faithful distribution of wealth. The Bible has a prescription: share so that no one has too little while others have more than enough. God's design for human flourishing is that everyone has enough. This can be championed through fighting for equitable and ethical business practices and legislation. It can also be championed in our own lives by distributing our abundance to the poor and destitute. God wants us all to have enough.

How does this lesson motivate you to care for the earth or fight for economic justice?

Make It Happen

• Using a Monopoly board, discuss how the rules of the game would change if based on Leviticus 25.

• Evaluate whether you have more than enough in the areas of food and clothing and decide whether to donate the excess to a charity organization, or to someone right in your church.

• Commit to sponsor a child through Compassion International: www.compassion.com.

Follow the Spirit

What God wants me to do:

_____

_____

_____

_____

Remember Your Thoughts

Special insights I have learned:

_____

_____

_____

_____

More Light on the Text
Leviticus 25:1–12

1 And the LORD spake unto Moses in mount Sinai, saying.

After leaving Egypt, the Israelites arrived at Mount Sinai three months later under Moses' leadership. The building of the Tabernacle and the Ark of the Covenant was completed the second year after their departure from Egypt (Exodus 40:17). From the Tabernacle, the Lord gave Moses the laws.

2 Speak unto the children of Israel, and say unto them, when ye come into the land which I give you, then shall the land keep a sabbath unto the LORD.

Some laws were to be implemented right there in the desert, but other laws had to be practiced once in the Promised Land. The Lord decided to give the land of Canaan to the descendants of Abraham after they stayed in a foreign land as slaves for four hundred years (Genesis 12:7, 15:13–21). Now they were in the wilderness, expecting to take possession of the land. The Lord therefore gives them instructions, as the real owner of the land, how to live in and take full advantage of all the blessings linked to it.

The Israelites must not work the land during the sabbatical year; it should be left fallow. The sabbatical year is built on the concept of rest after six days of work, as God did in Creation (Genesis 2:1–3). The will of God by this concept is to free the people from continuous labor so they could enjoy their new land and His blessing. It also acknowledges God's ownership of the land and boldly demonstrates the people's faith in Him for their food.

3 Six years thou shalt sow thy field, and six years thou shalt prune thy vineyard, and gather in the fruit thereof; 4 But in the seventh year shall be a sabbath of rest unto the land, a sabbath for the LORD: thou shalt neither sow thy field, nor prune thy vineyard.

Just as humans need rest, the land also needs a rest of one year after six years of being plowed. The sabbatical year is meant to honor God. Sowing and pruning of vineyards was forbidden.

As a theocracy, a nation governed by God, Israel integrated God in all the aspects of their lives. There was no separation between sacred and secular life as we have today. Besides the spiritual aspects of rest, lying a land fallow also has benefits in that it reduces the quantity of harmful mineral deposits in the soil. This legislation about the land is both good agricultural and ecological practice. This one year period allows the land to replenish its nutrients and be more fertile for the other six years to come.

5 That which groweth of its own accord of thy harvest thou shalt not reap, neither gather the grapes of thy vine undressed: for it is a year of rest unto the land. 6 And the sabbath of the land shall be meat for you; for thee, and for thy servant, and for thy maid, and for thy hired servant, and for thy stranger that sojourneth with thee, 7 And for thy cattle, and for the beast that are in thy land, shall all the increase thereof be meat.

"That which groweth of its own accord" (Heb. *safiakh*, **sah-FEE-akh**) is a reference to what grows naturally the season after seeds

fall to the ground. While verse 5 says that they shall not reap nor gather the grapes of the vine, verse 6 states that what grows by itself should be food for the slave, the foreigner, the landowner, and even domestic and wild animals. These two verses seem to contradict, but the intent is made clear when one realizes what was forbidden is the regular harvest work involving the servants and storage.

There should be no organized farming, sowing, pruning, or reaping. What grows by itself in the seventh year does not belong to anyone in particular, but has been given by the Lord for the benefit of all. The sabbatical year therefore also served as a time of alleviating the suffering of the poor.

This cycle of seven years is seen several other places in the Old Testament Law. The sabbatical year was a year of freedom for slaves (Exodus 21:2; Jeremiah 34:14). Unfortunately, Israel fails to keep the instructions of the covenant, which is part of the reason for their deportation to Babylon (Jeremiah 34:16–21). Debts were to be canceled during the sabbatical year (Deuteronomy 15:1–3), and the Law should be publicly read during the Feast of Tabernacles (Deuteronomy 31:10–12).

8 And thou shalt number seven Sabbaths of years unto thee, seven times seven years; and the space of the seven Sabbaths of years shall be unto thee forty and nine years. 9 Then shalt thou cause the trumpet of the jubilee to sound on the tenth day of the seventh month, in the day of atonement shall ye make the trumpet sound throughout all your land.

Seven Sabbaths of years, or seven cycles of sabbatical years, were times of celebration. On the Day of Atonement, a trumpet was blown to mark the beginning of the Year of Jubilee. The English word "jubilee" is derived from the Hebrew word used here, *yovel* (**yo-VEL**), which means ram or ram's horn. The Israelites used the ram's horn as a trumpet, sounded at the beginning of the year. It is from the same root as the name Jubal, the first person ever to play the harp and the flute (Genesis 4:21).

10 And ye shall hallow the fiftieth year, and proclaim liberty throughout all the land unto all the inhabitants thereof: it shall be a jubile unto you; and ye shall return every man unto his possession, and ye shall return every man unto his family.

The Year of Jubilee was a proclamation of freedom throughout the land of Israel. As in a sabbatical year, slaves were released. "Liberty" (Heb. *deror*, **deh-ROAR**) designates an edict of release and refers to the freedom granted to those bound by servitude. The Hebrew word carries the idea of flowing freedom of movement. This idea of freedom for the captive remains a key issue with God, as Jesus proclaims in His first public sermon that He has came to set the captives free (Luke 4:18).

Jubilee also granted a redemption of property. God, who owns the whole earth, granted the land to Israel as an everlasting possession. Each tribe, clan, and family's land was not secured by individual military prowess, but rather divided by sacred lot. The rest of Leviticus 25 (vv. 13–55) details how land, houses, debts, and slaves should be dealt with in light of the Year of Jubilee. For example, the jubilee requires any purchaser of land to return it to the original owner, so the purchase price must be proportional to the number of years to the next jubilee (vv. 15–16).

11 A jubile shall that fiftieth year be unto you: ye shall not sow, neither reap that which groweth of itself in it, nor gather the grapes in it of thy vine undressed. 12 For it is the jubile; it shall be holy unto you: ye shall eat the increase thereof out of the field.

Scholars debate whether the forty-ninth year, which is a sabbatical year (v. 8), and the fiftieth year, which is a jubilee year (v. 11), are the same. If they were two different years, it means that the people had to leave the land unplowed and unharvested for two consecutive years. However, the Hebrews, along with several other cultures of the region at the time, counted inclusively, so that it is likely the forthninth year was the Year of Jubilee.

As in the sabbatical year, sowing and reaping were not allowed during the jubilee. But, again like the sabbatical year, what grows by itself from the previous harvest constitutes food. The people are not to work diligently in a harvest to make sure all the crop was brought in, but they could bring in enough to satisfy themselves for the year.

The whole Year of Jubilee was to be seen as holy (Heb. *qodesh*, **ko-DESH**) for the Israelites, meaning it was set apart for God. This was a year to remember how God provided for their physical needs (land and harvest), as well as for their economic needs (freedom from slavery and return of property). The sabbatical year and the Year of Jubilee were a program of agricultural economy and social justice meant to reduce social inequalities and promote a community of mutual support.

Sources:
Harris, L.R. *Leviticus. In F. E. Gabelein, The Expositor's Bible Commentary vol. 2.* Grand Rapids, MI: Zondervan, 1990. 501–654.
Harrison, R.K. *Tyndale Old Testament Commentaries.* Edited by D.J. Wiseman. Downers Grove, IL: InterVarsity Press, 1980.
Hartley, J.E. *Word Biblical Commentary: Leviticus.* Dallas: Word Books, 1992.
Levine, B.A. *The Jews Publication Society:Leviticus.* Edited by N. M. Sarna. Philadelphia: The Jews Publication Society, 1989.
Péter-Contesse, R., & Ellington, J. *A Handbook on Leviticus.* Broadway: United Bible Societies, 1990.
Wenham, G.J. *The New International Commentary on the Old Testament.* Grand Rapids, MI: W. B. Eerdmans, 1979.

Say It Correctly

Jubile. joo-bi-**LEE**.
Sojourneth. so-**JER**-nith.

Daily Bible Readings

MONDAY
Keeping the Sabbath Yields Good Crops
(Leviticus 26:3–6)

TUESDAY
Lands and Houses Shared with All
(Acts 4:32–37)

WEDNESDAY
Bear Each Other's Burdens
(Galatians 6:1–5)

THURSDAY
I Will Maintain Covenant with You
(Leviticus 26:9–13)

FRIDAY
Fairness in Buying and Selling Property
(Leviticus 25:13–17)

SATURDAY
Helping One Another Face Difficulties
(Leviticus 25:35–38)

SUNDAY
Sabbatical Year and Year of Jubilee
(Leviticus 25:1–12)

Notes

_____

_____

_____

_____

Teaching Tips

Words You Should Know

A. Fears (Psalm 34:4) *megura* (Heb.)—Terrors, horrors, an entity that causes pain or terror.

B. Fear (v. 7) *yare* (Heb.)—To reverence, to fear, to hold in awe.

Teacher Preparation

Unifying Principle—More than Good. People want relief from their fears and brokenness. Where does such hope come from? Hopes for restoration are found through God's gift of Jesus Christ and His sacrifice.

A. Read the Bible Background and Devotional Readings.

B. Pray for understanding and clarity.

C. Read the Focal Verses in two or more translations.

O—Open the Lesson

A. Ask a volunteer to open the class with prayer.

B. Have a volunteer read the In Focus story. Discuss the impact ungodly behavior has on personal relationships, family members, and other innocent people.

C. State the Aim for Change.

P—Present the Scriptures

A. Ask for a volunteer to read the Focal Verses.

B. Examine the verses, utilizing Words You Should Know; The People, Places, and Times; Background; the At-A-Glance outline; and More Light on the Text sections.

E—Explore the Meaning

A. Answer the Search the Scriptures questions.

B. Answer questions from the Discuss the Meaning section.

C. Summarize the Lesson in Our Society section and relate it to today's theme.

N—Next Steps for Application

A. Summarize the lesson and encourage students to apply the Make It Happen section to their lives.

B. Remind students to read and meditate on their Daily Bible Readings.

C. Solicit prayer requests and close in prayer.

Worship Guide

For the Superintendent and Teacher
Theme: Rejoicing in Restoration
Song: "Trouble Don't Last Always"
Devotional Reading: Hebrews 7:20–28

Rejoicing in Restoration

Bible Background • LEVITICUS 16; PSALM 34; HEBREWS 2:5–18
Printed Text • PSALM 34:1–10; HEBREWS 2:17–18 | Devotional Reading • HEBREWS 7:20–28

—————— Aim for Change ——————

By the end of this lesson, we will: IDENTIFY the mercy and faithfulness of God; APPRECIATE the faithfulness of God; and PRAY for God's will for restoration for all people to be realized.

————————  In Focus ————————

Jamal never thought he would see this day. It had been ten years since he had been sentenced for a crime he didn't commit. Walking outside was like experiencing a whole new world. He couldn't help but smile as he saw his brother Jerome waiting in a car to pick him up. Just ten years ago, he was riding along in a car with a neighborhood friend when they were stopped by the police. His friend had stolen the car, but while they were being interrogated, he told the police that Jamal was an accomplice. Jamal was angry when he found out. *How could something like this happen to me?* he thought. He was on his way to college and couldn't have imagined being caught up in something like this.

Instead of being bitter, Jamal turned to faith. He found some men who were following the Lord and decided to do all he could to lean on Him while in prison. It wasn't easy. There were times when Jamal wanted to die. He faced so many dark days, but God had always been his light.

Now that he was free, Jamal had a sense of purpose. He didn't want to see any more young Black men caught up in the system, especially when they didn't deserve it. He knew he couldn't do it alone. That's why on Sunday morning, he would be the first one there to give God praise for bringing him through such a difficult time.

God's mercy and faithfulness are there for us even during times of crisis. Describe a time when you had to trust God in a difficult situation.

—————— Keep in Mind ——————

"O taste and see that the LORD is good: blessed is the man that trusteth in him"
(Psalm 34:8).

"O taste and see that the LORD is good: blessed is the man that trusteth in him" (Psalm 34:8).

Focal Verses

KJV **Psalm 34:1** [A Psalm of David, when he changed his behaviour before Abimelech; who drove him away, and he departed.] I will bless the LORD at all times: his praise shall continually be in my mouth.

2 My soul shall make her boast in the LORD: the humble shall hear thereof, and be glad.

3 O magnify the LORD with me, and let us exalt his name together.

4 I sought the LORD, and he heard me, and delivered me from all my fears.

5 They looked unto him, and were lightened: and their faces were not ashamed.

6 This poor man cried, and the LORD heard him, and saved him out of all his troubles.

7 The angel of the LORD encampeth round about them that fear him, and delivereth them.

8 O taste and see that the LORD is good: blessed is the man that trusteth in him.

9 O fear the LORD, ye his saints: for there is no want to them that fear him.

10 The young lions do lack, and suffer hunger: but they that seek the Lord shall not want any good thing.

Hebrews 2:17 Wherefore in all things it behoved him to be made like unto his brethren, that he might be a merciful and faithful high priest in things pertaining to God, to make reconciliation for the sins of the people.

18 For in that he himself hath suffered being tempted, he is able to succour them that are tempted.

NLT **Psalm 34:1** [A psalm of David, regarding the time he pretended to be insane in front of Abimelech, who sent him away.] I will praise the LORD at all times I will constantly speak his praises.

2 I will boast only in the LORD; let all who are helpless take heart.

3 Come, let us tell of the LORD's greatness; let us exalt his name together.

4 I prayed to the LORD, and he answered me. He freed me from all my fears.

5 Those who look to him for help will be radiant with joy; no shadow of shame will darken their faces.

6 In my desperation I prayed, and the LORD listened; he saved me from all my troubles.

7 For the angel of the LORD is a guard; he surrounds and defends all who fear him.

8 Taste and see that the LORD is good. Oh, the joys of those who take refuge in him!

9 Fear the LORD, you his godly people, for those who fear him will have all they need.

10 Even strong young lions sometimes go hungry, but those who trust in the LORD will lack no good thing.

Hebrews 2:17 Therefore, it was necessary for him to be made in every respect like us, his brothers and sisters, so that he could be our merciful and faithful High Priest before God. Then he could offer a sacrifice that would take away the sins of the people.

18 Since he himself has gone through suffering and testing, he is able to help us when we are being tested.

The People, Places, and Times

Psalmist. Many different people composed the Psalms, but King David is thought to have written most of them. No one knows how many unattributed psalms David wrote, but since he was known for writing psalms and playing the harp, his name is significantly attached to the book. Others were written by the sons of

Korah, who were leaders in Temple worship. Some psalms are also attributed to Moses, Asaph, and Solomon.

Achish/Abimelech. The Philistine king of Gath during the time of Saul was a man named Achish. Once, David had to pretend to be insane to avoid him (1 Samuel 21:10–15). Later, Achish hired David as a mercenary fighter (1 Samuel 27:1–4) but excused him from participating in a war against Israel (1 Samuel 29). He also gave David the city of Ziklag (1 Samuel 27:6). Achish seems to be his personal name, while Abimelech, which means "my father is king," is probably the royal title for Philistine kings.

What is your favorite psalm?

Background

In Psalm 34, David praises God for helping him narrowly escape the clutches of King Abimelech. During this time, David was on the run from Saul and had recently left the scene of Doeg the Edomite's slaughter of the priests. With nowhere to go, he decides to head into Philistine territory. While there, David could not escape his identity as an Israelite. The Philistine commanders recounted the songs sung about David and his victories against the Philistines. Overhearing this, David begins to drool and scratch on the doors. King Achish refuses to allow David to remain in his court. In this way, David narrowly escapes the Philistines' wrath.

Psalm 34 is an acrostic based on all the letters of the Hebrew alphabet except one. The first part (vv. 1–10) is David's testimony in regards to God's loving care and deliverance. The second part (vv. 11–20) includes the truths that anyone can stand on during a time of crisis like he experienced, running from not only Saul but also being saved from the Philistines.

Have you ever experienced a time where you narrowly escaped trouble or death?

At-A-Glance

1. The Call to Worship (Psalm 34:1–3)
2. The Recall of Deliverance (vv. 4–6)
3. Calling Out the Faithful (vv. 7–10)
4. Call on Jesus (Hebrews 2:17–18)

In Depth

1. The Call to Worship (Psalm 34:1–3)

At the beginning of Psalm 34, David expresses his praise and celebration on a personal level and invites others to join in. First he speaks of his own attitude and lifestyle of praise. His praise of the Lord is constant and ongoing, and he will boast only in the Lord. His boasting is exclusively about all that God can do and accomplish. As a result, the humble, or those who need help, will be glad because they will hear of the only One who can ultimately help them. Our praise can lift other people up as well. Lastly, he invites worshipers to speak of God's goodness and to worship Him corporately.

How can we encourage others to worship God with enthusiasm?

2. The Recall of Deliverance (vv. 4–6)

Next, David tells his personal testimony of his deliverance from King Achish of Gath. David recalls how he prayed to the Lord for deliverance from the Philistine king, and how the Lord freed him from all his fears. It shows that David was a man of prayer, even while faced with immediate danger. This is how we ought to be as well. We do not need to wait until a formal occasion to pray. Every occasion is an opportunity to ask God for help.

What would be the three main points in your personal testimony of God's goodness?

3. Calling Out the Faithful (vv. 7–10)

David then turns his attention to those who also worship the God of Israel. He lets them know that God's angel is there to protect them, and there is no better position to be in than to be able to experience God's goodness. David uses the figurative language of taste and sight to show how to truly enjoy His goodness.

People who fear God can enjoy this goodness and are delivered from all their fears. They will never want for any provision. He further reiterates God's care for the faithful by stating that they will not lack any good thing. David knows from experience that God will take care of him and anyone else who fears Him.

Is it hard to believe that those who are faithful and fear God are delivered from their fears and experience no lack? Why or why not?

4. Call on Jesus (Hebrews 2:17–18)

The writer of Hebrews lets his audience know that Jesus was made like us in His humanity. This was necessary so that He could not only experience our pain and weakness, but so that He could also be offered as a sacrifice for sin. Jesus is the High Priest as well as the sacrifice. Since He has gone through suffering, He can help whoever is going through a trial. He is the High Priest we can count on for help. When we face a trial like David, where we have no place to turn, we can call on Jesus for help.

Why is Jesus usually our last resort to turn to for help?

Search the Scriptures

1. Why does our boasting only in the Lord cause those who are helpless to be glad (Psalm 34:2)?

2. How can you taste and see that the Lord is good (v. 8)?

Discuss the Meaning

David trusted God and leaned on Him during hard times. He also used whatever means were at his disposal to get out of his situation. How can we discern whether our action is faith-based or fear-based?

Lesson in Our Society

It is certainly not hard to be overwhelmed by fear and brokenness. So many different news stories describe political conflict and oppression. Sometimes the violence and brutality shows up in our own neighborhoods from gangs or even the police who are supposed to protect us. On top of that, you might have to deal with your own personal family and finance issues. It's hard not to crack under the pressure of just trying to put food on the table and make ends meet.

This is why it is important to do what David did—call on God in times of crisis. This includes prayer and also rejoicing in God's goodness. For those of us who have tasted and seen His goodness, we can testify about it! He is the One who lifts our spirits up, even in times of crisis.

How have you experienced God's presence in the midst of suffering around you?

Make It Happen

- List three ways you have experienced God's goodness. Meditate on these throughout the week.
- Call or text someone who is going through a difficult time and encourage them.
- Write in your journal about the ways that God has delivered you in a time of crisis.

Follow the Spirit

What God wants me to do:

_____

_____

_____

_____

Remember Your Thoughts

Special insights I have learned:

_____

_____

_____

_____

More Light on the Text

Psalm 34:1–10

1 [A Psalm of David, when he changed his behaviour before Abimelech; who drove him away, and he departed.] I will bless the LORD at all times: his praise shall continually be in my mouth. 2 My soul shall make her boast in the LORD: the humble shall hear thereof, and be glad. 3 O magnify the LORD with me, and let us exalt his name together.

This psalm is an acrostic. The verses start by the successive letters of the Hebrew alphabet (with the exception of waw). Scholars think this form allows a free movement from theme to theme without losing coherence. The psalm's context is given in its title, while the full story is found in 1 Samuel 21:10–15. While on the run from King Saul, David ran to King Abimelech. However, the Philistine's princes doubted his sincerity because of his past record. David was in a very uncomfortable situation. Banished from his country and unwelcome in the land, he went to seek asylum.

In this very situation, David blesses and praises the Lord. The praise to God is continual, God-centered, and a product of a grateful heart. His words continually reflect the constancy of his attitude toward the Lord. In every circumstance, we should praise Him (Philippians 4:4).

David also gives a proclamation of the goodness of God. Praising the Lord is an individual undertaking as well as a collective endeavor. He calls on others, therefore, to help him magnify the Lord.

David's boasting (Heb. *halal*, **ha-LOL**) juxtaposes with humility. The Hebrew word here for boast is related to words for shine and praise, and David is perhaps making a play on words to have those ideas in mind along with his boast. David's boast is the Lord, even in his humiliating situation, therefore others who are humbled can see too that the Lord is still worth praising and be glad to know such a great God.

4 I sought the LORD, and he heard me, and delivered me from all my fears. 5 They looked unto him, and were lightened: and their faces were not ashamed. 6 This poor man cried, and the LORD heard him, and saved him out of all his troubles.

The word "fears" (v. 4) addresses the concerns that terrorize one's soul and occupy their thoughts. The Hebrew rendering is *megurah* (**meh-goo-RAH**), which means "terror" or "dread." When we seek the Lord in face of danger, He has the power to deliver us from all threatening situations in our lives.

Every time we look to God, He listens to us, even when we are suffering from our own wrongdoings (Psalm 107:8–12). In dire oppression, like in the case of the Israelites in Egypt, God heard their cries and came to their rescue.

When one turns to the Lord in times of trouble, he or she is "lightened" like the brightness of a happy face. It does not mean that the issue is necessarily taken away. In response to prayers, the peace of God that surpasses understanding keeps our hearts and minds in Christ (Philippians 4:7). That brightens our face, even in challenging times.

7 The angel of the LORD encampeth round about them that fear him, and delivereth them. 8 O taste and see that the LORD is good: blessed is the man that trusteth in him.

Some scholars believe the "angel of the LORD" is a term to designate God Himself coming down in flesh. He protects those who honor and trust in Him. The expression of God's goodness depends on a life of godliness. Angels are also instructed to keep watch over those who take refuge in the Lord (Psalm 91:11). Both "taste" (Heb. *ta'am*, **ta-AM**) and "see" (Heb. *ra'ah*, **ra-AH**) literally refer to using these senses to perceive God's goodness, because that is how real and substantive it is. This is not a call to check God's credentials, but instead an invitation to experience His goodness in a real, tactile sense.

9 O fear the LORD, ye his saints: for there is no want to them that fear him. 10 The young lions do lack, and suffer hunger: but they that seek the LORD shall not want any good thing.

The call to fear the Lord is once more repeated. Fear of the Lord is a demonstration of an attitude of humility and genuine worship, because those who fear Him lack for nothing. David elsewhere declares that the Lord is his shepherd, so he will not lack anything (Psalm 23:1). Young lions are contrasted with the saints who fear the Lord. The word "lion" may be used metaphorically to describe those who

are strong, oppressive, and evil (Psalms 17:12 and 35:17).

11 Come, ye children, hearken unto me: I will teach you the fear of the LORD. 12 What man is he that desireth life, and loveth many days, that he may see good?

The style of these verses is that of "wisdom instruction," as seen in Proverbs and Ecclesiastes. The students in wisdom literature are often called "children" (Heb. *ben*, **BEN**) (Proverbs 2:1). The focus is placed on the fear of the Lord. A reward of wisdom is already in this life. First Peter 3:10 repeats almost exactly the expression of verse 12.

Hebrews 2:17–18

17 Wherefore in all things it behoved him to be made like unto his brethren, that he might be a merciful and faithful high priest in things pertaining to God, to make reconciliation for the sins of the people. 18 For in that he himself hath suffered being tempted, he is able to succour them that are tempted.

On the Day of Atonement, the high priest was required to identify himself with the sacrifice by laying his hands on its head. Christ as High Priest had to be identified to His brothers. Many Scriptures reiterate the fact that Jesus came in the flesh to make atonement for our sins (Romans 1:3; 1 Timothy 3:16; Hebrews 5:7; 1 Peter 4:1). The application of the term "high priest" to Jesus appears only in Hebrews (Hebrews 4:14–16).

In Jesus' earthly ministry, He suffered in many instances. He faced temptation (Matthew 4:1–11), and in agony before the Cross He prayed earnestly (Luke 22:44), the paroxysm of His suffering He bore on the Cross when He was carrying our sins (1 Peter 2:24). This is what qualifies Him to intercede on our behalf in our daily ordeals.

Sources:

Kidner, D. Tyndale Old Testament Commentaries: Psalms 1–72. Edited by D. J. Wiseman. London: InterVarsity Press, 1973.

Life Application Study Bible: New Living Translation. Tyndale House Foundation, 2007.

Morris, L. Hebrews. In F.E. Gabelein, The Expositor's Bible Commentary; vol. 12, Grand Rapids, MI: Zondervan, 1981. 3–158

VanGemeren, W.A. The Expositor's Bible Commentary: Psalms vol. 5. (F.E. Gabelein, Éd.) Grand Rapids, MI: Zondervan, 1991.

Say It Correctly

Encampeth. En-**KAM**-pith.
Succour. **SU**-koor.

Daily Bible Readings

MONDAY
The Atoning Sacrifice for the People
(Leviticus 16:15–19)

TUESDAY
The Lord Hears the Righteous Cry
(Psalm 34:11–18)

WEDNESDAY
Jesus Tasted Death for Everyone
(Hebrews 2:5–9)

THURSDAY
Jesus Brings Salvation Through Suffering
(Hebrews 2:10–13)

FRIDAY
Jesus Destroys the Devil's Power
(Hebrews 2:14–16)

SATURDAY
Jesus, the People's High Priest Forever
(Hebrews 7:18–28)

SUNDAY
Jesus, Our Redeemer and Deliverer
(Psalm 34:1–10; Hebrews 2:17–18)

Notes

Justice in the New Testament

The study this quarter focuses on justice as presented in the New Testament. Justice is portrayed as a primary characteristic of God's nature. Human beings are called to emulate God's justice toward one another.

UNIT 1 • GOD IS JUST AND MERCIFUL

This first section includes four lessons that remind us that human interpretations of the Law must not conflict with mercy and justice as acted out in our daily lives. The lessons from Matthew look at conflicts between Jesus and the Pharisees on questions of mercy and justice. The lesson from Luke looks at how God dispenses justice and mercy.

Lesson 1: June 3, 2018
Justice and Sabbath Laws
Matthew 12:1–14

Our justice system was established to provide equity. What should we do when certain interpretations of the law interfere with responding to human need? Two events in Jesus' life, plucking grain and healing a man with a withered hand on the Sabbath, illustrate the priority of responding to human need.

Lesson 2: June 10, 2018
Parables of God's Just Kingdom
Matthew 13:24–33

People want to experience living in a world filled with justice. Where can we find justice? Jesus' parables describe the kingdom of heaven, where God's justice is merciful, pervasive, and certain.

Lesson 3: June 17, 2018
Jesus Teaches About Justice
Matthew 15:1–9

Sometimes things we do out of tradition are not fair to others. How do we act with true fairness and justice? When the Pharisees confronted Jesus on a question of ritual observance, He challenged them to do what is truly fair and just, and not merely talk about it.

Lesson 4: June 24, 2018
Reaping God's Justice
Luke 16:19–31

There is great concern for the inequities in the lives of the poor versus the rich. How will these inequities be resolved? The story of the rich man and Lazarus tells us that the poor will receive their reward.

UNIT 2 • JESUS CALLS FOR JUSTICE AND MERCY

This second section contains five Scripture lessons that explore Jesus' teachings on God's justice in Matthew and Luke. Included is Jesus' demand for leaders to practice justice as well as to understand the universality of God's justice and mercy.

Lesson 5: July 1, 2018
Parable of the Unforgiving Servant
Matthew 18:21–35

People desire forgiveness even though they refuse to forgive. What are the consequences of an unforgiving heart? The parable of the unforgiving servant teaches us to forgive as we have been forgiven.

Lesson 6: July 8, 2018
Jesus Criticizes Unjust Leaders
Matthew 23:1–8, 23–26

We encounter leaders who expect people to do one thing while they do something else. What is a fair response to such an expectation? Jesus challenges unjust leaders to change or experience destruction.

Lesson 7: July 15, 2018
The Widow and the Unjust Judge
Luke 18:1–8

People become discouraged when their requests for relief seem to go unanswered. Why should we persist? Jesus promises justice to those who persistently request relief from unjust treatment.

Lesson 8: July 22, 2018
Entering God's Kingdom
Luke 13:22–30

People desire to be rewarded for what they consider acceptable behavior. What kind of behavior is acceptable? Jesus taught that we must bear good fruit and come to him through a narrow way.

Lesson 9: July 29, 2018
Parable of the Great Dinner
Luke 14:15–24

Some people eagerly accept invitations to important events while others feel that they have better things to do. What are the consequences of rejecting such invitations? Jesus declares that those who reject His invitation will not be allowed in His kingdom.

UNIT 3 • PAUL TEACHES ABOUT NEW LIFE IN CHRIST

The third section has four lessons that offer Paul's teachings about just and merciful behaviors. Those who live the new life in Christ are called to imitate God's just and merciful nature through their actions toward others, including their enemies.

Lesson 10: August 5, 2018
God's Justice
Romans 2:1–12

It is very easy to judge others, condemning them for doing the same thing we have done. How can we avoid being judgmental? Paul teaches that God's kindness, forbearance, and patience lead us to repentance and new life.

Lesson 11: August 12, 2018
Global Economic Justice
2 Corinthians 8:7–15

We want to be generous to those in need. What motivates true generosity when the needs seem so overwhelming? Paul encouraged the Corinthians' generosity in response to God's generous gifts to them.

Lesson 12: August 19, 2018
Loving and Just Behavior
Romans 12:9–21

We want to be loving people. What makes for genuine love in the world? Paul offers the marks of true love that are to be lived by the faithful.

Lesson 13: August 26, 2018
Practicing Justice
Colossians 3:5–17

People want to live lives that make a difference. What makes for living justly in the world? Paul encourages the faithful to clothe themselves with the love of Christ and let the peace of Christ rule in their hearts.

Fighting Injustice in an Unjust World

"Unjust" is a very fitting adjective to describe the world that we live in. Natural disasters take lives and damage property indiscriminately. Many suffer from abuse and oppression through no fault of their own. Wars are fought and innocent people die because of the greed and callousness of misguided leaders. From the day we are born, we recognize that the world doesn't just yield to our way and does not seem fair. Moreover, we recognize that the world is a dangerous place, hostile to our well-being. It seems as though evil has the last say and the scales are tipped in its favor.

So we search for justice. Many take up this quest and fight against those who would oppress and take advantage of others. Others seek to relieve the suffering caused by disease and natural disasters. Deep down within us, we know that the world is not right and the most noble of us seek to help heal it. This can be done through confronting those in authority who abuse their power or through establishing places of refuge for those whose lives have been ravaged. Something inside pulls us to not wallow in the mess but build a better world and be better people.

This oftentimes becomes a futile effort. We say to ourselves, "What can one person do to solve this problem?" Whether concerned about clean water or neighborhood gangs, we feel overwhelmed by the task at hand. This drives us to either give up and let the situation go on as it is, or become more determined and double our efforts. The first option leaves us in the same oppressive and unjust conditions. It not only keeps the condition the same, but makes it worse because now we are a part of the problem, not the solution. Why do gangs continue to dominate a neighborhood? Because good people don't speak up. This silence continues to multiply and increases the gang's power in the community. The second option soon makes us tired and self-righteous. We wonder why others are not joining the cause and helping us out. We become exhausted or equally as oppressive and unjust as the injustice we are fighting against. There has to be a better way.

A better way can be found in the pages of the Bible. God has the market cornered on justice. He is just and righteous inside and out. He saw the needs of this world long before you and I were ever thought of in our parents' minds. God knew that this world would need justice. His solution to this dilemma was not a homeless shelter or a rally in the streets. It wasn't a boycott or a voter's drive. God's solution to the injustice of this world is Jesus Christ. Jesus Christ came to bring justice to a world that was unjust. Throughout His ministry, Jesus healed the sick and raised the dead. He fed the poor and taught people how to live righteously and not oppress others. Jesus spoke out against the unjust systems in first-century Palestine. It was His stance against injustice that finally caused

Him to be executed by the Romans on a cross outside Jerusalem. The Bible speaks of Jesus' pursuit of justice this way:

> "He will not fight or shout or raise his voice in public. He will not crush the weakest reed or put out a flickering candle. Finally he will cause justice to be victorious. And his name will be the hope of all the world" (Matthew 12:19–21, NLT).

These verses say that Jesus will make justice victorious. Justice will be realized through His pursuit of it. How is that possible when Jesus died as an outcast criminal and an enemy of Rome? The answer can be found in some verses Paul wrote in Romans. Here Paul addresses our unrighteousness and sin and how God made atonement for our sins through Jesus, saying:

> "For God presented Jesus as the sacrifice for sin. People are made right with God when they believe that Jesus sacrificed his life, shedding his blood. This sacrifice shows that God was being fair when he held back and did not punish those who sinned in times past, for he was looking ahead and including them in what he would do in this present time. God did this to demonstrate his righteousness, for he himself is fair and just, and he declares sinners to be right in his sight when they believe in Jesus" (Romans 3:25–26, NLT).

Paul says that it was through Jesus that God demonstrated His righteousness and justice toward the world. Through Christ's death on the Cross, all of us who are sinners can be made right in His sight. That's true justice. Jesus could rest in not solving all the world's problems and dying on the Cross because His death is what brought genuine justice to the world. Poverty, crime, sickness, and government corruption are all symptoms of a deeper problem. The sacrifice of Jesus on the Cross attacked the root of injustice: sin.

When sin was released into the world, everything was thrown off balance. We see a small glimpse of this as the Lord curses the ground, which is symbolic of the whole created order (Genesis 3:17–19). We also see that creation is groaning, waiting for our redemption in order to be freed from decay and corruption (Romans 8:20–22). Man and woman's bond is also cursed as strife and conflict become their normal way of relating. This then becomes the normal relationship for coming generations. This is why we have natural disasters, sickness, and disease. This is why there is corruption and oppression and an abuse of power. The curse of sin is the root of all these problems.

Jesus' death released us from sin so we can fight against injustice. We do not have to give up and throw in the towel, because we have His Spirit empowering us. We do not have to become exhausted and burned out, because we can rest in His promise of a new heaven and earth. We can fight for injustice, because Jesus has already destroyed the root of injustice on the Cross. He has given us His Spirit so we can fight injustice with His energy and wisdom. He has given us the promise of victory so we can rest in His work and not our own.

There are many problems to tackle out there. Injustice is pervasive throughout society and many are affected by it, whether they are the oppressors or the oppressed. As followers of Jesus, we must take hold of His promise and receive His Spirit for daily empowerment to fight for a just and fair world. Only then can we model and imitate our Savior, who caused justice to triumph on the Cross.

Fostering Justice in Christian Education

by Melvin Banks Sr., Litt.D.

After teaching a Bible lesson that focused on God's desire that His people show justice to the poor, the Sunday School teacher led a brainstorming session on what the class members might do to show their concern for the poor and less fortunate. Someone remembered injustice that a racist group of people had inflicted on a community two hundred miles away. A class member suggested that their group might consider doing something for the families in that oppressed community.

With encouragement from their teacher, the class formed a committee, drove to the community, and interviewed families to determine their needs. They brought back to their Sunday School class a list of needs that included food, clothing, and shoes for children. The class raised funds and purchased clothes and supplies. Then the group drove the two hundred miles back to the community to deliver the items they had purchased. This is just a tangible way one Sunday School class put into practice a lesson on justice they gleaned from the study of God's Word.

Not only did the class learn that a study of God's Word could have tangible outcomes, they also discovered that they could experience a great sense of fulfillment in doing it. UMI Lesson Aims always include a component that we not only KNOW a truth and FEEL deeply about it, but also that we DO something to put that truth into practice. The DOING leaves a long-lasting impact on our memory and character development. It helps fulfill the biblical injunction, "Anyone who *does* what pleases God will live forever" (from 1 John 2:17, NLT, emphasis added). The Gospel of Matthew records that after Jesus spent considerable time teaching and demonstrating ministry principles to His disciples, He sent them out to preach, heal, and cast out demons from people (Matthew 10). We can profitably follow Jesus' example.

Addressing injustice and fostering justice can take multiple forms. The goal of justice is to right wrongs and foster fairness. Sometimes in Scripture, the focus is on how we ourselves treat others fairly. At other times, it might mean we come to the rescue of those whom others have mistreated. It might involve writing letters or voting for people who will work for justice.

Someone has developed this list of guidelines that both young and older people can use as a sort of checklist for practicing fairness in one-on-one relationships:

- Treat people how you want to be treated
- Take turns
- Tell the truth
- Think how your actions will affect others
- Listen to others with an open mind
- Do not blame others for your mistakes
- Do not take advantage of other people
- Do not play favorites

Let us take a closer look at justice...

Justice—What is It?

Justice is an objective standard of righteousness and right behavior that has its origin in God. Our Lord Jesus both personified and exemplified His passion for justice as He "went around doing good" (from Acts 10:38, NLT). In His life, teachings, ministry, and atoning sacrifice, Christ reversed the wrongs that Satan and his demons and followers had inflicted upon people.

Why is Justice Important for Us to Address?

God calls us to practice righteousness and fairness because He is righteous and fair. Jesus said, "But you are to be perfect, even as your Father in heaven is perfect" (Matthew 5:48, NLT). God Himself is our model. Jesus tells us to "do to others as you would like them to do to you" (Luke 6:31, NLT).

How Can We Convey the Idea of Justice to Others?

As teachers, we transmit to others best what we firmly believe and practice ourselves. Of course, we know some people in the role of "teacher" might attempt to burden others with what they do not firmly believe or model, but Jesus calls them hypocrites (Matthew 23:1–4).

We best communicate justice and righteousness when it becomes a burning desire in us. Then that fire for justice in us will likely ignite a desire in those we touch. As Christian educators, we can proceed to fashion a teaching plan that seeks to communicate justice to our students. Bear in mind that one can extend the outline below to be not only a plan for a class but also for a church-wide initiative.

We create an instructional or teaching aim.

For example: By the end of our teaching session, we will know that Christ expects His followers to practice fairness and justice; be deeply convinced that showing fairness is both a personal and corporate duty; and identify and implement a project where we can foster justice.

We plan an attention-getting way to focus the class on the issue of justice.

Pair up students and have them share an example of injustice. After three minutes, get their responses to build a list of situations they have identified.

We make a promise to the class.

With a list of unjust situations, the teacher can now make a promise to the class. For example: Today, we will explore what God has to say about justice and what we might possibly do to right some wrong or encourage righteous behavior.

We present biblical facts about justice.

We derive our objective standard of justice from God and His revelation of truth recorded in the Scriptures. Here are a few biblical texts that highlight God's concern for justice:

"Should not the Judge of all the earth do what is right?" (from Genesis 18:25, NLT).

"He will judge the world with justice and rule the nations with fairness" (Psalm 9:8, NLT).

"All he does is just and good, and all his commandments are trustworthy. They are forever true, to be obeyed faithfully and with integrity" (Psalm 111:7–8, NLT).

"Look at my servant, whom I strengthen. He is my chosen one, who pleases me. I have put my Spirit upon him. He will bring justice to the nations. He will not shout or raise his voice in public. He will not crush the weakest reed or put out a flickering candle. He will bring justice to all who have been wronged. He will not falter or lose heart until justice prevails throughout the earth. Even distant lands beyond the sea will wait for his instruction" (Isaiah 42:1–4, NLT).

"No, O people, the LORD has told you what is good, and this is what he requires of you: to do what is right, to love mercy, and to walk humbly with your God" (Micah 6:8, NLT).

We ask questions about each of these texts.
- What does this text say?
- What does this text mean by what it says?
- What does this text mean for us today?
- What might we do differently if we were to take this text seriously?

We apply the truth.

Go back to your list of unjust situations and ask students to pick one situation that disturbs them most and that they would like to address individually or as a class. Discuss what they might possibly do. Then ask who would like to serve on a project committee to address the issue. Appoint someone to serve as temporary chairperson until the group convenes its first meeting and selects a chairperson. Urge the class to complete a "justice project." Monitor the progress of the group and ask them to report their results to the class. Depending on the project, the committee might complete it by the following week, or might require several weeks to complete.

NOTE: This project would not replace the church's Commission for Social Justice, unless there is no such provision at present. This project is just a teaching device to show how we can translate learning into doing, to make it a part of our experience. It may or may not become an ongoing commission for the church.

So go ahead, make it happen!

Perspective

Justice: Just Live It

by Kimberly Gillespie

No Justice. No Peace. We want justice!!!
Justice for _____!!!

Justice.

We chant, protest, and fight for it. But, what is "justice"? Why do we insist on it? Justice is the principle or action of treating people in a way that is good, fair, moral, and unbiased.

Good. Fair. Moral. Unbiased.

Individually, we all want this, and fight for aspects of it, daily. While driving, someone cuts you off, causing you to miss the light. You get frustrated because what she did was not good. You have been overcharged on a bill, and you call to reconcile it, because the charges were not fair. A co-worker takes credit for a task you completed, so you confront him because it was not morally right. You enter into a restaurant at the same time as another customer of a different ethnicity, but they are served, while you are left waiting. You complain, because you believe the server was biased. We all want our form of justice. But true justice, specifically godly justice, is much loftier than our individual ambitions.

We live in a world of injustices. I have lived on the East and West coasts, in the South and the Midwest, and have traveled several times to Africa. Let me assure you, injustice is everywhere. Wherever I am, I notice that the common thread that connects the oppressed—whether children, various ethnic groups, the homeless, etc.—is poverty. When people lack financial resources, they are left without a voice. As a result, they are susceptible to being overlooked, exploited, judged, and treated unfairly. Briefly consider some of the topics that are prevalent these days: education, childhood obesity, immigration, human trafficking, universal health care, taxes, unemployment. Woven throughout these debates are the injustices often experienced because people lack sufficient resources.

Over the years, I have had the opportunity to teach in schools and organizations that serve the underprivileged. While a certain level of compassion developed as I served, a greater understanding came as a result of recent experiences. A year ago, my family relocated from a suburb of Nashville, Tennessee, to Richmond, California, to serve at an urban neighborhood church being revitalized. Prior to relocating, we prayed, researched, saved, and planned. However, our best-laid plans fell by the wayside. Six weeks after arriving in California, we found ourselves homeless and jobless with a 22-month-old son, and twins on the way.

Over the course of seven months, we stayed in five different homes. We applied for and received various resources allocated for "the poor." While we were grateful for the provision, those experiences were overwhelming, humbling, and quite educational. Unfortunately, we became well acquainted with certain injustices.

For one thing, all things are not created equal. Many of the resources allocated for the poor are substandard—from spoiled food to overcrowded and undersupplied classrooms to segregated medical facilities with inadequate, dirty, and outdated medical equipment.

Next, a certain bias against the poor has developed as a result of the vicious cycle of poverty. Ignorance begets ignorance, but not knowing is not necessarily a reflection of lack of capacity, but lack of exposure and often fear. However, those who lack resources are often treated as if they are unintelligent, lazy, and incapable of or uninterested in learning. Therefore, there can be a mentality of governing, but not educating.

While resources are available, accessing them can be a daunting task, requiring knowledge, access, time, and support, among other things. For example, some employers require a physical address—impossible if a person is homeless. Some resources require completing lengthy applications, and providing "proof" of various things—a challenge for those who cannot read, refugees and immigrants who speak other languages, or transients who travel with their entire lives in a cart, suitcase, or vehicle.

Poverty subjects people to situations they would normally not consider. For example, in recent years, more attention has been given to human trafficking. Previously, it was considered a foreign vice, as stories were told of families giving children over to "employers" in hopes of better lives and money. However, over time, it has been revealed that the United States is a destination for traffickers.

Injustice is everywhere. And God is not silent.

God's View of Justice

"For the LORD loves justice, and he will never abandon the godly. He will keep them safe forever, but the children of the wicked will die" (Psalm 37:28, NLT).

"He gives justice to the oppressed and food to the hungry. The LORD frees the prisoners" (Psalm 146:7, NLT).

"The LORD gives righteousness and justice to all who are treated unfairly" (Psalm 103:6, NLT).

"He ensures that orphans and widows receive justice. He shows love to the foreigners living among you and gives them food and clothing" (Deuteronomy 10:18, NLT).

"Even common people oppress the poor, rob the needy, and deprive foreigners of justice" (Ezekiel 22:29, NLT).

So, He makes provisions. God sees what we refuse to see, and commands in principle and in practice what is good, fair, moral, and unbiased.

Good

"When you are harvesting your crops and forget to bring in a bundle of grain from your field, don't go back to get it. Leave it for the foreigners, orphans, and widows. Then the LORD your God will bless you in all you do" (Deuteronomy 24:19, NLT).

Fair

"Do not twist justice in legal matters by favoring the poor or being partial to the rich and powerful. Always judge people fairly" (Leviticus 19:15, NLT).

"True justice must be given to foreigners living among you and to orphans, and you must never accept a widow's garment as security for her debt. Always remember that you were slaves in Egypt and that the LORD your God redeemed you from your slavery. That is why I have given you this command" (Deuteronomy 24:17–18, NLT).

Moral

"Never take advantage of poor and destitute laborers, whether they are fellow Israelites or foreigners living in your towns. You must pay them their wages each day before sunset because they are poor and are counting on it. If you don't, they might cry out to the LORD against you, and it would be counted against you as sin" (Deuteronomy 24:14–15, NLT).

Unbiased

"My dear brothers and sisters, how can you claim to have faith in our glorious Lord Jesus Christ if you favor some people over others? For example, suppose someone comes into your meeting dressed in fancy clothes and expensive jewelry, and another comes in who is poor and dressed in dirty clothes. If you give special attention and a good seat to the rich person, but you say to the poor one, 'You can stand over there, or else sit on the floor'—well, doesn't this discrimination show that your judgments are guided by evil motives?" (James 2:1–4, NLT).

But how does this apply to us?

The unfortunate reality is that we have ample opportunities to fight for true justice.

Perhaps your heart is pricked when you hear of orphans' struggles, both here and abroad: "Learn to do good. Seek justice. Help the oppressed. Defend the cause of orphans" (from Isaiah 1:17, NLT).

Maybe you are burdened by the ill treatment of senior citizens because of a bad experience with a parent or grandparent: "Fight for the rights of widows" (from Isaiah 1:17, NLT).

You weep when you hear of those involved in trafficking: "Speak up for those who cannot speak for themselves; ensure justice for those being crushed" (Proverbs 31:8, NLT).

You wonder what can be done about the homeless family you pass daily: "Give justice to the poor and the orphan; uphold the rights of the oppressed and the destitute" (Psalm 82:3, NLT).

You are angered when you see or hear of any injustice. "Yes, speak up for the poor and helpless, and see that they get justice" (Proverbs 31:9, NLT).

At any rate, as followers of Christ, James reminds us that we do not have the option of doing nothing: "What good is it, dear brothers and sisters, if you say you have faith but don't show it by your actions? Can that kind of faith save anyone? Suppose you see a brother or sister who has no food or clothing, and you say, 'Good-bye and have a good day; stay warm and eat well'—but then you don't give that person any food or clothing. What good does that do? So you see, faith by itself isn't enough. Unless it produces good deeds, it is dead and useless. Now someone may argue, 'Some people have faith; others have good deeds.' But I say, 'How can you show me your faith if you don't have good deeds? I will show you my faith by my good deeds'" (James 2:14–18, NLT).

I part with these words from Micah 6:8: "No, O people, the LORD has told you what is good, and this is what he requires of you: to do what is right, to love mercy, and to walk humbly with your God" (NLT).

Justice—Just live it.

Kimberly Gillespie has been teaching training in underserved communities in various capacities for over 15 years—a journey that began while at Dallas Theological Seminary. She and her husband have 1 son and twin daughters and reside in Atlanta, GA.

Lucille Clifton

(June 27, 1936 – February 13, 2010)

Lucille Clifton (June 27, 1936–February 13, 2010) was an accomplished writer, distinguished poet, and educator who has been as dubbed one of the most prolific voices of our time. Her work is best remembered for capturing the heart of African American life and culture. Through brilliant use of colloquial vernacular and creative word images, her work carried the heart and spirit of the community.

Born Thelma Lucille Sayles, Clifton inherited her passion for writing from her mother, who wrote poetry as a hobby. Although not educated past grade school, her mother wrote poetry in secret until her husband forbade her. At age 12, Lucille witnessed the death of her mother's gift. As her mother burned her work, it fueled Ms. Clifton's ambition and passion to share her voice with the world.

Ms. Clifton's talent was first recognized by Langston Hughes, who included her poems in his anthology *The Poetry Of The Negro* in 1966. Her first poetry collection release was *Good Times*, published in 1969 and listed among the *New York Times*' 10 best books for that year. Her work captured the continuing struggle for equality for Blacks and women, painting the political landscape of the times, while also reflecting the realities of the African American family, often with sharp wit and rhetorical insight. The *New York Times* noted that her work was widely anthologized and her cultural influence on the arts is unmistakable. Writing was her way of seeing and interpreting the world.

The mother of six children, Clifton wrote a number of children's books including a series featuring the character Everett Anderson. These books were used as a vehicle to remind children that God loves them, provide a positive view of the world, and help children deal with difficult situations.

Clifton won numerous literary awards throughout her career, including the prestigious Ruth Lilly Poetry Prize in 2007, as well as the National Book Award for *Blessing the Boats: New and Selected Poems, 1988–2000* (2000). She was also the first author to have two books of poetry chosen as finalists for the Pulitzer Prize, *Good Woman: Poems and a Memoir, 1969-1980* (1987) and *Next: New Poems* (1987). In 1984, she won the Coretta Scott King Award for *Everett Anderson's Goodbye*. She also served as the state of Maryland's poet laureate from 1974 to 1985.

As an educator, Clifton began her career at Coppin State College, Baltimore, MD, as poet-in-residence (1974–79). She would later hold various teaching posts: University of California, Santa Cruz, as professor of literature and creative writing (1985–89); St. Mary's College of Maryland, St. Mary's City, MD, as a Distinguished Professor of Literature (1989–91) and Distinguished Professor of Humanities (1991); Columbia University School of the Arts, as visiting professor (1995–99); and many others.

Teaching Tips

Words You Should Know

A. Corn (Mathew 12:1) *sporimos* (Gk.)—Sown fields, growing crops.

B. Mercy (v. 7) *eleos* (Gk.)—Kindness or goodwill toward the miserable or afflicted joined with a desire to help them.

Teacher Preparation

Unifying Principle—Compliance vs. Compassion. Our justice system was established to provide equity. What should we do when certain interpretations of the law interfere with responding to human need? Two events in Jesus' life—plucking grain and healing a man with a withered hand on the Sabbath—illustrate the priority of responding to human need.

A. Pray that the Lord will open your heart and your mind to allow you to better understand and follow His plan for this lesson.

B. Seek deeper understanding of the meaning of the lesson by studying the Background Scripture and Devotional Reading in several different translations of the Bible.

C. Complete Lesson 1 in the *Precepts For Living®* Personal Study Guide.

O—Open the Lesson

A. Open with prayer. Remember to invite the Holy Spirit to lead your Bible study.

B. Read Aim for Change and Keep in Mind verse in unison.

C. Have your class read the In Focus story silently. Invite discussion.

P—Present the Scriptures

A. Have class members read the Focal verses.

B. Ask for volunteers to read The People, Places, and Times, Background, and In Depth sections. Encourage discussion.

E—Explore the Meaning

A. Answer the questions in the Search the Scriptures and Discuss the Meaning sections.

B. Ask a volunteer to read the Lesson in Our Society section.

N—Next Steps for Application

A. Encourage students to apply the Make It Happen section.

B. Close in prayer.

Worship Guide

For the Superintendent or Teacher
Theme: Justice and Sabbath Laws
Song: "Leaning on the Everlasting Arms"
Devotional Reading: Psalm 10

Justice and Sabbath Laws

Bible Background • MATTHEW 12:1–14
Printed Text • MATTHEW 12:1–14 | Devotional Reading • PSALM 10

—————— Aim for Change ——————

By the end of this lesson, we will: EXPLORE Jesus' approach to questions of how properly to observe the Sabbath; AFFIRM the importance of responding to human needs; and IDENTIFY ways believers can prioritize compassionate service over external religious obligations.

———— In Focus ————

Tasha walked by church every Sunday shortly after noon while the deacons finished giving out food from the food pantry. She was afraid to get in line or ask for help because she knew the rule: People who arrived by 12 noon received assistance from the pantry. Her quiet disappointment did not escape the notice of Doris, however. Doris had been working in the food pantry for about a month. She always saw Tasha and wanted to reach out to her, but she felt limited by the rule. This particular Sunday, Doris was overwhelmed with compassion. She knew she needed to do something to help Tasha. So she filled a box of groceries and gave it to Tasha along with a warm embrace.

Tears started to roll down Tasha's cheek. She finally opened her mouth to say, "Thank you so much. I know the rules. I want to make it on time, but Sunday morning is the only time the state allows me to visit my children."

Doris looked at her with reassurance. "We are here to help."

Jesus placed more of a priority on meeting human needs than on satisfying human rules. Have you ever challenged a human rule to help someone in need?

—————— Keep in Mind ——————

"But if ye had known what this meaneth, I will have mercy, and not sacrifice, ye would not have condemned the guiltless" (Matthew 12:7).

"But if ye had known what this meaneth, I will have mercy, and not sacrifice, ye would not have condemned the guiltless" (Matthew 12:7).

Focal Verses

KJV **Matthew 12:1** At that time Jesus went on the sabbath day through the corn; and his disciples were an hungred, and began to pluck the ears of corn and to eat.

2 But when the Pharisees saw it, they said unto him, Behold, thy disciples do that which is not lawful to do upon the sabbath day.

3 But he said unto them, Have ye not read what David did, when he was an hungred, and they that were with him;

4 How he entered into the house of God, and did eat the shewbread, which was not lawful for him to eat, neither for them which were with him, but only for the priests?

5 Or have ye not read in the law, how that on the sabbath days the priests in the temple profane the sabbath, and are blameless?

6 But I say unto you, That in this place is one greater than the temple.

7 But if ye had known what this meaneth, I will have mercy, and not sacrifice, ye would not have condemned the guiltless.

8 For the Son of man is Lord even of the sabbath day.

9 And when he was departed thence, he went into their synagogue:

10 And, behold, there was a man which had his hand withered. And they asked him, saying, Is it lawful to heal on the sabbath days? that they might accuse him.

11 And he said unto them, What man shall there be among you, that shall have one sheep, and if it fall into a pit on the sabbath day, will he not lay hold on it, and lift it out?

12 How much then is a man better than a sheep? Wherefore it is lawful to do well on the sabbath days.

13 Then saith he to the man, Stretch forth thine hand. And he stretched it forth; and it was restored whole, like as the other.

NLT **Matthew 12:1** At about that time Jesus was walking through some grainfields on the Sabbath. His disciples were hungry, so they began breaking off some heads of grain and eating them.

2 But some Pharisees saw them do it and protested, "Look, your disciples are breaking the law by harvesting grain on the Sabbath."

3 Jesus said to them, "Haven't you read in the Scriptures what David did when he and his companions were hungry?

4 He went into the house of God, and he and his companions broke the law by eating the sacred loaves of bread that only the priests are allowed to eat.

5 And haven't you read in the law of Moses that the priests on duty in the Temple may work on the Sabbath?

6 I tell you, there is one here who is even greater than the Temple!

7 But you would not have condemned my innocent disciples if you knew the meaning of this Scripture: 'I want you to show mercy, not offer sacrifices.'

8 For the Son of Man is Lord, even over the Sabbath!"

9 Then Jesus went over to their synagogue,

10 where he noticed a man with a deformed hand. The Pharisees asked Jesus, "Does the law permit a person to work by healing on the Sabbath?" (They were hoping he would say yes, so they could bring charges against him.)

11 And he answered, "If you had a sheep that fell into a well on the Sabbath, wouldn't you work to pull it out? Of course you would.

12 And how much more valuable is a person than a sheep! Yes, the law permits a person to do good on the Sabbath."

13 Then he said to the man, "Hold out your hand." So the man held out his hand, and it was restored, just like the other one!

14 Then the Pharisees went out, and held a council against him, how they might destroy him.

14 Then the Pharisees called a meeting to plot how to kill Jesus.

The People, Places, and Times

Shewbread. This bread was a small round or oblong loaf. It was to be made every Sabbath and set near the lampstand and the altar of incense. At the end of the week the priests would eat this bread. The shewbread consisted of twelve loaves, which represented the twelve tribes of Israel. No one but the priests were permitted to eat this bread; however David and his men were given the old loaves by Ahimelech when they were on the run from Saul (1 Samuel 21:1–7).

Sabbath. The Jewish day of rest, based on God's act of resting on the seventh day after creation. Its observance has been practiced by Jewish people from the time of Moses. Keeping the Sabbath was a very critical issue in separating Jews from Gentiles and maintaining purity. It was so important that the Jewish leaders created 39 laws to make sure they were not violating the Sabbath. Multiple laws governed what constituted work on the Sabbath, and these laws were hotly debated by the Pharisees and other religious groups in first-century Palestine.

What are the hotly debated issues in the church today?

Background

In the chapters prior to this passage, Jesus has instructed the twelve disciples about preaching about the kingdom to the Jews. After outlining their method and message, John's disciples approach Jesus on whether He is the expected Messiah. Jesus responds and lets them know that His works speak for themselves. He is the Messiah and John was His forerunner. Furthermore, Jesus announces that those who do not believe in Him will face a worse judgment than the cities of Sodom and Gomorrah or Tyre and Sidon. Jesus then says a prayer of thanksgiving for God's grace in revealing Himself to the disciples who are not wise and clever. Next comes an invitation to come to Jesus, and those who do will find rest for their souls.

This is significant because in the story that begins the next chapter, Jesus shows how His yoke is easy and His burden is light. This is true especially in relation to the traditions of the Pharisees. Their many religious traditions were burdensome, especially in regards to the Sabbath. Many ordinary things were considered to be violations of the Sabbath, including such things as lighting a lamp. Unfortunately, many of these extra laws often got in the way of actually obeying the law of God and showing love to others. Jesus shows how backwards this way of thinking and living really is.

What religious traditions can be burdensome for us in the 21st century?

At-A-Glance

1. Conflict on the Sabbath (Matthew 12:1–8)
2. Clarity on the Sabbath (vv. 9–13)
3. Conspiracy on the Sabbath (v. 14)

In Depth

1. Conflict on the Sabbath (Matthew 12:1–8)

Jesus' disciples experienced one of the most basic human needs: hunger. In order to meet this need, they broke one of the Pharisees' Sabbath-keeping rules, causing the Pharisees to question His disciples' actions. Jesus responded by pointing out a similar situation that David and his friends faced when they were on the run from Saul. David and his men were hungry and the only bread available was the shewbread that was displayed in the tabernacle. This bread was holy and was not to be eaten by anyone except the priests—and only after new bread replaced it every week. Ahimelech the priest gave them this bread to meet their needs, showing that human needs are more of a priority than keeping rules.

Why would God put meeting human needs above keeping rules?

2. Clarity on the Sabbath (vv. 9–13)

Jesus went a step further in meeting human needs by settling the debate on whether it was lawful to heal on the Sabbath; He healed the man with the withered hand. He gave them an example from everyday life to further back up His point. If they had a sheep that fell in a pit, they would help it up out of the pit on the Sabbath. Human life is obviously more valuable than animal life, so therefore the healing is valid. Jesus showed justice and mercy to the man with the withered hand by healing him on the Sabbath. It is right to do good no matter what day it is.

How can we ensure that human tradition is not hindering our pursuit of doing good?

3. Conspiracy on the Sabbath (v. 14)

Then the Pharisees began plotting how they would kill Jesus. They believed that strict observance of the Sabbath was a way to merit God's favor. Because of their generational history of breaking God's covenant and losing their blessings, they believed if the Jewish people stayed ceremonially pure, God would break the yoke of Roman oppression and give them their land again. They thought that keeping the Sabbath was a means to that end, so they devised many rules to get there. On top of that,

they wanted to murder Jesus for undermining their rules, even though He was actually doing a good deed. This is religion that is twisted and deformed, and Jesus turned this concept on its head. The Sabbath was a means to attain the end of doing good and showing justice and mercy. This is what people need. Sabbath was not designed to oppress people, but to liberate them and set them free.

How have you seen something that was designed to liberate people twisted to oppress people?

Search the Scriptures

1. Why was it acceptable for David and his friends to eat the shewbread (Matthew 12:3–4)?

2. Why did the Pharisees plot together to kill Jesus (v. 14)?

Discuss the Meaning

1. In this lesson we are confronted with the fact that Jesus is Lord of the Sabbath. How do we make Him Lord of the Sabbath and every other aspect of our lives?

2. How can we meet human needs in our daily lives? Are there any rules that keep us from loving others and showing mercy?

Lesson in Our Society

Many times in the Black church, we can get caught up in going from church activity to church activity and forget the purpose behind what we're doing. In the quick pace of a church calendar, we must remember the reason why we were created: to love God and to love people. This is a higher priority than Bible studies, choir practices, or church anniversaries. If our church activities keep us from seeking justice for the oppressed and loving our fellow man, then we have lost sight of God's higher purpose.

Jesus' words in this passage highlight the attitude we should have toward any of our religious traditions. The concern for human life is more important than the external trappings of religion. While the various aspects of worship are important, they are negated if we do not love our neighbor as ourselves. God desires relentless love and abounding compassion more than religious sacrifice.

In what way have you seen a church corporately display God's love and compassion?

Make It Happen

• List three ways you can make the Sabbath a time of seeking justice.

• As a class, brainstorm ways to help those who are oppressed because of religious traditions or prejudices.

• Create a list of things that are helpful in valuing human needs when it comes to the Sabbath.

Follow the Spirit

What God wants me to do:

_____

_____

_____

_____

Remember Your Thoughts

Special insights I have learned:

_____

_____

_____

_____

More Light on the Text
Matthew 12:1–14

An important mark that distinguished the Jews from non-Jews (often referred to as Gentiles), particularly during the times of Jesus, was the Sabbath. The Jews took Sabbath observance very seriously and the Pharisees were especially rigid about it. When the enemy attacked on the Sabbath in the days of the Maccabees during the period between the Old and New Testaments, the Jews let themselves be slaughtered—men, women, and children—rather than break the Sabbath by defending themselves (1 Maccabees 2:31–38). At a later time, Pompey was able to erect the earthworks that made his siege of Jerusalem successful because he did it on a Sabbath day. The Jews were ready to suffer rather than break the Sabbath. The passage today deals with two Sabbath controversies. The first section, 12:1–8, deals with the harvesting of grain on the Sabbath and the second section, 12:9–14, addresses the issue of healing on the Sabbath. These two issues essentially deal with where authority lies.

1 At that time Jesus went on the sabbath day through the corn; and his disciples were an hungred, and began to pluck the ears of corn and to eat. 2 But when the Pharisees saw it, they said unto him, Behold, thy disciples do that which is not lawful to do upon the sabbath day. 3 But he said unto them, Have ye not read what David did, when he was an hungred, and they that were with him. 4 How he entered into the house of God, and did eat the shewbread, which was not lawful for him to eat, neither for them which were with him, but only for the priests? 5 Or have ye not read in the law, how that on the sabbath days the priests in the temple profane the sabbath, and are blameless. 6 But I say unto you, That in this place is one greater

than the temple. **7 But if ye had known what this meaneth, I will have mercy, and not sacrifice, ye would not have condemned the guiltless. 8 For the Son of man is Lord even of the sabbath day.**

Here we see the Pharisees in their characteristic manner, following Jesus not to receive His help, but to spy on Him with the intention of getting Him into trouble. The disciples were hungry and their action was much in line with Deuteronomy 23:24, "When you enter your neighbor's vineyard, you may eat your fill of grapes, but you must not carry any away in a basket," a humanitarian legislation intended to sustain the needy without giving them permission to pile up extras. But there was no mention of Sabbath in these cases. When the Pharisees saw Jesus' disciples picking food to eat, they seized the opportunity and immediately accused them of harvesting grain on the Sabbath. They complained that Jesus' disciples, with His implicit sanction, were doing what was "not lawful" (Gk. *exesti*, **EX-ess-ti**) to do on the Sabbath day. The Greek word here does not necessarily refer to the Law, but could be translated "is allowed or permitted." The Pharisees saw the action of the disciples as an infringement on Exodus 34:21, an injunction that demands the day of Sabbath to be a day of rest, and prohibits harvesting. They also interpreted it as a violation of the fourth commandment, which requires Sabbath observation (Exodus 20:8–11). Although the fourth commandment forbids the doing of "any work" on the Sabbath day, the question is, what constitutes "work"? The Pharisees spelled this out in minute detail in their regulations.

Jesus responded to the Pharisees by citing the case of David, who with the band of his hungry followers ate the shewbread (1 Samuel 21:1–6), which was only meant for the priests (v. 3). The common point between the incident Jesus cited and that of His disciples in Matthew 12:3–4 is satisfying the hunger of the followers of David and those of Christ, who is the Son of David. In citing this case, Jesus shows that love is the greatest law in the universe and supersedes all other regulations. Does this mean love requires that human needs be met, even if some legal technicalities have to be jettisoned in the process?

He further appeals to the Old Testament sacrifice where there is an explicit command that two lambs be offered every Sabbath (Numbers 28:9–10), so that Temple service takes precedence over Sabbath observance. Jesus draws attention to the fact that in the Law, it was prescribed that on every Sabbath, the priests should offer the sacrifice of two lambs as well as the normal daily offerings. Although the command does not specially mention the priests, since they were the only ones who could offer sacrifices, they would be the ones working on the Sabbath. As such, the mere fact that the priests performed work on the Sabbath—every Sabbath—should give cause for those who revered Scripture to think hard about what God meant the Sabbath to be and what people should do to keep it holy. They had too easily accepted views that made the Sabbath a burden and had overlooked the fact that Scripture did not fit into their pattern.

Jesus makes His main point in verse 6. There was someone now greater than the Temple. The True Temple, the meeting place between people and God, is Christ Himself. Since Jesus is greater than the Temple, then He must also be of more importance than the Sabbath. He quotes Hosea 6:6 to show that true religion consists of a right attitude rather than ritual acts (v. 7), thereby declaring that needy people who pluck grain to eat on the Sabbath are guiltless (Gk. *anaitios*, **ann-EYE-tee-oce**), which means without blame and innocent of a crime.

9 And when he was departed thence, he went into their synagogue: 10 And, behold, there was a man which had his hand withered. And they asked him, saying, Is it lawful to heal on the sabbath days? that they might accuse him. 11 And he said unto them, What man shall there be among you, that shall have one sheep, and if it fall into a pit on the sabbath day, will he not lay hold on it, and lift it out? 12 How much then is a man better than a sheep? Wherefore it is lawful to do well on the sabbath days. 13 Then saith he to the man, Stretch forth thine hand. And he stretched it forth; and it was restored whole, like as the other. 14 Then the Pharisees went out, and held a council against him, how they might destroy him.

The miracle in verses 9–14 is another item in Jesus' conflict with the Pharisees over proper Sabbath observance and what constitutes "work" on the Sabbath day. There was a man in the synagogue with his hand "withered" (Gk. *xeros*, **ksay-ROCE**), that is, literally "dried up," and they asked Jesus whether it was right to heal him on the Sabbath day (vv. 9–10). Though provoked by the presence of the disabled person, the question is general in form. Their purpose was to secure evidence against Jesus for violating the Sabbath, so as to accuse Him. For the Pharisees, complying with Sabbath regulations was more important than healing the person with the withered hand (he could seek healing on another day). The man's healing did not seem urgent because his life was not in danger.

In answer to their question, Jesus asked them whether it was proper to do good on the Sabbath, or to do evil. To clinch His point, He asked them if they would pull a sheep out of a pit on the Sabbath (v. 11). A man must definitely be more worth saving than a sheep. "Wherefore it is lawful to do well on Sabbath days" (v. 12). Jesus the Creator told the man to stretch his hand (v. 13). The man demonstrated his belief by his obedience, and his hand was restored "whole" (Gk. *hugies*, **hoo-gee-ACE**), which is also translated "healthy" and "sound."

Unfortunately, the miracle was not compelling enough to make the Pharisees believe in Jesus. From their intransigence, it is evident that there is nothing more unreasonable than religious fanaticism. Perverted and legalistic piety does nothing but blind people. The miraculous healing of the man with the withered hand did not impress them. Rather, they were concerned with a violation, not of the commands of God, but of their own understanding and interpretation of what God's command required. They took counsel so that they could destroy Him, an expression that indicates a determination to explore all the possibilities. The Pharisees' council (Gk. *sumboulion*, **soom-BOW-lee-on**) was not necessarily a formal body that usually met; the word is used for advising bodies comprised of a variety of people, e.g., Pharisees, Herodians, elders, scribes. Their rejection of Christ was total and their opposition was so bitter that nothing less than Jesus' death for satisfy them, a curious reaction to a miracle of healing, and a curious action for men who were so keen on keeping the Sabbath lawfully.

Sources:
Hahn, Roger L. *Matthew: A Commentary for Bible Students.* Indianapolis, IN: Wesleyan Publishing House, 2007 .
Earle, Ralph. *The Gospel According to Matthew.* Beacon Bible Commentary. Kansas City: Beacon Hill Press, 1964.
France, R.T. *Matthew.* Tyndale New Testament Commentaries. Grand Rapids, MI: Eerdmans, 1985.
Harrington, Daniel J. *Sacra Pagina: The Gospel of Matthew.* Collegeville, MN: Liturgical Press, 1991, 2007.
Nolland, John. *The Gospel of Matthew: A Commentary on the Greek Text.* New International Greek Testament Commentary. Grand Rapids, MI; Carlisle: W.B. Eerdmans; Paternoster Press, 2005.

Say It Correctly

Tyre. **TIE**-er.
Sidon. **SIGH**-don.
Abiathar. ah-**BYE**-ath-are.

Daily Bible Readings

MONDAY
David Eats the Bread of Presence
(1 Samuel 21:1–6)

TUESDAY
Lord Desires Mercy, Not Sacrifice
(Hosea 6:1–6)

WEDNESDAY
Plucking Grain
(Leviticus 19:9–10; Deuteronomy 23:25)

THURSDAY
The Sabbath is for Merciful Acts
(Luke 14:1–6)

FRIDAY
The Father and I Are Working
(John 5:9–18)

SATURDAY
Deliver Justice for the Oppressed
(Psalm 10:12–18)

SUNDAY
Meet Human Need on the Sabbath
(Matthew 12:1–14)

Notes

_____

_____

_____

_____

Teaching Tips

Words You Should Know

A. Tares (Matthew 13:25) *zizanion* (Gk.)—A kind of weed resembling wheat except the grains are black.

B. Leaven (v. 33) *zume* (Gk.)—Any substance that produces fermentation when added to dough.

Teacher Preparation

Unifying Principle—You Reap What You Sow. People want to experience living in a world filled with justice. Where can we find justice? Jesus' parables describe the kingdom of heaven, where God's justice is merciful, pervasive, and certain.

A. Pray for lesson clarity and understanding.

B. Read the selected Scripture passage in two or more modern translations.

C. Read More Light on the Text for a better understanding of context of the passage.

D. Complete the lesson in the *Precepts For Living®* Personal Study Guide.

O—Open the Lesson

A. Ask a volunteer to pray for the class.

B. State the title of the lesson and ask someone to read Aim For Change.

C. Ask for a volunteer to read the In Focus story and discuss as a class.

P—Present the Scriptures

A. Read the Focal Verses.

B. Have volunteers read The People, Places, and Times, Background, and In Depth sections and discuss.

E—Explore the Meaning

A. Answer the questions in the Search the Scriptures and Discuss the Meaning sections.

B. Have a volunteer read the Lesson in Our Society section and discuss.

N—Next Steps for Application

A. Encourage the class to apply the Make It Happen section during the following week.

B. Summarize the lesson and close in prayer.

Worship Guide

For the Superintendent or Teacher
Theme: Parables of God's Just Kingdom
Song: "All Hail the Power of Jesus' Name"
Devotional Reading: Psalm 78:1–8

459

Parables of God's Just Kingdom

Bible Background • MATTHEW 13:24–43
Printed Text • MATTHEW 13:24–33 | Devotional Reading • PSALM 78:1–8

—————— Aim for Change ——————

By the end of this lesson, we will: EXPLAIN how each of the parables teaches that God's kingdom is established on justice; GIVE thanks for being included as a citizen in God's just kingdom; and DECIDE to practice justice in all relationships with others in and out of God's kingdom.

———— In Focus ————

Clarence was infuriated as he drove from church on Sunday morning. He suspected certain deacons were not being honest with the offerings. Two weeks ago, he voiced his concern to the pastor and the board. They shrugged it off and refused to even investigate it. Clarence couldn't understand how they could not see what was happening right in front of their eyes. Their reasoning was that they knew the deacons in question and had no doubt about their integrity.

Clarence's wife, Veronica, assured him that justice would come in God's time and in God's way. At first Clarence couldn't accept her perspective, but then he decided to pray about it. While down on his knees, God reassured him that He was not blind to the injustice that was going on. For this particular situation, all Clarence had to do was continue to do his part and speak up.

The following Thursday, Clarence was watching the news. A journalist was reporting on an investigation regarding a local political office and embezzlement of government funds. He couldn't believe it—it was one of the deacons! He was not only dishonest with the church's money, but also dishonest with the city's money. Justice was finally served.

Sometimes it may seem like people are allowed to continue to do their bad deeds without consequences. It is more alarming when it happens among the people of God. Have you ever seen God deal out justice to those who portray themselves as innocent?

—————— Keep in Mind ——————

"Let both grow together until the harvest: and in the time of harvest I will say to the reapers, Gather ye together first the tares, and bind them in bundles to burn them: but gather the wheat into my barn" (Matthew 13:30).

"Let both grow together until the harvest: and in the time of harvest I will say to the reapers, Gather ye together first the tares, and bind them in bundles to burn them: but gather the wheat into my barn" (Matthew 13:30).

Focal Verses

KJV **Matthew 13:24** Another parable put he forth unto them, saying, The kingdom of heaven is likened unto a man which sowed good seed in his field:

25 But while men slept, his enemy came and sowed tares among the wheat, and went his way.

26 But when the blade was sprung up, and brought forth fruit, then appeared the tares also.

27 So the servants of the householder came and said unto him, Sir, didst not thou sow good seed in thy field? from whence then hath it tares?

28 He said unto them, An enemy hath done this. The servants said unto him, Wilt thou then that we go and gather them up?

29 But he said, Nay; lest while ye gather up the tares, ye root up also the wheat with them.

30 Let both grow together until the harvest: and in the time of harvest I will say to the reapers, Gather ye together first the tares, and bind them in bundles to burn them: but gather the wheat into my barn.

31 Another parable put he forth unto them, saying, The kingdom of heaven is like to a grain of mustard seed, which a man took, and sowed in his field:

32 Which indeed is the least of all seeds: but when it is grown, it is the greatest among herbs, and becometh a tree, so that the birds of the air come and lodge in the branches thereof.

33 Another parable spake he unto them; The kingdom of heaven is like unto leaven, which a woman took, and hid in three measures of meal, till the whole was leavened.

NLT **Matthew 13:24** Here is another story Jesus told: "The Kingdom of Heaven is like a farmer who planted good seed in his field.

25 But that night as the workers slept, his enemy came and planted weeds among the wheat, then slipped away.

26 When the crop began to grow and produce grain, the weeds also grew.

27 The farmer's workers went to him and said, 'Sir, the field where you planted that good seed is full of weeds! Where did they come from?'

28 'An enemy has done this!' the farmer exclaimed. 'Should we pull out the weeds?' they asked.

29 'No,' he replied, 'you'll uproot the wheat if you do.

30 Let both grow together until the harvest. Then I will tell the harvesters to sort out the weeds, tie them into bundles, and burn them, and to put the wheat in the barn.'"

31 Here is another illustration Jesus used: "The Kingdom of Heaven is like a mustard seed planted in a field.

32 It is the smallest of all seeds, but it becomes the largest of garden plants; it grows into a tree, and birds come and make nests in its branches."

33 Jesus also used this illustration: "The Kingdom of Heaven is like the yeast a woman used in making bread. Even though she put only a little yeast in three measures of flour, it permeated every part of the dough."

The People, Places, and Times

The Kingdom of Heaven. The phrase "Kingdom of Heaven" in Matthew is synonymous with the term "Kingdom of God" in Mark and Luke's Gospels. In the first century, the Jewish people expected the coming of a Messiah who would defeat their oppressors and rule the earth. Throughout the Gospels, Jesus expands this definition to mean the dynamic rule and reign of God.

Parable. A parable is a story that illustrates a spiritual truth. It literally means something thrown alongside something else. Jesus employed this method of teaching quite frequently. Forty-six parables are found in the Gospels. Parables were a way to use examples from everyday life in order to illuminate people's minds regarding an abstract reality.

What would it look like to see Jesus rule and reign in justice over our world right now?

Background

Matthew 13 is dedicated to the parables of the kingdom. In eight parables, Jesus explains how to understand the kingdom of God to a large crowd that had followed Him to the sea. He used analogies that His listeners would understand pretty well, such as the tasks of a sower (1–8 and 18–23) or the result of yeast in dough (33). Thus, the revelation of the kingdom of God is hidden in plain sight, which is the nature of the kingdom; its progress in the world is not so obvious, but rather hidden like the meaning of a parable. It is probably for this reason that Jesus speaks to them in parables—usually simple stories used to communicate something that can only be understood if the listener pays close attention. They can hide the truth in plain sight from those who are uninterested or inattentive. Earlier in the chapter (v. 10), one of the disciples asked Jesus why He used parables to communicate these great mysteries of the kingdom. In response, Jesus said,

"because it is given unto you to know the mysteries of the kingdom of heaven, but to them it is not given." His speaking of the kingdom in parables draws a parallel to the audience of the book of Isaiah, which read, "Listen carefully, but do not understand. Watch closely, but learn nothing" (Isaiah 6:9). Parables invite those who can to hear what the Spirit is saying. Jesus would often take time to interpret some of the parables to the disciples, usually in private.

The text before us focuses on three of the eight parables in Matthew 13—the wheat and the weeds, the mustard seed, and the leaven. In the first parable, we hear of two sowers; one is the owner of a field and he sows wheat. The other is an enemy of the owner who comes in the night to sow weeds among the wheat. The second parable is about a mustard seed, which is a small seed that can grow into a tree on which birds can perch. The third is about leaven hid inside a meal.

How can parables help us to understand the dynamics of God's kingdom and how He operates?

At-A-Glance

1. Kingdom Sowing (Matthew 13:24–26)
2. Kingdom Harvest (vv. 27–30)
3. Kingdom Growing (vv. 31–33)

In Depth

1. Kingdom Sowing (Matthew 13:24–26)

Jesus turns from describing people's response to parables, to another parable regarding the kingdom of God. This time He uses the illustration of a farmer with a rival. When the farmer sows his seeds, his rival sneaks in and sows weeds in his field. The allusion to Satan is probably not lost on His listeners. While the good seeds grew and produced wheat, the other seeds grew alongside it but produced weeds.

This more than likely represents those who would seem to be aligned with the kingdom, but produce bad fruit. They are, in effect, not a part of the kingdom and not children of the kingdom. The truth Jesus illustrates is that there will be good and bad seed on the earth, but His kingdom will ultimately right every wrong.

How does it make you feel to know that even though there will be injustice, Jesus will ultimately right every wrong?

2. Kingdom Harvest (vv. 27–30)

The farmer's workers come and alert him to the problem. This doesn't alarm the farmer. He tells them to let everything grow until the harvest, when the wheat will be separated from the weeds. This harvest speaks of the end of the age, when God's kingdom will be fully realized. This time is when God will judge those who are in the kingdom and producing the fruit of the kingdom, and those who do not.

Today, we may see those who commit acts of injustice and all sorts of evil. We may be tempted to take the attitude of the workers who wanted to uproot the weeds right away. Jesus lets us know that it's not our job. He will deliver justice in His time. It is His kingdom and His harvest.

Does waiting for justice to be delivered in God's time mean that we do not work for justice here and now? Why or why not?

3. Kingdom Growing (vv. 31–33)

Now Jesus lets the listeners know how the kingdom of God grows in influence. The kingdom is not a big massive enterprise, not something that the world would look at and admire. He says that it's the size of a mustard seed. The very small and unassuming mustard seed serves as an example of the subversive nature of the kingdom of God. It starts off small, but grows big in influence, just like the mustard tree grows and provides shelter for birds.

Jesus also explains that the kingdom is hidden, like leaven mixed in dough. You can't see it in the dough, but you see its effects. Without leaven, the dough never rises. This is the same with the kingdom of God. It is hidden, but it impacts everything that it contacts. This applies to kingdom justice as well. God's justice might seem to be invisible, but in His timing, it will be fully realized.

What are the effects of God's kingdom that you can see right now?

Search the Scriptures

1. What was the reason the farmer let the wheat and tares grow together (Matthew 13:29)?

2. How do the qualities of the leaven and the mustard seed represent the kingdom of God (vv. 31–33)?

Discuss the Meaning

1. How does it feel to hear that God will judge people ultimately at the end of the age? Do you think it makes people passively wait for justice? Why or why not?

2. How can we discern the activity of God's kingdom even though it starts off small and invisible?

Lesson in Our Society

We often look to outward signs as proof that God is at work. We can look for churches to be filled with showy displays of spiritual power, well-dressed people, and smooth words. Similarly, we expect to see God's justice immediately when it comes to police brutality, corrupt politics, and extreme poverty. In reality, the way people dress or how they talk does not signal that the kingdom of God is near, and His justice is not always immediately seen.

The issue is that we do not understand the way God's kingdom works. The dynamics of the kingdom are the opposite of this world. We look through our human perception and expect things to be worked out in big and bold ways. In contrast, God uses the small and invisible to actually show His power and bring about change. God displays His power by using what seems insignificant to subvert the power of what the world sees as mighty. That is how the kingdom of heaven works.

What is your understanding of how the kingdom of God works?

Make It Happen

• Research potential issues of injustice in your local area.

• Make a list of the issues where you want to see God's justice, and make a similar list of the different ways He is using people to bring about justice concerning those issues.

• Write in your journal about the ways in which God's kingdom is small and insignificant while at the same time growing in its influence in your own life.

Follow the Spirit

What God wants me to do:

_____

_____

_____

_____

Remember Your Thoughts

Special insights I have learned:

_____

_____

More Light on the Text
Matthew 13:24–33

24 Another parable put he forth unto them, saying, The kingdom of heaven is likened unto a man which sowed good seed in his field: 25 But while men slept, his enemy came and sowed tares among the wheat, and went his way. 26 But when the blade was sprung up, and brought forth fruit, then appeared the tares also.

This was a rather long day in which Jesus had a large crowd following Him. Being a great rabbi, He would make sure that He shares something with them that would stay. Living in an oral Middle Eastern culture, parables make a great tool for communication. They are memorable and fluid. They do not render themselves to only one interpretation, which means they can stay on the mind of the hearers long after they have been told. Many African cultures are similar. They value parables, proverbs, and folk stories, they are an excellent way of communicating.

Here Jesus has several parables lined up. Some scholars have asserted that He did not teach them all at once but Matthew collected them all in one chapter. The chapter started with the parable of the sower whose seeds fell on four different kinds of grounds. And now He puts before them another parable. In this one, He talks about wheat and tares sown in the same field. Thus, Jesus is continuing with the agricultural theme started in the previous parable, but here the message is different. While the first parable of the sower is about how hearers respond to God's Word, this second one is about the ongoing presence of evil in a world that is supposed to be the kingdom of God.

This kingdom, He says, is like a field in which the owner sows wheat and his enemy secretly sows tares. The owner's servants discovered the ploy much later, when both the wheat and the weeds have produced their fruit, by which time the roots of the wheat and the weeds have intertwined. The word used here for tares (Gk. *zizania*) is a common term for weeds, wild rice grasses, or false grain. Many scholars agree it is the plant darnel which looks very much like wheat and can be poisonous.

27 So the servants of the householder came and said unto him, Sir, didst not thou sow good seed in thy field? from whence then hath it tares? 28 He said unto them, An enemy hath done this. The servants said unto him, Wilt thou then that we go and gather them up? 29 But he said, Nay; lest while ye gather up the tares, ye root up also the wheat with them. 30 Let both grow together until the harvest: and in the time of harvest I will say to the reapers, Gather ye together first the tares, and bind them in bundles to burn them: but gather the wheat into my barn.

The owner of the field is now identified as the master of the household. Here, we learn also that he has slaves (or servants). When these servants notice the weeds growing in the field where only wheat was expected, they ask their master where the weeds came from. The master calmly replies that an enemy has sown the weeds. It does not seem the master is surprised at all. He is not surprised at the efforts of the enemy at sabotaging the field. The servants are anxious to take care of the problem as soon as possible. They want to root the weeds out immediately so that the wheat can bring forth its grain without being choked by the weeds. However, the master warns that they cannot take the weeds out without uprooting the wheat as well, for their roots are intertwined. The only way justice can be done is by patiently waiting for harvest time when the weeds will be burned. In the meantime, the master orders his servants to let both the wheat and the weeds grow together.

Later in the chapter, and in the privacy of their house, Jesus offers the disciples the interpretation of the parable. "He that soweth the good seed is the Son of man; The field is the world; the good seed are the children of the kingdom; but the tares are the children of the wicked one; the enemy that sowed them is the devil; the harvest is the end of the world; and the reapers are the angels" (from vv. 37–39). It is important to note that many Christians have mistaken the parable to be about the church and her members. That interpretation suggests that the field is the church, the seed is the word of God, and the servants are good Christians while the enemy are nominal or bad Christians. This is far from what Jesus says.

The message of the parable is that in the world today, there will be wheat or good seeds (children of the kingdom) and there will be weeds or bad seeds (children of the evil one). And these two "seeds" are systemically intertwined in the circle of life such that ultimate separation and judgment will only be possible at the end of time. While Jesus Himself is the Son of Man who sows good seeds—children of the kingdom—the devil is also active in the world sowing his own seeds—children of the evil one. Thus, just like the wheat and the weeds coexist in the field, children of the kingdom and children of the evil one exist together in the world, not waiting for the destruction of the children of the evil, but also for the children of the kingdom to transform the world like leaven transforms dough.

Reapers will come to do the separation and give the tares to destruction (v. 30). The word used here for "burn" (Gk. *katakaio*, **ka-ta-KIE-oh**) connotes completely burning something up so there is nothing left, and is often used to refer to end-times judgment. But for now, the workers are told to let the wheat and the weeds grow together because the judgment and the weeding belong to God.

In the parable, Christ does not hesitate to say that the enemy is the devil. Christians will do well to note the presence of a real enemy in the world. The devil, though not being an opposite equal with God, is the enemy who sows his children into the world. He is the father of lies who only comes to steal, kill, and destroy (John 8:44, 10:10). He leads a spiritual kingdom of rebellion. His children—the children of evil—fight against the progress of the kingdom of God.

31 Another parable put he forth unto them, saying, The kingdom of heaven is like to a grain of mustard seed, which a man took, and sowed in his field: 32 Which indeed is the least of all seeds: but when it is grown, it is the greatest among herbs, and becometh a tree, so that the birds of the air come and lodge in the branches thereof.

Again, He put before them another parable. This time it is about a mustard seed that, when planted, grows into a tree. This is one of the two small parables that Matthew inserts between the parable of the wheat and weeds and its interpretation (v. 36). The second one is about yeast that, when put into dough, leavens it. Both these parables demonstrate that even though the kingdom of God may seem small and contemptible in its beginning, its growth and influence is inevitable. Zechariah once prophesied, "Who hath despised the day of small things?" (from Zechariah 4:10). Of course, this is the story of the manifestation of the kingdom through the ministry of Jesus, which started with an initial gathering was of twelve disciples, but continues to grow until it reaches its full potential in God.

The kingdom of God is like a mustard seed that someone planted. Thus, in this parable, just like the previous one, there is a sower (Jesus), the seed that he sows (the children of His kingdom—the community of His followers, the church), and the sower's field (which is the world). When planted, the mustard plant would grow to be "the greatest of shrubs to become a tree." Size represents significance. The kingdom would grow both in its earthly significance and its spiritual impact.

The plant that is referred to here as mustard has been a subject of theological discourse for ages. Most probably, it is the black mustard, *sinapis nigra*, a plant that can grow up several feet tall, but whose seed is proverbially known to be the smallest of the earth. Of course, the *sinapis* seed was not the smallest—but the mustard seed was, in Jewish tradition, proverbial for smallness. It is mentioned five times in the Gospels, generally in relation to its smallness in size, and is connected to either the kingdom of God (as in this parable, repeated in Mark 4:30–32 and Luke 13:18–19) and the smallness of the faith needed to move either a mountain (Matthew 17:20) or a mulberry tree (Luke 17:5–6). And this smallness is the main thrust of the parable. That the kingdom of God would grow extremely big should not be a surprise to people who expected a messiah so powerful that he would deliver them from Roman rule. However, it is the humble beginnings of the kingdom, that it would start small—like a mustard seed—that would a ground-breaking revelation.

33 Another parable spake he unto them; The kingdom of heaven is like unto leaven, which a woman took, and hid in three measures of meal, till the whole was leavened.

Matthew introduces this parable with yet again, "He told them another parable." And this is the final parable before they retreat from the beach to the house where Jesus would interpret the parable of the wheat and weeds. The kingdom of God is like leaven, or yeast (Gk. *zume*, **ZOO-may**), which is used in both positive (v. 33) and negative (Mark 8:15) contexts to metaphorically refer to behavior that spreads from person to person. A small amount of yeast is mixed with flour, and when placed under the right circumstances, transforms a small dough into larger dough. So, while the previous parable of the mustard seed highlights something big like a tree coming out of a small seed, this parable of the yeast emphasizes the pervasive and transformative nature of the yeast. And, indeed, the yeast can make something small, big.

However, as the KJV puts it, the woman hid the yeast in the dough. The Greek word is *enkrupto* (**en-KROOP-to**) which means "to cover or to conceal in something, to mingle one thing with another and thus to hide one thing in another." Its root gives us the word "encrypt," which in our day connotes a mixing of letters to hide the message. The yeast had to be mixed well in the dough as to be hidden. It is this hidden nature of the transformative work of the kingdom that stands out in this parable. It is after being so mixed that it causes the dough to ferment and rise. Outside the dough, the yeast can do nothing. Inside the dough, the transformative power of the yeast is unleashed, though concealed to the eye. It spreads slowly throughout the dough until it is leavened. This is a picture of the kingdom of God which is hidden but pervasively transforming the world.

Say It Correctly

Leaven. **LEH**-vin.
Tare. **TAIR**.

Daily Bible Readings

MONDAY
Rehearse the Deeds of the Lord
(Psalm 78:1–8)

TUESDAY
God's Tree of Justice for All
(Ezekiel 17:22–24)

WEDNESDAY
Jesus Affirmed as Son of Man
(Matthew 16:13–20)

THURSDAY
Jesus Not Believed in Hometown
(Matthew 13:54–58)

FRIDAY
Will Son of Man Find Faith?
(Luke 18:1–8)

SATURDAY
Jesus Explains Parable of the Weeds
(Matthew 13:34–43)

SUNDAY
Defer Judgment Until the Final Day
(Matthew 13:24–33)

Sources:
Adeyemo, Tokunboh, *Africa Bible Commentary: A One-Volume Commentary*. Nairobi, Kenya: WordAlive Publishers, 2006.
Dunn, James D. G., and J. W. Rogerson. *Eerdmans Commentary on the Bible*. Grand Rapids, MI: W.B. Eerdmans, 2003.
Green, Michael. *The Message of Matthew: The Kingdom of Heaven*. Rev ed. Leicester: InterVarsity, 2000.
Hagner, Donald Alfred. *Matthew 1–13*. Word Biblical Commentary V. 33a. Edited by Bruce M. Metzger. Dallas, TX.: Word Books, 1993.
Keener, Craig S. *A Commentary on the Gospel of Matthew*. Grand Rapids, MI.: W.B. Eerdmans Publishers, 1999.

Teaching Tips

Words You Should Know

A. Scribes (Matthew 15:1) *grammateus* (Gk.)—Interpreters and teachers of the Mosaic Law.

B. Hypocrites (v. 7) *hupokrites* (Gk.)—People who are pretentious, pretending to be better than they really are.

Teacher Preparation

Unifying Principle—More Than Lip Service. Sometimes things we do out of tradition are not fair to others. How do we act with true fairness and justice? When the Pharisees confronted Jesus on a question of ritual observance, He challenged them to do what is truly fair and just and not merely talk about it.

A. Read the Bible Background and Devotional Readings.

B. Complete Lesson 3 in the *Precepts For Living®* Personal Study Guide.

C. Read the Focal Verses in two or more modern translations.

O—Open the Lesson

A. Ask a volunteer to open the class with prayer.

B. Ask a volunteer to read the In Focus story and Aim for Change.

P—Present the Scriptures

A. Ask for volunteers to read the Focal Verses.

B. Unpack the lesson using The People, Places, and Times; Background; At-A-Glance; and In Depth sections.

E—Explore the Meaning

A. Discuss the Search the Scripture questions.

B. Work through the Discuss the Meaning, Lesson in Our Society, and Make It Happen sections.

N—Next Steps for Application

A. Complete the Follow the Spirit and Remember Your Thoughts sections.

B. Close in prayer.

Worship Guide

For the Superintendent or Teacher
Theme: Jesus Teaches About Justice
Song: "Give Me a Clean Heart"
Devotional Reading: Mark 7:1–13

469

Jesus Teaches About Justice

Bible Background • MATTHEW 15:1–9; MARK 7:1–13
Printed Text • MATTHEW 15:1–9 | Devotional Reading • MARK 7:1–13

—————— Aim for Change ——————

By the end of this lesson, we will: CONTRAST Jesus' concept of obedience to God with that of the Pharisees; REPENT of offering lip service to God while neglecting to honor God inwardly; and COMMIT to follow God wholeheartedly and not merely conform to outward religious traditions.

———————— In Focus ————————

Dayshawn had grown up in church. He could not remember if he had ever missed a Sunday. He was so active in church that he was in the building at least four to five days a week. If it wasn't Bible study or midweek service, it was choir rehearsal or Sunday night youth service. Besides that, when things were slow at his home church, Dayshawn would travel around to other churches, especially when a famous preacher was in town.

One day Dayshawn's friend Darren came by to ask him to play basketball. Dayshawn told him it was almost time for church and he didn't want to miss it. "Man, you go to church every day. You practically live there," Darren said.

"When the Spirit is moving, it's a privilege. I don't want to take that for granted," Dayshawn replied.

Just then, Dayshawn's neighbor, Deacon White, came by and asked them if they wanted to go volunteer at the soup kitchen. "I can't do it tonight," Dayshawn said. "I got church. The Spirit is moving."

"If that's what the Spirit is moving you do, I don't know what kind of spirit that is. The Spirit is moving me to make a difference," Deacon White said.

Dayshawn thought about what Deacon White said. He always thought that the Holy Spirit was moving when he had goosebumps, not when he actually served others. The next week, both Darren and Dayshawn decided to volunteer at the soup kitchen.

Sometimes our religious tradition can make us blind to God's demands of obedience. Describe a time when you realized you were neglecting to obey one of God's commands.

—————— Keep in Mind ——————

"This people draweth nigh unto me with their mouth, and honoureth me with their lips; but their heart is far from me" (Matthew 15:8).

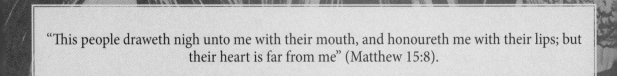

"This people draweth nigh unto me with their mouth, and honoureth me with their lips; but their heart is far from me" (Matthew 15:8).

Focal Verses

KJV **Matthew 15:1** Then came to Jesus scribes and Pharisees, which were of Jerusalem, saying,

2 Why do thy disciples transgress the tradition of the elders? for they wash not their hands when they eat bread.

3 But he answered and said unto them, Why do ye also transgress the commandment of God by your tradition?

4 For God commanded, saying, Honour thy father and mother: and, He that curseth father or mother, let him die the death.

5 But ye say, Whosoever shall say to his father or his mother, It is a gift, by whatsoever thou mightest be profited by me;

6 And honour not his father or his mother, he shall be free. Thus have ye made the commandment of God of none effect by your tradition.

7 Ye hypocrites, well did Esaias prophesy of you, saying,

8 This people draweth nigh unto me with their mouth, and honoureth me with their lips; but their heart is far from me.

9 But in vain they do worship me, teaching for doctrines the commandments of men.

NLT **Matthew 15:1** Some Pharisees and teachers of religious law now arrived from Jerusalem to see Jesus. They asked him,

2 "Why do your disciples disobey our age-old tradition? For they ignore our tradition of ceremonial hand washing before they eat."

3 Jesus replied, "And why do you, by your traditions, violate the direct commandments of God?

4 For instance, God says, 'Honor your father and mother,' and 'Anyone who speaks disrespectfully of father or mother must be put to death.'

5 But you say it is all right for people to say to their parents, 'Sorry, I can't help you. For I have vowed to give to God what I would have given to you.'

6 In this way, you say they don't need to honor their parents. And so you cancel the word of God for the sake of your own tradition.

7 You hypocrites! Isaiah was right when he prophesied about you, for he wrote,

8 'These people honor me with their lips, but their hearts are far from me.

9 Their worship is a farce, for they teach man-made ideas as commands from God.'"

The People, Places, and Times

Pharisees. As one of the largest groups of Jewish religious leaders in the New Testament, the Pharisees transformed the focus of Judaism from sacrifice to law. They accepted the Scripture (our Old Testament) as the authority because they believed the way to God was obedience to the Law. Problems arose, however, because over the years they added hundreds of religious traditions to the Law and then made those traditions as important as the Law.

They were fierce opponents of Jesus because He refuted their interpretation of the Law and many of their traditions.

Hypocrite. A Greek word, its original meaning was to give an answer. The meaning later shifted to describe one who is pretentious or believes he is a better person than he really is. The Gospels describe Jesus' opposition to the religious leaders who acted like hypocrites (see Matthew 6, 15, 22–24; Mark 7; Luke 11–12).

How has hypocritical behavior amongst so-called "Christians" affected our ability to witness and develop positive relationships with those outside the church?

Background

As the first book of the New Testament, Matthew introduced Jesus Christ: "This is a record of the ancestors of Jesus the Messiah, a descendant of David and of Abraham" (Matthew 1:1, NLT). Presented as a proclamation of Good News, the Gospel of Matthew establishes Jesus Christ as the Son of God, the long-awaited Messiah of Israel, and the world's Savior.

The Gospel of Matthew records the birth of Jesus by Mary, who was a virgin; her subsequent marriage to Joseph; the wise men who came to visit the infant Jesus; and the flight of Joseph and Mary to Egypt after an angel of the Lord warned Joseph to take his family there for protection. The Gospel of Matthew describes the birth of Jesus as fulfilling prophecy: "All of this occurred to fulfill the Lord's message through his prophet: 'Look! The virgin will conceive a child! She will give birth to a son, and they will call him Immanuel'" (from vv. 22–23, NLT).

Jesus taught His disciples and, through the Word of God, teaches us how to live and then how to share with others the way to become His followers. "Therefore, go and make disciples of all the nations, baptizing them in the name of the Father and the Son and the Holy Spirit. Teach these new disciples to obey all the commands I have given you" (from 28:19–20, NLT).

How can personal beliefs cause us to disagree and argue about the proper interpretation God's Word?

At-A-Glance

1. The Question (Matthew 15:1–3)
2. The Confrontation (vv. 4–6)
3. The Condemnation (vv. 7–9)

In Depth

1. The Question (Matthew 15:1–3)

In verses 1 and 2, the scribes and Pharisees questioned Jesus' authority because His statements and teachings contrasted with their interpretation of the Law. They asked Him why His disciples did not ritually wash their hands prior to eating bread. Jesus did not immediately respond, but instead asked them how they could justify not taking care of their parents, which is a commandment of the Law. He turned their question about something minor into a larger question of faithfulness to the Law.

Why do we have a tendency to focus on trivial matters and traditions versus larger issues of faithfulness?

2. The Confrontation (vv. 4–6)

Jesus further elaborates on His question by pointing out their inconsistency. He confronts them with the Word of God. The commandments say "Honor your father and your mother" and "He who curses father or mother, let him be put to death." What they were doing by not honoring their father was not trivial. They were committing a capital offense according to the Law. Although dishonoring one's parents was a capital offense, tradition made it acceptable.

The "tradition" to which Jesus referred was called Corban. A person who made a Corban vow was dedicating money to God's Temple. Unfortunately, some would make a Corban vow and then hold the money and continue to use it as they saw fit. But they could refuse to help their parents, ostensibly because the money was "spoken for." Jesus pointed out that this was putting tradition above the Law to help one's parents. In following this tradition, one would be committing injustice against their own flesh and blood.

Have religious traditions superseded the authority of the Word in our churches and personal lives? Why or why not?

3. The Condemnation (vv. 7–9)

Next, Jesus follows up with a condemnation of their actions. He not only condemns them, but He uses the prophet Isaiah for support. The Pharisees are people who "draw nigh" with their mouth and honor "with their lips." In reality, they are far from God. They teach their own traditions as law and violate the Law of God. This is a supreme form of idolatry as it uses what is supposed to be good as a way of avoiding obedience to God. Traditions are good, but they are sometimes in opposition of the right thing to do.

Many times it's easier to go along with "how we have always done things" than to pursue what is just and right. Jesus holds a mirror up to this hypocritical attitude and shows us that if our traditions obstruct justice and human flourishing, then they are worthless. God is only pleased with our obedience to Him, not man-made rules.

What can we do to ensure we are fulfilling Jesus' commands and not following empty traditions?

Search the Scriptures

1. How were the religious leaders using tradition to excuse breaking God's Law (Matthew 15:5)?

2. What does it mean to make "the commandment of God of none effect" (v. 6)?

Discuss the Meaning

Jesus confronted the religious leaders on their traditions. Does today's church have traditions that have a negative impact on pursuing justice for others?

Lesson in Our Society

Many young people are pursuing justice through organizations outside the church. The question then becomes, has the Black church lost its prominence on issues? Are there traditions within our churches that keep us from connecting with young people as well as actually pursuing justice?

Jesus knew that man-made traditions were not as important as obeying God's Word and walking in righteousness. Many things are minor and we as humans have a tendency to make them major. It is our responsibility to examine ourselves and see whether we have let less than important traditions become idols that keep us from pursuing God's heart. Justice for all trumps traditions that benefit a few.

How can we discern between a positive and negative tradition?

Make It Happen

• Review church traditions that might be a hindrance to advocating for justice.

• Examine when the tradition transitioned from being a meaningful remembrance or celebration to an event without meaning.

• Once that transition has been identified, examine steps to redirect the tradition toward loving others and seeking the welfare of the community.

Follow the Spirit

What God wants me to do:

_____

_____

_____

_____

Remember Your Thoughts

Special insights I have learned:

_____

_____

_____

_____

More Light on the Text

Matthew 15:1–9

1 Then came to Jesus scribes and Pharisees, which were of Jerusalem, saying, 2 Why do thy disciples transgress the tradition of the elders? for they wash not their hands when they eat bread. 3 But he answered and said unto them, Why do ye also transgress the commandment of God by your tradition?

The Pharisees in Jerusalem felt that it was their responsibility to see that the Israelites obeyed the Law as they thought it should be done. Generation after generation, the Pharisees and various rabbis had interpreted the Law with very detailed explanations about how to obey the smallest phrase. In Exodus 30:18–21, the priests were commanded to wash before they offered sacrifices to the Lord, but somehow this got magnified to having everyone wash before, during, and after eating. Even the individual washing routines were spelled out differently. The Pharisees took baths after they went to market, because they thought that maybe the dust from a Gentile or some other unclean person or thing might contaminate them. In many religions, people avoid doing or touching some things because they think it will make them impure or even unlucky. To disobey the hand-washing regulations devised by the Pharisees was considered transgressing (Gk. *parabaino*, **pa-ra-BYE-no**), which means "to walk beside or across," violating a command. In this context, the Pharisees were "walking across" the boundaries established by God.

So the Pharisees sent the equivalent of the religious police to check out this new teacher called Jesus. One of the first things they noticed was that His disciples were not washing their hands with the specific directions passed down by the Pharisees' traditions. The traditions (Gk. *paradosis*, **pa-RA-do-sees**, "that which is handed down") had come to have the same weight as the precepts written in the Old Testament.

The word "also" (Gk. *kai*, **KIE**) should not be overlooked here. When Jesus used this word, He was admitting that His disciples were not obeying the hand-washing customs—but He accused the Pharisees of far worse. They were disobeying God's commandments plainly written in the Scripture. Jesus was really putting the Pharisees on the spot. They thought they were politely (although with their noses in the air) correcting this upstart teacher, but Jesus was boldly accusing them—the moral police of Judaism—of sinning against God's Law.

4 For God commanded, saying, Honour thy father and mother: and, He that curseth father or mother, let him die the death. 5 But ye say, Whosoever shall say to his father or his mother, It is a gift, by whatsoever thou mightest be profited by me; 6 And honour not his father or his mother, he shall be free. Thus have ye made the commandment of God of none effect by your tradition.

The King James Version translates the Greek phrase *thanato teleutato* (**tha-NA-toe te-lew-TAH-to**) as "to die the death," reversing the order of the words for English readers. This comes from the Hebrew idiom found in the verses Jesus quotes here, "he shall certainly be executed," which shows the seriousness with which God's Word treats disrespecting one's parents (Exodus 21:17; Leviticus 20:9). The command to honor one's parents was the fifth commandment (Exodus 20:12), the first with a promise for obedience attached to it (Ephesians 6:2). After the commandments were stated, the book of Exodus elaborated upon them with punishments for disobedience: death (Exodus 21:15, 17).

Scripture has no record of this ever being carried out, but it does emphasize that God holds obedience and respect within the family as an absolute value. The family is meant to be a picture of the relationship that God desires to have with us—He as our Father and we as His children. Disobedience or disrespect of our Heavenly Father deserves eternal punishment. Perhaps the grandest story of the son who disrespected his father was the prodigal son, but in the end, the father graciously forgave his son, just as our loving heavenly Father desires to forgive our sins and restore the relationship with Him that has been broken by our sin (Luke 15:11–32).

The command to honor one's parents was not meant just for children still living at home with their mother and father, but also extended to adult children as well. Understand that this is not about "obedience" to parents, but "honoring" them—something children should do their entire lives. The Jews clearly understood that grown children were responsible for the financial welfare of the parents who raised them, which is what Jesus was pointing out. The Pharisees had a tradition that allowed adult children to get out of their financial responsibilities to their elderly parents. The Greek word for gift is *doron* (**DO-ron**), referring in this instance specifically to an offering or sacrifice. This was just a tricky bit of semantics, because

the one making this oath was not promising to give it to the Temple, but because it was an oath, his wealth was placed out of the reach of his financially needy parents. Thus, he did not have to do anything with his money except keep it for himself.

When an adult son or daughter uttered the phrase, "It is a gift," it was an oath. God's people are commanded to keep any oaths they make (Numbers 30:2). In Mark's parallel to this Scripture, he uses the word "Corban" instead of "gift" (Mark 7:1–23). Corban is the actual Greek word (**kor-BAN**), and referred to a gift designated as an offering for the Lord. In the situation that Jesus was referring to, however, it was not actually given to the Lord. An oath should be kept, but Jesus taught that it is more important to obey the Lord's direct commands.

7 Ye hypocrites, well did Esaias prophesy of you, saying, 8 This people draweth nigh unto me with their mouth, and honoureth me with their lips; but their heart is far from me. 9 But in vain they do worship me, teaching for doctrines the commandments of men.

"Well" conveys the meaning of "honestly" (Gk. *kalos*, **ka-LOCE**), so Jesus was telling the Pharisees that Isaiah was correct in what he said: "Wherefore the Lord said, Forasmuch as this people draw near me with their mouth, and with their lips do honour me, but have removed their heart far from me, and their fear toward me is taught by the precept of men" (Isaiah 29:13).

The phrase "their heart is far from me" means to hold off from, to deliberately hold oneself far from God. So the picture Isaiah presented is of a hypocritical religion in which people say they are close to God, but inwardly their hearts are far from Him. Instead of teaching people to obey God's Word, the religious leaders raised their own interpretations above the Law given to their ancestors—and then taught the people to do the same. This is in opposition to the real heart behind God's Law. God is far more concerned with our relationships with one another and with Him than displays of religious tradition.

Sources:

Barclay, William. *The Gospel of Matthew*, Volume 2. Philadelphia, PA: Westminister Press, 1975.

France R. *The Gospel of Matthew*. Grand Rapids, MI: Wm. B. Eerdmans Publishing, 2007.

Guzik, David. *Matthew*. Santa Barbara, CA: Enduring Word Media, 2012.

Harney, Kevin G. *Seismic Shifts Little Changes That Make a Big Difference in Your Life*. Grand Rapids, MI: Zondervan, 2007.

Stern D.H. *Jewish New Testament Commentary, A Companion Volume to the Jewish New Testament*. Clarksville, MD: Messianic Jewish Publisher, 1992.

Say It Correctly

Esaias. eh-**SAI**-ahs.
Hypocrite. hi-puh-**KRIT**.

Daily Bible Readings

MONDAY
Wash Away Your Evil Ways
(Isaiah 1:12–17)

TUESDAY
Let Justice Roll Like Water
(Amos 5:18–24)

WEDNESDAY
Honor Your Father and Mother
(Exodus 20:12; Deuteronomy 5:16)

THURSDAY
The Spirit Gives Life
(2 Corinthians 3:1–6)

FRIDAY
Call No One Profane or Unclean
(Acts 10:23–33)

SATURDAY
What Defiles Comes from the Heart
(Mark 7:14–23)

SUNDAY
Treat Your Parents Justly
(Matthew 15:1–9)

Notes

_____

_____

_____

_____

Teaching Tips

Words You Should Know

A. Rich (Luke 16:19) *plousios* (Gk.)—Wealthy, abounding with.

B. Beggar (v. 20) *ptochos* (Gk.)—Poor and helpless; one who in his abjectness needs lifting.

Teacher Preparation

Unifying Principle—The Tables Are Turned. Many are greatly concerned about the inequities in the lives of the poor versus the rich. How will these inequities be resolved? The story of the rich man and Lazarus tells us that the poor will receive their reward.

A. Pray for clarity as you study the lesson.

B. Read the selected passage in two or more translations.

C. Read More Light on the Text for additional understanding.

O—Open the Lesson

A. Open the lesson with prayer and ask a student to especially intercede on behalf of those who are impoverished as well as the rich. Ask, "Why do we need to pray for both?"

B. Show contrasting images of the rich and the poor in today's world. How are they treated differently? Discuss.

C. Review the Aim for Change and reflect on how you consider the poor of the world. How does this lesson affect you personally?

P—Present the Scriptures

A. Ask for a volunteer to read the lesson.

B. Lead students in answering the Search the Scriptures, Discuss the Meaning, or any other questions that may arise from your study.

C. Incorporate corresponding Scriptures that further illuminate the text to add to the discussion.

E—Explore the Meaning

A. Have students create a skit using the lesson in today's context. Ask who would be the rich man and Lazarus today.

B. Discuss why Jesus would use this parable to explain how God views justice for the poor.

N—Next Steps for Application

A. Read the Lesson in Our Society and Make It Happen sections aloud.

B. Encourage your students pray for opportunities to individually share Christ this week by giving to those less fortunate domestically or abroad.

Worship Guide

For the Superintendent and the Teacher
Theme: Reaping God's Justice
Song: "Pass Me Not"
Devotional Reading: Luke 6:20–26

Reaping God's Justice

Bible Background • LUKE 16:19–31; JOHN 5:24–30
Printed Text • LUKE 16:19–31 | Devotional Reading • LUKE 6:20–26

———— Aim for Change ————

By the end of this lesson we will: UNDERSTAND what the parable of the rich man and Lazarus teaches about God's definition of justice; SENSE how this passage challenges simplistic understandings of who is or is not included in God's kingdom; and IDENTIFY with the most vulnerable members of society in order to minister to them in Jesus' name.

⤳ In Focus

Jay has lived a very privileged life. His family always took pride in sponsoring events to help the less fortunate, but at the dinner table, he often heard both his grandfather and father say that people in poverty live that way because they are lazy and worthless. His family felt that life would be better off if those people were hidden away somewhere. Jay secretly agreed and felt a sense of arrogance and pride that his family was not in that position. They weren't loafing off of others, but had made their money by working hard. He planned to continue that legacy.

Then one day while walking downtown, Jay ran into Clarence, a former corporate attorney for a major energy company. Having achieved his dream, Clarence had thought he had it all—until disaster struck. On his watch, the company came under a major federal investigation, which cost him his career. Clarence lost everything and was homeless, living on the street.

Jay knew Clarence through his father, so when Jay saw him, he was in shock. After exchanging some pleasantries, Jay asked what happened to him. All Clarence could muster up was, "One bad decision and I lost everything." Jay slipped some money into Clarence's pocket as well as his business card. Jay was totally shaken when he left Clarence.

The rich and poor will both be judged by God. What kind of perceptions do most people have about those who are rich and those who are poor?

———— Keep in Mind ————

"But Abraham said, Son, remember that thou in thy lifetime receivedst thy good things, and likewise Lazarus evil things: but now he is comforted, and thou art tormented" (Luke 16:25).

"But Abraham said, Son, remember that thou in thy lifetime receivedst thy good things, and likewise Lazarus evil things: but now he is comforted, and thou art tormented" (Luke 16:25).

Focal Verses

KJV **Luke 16:19** There was a certain rich man, which was clothed in purple and fine linen, and fared sumptuously every day:

20 And there was a certain beggar named Lazarus, which was laid at his gate, full of sores,

21 And desiring to be fed with the crumbs which fell from the rich man's table: moreover the dogs came and licked his sores.

22 And it came to pass, that the beggar died, and was carried by the angels into Abraham's bosom: the rich man also died, and was buried;

23 And in hell he lift up his eyes, being in torments, and seeth Abraham afar off, and Lazarus in his bosom.

24 And he cried and said, Father Abraham, have mercy on me, and send Lazarus, that he may dip the tip of his finger in water, and cool my tongue; for I am tormented in this flame.

25 But Abraham said, Son, remember that thou in thy lifetime receivedst thy good things, and likewise Lazarus evil things: but now he is comforted, and thou art tormented.

26 And beside all this, between us and you there is a great gulf fixed: so that they which would pass from hence to you cannot; neither can they pass to us, that would come from thence.

27 Then he said, I pray thee therefore, father, that thou wouldest send him to my father's house:

28 For I have five brethren; that he may testify unto them, lest they also come into this place of torment.

29 Abraham saith unto him, They have Moses and the prophets; let them hear them.

30 And he said, Nay, father Abraham: but if one went unto them from the dead, they will repent.

NLT **Luke 16:19** Jesus said, "There was a certain rich man who was splendidly clothed in purple and fine linen and who lived each day in luxury.

20 At his gate lay a poor man named Lazarus who was covered with sores.

21 As Lazarus lay there longing for scraps from the rich man's table, the dogs would come and lick his open sores.

22 Finally, the poor man died and was carried by the angels to sit beside Abraham at the heavenly banquet. The rich man also died and was buried,

23 and he went to the place of the dead. There, in torment, he saw Abraham in the far distance with Lazarus at his side.

24 The rich man shouted, 'Father Abraham, have some pity! Send Lazarus over here to dip the tip of his finger in water and cool my tongue. I am in anguish in these flames.'

25 But Abraham said to him, 'Son, remember that during your lifetime you had everything you wanted, and Lazarus had nothing. So now he is here being comforted, and you are in anguish.

26 And besides, there is a great chasm separating us. No one can cross over to you from here, and no one can cross over to us from there.'

27 Then the rich man said, 'Please, Father Abraham, at least send him to my father's home.

28 For I have five brothers, and I want him to warn them so they don't end up in this place of torment.'

29 But Abraham said, 'Moses and the prophets have warned them. Your brothers can read what they wrote.'

30 The rich man replied, 'No, Father Abraham! But if someone is sent to them from

31 And he said unto him, If they hear not Moses and the prophets, neither will they be persuaded, though one rose from the dead.

the dead, then they will repent of their sins and turn to God.'

31 But Abraham said, 'If they won't listen to Moses and the prophets, they won't be persuaded even if someone rises from the dead.'"

The People, Places, and Times

Hades. Also known as Sheol or "place of the dead" in the Old Testament, it is believed to be the region of departed spirits for those who died. Its translated meaning denotes the underworld and was believed to be the immediate state between death and resurrection. In Jesus' parable, it is an impassible gulf or chasm that separates the lost from the righteous.

Abraham's Bosom. Believed to be the compartment of Hades for those who died in right standing with God due to their faith and obedience to the Law. In the Talmud, a collection of rabbinic commentary of the Hebrew Scripture, it is mentioned as the place where the soul rests after death. It is a place of privilege for Abraham's righteous children.

How can you discern whether someone is poor because of their own choices or because of oppression?

Background

The book of Luke features more parables than any of the other Gospels. Jesus used these illustrations to convey key principles of kingdom living. Early on in Luke 16, Jesus told the parable of the dishonest manager to make the point that to be true kingdom believers, we cannot serve both God and wealth (v. 13). After hearing this parable, the Pharisees—because of their own power and wealth—ridiculed Jesus in an attempt to discredit Him. In response, He told the Pharisees that they were good at appearing righteous, but their hearts were not. In their minds, their great wealth showed that

they were blessed by God, but Jesus pointed out that they were only wealthy through dishonest gain. Jesus declared that the kingdom of God runs counter to the dominant culture. The Pharisees relished their wealth and power, but Jesus warned them that they fell short of God's standards. He further bruised their egos by letting them know that God reads the heart, so it was useless to justify themselves based on their works (v. 15).

What do you think is the reason for the widespread association with riches and righteousness in our church culture?

At-A-Glance

1. A Picture of Life (Luke 16:19–21)
2. A Picture of the Afterlife (vv. 22–26)
3. A Picture of a Final Plea (vv. 27–31)

In Depth

1. A Picture of Life (Luke 16:19–21)

In opening this parable, Jesus gave a vivid contrast between the rich man and Lazarus, a poor beggar. He didn't give the rich man a name but gave great detail about his way of life. The rich man was dressed in purple and fine linen, showing his outward wealth and his ability to afford the best. He also noted that the rich man didn't just eat well, but that he "fared sumptuously every day," a signal to the listener that this man did not eat to live but lived to eat. In this context, the ability to buy and enjoy rich foods was a symbol of wealth and abundance.

Jesus sought to drive home the stark contrast between the beggar and the rich man as He spoke to an audience who could relate to each character—they had seen plenty of very wealthy people and plenty of poor and destitute people.

Next, Jesus introduced Lazarus, a homeless beggar who stayed at the gate. As a part of the lowest social caste, he relied on the mercy and kindness of others to even receive crumbs to eat. Unlike the rich man, his existence was truly survival mode. He was unhealthy and malnourished; his clothes were tattered and worn; he lived in constant pain from sores that covered his body. Because he was an outcast, the only touch he experienced was from the dogs that would lick his wounds. Lazarus lived in a constant state of need. Jesus took great time and care to set up this story to communicate a message that is consistent with God's love and care for the poor and His disdain for those who would mistreat them. God commands His people to be a blessing to those in need and to show the same compassion He has shown. Their abundance was never meant to be hoarded, but to be given freely so that no one would be in lack.

What prohibits people from sharing their abundance with others?

2. A Picture of the Afterlife (vv. 22–26)

In this parable, both Lazarus and the rich man died. Jesus then gave a glimpse of the afterlife. Some scholars argue whether Jesus meant to give a portrait of the afterlife or was simply telling a story, but He convincingly made the point that the soul exists after death. Lazarus died and was carried away by angels to Abraham's bosom, which, according to Jewish tradition, was the place of rest for those who died in the faith of Abraham. According to early rabbis, Abraham's bosom was believed to be "paradise."

While Lazarus was carried away by angels, Jesus let the listeners know that the rich man was buried and went to hell. To add insult to injury, the rich man looked up and could see Lazarus in heaven. While the rich man was in torment, the very man he had scoffed and ignored on earth was now in comfort at Abraham's side. Thinking he could use his influence as a descendant of Abraham, the rich man sought to draw upon his lineage to receive mercy. In his continued arrogance, the rich man pleaded with Abraham to allow Lazarus to serve him by providing relief from his agony. Now the roles had been reversed: Lazarus was in comfort and the rich man was in agony. Abraham spoke to the rich man, noting that a gulf or chasm separated them and no one could pass between.

What causes people to seek their paradise in this life?

3. A Picture of a Final Plea (vv. 27–31)

Jesus closed out this parable with the rich man making a final appeal to Abraham on behalf of those he left behind. The rich man asked for Lazarus to be sent back among the living to warn his brothers of the torment to come if they do not make things right (i.e., repent). However, Abraham responded that the rich man's brothers should listen to Moses and the prophets, who already gave warnings and calls to repentance. The rich man continued to plead with Abraham, saying that someone coming from the grave who had experienced the afterlife would be more believable. But his request was denied. Abraham responded: "If they hear not Moses and the prophets, neither will they be persuaded, though one rose from the dead" (from v. 31).

Do you think it's hard for rich people to listen to words of discipline? Why or why not?

Search the Scriptures

1. Where did Lazarus and the rich man go when they died? What was different about their passing (Luke 16:22–23)?

2. Why did the rich man decide to appeal to Abraham (vv. 27–28)?

Discuss the Meaning

1. What does this parable say about how we should view our lives and the value we place on the things we have on this side of eternity?

2. How should we view those who are poor and in need? How can we also help the rich who may be poor in spirit?

Lesson in Our Society

Even in our churches, we often measure people by what they do, what they have, and whom they know rather than their display of Christ-like character. This is not the way of the kingdom. We live in a self-centered, entertainment-driven, overstimulated world where we are raising a generation of young people who have no regard for the sacrifices made to enjoy the freedoms we have today. In striving for a better life, we have forgotten that in our struggle as African Americans, we banded together as a people and that this is the very foundation of our dignity—the heart of compassion to look at each other as brother and sister.

Today's lesson reminds us that God does not want us to shut our eyes, close our ears, and cover our mouths when we see social injustices. We have a mandate from our Lord to care for the poor, the disenfranchised, and the marginalized. In the end, God will see to it that those who honor the poor honor Him and will be richly rewarded.

How can you cultivate a compassionate Christlike attitude toward the less fortunate?

Make It Happen

• Fast one meal a day as a way to show solidarity with the poor.

• Consider the ways you can include those who are less fortunate in your church.

• Make a list of the people you believe are included and excluded from God's kingdom.

Follow the Spirit

What God wants me to do:

_____

_____

_____

_____

Remember Your Thoughts

Special insights I have learned:

_____

_____

_____

_____

More Light on the Text

Luke 16:19–31

19 There was a certain rich man, which was clothed in purple and fine linen, and fared sumptuously every day.

Purple was a royal color in Jesus' time, such as the purple "kingly" robe mockingly tossed around His bleeding body to match his "crown" of thorns (John 19:2, 5). "Fine linen" refers to high-quality undergarments made in Egypt. The Greek word for "fared" (*euphraino*, **ew-FRI-no**) is elsewhere translated "made merry" and "rejoiced." To this is added "sumptuously" (Gk. *lampros*, **lamp-ROCE**), which can also be translated "brightly" or "magnificently." This clearly includes feasting, along with other kinds of merriment found at a bright party. A familiar concept in any time period, the set-up of the parable clearly is a person living in the lap of luxury and enjoying the finest of everything.

20 And there was a certain beggar named Lazarus, which was laid at his gate, full of sores, 21 And desiring to be fed with the crumbs which fell from the rich man's table: moreover the dogs came and licked his sores.

Unique among all of Jesus' parables, here He named one of His characters. That He named the poor man and left the rich man unnamed underscores the most important figure in the story since, normally, the rich would be named and the poor would be nameless. That the man was "full of sores" (Gk. *helkoo*, **hel-KO-oh**) indicates a truly pitiful state.

22 And it came to pass, that the beggar died, and was carried by the angels into Abraham's bosom: the rich man also died, and was buried; 23 And in hell he lift up his eyes, being in torments, and seeth Abraham afar off, and Lazarus in his bosom. 24 And he cried and said, Father Abraham, have mercy on me, and send Lazarus, that he may dip the tip of his finger in water, and cool my tongue; for I am tormented in this flame.

In the reversal, angels escorted the once lowly Lazarus to Abraham's bosom or side (Gk. *kolpos*, **KOL-pos**), which is the ultimate reward for believing Jews, to share in the same contentment as Abraham (cf. Matthew 8:11). The same Greek word is used to describe how Jesus was in the Father's "bosom" (John 1:18), and John leaned on Jesus' "bosom" (John 13:23).

No one really knows all that happens on the other side, but Jesus provides a comforting picture of a gracious escort. For those who

manage to escape judgment for their evil deeds in this life, it is also comforting to know that they will not escape ultimate justice. Paul tells us that those believers who "fall asleep" are with Christ (2 Corinthians 5:8; Philippians 1:23). In contrast, biological Jews are not guaranteed a place at Abraham's bosom by their bloodline alone—rather, along with the rest of unrepentant humanity, they also will face divine judgment.

Lazarus' joining with Abraham contrasted with his previous life with dogs for company. Meanwhile, the rich man's former luxury not only ended but was replaced with torment—an even more serious condition than Lazarus' former humiliation. Another aspect of Lazarus' new reality of blessing was his joining with the patriarchs of the faith (cf. John 8:39), much like the modern future hope of being rejoined with loved ones as well as saints who passed before. The reversal continued with Lazarus' future in heaven compared with the rich man's polar opposite future in hell (Gk. *hades*, **HA-dees**), which is the name from Greek mythology for the underworld, but also just the word used generally for the place where spirits (often evil or unrighteous spirits) dwell after death. In life, the rich man was blessed and Lazarus suffered, but both temporarily. In death, Lazarus was blessed and the rich man suffered, now eternally (cf. the contrasts of the poor versus the rich in the Beatitudes, Luke 6:20–26). Whatever hell actually looks like, clearly there is terrible torment, and fire is a perfect depiction.

25 But Abraham said, Son, remember that thou in thy lifetime receivedst thy good things, and likewise Lazarus evil things: but now he is comforted, and thou art tormented.

Like the rich man in the parable, the rich Pharisees whom Jesus often addressed lived for themselves, not God, and they followed their own wisdom, not God's. They were more concerned with appearing religiously right than actually being right with God in the most important ways. Misusing Scripture for their own benefit, and they also scorned the poor. It is no wonder that they hated Jesus, because He exposed their wrong and self-centered interpretation of the Old Testament (see Deuteronomy 28:1–14; Psalm 1:3–4). Along with material preceding this parable, the story of Lazarus and the rich man is another example of their wrong and self-serving twisting of God's Word.

Jesus' message to the Pharisees is clear: Just as the rich man was fatally wrong to ignore Lazarus and have no compassion on him, so the Pharisees were just as fatally wrong in their self-righteous and cold-hearted lifestyle. Other Old Testament laws pointed to having mercy on the poor and transients (e.g., Leviticus 19:9–10; Deuteronomy 15:7–11 even speaks of a gate like the rich man's). In fact, Isaiah 58:6–7 expressly directs the sharing of bread with the hungry, housing the homeless, and clothing the naked (cf. Matthew 25:35–36). Thus the Pharisees—like some prosperity preachers today—severely miss, to their peril, the point of material blessing. It is not earthly reward for human righteousness to be squandered in unrighteousness; rather, it is earthly seed to be generously sown in humility for heavenly reward.

26 And beside all this, between us and you there is a great gulf fixed: so that they which would pass from hence to you cannot; neither can they pass to us, that would come from thence.

Not only did Jesus state unequivocally that hell is real, but also that there is an unbridgeable, uncrossable chasm between it and Abraham's bosom; no one can cross from one to the other.

The fate of the two men ends with an "utter and unchangeable finality" (Craddock, 192). Death visits ten out of ten people and strikes both the poor and the rich—for one, the trials end; for the other, the blessings end; and for both, judgment begins.

27 Then he said, I pray thee therefore, father, that thou wouldest send him to my father's house: 28 For I have five brethren; that he may testify unto them, lest they also come into this place of torment. 29 Abraham saith unto him, They have Moses and the prophets; let them hear them.

According to Craddock, the Pharisees did not follow their own Scripture, the "law and the prophets" (v. 16), which made them no better than the rich man's brothers who "have Moses and the prophets" (v. 29). The rich man found out the hard way just how far off was his and his family's interpretation of Scripture. Abraham informed him that the Scriptures would be sufficient to teach his brothers properly if only they would be willing to listen. Speaking through Abraham to the Pharisees via the parable, Jesus exposed both their flawed beliefs and their empty hearts.

30 And he said, Nay, father Abraham: but if one went unto them from the dead, they will repent. 31 And he said unto him, If they hear not Moses and the prophets, neither will they be persuaded, though one rose from the dead.

The rich man desperately believed that if his brothers only saw Lazarus alive, they would repent. Yet Jesus clearly stated that not even a dead person raised to life would persuade the hard-hearted (v. 31). Indeed, the Pharisees soon would personally witness this event twice, and their hearts not only would remain stone cold but would grow even more evil. Everything Jesus did was true to Scripture and, most importantly, according to a proper understanding of it—about which He was intentional in teaching His disciples (24:25–27, 44–47).

Scholars speculate whether Jesus referred prophetically to the same Lazarus who would be the next person to be raised from the dead (John 11:43)—certainly, the name coincidence and the mention of resurrection in verse 31 make such an argument compelling. On the other hand, Lazarus was a common name in the day, and most scholars agree that Jesus was probably making reference to His own resurrection, which would forever seal the fate of the Pharisees and all like them—much like the fate of the heartless rich man.

This parable contains a strong warning to heed the Word when it brings conviction and to not harden your heart, because your decisions in life have consequences on the inevitable judgment day. Jesus made it clear that the rich man's eternal demise came from his own decisions and hardness of heart—just as the Pharisees had consciously and selectively rejected the words of Moses and the prophets (Luke 16:29; cf. John 5:46). He might have prophesied about His own resurrection, knowing that not even that miracle of miracles would cause them to repent and change their ways.

A final note is that the rich man's wealth did not condemn him; it is not evil to be blessed with wealth. Rather, his lack of compassion was his undoing. Like the rich fool mentioned earlier, he had no eternal wealth and lost his soul to the deceitfulness of temporal wealth (cf. Luke 12:21, 33, 16:11) and a crucially flawed misunderstanding of Scripture. In the New Testament, Jesus summarized the entire Old Testament in words that could not possibly be clearer—yet, most assuredly, many will continue to fatally miss the plain meaning: "Jesus said unto him, Thou shalt love the Lord thy God with all thy heart, and with all thy soul, and with all thy mind. This is the first and great commandment. And the second is like unto it, Thou shalt love thy neighbour as thyself. On these two commandments hang all the law and the prophets" (Matthew 22:37–40).

Sources:

Bock, Darrell L. *Luke*. The NIV Application Commentary. Grand Rapids, MI: Zondervan, 1996.

Craddock, Fred B. *Luke: Interpretation: A Bible Commentary for Teaching and Preaching*. Louisville: John Knox Press, 1990.

Hebrew Greek Key Word Study Bible. KJV, 2nd ed. Chattanooga, TN: AMG Publishers, 1991.

Say It Correctly

Sumptuously. **SUMP**-choo-us-lee.
Receivedst. re-**SEE**-vidst.

Daily Bible Readings

MONDAY
The Folly of Riches
(Psalm 49:1–4, 16–20)

TUESDAY
Oppressing the Poor Leads to Loss
(Proverbs 22:1–2, 7–9, 16)

WEDNESDAY
Both Oppressors and Righteous Receive
Justice
(James 5:1–5)

THURSDAY
Blessed are the Poor
(Luke 6:20–26)

FRIDAY
Two Responses to the Light
(John 3:16–21)

SATURDAY
Entry into the Kingdom of Heaven
(Matthew 19:23–30)

SUNDAY
Lazarus Cannot Help the Rich Man
(Luke 16:19–31)

Notes

Teaching Tips

Words You Should Know

A. Forgive (Matthew 18:21) *aphiemi* (Gk.)—To let go, let alone, give up a debt, or give up a thing to a person.

B. Heart (v. 35) *kardia* (Gk.)—The middle, central, or inmost part of anything, including our spiritual core.

Teacher Preparation

Unifying Principle—Consequences of Unforgiveness. People desire forgiveness even when they refuse to forgive. What are the consequences of an unforgiving heart? The parable of the unforgiving servant teaches us to forgive as we have been forgiven.

A. Seek God regarding anything or anyone in your own life that you have not fully addressed and reconciled with forgiveness.

B. Pray for your students and the message God wants to impart into them.

C. Read Matthew 18:21–35 in two or more translations.

D. Be prepared to talk about a news event or personal story where forgiveness (or a lack of forgiveness) directly impacted what happened.

O—Open the Lesson

A. Open with prayer, including the Aim for Change.

B. Introduce today's lesson title.

C. Have your students read the Aim for Change and Keep in Mind verse together. Discuss.

D. Share your news event or personal story regarding forgiveness with the class. Discuss.

E. Ask, "When have you seen the difference forgiveness makes, either on the giving or receiving end?"

F. Allow students to share their responses.

G. Tell the class to read the In Focus story silently, then discuss it.

P—Present the Scriptures

A. Have volunteers read the Focal Verses.

B. Use The People, Places, and Times; Background; Search the Scriptures; At-A-Glance outline; In Depth; and More Light on the Text to clarify the verses.

E—Explore the Meaning

A. Divide the class into groups to discuss the Discuss the Meaning, Lesson in Our Society, and Make It Happen sections. Tell the students to select a representative to report their responses.

B. Connect these sections to the Aim for Change and the Keep in Mind verse.

N—Next Steps for Application

A. Summarize the lesson.

B. Close with prayer.

Worship Guide

For the Superintendent or Teacher
Theme: Parable of the Unforgiving Servant
Song: "Jesus Paid It All"
Devotional Reading: Colossians 3:12–17

Parable of the Unforgiving Servant

Bible Background • MATTHEW 18:21–35
Printed Text • MATTHEW 18:21–35 | Devotional Reading • COLOSSIANS 3:12–17

———— Aim for Change ————

By the end of this lesson, we will: CONTRAST the type of answer Peter expected in his question about forgiveness with the type of answer that Jesus gave him; ASPIRE to forgive as Jesus said to forgive; and EXHIBIT a forgiving spirit that realizes how much God has forgiven us of.

In Focus

Tim summoned up his courage and knocked on his neighbor's apartment door.

The door opened and a man stood on the other side of the doorway. "Yeah?"

"Hi, Fred," Tim began. "It's Tim. Your neighbor. I accidentally hit your car with my car. I think I only really damaged your bumper. I'd be more than willing to pay for it. Can I show you?" The two men walked out together and surveyed the damage. Tim continually apologized for the error while Fred remained somewhat quiet. Finally, Fred spoke up.

"Tell you what," Fred began, "let's just call it good. I have a buddy who owns a body shop and it'd be easier to get him to fix the bumper in an hour than for us to get our insurance companies involved."

Tim couldn't believe Fred's response. "Are you sure? I'll happily pay for his time."

"He owes me a big favor," Fred affirmed. "No worries."

The two men shook hands and concluded their conversation. Tim again thanked Fred for how gracious he'd been, while Fred was equally appreciative for Tim's integrity. Tim eventually headed back into his apartment to tell his family what had happened.

He walked through the door. Within seconds, he walked into and tripped over a pile of toys his son had left near the door. Tim began shouting, "WHAT IS WRONG WITH YOU?"

Have you been forgiven after offending or hurting someone deeply? Have you been unforgiving over something small?

———— Keep in Mind ————

"Shouldest not thou also have had compassion on thy fellowservant, even as I had pity on thee?" (Matthew 18:33).

"Shouldest not thou also have had compassion on thy fellowservant, even as I had pity on thee?" (Matthew 18:33).

Focal Verses

KJV **Matthew 18:21** Then came Peter to him, and said, Lord, how oft shall my brother sin against me, and I forgive him? till seven times?

22 Jesus saith unto him, I say not unto thee, Until seven times: but, Until seventy times seven.

23 Therefore is the kingdom of heaven likened unto a certain king, which would take account of his servants.

24 And when he had begun to reckon, one was brought unto him, which owed him ten thousand talents.

25 But forasmuch as he had not to pay, his lord commanded him to be sold, and his wife, and children, and all that he had, and payment to be made.

26 The servant therefore fell down, and worshipped him, saying, Lord, have patience with me, and I will pay thee all.

27 Then the lord of that servant was moved with compassion, and loosed him, and forgave him the debt.

28 But the same servant went out, and found one of his fellowservants, which owed him an hundred pence: and he laid hands on him, and took him by the throat, saying, Pay me that thou owest.

29 And his fellowservant fell down at his feet, and besought him, saying, Have patience with me, and I will pay thee all.

30 And he would not: but went and cast him into prison, till he should pay the debt.

31 So when his fellowservants saw what was done, they were very sorry, and came and told unto their lord all that was done.

32 Then his lord, after that he had called him, said unto him, O thou wicked servant, I forgave thee all that debt, because thou desiredst me:

NLT **Matthew 18:21** Then Peter came to him and asked, "Lord, how often should I forgive someone who sins against me? Seven times?"

22 "No, not seven times," Jesus replied, "but seventy times seven!

23 Therefore, the Kingdom of Heaven can be compared to a king who decided to bring his accounts up to date with servants who had borrowed money from him.

24 In the process, one of his debtors was brought in who owed him millions of dollars.

25 He couldn't pay, so his master ordered that he be sold—along with his wife, his children, and everything he owned—to pay the debt.

26 But the man fell down before his master and begged him, 'Please, be patient with me, and I will pay it all.'

27 Then his master was filled with pity for him, and he released him and forgave his debt.

28 But when the man left the king, he went to a fellow servant who owed him a few thousand dollars. He grabbed him by the throat and demanded instant payment.

29 His fellow servant fell down before him and begged for a little more time. 'Be patient with me, and I will pay it,' he pleaded.

30 But his creditor wouldn't wait. He had the man arrested and put in prison until the debt could be paid in full.

31 When some of the other servants saw this, they were very upset. They went to the king and told him everything that had happened.

32 Then the king called in the man he had forgiven and said, 'You evil servant! I forgave you that tremendous debt because you pleaded with me.

33 Shouldn't you have mercy on your fellow servant, just as I had mercy on you?'

33 Shouldest not thou also have had compassion on thy fellowservant, even as I had pity on thee?

34 And his lord was wroth, and delivered him to the tormentors, till he should pay all that was due unto him.

35 So likewise shall my heavenly Father do also unto you, if ye from your hearts forgive not every one his brother their trespasses.

34 Then the angry king sent the man to prison to be tortured until he had paid his entire debt.

35 "That's what my heavenly Father will do to you if you refuse to forgive your brothers and sisters from your heart."

The People, Places, and Times

Jesus in the First Century. The culture Jesus taught in reflected multiple tensions Bible readers might miss at first glance. The Roman government had conquered much of the known world and sought to transform things into its image, after the Greeks had first done the exact same thing to change the language, thinking, and way of life. Underneath all of that, the Jewish culture wrestled with furthering what God had started in them centuries earlier. This massive collision of worldviews left everyone not only trying to understand what was happening worldwide, but also what was true within their own unique cultures.

The Question of Truth. The geographical and cultural tensions of the first century consequently blurred the lines of truth. People commonly turned to thought leaders both inside and outside of their traditions to adequately sort out truth in a collision of culture and theology. The Pharisees were the dominant religious voices for the Jews, and these leaders famously gave detailed answers full of multiple rules. Still, the average person wondered what everyday practices like forgiveness actually looked like when lived out.

Whom do you classify as trustworthy enough to give you counseling and wisdom in reference to God's truths?

Background

Jesus had a way of seeing through the questions people asked Him, even if they weren't aware of their motivations themselves. It enabled Him to cut to the real heart of an issue. For example, at the beginning of Matthew 18, when the disciples asked, "Who is the greatest in the kingdom of heaven?" Jesus replied to their attempt at position by sharing about how a little child might humbly come to Him (Matthew 18:1–5).

Jesus regularly used symbols, metaphors, and stories to draw people in so they could better understand how they had boxed God out. It was actually a common rabbinical teaching tool, with multiple teachers often telling the same parables with slight adaptations to suit their purposes. The parable of the prodigal son in Luke 15 is such an example, as first-century listeners might have commonly heard an ending of the father righteously holding the son accountable for his rebellious choices and not letting him back into the home. Jesus instead shared an ending that spoke about forgiveness, restoration, and mercy. Both versions of this story arguably have moral value, even though the biblical version we're more familiar with expressed what Christ wanted to speak into that audience (and future audiences who read it as Scripture).

The parable of the unmerciful servant definitively highlights both values of righteousness and grace. It shows God having a heart to set people free from their sin or debt while also wanting us to become people who make it possible for others to experience such grace.

How does choosing storytelling or role playing impact our ability to understand the Word?

At-A-Glance

1. The Limits of Forgiveness (Matthew 18:21–22)
2. The Example of Forgiveness (vv. 23–27)
3. The Accountability of Forgiveness (vv. 28–35)

In Depth

1. The Limits of Forgiveness (Matthew 18:21–22)

The question of forgiveness and its limits is something people have been asking about for centuries. We feel it when we have a conflict in our life with someone else, if our neighbors live at odds with each other, or as a tension between groups of people in society. It's uncomfortable to live in this tension, but it's also uncomfortable to forgive—especially if you believe you're correct. This may be why when people approached rabbis on this topic, they specifically asked what the limits of forgiveness actually looked like.

Some teachers offered that if you forgave someone three times, you had gone as far as you really needed to go. Others recognized a symbolism to certain numbers, such as seven representing wholeness or completeness. Whether Peter's reason in asking Jesus about this specific number was noble, intellectual, or a bureaucratic attempt to appear righteous, his question invites us to realize our own temptation to put limitations on forgiveness.

When you choose to repeatedly forgive someone who has offended you, what type of spiritual and personal transformation happens within you?

2. The Example of Forgiveness (vv. 23–27)

The parable Jesus told begins with a king in authority representing God, a man in debt representing the average person, and a financial balance due that represents sin. The debt owed is listed as a financial amount, but it's akin to a hyperbole—like saying that we owe someone a billion dollars or that overcoming such a gap would be like trying to jump across the Grand Canyon. Nonetheless, God is in the forgiving business, even when it means forgiving a seemingly unpayable debt. Only a grace-giving, all-powerful God can declare our slate clean and expect us to do the same for others who owe us even something small.

When was the last time you chose to extend forgiveness and grace toward someone?

3. The Accountability of Forgiveness (vv. 28–35)

If the first man in the story owed the king millions, the second man owed the first man a few thousand dollars. That's not to say the amount wasn't significant, because it was what the average person in a poor economy might earn over three months. Such a debt can seem significant to someone living on meager provisions.

Forgiving people is somewhat similar in scale. As we've been forgiven by God for a significant eternal debt beyond words, so should we offer forgiveness to people we feel owe us something. If we instead expect a payment of respect or elevation, the debt's legality will become even more complicated, with no hope of real forgiveness in sight. This is what happened to the first man; he seemed not to recognize his own hypocrisy but was held accountable through the consciences of his fellow servants who told the master.

The analogy is clear: holding grudges doesn't reflect the heart of God, but is the way of the world. God has forgiven our great debt with such tremendous grace that He expects us to pass it on. If we don't, He is justified to use as much discipline as needed to put us in our place.

Imagine if in the story, the first man opted to take time to understand what the master had done for him, and let that grace transform his own life. Similarly, we often just take from God without letting our character be conformed to His. Jesus' reply to Peter was to show that this was the master's real invitation—for only God can give us the power to forgive and move us past what we legalistically think we deserve from others. Forgiveness is not a matter of numerical limits and record-keeping, but must come from a transformed heart.

How can unforgiveness break down our relationship with God and others?

Search the Scriptures

1. What do you think Jesus meant when He told the disciples to forgive "seventy times seven" (Matthew 18:22)?

2. What might be the significance of the forgiven man putting his hands on the throat of the man who owed him a lesser amount (v. 28)?

Discuss the Meaning

We all desire forgiveness when we've done something wrong, even though we find it difficult to forgive others. We may even opt to dispense large doses of revenge or punishment against people who have only wronged us in small ways. Why might God want to set us free from this cycle and even hold us accountable to it?

Lesson in Our Society

Many individuals and groups today seem to receive a lot of hurt and negative attention. Whether it's a pop star, an outspoken person, or groups that get singled out such as Black people or immigrants, sometimes it seems like they can't catch a break. When people keep getting knocked down over and over again, the urge can be to dish out retribution with that much more intensity and anger. The transformation we're hoping to see in the world begins in us, not by ignoring injustices but by naming them and working toward reconciliation through Jesus' example.

Whom do you think you need to forgive and be reconciled with?

Make It Happen

One amazing benefit to being a Christian is growing into a rooted community of believers who help each other walk through life with Jesus. Your church family is made up of other flawed individuals meant to forgive one another because they have all been forgiven by Christ. Unfortunately, we can focus on their flaws and hypocrisy while overlooking or excusing our own.

Mentally role-play the parable Jesus told. Expand the dialogue to include Jesus forgiving you for your sin, but then you harboring resentment in a situation toward someone whom you feel has somehow wronged you. Play the dialogue out with two different endings: first, with you being held accountable by God like the king held the man in the parable; second, with you being commended by God for extending grace as you've experienced it yourself. Finally, take action on living out the latter example by tangibly reaching out to a person whom you feel offended you.

Follow the Spirit

What God wants me to do:

_____

_____

_____

_____

Remember Your Thoughts

Special insights I have learned:

_____

_____

_____

_____

More Light on the Text
Matthew 18:21–35

Jesus has just finished teaching the disciples how to deal with disputes where one believer has offended another. First, the one who has been offended should approach the offender to solve it. If that does not work, then bring other people to help settle the matter. If the issue is still not resolved, the church should get involved. If the brother refuses to change, then he should be disciplined (vv. 15–17). In verses 18–20, Jesus speaks of the power that the church has because of His permanent presence.

21 Then came Peter to him, and said, Lord, how oft shall my brother sin against me, and I forgive him? Till seven times? 22 Jesus saith unto him, I say not unto thee, Until seven times: but, Until seventy times seven.

Matthew introduces the next sequence of events with the conjunction "then" (Gk. *tote*, **TOE-tay**), and links the preceding event with the ones that follows. The word is used to introduce something that follows in time, and can be rendered "at that time" or "after that." Perhaps, prompted by the teaching of forgiveness, Peter approaches Jesus and asks a follow-up question, using a practical example. The issue is not referring to decisions by the church, but personal forgiveness (Matthew 6:14–15; Mark 11:25; Luke 17:3–4): "How oft shall my brother sin against me, and I forgive him?" Peter asks. "Till seven times?" In the rabbinical community, the agreement was that a brother might be forgiven for a repeated sin three times, and after that came no forgiveness. Why did Peter come up with seven? Was he trying to be magnanimous by suggesting seven times? Alternatively, was he following a common thread of the use of seven in the Bible? Some scholars suggest that the number seven indicates completeness, using the Genesis creation account as the basis (Genesis 2:1–3; compare Leviticus 4:6; 26:21; Joshua 6:4; Proverbs 24:16). The Greek word, translated "my brother," is *adelphos* (**ah-DEL-foce**) and could be a blood-related sibling, or anyone of the same religious society (Matthew 18:15). Jesus' reply, "I say not unto thee," suggests that this situation has been discussed earlier, and perhaps Peter did not understand it clearly. Jesus then says not seven times, but seventy times seven. This is similar to elsewhere that Jesus says, "If thy brother trespass against thee …, forgive him. And if he trespass against thee seven times in a day, and seven times in a day turn again to thee, saying, I repent; thou shalt forgive him" (from Luke 17:3–4).

What does Jesus mean by seventy times seven? Reading it with a Greek or English understanding, 70 times 7 equals 490, but with a Hebrew understanding, the phrase means

70 plus 7 equals 77. Jesus perhaps alludes to Genesis 4:24, transforming Lamech's revenge into a principle for forgiveness. In this context, Jesus is not setting 490 or 77 times as the upper limit for forgiveness, but teaches that frequency or quantity should not limit forgiveness. The parable that follows vividly illustrates the extent, rather than the frequency of forgiveness. It further shows that we are forgiven far more than we can ever forgive.

23 Therefore is the kingdom of heaven likened unto a certain king, which would take account of his servants.

Jesus illustrates His point with a parable. Since He requires His disciples to forgive those who offend them, He compares the kingdom of heaven with a king who removes the record of his debtors. "The kingdom of heaven" means the sovereignty of God over the universe and is paralleled with His kingdom. The kingdom of heaven is personified and refers to God, who is represented in the parable by an earthly king. Those in the kingdom are the king's servants (Gk. *douloi*, **DOO-loy**, "slaves"); they might include high-ranking officials in a huge colonial empire, since the amount some owed was huge (v. 24). The king decides to take account (Gk. *sunairo*, **soon-EYE-row**), or settle accounts with (cf 25:19), his servants.

24 And when he had begun to reckon, one was brought unto him, which owed him ten thousand talents. 25 But forasmuch as he had not to pay, his lord commanded him to be sold, and his wife, and children, and all that he had, and payment to be made. 26 The servant therefore fell down, and worshipped him, saying, Lord, have patience with me and I will pay thee all.

One of the officials who owes ten thousand talents is brought to the king's attention. Some people have estimated the dollar value of one talent of gold to be about $29,085, and 10,000 talents would be $290,850,000. A talent of silver is estimated at $1,920 and 10,000 talents would be $19,200,000. An idea of the debt's size can be compared with the donation for the construction of the Temple, where King David gave 3,000 talents of gold and 7,000 talents of silver, and the princes donated 5,000 talents of gold and 10,000 talents of silver (1 Chronicles 29:4, 7). In today's currency, with the fluctuating price of precious metals, coupled with inflation, these figures would run into billions or trillions of dollars. However, the amount is used to compare the extent of the forgiveness and mercy shown to the servant-debtor, and the amount owed to him by his fellow servant whom he shows no mercy to.

The servant appears before the king and is not able to pay what he owes. The king orders that he and his family (his wife and children), with all their possessions, be sold into slavery in order to recover the debt. The practice of being sold for a debt is consistent with the practice in the Old Testament (Leviticus 25:39; 2 Kings 4:1). It is the most severe and humiliating punishment for anyone to endure; the aim of selling the entire family is not to recover the full amount owed, but to punish. If top price for a slave would fetch one talent or less, as some suggest, then the total price of the family would not be enough to cover the debt. This is a punishment and such slaves, therefore, must be freed in the Year of Jubilee, every fifty years (Leviticus 25:10, 28). The servant, desperate and hopeless, falls down on his knees and pleads for time. The word "worshipped" is from the Greek verb *prosekuneo* (**pro-se-koo-NEH-oh**), which is to go on one's knees, to kneel before someone, or to prostrate oneself in homage (cf Matthew 20:20). The servant falling down and worshiping him serves the purpose of paying homage as a desperate plea to his lord (master). This honor is reserved for kings and people of higher positions in society.

27 The lord of that servant was moved with compassion, and loosed him and forgave the debt.

Seeing his desperation, helplessness, and inability to pay such a huge amount, the king is moved with compassion and forgives him of the whole amount owed. To be "moved with compassion" is to have sympathy, or to pity. The lord is moved with pity and forgives the "debt" (Gk. *daneion*, **DAH-nay-on**), which is better translated "loan." The lord treats the debt as a bad loan and writes it off. The servant doesn't have to pay it back, and is totally freed from any obligation. The phrase "loosed him" (Gk. *luo*, **LOO-oh**, to untie) suggests that he was arrested and bound before they brought him before the king, and has now been completely released when the lord forgave him. In this case, the debt was treated, at first, as embezzlement, but now the king cancels it and forgives the servant.

28 But the same servant went out and found one of his fellow servants, which owed him an hundred pence: and he laid his hands on him, and took him by the throat, saying, Pay me that thou owest. 29 And his fellow servant fell down at his feet, and besought him, saying, Have patience with me, and I will pay thee all. 30 And he would not, but went and cast him into prison, till he should pay the debt.

Verses 28–31 gives a complete opposite picture of verses 24–27. The servant who received mercy from his master for the huge debt shows no mercy to his fellow servant who owed a few pence. The Lord links the preceding story with the conjunction "but," which immediately strikes a note of contrast with and introduces the next phase of the parable. Having been

forgiven his debt, the servant probably rushes out of the king's court in celebration. He finds another servant, lower in rank than him, in the outer courtyard, who owes him 100 "pence." Scholars have calculated one hundred pence to equal about $17. The amount might be high in their standard, but very insignificant compared with the amount forgiven him. Immediately, he mercilessly grabs the servant by the throat, choking him, and demands that the debt be paid immediately. His fellow servant pleads with him for patience, that he would eventually pay him everything he owes. The similarity of this man's plea (v. 29) to his own plea to the king (v. 26) did not move this unforgiving man. Rather than show mercy, he has him thrown into a debtor's prison and ordered that he be kept there until he pays the amount in full.

31 So when his fellow servants saw what was done, they were very sorry, and came and told unto their lord all that was done.

The other servants, who witnessed what had happened, are distressed because of such cruelty, and go out to report to the master. The phrase "they were very sorry" is from the Greek words *lupeo sphodra* (**loo-PEH-oh SFO-dra**), which means "to be greatly grieved." They are not merely sorry, but are severely touched in the heart to the point of grieving. They are not merely sympathetic, they empathize with the fellow-servant, and show it by reporting it to their master. The word rendered "told" (Gk. *diasapheo*, **dee-ah-sah-FEH-oh**) means to explain, or to narrate. They explain in detail what the unforgiving servant has done.

32 Then his lord, after that he had called him, and said unto him, O thou wicked servant, I forgave thee all that debt, because thou desirest me: 33 Shouldest not thou also have had compassion on thy fellow servant, even as I had pity on thee? 34 And his lord

was wroth, and delivered to the tormentors, till he should pay all that was unto him.

On hearing this report, the master calls in the unforgiving servant, and reprimands him, denouncing him for what he has done and calls him a "wicked servant." He asked him why he could not forgive his fellow servant as he was forgiven. Of course, he has no answer, and the master expects no answer. No amount of explanation would exonerate him for his wicked action. The master is so upset that, instead of selling him (v. 25), he turns him to the tormentors. The word "tormentors" (Gk. *basanistes*, **ba-sa-neese-TAYS**) refers to jailers who have charge of the prisoners and torture them when asked to do so. The servant was to be tortured in prison until he paid back all that he owed, which was impossible.

35 So likewise shall my heavenly Father do also unto you, if ye from your hearts forgive not every one his brother their trespasses.

Jesus concludes the parable by comparing the master's reaction to the unmerciful servant with what God will do to those who do not forgive others' trespasses. This parable demonstrates the necessity of forgiveness and how we should treat one another. Jesus advocates that we forgive from our "hearts" those who have wronged us. "From the heart" here means genuine and sincere forgiveness. Concluding His teaching on prayer, Jesus tells His disciples that they ought to forgive others, as they have been forgiven, lest our "Father will not forgive your sins" (Matthew 6:12, 14–15).

This parable, as we have already said, does not deal with frequency, but illustrates the extent of forgiveness we have received from our Heavenly Father through the death of His Son. We are forgiven far more than we can ever forgive. Certain questions arise from this parable. When do we forgive our brother: before or after they have confessed? Do we have to forgive whether they repent or not? What does it mean to love your enemies and do good to those who hate you? As Christians, we have been forgiven much, and we should forgive much.

Sources:

France, R. *The Gospel of Matthew*. Grand Rapids, MI: Wm. B. Eerdmans Publishing, 2007.

Guzik, David. *Matthew*. Santa Barbara, CA: Enduring Word Media; 2012.

Harney, Kevin G. *Seismic Shifts Little Changes That Make a Big Difference in Your Life*. Grand Rapids, MI: Zondervan, 2007.

Stern D.H. *Jewish New Testament Commentary, A Companion Volume to the Jewish New Testament*. Clarksville, MD: Messianic Jewish Publisher, 1992.

Say It Correctly

Rabbinical. ra-**BIN**-ih-cul.
Wroth. **ROTH**.

Daily Bible Readings

MONDAY
Joseph Forgives His Brothers
(Genesis 50:15–21)

TUESDAY
Forgiveness and Healing of the Land
(2 Chronicles 7:12–16)

WEDNESDAY
Forgiving and Consoling the Offender
(2 Corinthians 2:5–11)

THURSDAY
Forgive Each Other's Complaints
(Colossians 3:12–17)

FRIDAY
Keep Forgiving Each Other
(Luke 17:1–4)

SATURDAY
God's Forgiveness Depends on Us
(Matthew 6:9–15)

SUNDAY
Offer Mercy and Forgiveness Freely
(Matthew 18:21–35)

Notes

_____

_____

_____

_____

Teaching Tips

Words You Should Know

A. Hypocrites (Matthew 23:23) *hupokrites* (Gk.)—One who answers, an actor, a pretender.

B. Cleanse (v. 26) *katarizo* (Gk.)—To clean of physical dirt and stains, or in a moral sense.

Teacher Preparation

Unifying Principle—Hypocrites! We encounter leaders who expect people to do one thing while they do something else. Is there a fair response to such an expectation? Jesus challenges unjust leaders to change or experience destruction.

A. Seek God regarding blind spots of hypocrisy in your own life.

B. Pray for your students and the message God wants to impart into them.

C. Read the selected passage in two or more modern translations.

O—Open the Lesson

A. Open with prayer, including the Aim for Change.

B. Introduce today's lesson title.

C. Have your students read the Aim for Change and Keep in Mind verse together. Discuss.

D. Tell the class to read the In Focus story silently, then discuss it together.

P—Present the Scriptures

A. Have volunteers read the Focal Verses.

B. Use The People, Places, and Times; Background; Search the Scriptures; At-A-Glance outline; and In Depth sections to clarify the verses.

E—Explore the Meaning

A. Divide the class into groups to engage the Discuss the Meaning, Lesson in Our Society, and Make It Happen sections. Tell the students to select a representative to report their responses.

B. Connect these sections to the Aim for Change and the Keep in Mind verse.

N—Next Steps for Application

A. Summarize the lesson.

B. Close with prayer.

Worship Guide

For the Superintendent or Teacher
Theme: Jesus Criticizes Unjust Leaders
Song: "What a Friend We Have in Jesus"
Devotional Reading: Luke 14:7–14

Jesus Criticizes Unjust Leaders

Bible Background • MATTHEW 23
Printed Text • MATTHEW 23:1–8, 23–26 | Devotional Reading • LUKE 14:7–14

—— Aim for Change ——

By the end of this lesson we will: EXPLAIN the difference between just and unjust actions; REJECT becoming like the hypocritical scribes and Pharisees; and EXPLORE ways to implement just leadership in our own lives.

✎ In Focus

Brandy was distraught after saying goodbye to the guest speaker her church had invited to speak this weekend. Kevin was still cleaning up from the events of the weekend and noticed her. "Are you okay?" he asked her, setting down his broom.

"I just had a weird conversation with our speaker over lunch. I shared a story with him about a girl I'd spoken to who I was able to lead to Jesus, and how she went home and flushed her drugs down the toilet."

"Wow, that's powerful!"

"That's what our speaker thought," Brandy continued. "He then asked me if I'd sell him that story so he could tell it as if he was the one who spoke with her. He said he likes sharing stories like mine, but in the first person so he can use them to inspire people in his messages. When I questioned him about it, he said it's just part of being a public speaker."

"What?" Kevin exclaimed. "That ain't right!"

"I know. Could we talk about it when everyone leaves? I'm really rattled."

"Sure," Kevin said. "But we're here by ourselves, though. You know we have that church policy about two people of the opposite sex not being alone in the building with each other."

"Oh, yeah," she said. "Well, maybe we could just lock the door and not make it that big of a deal. It's a silly rule, anyway."

Jesus gave His sharpest criticism to hypocrites. Sometimes being aware of our own hypocrisy is a difficult thing. How do we make sure we are not involved in hypocritical actions?

—— Keep in Mind ——

"The scribes and the Pharisees sit in Moses' seat: All therefore whatsoever they bid you observe, that observe and do; but do not ye after their works: for they say, and do not" (from Matthew 23:2–3).

"The scribes and the Pharisees sit in Moses' seat: All therefore whatsoever they bid you observe, that observe and do; but do not ye after their works: for they say, and do not" (from Matthew 23:2–3).

Focal Verses

KJV **Matthew 23:1** Then spake Jesus to the multitude, and to his disciples,

2 Saying The scribes and the Pharisees sit in Moses' seat:

3 All therefore whatsoever they bid you observe, that observe and do; but do not ye after their works: for they say, and do not.

4 For they bind heavy burdens and grievous to be borne, and lay them on men's shoulders; but they themselves will not move them with one of their fingers.

5 But all their works they do for to be seen of men: they make broad their phylacteries, and enlarge the borders of their garments,

6 And love the uppermost rooms at feasts, and the chief seats in the synagogues,

7 And greetings in the markets, and to be called of men, Rabbi, Rabbi.

8 But be not ye called Rabbi: for one is your Master, even Christ; and all ye are brethren.

23 Woe unto you, scribes and Pharisees, hypocrites! for ye pay tithe of mint and anise and cummin, and have omitted the weightier matters of the law, judgment, mercy, and faith: these ought ye to have done, and not to leave the other undone.

24 Ye blind guides, which strain at a gnat, and swallow a camel.

25 Woe unto you, scribes and Pharisees, hypocrites! for ye make clean the outside of the cup and of the platter, but within they are full of extortion and excess.

26 Thou blind Pharisee, cleanse first that which is within the cup and platter, that the outside of them may be clean also.

NLT **Matthew 23:1** Then Jesus said to the crowds and to his disciples,

2 "The teachers of religious law and the Pharisees are the official interpreters of the law of Moses.

3 So practice and obey whatever they tell you, but don't follow their example. For they don't practice what they teach.

4 They crush people with unbearable religious demands and never lift a finger to ease the burden.

5 "Everything they do is for show. On their arms they wear extra wide prayer boxes with Scripture verses inside, and they wear robes with extra long tassels.

6 And they love to sit at the head table at banquets and in the seats of honor in the synagogues.

7 They love to receive respectful greetings as they walk in the marketplaces, and to be called 'Rabbi.'

8 "Don't let anyone call you 'Rabbi,' for you have only one teacher, and all of you are equal as brothers and sisters.

23 What sorrow awaits you teachers of religious law and you Pharisees. Hypocrites! For you are careful to tithe even the tiniest income from your herb gardens, but you ignore the more important aspects of the law—justice, mercy, and faith. You should tithe, yes, but do not neglect the more important things.

24 Blind guides! You strain your water so you won't accidentally swallow a gnat, but you swallow a camel!

25 What sorrow awaits you teachers of religious law and you Pharisees. Hypocrites! For you are so careful to clean the outside of the cup and the dish, but inside you are filthy—full of greed and self-indulgence!

26 You blind Pharisee! First wash the inside of the cup and the dish, and then the outside will become clean, too."

The People, Places, and Times

Scribes and Pharisees. The Hebrew Scriptures had been preserved for centuries by God and humanity, being passed down from one generation to another, with various people in authority responsible for them. For example, what began in Moses' generation was passed down to Joshua's generation. In turn, various kings, priests, and prophets kept watch over these divine words, even through conflicts and captivity with other nations. During the era Jesus walked the earth, the scribes and Pharisees were among the religious leaders people looked to for communication and interpretation of the Scriptures.

Two Kinds of Authority. When Jesus spoke to these leaders, it was noted that He spoke with a deeper authority. While He ministered among people who knew Scripture by memory and passionately debated the intellectualism of their conclusions, Christ somehow knew the "truth under the truth" intimately. It's why in the Sermon on the Mount (Matthew 5–7), He revealed the larger value that trumped the traditions the Pharisees had been promoting. For this reason, Jesus said that His "yoke" (or true teaching of the Hebrew Scriptures) was light in comparison with the interpretation of the Pharisees, who manufactured authority by creating their own traditions.

What can we recommend as a way to hold religious leaders accountable for their teachings?

Background

The ancient world was famously filled with deep symbolism, especially with each culture trying to assert itself over the others. While the Romans and Greeks were known for their stunning architecture, the Jews were passionate about telling God's story through their places and objects of worship. The Jewish religious leaders in the first century furthered this by finding stories and truth in the Scriptures that they could turn into something tangible. In some instances, it was an unintended saving grace for the people.

For example, the "seat of Moses" is historically understood to have been a physical place that the Pharisees and scribes sat upon when they gathered together. Much like modern courtrooms all have an area set aside for a judge to sit down and preside, this "seat of Moses" represented how the Pharisees had inherited the succession of religious authority on God's behalf through the institutions established under Moses.

The Pharisees had many forms of tangible symbolism that they enjoyed, from the details of how they dressed to publicly showing off their spiritual practices before others. Time and time again, Jesus could be found rebuking them for getting off track, and warning people to beware as they present themselves before these leaders. We see this in Mark 12:38–40 and Luke 20:45–47 as they parallel a rebuke to the scribes, adding a condemnation that they "devour widows' houses." It would seem our challenge isn't to become cynical toward people in spiritual authority nor to wait for them to fall, but to use even their flaws to dig deeper at where God is at underneath all of the hypocrisy, and to show us the takeaway in our own lives.

How can focus on external symbolism separate us from God?

At-A-Glance

1. The Authority God Creates
(Matthew 23:1–4)
2. The Authority Humanity Promotes
(vv. 5–8)
3. The Authority Eternity Reveals (vv. 23–26)

In Depth

1. The Authority God Creates (Matthew 23:1–4)

Jesus begins a scathing criticism against the scribes and Pharisees. He basically lets the crowd and His disciples know that the scribes and Pharisees talk a good talk, but don't walk a good walk. Not only did they not do what they taught, but they also oppressed others with their religious demands.

God wants our actions to match our words. The reason why the scribes and Pharisees were accused of living hypocritical lives is because they focused on minor things and did not simply obey what God has plainly revealed. Just like the scribes and Pharisees were concerned about minor things at the expense of major things, so too can we become distracted by a leader's flaws and miss the purpose behind why God has put that authority into our lives through that person.

Why do we criticize and stand in judgment of our leaders but disregard our own flaws?

2. The Authority Humanity Promotes (vv. 5–8)

The Pharisees only furthered this hypocrisy by relying on their "script" of tradition and added laws to inflect a tone of authority over people. Even their clothing reflected an over-the-top "rock star" persona, including vibrant colors of costly clothing, ointments that made them smell unique, jewelry that caught the attention of others, enlarged objects they wore on their heads, and detailed fringes on the corners of their shawls. They would argue they were basing such things on interpretations of the Hebrew Scriptures, but Jesus felt the display had become louder than the Lord they were attempting to put on display.

What false displays do we need to point out and remove in our lives and the church?

3. The Authority Eternity Reveals (vv. 23–26)

Jesus warns the Pharisees that their current run at having authority over people means that they will be held to a greater accountability in the grand scheme of things. Their consistency with tithing, as important as it was and is, was never meant to overshadow the larger values of healthy judgment, generous mercy, and contagious faith.

We are just as accountable as the Pharisees regarding what we do with the charge God has given us. We are called to simply love God and love others. By adhering to this law of love, we can explain the difference between just and unjust actions. Then we will avoid becoming like the hypocritical scribes and Pharisees. Through the Spirit we can become just leaders.

Can you explain what it means to "but to do justly, and to love mercy, and to walk humbly with thy God" (Micah 6:8, KJV)?

Search the Scriptures

1. Jesus points out how the Pharisees have made it a burden for people to follow God. What do you imagine was their reaction to this (Matthew 23:4)?

2. What do you think is the difference between when something spiritual is a primary issue versus a secondary issue (v. 23)?

Discuss the Meaning

Hypocrisy isn't just an individual matter, but one that affects countless others. When we're blind to how our positions of authority affect others, it's like poisoning a water source that others will drink out of. In what ways has this been true of others whose actions affected you, and how have your actions made it harder for someone else to see God?

Lesson in Our Society

It's more common to distrust leaders than to put our trust into following them. Perhaps some of the political drama that's played out over decades is responsible for this, but we can add to the damage when our reaction swings so hard toward skepticism that we overlook the beauty in the authority God has established over us (Romans 13:1–7). Sometimes in our attempt to protect ourselves against blind trust, we stop trusting altogether.

Jesus points out that the Pharisees' actions should not be followed, but the Law of Moses is absolutely valid. This means that we cannot just throw away the Word of God and the standards that He has plainly laid out for us. Whenever a leader points us toward this standard, that is commendable. Man will have failures. Ultimately, Jesus is the true and just leader that we need to follow.

When choosing a leader (political, religious, organizational), can we assess how trust is a factor in our selection?

Make It Happen

• List three examples of good leadership and contrast them with three examples of bad leadership.

• If you know someone who is leading well, give them a word of encouragement.

• Write in your journal about which things in your spiritual life are major and which are minor.

Follow the Spirit

What God wants me to do:

_____

_____

_____

_____

Remember Your Thoughts

Special insights I have learned:

_____

_____

_____

_____

More Light on the Text

Matthew 23:1–4, 23–26

1 Then spake Jesus to the multitude, and to his disciples, 2 Saying The scribes and the Pharisees sit in Moses' seat: 3 All therefore whatsoever they bid you observe, that observe and do; but do not ye after their works: for they say, and do not.

The Pharisees were the largest of the three major religious groups in Palestine at Jesus' time, the others being the Sadducees and the

Essenes. A lay organization, they feared Jewish sins were delaying the coming of the Messiah. They hoped to prevent such sins through strict interpretation of the Law. This interpretation acted as a "hedge" or "fence" around the Law to keep the people from breaking it. For the Pharisees, the consequence would not simply be divine punishment of the offender, but also divine judgment against the whole people of Israel.

Jesus uses this moment to talk about the scribes and Pharisees, and the level of adherence His followers should give to their teachings. He describes the teachers as sitting in "Moses' seat." Some scholars have said that this term was an important seat in the synagogue. Others say this is a figurative expression. It is meant to highlight that the scribes and Pharisees believed their tradition to be rooted in Moses and the Law. This is what gave them their authority to teach others. They believed they were continuing the legacy of Moses.

Because of this authority, the people were to follow their teaching. But, Jesus warned, the people were not to follow their example, because they did not follow their own teaching. This is in opposition to what many of the Pharisees believed at the time. The common sentiment among the scribes and Pharisees was that a person was to first focus on knowing what the Law says before they obeyed it. However, they would not outright say that a person should not obey the Law or that obedience was not important.

4 For they bind heavy burdens and grievous to be borne, and lay them on men's shoulders; but they themselves will not move them with one of their fingers.

The image of someone tying or binding up heavy burdens fits the Pharisees and scribes' method of instruction. These instructions were "grievous to be borne" (Gk. *dusbastaktos*,

doos-BAS-tak-toce), or intolerable. What is interesting when examining the Pharisees' way of teaching is that they load men with heavy burdens—strict and legalistic interpretations of the Law—but will not carry these same burdens themselves. Here, Jesus is pointing back to His statement "they say, and do not" (v. 3).

5 But all their works they do for to be seen of men: they make broad their phylacteries, and enlarge the borders of their garments,

The Pharisees' goal in doing anything is not obedience to God, but the applause of men. Jesus highlights that they make larger their phylacteries (Gk. *phylakterion*, **fi-lak-te-REE-ahn**) or prayer-bands. These were small boxes that had a leather strap. These boxes included Scripture that was recited during the morning and evening prayers. The leather strap was used to tie the phylacteries to the left hand or to the forehead. Not only did they widen their phylacteries, they also made their fringes (Gk. *kraspedon*, **kra-spe-DAHN**) longer so as to be seen by others. The fringes that Jesus speaks of are the tassels which all Jews were required to wear on the end of their clothing. These tassels were intended to be reminders for them of God and a way to meditate on His glory. It is ironic that instead of focusing people's attention on God, they are more focused on being seen and recognized as religious.

6 And love the uppermost rooms at feasts, and the chief seats in the synagogues,

Seating position was very important in the ancient world. Ancient evidence indicates that people were not pleased when placed in seats for those of lower status. This was especially true at banquets. The Pharisees desired the uppermost (Gk. *protoklisia*, **pro-to-KLEE-see-ah**) rooms, or the places of honor, at the reclining table of the banquet. They also desired the chief seats (Gk. *protokathedria* pro-to-ka-the-DREE-ah), or seat of preeminent honor, in the synagogue (Gk. *synagogue*) or assembly. The synagogue was more than just an assembly; it was a building where the Israelites and those who trusted in the God of Israel would gather to worship. The synagogue was created to teach the Law to all of Israel as a reaction to their neglect in obeying the Law, which led to their exile. No one knows exactly when the first synagogue was created, but by the time of the first century, they were prevalent throughout the Greco-Roman world where the Jews had been taken into exile.

Seating arrangements in the synagogues of the first century do not show seating rank; however, a seat of preeminent honor would more than likely be in the front of the synagogue assembly. This was the area closest to the bema, the platform where the Law would be read. Important dignitaries would be given chairs while the other hearers would sit on mats.

7 And greetings in the markets, and to be called of men, Rabbi, Rabbi.

Greeting and saluting others was a very important thing in Jewish and Greek cultures. Specific rules dictated how to greet different types of people on different occasions. In Jewish culture, to not greet a person who was well versed in the Mosaic Law was offensive. The scribes and Pharisees wanted to be greeted in the marketplaces, which were the most populated places in any town at the time. This would increase their fame and pride as people would know not only who they were, but that they were important, pious men. This is indicated by the title of "rabbi." This word is actually a borrowing from Aramaic and means "my great one." Eventually the term meant "teacher." The scribes and Pharisees prided themselves on being teachers of the Law for the masses.

8 But be not ye called Rabbi: for one is your Master, even Christ; and all ye are brethren.

Jesus warns that no one is supposed to be called "rabbi" because there is only one Master (Gk. *didaskalos*, **dee-dah-ska-LAHS**). This word means teacher and in this context signifies the role of the rabbi as a master in the sense of the Mosaic Law as well as over his pupil. In contrast to contemporary Western forms of education, the rabbinical teaching style placed a lot of weight on following the teacher's example and instruction. As such, one could be called a "master" of the students.

The only one who is to be called master, and who actually is the Master, is Christ. Here, Jesus says that He is the Master. Although He has not yet proven to be Christ by His resurrection, the disciples who have witnessed Him affirm this as His identity (Matthew 16:13–21). With these words, Christ levels the playing fields. There are not many masters—only one. There is no hierarchy among believers in the kingdom of God. All those who follow Him are brothers and sisters.

23 Woe unto you, scribes and Pharisees, hypocrites! for ye pay tithe of mint and anise and cummin, and have omitted the weightier matters of the law, judgment, mercy, and faith: these ought ye to have done, and not to leave the other undone.

This is the fourth woe in Jesus' famous seven woes to the Pharisees (Matthew 23:13–30). "Woe" (Gk. *ouai*, **oo-AYE**) is an expression of grief, pity, or concern that has its origin in the prophetic literature of the Old Testament. It can be considered prayers or even a curse. In this context, it can be translated as a warning, such as, "What great disaster will come to you." Jesus denounces the scribes and Pharisees, although He does not mean all of them. Later rabbinical literature makes clear that many

Pharisees also condemned what Jesus condemned in these woes. There was no tolerance for hypocritical behavior.

Hypocrite (Gk. *hupokrites*, **hoo-po-kree-TASE**) was a term employed for the actors in Greek drama who wore masks. Eventually it became a way to describe a two-faced person. In this sense, the Pharisees and scribes wear the mask of religiosity in their scrupulous tithing, but neglect the "weightier matters." Jesus actually encourages them to tithe their spices, but also to not forsake justice, mercy, and faith. It is not that what they are doing is wrong, but that they have pursued the good only to neglect what is best.

24 Ye blind guides, which strain at a gnat, and swallow a camel.

Jesus continues His scathing criticism of the scribes and Pharisees. They are blind (Gk. *tuphlos*, **too-FLOCE**) guides. The use of the word "blind" here does not refer to physical blindness, but means "not able to understand." They are leading others while they themselves are not able to truly understand the purpose of the Law. They strain at gnats and swallow camels. Here Jesus uses hyperbole to highlight their approach to the Law. Straining a gnat indicates that they treat minor details as major. Swallowing a camel indicates that they treat major issues as minor.

25 Woe unto you, scribes and Pharisees, hypocrites! for ye make clean the outside of the cup and of the platter, but within they are full of extortion and excess. 26 Thou blind Pharisee, cleanse first that which is within the cup and platter, that the outside of them may be clean also.

Next, their behavior is exposed as backward and not in line with true religion. They clean the outside of the cup, but the inside is full of extortion (Gk. *harpage*, **har-pah-GAY**)

and excess (Gk. *akrasia*, **ah-kra-SEE-ah**). The word for extortion means a violent acquisition of goods or wealth, such as raping or pillaging. While the word for excess meant a general lack of ability, but more specifically, a lack of self-control. The Pharisees basically failed at being model examples of teachers of the Law and instead had shown they were self-indulgent and greedy sinners who used religion as their means of gratification.

Sources:
Earle, Ralph. *The Gospel According to Matthew.* Beacon Bible Commentary. Kansas City: Beacon Hill Press, 1964.
France, R.T. *Matthew. Tyndale New Testament Commentaries.* Grand Rapids: Eerdmans, 1985.
Hahn, Roger L. *Matthew: A Commentary for Bible Students.* Indianapolis, IN: Wesleyan Publishing House, 2007.
Harrington, Daniel J. *Sacra Pagina: The Gospel of Matthew.* Collegeville, MN: Liturgical Press, 1991, 2007.

Say It Correctly

Anise. **AH**-niss.
Cummin. **CUE**-men.

Daily Bible Readings

MONDAY
Visual Reminder of the Commandments
(Numbers 15:37–41)

TUESDAY
Jesus Fulfills the Law and Prophets
(Matthew 5:17–20)

WEDNESDAY
Craving Attention While Cheating Widows
(Luke 20:45–47)

THURSDAY
Doing is More Important Than Speaking
(Matthew 23:5–12)

FRIDAY
Keeping People Away from the Kingdom
(Matthew 23:13–15)

SATURDAY
Blind Guides Confuse Meaning of Oaths
(Matthew 23:16–22)

SUNDAY
Jesus is Critical of Scribes and Pharisees
(Matthew 23:1–4, 23–26)

Notes

_____

_____

_____

_____

Teaching Tips

Words You Should Know

A. Parable (Luke 18:1) *parabole* (Gk.)—A (symbolic) fictitious narrative of common life conveying a moral, or adage.

B. Avenge (v. 3) *ekdikeo* (Gk.)—To vindicate one's right, do justice; to protect, defend one person from another.

Teacher Preparation

Unifying Principle—Persistence Pays Off. People become discouraged when their requests for relief seem to go unanswered. Why should we persist? Jesus promises justice to those who persistently request relief from unjust treatment.

A. Pray for your students' understanding of today's lesson.

B. Read Luke 18:1–8 in two or more modern translations.

C. Research and introduce an article about a person or people who have persisted in the face of injustice and were vindicated in the end (e.g., anything related to the Civil Rights Movement of the 1960s).

O—Open the Lesson

A. Open with prayer.

B. Introduce today's lesson title.

C. Have your students read the Aim for Change and Keep in Mind verse together.

D. Share your article with your students. Have them read together. Discuss.

E. Ask, "When is it enough to pray for God to bring justice, and when is it incumbent on God's people to do more than pray, and to take action led by the Spirit?" Discuss.

P—Present the Scriptures

A. Have volunteers read the Focal Verses.

B. Have students act out the parable of the widow and the unjust judge.

C. Use the Background; Search the Scriptures; At-A-Glance outline; and In Depth sections to clarify the verses.

E—Explore the Meaning

A. Divide the class into groups to explore the Discuss the Meaning, Lesson in Our Society, and Make It Happen sections.

B. Connect these sections to the Aim for Change and the Keep in Mind verse.

N—Next Steps for Application

A. Summarize the lesson.

B. Close in prayer.

Worship Guide

For the Superintendent or Teacher
Theme: The Widow and the Unjust Judge
Song: "Victory in Jesus"
Devotional Reading: Psalm 145:13b–20

The Widow and the Unjust Judge

Bible Background • LUKE 18:1–8
Printed Text • LUKE 18:1–8 | Devotional Reading • PSALM 145:13b–20

———— Aim for Change ————

By the end of this lesson we will: EXAMINE the relationship between persistence and justice; VALUE the need for faithful persistence today; and BECOME persistent in prayer.

———— 🔍 In Focus ————

Jonathan never thought this day would come. After spending twenty years in prison for a crime he didn't commit, Jonathan was vindicated after a DNA test proved his innocence. Through the persistent prayers of his loving mother, Evelyn, Jonathan was finally free.

At age seventeen, Jonathan had been falsely accused of robbing a convenience store and shooting the store owner. He fit the description of the shooter, and Jonathan's clothes had the owner's blood on them because he had attempted to help the victim. Despite Jonathan's defense, the jury found him guilty of the charges.

Devastated by the conviction, Evelyn made it her mission to seek her son's vindication. A Christian woman of prayer and action, Evelyn spent the next twenty years seeking justice for her son. While raising her other three children, she researched the background of Jonathan's case, noticing inconsistencies in witness testimonies and police reports. She sought the help of many lawyers, but to no avail. Yet Evelyn never gave up.

With God's help, Evelyn went to a local law school and earned a law degree. She joined a legal advocacy group that sought to overturn false convictions. Evelyn and her legal team gathered enough evidence, including DNA evidence, to request a judge to review the case. After many years of many setbacks, a judge exonerated Jonathan of the crime. Jonathan now advocates alongside his mother for seeking justice for the falsely accused.

In today's lesson, Jesus reminds believers to persist in prayer and faithful action.

———— Keep in Mind ————

"And shall not God avenge his own elect, which cry day and night unto him, though he bear long with them?" (Luke 18:7).

"And shall not God avenge his own elect, which cry day and night unto him, though he bear long with them?" (Luke 18:7).

Focal Verses

KJV **Luke 18:1** And he spake a parable unto them to this end, that men ought always to pray, and not to faint;

2 Saying, There was in a city a judge, which feared not God, neither regarded man:

3 And there was a widow in that city; and she came unto him, saying, Avenge me of mine adversary.

4 And he would not for a while: but afterward he said within himself, Though I fear not God, nor regard man;

5 Yet because this widow troubleth me, I will avenge her, lest by her continual coming she weary me.

6 And the Lord said, Hear what the unjust judge saith.

7 And shall not God avenge his own elect, which cry day and night unto him, though he bear long with them?

8 I tell you that he will avenge them speedily. Nevertheless when the Son of man cometh, shall he find faith on the earth?

NLT **Luke 18:1** One day Jesus told his disciples a story to show that they should always pray and never give up.

2 "There was a judge in a certain city," he said, "who neither feared God nor cared about people.

3 A widow of that city came to him repeatedly, saying, 'Give me justice in this dispute with my enemy.'

4 The judge ignored her for a while, but finally he said to himself, 'I don't fear God or care about people,

5 but this woman is driving me crazy. I'm going to see that she gets justice, because she is wearing me out with her constant requests!'"

6 Then the Lord said, "Learn a lesson from this unjust judge.

7 Even he rendered a just decision in the end. So don't you think God will surely give justice to his chosen people who cry out to him day and night? Will he keep putting them off?

8 I tell you, he will grant justice to them quickly! But when the Son of Man returns, how many will he find on the earth who have faith?"

The People, Places, and Times

Widows. In ancient Israel, women were dependent upon their husbands for their social status, well-being, and protection. When husbands died, the inheritance was bestowed to the next male relative, starting with the first-born son. If there were no immediate surviving male relatives, the inheritance was given to the next male kin in the clan, leaving widows totally vulnerable to neglect and abuse from society if they didn't have the protection of a male relative. In the Old Testament, God instructed Israel to care for the widow, the orphan, and the foreigner in the Law (see Deuteronomy 24:17–18) and promises judgment against those who would break His commandment (Psalm 68:5).

Judges. In ancient Israel, magistrates resolved conflicts between Israelites. God called Moses to appoint judges from among the people to handle minor matters among the Israelites. In the book of Deuteronomy, Moses admonishes judges to hold impartiality, not preferring the rich and privileged over the orphan, the widow, and the foreigner among them (see Deuteronomy 1:16–18). If matters were too great for the judges to assess, they deferred to Moses. Judges might have served as chieftains or tribal leaders during times of crisis, as we see in the book of Judges. In the book, the prophet Deborah and the military leaders Othniel and Gideon are notable figures who "judged Israel" in the midst of fighting the Philistines.

If we analyze our current court system, how fair and impartial are the sentences handed down by judges?

Background

As Jesus was journeying to Jerusalem from Galilee to carry out His divine mission, He and His disciples made stops along the way in Samaria to minister to the people. Jesus performed many miracles and spoke many parables. As He was heading toward Jerusalem (Luke 9:52–54), Jesus passed through Samaria, a region north of Judea whose people were notably despised by many Jews during Jesus' day. The Samaritans were the descendants of the people of the Northern Kingdom of Israel, which fell to the Assyrian Empire in 722 BC. During that time, the Assyrians intermarried with the Israelite inhabitants. Consequently, the Samaritans were half-Jewish and half-Gentile. The Samaritans' faith tradition was similar to Jewish faith, but strikingly different in the part that mattered most to Jews: the holy dwelling place of God. For Jews, the house of God was the Temple in Jerusalem, while for Samaritans, the presence of God dwelt on Mt. Gerazim in the region of Samaria, One village did not receive Jesus' ministry (Luke 9:51–53), but He continued to teach, heal, and exorcise demons within Samaria.

On His way to Jerusalem, Jesus cleanses ten lepers (Luke 17:11–19), and some Pharisees ask Him about the coming of God's kingdom (Luke 17:20–21). After Jesus admonishes the Pharisees to recognize God's work among them, He urges the disciples to prepare for the coming of God's kingdom, although Jesus does not indicate when God will bring all things to fulfillment. However, there will be signs of its inbreaking (Luke 17:22–37).

What connection is there between the kingdom of God and our need to pray consistently?

At-A-Glance

1. The Persistent Widow (Luke 18:1–3)
2. The Unjust Judge Relents (vv. 4–5)
3. God's Justice (vv. 6–8)

In Depth

1. The Persistent Widow (Luke 18:1–3)

After Jesus discusses the coming of the Son of Man with His disciples (Luke 17:22–37), He tells them a parable to instruct them to persist in prayer during the present ordeal, which might include suffering for the sake of God's reign. Jesus introduces a widow who persistently seeks justice from a judge against an unspecified enemy. Here the widow's persistence serves as a model for the disciples. What is striking is that the widow, whose gender excluded her from being a credible witness in the ancient Jewish court, defies social conventions and pursues justice for herself without depending on a male relative to corroborate her claim. However, this judge "feared not God, neither regarded man." The judge's lack of interest toward the widow violated the judicial code of conduct outlined in the Old Testament. Despite this judge's lack of concern for God or the woman, the widow persists on coming to him to seek vindication.

How often do we choose to go the extra mile for those treated unjustly by others?

2. The Unjust Judge Relents (vv. 4–5)

At first, the judge simply refused the widow's petition. After a while, the judge relents and grants the persistent widow judgment, not because he repented from not fearing the God of justice or suddenly developed compassion for the widow. Rather, the judge grants her vindication because she continually troubles him. The judge becomes astonished at the widow's persistence; the widow, according to societal norms, should have accepted her fate. However, the widow defies these norms by demanding the judge to carry out his responsibility. The relentless widow "wears out" the judge by her actions. Thus, he reluctantly grants her justice.

How can persistent faith and actions create a change in our circumstances?

3. God's Justice (vv. 6–8)

Jesus tells His disciples to heed the words of the unjust judge: if he, an unjust man, can grant the widow vindication, surely God, who is the Righteous Judge (Psalm 7:11; 2 Timothy 4:8), will vindicate the elect, or "chosen people who cry to Him day and night." Yet the promise of God's quick vindication comes with a bit of irony. Although God promises to come quickly (Revelation 22:12), the people of God will endure the present ordeal. In the present ordeal, as Jesus relays, the disciples will incur suffering at the hands of unjust people. Hence, the people of God cry out to Him for their liberation. Given this present reality, the disciples must follow the example of the persistent widow and continue to pray fervently until the Son of Man comes. The Lord will not delay; however He seeks to find signs of faith on earth signified by the persistence in prayer that is exemplified in the widow's pursuit of justice.

Why is persistence in prayer distinguished as the key to liberation from injustices and oppression?

Search the Scriptures

1. What does the widow do to provoke a change in the unjust judge's treatment of her (Luke 18:4–5)?

2. What does Jesus mean when He says, "shall [the Son of Man] find faith on the earth" (v. 8)?

Discuss the Meaning

Jesus reminds us that prayer is a lifelong practice for every believer. We pray with the knowledge that God is faithful to His promise to save His people when we call on Him in the midst of unjust situations.

Lesson in Our Society

Prayer is fundamental to the life of every believer. It comes in many forms—thanksgiving, lament, petition, praise, confession, and intercession. Persistence in prayer is a characteristic of the Black Christians who participated in the Civil Rights Movement. They understood that prayer was a necessary act of resistance against the segregationist policies of the Jim Crow South. They endured many trials, but understood that in the end God's justice would come to pass and God's people would be vindicated.

How can prayer produce an impact against the current racial injustices and brutality Black people endure today?

Make It Happen

With as many forms of injustice that remain in the world today, we must adopt a regular practice of intercession and petition for God's justice to take root within our society. We also should practice pursuing justice within our spheres of influence. Whenever and wherever we see injustice, believers can pray for God's strength and power to defend those who are the most vulnerable among us.

Follow the Spirit

What God wants me to do:

_____

_____

_____

_____

Remember Your Thoughts

Special insights I have learned:

_____

_____

_____

_____

More Light on the Text

Luke 18:1–8

1 And he spake a parable unto them to this end, that men ought always to pray, and not to faint.

The context of this parable must be examined in conjunction with the parable itself. Just before this, Jesus spoke to His disciples about His Second Coming (Luke 17). Afterward, He presented the parable to them.

Luke immediately tells us Jesus' purpose for relaying this parable: to teach that men should always pray without ceasing (1 Thessalonians 5:17). Our prayers should be constant and consistent, not born of doubt or indecision. Evil temptations, fleshly desires, bad days, and a lack of patience will discourage us from praying earnestly, but Jesus wants to show His disciples—including us—that "the effectual fervent prayer of a righteous man availeth much" (from James 5:16).

2 Saying, There was in a city a judge, which feared not God, neither regarded man: 3 and there was a widow in that city; and she came unto him, saying, Avenge me of mine adversary.

This judge has no respect for either God or any other man. He is arrogant, proud, and reliant upon himself to meet all his needs—trademarks of people of the world, who often believe they don't need God or anyone else.

Widows of this era were symbols of helplessness. They were vulnerable to exploitation because they had no husbands to defend them. Apparently, the religious leaders of the time could not be trusted, as Jesus' indictment of the scribes and Pharisees suggests (Matthew 23:14). Here, the widow turns to the judge to avenge her (Gk. *ekdikeo*, **ek-dik-EH-oh**), meaning "to give justice" against her enemy. She was not seeking revenge through the judge, for Jesus would not honor such a petition. Instead, she wanted relief from the persecution she endured at the hands of her adversary, and she went through the correct channels of the justice system to pursue her vindication.

4 And he would not for a while: but afterward he said within himself, Though I fear not God, nor regard man; yet because this widow troubleth me, I will avenge her, lest by her continual coming she weary me.

The judge, because of the hardness of his heart and his concern only for himself, ignored the widow's pleas for some time. Eventually, he became annoyed with the woman's nagging requests. He reaffirms to himself that he is not accountable to anyone, but then relents because of the widow's persistence. "Troubleth me" would be more directly translated as "maketh trouble for me." The Greek word for trouble here is *kopos* (**KOP-os**), which refers to wearisome labor; beating one's breast in sorrow; and hardship amid turmoil and trials.

The widow's refusal to give up began to weigh on the judge's mind because his peace was disturbed greatly.

The judge appears wary of more than the widow's endless trips to his chambers. There is the possibility of physical assault, evidenced by the phrase, "lest … she weary me." The Greek word translated "weary" is *hupopiazo* (**hoo-poe-pee-AD-zo**), which could mean one of two things, depending on its derivation. It could be an intensified from of a verb meaning "to oppress, stifle, or exhaust," which is the understanding of the KJV translation. Alternatively, it could be a compound of the words "under-eye," which is a word used elsewhere to refer to striking someone under the eye. If this is the origin, the text could be dynamically translated as, "Lest … she give me a black eye." The judge might have feared that the widow would be driven to physical blows. The point is that she wore him down to the point of submission.

6 And the Lord said, Hear what the unjust judge saith. 7 And shall not God avenge his own elect, which cry day and night unto him, though he bear long with them?

Jesus wanted His disciples to take note of the judge's change of heart. By calling him unjust (Gk. *adikia*, **ah-dee-KEE-ah**, "unrighteous") the Lord accentuated the magnitude of the situation. If a man who knew no righteousness would grant an increasing petition, why wouldn't a righteous God do the same? The elect (Gk. *eklektos*, **ek-lek-TOCE**) are those chosen by God. They belong to Him and no one else. In the parable, God's elect are contrasted with the widow, who had no ties with the judge. He cared for her no more or less than he did for any other citizen.

Notice the extent of the cries of God's elect: "day and night." Jesus paints a picture of incessant prayers and supplication to the Father that cease only when the need is satisfied. He also hints at the emotion and longing that drive them. God responds to the sincere, genuine prayers of those who endure patiently.

But God is longsuffering. He waits before acting. God has promised to avenge His people against their adversary when He's ready. However, our ignorance of God's time should not erode our prayer life. Persistent prayers are a sign of faithfulness, and God never fails to reward our faithfulness. The widow also showed that our continual coming to the Lord might be our only weapon in spiritual warfare.

God's forbearance with His people serves as a blessing. Though it would be easy for Him to provide quick answers, that would prevent us from experiencing His grace, mercy, and strength. By bearing long, God teaches us patience and appreciation. When God waits to bless His people, they tend to value those gifts more. The longer it seems our prayers go unanswered, the more joy we feel when we receive our answers.

8 I tell you that he will avenge them speedily. Nevertheless when the Son of man cometh, shall he find faith on the earth?

Again, we must read this passage in context with the last verses of chapter 17. Here, Jesus foreshadows His Second Coming as God's method of vengeance. He then asks about the faith of those who will be waiting for Him. Will they have faith that prays always, suffers long, faints not, cries day and night, and waits expectantly for God's consent? He wanted His disciples to understand that the persecution and tribulations they would undergo would be validated when He came back to rule the earth.

Sources:

Bock, D. *Jesus According to Scripture: Restoring the Portrait from the Gospels.* Grand Rapids, MI: Baker Academic, 2002. 291-294.

Cone, J. H. *God of the Oppressed*, revised edition. Maryknoll, NY: Orbis Books, 1997. 158-159.

Keck, L., gen. ed. *The New Interpreter's Bible: Luke - John*, vol. 9. Nashville, TN: Abingdon Press, 1996. 278-279.

Migliore, D. L. Faith Seeking Understanding: An Introduction to Christian Theology, third edition. Grand Rapids, MI: Wm. B. Eerdmans Publishing Co., 2014.

The New Interpreter's Study Bible, New Revised Standard Version with the Apocrypha. Nashville, TN: Abingdon Press, 2003. 1887-1888.

Verhey, A. Remembering Jesus: Christian Community, Scripture, and the Moral Life. Grand Rapids, MI: Wm. B. Eerdmans Publishing Co., 2014.

Say It Correctly

Adversary. ad-ver-sa-**REE**.
Troubleth. **TRU**-bi-lith.

Daily Bible Readings

MONDAY
Ask, God Will Respond
(Luke 11:5–13)

TUESDAY
I Always Remember You in Prayer
(Romans 1:7–15)

WEDNESDAY
Unceasing Prayer
(1 Thessalonians 5:12–18)

THURSDAY
God's Justice for the Widow
(Deuteronomy 10:17–21)

FRIDAY
Take Care of Widows Now
(Acts 6:1–6)

SATURDAY
The Lord Watches His People
(Psalm 33:18–22)

SUNDAY
Keep Insisting until Justice Comes
(Luke 18:1–8)

Notes

Teaching Tips

Words You Should Know

A. Saved (Luke 13:23) *sozo* (Gk.)—To save, deliver or protect (literally and figuratively); heal, preserve, save (self), do well, to be whole.

B. Kingdom of God (v. 28) *basileia tou theou* (Gk.)—Jesus' central message; God's sovereign rule over all of His creation decisively enacted in the life, ministry, death, and resurrection of Jesus.

Teacher Preparation

Unifying Principle—Come In. People desire to be rewarded for what they consider acceptable behavior. What kind of behavior is acceptable? Jesus taught that we must bear good fruit and come to Him through a narrow way.

A. Pray for your students' understanding of today's lesson.

B. Read Matthew 7:15–23 and Luke 13:22–30 in two or more translations

O—Open the Lesson

A. Open with prayer, including the Aim for Change.

B. Introduce today's lesson title, "Entering God's Kingdom."

C. Have students read and discuss the Aim for Change and Keep in Mind verse together.

D. Discuss, "How does one enter the narrow door?" In the course of the discussion, provide opportunity (perhaps privately, after class) for anyone who wants to make a decision to be a part of God's kingdom.

P—Present the Scriptures

A. Have volunteers read the Focal Verses.

B. Use The People, Place, and Times; Background; Search the Scriptures, At-A-Glance outline; and In Depth to clarify the text.

C. Show other examples in Scripture where Jesus speaks about the "narrow door" and "weeping and gnashing of teeth" using a Bible concordance.

E—Explore the Meaning

A. Divide the class into groups to explore Discuss the Meaning, Lesson in Our Society, and Make It Happen.

B. Connect these sections to the Aim for Change and the Keep in Mind verse.

N—Next Steps for Application

A. Summarize the lesson.

B. Close in prayer.

Worship Guide

For the Superintendent or Teacher
Theme: Entering God's Kingdom
Song: "To the Utmost, Jesus Saves"
Devotional Reading: Psalm 1

Entering God's Kingdom

Bible Background • MATTHEW 7:15–23; LUKE 13:22–30
Printed Text • LUKE 13: 22–30 | Devotional Reading • PSALM 1

Aim for Change

By the end of the lesson, we will: IDENTIFY the sense and reference of the narrow door; APPRECIATE the difference between human and divine expectations regarding eternal reward; and SEEK to enter through the narrow door.

In Focus

Candace regularly attended church. She read her Bible daily. She sang alto in the choir and on the praise team. Candace volunteered at the local soup kitchen. She also taught Sunday School for the youth. Candace loves the Lord.

One morning as Candace walked to the bus stop, she encountered a young woman named Tameka. Candace thought Tameka's clothes were too provocative. Candace also noticed her nose ring and the tattoos on her arm. Further, she overheard hip-hop music blaring from Tameka's headphones. Candace shook her head and sneered to herself. *Poor child. She needs to get saved!* So she approached Tameka and asked, "Excuse me, young lady. Do you know the Lord?"

Tameka replied, "Yes, ma'am, I know Him. I am a child of God!" Despite Tameka's confession, Candace insisted on telling her about Jesus. "Ma'am, thank you, but I do know Jesus as my Savior," Tameka reiterated.

Candace didn't believe it. "Young lady, by the way you're dressed and the music you're listening to, it's clear you have fallen from the faith. Repent, and rededicate your life to Jesus today!" She fervently grabbed Tameka's arm. Scared, Tameka ran away from the bus stop and missed her bus. Saddened, Candice asked, "Lord, what did I do wrong?"

In today's lesson, we will learn that many who strive to enter God's kingdom will be surprised by who will enter it first.

Keep in Mind

"Strive to enter in at the strait gate" (from Luke 13:24).

"Strive to enter in at the strait gate" (from Luke 13:24).

Focal Verses

KJV **Luke 13:22** And he went through the cities and villages, teaching, and journeying toward Jerusalem.

23 Then said one unto him, Lord, are there few that be saved? And he said unto them,

24 Strive to enter in at the strait gate: for many, I say unto you, will seek to enter in, and shall not be able.

25 When once the master of the house is risen up, and hath shut to the door, and ye begin to stand without, and to knock at the door, saying, Lord, Lord, open unto us; and he shall answer and say unto you, I know you not whence ye are:

26 Then shall ye begin to say, We have eaten and drunk in thy presence, and thou hast taught in our streets.

27 But he shall say, I tell you, I know you not whence ye are; depart from me, all ye workers of iniquity.

28 There shall be weeping and gnashing of teeth, when ye shall see Abraham, and Isaac, and Jacob, and all the prophets, in the kingdom of God, and you yourselves thrust out.

29 And they shall come from the east, and from the west, and from the north, and from the south, and shall sit down in the kingdom of God.

30 And, behold, there are last which shall be first, and there are first which shall be last.

NLT **Luke 13:22** Jesus went through the towns and villages, teaching as he went, always pressing on toward Jerusalem.

23 Someone asked him, "Lord, will only a few be saved?" He replied,

24 "Work hard to enter the narrow door to God's Kingdom, for many will try to enter but will fail.

25 When the master of the house has locked the door, it will be too late. You will stand outside knocking and pleading, 'Lord, open the door for us!' But he will reply, 'I don't know you or where you come from.'

26 Then you will say, 'But we ate and drank with you, and you taught in our streets.'

27 And he will reply, 'I tell you, I don't know you or where you come from. Get away from me, all you who do evil.'

28 There will be weeping and gnashing of teeth, for you will see Abraham, Isaac, Jacob, and all the prophets in the Kingdom of God, but you will be thrown out.

29 And people will come from all over the world—from east and west, north and south—to take their places in the Kingdom of God.

30 And note this: Some who seem least important now will be the greatest then, and some who are the greatest now will be least important then."

The People, Places, and Times

Galilee. Galilee is a region that lies in Northern Israel. In the book of Joshua, the tribes of Asher, Zebulun, Isaachar, and Naphtali received allotments in the region. In the time of the judges, the tribe of Dan moved to the uppermost part of the region (Joshua 19:40–48; Judges 18). In the time of Jesus, Galilee was one of three regions that made up Palestine, Samaria and Judea being the other two. Jesus, although born in Bethlehem, came out of Nazareth, a city within Galilee (Mark 6:1; John 1:46; see also Mark 16:7). Jesus spent most of His ministry career traveling throughout the region, teaching in the synagogues, and performing healings and exorcisms.

Pharisees. The Pharisees were a prominent group within the Jewish tradition that existed during the period of Second Temple Judaism (2nd century BC—1st century AD). The Pharisees were members of the laity who were experts in the Law. The Pharisees emphasized the importance of adhering to tithing, purity laws, and rituals. They developed and promoted a robust oral tradition which they followed in addition to the Law (even using the tradition to interpret it). Pharisees also believed in the afterlife, divine judgment, and a spiritual realm. The New Testament portrays the Pharisees as religious opponents of Jesus.

In today's society, how can we prepare to handle religious leaders like the Pharisees, who are legalistic?

Background

Along His journey to Jerusalem, Jesus ministered throughout the region of Galilee. Galilee was the region where Jesus was raised and began His ministry. In several cities, Jesus performed healings, told parables, taught, and answered questions concerning the kingdom of God. In the moments leading up to today's passage, Jesus has several interactions with three audiences: 1) a group of Galileans who ascribed to Him the tragedy of some Galileans who were killed by Pilate while offering sacrifices (Luke 13:1–5); 2) a severely crippled woman whom Jesus healed in the synagogue (Luke 13:10–13); and 3) the leaders of the synagogue, his religious opponents, and the crowd who witnessed the healing (Luke 13:14–17).

After rebuking His opponents, Jesus told two parables concerning God's kingdom; one on the mustard seed (vv. 18–19), and another on the yeast (vv. 20–21). Whenever Jesus spoke on the kingdom of God, He told parables. Parables were literary forms or figures of speech which gave comparisons to illustrate a point or single idea. Although not a parable

in the technical sense, Jesus' discussion on the entry to the kingdom is filled with metaphor.

What do these parables explain about the expansion of the kingdom?

At-A-Glance

1. Strive to Enter (Luke 13:22–25)
2. We Ate and Drank With You (vv. 26–27)
3. The Last Will Be First and the First Will Be Last (vv. 28–30)

In Depth

1. Strive to Enter (Luke 13:22–25)

The question posed to Jesus in v. 23 echoes His own earlier teaching: "Because strait is the gate, and narrow is the way, which leadeth unto life, and few there be that find it" (Matthew 7:14). Yet Jesus does not give a direct answer to the concerned person's question. Instead, Jesus exhorts the crowd to "strive to enter through the narrow door." This admonition invokes the task an athlete engages in order to win a race. In this context, one must take on this task to enter God's kingdom by living a life of right action. Jesus warns that once the door is shut, many will stand outside of the door begging the owner to let them in.

What changes do you have to make to prioritize God's kingdom and work in your life?

2. We Ate and Drank With You (vv. 26–27)

Table fellowship is a central theme in the Gospel of Luke. Here Luke echoes the prophet Isaiah's imagery of the heavenly banquet God hosts for the peoples of all nations (Isaiah 25:6–9). Those who stand outside will claim to have had table fellowship with Jesus and heard Him teach. In Matthew 7, those who stand on the outside will claim to have prophesied and exorcised demons in the Lord's name. In both instances, Jesus will claim ignorance of them, "I never knew you" (v. 23; cf. Luke 13:27: "I know you not whence ye are"), and send them away as evildoers.

How can we compare and contrast ritualistic acts versus faithful service?

3. The Last Will Be First and the First Will Be Last (vv. 28–30)

The warning of "weeping and gnashing of teeth" comes to those among the Jewish crowd who rejected Jesus' message. They will stand on the outside and view the inclusion of the Gentiles—those who will come "from the east, and from the west, and from the north, and from the south"—into the kingdom of God along with their ancestors Abraham, Isaac, Jacob, and the prophets of old. Their status as God's people by circumcision alone no longer affords them privilege to access the kingdom. There is a great reversal! The kingdom includes all those once considered "last"—the Gentiles, the poor, the social outcasts, and sinners. The supposed righteous or "the first" will now enter the kingdom last, if at all.

How can personal bias influence the reason we choose not to witness to certain populations?

Search the Scriptures

1. Why does Jesus refer to God's kingdom having a "narrow door" (Luke 13:24)?

2. Why does Jesus say "I don't know you or where you come from" to those pleading to enter the kingdom (v. 25)?

Discuss the Meaning

Jesus Himself is the "door" and the "owner of the house." Those who put their faith in Him and heed His commandments will enter into the kingdom of God. In the 21st century, what prevents many from entering through the door? How can we make sure we have entered through the door?

Lesson in Our Society

As African Americans, we share a tragic history of being denied entrance into different places. Sometimes those doors have been visible, such as the doors to all-White organizations or institutions. Sometimes the doors have been invisible, such as the chance for a promotion or a loan signing thwarted by prejudice or bias. That being the case, we can appreciate Jesus' words as we who have been historically last can be first in God's kingdom. This calls us to be inclusive in our outreach and our witness. God's kingdom is open to all who go through the narrow door.

Many believers share the Good News of Jesus Christ in word only, but not in deed. In other words, right behavior is a testament to our faith as Christians. We cannot presume to deem others as unacceptable because they do not fulfill our expectations. As we strive to share our faith with our neighbors, we cannot deny the love and respect that is due to them as God's image bearers. We must show people the way to the narrow door, but we must do so with humility because we, like our neighbors, received grace to enter God's kingdom.

What can we do to develop more inclusiveness when we share our faith?

Make It Happen

• Create a list of the non-believers in your life. Pray for each of them specifically.

• Ask them why they haven't chosen to accept Christ. Be sure to continue the conversation without being pushy.

• Write in your journal the ways that you can show them love and lead them toward Christ.

Follow the Spirit

What God wants me to do:

_____

_____

_____

_____

Remember Your Thoughts

Special insights I have learned:

_____

_____

_____

_____

More Light on the Text

Luke 13:22–30

22 And he went through the cities and villages, teaching, and journeying toward Jerusalem.

Jesus is aware at this time that His ministry on earth is about to come to a close. This is the reason He is headed toward Jerusalem—to bring everything to a crescendo on the Cross according to the purposes and plans of the Father. While Luke shows some urgency in Jesus' going down to Jerusalem, and Jesus is determined to be in Jerusalem for Passover, He is also determined to preach and teach in as many towns and villages as possible. Thus, He makes constant stops in villages and towns to preach. The heaviness of the situation awaiting Him in Jerusalem does not discourage Him from the task at hand. Instead, it seems to make Him more resolute to preach in every town and village along the way.

23a Then said one unto him, Lord, are there few that be saved?

In this context of trying to teach in as many places as possible—with the intent to save as many as possible—someone (probably a member of the crowds and not one of the disciples) asked Jesus a question: "Lord, are there few that be saved?" By "saved" (Gk. *sozo*, **SODE-zo**), Luke points to the salvation that happens at the end of time—which is tantamount to entering the kingdom of God or gaining eternal life, and this is something that Jesus uses to give an indirect answer to the question. At the surface, this is a straightforward question: "Are you doing all this work to save only a few?" Today, mission strategists and evangelism team leaders will continue with other questions like, "Why bother to do all this when the results are already destined to be small?" or, "Is there a more effective way to maximize the ministry so that many (and not only a few) will be saved?" or even, "Could we simply have big preaching campaigns in several strategic locations to save us the trouble of going from one place to another?"

However, there is also a deeper theological question here. Probably, the person was asking about how many Jews would be saved at the end of time. Or even if the Gentiles would be saved as well.

The question was very relevant in view of the confused religious state of that day. Evidence exists that it was discussed and the rabbis held widely differing views. But it seems to have been firmly held that all Israel would be saved, except for a few blatant sinners who excluded themselves.

23b And he said unto them, 24 Strive to enter in at the strait gate: for many, I say unto you, will seek to enter in, and shall not be able.

Jesus begins to engage the questioner, but He engages more than just the question; He spoke to them. He did not answer the question directly, and actually avoided talking about the statistics and figures. Instead, He shifted the conversation from being a theological debate about who will be saved to a direct prophetic challenge to those listening to Him. Rather than speculate about the fate of others, Jesus would have His hearers enter the gate, no matter how narrow and difficult, rather than put off the decision until it is too late. Essentially, it is no longer a conversation about "them," but about "you." More importantly, it is not about how many will be saved, but whether the hearers respond to the message by entering the narrow gate before it is shut. Right now, the gate is open, but soon, it will be shut. The numbers are not limited; the time is.

Jesus admonished His audience to "strive" to enter through the narrow door. The word "strive" is an athletic term that comes from the Greek word *agonizomai* (**ah-go-NEED-zo-my**), which is also translated "to fight" and "to labor fervently." From it, we get the words "agonize" and "agony." In general language, it translates to contend with adversaries or struggle with difficulties and dangers as in athletic competitions. Jesus invites His listeners to make every effort to enter the kingdom—there is no room for half-heartedness. They must strain every nerve to be in the number of those who make it through the door, however large or small it will be.

The narrow door leads into the house. Matthew 7:13 talks about a similar narrow gate that leads to eternal life, but that seems to be an outside gate, while for Luke, the door is narrow and leads straight into a house where, it seems, there is a banquet going on. But for Luke as well, the door leads to entering the kingdom of God (v. 28). Only those who strive can enter, and Jesus' words seem to suggest that many of His hearers will not make it into the door. Many—who do not strive to enter the narrow door today—will, in the future, seek to enter, but it will be too late.

25 When once the master of the house is risen up, and hath shut to the door, and ye begin to stand without, and to knock at the door, saying, Lord, Lord, open unto us; and he shall answer and say unto you, I know you not whence ye are: 26 Then shall ye begin to say, We have eaten and drunk in thy presence, and thou hast taught in our streets. 27 But he shall say, I tell you, I know you not whence ye are; depart from me, all ye workers of iniquity.

Luke shifts the narrative—the narrow door will soon be shut. The "master of the house" (Gk. *oikodespotes*, **oy-ko-des-PO-tes**, literally "house-master," later "lord," Gk. *kyrios,* **KOO-ree-oce**) rises to shut the door. Luke does not say how the house owner determines when to shut the door, but it seems more likely that He is watching the time. When the hour strikes, whether few or many will have gotten inside the door, He will rise and shut the door. When that happens, Jesus is certain that many would be left outside, and among these will be some of His listeners.

Jesus anticipates that once the door is shut, those outside will knock at the door calling the master of the house—addressing Him as Lord—to open for them. It is very likely that even though Jesus describes this exchange between the owner of the house and those standing outside in the third person, when this happens, He is the master of the house and the Lord who will shut the door when the time comes. Those outside the house have no possibility of entering the house. However, from outside, they are able to talk to the master inside, and they are also able to see and recognize the people inside (v. 28). In reply to their plea to be allowed entry, the master will say he doesn't know who they are or where they are from. In essence, He refuses to acknowledge them. Matthew's accounts of similar exchanges get a sterner response from Jesus, "I never knew you; go away from me, you evildoers" (Matthew 7:23, NIV) and "Truly I tell you, I do not know you" (Matthew 25:12, NIV).

28 There shall be weeping and gnashing of teeth, when ye shall see Abraham, and Isaac, and Jacob, and all the prophets, in the kingdom of God, and you yourselves thrust out.

Having been denied entry into the kingdom, those outside will wail and gnash their teeth in sorrow and rage. Sorrow because of the missed opportunity—they could be inside the house if they had responded to the invitation before the door was shut. Rage because now the Master whom they believed knew them has declared He does not know them (or where they come from, even though they say they saw Him teaching in their streets). Even more, when they look inside, they see the heroes of the faith. Where Old Testament saints are welcome, contemporaries of Jesus are denied entry. And, of course, they consider themselves sons and daughters of Abraham who should not be excluded from the banquet. As a matter of fact, they were thrown out, which means they possibly tried to force their way through.

29 And they shall come from the east, and from the west, and from the north, and from the south, and shall sit down in the kingdom of God. 30 And, behold, there are last which shall be first, and there are first which shall be last.

Here, Luke uses the phrase "eat in the kingdom of God" to describe a future heavenly banquet. Thus, those left outside—who ate and drank in the presence of Jesus on earth—only see the real banquet of the kingdom from a distance. While they are surprised, disappointed, and frustrated at the sight of the patriarchs at the table from which they have been excluded, Jesus adds that they will find many more surprises in the kingdom of God. In addition to the patriarchs, prophets, and many other saints of the Old Testament, Gentiles will also sit at the table. Those who are locked outside will see many people from all over the earth enjoy the banquet, and this will make their sorrow and anger even worse. All in all, Gentiles who enter the narrow door before the closing time will find their way to the banquet, while those Jews who saw and heard Jesus teach in their towns and villages but did not enter the narrow door while it was open, will be outside.

Here lies the climax of the conversation. Jesus says to His listeners, "there are last which shall be first, and there are first which shall be last." They were worried about how many will be saved, but Jesus wanted to assure them that not many of those who saw Him, or ate and drank with Him, or heard Him teach in their streets would enter the narrow door before it closes. However, Gentiles who respond to His message in time will enter the kingdom. Thus, the first (the Jews who would generally believe they belong in the kingdom) would be left out when the last (the despised Gentiles) enter in. The Gentiles are enjoying bliss at the banquet with the patriarchs while Jews are outside gnashing their teeth. This is the exact opposite of what the Jews would have expected.

Sources:

Bock, D. *Jesus According to Scripture: Restoring the Portrait in the Gospels.* Grand Rapids, MI: Baker Academic, 2002. 275-276.

Bosch, D.J. *Transforming Mission: Paradigm Shifts in Theology of Mission.* Maryknoll, NY: Orbis Books, 2011.

Cosby, Michael R. *Portraits of Jesus: An Inductive Approach to the Gospels.* 1st ed. Louisville, KY: Westminster John Knox Press, 1999. 86-87.

Dunn, James D. G., and J.W. Rogerson. *Eerdmans Commentary on the Bible.* Grand Rapids, MI: W.B. Eerdmans, 2003.

Freedman, D.N., ed. *Eerdmans Dictionary of the Bible.* Grand Rapids, MI: Wm. B. Eerdmans Publishing Co, 2003. 478-480, 1043-1044.

Keck, L., gen. ed. *The New Interpreter's Bible: Matthew–Mark.* Vol. 8. Nashville, TN: Abingdon Press, 1996. 216-217.

Keck, L., gen. ed. *The New Interpreter's Bible: Luke–John*. Vol. 9. Nashville, TN: Abingdon Press, 1996. 335-340.

Marshall, I. Howard. *The Gospel of Luke: A Commentary on the Greek Text*. Grand Rapids, MI: Eerdmans, 1978. 440-450.

Morris, Leon. *The Gospel According to St. Luke: An Introduction and Commentary*. The Tyndale New Testament Commentaries. 1st American ed. Grand Rapids, MI: Eerdmans, 1974.

The New Interpreter's Study Bible: New Revised Standard Version with the Apocrypha. Nashville, TN: Abingdon Press, 2003. 1759, 1881.

Plummer, Alfred. *A Critical and Exegetical Commentary on the Gospel According to St. Luke*. 5th ed. Edinburgh: T. & T. Clark, 1975. 283-288.

Thompson, Richard P., and Thomas E. Phillips. *Literary Studies in Luke-Acts: Essays in Honor of Joseph P. Tyson*. Macon, GA: Mercer University Press, 1998. 317-320.

Wilcock, Michael. *The Savior of the World: The Message of Luke's Gospel*. The Bible Speaks Today. Downers Grove, IL: InterVarsity Press, 1979.

Say It Correctly

Gnash. **NASH.**

Patriarch. **PAY**-tree-ark.

Daily Bible Readings

MONDAY
Enter by the Narrow Gate
(Matthew 7:13–14)

TUESDAY
Jesus, Gate of Salvation
(John 10:1–10)

WEDNESDAY
Stay Connected to Jesus
(John 15:1–11)

THURSDAY
By Their Fruits You Will Know
(Matthew 7:15–23)

FRIDAY
Hear and Act on the Word
(Matthew 7:24–29)

SATURDAY
Abundant Life Today and Eternally
(Mark 10:28–31)

SUNDAY
Strive to Enter God's Kingdom
(Luke 13:22–30)

Notes

_____

_____

_____

_____

Teaching Tips

Words You Should Know

A. Come (Luke 14:17) *erchomai* (Gk.)—To appear, to make oneself known; to follow; to return.

B. Room (v. 22) *topos* (Gk.)—A place, space; opportunity.

Teacher Preparation

Unifying Principle—Join the Party. Some people eagerly accept invitations to important events while others feel that they have better things to do. What are the consequences of rejecting such invitations? Jesus declares that those who reject His invitation will not be allowed in His kingdom.

A. Pray for your class and spiritual illumination in the lesson.

B. Read Luke 14 in two or more modern translations.

C. If time and space allows, try teaching this lesson at a table, around a small meal, or in a large circle where all students feel comfortable and present.

D. Bring newspaper articles or video clips to help students identify marginalized people, and brainstorm ways they may welcome and embrace them.

O—Open the Lesson

A. Open the Lesson with prayer.

B. Introduce the lesson's title.

C. Ask students to review the Aim for Change and discuss the Keep in Mind verse together.

D. Have the class read the In Focus story and discuss it.

P—Present the Scriptures

A. Ask a few volunteers to act out the verses. You will need seven major characters: Jesus, dinner party guest, host, servant, and 3 invitees. The remainder of the class may serve as the large crowd of people on the margins whom the servant compels to come to the dinner party.

B. Use The People, Places, and Times; Background; Search the Scriptures; At-A-Glance outline; and In Depth sections to illuminate the verses.

E—Explore the Meaning

A. Present current events (e.g., news articles or video clips) to help the class frame a group dialogue of marginalized people, and to go over Discuss the Meaning and Lesson in Our Society.

B. Link the Make It Happen section to the Keep in Mind verse and Aim for Change.

N—Next Steps for Application

A. Summarize the lesson.

B. Close with prayer.

Worship Guide

For the Superintendent or Teacher
Theme: Parable of the Great Dinner
Song: "At the Table"
Devotional Reading: Luke 14:25–33

Parable of the Great Dinner

Bible Background • LUKE 14:15–24
Printed Text • LUKE 14:15–24 | Devotional Reading • LUKE 14:25–33

Aim for Change

By the end of this lesson, we will: EVALUATE the excuses people gave for not responding appropriately to the invitation to the banquet; AVOID being like one of the invitees who gave excuses; and SHARE with others Jesus' invitation to the great banquet.

In Focus

Faith and Nicholas invited their closest family and friends to attend their wedding. Faith and Nicholas' budget would only allow 200 guests, which meant they could not invite their entire church family. Two weeks before the ceremony, the church clerk read their wedding announcement, but did not extend an invitation to members. Faith overheard whispers among the congregation. Some congregants who received personal invitations bragged that they would attend. Some were not bothered because they did not know the couple well. Still others felt saddened that they were overlooked and uninvited. Faith knew their budget could not afford a larger party, but she did not want anyone to feel left out.

As the ceremony drew closer, many of the very special guests Faith originally invited failed to RSVP. Faith included in the next church announcement that all who desired to come could attend. She focused her attention on the company of those who wanted to share in the celebration of her and Nicholas' union. Once the invited wedding guests and those welcomed from the congregation were seated, there were still seats available for guests who just showed up to join the party.

There is enough room for all who desire to come and fellowship in the kingdom of God. In today's lesson, we will examine welcoming and embracing the least. Describe a time when you were invited to a very important party or event.

Keep in Mind

"So that servant came, and shewed his lord these things. Then the master of the house being angry said to his servant, Go out quickly into the streets and lanes of the city, and bring in hither the poor, and the maimed, and the halt, and the blind" (Luke 14:21).

"So that servant came, and shewed his lord these things. Then the master of the house being angry said to his servant, Go out quickly into the streets and lanes of the city, and bring in hither the poor, and the maimed, and the halt, and the blind" (Luke 14:21).

Focal Verses

KJV **Luke 14:15** And when one of them that sat at meat with him heard these things, he said unto him, Blessed is he that shall eat bread in the kingdom of God.

16 Then said he unto him, A certain man made a great supper, and bade many:

17 And sent his servant at supper time to say to them that were bidden, Come; for all things are now ready.

18 And they all with one consent began to make excuse. The first said unto him, I have bought a piece of ground, and I must needs go and see it: I pray thee have me excused.

19 And another said, I have bought five yoke of oxen, and I go to prove them: I pray thee have me excused.

20 And another said, I have married a wife, and therefore I cannot come.

21 So that servant came, and shewed his lord these things. Then the master of the house being angry said to his servant, Go out quickly into the streets and lanes of the city, and bring in hither the poor, and the maimed, and the halt, and the blind.

22 And the servant said, Lord, it is done as thou hast commanded, and yet there is room.

23 And the lord said unto the servant, Go out into the highways and hedges, and compel them to come in, that my house may be filled.

24 For I say unto you, That none of those men which were bidden shall taste of my supper.

NLT **Luke 14:15** Hearing this, a man sitting at the table with Jesus exclaimed, "What a blessing it will be to attend a banquet in the Kingdom of God!"

16 Jesus replied with this story: "A man prepared a great feast and sent out many invitations.

17 When the banquet was ready, he sent his servant to tell the guests, 'Come, the banquet is ready.'

18 But they all began making excuses. One said, 'I have just bought a field and must inspect it. Please excuse me.'

19 Another said, 'I have just bought five pairs of oxen, and I want to try them out. Please excuse me.'

20 Another said, 'I just got married, so I can't come.'

21 The servant returned and told his master what they had said. His master was furious and said, 'Go quickly into the streets and alleys of the town and invite the poor, the crippled, the blind, and the lame.'

22 After the servant had done this, he reported, 'There is still room for more.'

23 So his master said, 'Go out into the country lanes and behind the hedges and urge anyone you find to come, so that the house will be full.

24 For none of those I first invited will get even the smallest taste of my banquet.'"

The People, Places, and Times

Parables. Jesus traveled from place to place preaching and teaching to all who would listen. He used parables as a primary tool to convey His messages. A parable is a short narrative aimed at teaching a spiritual principle or moral lesson. On numerous occasions, Jesus' followers would come to Him with questions or insight about a spiritual practice, and He often responded with parables to enhance the followers' understanding. The parable of the great dinner is told in both Matthew 22:1–14 and Luke 14:15–25. Whereas Matthew uses the parable to reveal good treatment toward new believers, Luke's writing emphasizes God's open invitation to all people. When the host opens the dinner to include all people in Luke 14:21–25, the people least considered were the very ones willing to attend, and there was still more room for others.

Meal Fellowship. One sacred Christian ritual is fellowship around a meal. On the journey to Jerusalem, Jesus and His disciples were often greeted by hosts who welcomed them into their home and prepared a meal for them. Much of Luke's Gospel features Jesus eating and drinking with unlikely people (Luke 5:27–32, 7:36–50, 10:38–42, 19:1–10). Meal fellowship in this passage is symbolic of the Great Banquet, a heavenly feast of believers upon the messianic return of the Lamb of God (Revelation 19:9). Everyone invited to the table of fellowship of believers must accept the invitation in order to join the party. Believers accept this invitation through belief in Jesus Christ as Savior who will return to redeem the people of God. As the dinner guest announces in Luke 14:15, "What a blessing it will be to attend a banquet in the Kingdom of God!"

What do you imagine will be on the menu at the banquet in the kingdom of God?

Background

The Gospel of Luke presents Jesus as the Savior of the world. Luke's Jesus shows a deep concern for the dispossessed. Jesus reverses the social power dynamics to reveal the order of God. In Luke 14:1, Jesus is present at a dinner in the house of a Pharisee, a member of a Jewish sect who practiced strict observance of the Law. Those present at the dinner party were eager to hear and see Jesus' actions. On two other occasions in Luke (6:6–11, 13:10–17), Jesus infuriates religious leaders by healing on the Sabbath, a holy day observed by the Jewish

community to honor God. Jesus redefines the socio-religious order by performing a healing on the man suffering from swollen arms and legs on the Sabbath at the dinner in Luke 14:1–6, thus exposing that the rule of God is to extend care and concern for those in need.

As an invited dinner guest, Jesus gives lessons on humility and hospitality (vv. 7–14). He teaches on shame and honor associated with banquets because of who is invited and where one sits as a guest. Jesus encourages guests to maintain humility at all times because the esteemed will be brought low and the humble exalted (v. 11) in God's reign.

Appropriate dinner party etiquette in those times was to invite someone who could return the favor (vv. 12–14). By inviting people shunned by society, the host could not expect such a courtesy in return. Jesus offers a new paradigm of invitation in the kingdom of God whereby the nobodies of society are given place at the table. At the Lord's table, no one can repay the host, but we can make room for others to come join in the glorious feast.

How does it feel to know that you have been invited to God's kingdom banquet?

At-A-Glance

1. Dinner is Served (Luke 14:15–17)
2. Excuses, Excuses, Excuses (vv. 18–21)
3. There is Still Room (vv. 22–24)

In Depth

1. Dinner is Served (Luke 14:15–17)

The parable of the great dinner begins as a response from Jesus to a dinner party guest proclaiming the honor of feasting in the kingdom of God. The kingdom of God pronounces His eternal rule or reign. Jesus uses this parable to illustrate that the Lord's table is not restricted to a particular few, but rather open and inclusive for all who desire to come and partake.

Hosting a large group for a meal is no easy task. Such a task requires an extended period of preparation by the host to make the space ready and arrange the meal. Once all elements are put in place at a dinner party, the host will announce, "Dinner is served," which is an invitation for all guests to join the party and participate in the lavish feast that is prepared. In this parable, the host sends a servant out as a messenger and invites guests to attend and alert invitees that the feast is ready.

How can you alert others to Jesus' invitation to the kingdom feast?

2. Excuses, Excuses, Excuses (vv. 18–21)

Today we have a whole industry devoted to preparing invitations, from paper notes and e-vites, to websites and video messages. Can you imagine preparing a large dinner and on the day of, your invited guests one by one send notice that they cannot attend? Can you imagine the hurt feelings? In this parable, the invited guests turned down the invite and offered an array of excuses for why they could not attend the prepared dinner. Angered by the excuses, the host instructs the servant to find anyone who would accept the invitation to come.

Likewise, God calls humanity to join and experience His kingdom. He prepares and makes ready all that we need in advance. God sends messengers to us to share the good news of His call. All excuses to ignore God's invitations are trivial. It disturbs Him when we deny His welcome.

What are some excuses that people give for rejecting God's invitation?

3. There is Still Room (vv. 22–24)

The servant goes out into the hills and highways to invite those least likely to join the party. The lowly guests begin pouring in, but still there is room at the banquet. The host then instructs the servant to spread the news to everyone everywhere and bid them to come and fill the house. This parable's irony is that the esteemed few were unable to show, but the lowly were willing to come and attended in large numbers.

One of the major reasons a host invites certain guests to any party is the potential of scarcity. No host wants the food to run out or the space to become overpopulated and too crowded for guests. In the kingdom of God, the Lord's table has more than enough space. We serve a God who specializes in sufficiency and abundance. One's position or status in society does not matter; there is always room in the kingdom of God.

Why would someone think there is no room in the kingdom of God for them?

Search the Scriptures

1. Do you believe the excuses to reject the invitation were valid? Why or why not (Luke 14:18–20)?

2. Who is welcome to the feast of the kingdom (v. 21)?

Discuss the Meaning

It is easy to honor and welcome people who we think are of high esteem. The real test of our Christian character is whether we can value and embrace those who are the least, the left out, the outcasts and the unwanted. This lesson teaches us that the ones who are cast down are often the ones who should be raised up. Who in your community are the people on the margins? Have you overlooked or uninvited these people to the table of the fellowship of believers?

Lesson in Our Society

The African American community can relate to the experience of marginalization historically and today. Blacks have fought for centuries to sit at the American table of democracy with equal representation and recognition. In a world where Black lives struggle to matter globally, there is hope in the table of fellowship in the kingdom of God which remains open to all, especially the ostracized. Just as we are welcomed and embraced by God, we are called to receive and accept others with open arms.

Make It Happen

• As Christians, we are called to serve as messengers of God by sharing with others the invitation to His kingdom.

• There is no excuse that can release us from the Christian duties of humility and hospitality. It is our responsibility to make room for others, particularly at the tables of power and privilege that we occupy. Consider in your church, your committees, your professional societies, and your civic organizations, how you can make room for others.

• Make a commitment to opening the doors of opportunity for the least likely: the young, the old, the poor, the sick, the disenfranchised, etc.

Follow the Spirit

What God wants me to do:

_____

_____

_____

_____

Remember Your Thoughts

Special insights I have learned:

_____

_____

_____

_____

More Light on the Text

Luke 14:15–24

15 And when one of them that sat at meat with him heard these things, he said unto him, Blessed is he that shall eat bread in the kingdom of God.

Jesus was at the home of a Pharisee and had finished telling the host who should be invited to any of his luncheons or dinners. Jesus included the poor, the crippled, the lame, and the blind. He added that since these impoverished people could in no way repay the host, at the resurrection of the godly, God would reward the host for inviting those who could not repay him (14:12–14). When a man sitting at the table with Jesus heard these things, he saw the glory of God's kingdom and said, "Blessed is he that shall eat bread in the kingdom of God."

The word "blessed" in Greek is *makarios* (**mah-KAH-ree-oce**) and means "supremely favored, happy, well off." The phrase "kingdom of God" refers to a time and place when God rules over all hearts and provides richly for His people. In essence, the man said that a person is supremely fortunate to sit at the Lord's table and partake of what He offers, which is everlasting life.

16 Then said he unto him, A certain man made a great supper, and bade many:

Now the Lord tells a parable of a great supper that a certain man had. The word "supper" in Greek is *deipnon* (**DAYP-known**), referring to the last meal of the day, which was usually the main meal. This one being a "great" supper implies it was closer to a feast than an evening meal. In the illustration that Jesus gave, this man had a great banquet or dinner and invited different people to attend and share from his table. Of course, Jesus is that "certain man" inviting all to come to His supper or great feast and partake of what He is offering—eternal life in the kingdom of God, which can only be found at the Lord's table.

17 And sent his servant at supper time to say to them that were bidden, Come; for all things are now ready. The man's servant obeyed and went and told the invited guests that the feast was ready and they should come. 18 And they all with one consent began to make excuse. The first said unto him, I have bought a piece of ground, and I must needs go and see it: I pray thee have me excused. 19 And another said, I have bought five yoke of oxen, and I go to prove them: I pray thee have me excused. 20 And another said, I have married a wife, and therefore I cannot come.

However, as though with one voice ("with one consent"), the invitees presented reasons not to attend the banquet (v. 18). They wanted to be excused. The excuses vary, but the basic reason is similar—either financial or familial concerns. Something else is ultimately more important than attending. The excuses went on and on as to why the invited guests could not and would not attend the feast.

One said that he had bought a yoke of oxen and had to prove them. The word "prove" in Greek is *dokimazo* (**do-kee-MOD-zo**) and means "to test, examine." His excuse was that he had to find out if the oxen were any good. Apparently, he bought them without first examining them. Another invitee said that he had gotten married and could not come. Since Christ was speaking of the end-times banquet, He was making the point that other concerns get in the way of deciding for Jesus and sharing

the hope of the eschaton (Gk. **es-ka-TAHN**), which is the Greek word for the end of the age. Such excuses are poor, even insulting, in light of the occasion and their previous willingness to come.

Today, people use many excuses to reject Christ's offer of salvation. Some feel that they are too young to get saved now and will do so later. Others feel that they are too old or too bad to be forgiven. Still others feel that salvation is not for them, while some think that there are ways of salvation apart from Christ.

21 So that servant came, and showed his lord these things. Then the master of the house being angry said to his servant, Go out quickly into the streets and lanes of the city, and bring in hither the poor, and the maimed, and the halt, and the blind.

The servant told his master what the invitees said. The master was angry about all the excuses and rejections, and he sent his servant into the streets to invite the outsiders to the banquet—those who had been overlooked by the elite, the marginalized of society. Translated from the Greek, "the poor" is *ptochos* (**pto-KHOS**) and means "beggars, paupers"; "the maimed" (Gk. *anaperos*, **ah-NA-pay-roce**) means "crippled"; the "halt" in Greek is *cholos* (**kho-LOS**), and it means "limping, crippled, lame." The parable extends the invitation beyond expected boundaries. In essence, God sent His one and only Son to a whole world of spiritually needy people—to those who recognize it as well as those who are less aware.

22 And the servant said, Lord, it is done as thou hast commanded, and yet there is room. 23 And the lord said unto the servant, Go out into the highways and hedges, and compel them to come in, that my house may be filled.

Since there was still room at what must have been a huge table, the master in the story sent his servant to the highway and hedges to invite more people—those outside of the church, the street people—to come so that God's house would be filled. The idea that this master had enough room for everyone equals the belief that God turns no one away from joining His kingdom—all can be saved! God's people must be sought and found in surprising places. Whosoever will may come.

24 For I say unto you, That none of those men which were bidden shall taste of my supper.

Jesus now summarizes the parable for His audience. Those whom the man had invited to come to the supper in the first place were really missing out; they would never "taste" (Gk. *geuomai*, **GEW-oh-my**), which here has the double meaning of literal eating and figurative experiencing, his feast. In essence, those who reject Jesus Christ as their personal Savior will never experience His wonderful salvation—be a part of His kingdom that will reign forever and ever. In other words, the rejecting ones will experience death—eternal separation from a holy God.

Sources:
Crowder, Stephanie Buckhanon. "Luke." *True to Our Native Land: African American Commentary.* Edited by Brian K. Blount, Cain Hope Felder, Clarice J. Martin and Emerson B. Powery. Minneapolis, MN: Augsburg Fortress Press, 2007. 158–185
deSilva, David. *An Introduction to the New Testament: Contexts, Methods, and Ministry Formation.* Downers Grove, IL: InterVarsity Press, 2004. 298–347.
Green, Joel B., ed. *The CEB Study Bible with Apocrypha.* Nashville, TN: Common English Bible, 2013. 103–165.
Levine, Amy-Jill and Marc Zvi Brettle., ed. *The Jewish Annotated New Testament: New Revised Standard Version.* New York: Oxford University Press, 2011. 96–151.

Say It Correctly

Hither. hi-**THUR**.
Bidden. bi-**DEN**.

Daily Bible Readings

MONDAY
Exemptions from Military Service
(Deuteronomy 20:5–8)

TUESDAY
The Wealthy and Kingdom Membership
(Luke 18:18–25)

WEDNESDAY
Take Up the Cross and Follow
(Matthew 16:24–28)

THURSDAY
My True Mother and Siblings
(Mark 3:31–35)

FRIDAY
The Gentiles Will Listen
(Acts 28:23–28)

SATURDAY
Count the Cost, Then Follow Me
(Luke 14:25–33)

SUNDAY
Everyone Invited to the Great Dinner
(Luke 14:15–24)

Teaching Tips

Words You Should Know

A. Longsuffering (Romans 2:4) *makrothumia* (Gk.)—A Christian virtue of patience; a fruit of the Spirit that manifests in Christian behavior and character.

B. Wrath (v. 5) *orge* (Gk.)—Strong anger or indignation.

Teacher Preparation

Unifying Principle—Equity for All. It is very easy to judge others, condemning them for doing the same thing we have done. How can we avoid being judgmental? Paul teaches that God's kindness, forbearance, and patience lead us to repentance and new life.

A. To prepare for today's lesson, read the Bible Background and The People, Places, and Times sections.

B. Read the Focal Verses in several Bible translations to help you understand the meaning of the verses.

O—Open the Lesson

A. Open the class with prayer.

B. Share the Words You Should Know with the students.

C. Read the In Focus story and discuss.

P—Present the Scriptures

A. Ask for a volunteer to read the People, Places, and Times and Background sections. Discuss briefly.

B. Read Focal Verses and the Keep in Mind verse together in class. Ask each student to read two paragraphs of the In Depth sections and discuss.

E—Explore the Meaning

A. Ask the students to answer the Search the Scriptures and Discuss the Meaning questions.

B. Ask a volunteer to read the Lesson in Our Society and discuss as a class.

N—Next Steps for Application

A. Encourage the students to apply the Make It Happen section.

B. Challenge the students to read the Daily Bible Readings for the week.

C. Ask if there are any prayer concerns and then end the session with prayer.

Worship Guide

For the Superintendent or Teacher
Theme: God's Justice
Song: "We Shall Overcome"
Devotional Reading: Psalm 32

God's Justice

Bible Background • ROMANS 2:1–16
Printed Text • ROMANS 2:1–12 | Devotional Reading • PSALM 32

—————— Aim for Change ——————

By the end of this lesson we will EXPLORE Paul's convictions regarding living generous and just lives before God in community; ASPIRE to refrain from judgmental attitudes that only serve to condemn us; and PRACTICE repentance that leads to new life in Christ.

————— In Focus —————

Mike admired his new car. He housed it safely in his parents' garage. Over the summer, he had worked long hours to save money to purchase his used but beautiful Ford Mustang. His younger brother, Josh, would frequently hint around to Mike that he wanted to take the car for a joyride. Mike insisted the car was not to be moved or driven by his younger brother.

One evening, Mike accidentally left the garage door unlocked and a kid from down the street walked in and stole his car. The next morning, Mike noticed the car was missing and accused Josh of stealing his car. Josh repeatedly denied having anything to do with Mike's missing car; nonetheless, after their parents called the police to report the car missing, Josh was unfairly punished. No matter how much he tried to defend himself, he definitely seemed to be guilty.

Two weeks later, the police came to the house and reported that the car had been confiscated. The perpetrator who stole the car had been arrested and was in police custody. Mike and his parents realized they had accused Josh unjustly and apologized. Josh's feelings were hurt; however, he forgave them.

God's justice is always fair and He is no respecter of persons. In this lesson, we will look at the ways God judges people. Have you ever judged someone wrongly based on your own human perception?

—————— Keep in Mind ——————

"But glory, honour, and peace, to every man that worketh good, to the Jew first, and also to the Gentile: For there is no respect of persons with God" (Romans 2:10–11).

"But glory, honour, and peace, to every man that worketh good, to the Jew first, and also to the Gentile: For there is no respect of persons with God" (Romans 2:10–11).

Focal Verses

KJV **Romans 2:1** Therefore thou art inexcusable, O man, whosoever thou art that judgest: for wherein thou judgest another, thou condemnest thyself; for thou that judgest doest the same things.

2 But we are sure that the judgment of God is according to truth against them which commit such things.

3 And thinkest thou this, O man, that judgest them which do such things, and doest the same, that thou shalt escape the judgment of God?

4 Or despisest thou the riches of his goodness and forbearance and longsuffering; not knowing that the goodness of God leadeth thee to repentance?

5 But after thy hardness and impenitent heart treasurest up unto thyself wrath against the day of wrath and revelation of the righteous judgment of God;

6 Who will render to every man according to his deeds:

7 To them who by patient continuance in well doing seek for glory and honour and immortality, eternal life:

8 But unto them that are contentious, and do not obey the truth, but obey unrighteousness, indignation and wrath,

9 Tribulation and anguish, upon every soul of man that doeth evil, of the Jew first, and also of the Gentile;

10 But glory, honour, and peace, to every man that worketh good, to the Jew first, and also to the Gentile:

11 For there is no respect of persons with God.

12 For as many as have sinned without law shall also perish without law: and as many as have sinned in the law shall be judged by the law.

NLT **Romans 2:1** You may think you can condemn such people, but you are just as bad, and you have no excuse! When you say they are wicked and should be punished, you are condemning yourself, for you who judge others do these very same things.

2 And we know that God, in his justice, will punish anyone who does such things.

3 Since you judge others for doing these things, why do you think you can avoid God's judgment when you do the same things?

4 Don't you see how wonderfully kind, tolerant, and patient God is with you? Does this mean nothing to you? Can't you see that his kindness is intended to turn you from your sin?

5 But because you are stubborn and refuse to turn from your sin, you are storing up terrible punishment for yourself. For a day of anger is coming, when God's righteous judgment will be revealed.

6 He will judge everyone according to what they have done.

7 He will give eternal life to those who keep on doing good, seeking after the glory and honor and immortality that God offers.

8 But he will pour out his anger and wrath on those who live for themselves, who refuse to obey the truth and instead live lives of wickedness.

9 There will be trouble and calamity for everyone who keeps on doing what is evil—for the Jew first and also for the Gentile.

10 But there will be glory and honor and peace from God for all who do good—for the Jew first and also for the Gentile.

11 For God does not show favoritism.

12 When the Gentiles sin, they will be destroyed, even though they never had God's written law. And the Jews, who do have God's law, will be judged by that law when they fail to obey it.

The People, Places, and Times

Gentile. This name is given to any ethnic group other than the Jewish race. The Jews looked down upon other races as barbarous and unclean. In the Old Testament, Jews referred to themselves as "God's chosen people" or "God's elect." In the New Testament, salvation is offered to Jews and Gentiles alike.

The Law. The Law is also referred to as the Law of Moses. It is the authoritative rule of conduct spelled out in the Ten Commandments and the Pentateuch (the books of Genesis, Exodus, Leviticus, Numbers, and Deuteronomy). The Lord revealed this code to Moses on Mt. Sinai (Deuteronomy 5:1–2). While many of the regulations are ceremonial and procedural in nature, the moral law embodied in the Law of Moses is eternal, unchangeable (Romans 7:7–12), and fulfilled through Jesus Christ (Matthew 5:17–18).

Have you seen rules that are too harsh?

Background

The Apostle Paul is writing to the church in Rome. The congregation consists of Jewish and Gentile believers. Paul and the other apostles had heard of the church in Rome but never been there. It is believed that Jewish believers who were present on the Day of Pentecost established the church. These believers were among the 3,000 who were added to the church and took the Gospel to Rome. Paul's comment in his letter shows evidence that the Gospel had gone out to the Gentiles and that their presence was visible in the Roman church (Romans 1:13–15). During New Testament times, Rome was the capital of the Roman Empire. It was a cultural center, experiencing prosperity along with literary and artistic advancement. Yet, it was surrounded by moral decay. Roman citizens worshiped idols and practiced acts of perversion. In the prior chapter (Romans 1:18–32), Paul goes into great detail describing the depth of man's depravity and the evil acts committed against God; these acts included violence, greed, envy, murder, strife, malice, arrogance, boastfulness, disobedience, and every form of ungodly behavior imaginable to man. Because of man's wretched condition and his refusal to acknowledge and obey God's commandments, God gave man over to his corrupt thinking and ways. Paul goes on to say in Romans 2:1–16 that Jews or Christian believers are in no position to judge others. He explains how God's long-suffering is purposeful, allowing plenty of time for human repentance and giving mankind time to draw closer to God. Nevertheless, humanity tends to take God's grace for granted. In his letter, Paul makes a strong case for repentance by unfolding the consequences of sin and the inevitable destruction of those who continue to do evil.

In this lesson, we will learn why God's punishment for sin is just, impartial, and inevitable.

How have you experienced mercy?

At-A-Glance

1. God's Judgment is Just (Romans 2:1–4)
2. God's Judgment is Impartial (vv. 5–12)

In Depth

1. God's Judgment is Just (Romans 2:1–4)

Paul explains why believers are guilty and sternly cautions the believer. He warns us to be careful how we judge others, especially when we become angry at someone else's sin, because the sin that we recognize in the lives of others may be the same sin at work in our own lives. For example, people who gossip have a tendency to become extremely irritated when others talk behind their backs, and individuals who are self-promoting tend to be very critical of others who seek the spotlight. God's Word reveals to us the necessity of examining our own behavior, not against the conduct of others, but against the Word of God—adjusting our lifestyles so that they line up with His perfect will.

Paul is not suggesting that everyone who judges the sinner is actively involved in the same sin. What Paul is saying is that those who point an accusatory finger—for instance, at the adulterer—might be involved in a similar sin, but one deemed more "socially acceptable." For example, one might cruise the Internet for pornographic material, watch X-rated movies in the privacy of their own home, or read books or watch sitcoms with sexually explicit stories centered around adultery. The point here is that sin is sin, and the Bible tells us that anyone who looks at a woman lustfully "has committed adultery with her in his heart already" (Matthew 5:28). Sin begins in our minds and hearts. It is important to bathe our minds on a daily basis with the Word of God. What we see, think, and meditate on will eventually become visible through our actions. God's Word must transform us, cleansing our hearts and minds of all impurities.

Have you seen examples of people judging private sin as less offensive than public sin?

2. God's Judgment is Impartial (vv. 5–12)

When we purposely continue to sin against God, we are storing up wrath against ourselves (v. 5). A believer can store up wrath by possessing an unrepentant and hardened heart. A hardened heart can be filled with unforgiveness, envy, jealousy, anger, bitterness, and other sinful attitudes. These hindrances make it difficult for God's Word to grow and mature in our hearts. As we pray and meditate on God's Word, our hearts can be restored. When we ask God to forgive us, His redemptive Word heals our brokenness and restores our hearts to a purified condition. God's will is that we serve Him with a clean heart, which allows us to rest in knowing we have security in Him, and allows us to see and treat others the way He intended us to.

God will give to each person what they deserve based on how they live, including their attitudes (v. 6). He will grant immortality, blessings, and eternal life to every believer who continues to serve the Lord and do His will (vv. 7, 10). We all stand guilty before God. Paul's letter gives us a clear indication of the importance of godly obedience. Tribulation, anger, and wrath are the future reality for those who insist on living selfish, disobedient lives (vv. 8–9). God makes no distinction between Jew and Gentile; all are subject to His penetrating eye. Every human being will be judged accordingly. God is fair and accurate in His assessment of human behavior (vv. 11–12).

How does knowing we have all sinned help us to stay humble and seek God?

Search the Scriptures

1. What will be the reward for those who are contentious and unrighteous (Romans 2:8–9)?

2. What is meant by, "For there is no respect of persons with God" (v. 11)?

Discuss the Meaning

1. The Bible says that God will judge man's secrets (v. 16). What does this tell us about the things we try to keep secret from God?

2. Explain in your own words what the following Scripture means to you: "[God] will render to every man according to his deeds" (Romans 2:6).

Lesson in Our Society

The death of Michael Brown Jr. in Ferguson, Missouri at the hands of a law enforcement officer became a catalyst for public protest around the country in the weeks following. In the immediate aftermath, there was division about what actually happened, who was to blame, and how to respond.

Did you rush to judgment? Whom did you blame? How did you view this horrendous incident? Did you judge the victim? The perpetrators? How did you feel about God when it happened? And why do you think God allows things like this to happen in our society?

Make It Happen

• Write a list of those you might judge based on personal bias or prejudice. Pray for God to change your heart.

• Take an Implicit Bias test here: https://implicit.harvard.edu/implicit/takeatest.html

• Write in your journal the ways you see God's justice working out in the world.

Follow the Spirit

What God wants me to do:

_____

_____

_____

_____

Remember Your Thoughts

Special insights I have learned:

_____

_____

_____

_____

More Light on the Text

Romans 2:1–12

1 Therefore thou art inexcusable, O man, whosoever thou art that judgest: for wherein thou judgest another, thou condemnest thyself; for thou that judgest doest the same things.

How easy it is to fall into the habit of judging others, yet Paul calls it "inexcusable" (Gk. *anapologetos*, **an-ah-po-LO-gay-toce**), which means one cannot give an adequate defense. We live in a society that encourages competition, and this reality makes it easy for people to develop the habit of judging others. God is perfectly holy and wants us to understand that all human beings are flawed and damaged because of sin. For that reason, we should not judge anyone without subjecting ourselves to the same standard. To do so only causes us to condemn ourselves, because even if we don't commit the same sin as someone else, we still are guilty of our own sin and God will hold us accountable.

2 But we are sure that the judgment of God is according to truth against them which commit such things. 3 And thinkest thou this, O man, that judgest them which do such things, and doest the same, that thou shalt escape the judgment of God?

This Scripture passage should cause each one of us to pause and consider the things we permit ourselves to embrace. Unlike sinful human beings, there is no falsehood in God. He is the very essence of truth (see Titus 1:2, John 14:6). Therefore, we should not expect Him to see our actions and activities in the same fashion as we do. God formed us; He knows every part of us—our desires, our intentions, even the thoughts that motivate us. None of us can deceive Him, nor should we expect to avoid standing before Him in judgment.

4 Or despisest thou the riches of his goodness and forbearance and longsuffering; not knowing that the goodness of God leadeth thee to repentance? 5 But after thy hardness and impenitent heart treasurest up unto thyself wrath against the day of wrath and revelation of the righteous judgment of God.

Our desire to live for ourselves and satisfy our sinful nature results in our rejecting God's kindness toward us. We seem to hold His good qualities in contempt and "despise" them (Gk. *kataphroneo*, **ka-ta-fro-NEH-oh**). This word has the sense of thinking of something as little or looking down on it. We don't want to believe that God is good and that He loves us despite the fact that we don't know how to love ourselves most of the time. God doesn't desire to be angry with us; that's why He is long-suffering.

6 Who will render to every man according to his deeds:

There does come a point when God will accept a person's rejection and deal with them in righteous judgment. Each person will stand before God to review the life he or she lived. When the examination of his or her life is ended, He judges the motives of our hearts in giving and well-doing. The person who has rejected God's saving grace will understand that he or she never came close to meeting the standard that would please Him. It is impossible for any human to do so without Christ.

7 To them who by patient continuance in well doing seek for glory and honor and immortality, eternal life: 8 But unto them that are contentious, and do not obey the truth, but obey unrighteousness, indignation and wrath.

God rewards those godly attributes that He has established in those He loves. These rewards include glory, honor, and eternal life. It is not possible for a person to earn these things; our sin nature ensures that we will always fall short of God's standard. Rather, these rewards are gifts from God given in recognition of the changes occurring in one's life. By the same token, those individuals who are contentious (Gk. *eritheia*, **eh-re-THAY-ah**) and do not obey God will receive His wrath and indignation. This word for contentiousness is used in earlier Greek sources to refer to people who pursue political office by unfair means and for selfish reasons. In its use here, the ideas of unfairness and selfishness continue to be vices in the Christian church, as is partisan jockeying for position in the church (though Paul might not have that in mind here).

9 Tribulation and anguish, upon every soul of man that doeth evil, of the Jew first, and also of the Gentile; 10 But glory, honour, and peace, to every man that worketh good, to the Jew first, and also to the Gentile:

It has been suggested that with great privilege comes great responsibility. The Jews are a living example of what happens when people, even those specially chosen and set apart by God, fail to live up to their God-given privileges. The Jewish nation's rejection of God's Son, Jesus Christ, as their Messiah resulted in God's rejection of them as His corporate people. Now, the privilege of being God's chosen people is offered to all of humanity. However, each of us must respond by either accepting God's offer and allowing the Holy Spirit to guide us into good works, or rejecting it and incurring God's great anger.

11 For there is no respect of persons with God. 12 For as many as have sinned without law shall also perish without law: and as many as have sinned in the law shall be judged by the law.

God does not "respect" (Gk. *prosopolepsia*, **pro-so-po-lape-SEE-ah**), or favor, one person or nation above another. We are all the same in His eyes. Because we are all the same, we can expect that His judgments will be fair and impartial. God shows no concern for the outward appearance or circumstances when considering the deeds of human beings. Instead, God's grace prevails when He considers the sins of man.

The Mosaic Law was given to the Jews by Moses. In verse 12, Paul is saying that the Gentiles who sin will perish, but the Law of Moses will not be used as a standard of judgment against them. However, the Jews, who were given the law, will be judged by the law.

Sources:
Cottrell, Jack. Romans. *College Press NIV Commentary.* 2 vols. Joplin, MO: College Press, 1996.
Dunn, James D. G., and J.W. Rogerson. *Eerdmans Commentary on the Bible.* Grand Rapids, MI: W.B. Eerdmans, 2003.
Stott, John R. W. *The Message of Romans: God's Good News for the World.* The Bible Speaks Today. Leicester, England: InterVarsity Press, 2001

Say It Correctly

Inexcusable. in-eks-**CYOO**-su-bul.
Impenitent. im-**PI**-ni-tint.

Daily Bible Readings

MONDAY
The Power of the Gospel
(Romans 1:16–17)

TUESDAY
Bear Fruit of Repentance
(Luke 3:7–14)

WEDNESDAY
Genuine Christian Behavior
(Romans 12:14–21)

THURSDAY
Gentiles Experience Repentance
(Acts 11:15–18)

FRIDAY
Paul's Joy at Corinthians' Repentance
(2 Corinthians 7:9–11)

SATURDAY
Doers of the Law are Justified
(Romans 2:12–16)

SUNDAY
God's Righteous, Impartial Judgment
(Romans 2:1–12)

Teaching Tips

Words You Should Know

A. Poor (2 Corinthians 8:9) *ptocheuo* (Gk.)—To be destitute financially or spiritually.

B. Rich (v. 9) *plouteo* (Gk.)—To be prosperous financially or spiritually.

Teacher Preparation

Unifying Principle—Charitable Equity For All. We want to be generous to those in need. What motivates true generosity when the needs seem so overwhelming? Paul encouraged the Corinthians' generosity in response to God's generous gifts to them.

A. Pray for your preparation and individuals who will attend.

B. Read the Focal Verses in two or more modern translations.

C. Complete the companion lesson in *Precepts For Living®* Personal Study Guide.

O—Open the Lesson

A. Introduce the lesson title and ask a volunteer to begin with prayer.

B. Have students read the Aim for Change and Keep in Mind silently.

C. Ask for a volunteer to read In Focus and discuss.

P—Present the Scriptures

A. Ask participants to read along silently as you read the Focal Verses aloud.

B. Utilize The People, Place and Times; Background; Search the Scriptures; and In Depth sections.

E—Explore the Meaning

A. Divide the class into groups to complete Lesson in Our Society. Come back together and discuss as a class.

B. Have participants complete Discuss the Meaning individually. Ask for a few volunteers to share their responses.

N—Next Steps for Application

A. Instruct participants to complete Make It Happen as an individual meditation exercise. Do not ask them to share answers the exercise is for personal reflection.

B. Ask each student to share one take away from the lesson.

C. Close in prayer.

Worship Guide

For the Superintendent and the Teacher
Theme: Global Economic Justice
Song: "Give of Your Best to the Master"
Devotional Reading: Proverbs 3:9–10, 13–20, 27–28

Global Economic Justice

Bible Background •2 CORINTHIANS 8, 9
Printed Text • 2 CORINTHIANS 8:7–15 | Devotional Reading • PROVERBS 3:9–10, 13–20, 27–28

—————— Aim for Change ——————

By the end of the lesson, we will: IDENTIFY ways of living generous lives in Christ; FEEL greater compassion for the poor and oppressed; and DECIDE to practice equity and justice toward other people.

———————— 🔍 In Focus ————————

Vanessa came home with her arms full of shopping bags. She had always loved to wear the latest fashions. After getting a raise this year, she decided it was time to splurge. Soon she found herself on the couch being exhausted from a day at the mall. As she was going through the clothes that she bought and plotting when and on what occasion she would wear her new outfits, the phone rang. It was one of the church members, Sister Rosie.

Sister Rosie reminded Vanessa about the fundraising they were doing for Haiti and that all the money would be due on this coming Sunday. As Sister Rosie described the conditions the people were living in, Vanessa felt convicted. How could she buy more clothes that she didn't even need when so much of the world was in serious poverty?

Soon Vanessa was on the road to the mall. She packed her car up with all of the outfits that she bought and returned every last one of them. She had enough. There was no reason for her to buy more things that she didn't need. Now she was going to do something to help those who were barely making it.

Many people around the world and in our own local communities are struggling to meet their daily needs. God is challenging the church to do something about it. Have you ever taken part in an activity to help those in other countries who are suffering?

——————— Keep in Mind ———————

"For ye know the grace of our Lord Jesus Christ, that, though he was rich, yet for your sakes he became poor, that ye through his poverty might be rich" (2 Corinthians 8:9).

"For ye know the grace of our Lord Jesus Christ, that, though he was rich, yet for your sakes he became poor, that ye through his poverty might be rich" (2 Corinthians 8:9).

Focal Verses

KJV **2 Corinthians 8:7** Therefore, as ye abound in every thing, in faith, and utterance, and knowledge, and in all diligence, and in your love to us, see that ye abound in this grace also.

8 I speak not by commandment, but by occasion of the forwardness of others, and to prove the sincerity of your love.

9 For ye know the grace of our Lord Jesus Christ, that, though he was rich, yet for your sakes he became poor, that ye through his poverty might be rich.

10 And herein I give my advice: for this is expedient for you, who have begun before, not only to do, but also to be forward a year ago.

11 Now therefore perform the doing of it; that as there was a readiness to will, so there may be a performance also out of that which ye have.

12 For if there be first a willing mind, it is accepted according to that a man hath, and not according to that he hath not.

13 For I mean not that other men be eased, and ye burdened:

14 But by an equality, that now at this time your abundance may be a supply for their want, that their abundance also may be a supply for your want: that there may be equality:

15 As it is written, He that had gathered much had nothing over; and he that had gathered little had no lack.

NLT **2 Corinthians 8:7** Since you excel in so many ways—in your faith, your gifted speakers, your knowledge, your enthusiasm, and your love from us—I want you to excel also in this gracious act of giving.

8 I am not commanding you to do this. But I am testing how genuine your love is by comparing it with the eagerness of the other churches.

9 You know the generous grace of our Lord Jesus Christ. Though he was rich, yet for your sakes he became poor, so that by his poverty he could make you rich.

10 Here is my advice: It would be good for you to finish what you started a year ago. Last year you were the first who wanted to give, and you were the first to begin doing it.

11 Now you should finish what you started. Let the eagerness you showed in the beginning be matched now by your giving. Give in proportion to what you have.

12 Whatever you give is acceptable if you give it eagerly. And give according to what you have, not what you don't have.

13 Of course, I don't mean your giving should make life easy for others and hard for yourselves. I only mean that there should be some equality.

14 Right now you have plenty and can help those who are in need. Later, they will have plenty and can share with you when you need it. In this way, things will be equal.

15 As the Scriptures say, "Those who gathered a lot had nothing left over, and those who gathered only a little had enough."

The People, Places, and Times

The Jerusalem Church. Jerusalem is considered the political and religious capital for the Jewish people. During the Day of Pentecost, the Apostle Peter preached and 3,000 people were saved. Day by day, the Lord increased the number of believers. The believers in Jerusalem developed into the first church (Acts 2).

Macedonia. This was a province located between the north of Greece and the highlands of the Balkans. Macedonia enters into the biblical scene as Paul saw a vision of a man from Macedonia (Acts 16:9). Eventually he and Silas traveled to Philippi, which is on the eastern coast of Macedonia. This was the first city in Europe where the Gospel was preached and a local church was formed.

What do you believe about giving to foreign missions?

Background

After Paul's conversion, he visited Jerusalem on many occasions. At one time, he met with the leaders of the Jerusalem Council to get their approval of his preaching to the Gentiles (Galatians 2). Barnabas and Titus were also present during this visit. The leaders gave their approval and requested that Paul remember the poor. The Jerusalem church was suffering from a serious food shortage due to a drought in Palestine (Acts 11:28–30). Many of the other Gentile churches were financially stable and prospering. During Paul's missionary journeys, he took collections for the poor in Jerusalem.

Paul, who had written this letter from Macedonia, was appealing to the Corinthians to participate in collecting for the poor in Jerusalem. This letter tried to build on the success of an earlier harsh letter which has been lost. It led to forgiveness and reconciliation among the believers in Corinth. He was building upon the foundation that they had realigned themselves with him and obeyed his commands (2 Corinthians 2:9). Since they had been obedient to his directions before, Paul wanted the Corinthians to continue in their allegiance to him. His goal was their full participation in the collection for the saints in Jerusalem.

What is your reason for giving or not giving to causes of economic injustice?

At-A-Glance

1. Give as You Promised (2 Corinthians 8:7–8)
2. Give in Response to God's Grace (v. 9)
3. Give According to Your Ability (vv. 10–15)

In Depth

1. Give as You Promised (2 Corinthians 8:7–8)

Titus, who was Paul's representative, had previously encouraged the Corinthians to give toward the collection for the poor. But in light of their recent conflict with Paul, they had lost their zeal for collections (7:2–15). When affliction abounds in our lives, we should still be committed to God and ministering to others. The Macedonians were rejoicing in the midst of their troubles. Paul was encouraging the Corinthians to do the same. He told Titus to complete the gathering of collections from the Macedonians. Paul wanted them to prove their allegiance to him and their love for others.

The Corinthian believers excelled in many things. They had strong faith, knowledge, enthusiasm, and love. Paul appealed to them to have the same passion and commitment for the collections. For him, the offering is a remembering of the poor (Galatians 2:10), a collection of money (1 Corinthians 16:1–2), a ministry (Romans 15:25), and a gift (2 Corinthians 8:6). He was not commanding them to give, but urging them to prove that their love was sincere. This is a challenge to us as well. There are many needs locally and globally. It is up to us to do our part to eliminate economic injustice much like the Corinthian church. Our finances show where our devotion and affection are focused.

Is it possible to eliminate economic injustice? Why or why not?

2. Give in Response to God's Grace (v. 9)

The grace of our Lord Jesus Christ is the greatest example for all believers to follow. Jesus gave up His position and became a human (Philippians 2:6–7). He was born in poor circumstances, lived a poor life, and died in poverty—all so that He could bestow His favor upon us. "In whom we have redemption through his blood, the forgiveness of sins, according to the richness of his grace" (Ephesians 1:7). Jesus is our model, not the American dream. We must follow Him in giving to those who need it most.

How can we follow in Jesus' footsteps by becoming poor in order to make others rich?

3. Give According to Your Ability (vv. 10–15)

Paul urged the Corinthians to complete the collections for the poor that they had planned a year earlier (2 Corinthians 9:2). The gifts offered should be in proportion to what they are able to give. God does not want us to be burdened by giving that which we cannot sacrifice. Whatever we give, we should do it willingly, "for God loveth a cheerful giver" (from 2 Corinthians 9:7).

When you have given to others, it is an act of justice. In speaking of the balance that comes from a culture of generosity, Paul could be reflecting on the charity of the early Jerusalem church. The believers shared voluntarily in Jerusalem (Acts 4:32–37). Everyone shared possessions equally so no one lacked anything. Believers should willingly share with others. The collection symbolizes for Paul a unified people of God, in whom there is no Jew or Gentile (Galatians 3:28). We are of one body in Christ. If we are of one body, it is an injustice to see the needs of this world and refuse to offer assistance.

How can you practice and display an attitude of cheerful giving?

Search the Scriptures

1. How did Jesus become poor "so that by His poverty he could make you rich" (2 Corinthians 8:9)?

2. Why did Jesus say that giving should not be "that other men be eased, and ye burdened" (v. 13)?

Discuss the Meaning

Around the globe, there are many different needs, as well as in some of our own cities. In your opinion, should we attend to local needs first and then global needs? Why or why not?

Lesson in Our Society

In today's society, some people give out of a sense of obligation. Their motivation is to strictly adhere to the law as commanded in the Word and by the pastor. However, God wants us to give liberally, not under compulsion, but as an acknowledgment of His love and favor.

Others give out of selfish reasons. They give just to get something in return. However, our focus in giving to others should be remembering all God has given to us through His Son, Jesus Christ. Jesus gave His life for us so we should give generously to others.

If you live in America, you live in one of the wealthiest nations on Earth when it comes to wealth; billions of people live on less than two dollars a day. This wealth wasn't given so we could spend it on luxuries and comforts, but so we could be a blessing to others.

Giving is not limited to financial gifts. We can also share our time and skills. We can volunteer at homeless shelters, schools, hospitals, and prisons. Every day we have opportunities to give to others. We should give, within our ability, as the occasion allows.

How does it feel to know that you live in one of the wealthiest nations on Earth?

Make It Happen

• Go to the globalrichlist.com website and discover where you stand in regards to the wealthy of the world.

• Write in a journal about how you feel about being considered one of the wealthiest people in the world by virtue of living in the United States.

• Create a plan for giving to someone in need. Determine how much and how often you will give (beyond tithing to your local church).

Follow the Spirit

What God wants me to do:

_____

_____

_____

_____

Remember Your Thoughts

Special insights I have learned:

_____

_____

_____

_____

More Light on the Text

2 Corinthians 8:7–15

7 Therefore, as ye abound in every thing, in faith, and utterance, and knowledge, and in all diligence, and in your love to us, see that ye abound in this grace also.

Many of the Greek words used here provide insight into Paul's full meaning. The Greek word for "abound" is *perisseuo* (**peh-reese-SYOO-oh**), which means to excel, to have enough plus leftovers. The word for "utterance" is *logos* (Gk. **LOG-os**), which can also be translated as "word," referring to either the Corinthains' own speaking prowess or to the Word of God. *Spoude* (**spoo-DAY**) is the Greek word for "diligence"; it means earnestness, putting one's whole heart into a task. Paul says that the Corinthians have excelled in their faith, speech, knowledge of the Word, earnestness to follow Christ, and love for Paul and Titus. However, Paul wanted to make sure that they excelled at the grace of their giving as well.

8 I speak not by commandment, but by occasion of the forwardness of others, and to prove the sincerity of your love. 9 For ye know the grace of our Lord Jesus Christ, that, though he was rich, yet for your sakes he became poor, that ye through his poverty might be rich.

Paul assures the Corinthians that he is not making a decree that they must give more, but he wanted them to have the chance to prove the sincerity of their love. Paul also reminds the Corinthians of Christ's unselfishness in order to encourage them to remain unselfish as well. Paul says the Corinthians "know the grace of our Lord Jesus Christ." The Greek word for "know" is *ginosko* (**ghin-OCE-ko**), which connotes being sure of something by having experienced it personally. The word for "grace" in Greek is *charis* (**KHAR-ece**), which can be translated as "favor." The Corinthians, and every Christian, have a personal knowledge that Christ did the ultimate favor for us, by leaving His throne in heaven as King of kings and coming down to earth in the form of a child. Despite His eternal royalty, Christ came to earth as a baby born in a manger, who grew up having to work as a carpenter. Ultimately, Christ made the ultimate sacrifice by allowing Himself to be crucified on the Cross, to accomplish salvation for all who are in Him. Christ's poverty made us rich in grace and mercy.

10 And herein I give my advice: for this is expedient for you, who have begun before, not only to do, but also to be forward a year ago. 11 Now therefore perform the doing of it; that as there was a readiness to will, so there may be a performance also out of that which ye have.

Paul gives the Corinthians his advice on what to do with their giving. The word for "be forward" in Greek is *thelo* (**THEL-oh**), which means determined or willed. Paul wants them not only to continue to give, but he also wants the Corinthians to continue to be determined, just as they were a year ago. The Greek word for "perform" is *epiteleo* (**ep-ee-tel-EH-oh**), which means to bring to a finish. Paul challenged the Corinthians to finish their giving. He said that just as they had a readiness and determination to give before (the word for "will" is the same word used for "be forward" in the previous verse), the Corinthians should be determined to finish their giving according to what they have to give.

12 For if there be first a willing mind, it is accepted according to that a man hath, and not according to that he hath not.

Paul reminds the Corinthians that they can only give what they have. He emphasizes the importance of the right attitude in giving. The Greek word for "willing mind" is similar to the word for "readiness" in verse 11. *Prothumia* (**pro-thoo-MEE-ah**) is the Greek word used in this verse, and it can be translated as "forwardness of mind" or "readiness of mind." This text has a definite theme of willingness to give. The word for "accepted" in Greek is *euprosdektos* (**ew-PROS-dek-tos**), which means well-received. Paul suggested that the proper attitude in giving is more important than the amount given. He says that the gift is well-received according to what the Corinthians are able to give, not what they cannot give.

13 For I mean not that other men be eased, and ye burdened: 14 But by an equality, that now at this time your abundance may be a supply for their want, that their abundance also may be a supply for your want: that there may be equality.

Paul does not want to put the entire burden on the Corinthians to do all of the giving to the ministry. He also doesn't want them to give so much that they suffer from not having enough for themselves. Paul knows that others need to give as well, but he believed giving needs equality. The Greek word for "want" is *husterema* (**hoos-TEH-ray-mah**), which means lack or need. Paul says that the Corinthians should be able to meet others' needs now, so that in the future, if the Corinthians are ever in need, others can be a help to them. Since Christians shared supplies in tough times, this is entirely possible.

15 As it is written, He that had gathered much had nothing over; and he that had gathered little had no lack.

Paul quotes Exodus 16:18 in this verse. The Greek word for "no lack" is *elattoneo* (**eh-lat-toe-NEH-oh**), which is also translated as "fall short." Since everyone was working together and all that was gathered was put together, those who gathered a lot did not have too much, and those who could only gather a little did not fall short in supplies. This principle only worked if the children of God remained unselfish. The unselfishness of others is what helped the Christian church maintain the support it needed. Paul encouraged the Corinthians to not only continue giving, but also to give with the right attitude and perspective.

Sources:
Craig Evans, and Stanley Porter, ed. *Dictionary of New Testament Background*. Downers Grove, IL: IVP Academic, 2000.
Keener, Craig. *The IVP Bible Background Commentary: New Testament*. Downers Grove, IL: IVP Academic, 1994.
Richards, Lawrence O. *The Teacher's Commentary*. Wheaton, IL: Victor Books, 1989.

Say It Correctly

Diligence. **DIH**-li-jins.
Expedient. eks-**PEE**-dee-int.

Daily Bible Readings

MONDAY
God Provides Food to the People
(Exodus 16:13–17)

TUESDAY
The Widow's Generosity
(Mark 12:38–44)

WEDNESDAY
Generous Self-Giving of Jesus
(Philippians 2:5–11)

THURSDAY
Excel in Generosity
(2 Corinthians 8:1–6)

FRIDAY
Generosity Results in Mutual Thanksgiving
(2 Corinthians 9:11–15)

SATURDAY
Support the Ministry of Church Leaders
(2 Corinthians 8:16–24)

SUNDAY
Balance Need and Abundance Fairly
(2 Corinthians 8:7–15)

Notes

Teaching Tips

Words You Should Know

A. Dissimulation (Romans 12:9) *anypokritos* (Gk.)—Without hypocrisy, sincere.

B. Bless (v. 14) *eulogeo* (Gk.)—To speak well of by expressing good wishes upon another.

Teacher Preparation

Unifying Principle—Equity in Conduct. We want to be loving people. What makes for genuine love in the world? Paul offers the marks of true love that are to be lived by the faithful.

A. Pray that the Lord will open your heart and your mind to allow you to better understand and follow His plan for this lesson.

B. Seek deeper understanding of the meaning of the lesson by studying the Background Scripture and Devotional Reading in several different translations.

C. Complete Lesson 12 in the *Precepts For Living®* Personal Study Guide.

O—Open the Lesson

A. Open with prayer. Remember to invite the Holy Spirit to lead your Bible study.

B. Read Aim for Change and Keep in Mind verse in unison.

C. Have your class read the In Focus story silently. Invite discussion.

P—Present the Scriptures

A. Have class members read the Focal Verses.

B. Ask for volunteers to read The People, Places, and Times, Background, and In Depth sections. Encourage discussion.

E—Explore the Meaning

A. Answer the questions in the Search the Scriptures and Discuss the Meaning sections.

B. Ask a volunteer to read the Lesson in Our Society section and discuss.

N—Next Steps for Application

A. Encourage students to apply the Make It Happen section.

B. Close in prayer.

Worship Guide

For the Superintendent and the Teacher
Theme: Loving and Just Behavior
Song:"Victory Shall Be Mine"
Devotional Reading: Matthew 5:38–48

Loving and Just Behavior

Bible Background • ROMANS 12:9–21
Printed Text • ROMANS 12:9–21 | Devotional Reading • MATTHEW 5:38–48

Aim for Change

By the end of the lesson, we will: CONSIDER Paul's words about personal behaviors as indicative of a Christian way of life; AFFIRM human expressions of love for one another; and BECOME more loving, according to Paul's teaching.

In Focus

Long before Kim's next-door neighbors moved in, she prayed for them. She prayed that God would send neighbors who believed in Him, and imagined having regular Bible studies and being able to pray with her new neighbors. She went to meet every person who looked at the house. Most were nice, except for one woman who refused to acknowledge Kim. When Kim introduced herself, the woman asked, "May I help you?" Kim prayed not to have her as a neighbor, but was appalled to see her moving in a month later. Hadn't the Lord heard her prayer?

Things didn't get any better between them. Even though Kim made herself speak to the woman and her teenage daughter, neither of them spoke back. After a while, Kim began to hold bitterness and avoided having to bump into her new neighbors. Eventually, Kim felt convicted and began to pray for her neighbor. She decided to forgive them and brainstormed ways she could bless her and her daughter.

God calls us to practice loving and just behavior. Have you ever had to show love to someone who didn't deserve it?

Keep in Mind

"Let love be without dissimulation. Abhor that which is evil; cleave to that which is good" (Romans 12:9).

"Let love be without dissimulation. Abhor that which is evil; cleave to that which is good" (Romans 12:9).

Focal Verses

KJV **Romans 12:9** Let love be without dissimulation. Abhor that which is evil; cleave to that which is good.

10 Be kindly affectioned one to another with brotherly love; in honour preferring one another;

11 Not slothful in business; fervent in spirit; serving the Lord;

12 Rejoicing in hope; patient in tribulation; continuing instant in prayer;

13 Distributing to the necessity of saints; given to hospitality.

14 Bless them which persecute you: bless, and curse not.

15 Rejoice with them that do rejoice, and weep with them that weep.

16 Be of the same mind one toward another. Mind not high things, but condescend to men of low estate. Be not wise in your own conceits.

17 Recompense to no man evil for evil. Provide things honest in the sight of all men.

18 If it be possible, as much as lieth in you, live peaceably with all men.

19 Dearly beloved, avenge not yourselves, but rather give place unto wrath: for it is written, Vengeance is mine; I will repay, saith the Lord.

20 Therefore if thine enemy hunger, feed him; if he thirst, give him drink: for in so doing thou shalt heap coals of fire on his head.

21 Be not overcome of evil, but overcome evil with good.

NLT **Romans 12:9** Don't just pretend to love others. Really love them. Hate what is wrong. Hold tightly to what is good.

10 Love each other with genuine affection, and take delight in honoring each other.

11 Never be lazy, but work hard and serve the Lord enthusiastically.

12 Rejoice in our confident hope. Be patient in trouble, and keep on praying.

13 When God's people are in need, be ready to help them. Always be eager to practice hospitality.

14 Bless those who persecute you. Don't curse them; pray that God will bless them.

15 Be happy with those who are happy, and weep with those who weep.

16 Live in harmony with each other. Don't be too proud to enjoy the company of ordinary people. And don't think you know it all!

17 Never pay back evil with more evil. Do things in such a way that everyone can see you are honorable.

18 Do all that you can to live in peace with everyone.

19 Dear friends, never take revenge. Leave that to the righteous anger of God. For the Scriptures say, "I will take revenge; I will pay them back," says the LORD.

20 Instead, "If your enemies are hungry, feed them. If they are thirsty, give them something to drink. In doing this, you will heap burning coals of shame on their heads."

21 Don't let evil conquer you, but conquer evil by doing good.

The People, Places, and Times

Jews and Christians in Rome. Because Rome was the principal city of the empire, it was inevitable that both Christians and Jews should comprise large subgroups within the city. By the time Paul wrote the epistle to the

Romans (around mid first century AD), it had already become an important church (Romans 1:8). About the year AD 49, the emperor Claudius issued an edict expelling Jews from Rome. The fact that Christians were expelled as well (see Acts 18:2) indicates that at that time Roman officials did not differentiate between Christians and Jews, perhaps because the Christian community was not yet large enough to be significant.

Saul/Apostle Paul. A well-educated Roman citizen, Saul was a Pharisee who persecuted Christians as proof of his zeal for the Jewish faith and way of life (Philippians 3:4–6; Acts 26:4–5). On such a mission on the road to Damascus to carry out his mission, he had a remarkable encounter with Jesus. Shortly after, he learned of his call from God to take "[God's] message to the Gentiles and to kings, as well as to the people of Israel" (Acts 9:15, NLT). As an apostle, Paul's life exemplified one of great sacrifice and persecution. He wrote about his experiences in hopes of drawing people to Christ, and to strengthen and mature believers.

Why do you think today's passage was necessary for Jew and Gentile Christians living in Rome?

Background

The epistle to the Romans is the longest and arguably the most influential letter that the apostle Paul wrote. In fact, Romans is placed first among the other New Testament letters. The apostle wrote this letter with his apostolic mission to the Gentile world in mind.

In Romans 15:20, Paul's affirmation that he did not consider Rome as another apostle's specific territory or mission field has led another group of scholars to suppose it could be that the church at Rome was established by some of Paul's converts from Asia and Macedonia. However, if we look at Acts 2:10, we see that some of the Jews and proselytes that were converted on the Day of Pentecost were from Rome and could have also been instrumental in establishing the church.

Paul states that he often had plans to preach the Gospel to the believers in the city, but was hindered from doing so (Romans 1:13–15, 15:22). Paul wrote this book in order to prepare the way for his missionary trip to Rome and his anticipated mission trip to Spain. Paul also needed to address certain problems in the church between the Jews and Gentiles. Their attitudes were ungodly toward each other (see Romans 2, 11:11–36), and as their apostle, it was Paul's responsibility to correct them.

As believers, how does our attitude toward each other affect our witness to the outside world?

At-A-Glance

1. The Believer's Call to Love
(Romans 12:9–13)
2. The Believer's Call to Practical Living
(vv. 14–21)

In Depth

1. The Believer's Call to Love (Romans 12:9–13)

One of the spiritual "fruits" that we must have is love (see Galatians 5:22). Just as fruit must be ripened, so must our love be developed. This love, if it is to be a logical outcome from God's character, must be unconditional. How? When we experience God's love despite our failures and imperfections, we are better able to love others.

Out of this love for others grows an orientation toward respect, kindness, affection, and a show of sincere concern for the welfare of others. We may find ourselves desiring God's best for those with whom we interact. We don't mind helping others achieve their God-given goals. It is this love, grounded in God's transforming mercy, that Paul says reminds us that we are to "prefer" one another in honor. We are to look beyond the present to the possibility seen by God in others. Too often we focus on people's weaknesses. We are encouraged to look beyond their shortcomings and pray for their victories. Praying for others changes our attitude and affects positive change in their lives.

This dedication to love also challenges us not to be slothful in business, but fervent in spirit. Why? Because we are ambassadors for Jesus Christ. Our pursuit of excellence in everything, including our home, workplace, and ministry grows out of our deep love for the God who saved us. We cannot afford to be lazy or indifferent because we belong to a God who excels. When people are hopeless, we offer them hope. When we face times of testing, we patiently endure them because we know the love of God.

Why is it difficult to prefer others above ourselves?

2. The Believer's Call to Practical Living (vv. 14–21)

Paul tells believers how to demonstrate their Christianity in practical ways. He acknowledges that it is not easy to be a Christian in the world we live in. Many people will do us wrong just because we are Christians. Perhaps that is why he says, "bless them which persecute you: bless and curse not" (v. 14). God wants us to respond in a Christ-like manner since He has given us the Holy Spirit to enable us to overlook offenses.

Paul tells us how to react when others experience a "season" of joy. We must be happy for them and rejoice with them. On the other hand, we need to learn how to identify with another's pain and sorrow and weep with them. Every believer will go through seasons of joy and pain. We should be sensitive and available to the needs of others.

Finally, Paul reminds believers of our responsibilities in living out the Gospel: to feed our enemies, give them something to drink, and treat them well, "for in so doing, thou shalt heap coals of fire on his head" (v. 20). Those who have treated us wrong will be surprised that the evil they perpetuated against us did not overcome us and cause us to react negatively. They will be ashamed of how they have mistreated us. In fact, our goodness toward evildoers might motivate them to change their lives and become believers in Jesus Christ.

What is the most difficult thing about the command to do good to your enemies?

Search the Scriptures

1. What kind of love should believers demonstrate toward other people (Romans 12:10)?

2. Why shouldn't a believer avenge slights against them (v. 19)?

Discuss the Meaning

Is it possible for believers to live as the apostle Paul instructs? Why or why not? Paul points toward some pretty high standards given to us by God. Does He expect us to turn the other cheek every time another person mistreats us? Why or why not?

Lesson in Our Society

Today, people are looking for the "real thing" in every area of society, including the church of Jesus Christ. They want to know whether walking in the way of Jesus really makes a difference. We are called to be distinct and set apart from the world. Let us be the light He has called us to be, not just on Sunday but every day of our lives.

This is so necessary in our African American communities. Our focus has often been on justice, but we also need to turn the mirror on ourselves and ask whether we exhibit loving and just behavior toward each other. Many problems in our communities, such as gangs, joblessness, and the lack of mentors for the next generation, could be solved. It starts with simply committing to be a good neighbor. When we walk in love toward other people, we will treat them justly.

What is the ultimate benefit of overcoming evil with good?

Make It Happen

• Make a checklist of all of the practical instructions from Romans 12:9–21. Check off the ones that you actually put into practice.

• Create a plan to implement the instructions that weren't checked off on your list.

• After you complete your initial tasks, write in your journal about the results of your obedience.

Follow the Spirit

What God wants me to do:

_____

_____

_____

_____

Remember Your Thoughts

Special insights I have learned:

_____

_____

_____

_____

More Light on the Text

9 Let love be without dissimulation. Abhor that which is evil; cleave to that which is good.

Here Paul begins a general parenesis. A parenesis was a style of teaching used by ancient moral philosophers. This style incorporated various moral exhortations that were not necessarily connected; however, most of the exhortations in this section are centered around the theme of having good relationships.

First, Paul encourages the Christians in Rome to operate in sincere love—to show real kindness and unconditional affection to one another. This timeless message speaks to Christians from various settings, times, and cultures. We are challenged to love God and love our fellow men and women. It is not a love in word only, but grounded in word and action. It is not a love based on hypocrisy—saying one thing and doing the opposite—but sincere and from the heart. Paul gave the Roman Christians a list of ways to live out their faith in relationship to God and to others, even those who persecuted them. Paul exhorts the Christians to ways of practical living that reflect their humility (v. 3) and Christian virtue.

Love reverberated as the primary theme for the rest of this chapter (see also 1 Corinthians 13). Paul's use of polarization (i.e., abhor/cleave; evil/good) further clarifies the image of a Christian (see also 1 Thessalonians 5:21–24; Psalm 34:14). Their love is to be "without dissimulation" (Gk. *anupokritos*, **ah-noo-PO-kree-toce**) or without hypocrisy. The Christians will openly abhor evil and at the same time cleave (Gk. *kollao*, **ko-LAH-oh**), or associate with only the good. The word for cleave is normally associated with interpersonal relationships, so here Paul could refer to good people rather than just merely the abstract concept of good.

10 Be kindly affectioned one to another with brotherly love; in honour preferring one another; 11 Not slothful in business; fervent in spirit; serving the Lord; 12 Rejoicing in hope; patient in tribulation; continuing instant in prayer;

Brotherly love, the second kind of love mentioned (v. 10), helps us hold all Christians as family (Hebrews 13:1; 1 Peter 1:22, 2:17). The later half of the verse is Paul's command to show honor by preferring (Gk. *proegeomai*, **pro-eh-GEH-oh-my**, leading) one another.

The Romans are then exhorted to not be slothful (Gk. *okneros*, **oak-ner-OSE**) or idle. This statement has the sense of being reluctant or hesitant. They should not be reluctant or hesitant in business (Gk. *spoude*, **SPOO-day**) or in applying themselves as much as they can. The Christian must be eager to apply themselves to whatever task and fervent in spirit. Fervent (Gk. *zeo*, **ZEH-oh**) here means to be kept at boiling point. The Christian's spirit should be enthusiastic and bubbling over. This does not necessarily mean that we change our personalities, but that we give energy and passion to all that we do. Their entire disposition is affected by the fact that they are serving (Gk. *douleuo*, **doo-LEW-oh**) or a slave for the Lord (v. 11).

Paul exhorts the Roman Christians to rejoice in hope and be patient in tribulation. He also exhorts them to be "continuing instant" (Gk. *proskartereo*, **pro-scar-teh-REH-oh**), or persevere constantly in prayer. (Here the King James English uses "instant" in the old sense of "urgently.") Notice the Christian is not told to rejoice in good, or during good times; we are told to rejoice in hope. Paul also tells Christians to give thanks in everything (1 Thessalonians 5:18). Christians are able to rejoice in good times and bad times because their trust is not in circumstances, but in a God who is Lord of all. Therefore, we rejoice in bad times because we know that trouble will not last always.

The call to persevere in prayer reminds us that we are to live a life devoted to prayer. In good times, we acknowledge God in prayer as our source and give thanks for His grace and mercy. In bad times, we commit to persevering in prayer and to never waver in that commitment.

13 Distributing to the necessity of saints; given to hospitality. 14 Bless them which persecute you: bless, and curse not.

The importance of generosity is stressed in the injunction to "[distribute] to the necessity of saints" meaning to share in the needs of fellow Christians (cf. Ephesians 4:28; 1 Peter 4:3). Paul continues on how Christians ought to live with the exhortation to "bless" (Gk. *eulogeo*, **ew-lo-GEH-oh**, to speak well of) rather than "curse" (Gk. *kataraomai*, **ka-ta-RAH-oh-my**), which means to speak doom on someone (cf. Matthew 5:44; Luke 6:28).

15 Rejoice with them that do rejoice, and weep with them that weep. 16 Be of the same mind one toward another. Mind not high things, but condescend to men of low estate. Be not wise in your own conceits.

Paul continues to use opposites to clarify Christian behavior with the words "rejoice" and "weep." Continuing the idea of unity from v. 15, Paul encourages keeping a similar way of thinking among themselves in v. 16. The phrase "be not wise in your own conceits" parallels the thought in verse 3 where Paul reminds each of them not to think of themselves in more elevated terms than really apply.

17 Recompense to no man evil for evil. Provide things honest in the sight of all men. 18 If it be possible, as much as lieth in you, live peaceably with all men. 19 Dearly

beloved, avenge not yourselves, but rather give place unto wrath: for it is written, Vengeance is mine; I will repay, saith the Lord. 20 Therefore if thine enemy hunger, feed him; if he thirst, give him drink: for in so doing thou shalt heap coals of fire on his head. 21 Be not overcome of evil, but overcome evil with good.

Verses 17 and 18 note that responding in kind when we receive evil demonstrates the difference between the Christian and the world. He warns them against being vengeful, as vengeance belongs to the Lord who will avenge them.

Paul then deals with treatment of one's enemies (vv. 19–20). Christians should supply needs of hunger and drink—in other words, provide sustenance to their enemy. These words are direct quotes from Proverbs 25:21 and support Paul's line of thinking. Verse 21 goes back to verse 17, where the Christian is advised against handing out "evil for evil" received. As Christians, we should overcome evil with good (cf. Exodus 23:4–5; Matthew 5:44).

These verses are a picture of what a true Christian life should look like. It is a life of love, not hatred; a life of giving and placing the needs of others above your own; a life that repays evil with good. Such thoughts are contrary to this world system. It is what the world calls "killing your enemies with kindness." Enemies of the Christian are enemies of God. However, God is patient, not wanting anyone to perish but everyone to come to repentance. Therefore, Christians' responsibility is to exemplify Christ and draw their enemies to the love of God.

Sources:
Cottrell, Jack. Romans. *College Press NIV Commentary*. 2 vols. Joplin, MO: College Press, 1996.
Dunn, James D. G., and J.W. Rogerson. *Eerdmans Commentary on the Bible*. Grand Rapids, MI: W.B. Eerdmans, 2003.
Stott, John R. W. *The Message of Romans: God's Good News for the World*. The Bible Speaks Today. Leicester, England: InterVarsity Press, 2001.

Say It Correctly

Dissimulation. di-si-**MUH**-lay-shun.
Recompense. re-**KUHM**-pen(t)s.

Daily Bible Readings

MONDAY
Many Members in One Body
(1 Corinthians 12:12–26)

TUESDAY
Aim to Live by the Spirit
(Galatians 5:16–26)

WEDNESDAY
Respond to Abuse With a Blessing
(1 Peter 3:8–12)

THURSDAY
Treat Enemies With Love and Mercy
(Luke 6:27–36)

FRIDAY
Don't Act by Human Standards
(2 Corinthians 10:1–5)

SATURDAY
New Life in Christian Community
(Romans 12:1–8)

SUNDAY
Behavioral Action Goals of Christians
(Romans 12:9–21)

Teaching Tips

Words You Should Know

A. Anger (Colossians 3:8) *orge* (Gk.)—Feeling of discontent, displeasure, or indignation.

B. Malice (v. 8) *kakia* (Gk.)—General feeling of badness, a vicious disposition, prompting one to injure one's neighbor.

Teacher Preparation

Unifying Principle—Equity in Character. People want to live lives that make a difference. How can one live justly in the world? Paul encourages the faithful to clothe themselves with the love of Christ and let the peace of Christ rule in their hearts.

A. Pray that the Lord will open your heart and your mind to allow you to better understand and follow His plan for this lesson.

B. Seek deeper understanding of the meaning of the lesson by studying the Background Scripture and Devotional Reading in several different translations.

C. Complete Lesson 13 in the *Precepts For Living®* Personal Study Guide.

O—Open the Lesson

A. Open with prayer. Remember to invite the Holy Spirit to lead your Bible study.

B. Read Aim for Change and the Keep in Mind verse in unison.

C. Have your class read the In Focus story silently. Invite discussion.

P—Present the Scriptures

A. Have class members read the Focal Verses.

B. Ask for volunteers to read The People, Places, and Times, Background, and In Depth sections. Encourage discussion.

E—Explore the Meaning

A. Answer the questions in the Search the Scriptures and Discuss the Meaning sections together.

B. Ask a volunteer to read the Lesson in Our Society section and discuss.

N—Next Steps for Application

A. Encourage students to apply the Make It Happen section.

B. Close in prayer.

Worship Guide

For the Superintendent or Teacher
Theme: Practicing Justice
Song: "Lord Prepare Me to Be a Sanctuary"
Devotional Reading: Romans 8:1–11

Practicing Justice

Bible Background • EPHESIANS 4:25–5:2; COLOSSIANS 3:1–17
Printed Text • COLOSSIANS 3:5–17 | Devotional Reading • ROMANS 8:1–11

Aim for Change

By the end of this lesson we will: EXPLORE the symbolic significance of being clothed in Christ for living justly in the world; APPRECIATE ways others have demonstrated being clothed in Christ; and COMMIT to living justly.

In Focus

Jason couldn't believe it. He had just run into his old friend Brandon at the local grocery store. He hadn't seen him for three years. They had both gone their separate ways after college and failed to keep in touch. While in college, Jason and Brandon had both accepted Christ and were baptized at the same church.

As they stood there in the aisle catching up on old times, something about Brandon rubbed Jason the wrong way. Now Jason could see why they hadn't kept in touch. Brandon was a different person. He talked badly about immigrants and called women out of their names. He also ran schemes that cheated his customers out of money. Jason silently prayed for Brandon as he listened to him recap the last few years. "You know," Jason said, "one of the best things I remember about college was when we both began following Christ together." Brandon looked at him like a deer caught in headlights. "When we chose to follow Jesus, we chose to treat people as human beings made in the image of God. What happened?"

Brandon looked down. "I really can't tell you, life happens. Everything isn't always black and white, and it's hard when the world is against you."

Jason nodded and said, "It's true. But if something is wrong, making it right starts with you."

Justice is never absent of personal character. How has your relationship with Christ caused you to live justly?

Keep in Mind

"Put on therefore, as the elect of God, holy and beloved, bowels of mercies, kindness, humbleness of mind, meekness, longsuffering" (Colossians 3:12).

"Put on therefore, as the elect of God, holy and beloved, bowels of mercies, kindness, humbleness of mind, meekness, longsuffering" (Colossians 3:12).

Focal Verses

KJV **Colossians 3:5** Mortify therefore your members which are upon the earth; fornication, uncleanness, inordinate affection, evil concupiscence, and covetousness, which is idolatry:

6 For which things' sake the wrath of God cometh on the children of disobedience:

7 In the which ye also walked some time, when ye lived in them.

8 But now ye also put off all these; anger, wrath, malice, blasphemy, filthy communication out of your mouth.

9 Lie not one to another, seeing that ye have put off the old man with his deeds;

10 And have put on the new man, which is renewed in knowledge after the image of him that created him:

11 Where there is neither Greek nor Jew, circumcision nor uncircumcision, Barbarian, Scythian, bond nor free: but Christ is all, and in all.

12 Put on therefore, as the elect of God, holy and beloved, bowels of mercies, kindness, humbleness of mind, meekness, longsuffering;

13 Forbearing one another, and forgiving one another, if any man have a quarrel against any: even as Christ forgave you, so also do ye.

14 And above all these things put on charity, which is the bond of perfectness.

15 And let the peace of God rule in your hearts, to the which also ye are called in one body; and be ye thankful.

16 Let the word of Christ dwell in you richly in all wisdom; teaching and admonishing one another in psalms and hymns and spiritual songs, singing with grace in your hearts to the Lord.

17 And whatsoever ye do in word or deed, do all in the name of the Lord Jesus, giving thanks to God and the Father by him.

NLT **Colossians 3:5** So put to death the sinful, earthly things lurking within you. Have nothing to do with sexual immorality, impurity, lust, and evil desires. Don't be greedy, for a greedy person is an idolater, worshiping the things of this world.

6 Because of these sins, the anger of God is coming.

7 You used to do these things when your life was still part of this world.

8 But now is the time to get rid of anger, rage, malicious behavior, slander, and dirty language.

9 Don't lie to each other, for you have stripped off your old sinful nature and all its wicked deeds.

10 Put on your new nature, and be renewed as you learn to know your Creator and become like him.

11 In this new life, it doesn't matter if you are a Jew or a Gentile, circumcised or uncircumcised, barbaric, uncivilized, slave, or free. Christ is all that matters, and he lives in all of us.

12 Since God chose you to be the holy people he loves, you must clothe yourselves with tenderhearted mercy, kindness, humility, gentleness, and patience.

13 Make allowance for each other's faults, and forgive anyone who offends you. Remember, the Lord forgave you, so you must forgive others.

14 Above all, clothe yourselves with love, which binds us all together in perfect harmony.

15 And let the peace that comes from Christ rule in your hearts. For as members of one body you are called to live in peace. And always be thankful.

16 Let the message about Christ, in all its richness, fill your lives. Teach and counsel each other with all the wisdom he gives. Sing psalms and hymns and spiritual songs to God with thankful hearts.

17 And whatever you do or say, do it as a representative of the Lord Jesus, giving thanks through him to God the Father.

The People, Places, and Times

Barbarians. The Greeks used this as a term for those they deemed uneducated, that is, those who did not speak Greek or follow a Greek pattern of living. These people were also despised by the educated citizens and those living in areas eventually conquered by Greece and Rome.

Scythian. A native of Scythia, an area on the edge of the world known to the Romans, north and east of the Black Sea, controlling areas that are now Ukraine, Russia, and Kazakhstan. Scythians were considered savages, and the ultimate of barbarism. The Greeks despised the Jews; a barbarian scorned a Scythian. They were the lowest of the low.

How can labels and hatred create problems within the church and world?

Background

In the final two chapters of the book of Colossians, Paul challenged the Colossians to practically apply the doctrines he had been preaching. Paul believed Christians should not just know the truth and be able to defend it, but live out that truth in their daily lives as well.

The pagan religions of Paul's day said little or nothing about personal morality. Worshipers gave offerings to idols to pay them back for or to bribe them for favors. It was called "*do ut des*," Latin for "I give so that you might give." A worshiper could bow before an idol and put his offering on the altar, and it had no impact on how they lived. What a person believed had no direct relationship with how he behaved.

The Christian faith brought a whole new concept into the pagan society. Faith in Christ meant being united with Him. If Christians share His life, they must follow His example. If Christ lives in the believer, he or she cannot continue in sin. Thus, Paul concluded his letter to the Colossians with some specific instructions about Christian conduct.

How do we arrange to let Christ live within us and guide our lives?

At-A-Glance

1. New Life in Christ (Colossians 3:5–9)
2. Renewal Procedures (vv. 10–11)
3. Walking New (vv. 12–17)

In Depth

1. New Life in Christ (Colossians 3:5–9)

Paul speaks forthrightly about the demands of the new life and our urgent need to curb all of our old nature's degrading tendencies. The believer has to let the old life die. We are not simply to suppress or control evil acts and attitudes; we must wipe them out completely— exterminate the old way of life. The action is to be undertaken decisively and urgently. The request suggests a vigorous, painful act of personal determination. Paul is calling for a slaying of evil passions, desires, and practices that root themselves in our bodies.

Paul goes on to list sins. He warned that God's judgment would fall on the disobedient. He reminded the Colossians that this is the way they used to live. He said this ungodly life belongs to the past, and that the Christian should be done with it.

The phrase "but now" marks a new beginning. Paul firmly encourages them to "put off" this past life (v. 8). The Christian is to take off the filth of the past as one would a dirty shirt. Paul specifically names anger, wrath (a sudden and passionate outburst of displeasure), malice, and blasphemy (insulting talk against one's fellows). Filthy communication is "bad or abusive speech, foul-mouthed abuse." The sin of falsehood is particularly singled out; lying is given separate treatment and given a strong exhortation: "lie not one to another" (v. 9).

The Christian must have a totally new life change in which he or she has put off the old self with its practices, habits, or characteristics, and put on the new. This is like the resurrection of Christ, who pulled off the grave clothes and then left them behind in the tomb. Christians now have a new life in Christ; the old deeds and desires must be put off.

Why does fear of the wrath of God convince some to make changes while others do not?

2. Renewal Procedures (vv. 10–11)

Paul talked about becoming a new creature in Christ and taking off the old self, but how can that be done? Bad habits and ungodly conduct are not simply going to fall away like dirty clothes.

Paul used the word "knowledge" to explain how a person changes (v. 10)—not through knowledge of more rules and laws, but the knowledge of Christ. Our minds must be renewed. As believers grow in knowledge of the Word of God, when we learn, read, and study His Word, God's Spirit changes us. God transforms Christians by washing old thoughts, desires, and intentions out of our minds and replacing them with new ones.

Paul gives an example of this kind of mind change when he speaks about human distinctions and differences. In Christ, there are no nationalities (neither Greek nor Jew), religious differences (circumcised or non-circumcised), nor cultural differences (barbarian or Scythian).

The Greeks considered all non-Greeks to be barbarians and the Scythians to be the lowest savages of all. Yet, in Jesus Christ, a person's cultural status has no advantage or disadvantage. Nor is economic or political status helpful (bond or free). Slaves should try to get their freedom, but if they do not, that does not make them any less in Christ's sight. All of these kinds of distinctions belong to the old self and the old way of thinking.

How has the Word of God caused you to modify your behavior?

3. Walking New (vv. 12–17)

Christians are chosen, set apart, and loved by God. These are privileges God gave to His people in the Old Testament that are made available to Christians as well. Because God gave these blessings to His people, Paul encourages them to walk in compassion, kindness, goodness, graciousness, in humility, in gentleness, and in patience. Being chosen also means bearing with and forgiving one another (putting up with things we don't like). The final word is "charity," or divine love (v. 14). Love is unconditional giving and caring that goes beyond the call of duty. Peace is another characteristic that Paul exhorts the believer to put on—not just peace with each other, but peace of mind, unruffled by difficulties and confusion. As usual, Paul weaves an attitude of thanksgiving in this section of the letter. Thankfulness to God and to our brothers and sisters promotes inward and outward peace.

The Colossians are told to allow the Word of God, the Gospel, and the messages about Christ to be a rich treasure for them that becomes so deeply implanted that it controls their thinking, attitudes, and actions. When God's Word is deep down in our hearts, Christ's presence causes us to conduct ourselves wisely, influenced by His insight and instruction. Paul writes that God's Word dwelling in our hearts will also cause us to sing psalms from the Old Testament, and hymns and spirituals draw on that tradition today.

Paul concludes by saying to "Do all in the name of the Lord Jesus." We are to always act as Christ's representatives. Christ is to live through God's children, those who have trusted in Him for their salvation and are eternally thankful.

Do people conclude when they see you that Christ at work in your life? Explain.

Search the Scriptures

1. Why are forgiveness and love two key elements in a life that pleases God (Colossians 3:13–14)?

2. How can an attitude of thanksgiving help us in our relationship with God and with other people (v. 15)?

Discuss the Meaning

1. How do we continue to "put off our old selves" when it is so easy to forget that we are in constant need of renewal?

2. How can our personal moral actions help to advocate for justice?

Lesson in Our Society

For many today, justice has become a public thing, about the public display of protecting rights or enacting policies. Justice has been the focus of many marches and protests. This is good, but the New Testament espouses a view of justice that begins within and expresses itself outwardly in public places. The passage today exhorts the Christian to not only work for justice, but also live it. It is not enough for us to organize and fight for civil rights if our personal lives are not organized around

righteousness. Real advocacy for justice starts in our hearts and our lifestyle. It starts with the way we treat those around us, and boils down to Jesus' command to love our neighbor as ourselves.

For many people today, lying is common. Far too many people believe that if the truth is going to hurt, make you uncomfortable, ruin your reputation, get you in trouble, or cause you to pay money, then lying is acceptable. We justify lying or find creative ways to do it by calling it something else. In popular culture, how does it manifest itself, and how do we ourselves participate? In the midst of this, the Christian is exhorted to tell the truth. Lying in any form is considered part of our old life and needs to be discarded.

How can truth promote peace and harmony in our relationships with others?

Make It Happen

• Make a list of the virtues mentioned in this week's lesson. Check off the ones you believe you need to improve on.

• Write in your journal how you plan to improve on these things.

• Discuss your plan with a friend or spiritual leader.

Follow the Spirit

What God wants me to do:

_____

_____

_____

_____

Remember Your Thoughts

Special insights I have learned:

_____

_____

_____

_____

More Light on the Text

Colossians 3:5–17

5 Mortify therefore your members which are upon the earth; fornication, uncleanness, inordinate affection, evil concupiscence, and covetousness, which is idolatry: 6 For which things' sake the wrath of God cometh on the children of disobedience:

In view of the previous paragraph of his epistle (about being united with Christ and the hope of appearing with Him in glory when He comes), Paul calls the Colossians to action against evil and toward good. The word "mortify," used here as a command, is the verb *nekrosate* in the Greek, from *nekroo* (**neh-KRO-oh**), which means "put to death, to slay, or to kill." "Mortify" is used here metaphorically, suggesting that the reader should actively deal a deadly blow to sinful habits. Verse 3, "Ye are dead," and verse 5, "mortify therefore," contains a paradox: on one hand, Paul is saying that the Colossians are already dead, and on the other hand, he is asking them to put their body parts to death. Scholars have never easily understood and reconciled the two seemingly contradictory statements.

We can best explain this by understanding the concepts of grace and working faith. The moment we acknowledge that we are yielded to the Lord, He solicits our cooperation. As He works in us by making us uncomfortable in the midst of sinful practices, we start to obey Him and begin to unload our baggage of sin. We begin to live Christ-like lives, and all the worldly rudiments begin to dissipate. Our attitudes change, and new lifestyles and behaviors begin. A change in character becomes noticeable; our desires, passions, and aspirations change. This process is called sanctification, the work of the Holy Spirit. However, conscious and deliberate self-involvement is needed— and this is working faith (Philippians 2:12).

What parts of our bodies, or literally sinful characteristics, need to be slaughtered? "Fornication" (Gk. *porneia*, **por-NAY-ah**) includes all manner of illicit sexual relationships and intercourse outside of marriage, including adultery (Matthew 5:32, 19:9; 1 Corinthians 7:2, 10:8) and incest (1 Corinthians 5:1). Fornication does not apply only to single people, but to all sorts of sexual perversion. "Uncleanness" (Gk. *akatharsia*, **ah-ka-thar-SEE-ah**) is used to describe whatever is the opposite of purity, including thoughts and motives. The emphasis seems to lie on sexual immorality, which likely includes all forms of sexual seduction, homosexuality, and sodomy (Romans 1:26–27, 6:19; 2 Corinthians 12:21; Ephesians 5:3). In Colossians 3:5, the phrase "inordinate affection" (Gk. *pathos*, **PA-thoce**) describes out-of-control passion and lust (1 Thessalonians 4:5). The same Greek word is translated "vile affections" in Romans 1:26 where Paul refers to homosexuality. "Evil concupiscence" (Gk. *kakos epithumia*, **ka-KOCE eh-pee-thoo-MEE-ah**) is any strong or vehement desire associated mainly with evil and depraved lusts (John 8:44; Ephesians 2:3). Here again, it connotes illicit sexual immorality. "Covetousness" (Gk. *pleonexia*, **pleh-oh-nek-SEE-ah**) is a greedy desire to have more or take what belongs to someone else.

The first four sins mentioned in Colossians 3:5 (also listed in Romans 1:24–29 and

1 Thessalonians 4:3–7) can be related to sex outside of marriage. The fifth one seems to be the underlying evil that summarizes the rest of the vices—idolatry, essentially the worship of self rather than God, eventually replacing the Lordship of Christ.

"Member" is a translation of the Greek word *melos* (**MEL-oce**), meaning "limb or a member of the human body." The term is used figuratively here to describe the sins that have become attached to us, as limbs are attached. They have become such a part of our bodily experiences that we have become used to them as inherent parts of our being. Paul calls on the Colossians to not only mutilate these vices, but to kill them outrightly.

Having listed the evils, Paul reminds and warns the Colossians of the consequences of indulgence. These sins attract or invoke the wrath of God against those who indulge themselves in them, i.e., the children of disobedience. God's "wrath" (Gk. *orge*, **or-GAY**) or extreme displeasure refers to the coming judgment day (see Romans 2:5–11; Ephesians 2:2–3; 2 Thessalonians 1:8–10).

7 In the which ye also walked some time, when ye lived in them. 8 But now ye also put off all these; anger, wrath, malice, blasphemy, filthy communication out of your mouth. 9 Lie not one to another, seeing that ye have put off the old man with his deeds;

Paul compares the Colossians' former lifestyle with their present disposition as those who have been raised with Christ. In their previous state, they indulged in those vices, but now they have been reborn through Christ's death and sacrifice, so those vices should be abandoned. Paul now uses a different metaphor; instead of putting the sins to death, he urges them to put them off like worn-out garments or clothes that no longer fit. "Put off" translates from the Greek word *apotithemi*

(**ah-po-TEE-thay-me**), which means "to put away, to cast off." The idea here is more serious than the language seems to convey—to discard, never to be worn again.

The phrase in verse 8, "but now ye also put off all these," means that in addition to the listed vices that need to be mortified (v. 5), the believers need to also discard anger, wrath, malice, blasphemy, and filthy communication—another list of five vices related to attitudes toward others.

"Anger" is sometimes translated "wrath," and the words are used interchangeably. Anger indicates a instant, sudden feeling, whereas wrath is more of a state of mind. Paul also includes "malice" (Gk. *kakia*, **ka-KEE-ah**, evilness or wickedness) in his list of vices. These sins are related: extended anger develops into wrath, and wrath can grow into malice.

The first three vices deal with people's attitude toward others, and the next two relate to use of the tongue: blasphemy and filthy communication. The first three start from the heart, and manifest themselves vocally in blasphemy (slander) and foul or abusive language. The word "blasphemy" is a direct derivation of the Greek *blasphemia* (**blas-fay-ME-ah**), which means evil speaking. Although typically used to refer to evil words against God (Matthew 12:31), it also refers to speaking evil or slander against people (Ephesians 4:31). By "filthy communication," Paul refers to bad or foul language or vile conversation, the same idea he expressed in Ephesians 4:29 and 5:4.

Lying must also be discarded. With a third imperative, Paul says: "Lie not one to another" (v. 9). It carries the same idea as in the preceding verse and is included in the things to be discarded.

10 And have put on the new man, which is renewed in knowledge after the image of him that created him:

Continuing the clothing motif, Paul instructs the Colossians to "put on the new man" (v. 10), meaning to clothe oneself with the new nature, which results from our spiritual union with Christ through His death and resurrection (2 Corinthians 5:17). Putting on our new nature as Christ-followers renews us. The word "renewed" implies growth and changing from former corruption into new life.

When Christians receive Christ, we begin a new relationship. As it deepens, our lives and thought processes change, and we make new choices patterned according to Christ's example. Therefore, the standard of the renewal, or the new man, is God's image.

God's original plan in creating man and woman in His image was for them to fully know how to live according to His moral and spiritual likeness. Humanity severely damaged this understanding at the Garden of Eden through sin. Now God renews us and gives us the true knowledge through the new Adam— Christ Jesus (2 Peter 1:3–13).

11 Where there is neither Greek nor Jew, circumcision nor uncircumcision, Barbarian, Scythian, bond nor free: but Christ is all, and in all.

This progressive transformation into the image of God does not distinguish between racial, religious, cultural, and social boundaries. The introduction of this theme indicates that Paul is aware of the scandals in his time. The partition between the Greek and Jew was practically unbreakable, especially from the Jewish end. The Jews who were circumcised would look down on and refuse to acknowledge the uncircumcised Greeks or Gentiles. The word "barbarian" refers to all non-Greeks, those ignorant of the Greek language; the Greeks regarded them as the lower class in society. Barbarians were also regarded as uncultured, crude, and rough, hence our term

"barbaric." A Scythian was thought to be part of the lowest class of barbarians, rude and rough. They lived in Scythia, which included parts of modern-day Ukraine, Russia, and Kazakhstan.

Baseless social barriers continue today, including class discrimination, racial bigotry, and misogyny. Paul condemns all of these mindsets, and the same is true today. Paul sums it up by saying, "but Christ is all, and in all"—meaning Christ is all that matters. He lives in all believers, whether Greek or Jew, Barbarian or Scythian, slave or free. His Spirit works in every heart yielded to Him.

12 Put on therefore, as the elect of God, holy and beloved, bowels of mercies, kindness, humbleness of mind, meekness, longsuffering;

Paul returns to the theme of "putting on" from verse 10. The idea is because you have shed the old person and put on the new, then you should practice it as well. Paul uses a series of phrases to describe whom believers become when they receive Christ. First, they are "the elect of God," which means "the chosen ones of God." Secondly, they are "holy" (Gk. *hagios*, **HA-gee-oce**), meaning "set apart, special, or sacred." All true believers are holy in God's sight. Paul affirms the Colossians' position before God, a special place that all Christians now share with the ancient covenant people of Israel (see Isaiah 4:3; 1 Peter 2:9; Romans 9:25).

After affirming whom they are because of their relationship with God through Christ, Paul now enumerates the qualities expected of the Colossians. While the list in v. 8 consists of selfish sins, the list here indicates care for others' well-being.

These qualities are paired with some overlap. The first pair is "bowels of mercies" and "kindness." "Bowels of mercies" figuratively describes the spirit of compassion resididing in the heart of God's elect. The word "bowel"

(Gk. *splagchnon*, **SPLANKH-known**) refers to the intestines, stomach, or abdomen; here, it means pity, sympathy, or inward affection. For the Hebrews, bowels were the seat of kindness, compassion, and benevolence, which we now associate with the heart. Bowels and "mercies" (Gk. *oiktirmos*, **oik-tear-MOCE**), which mean "compassion" or "pity," go together. The phrase can be translated as "bowels in which compassion resides." The next word, "kindness" (Gk. *chrestotes*, **khray-STO-tace**), is synonymous with bowels of mercies and expresses moral goodness and compassion.

The next qualities the Colossians are asked to adopt are "humility of mind" (Gk. *tapeino-phrosune*, **tah-pay-no-fro-SOO-nay**), meaning lowliness, and "meekness" (Gk. *praotes*, **prah-OH-tace**). Both of these convey the spirit of gentleness and modesty. Humility was not always seen positively in the heathen world and is in opposition to pride, but to the Christian, it is an honorable quality to strive for and one Christ exhibited throughout His earthly ministry (Philippians 2:3).

Another quality that Paul mentions is "long-suffering" (Gk. *makrothumia*, **ma-kro-thoo-MEE-ah**), which is patience or "slowness in avenging wrongs." It characterizes self-control, refusing to yield to passion and rage when wronged. Patience is almost exclusively associated with relationships with others. However, one also needs patience to succeed in life in general.

13 Forbearing one another, and forgiving one another, if any man have a quarrel against any: even as Christ forgave you, so also do ye.

Closely associated with the five virtues is a pair of activities required of all believers. The first virtue, "forbearing" (Gk. *anecho*, **an-EKH-oh**), means "to hold oneself up against, to bear with, or to endure," suggesting tolerance or putting up with something negative. Paul adds the second activity, "forgiving one another," so as to follow in Christ's supreme example. Christ taught His disciples to pray, "And forgive us our debts, as we forgive our debtors" (Matthew 6:12), and sets no limit on how many times to forgive one another (Matthew 18:22). All the virtues Paul listed are apparent in Christ's life—a heart of compassion, humility, meekness, long-suffering, endurance or forbearance, and forgiveness. When believers manifest these virtues, they have put on Christ.

14 And above all these things put on charity, which is the bond of perfectness. 15 And let the peace of God rule in your hearts, to the which also ye are called in one body; and be ye thankful.

The word here for "love" is *agape* (Gk. **ah-GAH-pay**), which the KJV often translates as charity. It refers to unconditional love, not just almsgiving. Love ties together all the other virtues. "Perfectness" (Gk. *teleiotes*, **teh-lay-OH-tace**) means completeness, and "bond" (Gk. *sundesmos*, **SOON-des-moce**) is like a joint tie or ligament binding things together, particularly body .

Paul continues with his theme of unity; God's peace not only brings harmony to individual hearts, but also harmony and oneness within the larger body of Christ. Letting peace "rule" (Gk. *brabeuo*, **bra-BEW-oh**) suggests peace being an umpire, judge, or arbitrator that directs or controls. The "peace of God" means either "the peace that God gives" or "the peace that belongs to God." Paul adds that believers should be "thankful," an expression used frequently throughout the epistle. A grateful heart produces a peaceful mind; conversely, an ungrateful heart produces disharmony inside that overflows to others, breeding discord within the body of Christ.

16 Let the word of Christ dwell in you richly in all wisdom; teaching and admonishing one another in psalms and hymns and spiritual songs, singing with grace in your hearts to the Lord.

The Word of Christ should "dwell" (Gk. *enoikeo*, **en-oy-KEH-oh**), or inhabit, our hearts as well. The word "dwell" is used figuratively to suggest influencing one's life and activities. While the peace of Christ should control our lives, His Word should influence our activities, and both should dwell in our hearts. The Word of Christ dwelling within our hearts will produce all the wisdom we need in life. It will influence and govern our thoughts, deeds, and motivations, as well as help us make good, rational decisions in life. When we are abundantly equipped through the Word of Christ, we will be teaching and "admonishing" (Gk. *noutheteo*, **noo-theh-TEH-oh**, warning, cautioning or gently reproving) each other through psalms, hymns, and spiritual songs.

17 And whatsoever ye do in word or deed, do all in the name of the Lord Jesus, giving thanks to God and the Father by him.

In order to "do all in the name of the Lord Jesus," we must act according to His revealed will; we should be mindful of our relationship with Him; we will need to live subject to His authority and power; and we will do everything for His glory, not ours.

Paul adds, "giving thanks to God and the Father by him." We appreciate what God has accomplished for us through Christ's redemptive and atoning sacrifice, whereby we sinners receive forgiveness and are accepted by God as sons and daughters. Our lives should be motivated by the love of Christ in us to honor and glorify His name. Our lives and activities must be governed by the peace of God in our hearts (v. 15), influenced by the Word of Christ dwelling richly in wisdom (v. 16), and motivated by our relationship with Christ—with eternity in view.

Sources:
Hendriksen, William. *Exposition of Colossians and Philemon: New Testament Commentary*. Grand Rapids, MI: Baker Book House, 1964.
Unger, Merrill F. *The New Unger's Bible Dictionary*. Chicago, IL: Moody Press, 1988.

Say It Correctly

Concupiscence. con-**KYOO**-pi-sens.
Scythian. si-**THEE**-en.

Daily Bible Readings

MONDAY
Buried in Baptism; Raised with Christ
(Colossians 2:6–12)

TUESDAY
God's Example in All Relationships
(Matthew 5:43–48)

WEDNESDAY
Life with Christ in the World
(John 17:14–19)

THURSDAY
Life in the Spirit
(Romans 8:1–11)

FRIDAY
Speak Truthfully Always
(Ephesians 4:25–30)

SATURDAY
Replace Anger with Forgiveness
(Ephesians 4:31–5:2)

SUNDAY
Live the New Life in Christ
(Colossians 3:1–17)

A

Abomination: A foul and detestable thing

Affliction: Anguish, burden, persecution, tribulation, or trouble

Angel: A messenger of God, not eternal or all-knowing; specific types include cherubim and seraphim

Ascension: Raising up in authority or physical place. Can especially refer to the event forty days after Jesus' death, burial, and Resurrection, when He went returned to heaven to sit at the right hand of the Father (Acts 1:9–11)

Atone: To propitiate, satisfy the demands of an offended holy God; or reconcile to a holy God after sin

B

Baptize: To dip, immerse, or submerge

Blameless: Irreproachable, faultless, flawless

Blessedness: Happiness, joy, or prosperity, to be well spoken of by God or others

Bless the Lord: To bend the knee in praise to God

Blood of the Lamb: The blood that Jesus shed on the Cross that redeems humanity

Bowels: To ancient Middle Easterners, the place of emotion, distress, or love

C

Called by God: Appointed or commissioned to fulfill a task

Charge: Admonish, order, command

Chosen: To be approved and selected by God

Christ: The Anointed One, the expected Messiah the Jews hoped for and whom Christians believe came as Jesus of Nazareth

Commandments: God's mandates; the entire body of Laws issued by God through Moses for Israel

Conduct: Manner of living

Confess: To acknowledge or fully agree

Consider: To determine or make out

Covenant: An agreement or promise between God and humanity based on God's character, strength, and grace

Crucifixion: A method of Roman execution in which a criminal was hung on a cross

D

Decalogue: From "ten words" in Greek; the Ten Commandments

Desolation: The state of being deserted or uninhabited

Disciples: Learners, students, followers

Dominion: Rule or reign

Dwelling place: A person's refuge or home

E

El: The Hebrew word for "god" or "mighty one"

Evil: Bad, unpleasant, or displeasing things

Evil doer: A malefactor, wrongdoer, criminal, troublemaker

Evil spirits: Messengers and ministers of the devil

Exalt: To raise up to the highest degree possible

Exhortation: Giving someone motivation to change his or her behavior either by rebuke or encouragement

F

Faithfulness: Steadfastness, steadiness

Fear of the Lord: Reverence or awe of who God is, resulting in obedience to Him and abstaining from evil

G

Glory: Splendor, unparalleled honor, dignity, or distinction; praise and worship

God's bride: The church

God's own hand: God's strength, power

Gospel: The Good News of Jesus the Messiah's arrival and presence of His kingdom

Graven image: An idol cut (often from stone, wood, or metal) and worshiped as a god

Great Tribulation: A time of great suffering that has not been experienced since the world began (Matthew 24:21, Revelation 7:14)

H

Hallowed: Consecrated, dedicated, or set apart

Hear: Listen to, yield to, or obey

Hearken: Pay attention to, give attention to

Heart: The figurative place of emotion and passion

Heathens: The Gentiles, all those who are not a part of the people of God

Holy: Anything consecrated and set aside for sacred use; set apart from sin

Honor: To revere or value

Host: An army or vast number

I

Idolatry: The worship of anything other than God

Infidel: One who is unfaithful, unbelieving, and not to be trusted

Iniquity: Perversity, depravity, guilt, sin

J

Just: Righteous, that which is right and fair

Justice: Righteousness in government

K

Kingdom of Christ: The rule and reign of Christ as King both now and in the age to come

L

Law: Either the Mosiac Law or any human law; synonyms include commandments, ordinances, statutes, legal regulations, authoritative instructions, and teachings

Logos (LOG-os): (Gk.) Word; the Word of God, either the Bible or Jesus

M

Manna: Food from heaven baked into a kind of bread, which God miraculously gave to the Israelites in the wilderness

Messiah: The Anointed One

Minister: A servant, an attendant, one who executes the commands of another

Mosiac Law: The law passed down by Moses from God to the Hebrew people at Mt. Sinai

O

Omnipotent: All powerful

Omnipresent: All present, being everywhere

Omniscient: All knowing

Ordained: Established and founded by God; founded, fixed, or appointed

P

Parousia (par-oo-SEE-ah): (Gk.) presence, appearing; Christ's Second Coming

Peace: Wholeness, quietness, contentment, health, prosperity; more than an absence of conflict or problems, but every part of life being blessed

Pentateuch: The first five books of the Old Testament

Power: Boldness, might, or strength, especially God's

Prophets: People filled with the Spirit of God and under the authority and command of God, who pleaded His cause and urged humanity to be saved

Profit: To gain or benefit

Prosper: To succeed, especially in spiritual things; to move forward or succeed in one's efforts

Proved: Examined, tested, tried

Psalm: A piece of music or a melody, especially one dedicated to God or a god

Purity: Sinlessness, without blemish spiritually

R

Ransom: To buy back or pay a price for a person, buying their freedom

Redeem: To ransom or purchase

Refuge: A shelter from rain, storm, or danger; stronghold or fortress; a place to run to and be secure when the enemy threatens

Repent: To turn back from sin and turn to God in faith

Righteous: To be declared not guilty

Righteousness: Justness, rightness, especially God's, which He works as a gift in His people; the right way to live as opposed to a lifestyle that treats others unfairly or unjustly

S

Sabbath: From "ceasing (from work)" in Hebrew; the day set aside to worship God

Sanctuary: The holy place, either in the Tabernacle or the Temple

Salvation: Rescue, safety, or deliverance, especially from eternal punishment

Satan: A fallen angel who is opposed to God and His people

Savior: Defender, rescuer, or deliverer; a term applied to Christ as the rescuer of those who are in bondage to sin and death

Scribes: Secretaries, recorders, men skilled in the Law during Jesus' day

Selah (SEE-lah): (Heb.) A pause in singing to allow for an instrumental musical interlude or silent meditation

Septuagint: "Seventy" in Latin; the Greek translation of the Hebrew Old Testament made by 70 Jewish scholars beginning in the third century BC

Servant: A slave, subject, or worshiper

Shalom (sha-LOME): (Heb.) Peace, prosperity, blessing

Shekinah Glory: The awesome presence of the Lord; His honor, fame, and reputation

Shofar (sho-FAR): (Heb.) A ram's horn; commonly used in celebration, as well as in signaling armies or large groups of people in civil assembly

Soul: The immaterial part of a person (what leaves the body after death), or the whole being, the self, one's life

Stiffnecked: Obstinate and difficult

Strengthen: To secure, make firm

Strive: To struggle, to exert oneself

Supplication: Seeking, asking, entreating, pleading, imploring, or petitioning

T

Tabernacle: A tent; the name of the portable temple constructed by Moses and the people of Israel

Tetragrammaton: YHWH; the four consonants of God's name, as the Jews would often write it

Torah: (Heb.) Law, instrument, or direction; the first five books of the Old Testament

Transfiguration: A change or transformation. Often refers to Jesus' transformation while on the Mount of Olives with His disciples Peter, James, and John, when His face shone like the sun and His clothing was white as snow (Matthew 17:2; Mark 9:2; Luke 9:29)

Transgression: Sin, rebellion, breaking God's Law

Try: In the sense of a test: refined or purified

Trumpet: A ram's horn or simple metal tube used in celebration as well as in signaling armies or large groups of people in civil assembly

V

Vanity (vain): A waste, a worthless thing, or simply emptiness

W

Wisdom: Prudence, an understanding of ethics

Woe: Grief or sorrow

Worship: Bow down deeply, show obedience and reverence

Wrath: Burning anger, rage

Y

Yahweh: God's name, often spelled with consonants only (see Tetragrammaton)

Notes

Notes